CANADA AMONG NATIONS 2001

CANADA AMONG NATIONS 2001

The Axworthy Legacy

Edited by
Fen Osler Hampson, Norman Hillmer,
and Maureen Appel Molot

OXFORD
UNIVERSITY PRESS

OXFORD
UNIVERSITY PRESS

70 Wynford Drive, Don Mills, Ontario M3C 1J9
www.oupcan.com

Oxford University Press is a department of the University of Oxford.
It furthers the University's objective of excellence in research, scholarship,
and education by publishing worldwide in

Oxford   New York

Athens   Auckland   Bangkok   Bogotá   Buenos Aires   Cape Town
Chennai   Dar es Salaam   Delhi   Florence   Hong Kong   Istanbul   Karachi
Kolkata   Kuala Lumpur   Madrid   Melbourne   Mexico City   Mumbai   Nairobi
Paris   São Paulo   Shanghai   Singapore   Taipei   Tokyo   Toronto   Warsaw

with associated companies in Berlin   Ibadan

Oxford is a trade mark of Oxford University Press
in the UK and in certain other countries

Published in Canada
by Oxford University Press

Canadian Cataloguing in Publication Data

The National Library of Canada has catalogued this publication as follows:
Canada among nations

Annual.
1984–
Produced by the Norman Paterson School of International Affairs at Carleton University.
Each vol. Has also a distinctive title.
Published: Ottawa : Carleton University press, 1993?-1997; Toronto : Oxford University Press, 1998- .
ISSN 0832-0683
ISBN 0-19-541667-8 (2001)

1. Canada—Foreign relations—1945-   —Periodicals. 2. Canada—Politics and
government—1984   —Periodicals. 3. Canada—Politics and government—1980-1984 Periodicals. I.
Norman Paterson School of International Affairs.
FC242.C345   327.71   C86-031285-2
F1029.C3

1 2 3 4 - 05 04 03 02

This book is printed on permanent (acid-free) paper ∞.
Printed in Canada

CONTENTS

Part Two: After Axworthy: Emerging Issues in Canadian Foreign and Security Policy

CONTRIBUTORS

Susan Ariel Aaronson is Senior Fellow at the National Policy Association.

Chris Brown is an associate professor of Political Science at Carleton University.

Adam Chapnick is a Ph.D. candidate in the Department of History at the University of Toronto.

Daryl Copeland is a member of the Department of Foreign Affairs and International Trade.

Grant Dawson is a Ph.D. candidate in the History Department at Carleton University.

John English is a professor of History at the University of Waterloo.

James Fergusson is the Deputy Director of the Centre for Defence and Security Studies, and an associate professor in the Department of Political Studies at the University of Manitoba.

Earl H. Fry is a professor of Political Science and Endowed Professor of Canadian Studies at Brigham Young University.

Fen Osler Hampson is a professor in The Norman Paterson School of International Affairs at Carleton University.

Norman Hillmer is a professor of History at Carleton University.

Maureen Appel Molot is a professor and Director of The Norman Paterson School of International Affairs, at Carleton University.

Michael Pearson was a Senior Policy Adviser to two Canadian Foreign Ministers, 1993–7. He is an independent public/foreign affairs consultant based in Ottawa.

Vincent Rigby is a Policy Officer with the Department of National Defence.

Heather A. Smith is an assistant professor of International Studies at the University of Northern British Columbia.

Denis Stairs is McCulloch Professor in Political Science and a member of the Centre for Foreign Policy Studies at Dalhousie University.

Judith Teichman is a professor of Political Science at the University of Toronto.

Alison Van Rooy is a Research Associate with the North-South Institute in Ottawa.

ABBREVIATIONS

ABM	Anti-Ballistic Missile (Treaty)
APEC	Asia-Pacific Economic Cooperation
BANAMEX	Banco nacional de México
BMC³	battle management command, control, and communications
CAI	Core Area Initiative (Winnipeg)
CANMILSATCOM	Canadian Military Satellite Communications
CBD	Convention on Biological Diversity
CCFPD	Canadian Centre for Foreign Policy Development
CDM	Clean Development Mechanism
CEPAL	UN Economic Commission for Latin America and the Caribbean
CFCS	chlorofluorocarbons
CIDA	Canadian International Development Agency
CIIS	Canadian International Information Strategy
CMD	cruise missile defence
COP	Conference of Parties
COSENA	National Security Council (Mexico)
DEA	Department of External Affairs (Canada)
DEW	Distant Early Warning
DFAIT	Department of Foreign Affairs and International Trade
DND	Department of National Defence
DRC	Democratic Republic of Congo
ECOMOG	Economic Community of West African States Cease-Fire Monitoring Group
ECOSOC	UN Economic and Social Council
EU	European Union
EZLN	Zapatista Liberation Army
FAO	Food and Agriculture Organization
FCCC	Framework Convention on Climate Change
FTA	Canada-US Free Trade Agreement
FTAA	Free Trade Area of the Americas
GATT	General Agreement on Tariffs and Trade
GDP	gross domestic product
GHG	greenhouse gases
G-7	Group of Seven (Canada, France, Germany, Japan, Italy, UK, and US)

G-8	Group of Eight (Canada, France, Germany, Japan, Italy, Russia, UK, and US)
G-77	Group of 77 (developing countries)
ICBM	intercontinental ballistic missile
ICC	International Criminal Court
ICTY	International Criminal Tribunal for the former Yugoslavia
IGAD	Intergovernmental Authority on Development
IMF	International Monetary Fund
INTERFET	International Force in East Timor
ISLA	Information Services on Latin America
ITC	Department of Industry, Trade and Commerce
JUSCANZ group	Coalition of Japan, United States, Canada, Australia, and New Zealand
LMO	living modified organism
MAI	Multilateral Agreement on Investment
MFN	most favoured nation
MONUC	UN Organization Mission in the Democratic Republic of the Congo
MPLA	People's Movement for the Liberation of Angola
NAFTA	North American Free Trade Agreement
NATO	North Atlantic Treaty Organization
NIF	National Islamic Front
NGOs	Non-governmental organizations
NMD	National Missile Defense
NORAD	North American Aerospace Defence Command
OAS	Organization of American States
ODA	Overseas Development Assistance
OECD	Organization for Economic Co-operation and Development
PAN	Popular Action Party (Mexico)
PEMEX	Petroléos Mexicanos
PRD	Party of the Democratic Revolution (Mexico)
PRI	Institutional Revolutionary Party (Mexico)
PROGRESA	Education, Health and Nutrition Program (Mexico)
PRONASOL	National Solidarity Program (Mexico)
RCMP	Royal Canadian Mounted Police
RDMHQ	Rapidly Deployable Mission Headquarters
RDMU	Rapidly Deployable Management Unit
RSI	RADARSAT International

RUF	Revolutionary United Front/Party (Sierra Leone)
SDI	Strategic Defense Initiative (Star Wars; US)
SFOR	stabilization force
SHRIBRIG	Multinational Stand-by Forces High Readiness Brigade
SPLA	Sudanese People's Liberation Army
START	Strategic Arms Reduction Treaty
TELMEX	Télefonos de México
UN	United Nations
UNAMSIL	UN Mission in Sierra Leone
UNCED	UN Conference on Environment and Development
UNCHE	UN Conference on the Human Environment
UNDP	UN Development Program
UNESCO	UN Educational, Scientific and Cultural Organization
UNGA	UN General Assembly
UNITA	National Union for the Total Independence of Angola
UNMEE	UN Mission in Ethiopia/Eritrea
UNMIBH	UN Mission in Bosnia-Herzegovina
UNMIK	UN Interim Administration Mission in Kosovo
UNRRA	United Nations Relief and Rehabilitation Agency
UNTAET	UN Transitional Administration in East Timor
USTR	United States Trade Representative
WHO	World Health Organization
WTO	World Trade Organization

To the Memory of Anne Hillmer

Preface

Lloyd Axworthy assumed the position of Canada's Foreign Minister in January 1996 with a deep interest in international affairs and a determination to make a difference. His initiatives on landmines, the International Criminal Court, war-affected children, broad consultations with non-governmental organizations (NGOs), and Security Council reform contributed to his reputation as an innovative thinker and foreign policy activist and raised Canada's international profile to extraordinary—and controversial—heights. The central purpose of *The Axworthy Legacy* is to generate debate over Axworthy's term as Foreign Minister. A second is to recognize the impact of new presidents in the US and Mexico and evaluate what this new leadership in North America might mean for Canada. The third intent of the volume is to examine the Chrétien government's record in a number of important foreign policy areas and to look ahead to the challenges that the Prime Minister and his new team face; among these are Canada's relations with the United States, decisions on National Missile Defense, peacekeeping, the environment, and Africa.

The Axworthy Legacy is the seventeenth in the *Canada Among Nations* series published annually by The Norman Paterson School of International Affairs (NPSIA). The editors appreciate the support of the Security and Defence Forum of the Department of National

Defence and the Dean of the Faculty of Public Affairs and Management at Carleton University. Their assistance underwrote some of the costs of a workshop in December 2000, at which the contributors presented their papers and debated the policy issues discussed in the volume.

Once again many people at NPSIA contributed to the success of the volume. Brenda Sutherland input the text and demonstrated patience with the editors as they requested all too many changes. Janet Doherty organized yet another workshop and supervised the financial side of the project. Thanks to Vivian Cummins for her comments and assistance. Anita Symonds and Ed Gillis did some of the editing and proofreading, provided research assistance to the editors, and compiled the list of acronyms. We also acknowledge with pleasure the assistance of Phyllis Wilson and her staff at Oxford University Press and the superb work of the copy editor, Richard Tallman.

The editors very much enjoyed working with the contributors to *The Axworthy Legacy*. One sign of a healthy polity is debate over foreign policy. We hope this volume contributes to much heated discussion about the past and the future of Canadian foreign policy.

This edition of *Canada Among Nations* is dedicated to the memory of Anne Hillmer, a graduate of NPSIA who went on to a distinguished career in the Department of Foreign Affairs. Prime Minister Jean Chrétien said immediately after her death on 14 March 2001 that her work on development and international sport was 'legendary. Her dynamism and commitment will be sorely missed by all Canadians.'

Fen Osler Hampson
Norman Hillmer
Maureen Appel Molot

April 2001

1

The Return to Continentalism in Canadian Foreign Policy

FEN OSLER HAMPSON, NORMAN HILLMER, AND
MAUREEN APPEL MOLOT

Evaluating the Canadian foreign policy agenda at the beginning of April 2001, focused as it is on the relationship with the United States as well as broader hemispheric issues, it is remarkable how quickly Lloyd Axworthy's agenda has faded. Like the Cheshire Cat whose image faded from Alice's view, the key question is what remains of Axworthy's foreign policy priorities.

In debating Axworthy's impact, it is important to recall that when he was appointed Foreign Minister in January 1996 DFAIT's budget had shrunk by almost a third (in real terms) from what it was at the beginning of the decade. Not only were there fewer resources to manage and carry out Canadian foreign policy, but also no clear agenda had emerged from the government's exhaustive 1994–5 assessment of foreign policy. The parliamentary review of Canadian foreign policy that produced the 1994 Special Joint Committee Report failed to identify any particular priorities among the many issues that it discussed. In the government's response, *Canada and the World* (DFAIT, 1995), there was an emphasis on economic prosperity and employment through trade opportunities for Canadians, coupled with attention to the vast array of new security challenges that Canada faced, including global warming, pandemic diseases, the risks and opportunities presented by globalization, and the need to build lasting peace in countries emerging from civil war. Again, what Canadians got was a laundry list instead of a clear statement of priorities and foreign policy objectives. The only concrete institutional initiative to come out of the government's statement was the creation of the Global Issues Bureau (the brainchild of then Deputy Foreign Minister Gordon Smith), which was to deal with these new problems and to be more consultative with Canadians on these problems.

Under a different Foreign Minister, one would have expected retrenchment and a further downgrading of Canada's international profile and commitments. Instead, on becoming Foreign Minister, Axworthy moved to define his human security 'vision' and to push his new agenda vigorously.

This book, the seventeenth successive volume in the *Canada Among Nations* series, centres on Lloyd Axworthy and his foreign policy legacy. In choosing to focus on this theme, we are cognizant of the fact that Axworthy's four and a half years as Foreign Minister have sparked widely conflicting assessments of his achievements and of where Canada's real foreign policy interests lie. University of Toronto historian Robert Bothwell argues that Axworthy appealed 'to a long tradition of liberal interventionists, some Canadian, like Pearson, but also to figures like the 19th-century British prime minister William Ewart Gladsone and the American president Woodrow Wilson. Gladstone and Wilson stood for an active international conscience, and clung to a standard of international morality. Mr Axworthy did the same' (Bothwell, 2000: A18). Others charge that Axworthy's global crusades were an unwelcome distraction from more pressing national interests. For example, former Canadian ambassador to Washington, Derek Burney, suggested that in recent years Canada had spent too much time worrying about winning Nobel prizes instead of tending to its vital trade relationships with the United States (Baxter, 2000: A1, A2).

A number of the essays in the first section of this volume attempt to situate the Axworthy legacy within a broader historical context.

Even so, it is not surprising that historians continue to differ on what his tenure as Foreign Minister means for Canadian foreign policy. John English in Chapter 5 and Norman Hillmer and Adam Chapnick in Chapter 4 offer two starkly contrasting views of the Axworthy period. While English, like Bothwell, argues that Axworthy's policies stand firmly in the 'liberal' tradition, Hillmer and Chapnick argue that his legacy was much more revolutionary than even his partisan supporters are willing to admit.

Although Axworthy will be chiefly remembered for spearheading the Anti-Personnel Mines Convention, signed by 122 countries in Ottawa in December 1997, his agenda was considerably more ambitious. The landmines treaty renewed small arms control efforts and in early 1998 Canada co-sponsored a resolution in both the UN Commission on Crime Prevention and Criminal Justice and the UN Economic and Social Council calling on states to work towards the elaboration of an international instrument to combat the illicit manufacturing of and trafficking in firearms. Other initiatives included efforts to dramatize the plight of children in situations of armed conflict. The minister supported the creation of a joint committee on war-affected children that brought together government officials and non-governmental organizations (NGOs) to work on this issue and whose efforts led to the international conference in Winnipeg in the fall of 2000. Canada was also a leading voice in the negotiations leading to the Optional Protocol to the Convention on the Rights of the Child, which raised to 18 years the age of recruitment for and participation in hostilities.

Axworthy's human security agenda also involved a series of initiatives aimed at promoting international law and human rights. Foremost among them was the statute establishing a framework for the International Criminal Court, which was signed in July 1998. Canada also took the lead with Norway in developing a draft declaration on the right and responsibility of individuals, groups, and institutions to promote and protect universally recognized human rights and freedoms (otherwise known as the Declaration on Human Rights Defenders), which was approved at the 54th session of the UN Human Rights Commission in March-April 1998.

Michael Pearson argues in Chapter 7 that as a non-permanent, elected member of the Security Council, Canada used its seat (and the presidency when it was in the chair) to focus on threats to human security, particularly those arising from the 'civilianization' of armed conflict. Axworthy himself called on the Council to strengthen its role in the prevention of armed conflict through improved early warning, strengthened human rights institutions, and renewed efforts to control the flow of arms. As Chris Brown shows in Chapter 10, Axworthy's priorities for advancing human security—protection of civilians, peace support operations, conflict prevention, governance and accountability, and public safety—put Africa at the front of Canada's foreign policy agenda, raising the importance of the region to Canada in a way that would have been inconceivable without this template and the list of functional concerns and priorities that came with it. In placing such issues on the table as the protection of civilians in situations of armed conflict, in actively pursuing sanctions against rebel movements in Angola, in drawing the UN Security Council's attention to the humanitarian dimensions of conflict following the release of the report on Rwanda, the African dimension to these human security problems loomed large.

Axworthy also launched a vigorous and highly publicized series of public consultations with NGOs and members of civil society. Allison Van Rooy notes in Chapter 13 that these efforts were directed at making Canada's foreign policy more accountable and democratic. The Canadian Centre for Foreign Policy Development—an arm of the Foreign Minister's office—organized many of these public consultations.

Admittedly, and to the chagrin of both his critics and supporters, there were contradictions and inconsistencies in Axworthy's embrace of human security and soft power. Enthusiasts of the soft power of ideas and 'co-optation' were disappointed by Axworthy's support for NATO's bombing campaign to staunch the humanitarian crisis in Kosovo. Axworthy's failure to halt Talisman Energy's investments in Sudan, even after a government-sponsored report had unflattering things to say about Talisman's activities in helping the Sudanese government's military operations in the ongoing civil war, was also a matter of some contention. Within the Department of Foreign Affairs itself, as Daryl Copeland indicates in Chapter 8, there were mounting concerns about the lack of ministerial attention to the staple issues in Canadian foreign policy, especially Canada–US relations and broader hemispheric relations. One of the issues to which Foreign Minister Axworthy paid little attention was the environment, as Heather Smith points out in Chapter 11 in regard to problems of global warming, concern about the Arctic, and the difficulties with the Kyoto process, which now seems to have collapsed. Within the Department of National Defence, as Vincent Rigby notes in Chapter 3, there were serious concerns that Axworthy's decidedly civilian-oriented approach to human security ignored the long-standing role that Canada's military had played (and continues to play) in peace support operations and the pursuit of human security. And Grant Dawson in Chapter 15 argues convincingly that UN peacekeeping was relegated to the sidelines in many of Axworthy's human security initiatives, including those launched within a UN framework or context.

CONTINENTALISM VERSUS INTERNATIONALISM IN CANADIAN FOREIGN POLICY

The debate between Axworthy's critics and supporters underscores Canadians' long-standing ambivalence about what our role or mission on the international stage should be. In earlier times, this tension arguably expressed itself in the difference between an Atlanticist and a continentalist vision of our place in the world order—what the late John Holmes (1983) called the two sides of the dumbbell in Canadian foreign policy.

On the one hand, continentalists argue that Axworthy went out of his way to tweak the nose of the Americans on Cuba, on landmines, on the International Criminal Court. He needlessly and recklessly isolated and embarrassed the United States at a time when important demographic and regional shifts in the United States mean that the generation of US policy-makers who knew Canada well is being replaced by a younger generation of politicians from the South who do not.[1] Yet, as Earl Fry suggests in Chapter 6, in a number of respects Axworthy's agenda did address issues of concern to President Bill Clinton, most notably the International Criminal Court and landmines, even if the President had difficulty in bringing the US on board on these topics in the manner he might have wished. The tensions experienced in the Canada-US security relationship under Axworthy were not new; nor were they entirely of his own making. Historically, there have always been differences and points of contention—over NATO, NORAD, Vietnam, the Reagan Strategic Defense Initiative, cruise missile testing, Cuba, and now National Missile Defense, as James Fergusson shows in Chapter 12. Certainly, Axworthy could, at times, have shown greater sensitivity to US concerns in the interests of maintaining the bilateral relationship on an even keel, but this assessment tends to depend on whether one is a continentalist as opposed to internationalist on the Canadian foreign policy dumbbell.

On the other hand, internationalists welcomed Axworthy's special brand of internationalism, which championed the rights of the marginalized and disenfranchised in global politics—women, children, and the victims of armed conflict. As we wrote in the introduction to *Canada Among Nations 2000: Vanishing Borders*, Prime Minister Jean Chrétien came to office determined to distinguish himself from his predecessor, Brian Mulroney, whom he accused of having far too close a relationship with the Americans (Hampson and Molot, 2000). Despite a warm relationship with President Clinton, the Prime Minister's attitude towards Canada–US relations during his second term in office remained highly ambivalent. Axworthy's human security agenda made for good domestic politics, especially with the Liberals' left flank.

With Axworthy's departure, the pendulum has swung in the other direction—away from internationalism in favour of a decidedly continentalist orientation. Whether caused by his distance from Ottawa provoking some reflection on Canada's relationship with the United States, or the announcement that President George W. Bush's first trip abroad would not be to Canada,[2] or the statement by President Vicente Fox of Mexico that his country aspires to replace Canada as the Americans' most important trading partner, former Foreign Minister Axworthy himself commented from British Columbia in mid-February 2001 that 'the hemisphere has changed' and 'we can't continue to do business as usual' (Lindgren, 2001: A1, A2). Canada, he noted, could no longer take its relationship with the US for granted and had to devote more time, attention, and resources to the connection. By implication, he suggested that Canada should follow Mexico's lead and increase its consular presence in the United States. Axworthy's successor, John Manley, articulated the same priorities in interviews following his assumption of office. Canada's relations with the United States would be his primary focus. Top on the agenda are trade issues, as well as those of defence (Trickey, 2000: A1). Moreover, Manley will seek resources to augment the Canadian consular representation in the US. If the new minister has any longer-term goals for Canada's bilateral or trilateral relationships in North America, he has not revealed them in the initial months of his tenure.

What are we seeing with these comments? Is this simply the effort by a previous Foreign Minister to demonstrate his continuing attentiveness to issues and an acknowledgement that he left office before he could address what he began to recognize as an omission on his watch? Or is it a new incumbent determined both to follow his own instincts on what Canada's priorities should be—Manley had previously had responsibilities for Industry Canada and was thus sensitive to the concerns of Canadian business—and to distinguish quickly his priorities from those of his predecessor? There are also other possible explanations for this coincidence of views. One is economic reality: when the economy to which we send most of our exports slows down dramatically, there are immediate implications for Canada's economic well-being. A second might be the new administration in Washington and the importance of an early Canadian presentation of interests and priorities across a range of topics. A third might be the influence of senior DFAIT officials who, frustrated with Axworthy's lack of interest in Canada's most important relationship, were determined to ensure that the new minister demonstrate his attentiveness to it and think more creatively about Canada's place in North America and how it manages its continental connections. We will address each of these in turn.

During his tenure, Lloyd Axworthy did not completely ignore the United States. Yet he was certainly less sensitive to US interests than some of his predecessors and, by philosophical predisposition, strongly opposed to some US foreign policy positions. Axworthy's lack of attention to the larger aspects of the bilateral relationship may also have taken its cue from the Prime Minister. Foreign Minister Manley's early articulation of a priority on Canada–US relations very likely reveals his own personal preferences, his higher comfort level with economic issues as a result of his previous responsibilities, and perhaps a change of thinking in the Prime Minister's Office. It may also have been an effort to stake out territory with respect to his colleague Pierre Pettigrew, who has responsibilities for International Trade, and his successor in the Industry portfolio, Brian Tobin.

Of considerable importance in explaining the new focus on Canada–US relations may be the changing economic outlook in North America. It is now commonplace to note that more than $1.5 billion (Cdn) in goods moves back and forth across the Canada–US border on a daily basis. Approximately 85 per cent of Canadian exports go to the US and some 76 per cent of what we import comes from that country. About one-third of total Canadian economic activity is connected to, or dependent on, our relationship with the United States. Canada is also the most important trading partner of the US. The United States sells more to Canada than it does to either Japan or the European Union. Without question the Canada–US trading relationship is the largest in the world. In 2000, Canada had a $90 billion (Cdn) trade surplus with the United States. Given the intensity of the relationship, it is hardly surprising that any slowdown in the US economy causes concern in Canada. Statistics on US output at the end of calendar year 2000 and for the first quarter of 2001 indicate a demonstrable decline in economic growth, high producer inventories, and reduced consumer confidence. Whether the policies of Federal Reserve Board Chair Alan Greenspan can engineer the 'soft landing' so frequently mooted remains to be seen. What is happening in Canada is a parallel slowdown in output, as major producers of goods for export to the United States, for example, the auto industry, reduce production in an effort to lessen inventory and lay off workers, and predictions abound of lower Canadian economic growth for 2001 than had been anticipated in mid-2000.[3] Canadians enjoyed a shorter and less robust rebound from the recession at the beginning of the 1990s than did the US, lost ground to their American cousins in terms of standard of living, and were unsuccessful in closing the unemployment gap (Sharpe, 2000). Moreover, Canadian productivity across a range of industries has not yet caught up to US levels (Schwanen, 2000). If the slowdown in the US becomes something more, the potential for trade friction may rise as industries seek respite from falling sales and from what they see as unfair competition.

Given the complexity of the Canada–US economic relationship, there are remarkably few trade disputes between the two countries. As Michael Hart pointed out in *Vanishing Borders,* for the most part Canada and the US have been prepared to use the dispute settlement mechanisms, first under the Canada–US Free Trade Agreement (FTA) and then the North American Free Trade Agreement (NAFTA), as well as under the World Trade Organization (WTO), to resolve bilateral disputes (Hart, 2000: 114). One outstanding exception with the potential for generating considerable tension between Ottawa and Washington, softwood lumber, is again on the bilateral agenda. Softwood lumber has been the subject of three bilateral disputes over a 15-year period. Despite a favourable dispute settlement panel ruling, Canada agreed in 1996 to restrict softwood lumber exports to the US to defuse continuing differences over export levels. Under what was in effect an agreement to manage trade, Canada capped its exports at 14.7 billion board feet; shipments above this level were hit with escalating export fees. Canada exports close to $10 billion of lumber annually to the US, about 40 per cent of the US market. The export restraint agreement ended on 31 March 2001 and Canada decided not to seek a renewal.

Both sides are staking out their positions. At issue are differences over stumpage—the fees firms cutting lumber in Canada pay to provincial governments for permission to harvest timber on Crown lands. US lumber interests, which cut timber primarily on private land where prices are set at auction, have long maintained that the Canadian provinces illegally subsidize lumber exports by granting producers below-market timber-cutting rights; Canada has stipulated this is not the case and that no subsidization is occurring.[4] The US lumber lobby, aggressive in its determination to push its interests, has sought the imposition of anti-dumping and countervailing duties as high as 76 per cent. In a letter to President Bush, more than half the members of the US Senate[5] appealed to him to strictly enforce US trade law when the agreement ends (McKenna, 2001c: B1, B2). In an effort to ameliorate the dispute and to prevent additional stresses at the April Free Trade Area of the Americas (FTAA) summit in Quebec City, Canada suggested appointing special envoys to review the dispute, a request to which the US did not respond (MacKinnon, 2001: B3). Ottawa also asked United States Trade Representative (USTR) Robert Zoellick for assurances that softwood lumber and other Canadian exports would not be affected by a new US law that rewards firms for pursuing anti-dumping and countervailing duty cases (McKenna, 2001a). Zoellick's initial response appeared very sympathetic to US lumber interests (McKenna, 2001d). The future might hold costly suits or the conventional quiet diplomacy that normally governs the complex Canadian-American relationship. In an economic relationship already governed by free trade agreements, it seems reasonable to advocate free trade in lumber as in other resources. To get to this point, however, may require political choices that the new US administration, caught as always in a complex domestic environment, may not be prepared to make. Differing provincial perspectives will also play a role in determining how the issue evolves. While positions are being articulated on both sides,

Canada has taken some action to protect its interests by launching two challenges at the WTO to protect softwood lumber exporters from potential US countervailing duties.

Also on the bilateral economic agenda is energy, with some potential for differences of views and new questions about the direction of the relationship. During calendar year 2000 oil prices were higher than they had been for two decades. Moreover, California experienced a costly electricity shortage, which led to the search for alternative sources of supply. Prior to his inauguration, President Bush indicated his support for plans to drill for oil in the Arctic National Wildlife Refuge, a position strongly opposed by Ottawa. For Canada, the energy issue is two-sided: on the one hand, Canada is the most important supplier of US energy imports;[6] on the other, cognizant of the domestic environmental lobby and its commitment to protecting the Arctic, Canada is deeply concerned about a rush to undertake drilling in a sensitive habitat (Morton, 2001a: A10). One of the issues discussed by Prime Minister Chrétien in his February 2001 meeting with President Bush was the President's proposal for a continental energy pact. The subject was also discussed by Canadian Natural Resources Minister Ralph Goodale and US Energy Secretary Spencer Abraham at the end of February (Morton, 2001b: C1) and between Goodale and his Mexican counterpart in mid-March.

This is not the first time the US has proposed a common energy policy or that Canadian and US negotiators have considered the subject (see Mahant and Mount, 1999: 108-25). Under what was at the time a controversial article of the Canada–US FTA, Canada committed itself to treating US customers for oil and gas exports in the same way as it treated Canadian purchasers; there could be no unilateral price or export changes for the US unless Canadian consumers were handled the same way. For its part, the US agreed that Canadian energy exports would no longer be subject to safeguard procedures when imports rose too rapidly. In their classic study of the negotiation of the FTA, Doern and Tomlin (1991: 80–2) suggest that Canada would have preferred that energy be treated as simply another commodity, rather than in a separate chapter. The US insisted on a separate chapter, in part to persuade Americans of the value of the overall agreement. The US tried and could not persuade Mexico to agree to similar energy provisions during the NAFTA negotiations (Cameron and Tomlin, 2000). The still inchoate US energy plan may in fact be aimed more at Mexico than at Canada. The US may also want some guarantees about Canadian electricity exports.[7] In any negotiations that may occur over a possible continental energy pact, Canada will have to balance the interests of its exporters, on the one hand, and the environmental lobby and those who are suspicious of any closer connections with the United States, on the other.

The inauguration of a new President, one with limited familiarity with Canada, contributed to the new priority on bilateral relations and prompted a flurry of high-level visits by senior Canadian cabinet members to Washington. First to travel south was Foreign Minister John Manley, who met with US Secretary of State Colin Powell at the end of January 2001. He was followed by Prime Minister Chrétien, who squeezed in a visit to President Bush in early February prior to the PM's departure for the Team Canada mission to China and the President's visit to Mexico. In a world in which personal relationships now play a more significant role in diplomacy, a great deal of attention was focused on this first prime ministerial-presidential meeting. For all of the punditry, the meeting provided the obvious opportunity for the two men to get to know each other and to review the myriad of items on the bilateral agenda, among them softwood lumber, PEI potatoes, drilling in the Arctic and energy, National Missile Defense, and the FTAA. Although warm personal connections may make for excellent photo ops and a range of stories, what counts is the capacity to address issues. Both countries have an interest in ensuring that differences are resolved expeditiously and that opportunities for co-operation are exploited.

The management and perhaps refashioning of the Canada–US relationship has become a top priority for DFAIT officials who tried unsuccessfully to engage Foreign Minister Axworthy and Prime Minister Chrétien in long-range thinking about this issue prior to the November 2000 Canadian election. They are quick to point out that by 2005 more Americans will be living in the four states bordering Mexico than in the 13 bordering Canada. Moreover, US–Mexico trade is growing at a faster rate than US–Canada trade. For many US politicians, discussions about the border focus on the US–Mexico one, not the forty-ninth parallel. With a new Mexican President intent on shaping how his country relates to the United States, bilaterally and in the context of NAFTA (see Chapter 14 by Teichman), officials in Ottawa want to anticipate possibilities, not to be caught off guard as they were when former Mexican President Carlos Salinas approached the first President Bush a decade ago about negotiating a Mexico–US free trade agreement. In retrospect, senior DFAIT officials feel they missed an opportunity in the early years of NAFTA to develop a much closer working relationship with Mexico. They recognize, further, that initiatives on Canada–US relations have to come from Ottawa, not Washington. Should attention focus on removing government obstacles to cross-border bidding on procurement, on mutual recognition of standards, labelling requirements, and product testing, on regulatory requirements, on improving border capacity and procedures for clearance of goods? Can any arrangements be bilateral or must they be trilateral? In many respects this concentration on the future shape of the Canada–US relationship is reminiscent of the ferment of the early 1980s. How the choice will be made is not obvious. What is clear is that the momentum driven by the conjuncture of a new minister, a new American President, and old issues should not be lost.

Denis Stairs argues in Chapter 2 that, when stripped down to its essence, Canadian foreign policy is about trade. What better illustration of this than the Team Canada mission to China in February 2001 led by the Prime Minister, the second to that country. Try as he did to push the economic rationale for the mission and the benefits to Canada of the contracts that would be signed, for many Canadians the trip highlighted the new character of the trade agenda, the link between trade and human rights. Phrased differently, this was the clash between hard national interests and human security. What caught the attention of Canadians—as well as some members of the Liberal caucus—was China's poor human rights record, in particular the persecution of members of the Falun Gong.[8] The Prime Minister raised the human rights issue on a number of occasions, but the intensity of his remarks seemed to increase with his distance from China's leadership. Chrétien expressed official Canadian 'concern' about a range of human rights issues in a meeting with China's Premier Zhu Rongji, then spoke about the need for judicial reform and the right to a free trial and equal access to legal protection in a speech to China's National Judges College, and linked continuing foreign investment to the right of free expression in a talk to a university group in Shanghai (Alberts, 2001a: A1; 2001b: A1; 2001c: A1).

Yet another illustration of the centrality of trade in Canadian foreign policy is the conversion of Prime Minister Chrétien from an opponent to a strong proponent of free trade. The Liberal government not only has embraced NAFTA but also has negotiated free trade agreements with Israel and Chile.[9] Canada is also in the midst of negotiating a bilateral trade agreement with Costa Rica and is considering the feasibility of a free trade arrangement with Guatemala, El Salvador, Honduras, and Nicaragua (Pettigrew, 2001a). Even more critical is the commitment Canada has made to the Free Trade Area of the Americas. With the United States and Chile, Canada has been in the forefront of the FTAA process: Canada served as chair of the initial phase of the discussions, hosted the Trade Ministerial of the Americas in the fall of 1999, the meeting of the Organization of American States (OAS) in Windsor in June 2000, and, most significantly, the Third Summit of the Americas in Quebec City at the end of April 2001. In the words of Foreign Minister Manley, 'We have become more engaged in the Americas because it is in Canada's interest to be engaged. Our future prosperity is intimately linked to our ability not just to recognize opportunities, but to show leadership in the development of hemispheric relations' (Manley, 2001).

Without fast-track authorization from Congress for the US President (see Chapter 9 by Aaronson on US trade policy), there will be no hard bargaining on the FTAA. Nonetheless, working groups have met frequently and Canada, like other states, readied a draft text on a range of subjects[10] for consideration at the FTAA Ministerial in Buenos Aires that preceded the Quebec City summit. The Summit of the Americas agenda illustrates the acceptance of issue-linkage in trade talks. Despite some disquiet about loading onto a complex trade negotiation what might be seen as a legacy of the human security agenda, two of the three themes at Quebec City speak to human security topics: strengthening democracy and human rights and realizing human potential (health, education, cultural diversity). The third theme, creating prosperity, focuses on the original purpose of the hemispheric process, the promotion of free trade. Some six weeks before the summit Canada proposed adding to the agenda the consideration of initiatives for engaging the private sector, the multilateral development banks, and civil society in a dialogue around the principles of good corporate governance and social responsibility (Kilgour, 2001).

The more complex a summit agenda, the less likely agreement on substantive matters, whatever the communiqués say. A number of challenges faced the hemispheric presidents and prime ministers at the Quebec City summit.

(1) This was President Bush's first international gathering. The successful negotiation of an FTAA may rank high among the President's foreign policy priorities, but without fast track he can make no commitments. It remains to be seen whether trade comes to the forefront of the agenda, given the Bush administration's focus on tax cuts, education, and increased military spending (*Inside US Trade*, 2001: 4). Moreover, it may not be easy for the President to get fast-track authority through an evenly divided Senate in a period of slower growth economic; also unknown are the conditions that could be attached to any grant of fast-track authority.[11]

(2) The summit was the object of demonstrations by a range of groups opposed to what they see as globalization and the loss of state authority to unrepresentative international bodies (see Chapter 13 by Van Rooy, as well as Stairs, 2000). Although Canada strove to avoid the kind of embarrassment that occurred at the Asia-Pacific Economic Co-operation meeting in Vancouver in November 1997, the anti-globalization forces expended considerable energy and resources mobilizing for the event.

(3) Brazil, which sees itself as the leading player in South America and which has never been enthusiastic about the FTAA, has had an acrimonious trade dispute with Canada over the question of support for domestic aircraft manufacturers, Embraer of Brazil and Canada's Bombardier. The dispute is again before the World Trade Organization.

(4) Cuba remains outside the hemispheric process. Foreign Minister Manley justified Cuba's exclusion from Quebec City in terms of its lack of democracy. This position may signal a change in Canada's attitude to Cuba or could be another indication of Manley's effort to distinguish his stance from that of his predecessor.

(5) There is the real matter of the cost of lack of substantive progress and the likelihood of agreement on a FTAA by 2005. At one level the FTAA/hemispheric summit process has been useful in terms of governments' commitment to democracy, to trade liberalization, and to discussions on the linkages

between trade and other substantive issues. At the same time, there are many tough issues to be negotiated, among them the question of special treatment for the small economies of the hemisphere (Canadian Foundation for the Americas, 2000) and the inclusion of non-trade issues—labour and environment—in an agreement.

(6) For Canada, there is the need to weigh the costs and benefits of our continuing heavy involvement in the FTAA process. Although our trade with members of the hemisphere has increased notably in recent years, the reality is that our exports to non-NAFTA partners in the hemisphere amount to less than 1 per cent of our overall exports.

CONCLUSION

Lloyd Axworthy's legacy appears to be receding. Foreign Minister John Manley seems to be paying no more than lip service to the concept of human security. Even so, human security will outlive Axworthy mainly because it was not just his idea (and agenda) even though he was one of its most ardent champions. One need not look further than UN Secretary-General Kofi Annan's *Millennium Report* (2000) and the agenda of the Millennium General Assembly to see that others in the international community are mouthing many of the same concerns. Within DFAIT the Bureau for Global Issues and Human Security will carry through on many of the initiatives Axworthy started—although whether they continue to get the level of ministerial scrutiny and attention under Axworthy's successors is an open question.

Axworthy's chief influence, however, is that he raised the country's profile internationally, and it is indeed Canada's name that is associated with landmines and various other human security initiatives and not so much that of Axworthy himself. As Joseph Nye (1999) wrote in *Time* magazine, Canada has punched above its weight in international affairs, but the irony is that Axworthy raised our international stock when—measured in real terms—Canada had less to offer. With surpluses to spend, the foreign policy imperative will be to put real resources behind our rhetoric, even as foreign policy moves in a continental direction. This is the challenge for those who come after Axworthy, and this will be the real test of his legacy.

NOTES

1. Both candidates in the 2000 presidential election came from southern states. Perhaps even more significant is that in the most recent redistribution of seats in the US House of Representatives as a result of the 2000 census, Arizona, Texas, Florida, and Georgia each gained two seats, while New York and Pennsylvania each lost two. Texas has displaced New York as the second most populous state (Associated Press, 2000). See also discussion in Sands (2000).

2. A number of commentators noted that President Bush's three predecessors had each made Canada their first foreign destination. While true, the spin put on it suggested that Presidents Reagan, Bush, and Clinton each purposively visited Canada before going elsewhere. In fact, only President Reagan's visit was an official one; the elder President Bush's trip was a 'working visit' and President Clinton came to Vancouver to meet Russian President Yeltsin at a summit hosted by Prime Minister Mulroney.

3. US economic growth is anticipated at less than 2 per cent (annualized) in the first two quarters of 2001 and possibly at 2.4 per cent for 2001 as a whole. Canada's growth in 2000 was 4.7 per cent; in 2001 it is anticipated at no higher than 2.4 per cent overall. As a result of the economic slowdown in the US, the Canadian economy is expected to slow in the first half of 2001. Tax cuts and rising government spending will cushion somewhat the impact of slower US growth (Little, 2001: B12).

4. The issue is made more complex in Canada because the agreement to restrict lumber exports required provincial approval to divide up the duty-free export quota of 14 billion board feet among producers in BC, Alberta, Ontario, and Quebec. The quota allocated to each producer was based on the company's historic export level. Mills without quota cannot export to the US without paying duty and those without access cannot get a quota. This has cost jobs in Canada. Moreover, there are differences within the lumber industry in Canada. Producers in Ontario and Quebec are more prepared to defend against a US trade action while many large companies in BC want a negotiated settlement (McKenna, 2000: B7).

5. What makes the letter of even greater significance is the coalition of interests represented among the signatories. In addition to supporters of the lumber industry are Senators Ted Kennedy and Diane Feinstein, advocates of environmental and labour causes (McKenna, 2001b: B3).

6. More than 50 per cent of Canada's petroleum production and 90 per cent of Canada's total energy exports go to the United States. In calendar year 2000 the value of these exports was $50 billion (Cdn).

7. Negotiations over electricity exports could become complicated because some electricity rates fall under provincial jurisdiction.

8. The persecution of those who practise Falun Gong took on a decidedly Canadian face when the father of an Ottawa student was incarcerated for his practices and Liberal MP Irwin Cotler agreed to advocate on his behalf.

9. In speeches prior to the FTAA summit in Quebec City, Minister of International Trade Pierre Pettigrew highlighted the benefits to Canada of free trade with Chile. See, for example, Pettigrew (2001b).

10. Canadian proposals have been submitted to FTAA negotiating groups on market access, government procurement, agriculture, competition policy, and subsidies and anti-dumping/countervailing duties. These proposals are available on the DFAIT Web site at <www.dfait-maeci.gc.ca/tna-nac/ftaa_neg-e.asp>. Canada has not yet made submissions to the negotiating groups on investment, services, dispute settlement, and intellectual property rights.

11. One issue will be the role that commitments on labour and the environment will play in the negotiations over fast track. A second issue that could complicate fast track is the rising demand for aid to the steel industry (*Inside US Trade*, 2001: 5-6).

REFERENCES

Alberts, Sheldon. 2001a. 'Canada too "small" to lecture China: PM', *National Post*, 12 Feb., A1, A6.

———. 2001b. 'PM Urges China to Reform Courts', *National Post*, 13 Feb., A1, A10.

———. 2001c. 'PM Scolds China on Rights Abuses', *National Post*, 15 Feb., A1, A6.

Annan, Kofi. 2000. *Millennium Report of the Secretary General of the United Nations*, 3 Apr. Available at: <http://www.un.org/millennium/sg>.

Associated Press. 2000. 'Ariz., Texas, Fla., Ga. Gain Seats', 28 Dec.

Baxter, James. 2000. 'Advice to PM: Cut the Grandstanding', *Ottawa Citizen*, 19 Sept., A1, A2.

Bothwell, Robert. 2000. 'Lloyd Axworthy: Man of Principle', *National Post*, 19 Sept., A18.

Cameron, Maxwell, and Brian Tomlin. 2000. *The Making of NAFTA: How the Deal Was Done*. Ithaca, NY: Cornell University Press.

Canadian Foundation for the Americas (FOCAL). 2000. 'The Smaller Economies of the Americas: Making a Case for Hemispheric Integration', *policy paper*, May.

Department of Foreign Affairs and International Trade (DFAIT). 1995. *Canada in the World*. Ottawa: Government Communications Group.

Doern, G. Bruce, and Brian Tomlin. 1991. *Faith & Fear: The Free Trade Story*. Toronto: Stoddart.

Hampson, Fen Osler, and Maureen Appel Molot. 2000. 'Does the 49th Parallel Matter Any More?', in Molot and Hampson (2000: 1–23).

Hart, Michael. 2000. 'The Role of Dispute Settlement in Managing Canada–US Trade and Investment Relations', in Molot and Hampson (2000: 93–116).

Holmes, John W. 1983. 'Defending the West: The Dumbbell Won't Do', *Foreign Policy*, 50 (Spring): 3–22.

Inside U.S. Trade. 2001. 'Zoellick Signals Fast-Track Link to U.S. Jordan Trade Deal', 19, 9 (2 Mar.): 4–5.

Kilgour, David. 2001. 'Notes for an Address by The Honourable David Kilgour, Secretary of State (Latin America and Africa) at the First Canadian Open Business Forum on Building Corporate Social/Environmental Responsibility', Calgary, 8 Mar.

Lindgren, April. 2001. 'Canada Stuck in "time warp" ', *Ottawa Citizen*, 15 Feb., A1, A2.

Little, Bruce. 2001. 'Economists grow gloomier', *Globe and Mail*, 27 Mar., B12.

McKenna, Barrie. 2000. 'Canada aims to avoid U.S. lumber war', *Globe and Mail*, 16 Dec., B7.

——. 2001a. 'Relations with Bush regime in a knot', *Globe and Mail*, 1 Mar., A1.

——. 2001b. 'Lumber dispute heating up', *Globe and Mail*, 1 Mar., B3.

——. 2001c. 'Senators assailed over lumber', *Globe and Mail*, 3 Mar., B1, B2.

——. 2001d. 'Lumber dispute heads for full-scale trade war', *Globe and Mail*, 8 Mar., A1, A15.

MacKinnon, Mark. 2001. 'U.S. lets pass Canadian request for softwood envoys', *Globe and Mail*, 16 Mar., B3.

Mahant, Edelgard, and Graeme S. Mount. 1999. *Invisible and Inaudible in Washington: American Policies toward Canada*. Vancouver: University of British Columbia Press.

Manley, John. 2001. 'Notes for an Address by the Honourable John Manley, Minister of Foreign Affairs, to the Standing Committee on Foreign Affairs and International Trade "Canada and the Summit of the Americas"', Ottawa, 15 Mar. Available at: <bulletins@dfait-maeci.gc.ca>.

Molot, Maureen Appel, and Fen Osler Hampson, eds. 2000. *Canada Among Nations 2000: Vanishing Borders*. Toronto: Oxford University Press.

Morton, Peter, 2001. 'U.S. Moves To Open Alaska Refuge', *National Post*, 27 Feb., A10.

Nye, Joseph S., Jr. 1999. 'The Challenge of Soft Power', *Time Magazine* 153, 7 (22 Feb.): 30.

Pettigrew, Pierre. 2001a. 'Canada to Begin Consultations on Free Trade Agreement with Four Central American Nations', press release, DFAIT, 9 Jan. Available at: <bulletins@dfait-maeci.gc.ca>.

——. 2001b. 'Canada in the Americas', Notes for an Address by the Honourable Pierre S. Pettigrew, Minister for International Trade, to the Canada–Chile Chamber of Commerce, Montreal, 5 Mar.

Sands, Christopher. 2000. 'How Canada Policy Is Made in the United States', in Molot and Hampson (2000: 47–72).

Schwanen, Daniel. 2000. 'Catching Up Is Hard to Do: Thinking About the Canada–US Productivity Gap', in Molot and Hampson (2000: 117–44).

Sharpe, Andrew. 2000. 'A Comparison of Canadian and US Labour Market Performance in the 1990s', in Molot and Hampson (2000: 145–64).

Special Joint Committee. 1994. *Canada's Foreign Policy: Principles and Priorities for the Future*. Report of the Special Joint Committee Reviewing Canadian Foreign Policy. Ottawa: Public Works and Government Services Canada.

Stairs, Denis. 2000. 'Foreign Policy Consultations in a Globalizing World: The Case of Canada, the WTO, and the Shenanigans in Seattle', *Policy Matters/Enjeux publics* (Institute for Research on Public Policy) 1, 8 (Dec.).

Trickey, Mike. 2000. 'Putting Canada on US "radar screen" a Manley priority', *National Post*, 28 Dec., A1, A4.

2

The Changing Office and the Changing Environment of the Minister of Foreign Affairs in the Axworthy Era

DENIS STAIRS

For nearly five years, from January 1996 to October 2000, Lloyd Axworthy was Canada's Minister of Foreign Affairs. During his tenure he developed a deserved reputation for high-profile activism. In the context of a portfolio usually managed by those whose styles, roles, and circumstances incline them less to revolutionary initiatives than to the reactive exploitation of passing opportunities for marginally useful work, this may be cause for surprise. By the conventional standards of statecraft, after all, Canada's assets—the ones it enjoys, but more importantly the ones it does without—conspire in the end to limit its capacity to redirect the general course of world affairs. Its diplomatic representatives, occasionally acting alone but more often with the help of counterparts abroad (and increasingly now in close co-operation with private groups in both the domestic and international environments), can sometimes contribute to restoring a modicum of order, if not of amity, to communities or relationships in which tranquility has broken down. Sometimes, too, they can deploy brightly inventive ideas in support of what they conceive to be the wider common good, cultivating allies for their various causes in the process. Given the fortunate happenstance of Canada's geopolitical positioning in North America, moreover, they can safely assume that the fundamental security of their country will rarely be threatened head-on from abroad, and further that they will be able to protect its most vital interests (with the assistance, as needs be, of foreign friends) to reasonable effect most of the time. But no one expects them to fulfil by themselves a grand design of their own fabrication or to have much success in mobilizing the support of the world at large in pursuit of transformative global visions. In benign circumstances, middle powers do well to muddle benignly through. If they can do so in a way that occasionally has ameliorative effects abroad, this is a bonus, to be savoured as much for its garnish of novelty as for its substantive import.

Lloyd Axworthy displayed larger ambitions than this, and these ambitions led him to force-feed the development of a daunting international agenda for both the foreign service and the galaxy of non-governmental partners with whom Canada's officials now routinely, if sometimes uneasily, work. This agenda has come to be equated above all with the requirements of 'human security'. On Axworthy's own account, it has been manifested most obviously in the Ottawa Convention banning anti-personnel landmines and in the emergence of an International Criminal Court to prosecute individuals, irrespective of either their citizenship or their political or military station, for crimes against humanity.

The agenda that he and his department have defined,[1] however, is much more than a challenging list of 'things to do'. This is because it is founded on the explicitly declared notion that the proper objects of international politics are not, in the end, the sovereign states themselves, but the individuals who inhabit them. The security of the state may be one of the underlying prerequisites for the security of the individual, but it is not by itself sufficient. In the first place, secure states often mistreat their own citizens. In the second place, from the standpoint of the individual, the significant sources of misery in life are far more plentiful than the state-centric model connoted by the traditional conception of 'international peace and security' would suggest. An apparently increasing amount of gratuitous killing takes place *within* states, not just between them. In the case of failed states, it happens in spite of them. And superimposed on the killing, maiming, and destruction of property that too often emanate from an unrestrained humanity in bestial (or desperate) mood are comparable sufferings that derive from other forces—from ignorance, for example, or poverty, or famine, or disease, or despotic rule, or environmental decay, or any of a host of other mutually reinforcing manifestations of the tragedies and ailments of the commons and of the perennial exploitation of the weak by the strong. A *good* international politics, a politics led by well-intentioned states, must have as its primary objective the pursuit of remedies for these horrendous ills, for until they are gone, their victims, actual or potential, can never feel truly safe.

This is not as new a conception of the proper purposes of statecraft as is commonly supposed. For a start, it falls four-square within the long-standing liberal view of the functions of government—functions that liberal theory has always regarded as no more than instrumental. In the liberal tradition, the defence of the state rests entirely on its role as the servant of those who reside within it. It is a *means* only, and not an end in itself. The *true* 'end' is the welfare of the citizenry—what the Benthamite utilitarians described as the 'greatest happiness of the greatest number'. To the extent that the state must, *in extremis*, defend itself even by military means, and can reasonably claim to be just in doing so, this is only because the secure performance of its functions is essential to the public good and because it enjoys among its inhabitants, if it is properly constituted, a legitimacy and a confidence that all of its rivals will lack. It is *not*, however, because the state itself is founded, in the liberal view, on some sort of transcendental rationale. It is simply an artifact of convenience—an *important* artifact, but an artifact all the same.

In addition, many of the strains in the 'human security' argument have a long and well-established history in what used to be called 'idealist' commentary on international affairs. Antecedent roots in political philosophy and normative belief aside, such views found particularly lively expression in the period immediately following the horrors of World War I, and they could be detected even more concretely in the specialized agencies constructed in association with the United Nations after World War II. The encouragement that was presumed to be given to peace, and hence to security, by full stomachs (Food and Agriculture Organization [FAO]), secure health (World

Health Organization [WHO]), sound education (United Nations Educational, Scientific, and Cultural Organization [UNESCO]), economic prosperity (United Nations Relief and Rehabilitation Agency [UNRRA], Economic and Social Council [ECOSOC], United Nations Development Program [UNDP], the constructs of Bretton Woods), and good governance, especially when linked to indigenous (as opposed to imperial) roots and needs (Trusteeship Council)—the support for peace that was thought to derive from all these and more was a central feature of the rationale for the new international institutions that were part of the postwar 'creation'. It was a creation, moreover, that Canadians actively helped to construct.

Nonetheless, it is widely assumed by critics and supporters alike that Axworthy's leadership was something of a watershed in Canadian foreign policy. Its core elements had links to the past, and even with the embellishments that he gave to them they had well-developed precursors in the thinking of the putatively quite different government that immediately preceded his own.[2] But Axworthy assigned to these elements a new and more aggressive emphasis, and certainly he made use of innovative political stratagems in driving his agenda home. Where possible, he amplified his diplomatic influence abroad and his political influence within his own government (and even within his own departmental apparatus) by working at close quarters with vociferously activist transnational non-governmental organizations (NGOs), on the one hand, and with ad hoc combinations of like-minded sovereign states (albeit of the second, or third, order), on the other (Stairs, 1998: 44–7). From such improbable political cultivations emerged his 'coalitions of the willing', his benignly motivated assemblages of the modestly endowed. In addition, however, he was prepared in his diplomatic targeting to tackle even the most pre-eminently 'statist' of the custodians of *gravitas* in contemporary international politics, and to do so in their own lairs. He took advantage, for example, of Canada's two-year tenure on the UN Security Council to press his case not only on the transient ten, but also on the Permanent Five. And that 'case' included nothing less than a transformation of the norms upon which the politics of the state system has traditionally operated. The most systematic of his critics have accused him of 'pulpit diplomacy' (Hampson and Oliver, 1998). But none has accused him of want of activism, much less of invention. A discussion of the 'Axworthy doctrine' implies the presence of an 'Axworthy era'—an era guided from the top and displaying characteristics uniquely its own.

From that vantage point, much of the argument that follows may seem ill-founded and difficult to sustain, for it posits in the end that the office of the Minister of Foreign Affairs has actually been for some time in decline, and that for a variety of reasons it no longer controls the most important 'action' in foreign affairs. On this account, Canada's *real* foreign policies are engineered elsewhere, and they rest on different, and certainly more powerful, political foundations. Whether this is 'good' or 'bad' is a matter of political preference and judgement, and the argument is not designed to denigrate Axworthy's purposes or accomplishments. It does seek, however, to place them in somewhat broader perspective and to remind the attentive that in politics the surface sometimes obscures the core.

The argument itself rests on a series of observations about the changing contexts within which the Foreign Minister in recent years has increasingly been compelled to operate. Most of the changes in question have roots that were planted long ago, and some of the observations that are offered here with respect to them are highly subjective. A few may even reflect fairly arbitrary judgements about what is 'important' in government and what is not. But together they serve to qualify in some degree the 'watershed' interpretation of Axworthy's performance in office—an interpretation shared by his critics and supporters alike, even if there are those on both sides who think the direction in which he made the water flow may soon be reversed. The observations themselves are presented below. It cannot be said that they follow in any particular order.

THE ORGANIZATIONAL CONTEXT

In reflecting on the responsibilities of the Minister of Foreign Affairs, and on his capacity for dealing with them, it is useful to remember first that he does not possess a department he can call entirely his own. He must share it, instead, with the Minister for International Trade, and in a few additional respects, with the Minister for International Co-operation, who happens also to be the Minister Responsible for La Francophonie. The sharing with the latter is sometimes awkward, because only half of the responsibilities of the minister in question are served by the Department of Foreign Affairs and International Trade (DFAIT). The remainder fall within the purview of the Canadian International Development Agency (CIDA), with which DFAIT is perennially in conflict, if not openly at war. This complication of bureaucratic politics is compounded by the fact that DFAIT, with a very few exceptions, has money sufficient only to run itself, whereas CIDA has money to propagate programs, too (see discussion of 'the budget context' below).

DFAIT's bifurcation into a traditional foreign policy establishment, on the one hand, and an international trade establishment, on the other, is obviously not a new phenomenon. It dates to a major reorganization launched by the Trudeau government in 1982, nearly 20 years ago, when the trade components of the old Department of Industry, Trade and Commerce (ITC) were reassigned to the then Department of External Affairs. This was to some extent an afterthought, the trade commissioner service having emerged as a kind of half-forgotten residual—a 'leftover'—once the other 'economic development' units in the government apparatus had been rearranged. Nonetheless, it meant that the traditional foreign service now had to incorporate within its ranks a sizeable injection of trade-promotion personnel, whose mandate was narrowly focused on the pursuit abroad of Canada's economic interests and objectives. At the political level, there was even some hope that this would have a salutary effect on the priorities of the traditional diplomatic service, it being quite widely argued among political cognoscenti not only in Ottawa, but also in other capitals of the Western world, that diplomats could considerably enhance their utility to their respective governments by concentrating less on the arcane niceties of the international diplomatic environment and more on the encouragement of material prosperity—that is, on what really mattered in the end.

It might be assumed in retrospect that this organizational initiative was responsible by itself for the *volte face* in the government's position on the most important Canadian foreign policy question of the 1980s—namely, the issue of how Canada ought to manage its all-important economic relationship with the United States. In 1972, the favoured posture had been the 'third option', and the promotion of further economic integration with the US by public policy means had been effectively ruled out. It was, in effect, 'beyond the pale' (Sharp, 1972). Within a year of the organizational restructuring, however, the third option argument had been abandoned in favour of the case for selective, or sectoral, free trade, and a mere two years after that, in 1985, the government was committed to the pursuit of a bilateral free trade agreement more or less across the board.

Clearly, however, this policy transformation cannot be explained by reference to the rearrangement of the bureaucracy alone. Too many other factors were also at work. Indeed, it is difficult to investigate closely the politics of the free trade initiative in that period without coming to the conclusion that it was simply an idea whose time had come.[3] It could even be argued that the bureaucratic reorganization itself was more effect than cause—more the *result* of the prominence of the trade agenda than the *source* of it.

On the other hand, whether cause or effect, there can be little doubt that it was an integral part of an important process of change. A trade policy review that had been conceived in ITC came to be implemented in External Affairs (Doern and Tomlin, 1991: 18), and it constituted the early beginnings of what could now be described as the 'economization of Canadian foreign policy'.[4] In more concrete terms, what this means is that Canada's *real* foreign policy—the foreign policy grounded in deeply rooted constituency interests, the foreign policy that drives out other foreign policies whenever those other policies get in the way, the foreign policy about which the cabinet as a whole truly cares, the foreign policy to which domestic political imperatives ultimately apply—is Canada's *economic* foreign policy. And that is not the foreign policy with which the Minister of Foreign Affairs routinely deals.

Clearly this evolution (and it *is* an 'evolution') is not something that can be attributed to developments over the past five years alone. But when taken together with other forces, it has had the practical effect of imparting to the government's foreign policies outside the economic arena a cosmetic look—the look, that is, of the well-intentioned but not seriously sustained (which is to say, among other things, not *financially* sustained).

This phenomenon has been accelerated further, to the extent that it is a function of the way the government is organized to work, by the seemingly insistent intrusions of the Prime Minister into the practical conduct of the foreign policy agenda. The theme of prime ministerial dominance in foreign affairs has been a feature of several of the contributions to this series of volumes by John Kirton (1986, 1989, 1997), and from the perspective of so authoritative a student of summit diplomacy in the G-7/G-8 and elsewhere, it is an argument for which there is impressive supporting evidence. Kirton's interpretation has preceded, but certainly it parallels, the more general thesis recently advanced by Donald Savoie (1999) in drawing attention to the concentration of the powers of government as a whole in the hands of the Prime Minister and his office. In the field of foreign affairs, this development is to some extent a function of personal interest and inclination, and some prime ministers have been more content than others to delegate the management of the bulk of the external affairs agenda to the pertinent minister. But the various processes associated with globalization have made it increasingly difficult for heads of government to offload the foreign policy responsibility completely, and the option of doing so, even if they should wish to pursue it, becomes less and less realistic as more and more domestic interests are directly affected by developments abroad. Given that so many of these developments have an ever-more-direct bearing on the interests of those who play leading roles in the working of the economy, one of the consequences is a strengthening of the primacy of economics in the foreign policy agenda. Foreign ministers, some of the time, can think first of 'policy'. Prime ministers, all of the time, must think first of 'politics'. Hence, for example, the Prime Minister can often lend rhetorical support to the propagation of human rights abroad, knowing that in the absence of significant opportunity costs the gesture will be popular at home. But that support tends rapidly to disappear in cases where its deployment would put a substantial domestic economic interest at risk. In sum, the Foreign Minister is rivalled by peers in his own department. He is also rivalled by his boss.

THE BUDGETARY CONTEXT

The Foreign Minister's problem in finding effective room for manoeuvre is not merely, however, a function of his place in the organization of government. It comes in addition from the fact that he has at his disposal very little money with which to pay for the initiatives that he might otherwise like to take. There is a sense in which the Department of Foreign Affairs and International Trade is a *policy* department and a *representational* department, but not a *progam* department. It does administer a few programs aimed at performing what amount to promotional and public relations objectives either at home or abroad, and it manages a few more in fulfilment of certain dues-paying commitments to international organizations in which Canada happens to participate. None of these, however, amounts to very much, and the ones in the promotional category (for example, cultural and academic relations) are highly vulnerable to budget attack (1) because they are not regarded at the top as 'line' functions, and (2) because the department almost always finds it easier to eat them than to eat itself. Canada's missions abroad are extensions of its own governmental apparatus, and while contractions at the margins can and do sometimes occur (inessential missions are occasionally closed), there is enormous resistance to the notion that the on-site instruments of overseas representation can be abandoned without a penalty being paid by the state itself. Even where established missions appear not to provide a significant return on a daily basis, it is well understood that itinerant prime ministers and their political colleagues like to have resident diplomatic backup wherever they travel, and the accumulation of such travels over time continually reinforces the argument for breadth of coverage. The problem is further compounded by the fact that diplomatic insult may be taken whenever a mission is shut down. A constructive and amicable diplomacy thus does not sit well with 'stop-go' habits of budgetary management.

All of this means that the Minister of Foreign Affairs has very few program resources at his or her disposal. For this reason among others, creativity in the minister's office depends very heavily on policies whose essence is composed of bright ideas and persuasive talk. Hence Axworthy's attraction to a substantially modified version of Joseph Nye Jr's (1990) conception of 'soft power' may be explained in part by his need to make a virtue of necessity. In the absence of significant assets of the sort that 'hard power' requires, 'soft power' may be all there is. And if its deployment produces fruit in the end, it does so by bringing the politics of pressure, or the politics of persuasion (or some combination of the two), to bear on states for whom hard-power assets are not in such short supply.

In the early history of postwar Canadian foreign policy, this was not so serious a problem. In the first place, the Cold War then served to define the leading items on the foreign policy agenda in traditional politico-security terms, and the result was a hard-power response deployed in the company of allies with like-minded dispositions. In the second place, the ancillary ingredients of the security problem were not at first conceived in particularly ambitious terms. And where they were (as in the context of attempts in South and Southeast Asia to head off a radical politics of the left by triggering indigenous economic growth), it was generally assumed that the task was much too large for Canada to contemplate on its own, or even in tandem with its (Colombo Plan) Commonwealth cohorts. It would have to be taken up as well by the more richly endowed, who themselves would have little guarantee of success (Pearson, 1973: 107–12).

When ambitions are less restrained, however, the difficulty of launching significant initiatives in the absence of tangible program resources becomes immediately evident. The aspirations underlying what came to be defined as the 'human security' agenda were, and are, of that order. In their various ways, and in their varying degrees, they seek to promote fundamental transformations in the political, economic, and social circumstances of the communities they target. This may not be possible at all. Certainly it is not possible 'on the cheap'. This leaves the Minister of Foreign Affairs, as Axworthy soon discovered, with unpalatable and unrewarding options. The first is to try to extract money from the general public treasury by persuading the Prime Minister, the Minister of Finance, and the rest of the cabinet that expenditures of this sort abroad should be given a high priority at the expense of other things—a daunting challenge at a time when fiscal constraint is regarded as a primary requirement, and when everyone in the room knows that the most rewarding electoral calculus points to being stingy abroad in order to provide services at home. The second is to try to raid funds already assigned to overseas purposes, but under the auspices of other departments and agencies—a recourse that inevitably leads to inter-bureaucratic warfare with CIDA, the Department of National Defence (DND), and other irritated targets of opportunity. The third is to campaign jointly with like-minded public and private actors abroad in the hope of shaming other states (states, that is, with deeper pockets) into picking up the bill—a strategy that risks the alienation, and even the quiet contempt, of friends while arousing charges of hypocrisy, of being 'all talk and no action', of engaging in 'pinchpenny diplomacy', among both the disappointed and the fatalistic within Canada itself.[5]

The resource-constraint problem, when taken together with the other contextual factors at work, is thus a major limitation on the Foreign Minister's freedom of manoeuvre. Other ministers, of course, might be inclined to say much the same thing in reference to miseries of their own, particularly since many of their program expenditures are rendered inflexible by a combination of statutory requirements and political commitments. Nonetheless, they often have budgets that carry them far beyond the mere maintenance of their own departmental apparatus, and when they do, their expenditures have the very considerable political advantage that goes with catering directly to the needs of citizens at home as opposed to strangers overseas who do not vote in Canada.

THE AGENDA CONTEXT

This point, like the ones that succeed it below, may overlap with its predecessors, and it could well be controversial. But it warrants separate emphasis all the same. For the fact of the matter is that the primacy in the post-Cold War conduct of foreign policy has been given to economics, not to politico-security affairs. The reasons for the economic emphasis are many, and they are intricately interrelated. Quite apart from the impact of such underlying shifts as there may have been in the prevailing political culture and public policy fashion, and hence also in political will (see below), the focus on material welfare has been accelerated partly by the happy absence of a clear and present military threat to Canada's security, which has afforded everyone the luxury of being able to concentrate on the next most important thing. It has been enhanced as well by the much-trumpeted advance of globalization and the impact this has had on the international preoccupations of national governments. Even the critics and the disaffected know where the serious action really lies, as they have made colourfully clear by their responses (for example) in Paris in 1998 to the Organization for Economic Co-operation and Development (OECD) proposal for a Multilateral Agreement on Investment (MAI), and in Seattle in 1999 to the ministerial meeting of the World Trade Organization (WTO).[6]

If current trends continue, the agendas associated with international negotiations on economic matters will become increasingly intrusive and complex with the passage of time. This complexity, however, will be related for the most part to regulatory domains (like those bearing on environmental standards, labour codes, and agricultural practices), which are somewhat removed from the traditional core of the department's preoccupations and are led, in any case, by other ministries. To the extent that DFAIT retains the lead role in co-ordinating and executing the government's response, that role falls more to the Minister for International Trade than to the Minister of Foreign Affairs.

Again, this is not entirely a new development, and it is quite pos-sible to argue that the conduct of most international politics through-out history has really been about economics in the end. Nor is there anything very novel in pointing out that the transnational perme-ability of modern borders has meant that foreign affairs has become the business of almost everyone in government. In the developed states, certainly, foreign ministries lost their monopoly control of the foreign policy game a long time ago. Having said that, however, there is a sense in which the recent decline in the domestic salience of traditional politico-security concerns has taken the process to a higher stage, and the consequence for a country like Canada is that the Minister of Foreign Affairs is left more with the things that are 'nice to do', than with the things that have to be done.

This phenomenon is not unrelated to the increasing insistence of parliamentary committees, attentive publics, and government spokespersons alike that one of the primary purposes of Canada's foreign policy is to express Canadian values abroad. Those who take such a view tend to think unkindly of those who argue instead that the conduct of foreign policy ought to be tailored to the pursuit of interest. The latter respond by asserting that the former are confused or woolly-minded, or alternatively that they misunderstand what is really going on. Irrespective of one's personal preferences in this debate, a case can certainly be made that there really *is* a little room in a small corner of Canadian foreign policy for the expression of Canada's 'values' overseas. This is because not *all* of the room, given the unusually benign circumstances from which Ottawa can operate in the world at large, is taken up by the need to act on geopolitical imperatives. Perhaps another way of putting this is to say that the real imperatives, the imperatives that are politically driven, are largely economic, and in surprising measure they lie outside the Foreign Minister's assigned domain. In effect, the job of the Foreign Minister has come fortuitously to focus on voluntarist values, while his col-leagues elsewhere in government concentrate on the inescapable essentials, the unavoidable requirements.

THE GEOPOLITICAL CONTEXT

There may be a danger at this point of flogging a dead horse. But it is important to note that the impact on the minister's office of these mutually reinforcing realities is strengthened by a conjunction of other elements as well. It will be sufficient, perhaps, to deal with them in brief compass. We can start with the effect of geography, which places Canada next door to the United States and well away from everyone else. Given the disparity in the resources of the two countries as measured by almost all of the traditional dimensions of 'power' (population, gross domestic product, military capacity, and so on), the maintenance of an amicable working relationship with Washington is the primary foreign policy responsibility of any Canadian government. There can be disagreements in Ottawa and elsewhere over the details, and even over the tactics, but for Canada the need to adjust to what the Americans regard (rightly or wrongly) as vital to their interests is an implicit rule of the game. Nothing else in Canada's foreign affairs ultimately matters so much.

The impatient might be led here to interject that this is (a) obvious, (b) a long-standing condition, and (c) not by itself a challenge to the role of the Minister of Foreign Affairs. The problem, however, is that the US relationship is coming each day to matter more, and the stakes at issue bear as much on the business of other departments of government as on DFAIT itself. Once again, this is a pattern that has been developing more or less continuously since World War I, although it was greatly accelerated by World War II. At a more systemic level, it was first triggered by the decline of Great Britain and the rise of the United States as pre-eminent actors in world affairs. By the 1970s, even academicians were beginning to notice that the scope and variety of cross-border interactions between Canada and the United States were intensifying dramatically, and that this was generating an increasing array of 'transgovernmental' communications between various components of the American and Canadian governmental systems (Keohane and Nye, 1974). American states, Canadian provinces, and even the US Congress were contributing directly, moreover, to what was becoming a highly decentralized and uncontrolled process.[7] It was commonly rumoured that Canadian ambassadors in Washington, blind-sided time after time by developments triggered in other bureaucracies by other officials, were given to asking the trademark question of the office-holder who is ostensibly, but not really, in charge: 'Why am I always the last to know?' So serious was the problem becoming that, by the 1980s, keeping track of the inconveniences for Canada that might be emanating at any given time from the backroom log-rolling of congressional committees was being identified as one of the Washington embassy's principal tasks, and responding to it required new ways of performing the representational function.[8]

In themselves, these were surface phenomena—intensely interesting to inhabitants of the public service, and perhaps also to the more minutely attentive of academic onlookers, but not very arresting to anyone else. They did, however, point to an underlying reality, which was that the east-west linkages that Canadian governments with nation-building aspirations had worked so hard to create by public policy means were being overwhelmed by continental pull—by forces of market economics and communications technology that geography had made it impossible, or politically imprudent, to resist. The Canada–US Free Trade Agreement (FTA) was not the *cause* of this process, but the effect of it, and the forces involved are still at work. They are also overwhelmingly salient to Canadian politics and to Canadian interests, and in the present context what is interesting about them is that they lie, in surprising degree, outside the mandate of the Minister of Foreign Affairs (although they certainly act as a constraint on what the minister is free to do—or perhaps more often, *not* to do). Instead, they are dealt with by others, sometimes severally, sometimes in small groups, and sometimes in cabinet as a whole. This, too, contributes to the reality the minister confronts, which is that his room for manoeuvre is in voluntary and elective fields, rather than central to the Canadian interest as conventionally understood and politically interpreted. In such circumstances, once again, it may not be surprising to discover that these are the fields where 'values' are trumpeted, but resources are scarce.

THE PHILOSOPHICAL CONTEXT

Also at work in buttressing the various forces impinging on the Foreign Minister's job is a battery of philosophical premises and preferences, some of them at war with one another. Other analysts might prefer to think of them as manifestations of politics, pure and simple. In any case, the dominant ingredient is reflected in the primacy in our own time of American interpretations of the liberal idea, with the emphasis it gives, in particular, to the cultivation of market economics as one of the first priorities of state. This is not the place to dissect this phenomenon in detail, but it is important to note that market economics was at the root of the politics that led to the FTA, that it has much to do with the near-death condition of nationalism in English-speaking Canada (and perhaps also with its apparently weakening condition in Quebec), that it provides the theoretical foundation upon which the advocates and engineers of globalization rationalize their inherently decentralized and therefore largely uncontrolled endeavour, and that it stands also at the core of intergovernmental attempts to bring a measure of order and predictability to the workings of the international economy by negotiated regulatory means. Whether government behaviour here has followed the idea, or the idea has followed the behaviour, is a conundrum that good minds can debate at interminable length. Either way, however, the practical consequence is further reinforcement for the primacy that is given to economic issues in the foreign policy agenda, and hence for ministerial mandates that the Foreign Minister cannot call his own.

So dominant a philosophical position cannot, of course, go without challenge in a liberal democratic environment, and there are countervailing voices, some of them now becoming increasingly visible and insistent, even strident. Internationally, these have been manifested most obviously in the representations, noted above, that now routinely envelop the encounters of diplomats (and others) in multilateral conference. The ideas in contention vary, and so do the advocacies to which they lead, but at the root of many of them is the notion that governments have performance obligations that go far beyond the service of freewheeling economic exchange, and that they have a responsibility to deal also with the individual and communal casualties of a global capitalism in high flight. Governments need, as well, to direct their attention to problems of the global 'commons' (some of them very daunting) that profit-seeking players in the marketplace will routinely ignore.

Given his personal inclinations, this phenomenon (as already noted) occasionally gave Lloyd Axworthy opportunities for amplifying his political influence in areas in which he was badly in need of all the help he could get. He could do this by orchestrating political coalitions that included transnationally interconnected non-governmental organizations. To the extent, however, that the NGOs continue to identify their agendas with the defeat, or at least the taming, of the globalization process, the politics they create has tended in many cases to gravitate to other portfolios. It was Sergio Marchi, the Minister for International Trade, who presided over the collapse of the OECD conference on the MAI in Paris in 1998, and it fell to his successor, Pierre Pettigrew, together with Lyle Vanclief, the Minister of Agriculture and Agri-Food Canada, to cope with comparable excitements at Seattle in 1999.

Dealing with NGOs can work, in any case, both ways. Certainly they can provide useful supports. But they can also be the source of inconvenient demands—demands whose salience is greatly enhanced by the terror that seems now to grip the bureaucracy whenever there is critical coverage in the press. Increasingly adept in their handling of the electronic media in particular, the NGOs can certainly give a Foreign Minister political ammunition for use against his adversaries in government. But in politics, as in war, it is not unusual to be pinned down (or worse) by friendly fire. At the operational level, NGOs are fixated on their specific agendas. Their job is not to navigate a safe passage through a sea of competing considerations but to advance the particular causes they happen in each case to hold most dear. Their task, in short, is not to aggregate interests but to articulate them, not to govern but to nag. Hence their abiding fear of co-option, which they know leads directly to compromise. And hence, too, what the evidence shows, which is that co-option is exactly what the government will try to achieve. Thus, in the conflict of roles lies the guarantee that tensions will ensue.

CONCLUSION

It bears repeating that none of these various circumstances is completely new. Most 'conditions of work' with which foreign ministers have to cope have a very long history, and to the extent that these conditions have become more insistent in recent times, the underlying processes involved have been maturing for several decades at least. But in the past few years their combined impact on the Foreign Minister's room for manoeuvre has become much more evident. Perhaps this is partly due to the fact that Axworthy was determined to leave a mark, to make the most of his opportunity. The effort that ensued resulted in a number of accomplishments, one or two of them against very long odds. But his experience also demonstrated how powerful are the constraints on the Foreign Minister's office, and how pervasive its limits. In the light of the substance of his behaviour—which is assessed in detail elsewhere in this volume—it is possible to argue that he understood the realities of his position better than most. Perhaps he differed from his predecessor, André Ouellet, primarily in his refusal to be content with prudent strategies of 'con-structive response' and in his dedication, instead, to amplifying such slender political assets as he possessed in the pursuit of unusually ambitious initiatives. In effect, he was attempting to make what is 'peripheral' or 'optional' in Canadian foreign policy 'central'. The more hard-headed of analysts might be inclined to assert that this was a hopeless enterprise from the start, and that it succeeded to the lim-ited extent that it did only because its 'optics' worked well in the domestic polity and because for the most part it did not force a sig-nificant trade-off against a more immediate and tangible Canadian interest. It is for this reason, of course, that critics among the NGOs and on the left are drawn to the view that his initiatives were toler-ated by his colleagues in the government because they provided use-ful cosmetic cover for Canada's *real* foreign policy, a policy that was actually rooted in preoccupations of a material kind and that was focusing ever more tightly on the United States. Of this, the best indi-cator was the gap between the widely supported rhetoric of human security, on the one hand, and the actual allocation of public resources to its agenda, on the other. The argument could even be taken one step further: the government liked the human security agenda, and the alliance with the NGOs with which it was associated, because it made it possible to engage in highly visible humanitarian interventions abroad at relatively little cost. This was intervention by proxy, intervention that required no more than modest deployments of the real instruments of state.

This is harsh criticism, although it not so much a criticism of Axworthy himself as of the government for which he worked. It has to be acknowledged, moreover, that considered objections to the per-formance as a whole can be readily advanced:

- that its reach, for example, exceeded its grasp;
- that its rhetoric cultivated unrealistic expectations (followed by disillusionment) at home and an irritated cynicism among allies abroad;
- that it was predicated on ill-founded assumptions about our technical knowledge of how to go about changing both the world as a whole and the sovereign polities that reside within it;
- that it rested on an excessively optimistic assessment of the cur-rent state of 'progress' in the conduct of international politics;

- that, in particular, it overrated the significance of the assets that it linked to 'soft power' and underestimated the continuing importance of the ingredients of 'hard power';
- that it made too much of the notion that the behaviours (and more especially the *mis*behaviours) of states can soon be subordinated to the forces of a well-intended transnational populism;
- that it was sometimes irresponsible in leading people to think, in the context of cataclysms abroad, that a great deal could be done in a short time with very little.

But whatever one thinks of such controversies, and of others like them, the fact that so much activism could emanate from so tightly constrained an office is itself cause for surprise. The question now is whether the project itself will survive the departure of its architect, and if so, for how long.

NOTES

1. To what extent the term 'human security' was defined by Axworthy himself, to what extent by his political staff, and to what extent by permanent officials is not entirely clear. The concept has been refined over time, and the exposition of it has been more ambitiously conceived in some statements than in others. Certainly it reflects his own political tendencies, but its intellectual elaboration seems to have been prosecuted in officialdom.
2. Those who harbour doubts should examine some of the statements offered by Barbara McDougall in the final phases of the government of Brian Mulroney. McDougall's pronouncements were more cautious than those of Axworthy, and she was more inclined than he to stress the complexities of the task. But the basic assessment was not very different. See, for example, McDougall (1992–3).
3. Public opinion lagged behind, and there was vociferous opposition from trade unions, the cultural community, the more vulnerable sectors of the business community, the NDP, and even the Liberal Party. But by 1985 bilateral free trade with the US had been supported by the Economic Council of Canada, the Senate Committee on Foreign Affairs, and the Royal Commission on the Economic Union and Development Prospects for Canada (along with most of the witnesses who had appeared before it). The leading pressure groups of the business community, virtually all of the high-profile public policy think-tanks, the leading expositors of mainstream economics, and fully nine of the 10 provinces were also 'on side'. If the Prime Minister had put a wet finger to the wind, he would have had little difficulty in finding the direction of the strongest gusts.
4. Marxists and their offshoots would argue, of course, that foreign policy has *always* been guided in the end by the desire to serve the economic interest, as

defined by those in economic command. But that is a more sweeping argument than the one I want to offer here.

5. There is, of course, a fourth option—to lower the level of aspiration. And this is what most foreign ministers tend in practice to do, even if they do not admit it. But the strategy holds little appeal for a minister with seriously activist ambitions.

6. And as, at the time of writing (February 2001), they are gearing up to make clear again at the meeting of the Summit of the Americas in Quebec City in April.

7. By the early 1970s the phenomenon was becoming sufficiently intrusive to lead the US Department of State to commission Roger Frank Swanson to undertake an independent study of its scope and significance (Swanson, 1974).

8. Among practitioners, the principal innovator was Canada's Ambassador to Washington from 1981 to 1989, who later produced a vivid analysis of the problem as his experience led him to define it (Gotlieb, 1991). The leading academic dissection was probably that of Stephen Clarkson (1982). To the extent that it encourages low-level problem-solving by specialist officials, who are often willing to settle bilateral disputes 'on the merits' rather than on the basis of raw bargaining advantage, the decentralized way of proceeding sometimes has an advantage. But the advantage disappears when congressional politicians intrude.

REFERENCES

Clarkson, Stephen. 1982. *Canada and the Reagan Challenge: Crisis in the Canadian-American Relationship*. Toronto: James Lorimer for Canadian Institute for Economic Policy.

Doern, Bruce, and Brian W. Tomlin. 1991. *Faith & Fear: The Free Trade Story*. Toronto: Stoddart.

Gotlieb, Allan. 1991. *'I'll be with you in a minute, Mr. Ambassador': The Education of a Canadian Diplomat in Washington*. Toronto: University of Toronto Press.

Hampson, Fen Osler, and Dean F. Oliver. 1998. 'Pulpit diplomacy: A critical assessment of the Axworthy doctrine', *International Journal* 53, 3 (Summer): 379–406.

Keohane, Robert O., and Joseph S. Nye Jr. 1974. 'Introduction: The Complex Politics of Canadian-American Interdependence', *International Organization* 28, 4 (Autumn): 595–607.

Kirton, John. 1986. 'The Foreign Policy Decision Process', in Maureen Appel Molot and Brian W. Tomlin, eds, *Canada Among Nations 1985: The Conservative Agenda*. Toronto: James Lorimer, 25–45.

———. 1989. 'Foreign Policy Decision Making in the Mulroney Government', in Brian W. Tomlin and Maureen Appel Molot, eds., *Canada Among Nations: The Tory Record 1988*. Toronto: James Lorimer, 21–38.

———. 1997. 'Foreign Policy Under the Liberals: Prime Ministerial Leadership in the Chrétien Government's Foreign Policy-Making Process', in Fen Osler Hampson, Maureen Appel Molot, and Martin Rudner, eds, *Canada Among Nations 1997: Asia-Pacific Face-Off*. Ottawa: Carleton University Press, 21–50.

McDougall, Barbara. 1992–3. 'Canada and the New Internationalism', *Canadian Foreign Policy* 1, 1 (Winter): 1–6.

Nye, Joseph S., Jr. 1990. *Bound to Lead: The Changing Nature of American Power*. New York: Basic Books.

Pearson, The Right Honourable Lester B. 1973. *Mike: The Memoirs of The Right Honourable Lester B. Pearson - Volume 2: 1948–1957*. Toronto: University of Toronto Press.

Savoie, Donald J. 1999. *Governing from the Centre: The Concentration of Power in Canadian Politics*. Toronto: University of Toronto Press.

Sharp, Mitchell. 1972. 'Canada–U.S. Relations: Options for the Future', *International Perspectives*, Special Issue (Autumn).

Stairs, Denis. 1998. 'The Policy Process and Dialogues with Demos: Liberal Pluralism with a Transnational Twist', in Fen Osler Hampson and Maureen Appel Molot, eds, *Canada Among Nations 1998: Leadership and Dialogue*. Toronto: Oxford University Press.

Swanson, Roger Frank. 1974. *State/Provincial Interaction: A Study of Relations between U.S. States and Canadian Provinces Prepared for the U.S. Department of State*. Washington and Mosherville, Penn.: Canus Research Institute, for Office of External Research, Bureau of Intelligence and Research, Department of State.

3

The Canadian Forces and Human Security: A Redundant or Relevant Military?

VINCENT RIGBY

To many observers, the role of the Canadian Forces in human security policy over the past several years has been at best obscure and at worst non-existent or even hostile. Critics have argued that the government and the Department of Foreign Affairs and International Trade (DFAIT) have focused on the 'soft' aspects of human security while paying scant attention to the military. This misguided approach, they claim, was especially apparent in the early stages of the human security agenda. Moreover, they suggest that Canada's military, when called upon to support some of the policy's key initiatives, has been a reluctant participant, dragged along often against its will and complaining the whole way. This unflattering portrayal of the Canadian Forces suggests a tenuous link between the military and human security, as well as a strained relationship between the Department of National Defence (DND) and DFAIT.

Contrary to conventional wisdom, Canada's military establishment is a firm supporter of the government's human security agenda. To be sure, the role of the military is not always as clearly articulated in departmental statements as some would like, especially in the days before the 1999 Kosovo air campaign. However, the Canadian Forces have carried out a wide range of operations since the end of the Cold War—from traditional peacekeeping, to humanitarian intervention and disaster relief, to the use of force—that have implicitly or explicitly supported human security policy. Indeed, a strong case can be made that the Forces have long been in the human security business, if not in name then certainly in practice. These operations, while not always attracting the same public attention as the ban on anti-personnel landmines or the safety of war-affected children, have nonetheless provided a necessary complement to the diplomatic initiatives on the government's human security agenda.

This chapter examines some of the implications of human security for the Canadian Forces of the future. Despite Lloyd Axworthy's departure as Minister of Foreign Affairs, it is safe to assume that some, if not many, of the elements of his program will remain on the government agenda. This naturally raises questions about defence policy, force structure, operational tactics and training, and a host of other issues. At the very least, there is an argument that the Canadian Forces must remain combat-capable and multi-purpose if the government wishes to support human security across a broad spectrum of operations. This, in turn, means having a modern, flexible force capable of working closely with our allies.

HUMAN SECURITY AND 'HARD POWER': AXWORTHY AND HIS CRITICS

Axworthy's human security agenda generated immense debate in Canada and, to a lesser degree, internationally. Much of this discussion has focused on a simple question: what exactly *is* human security? Axworthy's definition, which evolved during his 1996–2000 tenure, drew criticism from some commentators for being either too nebulous or too broad—so much so that it has become open to virtually any interpretation. Others suggested that the definition is fine; the problem lies more in its implementation.

From a military perspective, two things are clear. First, the policy drew its inspiration more from development thinking than from what might be termed the 'traditional' security and defence community. The term 'human security', after all, was first used in the UN's 1994 *Human Development Report*, and Axworthy's early speeches on the subject clearly leaned in the direction of social, economic, and developmental issues. A typical definition can be plucked from 1997, when the Minister of Foreign Affairs stated that human security included 'security against economic privation, an acceptable quality of life, and a guarantee of fundamental rights. . . . [It] requires that basic needs are met, but it also acknowledges that sustained economic development, human rights and fundamental freedoms, the rule of law, good governance, sustainable development, and social equity are as important as arms control and disarmament' (Axworthy, 1997: 184). Many of the items on this list have, of course, long been traditional Canadian foreign policy objectives. The new policy, in this sense, was hardly revolutionary but more a repackaging of established ideas.

The second and related point is that the military appears to have had no defined role in the early stages of the human security agenda. In his public statements before 1999, the Minister of Foreign Affairs was at best inconsistent on this issue. Certainly, the Canadian Forces were rarely, if ever, mentioned. In April 1998, for example, Axworthy spoke to a Harvard audience about the 'new diplomacy' and made only passing reference to the role of military force; if anything, he downplayed the military as a foreign policy tool (Axworthy, 1998b). At this early juncture, he defined human security almost exclusively in terms of 'soft power', a term borrowed from Joseph Nye (Nye, 1990, 1998, 1999b). The Foreign Minister stated in October 1998 that 'the use of soft power—negotiation rather than coercion, powerful ideas rather than powerful weapons, public diplomacy rather than backroom bargaining—is an effective means to pursue the human security agenda' (Axworthy, 1998c). This approach was evident in the government's pursuit of such initiatives as the campaign to ban landmines, the establishment of the International Criminal Court, the protection of war-affected children, and the limiting of small arms, among others.

Inevitably, some commentators took exception to the emphasis on soft power with what they perceived to be barely a nod in the direction of 'hard' military power. At the core of much of this criticism was the view that Axworthy had taken Nye's model out of its American context. Nye argued that soft power also relied on military and economic assets. Soft power, in other words, was not a substitute for hard power; rather, the two were meant to complement one another, depending on the specific issue and the extent to which American interests came into play. Nye, who served in the CIA and then the US Department of Defense under the first Clinton adminis- tration, firmly believed that armed conflict was not an anachronism and that American armed forces still have a role to play. Some com- mentators argued that Axworthy made no effort to strike the delicate balance between hard- and soft-power assets. As one critic sug- gested, government references to this interrelationship were 'short, sharp and under-developed and convey no clear explication of what, for Nye, was a critical relationship; indeed, they contain little sub- stantive discussion of hard power at all' (Oliver, 1999: 2).

Political scientist Kim Richard Nossal criticized Axworthy for his soft power leanings. He argued that the minister's foreign policy left no room for the potential use of military assets when the going got tough, as Canada and its allies would inevitably be faced with those who would simply not be persuaded by our 'good ideas' about the world. 'In those cases, what you need is not *soft power*,' he claimed, 'but power, *period*; that is, the means to prevail over others. But that, of course, means summoning not just ideas "to get others to want what we want" but ideas about how best to prevail over others whose interests clash with ours. For this, you need a full array of "power tools" [including] military forces that can be deployed in peacekeeping missions to Rwanda or Kosovo' (Nossal, 1998). Nossal viewed Axworthy's human security program as a rejection of the Canadian Forces in foreign affairs.[1]

Others also argued that soft-power advocates neglected or down- graded the role of military power. They reminded the government of the large number of international crises in the 1990s, both of the interstate and intrastate variety, that had required a military response and hard military capability—from the Gulf War to the Balkans. These missions were increasingly dangerous, partly a result of a 'revolution in military affairs' that was helping to put high-tech weapons in the hands of smaller powers and paramilitary forces (Hampson and Oliver, 1998). They also pointed out the broad range of threats still facing Canada and the need, in this context, to link human security explicitly to physical security and armed defence (Ross, 1997; Bland, 1999). Even Nye himself reminded the Foreign Minister that 'states still matter, and hard power still matters in relations among states' (Nye, 1999a; Trickey, 1999).

Axworthy himself argued that in fact the military *had* a role to play in complementing these initiatives. In this sense, Canadian foreign policy was not for 'wimps'; it had teeth and, moreover, would ultimately require more resources for peacekeeping. 'We are pursuing an active foreign policy in resolving conflicts in such places as Haiti, Central Africa and Bosnia, using our skilled peacekeepers. We have developed a peace-building strategy. . . . We deployed our military resources as part of the UN coalition on Iraq, and we are actively participating in developing a security network in Southeast Asia' (Axworthy, 1998a). However, Axworthy did not specifically link these initiatives to human security. As well, most of these examples focused more on peacekeeping and humanitarian activities than on the use of coercive power to back up diplomacy in a crisis.

The differences between the two sides were definitional. For Nossal, hard power was viewed primarily in terms of military force aimed at forcing a recalcitrant enemy back into line. Armed forces were located at the coercive end of what Nye called the 'behavioural power continuum'. In contrast, Axworthy seemed more inclined, when pushed, to view hard power in the context of military forces conducting less coercive peacekeeping operations. At this early stage, he remained reluctant to acknowledge the need for hard military measures to defeat military opposition within the human security context. As one commentator has pointed out, there was an implicit danger that those who supported the military's traditional war-fighting capabilities might come to view the notion of soft power as contrary to the rationale of the Canadian Forces and neglect peacekeeping and humanitarian roles. On the other hand, those who might lean more in the direction of soft power could dismiss the Canadian Forces altogether as being solely 'instruments of war' (Smith-Windsor, 2000: 53–4).

THE CANADIAN FORCES AND HUMAN SECURITY: FORGING A LINK

Unfortunately, this early debate distorted the potential role of the Canadian Forces in support of human security. It had become an either/or question for Axworthy and his critics—peace support vs peace enforcement (i.e., war-fighting) operations. In reality, the Canadian military could provide a mix of hard-power capabilities to support human security right along Nye's 'behavioural power continuum'—starting with more moderate peacekeeping and humanitarian operations right up to coercion (read 'war-fighting') if necessary. Within such a framework, soft and hard power could be complementary in pursuit of the goal of human security.[2] The Canadian Forces were already putting this theory successfully to the test. Their participation in a broad range of multilateral operations during this period offered conclusive proof that the military could make a significant contribution to the government's human security agenda in a variety of ways.

To be sure, the early evolution of the human security agenda took place with limited defence input. This was partly the result of the 'soft' focus of Axworthy and his officials. However, there is also little doubt that some members of the Canadian Forces and the Department of National Defence were at times less than receptive to this new foreign policy outlook. This attitude reflected the anxiety that soft power might divert attention from the ultimate *raison d'être* of the Canadian Forces—to fight wars. This, in turn, might influence a government still occupied in paring the national deficit. When the Forces were mentioned in the same breath as human security before the Kosovo air campaign, it was usually in the context of perceived differences between National Defence and Foreign Affairs over specific initiatives. This was especially the case with landmines, although ultimately these differences were not as sharp as some have believed.

Few seemed to have noticed that the Canadian Forces were playing an increasingly important role in support of human security in a variety of regions around the globe. The key element of human security—the protection of people—has been at the core of Canada's military operations for some time. To the extent that Axworthy's agenda was but an extension of traditional Canadian foreign policy objectives, then the Canadian Forces have been carrying out human security operations for close to 50 years, if not longer. As one Canadian Forces member has commented, 'there is nothing new in this for Canada. From the North West Mounted Police to today's peacekeepers, human interests as much as state interests have guided and motivated the deployment of Canada's military assets' (Last, 1999: 1).

The 1994 Defence White Paper captured this concern. It identified a broad spectrum of operations that the Canadian Forces were prepared to undertake to support the government's foreign policy. They were human security operations in everything but name.

Reference was made not only to traditional peacekeeping and observer missions, but also to operations aimed at enforcing the will of the international community, such as the use of armed forces to create secure conditions for the delivery of aid and the protection of civilian populations and refugees. The description of these operations was revealing: 'the future nature of multilateral military operations must be multi-dimensional to address a full range of challenges. The goals of these missions—the protection of civilian populations and refugees, national reconstruction, upholding international law, and opposing aggression—are invariably unimpeachable' (DND, 1994: 32).

The White Paper made similar comments about post-conflict peacebuilding, a type of operation that has become synonymous with human security. The government argued that 'the rehabilitation of areas that have been the scene of armed conflict represents an important contribution that the training, skills and equipment of the Canadian Forces can make to security abroad.' The Forces could 'make an invaluable contribution in building a more durable peace' by delivering humanitarian relief supplies or rebuilding infrastructure and removing landmines (ibid., 32–3). The Canadian military could also take measures to enhance stability and build confidence internationally, whether through arms control initiatives or multilateral and bilateral contacts between civilian and military staffs of various countries. This latter type of activity was aimed at building transparency, confidence, and trust between militaries in those regions where the transition to democracy in the post-Cold War era remained a challenge. Civil-military relations are a key component of these activities, with a clear link to some of the themes, such as human rights and good governance, expressed in the human security agenda (ibid., 33).[3]

The authors of the White Paper had no idea just how busy the Canadian Forces would be in carrying out these operations in subsequent years. Prior to 1989, Canada's military carried out 25 international missions. Since then, they have participated in approximately 70. In early 2000, over 4,000 members of the Forces were deployed internationally, the largest number since the Korean War. Many of these operations reflected closely those identified in the White Paper, especially from a peacekeeping or humanitarian perspective—otherwise known as peace operations or 'operations other than war'. They included, for example, traditional UN peacekeeping in the Middle East and more recently the Horn of Africa; humanitarian intervention and peacebuilding in Haiti, Somalia, Cambodia, the Central African Republic, Rwanda, the Balkans, and East Timor; disaster relief in Turkey and Central America; and measures to enhance stability and confidence in Central and Eastern Europe.

The specific tasks carried out by the Canadian Forces as part of these operations are numerous, and virtually all have a human security dimension. They have included a multitude of short-term efforts aimed at mitigating some of the worst effects of wars and disasters. For example, the Forces have provided security and support for the delivery of humanitarian aid and, in many cases, have delivered the aid themselves, both by air (using, in particular, the Forces' Hercules fleet) and on the ground. They have carried out a wide range of peacebuilding efforts that have helped to establish trust between the military and local populations as well as to create a stable operational environment. These efforts have included reconstructing homes, schools, hospitals, roads, and bridges; restoring electricity and water; evacuating and housing refugees and assisting in the work of orphanages; providing medical care; helping UN and other aid agencies to rid countries of millions of unexploded landmines so that settlements can be rebuilt and arable land reclaimed; helping police maintain law and order; supporting elections; and resolving conflict.[4] The Disaster Assistance Response Team has provided emergency hospital and water-purification services to regions devastated by hurricanes and earthquakes, saving thousands of lives in the process. National Defence has also provided professional training to foreign militaries through a variety of measures such as the Military Training Assistance and Democratic Civil-Military Relations programs, the Canadian Forces Training System, and the Lester B. Pearson Canadian International Peacekeeping Training Centre. This has included French- and English-language training and programs covering such issues as refugees, human rights, international humanitarian law, and civil-military relations and co-operation. The aim of all these programs is to enhance the ability of armed forces in emerging democracies to carry out their legitimate defence responsibilities in keeping with democratic practices.[5]

As important as these tasks are, however, they have ultimately been secondary to the military's first priority in these situations: to create a stable and peaceful environment. Many of the more recent Canadian Forces operations have taken place in countries or regions where violence, anarchy, and human rights abuses have become endemic. The structures and institutions normally associated with civil society and government have all but collapsed. Somalia, Rwanda, and the Balkans are typical examples. These missions—second-generation peacekeeping, as they are sometimes called—have become more complex and dangerous. They typically involve a wide range of actors, including civilian groups whose primary purpose is to meet the long-term human security concerns of the population.

In these circumstances, the most important role of the Canadian military—whether operating under the auspices of the UN, a regional organization like NATO, or an ad hoc coalition—is to establish physical security for the individual and some form of law and order. As part of this mission, they conduct surveillance patrols to maintain a military presence, watch out for criminal activity, inspect weapons sites, and monitor disputes.[6] By carrying out these activities and playing a deterrence role, they stabilize a conflict situation and restore the conditions that allow for civil authorities to concentrate on specific human security measures. The premise is simple: all forms of human security—whether education, health, or economic prosperity—derive from physical or military security. As Robin Hay and Jean-François Rioux state, 'this relationship is of course most stark in war-torn societies where security of individual life and limb is the first order of business, with all other security needs flowing from it in a highly dependent fashion' (Hay and Rioux, 1999: 23). The military may be expensive to train for these operations, but only they have the skills and capabilities to perform them. Relations between military forces and humanitarian agencies in these missions have not always been smooth in recent years, but civilian groups have gradually come to recognize that soldiers can and must play a critical role in extreme human security situations. Indeed, several non-governmental organizations, working closely with the Conference of Defence Associations, have recently called for higher defence spending in Canada in support of human security goals (Belzile, 2000: 3).

The distinction between the military's roles in peace support operations—that is, short-term peacebuilding and humanitarian activities versus security *writ large*—is important. The military cannot, and should not, be a permanent solution. They are most effective when they establish secure and stable conditions and then leave the job of human security over the longer term to civilians. The 1994 White

Paper was very explicit on this point. It warned that the Canadian Forces had a critical role to play at the outset of these missions in the establishment of a secure environment and the provision of basic support, including transport, emergency medical assistance, logistics, and communications. However, over the long term, reconstructive activities—such as administration and the enforcement of civil law, provision of medical care, or distribution of humanitarian aid—was best left to civilian organizations (DND, 1994: 33). The training of the military for such tasks is limited, and it is too expensive to be cost-effective over many months or years. Moreover, the Forces are not blessed with so many personnel that they can spare them for long periods from their primary tasks.

The Canadian Forces have gained considerable experience in human security operations over the years. Lieutenant-General Bill Leach, former Chief of the Land Staff, has pointed out that in Kosovo, after the 1999 air campaign, 'you could see that the population was comfortable when the soldiers were present—stability, law and order, fairness is what the soldiers represent' (Leach, 1999: 3). Other commentators point out that in the same mission 'Canadian troops performed admirably, and were highly sought after. They were inherently objective and impartial, completely reliable, innovative, flexible and adaptable, and thus were able to work with any nation' (Ward, 2000: 69). There have also been failures, partly a result of the Canadian Forces tackling new experiences and learning on the job. But in almost every case, the military has been only part of the equation. Success in these types of missions almost always depends on military and civilian groups working together; this remains perhaps the greatest challenge.

HUMAN SECURITY AND KOSOVO: A TURNING POINT

Most of the military activities discussed above would not necessarily be placed at the coercive extreme of Nye's behavioural power continuum. In other words, they do not represent hard power in the same way that Nossal and others would have defined it. Indeed, as we have seen, critics of soft power had suggested since the early days of human security that Canada's 'new' foreign policy left no room for the use of military resources in a coercive manner.

This changed abruptly in 1999. The Kosovo air campaign represented hard power in its purest form—the use of military force to overcome a determined enemy. The North Atlantic Treaty Organization, firing shots in anger for only the second time in its history, unleashed a devastating air attack on the Federal Republic of Yugoslavia, and the Canadian Forces were front and centre. Canadian CF-18 pilots flew 678 combat sorties, or nearly 10 per cent of missions against fixed ground targets, and led about half the strike packages in which they took part. Canada was also among five countries delivering precision guided munitions. By almost any standard, Canada made an important contribution. Canadian participation, according to several experts, 'was a resounding success, and showed how magnificently Canadian service personnel can rise to a critical situation' (Bashow, 2000: 61).

Not only were Canadian military assets used in a coercive fashion, but the whole operation was portrayed by many in the international community, including Canada, as a classic case of human security. NATO member states had resorted to force not just for national interests but to restore human security for Kosovar Albanians in the face of ongoing Serb atrocities. It was humanitarian intervention with sharp teeth. As Vaclav Havel told the Canadian House of Commons at the time:

> This is probably the first war that has not been waged in the name of 'national interests' but rather in the name of principles and values. If one can say of any war that it is ethical, or that it is being waged for ethical reasons, then it is true of this war. Kosovo [unlike Kuwait] has no oil fields to be coveted; no member nation in the alliance has any territorial demands; Milosevic does not threaten the territorial integrity of any member of the alliance. And yet the alliance is at war. . . . it is fighting because no decent people can stand by and watch the systematic, state-directed murder of other people. . . . This war places human rights above the rights of the state. (Havel, 1999: 4–5)[7]

The Canadian government adopted the same tone. No longer was it possible to believe that human security was simply about soft power; it could also be about military intervention aimed at putting abusive bullies in their place. The Prime Minister made it clear that Canada had joined NATO in taking action against the former Yugoslavia because 'as Canadians—as world citizens—we could not sit and watch as people are displaced, their homes looted and burned. . . . Our participation in this NATO mission is just the most recent example of how our foreign policy is dictated not only by our interests but by our values' (Chrétien, 1999).

The Foreign Affairs Minister dropped hints in this direction in the months leading up to the air campaign. In early 1999, as NATO aircraft patrolled the skies over the former Yugoslavia and threatened air strikes, he made one of his first direct references to the role of the military, admitting that there would be occasions when the international community had to resort to 'robust action'. He made it clear that 'promoting human security can also involve the use of strong measures including . . . military force' (Axworthy, 1999a: 4). Once the air campaign began, Axworthy made the link between military force and human security even more explicit. Like Prime Minister Chrétien, he clearly identified Kosovo as a human security initiative, a war of values first and national interests second. The air campaign, he believed, addressed the security of individuals. The international community had left no stone unturned in its efforts to find a peaceful solution; when these efforts failed, there was no alternative but to resort to force. Axworthy was now expanding his definition of human security and accepting the role of the military in conducting not just 'peacekeeping' operations but actual combat missions. In a speech at Harvard University in April 1999, he called the crisis in Kosovo 'a concrete expression of [the] human security dynamic at work', adding that NATO's reaction:

> shows that the instruments for pursuing human security are diverse. In recent years, Canada has worked to move human security forward through different means based on negotiation and cooperation, building coalitions with other like-minded governments and civil society. Sometimes, however, hard power—in this case military force—is needed to achieve human security goals. NATO's air campaign should serve to dispel the misconception that military force and the human security agenda are mutually exclusive. Clearly, they are not. Pursuing human security involves using a variety of tools. Some rely more on persuasion—as with the campaign to ban anti-personnel mines, or with peacebuilding initiatives—while others are more robust, such as sanctions or military intervention. Similarly, support for military force does not mean abandoning human security. In Kosovo, clearly the opposite is true. The decision to pursue the military option was made precisely to ensure the security of Kosovo's population. (Axworthy, 1999b: 2)

Here was the ultimate expression of soft and hard power working together in pursuit of human security goals. This theme now became a staple of his speeches and public statements, as well as those of his senior officials. Paul Heinbecker, the assistant deputy minister for global and security policy at the Department of Foreign Affairs, echoed his minister's views when he stated bluntly that the crisis in Kosovo confirmed that 'a commitment to the protection of people also requires a commitment to back diplomacy with the threat of military force and, when necessary, with the use of force' (Heinbecker, 2000: 16).[8]

The Minister of National Defence, of course, needed no convincing of this view. Like the Foreign Affairs Minister, Art Eggleton saw hard and soft power as complementary; in his mind, military force had combined with diplomatic efforts to carry the day in Kosovo. At Harvard in September 1999, he explained to his audience that human security and humanitarian intervention were 'part of a continuum—one with both civil and military dimensions—and [we must] allocate our resources appropriately. Our response will sometimes be civil in nature, at other times it will be military and at other times a combination of both' (Eggleton, 1999: 3).

These themes soon became *de rigueur* in statements by Eggleton and his officials, both military and civilian. Not only was the linkage between soft power and hard power played up more than ever, but so, too, was the requirement for the Canadian Forces to have the resources necessary to support human security. The clearest expression came in Eggleton's appearance before the Standing Committee on National Defence and Veterans Affairs in November 1999:

> In the darkest moments, when human security is undone by forces beyond the influence of development programs and diplomacy, there is but one tool that is left in the box and then we turn to the Canadian Forces. In places like Bosnia, Haiti, Kosovo, and now East Timor, Canadians expected their country to respond. They were concerned about crises that threatened international stability, human security, or both. They wanted the international community to take action and they wanted Canada to do its share. These expectations were met by the Canadian Forces. Without them, our response would have been limited to aid and political support. If Canadians want this country to have an impact on human security and help promote peace and stability, Canada will continue to need capable military forces. It is vital that we strike the right balance between soft power initiatives and hard power capabilities. This is crucial if we want to deliver on our good intentions

when the limits of diplomacy and aid are reached. . . . It's not a question of either/or. Canada must do both. Soft power when suitable, stronger means when required. (Standing Committee, 1999a)

The very next day, the Chief of the Defence Staff, General Maurice Baril, echoed these sentiments before the same committee, stating that in the pursuit of human security, the government should have in its 'tool kit' a military capable of participating in coercive operations. He added that hard and soft power 'both make critical contributions to the human security agenda, often as two sides to the same coin. Diplomacy in pursuit of human rights or the prevention of humanitarian catastrophes sometimes needs to be backed up by military capability' (Standing Committee, 1999b).

While the most important priority for the Canadian Forces in Kosovo was the protection of civilians, the timing of the NATO air campaign in some respects could not have been more propitious for National Defence. Here was an organization that had been hit hard by government downsizing; between 1993–4 and 1998–9, the defence budget had been cut by 30 per cent in real terms. The Canadian Forces were looking for an opportunity to prove their worth to the government and stop the bleeding. Kosovo was such an opportunity, a high-profile operation that could help portray the Forces as an indispensable tool of a major government policy. It was also an operation that required modern forces that could be put in harm's way to help defeat a capable enemy. If the government wanted the Forces to continue to play this kind of role, capability was clearly an issue. In the wake of Kosovo, such documents as the Chief of Defence Staff's annual report and the department's Report on Plans and Priorities placed emphasis on the Forces' expertise not only in peace enforcement, but also in peacekeeping and peace-building, democratic civil-military relations, military training assistance, demining, and humanitarian assistance. All were clear examples of the military's 'important role' in the government's efforts to advance a more secure world and promote human security. The government, it would seem, also began to make the connection. In the 1999 Speech from the Throne, human security figured prominently, and the government committed itself to giving the Canadian Forces the resources necessary to support this policy. In February 2000, National Defence received a much-needed budget increase of $2.3 billion over four years.

The NATO air campaign was a turning point for Canada's human security policy. Kosovo demonstrated that traditional military force was sometimes required in the pursuit of human security's principles and objectives—notably, to protect people as some of Axworthy's critics had argued. Soft power and hard (coercive) power were not contradictory but part of the same human security continuum, one with both civil and military dimensions. No one in government was suggesting that, given the experience in Kosovo, every humanitarian crisis should now lead to such military intervention. It would not be warranted in every circumstance and, indeed, the international community might not possess the ability to resolve every problem in every circumstance. In the case of Kosovo, however, NATO's decision to intervene militarily was the right one.

HUMAN SECURITY AND THE FUTURE OF THE CANADIAN FORCES

The evolution of human security policy over the past several years has inevitably raised questions about the military forces Canada requires to participate in operations around the globe. Some have suggested that a combat-capable, multi-purpose force as identified in the 1994 White Paper was not the right model for human security operations, the trend instead pointing to less expensive 'niche' forces, small and lightly armed, working in a low-risk environment and capable of co-operating closely with civilian organizations. One commentator stated in 1998 that the human security agenda 'represents a challenge of some magnitude to Canada's existing defence policy, force structure and (possibly) international relationships. At the very least, it adds further legitimacy to small, low-capability, limited flexibility formations that were acknowledged, assessed, and rejected in the process leading to the 1994 Defence White Paper. This is a force for change which advocates of a status quo defence policy will be hard pressed to resist' (Oliver, 1999: 4).

In the wake of the Kosovo air campaign and other recent missions in the Balkans and Africa, one could make an equally compelling argument that the general tenets of current defence policy are a perfect fit for Canada's human security agenda. Canada must maintain combat-capable and multi-purpose sea, land, and air forces (perhaps lighter but also more mobile and rapidly deployable and packing no less a punch) to carry out the spectrum of activities supporting human security, whether peacekeeping, humanitarian assistance, disaster relief, or outright war. The government must retain the option of providing hard-power elements to complement soft power in pursuit of human security objectives—and, of course, to respond to more traditional security concerns, which, while not on the horizon, have not disappeared (including potential interstate wars). In this respect, the Canada 21 option of constabulary forces, which has been lurking in the shadows ever since the 1994 White Paper, remains a non-starter. The equipment and training for this type of force, which would be capable only of low-end peacekeeping, would simply not suffice in current operational environments. Canada would be unable to participate in another Kosovo air campaign, or even in UN Chapter 7 operations like those in Bosnia, Africa, or East Timor. In addition, it would be impossible to contribute to the more robust peacekeeping forces called for in the August 2000 report on UN peace operations (the Brahimi Report). The response of our allies, who have already expressed concerns over Canada's current defence capability, is also crucial; one of the major reasons why Canada has traditionally had armed forces is to guard sovereignty and maintain national self-respect.

At the same time, the Forces will certainly continue to participate in missions at the other end of the spectrum that will not necessarily require military force per se. To do so, they need a full range of military equipment, including supply ships, helicopters, and non-lethal weapons, as well as engineering and medical equipment. It is worth remembering, too, that high-end military equipment and forces designed to destroy an enemy can also protect people from militaries or paramilitaries that have the same purpose. CF-18s, frigates, armoured vehicles, artillery, and heavily armed soldiers may be 'tools of violence', in the words of David Last, but they can also manage violence and support human security (Last, 1999: 8). In short, they can serve as an effective deterrent. Canada's military must therefore have forces that can work at both the high and low ends of the spectrum. The 1994 White Paper recognized this reality when it noted that 'it would be misguided to invest in very specific forces and capabilities, whether at the higher end of the scale . . . or at the lower end. . . . To opt for either approach would be to forego the capability and flexibility that are inherent in a multi-purpose force' (DND, 1994: 14).

Directly related to the concept of a fully flexible force is the requirement to remain interoperable with allies and potential partners. Canada will never act alone in responding to international crises. It has never been part of our foreign policy tradition, nor do we have the military capability to act unilaterally beyond our borders. It is essential, therefore, that the government maintains robust forces that can operate fully alongside our allies and partners, especially the United States, in responding rapidly to humanitarian and other emergencies. Maintaining these forces will allow Canada to make a meaningful contribution in a variety of human security operations. It will also improve our reputation among allies. National Defence has recognized this reality; its *Strategy for 2020* document places considerable emphasis on interoperability, including joint and combined operations (DND, 1999: 10).

Interoperability touches on a wide range of issues, including similar concepts of operations and compatible doctrine. However, the key will ultimately be equipment. Canada was able to make an important contribution to the NATO air campaign against the Federal Republic of Yugoslavia for a simple reason: its CF-18s were combat-capable and our pilots were able to operate with other allied air forces, despite some limitations in such areas as anti-jam radios and night-vision goggles (Eggleton, 1999; Ward, 2000; Clark, 1999). For this reason, the Forces must keep pace with technological change in the context of the 'revolution in military affairs', especially on the communications side. Technology will not only help at the high end of combat operations. Sophisticated military sensor systems can locate enemy positions, but they can also save civilian lives. For example, they could provide accurate ground intelligence in humanitarian crises by tracking refugee flows and locating bodies hidden under rubble (Leach, 1999: 4).

All of this leads to a simple conclusion: if the military is to continue an active role in supporting an activist foreign policy, the Canadian Forces must be modern and properly equipped. This has been a DND refrain in recent years in the face of budget cuts and an increased operational tempo. In 1998, the Auditor General identified a $4.5 billion shortfall in National Defence's equipment budget over five years. Since then, an increasing number of military analysts have questioned whether the Canadian Forces can meet their specific White Paper commitments and continue to do the other jobs expected of them (Jockel, 1999). Recent signs—especially the 2000 federal budget—are encouraging, and National Defence hopes to increase its capital budget to 23 per cent of the total budget over the next five years (from a current level of about 18 per cent) (DND, 1999: 9). The Forces have already made excellent progress in acquiring new equipment since 1994, including search-and-rescue helicopters, armoured personnel carriers, submarines, light armoured reconnaissance vehicles, planned CF-18 upgrades, and the 'Clothe the Soldier' program.[9] National Defence has made the credible argument that the Forces are, in fact, more combat-capable today than they were 10 years ago (DND, 2000: 21; Standing Committee, 1999a; Sallot, 1999). But no one would deny that difficult decisions lie ahead.

These larger questions aside, the Canadian military must keep pace with operations that continue to evolve at a rapid pace. It is a truism that military missions have changed since the end of the Cold War; they are undoubtedly more dangerous, more complex, more demanding. They increasingly take place in operational environments involving combat, with the potential for individual confrontation greater than ever. The political and cultural issues are also different. Together these circumstances pose a dizzying array of challenges for Canadian soldiers:

> Every day, these young soldiers, Canadian men and women, have to deal with real human security issues. Sometimes they struggle to identify which group individuals belong to, individuals who wear no distinctive mark or uniform. Deciding what behaviour to adopt, and anticipating the reactions of individuals under these circumstances are quite difficult and require a totally different type of training than what was the norm just a couple of years ago. (Leach, 1999: 3)

Perhaps most important of all, the Canadian Forces must be prepared to work with a wide range of organizations—other armed forces, local officials, civilian police such as the RCMP, the media, non-governmental organizations, and humanitarian agencies (from CARE Canada to Doctors without Borders)—that are virtually all trying to maintain law and order, preserve the peace, or provide emergency relief.

To do their jobs properly in these environments, the military must first be clear about its role in relation to these other groups. This has not always been the case. As indicated earlier, most specific human security roles cannot and should not be performed by armed forces unless in an emergency. Military forces are most effective at guaranteeing security against organized military opposition. Their primary role, therefore, should be to arrive on the scene first and help establish a secure and stable environment in which other peacebuilding activities can take place. Once these tasks are completed, the military can take its leave (sometimes easier said than done in places like the Balkans, where violence has become endemic). The Canadian Forces are not experts in relief and development or democratization. These are civilian issues that should not distract soldiers from their primary function. In most human security activities, non-governmental organizations should take the lead; they are not only less expensive, but they are specifically trained and designed to do the job. Indeed, in some cases, soldiers can actually interfere with the efforts of qualified civilians and even militarize a situation that may then take longer to stabilize (Last, 1999: 3). As the new American National Security Council Adviser, Condoleezza Rice, has said in a slightly different context, 'we don't need to have the 82nd airborne escorting kids to kindergarten' (Traub, 2000).

That said, the Canadian Forces will inevitably be called upon to do some peacebuilding tasks. In the early stages of a crisis, before civilian organizations have arrived on the scene in sufficient numbers, the military often has no choice but to rebuild infrastructure, deliver aid, monitor human rights, conduct investigations into traffic accidents, or assist civilian police in controlling riots and civil disturbances. However, these tasks must be transferred to civilians as quickly as possible. Although few in the military would suggest that these roles should be expanded, the Forces must be able to perform them if called on to do so. This means that they must continue to remain flexible at the operational and tactical levels, adapt their training and doctrine as required, and pursue innovative ideas to meet the challenges of modern peace operations.

The Canadian Forces are at the leading edge of training for these new operations in the areas of peacebuilding, conflict prevention, or humanitarian support. Much progress was made in the wake of the Somalia affair. For example, the Forces have placed greater emphasis on human rights and military law training, and have also provided more intensive cultural training prior to deployments. A doctrine manual specifically designed for missions in support of rebuilding nations ravaged by war or other disasters has been produced, and all soldiers now carry Rules of Engagement cards to remind them of their limits in exercising force. As well, the Forces are trying to improve how they interact with local populations and civilian organizations. As the Brahimi Report recently pointed out, military-civilian communications are essential in second-generation peacekeeping,

Relations with NGOs are admittedly a sensitive area. The relationship is marked by both co-operation and friction. On the military side, it is not easy to adapt to the vast number of NGOs active in the field, not to mention their competitiveness, conflicting agendas, and varying degrees of competence. But progress has been made. The Forces have established a number of civil-military co-operation cells, for example in 1 Canadian Division Headquarters and the Joint Task Force Headquarters. There are also plans to create cells in National Defence Headquarters and the Reserves. A civil-military co-operation manual was published in 1999 (Pollick, 2000: 57–63; Ward, 2000: 70–1).

Much of this training is not only indispensable for participating in peace missions, but it also has the potential to enhance other skills. For example, such training in policing and crowd control can improve the ability to operate in domestic law-and-order duties. At the same time, the Forces have had the chance to hone such traditional skills as command and control, communications, and logistics. All of this can improve the military's reputation with allies, as well as with the Canadian public (Hay and Rioux, 1999: 29–30).

The Forces have not only worked hard to train their own people to meet the demands of post-Cold War operations, but they have also done much to prepare other militaries. This is an area where the Canadian military has a particular strength. Canada possesses a professional, modern, and well-educated military that has much to offer by way of expertise in a variety of fields, including human security. It should continue in this vein, through the Canadian Forces College, Pearson Peacekeeping Centre, Royal Military College, the Democratic Civil-Military Relations Program, and the Military Training Assistance Program.

Canada is a leader in efforts to improve the UN's capacity to plan, co-ordinate, deploy, fund, and train for operations. These efforts have focused most recently on the international community's ability to deploy quickly and efficiently to trouble spots around the world to carry out peace and humanitarian operations. The Stand-by High Readiness Brigade (in co-operation with Denmark) and a roster of military personnel on call for immediate deployment to UN missions are just two examples. The Canadian Forces are also exploring possible options for enhanced sealift and airlift capabilities to respond more quickly to international crises, an area that the government has identified as crucial in any human security operation. All of these efforts deserve continued attention.

CONCLUSION

Canada's human security policy continues to evolve. Democratization, human rights, developmental aid, conflict prevention, governance, peacebuilding, and humanitarian assistance—they have long been part of Canadian foreign policy, and they are not about to disappear anytime soon.

In the 2000 budget, the government committed $10 million annually over five years to the human security program. Some of its key elements include the protection of civilians, peace support operations, and conflict prevention. As the government moves forward in these areas, it has a number of different tools at its disposal—both of the soft- and hard-power variety. An Interdepartmental Program Advisory Committee has been established to oversee the human security program, and it includes representation from DND. The Interdepartmental Committee will build on and increase consultation between departments. In particular, it should allow DND to provide more input to the strategy and ensure that the military has a defined role in human security. In a 1999 Foreign Affairs publication on human security, military force still warranted but one sentence (DFAIT, 1999: 8).[10] An even more recent publication devoted two pages to peace support operations, but with an emphasis on rapid deployment and the role of CIDA and civilians (DFAIT, 2000: 5–6).

The Canadian Forces are an important element of the government's human security policy. As Kosovo and other recent operations prove, the Forces can contribute to human security across a broad range of potential operations. The former Chief of the Land Staff has put the role of the military in context: 'Much has changed in recent years, and things will continue to change, but I have yet to see anything that would lead me to think that my profession and the people who sustain it are heading for redundancy anytime soon. . . . "Soft power" and "hard power" can both make critical contributions to the human security agenda' (Leach, 1999: 3–4).

The Canadian Forces will continue to be in demand. We may witness even more deployments in the future as human rights in failed states and other such issues grab the spotlight; human security, after all, is an interventionist policy,[11] and the Prime Minister has referred to Canada as the world's 'Boy Scout'. This is not to say that national interest no longer plays a role in the government decision-making process. The government realizes that national security and human security go hand in hand. Situations are never so easy that one simply 'checks the boxes' and makes an automatic decision. It is a complex process and each case needs to be examined on its relative merits, and DND, of course, has its own guidelines as to whether the military should intervene (DND, 1994: 29). Nonetheless, we can expect the Canadian Forces to remain relatively busy.

Can they continue to meet the demand? Responding to the flood of operations over the last decade has not been easy. Budget cuts, high operational tempo, and equipment rust-out have put the Forces in a difficult position. Resources remain thinly stretched; the military cannot be everywhere at once. The Minister of National Defence captured the essence of this issue in his appearance before the Standing Committee on National Defence and Veterans Affairs in November 1999: 'If we want to restore human security where it is most at threat, if we want to continue to contribute in the areas where Canada has made its mark over the past 50 years, we will need . . . a strong and well-equipped Canadian Forces. Investing in them is an investment in the future of Canada' (Standing Committee, 1999a).

NOTES

The author is a policy officer with the Department of National Defence. The views expressed in this article are entirely his own and do not necessarily reflect those of the department. The author would like to thank Daniel Bon, Marc Whittingham, Brooke Smith-Windsor, David Last, Robin Hay, and James Lee for their assistance in the preparation of this article.

1. See also Nossal (1999). Given his previous reference to 'the means to prevail over others', Nossal's use of the term 'peacekeeping missions' is curious. As Smith-Windsor (2000) has pointed out, he probably means enforcement in this context.
2. See Regehr (1999: 5), who argues that the Canadian Forces can carry out human security operations in the spectrum between 'peacekeeping and war'.
3. For further discussion of the full range of operations carried out by the Canadian Forces, see the 'Spectrum of Conflict' in DND (2000: 5).
4. For examples of Canadian Forces peacebuilding activities in the Balkans, see Wallace (2000: 23–6).

5. See Government of Canada (1999) for specific examples of this type of training assistance.
6. For a detailed discussion of some of the tasks carried out by the Canadian Forces in establishing a secure environment, see Simiana (1999: 14).
7. This portrayal of the Kosovo air campaign as a human security operation has had its share of critics. See, for example, Owens and Arneil (1999: 7); Regehr (1999: 5).
8. Heinbecker was apparently less reluctant than his minister to make the link between human security and military power, even before Kosovo in some cases. See, for example, Heinbecker (1999a, 1999b).
9. The Clothe the Soldier program is aimed at providing the Canadian army with new operational clothing and 'personal protective equipment'. It includes such items as cold weather clothing (i.e., sweatshirts, sweatpants, parkas, overalls), gloves, boots, thermal underwear, combat hats, ballistic eyewear (for protection against ultraviolet radiation), etc. The project should be completed by 2004–5.
10. The sentence reads: 'Ensuring human security can involve the use of coercive measures, including sanctions and military force.'
11. This issue has generated considerable debate in both academic and government circles. See Stairs (2000) for a recent assessment.

REFERENCES

Axworthy, Lloyd. 1997. 'Canada and Human Security: the Need for Leadership', *International Journal* 52, 2 (Spring): 183–96.
———. 1998a. 'Why "soft power" is the right policy for Canada', *Ottawa Citizen*, 25 Jan., B6.
———. 1998b. 'Notes for an Address by the Honourable Lloyd Axworthy to a Conference on UN Reform at the Kennedy School, Harvard University, "The New Diplomacy: the UN, the International Criminal Court, and the Human Security Agenda" ', 98/30. Cambridge, Mass., 25 Apr.
———. 1998c. 'Notes for an Address by the Honourable Lloyd Axworthy, Minister of Foreign Affairs, to the Canadian Institute of International Affairs 1998 Foreign Policy Conference', 98/67. Ottawa. 16 Oct.
———. 1999a. 'Notes for an Address by the Honourable Lloyd Axworthy, Minister of Foreign Affairs, to the National Forum', 99/4. Montreal, 22 Jan.
———. 1999b. 'Notes for an Address by the Honourable Lloyd Axworthy, Minister of Foreign Affairs, to the Woodrow Wilson School of Public and International Relations, Princeton University, "Kosovo and the Human Security Agenda" '. 99/28. Princeton, NJ, 7 Apr.
Bashow, D., et al. 2000. 'Mission Ready: Canada's Role in the Kosovo Air Campaign', *Canadian Military Journal* 1, 1 (Spring): 55–61.
Belzile, C. 2000. 'The Broader Aspects of Human Security', letters to the editor, *Canadian Military Journal* 1 2 (Summer): 3.
Bland, D. 1999. 'A Sow's Ear from a Silk Purse: Abandoning Canada's Military Capabilities', *International Journal* 54, 1 (Winter 1998–9): 143–74.

Chrétien, J. 1999. Speech by the Prime Minister of Canada To a Luncheon of the Canadian Club of Winnipeg, Winnipeg, 25 Mar.

Clark, C. 1999. 'Campaign in Kosovo Highlights Allied Interoperability Shortfalls', *Defense News*, 16 Aug.

Department of Foreign Affairs and International Trade (DFAIT). 1999. *Human Security: Safety for People in a Changing World*. Ottawa, Apr.

———. 2000. *Freedom from Fear: Canada's Foreign Policy for Human Security*. Ottawa, Sept.

Department of National Defence (DND). 1994. 1994 Defence White Paper.

———. 1999. *Shaping the Future of Canadian Defence: A Strategy for 2020*. June.

———. 2000. *Building on a Stronger Foundation: Annual Report of the Chief of the Defence Staff, 1999–2000*.

Eggleton, Art. 1999. 'Speaking Notes for the Honourable Art Eggleton, Minister of National Defence, on "Canadian Lessons from the Kosovo Crisis" '. Harvard University, Cambridge, Mass., 30 Sept.

Government of Canada. 1999. News Release No. 237, 'Canada Announces $100 Million in New Initiatives for Kosovo and the Balkans', 1 Nov.

Hampson, Fen Osler, and Dean F. Oliver. 1998. 'Pulpit Diplomacy: A Critical Assessment of the Axworthy Doctrine', *International Journal* 53, 3 (Summer): 379–406.

Havel, V. 1999. 'Kosovo and the End of the Nation-State', an Address delivered to the Canadian Parliament, 29 Apr., reprinted in *New York Review of Books*, 10 June, 4–5.

Hay, R., and Jean-François Rioux. 1999. *Human Security and National Defence*. D Strat A Project Report No. 9916, Sept.

Heinbecker, P. 1999a. 'Human Security', *Canadian Foreign Policy* 7, 1 (Fall): 19–25.

———. 1999b. 'Human Security', *Behind the Headlines* 26, 2: 4–9.

———. 2000. 'Human Security: The Hard Edge', *Canadian Military Journal* 1, 1 (Spring): 11–16.

Jockel, J. 1999. *The Canadian Forces: Hard Choices, Soft Power*. Toronto: Canadian Institute of Strategic Studies.

Last, D. 1999. 'The Military Contribution to Human Security', Notes for a Presentation to the Club of Rome Association, Ottawa, 3 June.

Leach, W. 1999. 'CF Perspectives on Human Security', Talking Points for a Presentation to the 1999 Atlantic Canada Diplomatic Forum, St John's, 5 Nov.

Nossal, Kim Richard. 1998. 'Foreign Policy for Wimps', *Ottawa Citizen*, 23 Apr., A19.

———. 1999. 'Pinchpenny Diplomacy', *International Journal* 54, 1 (Winter 1998–9): 88–105.

Nye, Joseph, Jr. 1990. *Bound to Lead: The Changing Nature of American Power*. New York: Basic Books.

———. 1999a. 'The Challenge of Soft Power', *Time*, 22 Feb.

———. 1999b. 'Redefining the National Interest', *Foreign Affairs* (July-Aug.): 22–35.

———, with Robert O. Keohane. 1998. 'Power and Independence in the Information Age', *Foreign Affairs* (Sept.-Oct.): 81–94.

Oliver, D. 1999. 'Soft Power and Canadian Defence', Canadian Institute of Strategic Studies, Strategic Datalink #76, Feb.

Owens, H., and Barbara Arneil. 1999. 'The Human Security Paradigm Shift: A New Lens on Canadian Foreign Policy', *Canadian Foreign Policy* 7, 1 (Fall): 1–12.

Pollick, S. 2000. 'Civil-Military Cooperation: A New Tool for Peacekeepers', *Canadian Military Journal* 1, 3 (Autumn): 57–63.

Regehr, E. 1999. 'Defence and Human Security', *The Ploughshares Monitor* (Dec.): 2–6.

Ross, D. 1997. 'Canada and the World at Risk: Depression, War and Isolationism for the 21st Century?', *International Journal* 52, 1 (Winter 1996–7): 1–24.

Sallot, J. 1999. 'Forces take aim at lowly reputation', *Globe and Mail*, 10 Mar.

Simiana, J. 1999. 'CCSFOR Soldiers in Bosnia', *Vanguard* no. 4: 13–7.

Smith-Windsor, Brooke. 2000. 'Hard Power, Soft Power Reconsidered', *Canadian Military Journal* 1, 3 (Autumn): 51–6.

Stairs, D. 2000. 'Canadian Foreign Policy and Interventions Abroad', paper delivered to Institute on Research for Public Policy Conference, 'Challenges to Governance: Military Interventions Abroad and Consensus at Home', 17–19 Nov.

Standing Committee on National Defence and Veterans Affairs. 1999a. Evidence, 24 Nov.

———. 1999b. Evidence, 25 Nov.

Traub, J. 2000. 'W's World', *New York Times Magazine*, 14 Jan.

Trickey, M. 1999. '"Hard power" NATO win only way to retain credibility', *Ottawa Citizen*, 7 Apr., A4.

Wallace, S. 2000. 'CIDA in the Balkans', *Vanguard* no. 6: 23–6.

Ward, M. 2000. 'Task Force Kosovo: Adapting Operations to a Changing Security Environment', *Canadian Military Journal* 1, 1 (Spring): 67–74.

Part One

Assessing the Record

4

The Axworthy Revolution

NORMAN HILLMER AND ADAM CHAPNICK

Canada's style in foreign policy, the noted analyst James Eayrs has asserted, is the antithesis of revolution. Believing that problems can be managed or ameliorated, but not solved permanently, Canadians do not indulge in doctrines, spectacular gestures, or the long view. As Eayrs puts it, 'There has been little in Canadian experience to encourage the expectation that injuries to society may be healed in the same fashion and with the same hope of success as a machine is repaired or an appendix removed. It is the Canadian style to try to garden in the field of politics, not to dam or dredge' (Eayrs, 1961: 153–4). Careful, patient, compromising, flexible, workaday—these have been the watchwords of Ottawa diplomacy.

Not any more, or at least not recently. During his five years as Minister of Foreign Affairs, Lloyd Axworthy unleashed an ambitious doctrine of intrusive internationalism, transforming the tone and character of Canadian foreign policy. Axworthy's Canada was no longer 'a small, poky player on the international scene', a *New York Times* correspondent declared (DePalma, 1999). For the *Washington Post*, he was 'a moralizing foreign minister from a middle-power country', crusading for a 'touchy-feely approach to international relations that emphasizes negotiation over confrontation, "human security" over national security and the power of ideas over the power of weapons.' Moving 'boldly—some would say presumptuously—on the world stage', Axworthy seemed not to 'understand that Canada's foreign minister is supposed to walk softly and carry a little stick' (Pearlstein, 1999).

The Axworthy Revolution claimed that Canada could 'shape the world of the next century for the better', a comprehensive assertion of international moral leadership no Foreign Minister before him would have contemplated (Axworthy and Taylor, 1998: 203). On his watch, and untrammelled by close prime ministerial supervision, human security came to dominate the rhetoric and flavour of policy in a manner unprecedented in the Canadian experience.[1] Bidding farewell to 'Lloyd Axworthy: Man of Peace', the Winter 2001 issue of *Canada World View*, the official magazine of the Department of Foreign Affairs and International Trade (DFAIT), concentrated almost exclusively on the promotion of 'human priorities' in international relations. Canada's foreign policy took on the look and feel of single-issue politics.

Axworthy, moreover, changed the way policy was made and promoted. He systematically sought out and involved the elements of civil society, broadening Canada's foreign policy constituency and increasing exponentially the number of participating actors (see Chapter 13 by Van Rooy). He was also a shrewd tactician in the use of the non-governmental organization (NGO) community to do some of the heavy lifting on his issues. 'Being able to help mobilize civil groups behind various initiatives is a very productive use of our time and resources', he told the *Ottawa Citizen* late in his tenure (Trickey, 2000a). 'Canadian foreign policy has become a non-governmental organization', a senior Danish diplomat exclaimed at the end of 2000,[2] suggesting the extent to which Axworthyism had become linked to civil society.

If the rationale was human security, the instrument was Canada itself. Shortly after he left office, Axworthy told a CBC interviewer that the idea animating his diplomacy was very simple: 'it's that the risk to individuals is as important as the risk to nation-states. In today's world', he went on, 'I thought that Canada in particular had a special role to play simply because of who we are.' Canada was a country of rights, and identified itself as such; it was vital to express those values to the world, using 'our talents and our abilities and our resources to extend them'. When the tough questions about international roles and responsibilities were asked of Canadians, there had to be 'some basis for saying that we are all God's children, that there is some fundamental universal jurisdiction that we all have to honour' (Petrie, 2000).

The old way was the wrong way. If power politics and the competition of national interests were the sole criteria for international action, then 'the conservatives and reactionaries' would reject intervention in the internal problems of foreigners as 'none of our business'. 'Well, I can't do that as a practising Christian', said Axworthy, 'because it doesn't matter to me if a child is a Tutsi child from Rwanda or a child from a reserve in Manitoba, they still deserve the same respect and the same care and concern' (ibid.). The Axworthy foreign policy agenda flowed directly from this Christian perspective.

Axworthy did not invent the human security issue, although his relentless pursuit of it often made it seem completely his own. The impulses were everywhere, embedded in Canadian diplomatic history and practice, the post-Cold War transformation of the international environment, the priorities of DFAIT itself, and what political scientist Kim Richard Nossal describes as 'the culture of contemporary organizational leadership . . . that impels those who occupy leadership positions to take the initiative—any initiative' (Nossal, 2000: 7). Rising to a crescendo from the dying Cold War in 1990 through the interventionist fever of 1992–3, human security was implicit in the external policy of the Mulroney government. Instead of Axworthy's 'new diplomacy', External Affairs Secretary Barbara McDougall championed a 'new internationalism' of a similar oratorical ilk, where peoples' dignity mattered as much as, if not more than, state sovereignty (Hillmer and Oliver, 2001). McDougall's departmental advisers had a good deal to do with such notion-building.

Upon his appointment as Deputy Minister of Foreign Affairs in mid-1994, Gordon Smith began to assemble an expertise in the broad nexus of non-traditional security challenges he diagnosed as 'global' in scope. When Axworthy replaced André Ouellet as minister in early 1996, there was an active Global Issues Bureau waiting for him within

DFAIT, an institutional innovation of the Chrétien government's 1995 policy statement, *Canada in the World*. It had argued that the concept of security in international relations was evolving to incorporate the 'economic, social, and political needs of the individual' (Malone, 1999: 197–201; DFAIT, 1995).

Axworthy gave 'humanist activism' (Lee, 2000: 1) policy thrust and political saliency. Seldom have a minister and his message fit so naturally. As John English demonstrates in this volume, Axworthy came of political age in the 1960s, when nuclear weapons, military alliances, and American hegemony were concerns of the left and his concerns. He was a Canadian nationalist, campaigned against the Vietnam War, and began to develop ideas about the need to democratize public policy through the use of rapidly evolving technology. Travelling from the United States to a teaching position at the University of Winnipeg, he was commissioned by the government of Ontario's Committee on Productivity in 1971 to study the potential impact of communications technology on citizen participation in provincial affairs. He concluded that good government was informed government, and that officials should therefore make extensive use of the new media to improve their understanding of the needs of the electorate (Axworthy, 1971). Technology, he argued, could and should form the basis of new institutions dedicated to promoting a true people's government.

In preparation for the 1993 federal election, Axworthy—by now chair of the Liberal caucus on foreign affairs and national defence and Liberal critic for External Affairs—wrote the *Liberal Foreign Policy Handbook*. A summary of his thoughts on foreign affairs and an articulation of the party's platform, it took note of the decline of the absolute sovereignty of the state and the opportunity created by the end of the Cold War for progress in the promotion of human rights. A more independent Canadian foreign policy would be activist, inclusive, and grounded in an expanded concept of security beyond (and despite) borders and military might to include such issues as environmental protection and the alleviation of world poverty. As a state recognized for its forward thinking on social freedom, Canada was a natural leader in the redefinition of the international community's humanitarian agenda. Axworthy also argued in favour of a democratization of the foreign policy process to include a wider range of actors and to reflect more accurately national needs and concerns (Axworthy, 1993).

Following on this analysis, Axworthy as Foreign Minister and politician set out deliberately to expose his thinking in the written and spoken word, to attract and retain attention, to involve and proselytize. Like those of his hero, Lester B. Pearson, Axworthy's speeches and public pronouncements are an indispensable guide to the quite striking evolution of his ideas. Like Pearson, too, but uncommonly for a politician of the 1990s, Axworthy was intimately connected to the preparation, writing, and editing of what he said and what was said in his name. But the Pearsonian ethos was grounded primarily in interests, not values, and Pearson himself would never have suggested that war-affected children or victims of rape in faraway lands were the direct responsibility of Canadians or their government.

Once minister, Axworthy immediately hinted at dramatic changes to Canada's approach to foreign relations. Speaking in Geneva to the UN Commission on Human Rights in April 1996, he argued passionately for 'a new agenda around the definition of individual security'. State borders had become 'porous', national defence was of diminishing importance, and members of civil society—from the private sector, non-governmental organizations, or the general public—had begun 'contacting each other directly and shaping the agenda of their governments' to focus more strongly on the prevention of human suffering. Foreign policy was not simply the safe haven of diplomats, and vital decisions ought not to be taken without consultation with those individuals affected by them. As the power of civil society increased, human rights concerns, such as terrorism, the dissemination of hate literature, and the violation of the rights of children, would become even more central issues. 'Let us move the system', pleaded Axworthy, 'from one that is based solely around the interests, priorities and responsibilities of states, to one that responds to those of the citizenry as well.' As a concerned nation, Canada pledged to contribute by example. It would 'continue to work on the domestic front to eliminate violence and discrimination', and would maintain its active support of UN initiatives in collaboration with the Office of the High Commissioner for Human Rights (Axworthy, 1996d).

'Foreign Policy at a Crossroad', Axworthy called his first major report to the Standing Committee on Foreign Affairs and International Trade (Axworthy, 1996b). He cited 'four critical developments' on Canada's political landscape that made 'the creation of a coherent, integrated and focused foreign policy all the more important, yet challenging': the 'domestication' of foreign policy, as the line between foreign and domestic affairs blurred permanently; the proliferation of global bodies in an increasingly interdependent world community; the mounting international demand on Canadian resources; and the prospect of a reduction in the DFAIT budget to combat the federal deficit. In ranking future priorities, the protection of Canadians abroad came first, followed by the promotion of international trade to stimulate domestic employment and the defence of Canadian interests. Support for human rights, with an emphasis on Canada's leadership in the area of hate crimes—a subject he had mentioned in Geneva—came a lowly fourth, and was followed by other 'individual security' concerns such as international development, United Nations (UN) reform, peacekeeping, and youth outreach. Individual security priorities, or 'central missions', did outrank some of the more traditional security issues, but they remained clearly secondary.

For now, then, the official line did not stray from what had come to be expected: a healthy Chrétien government celebration of 'the instinct to stay home, cultivating one's own garden' (Cohen, 1995: 2). The surge of humanist activism in Axworthy foreign policy still lay in the future. As much as he might have believed that the world had changed, the minister had little to point to that would warrant a complete reorganization of the Canadian agenda. Canada seemed comfortable as a passive player in international politics—it supported humanitarian causes, but was more concerned with the health of its own economy. The failure of Axworthy's argument for a new focus to make an immediate impact on the policy level calls into question later accusations that the minister's human approach to foreign affairs was motivated primarily by national economic self-interest (Hampson and Oliver, 1998: 388; Nossal, 1998–9: 89), or that it was a deliberate diversion from the trade-centred policies of the Chrétien administration (Pearlstein, 1999). A government committed to limiting expenditures should have embraced Axworthy's humanism as an opportunity to justify reductions in strategic spending. But human security was not yet Canadian; it was merely Axworthyian, and the enthusiastic personal determination of the Foreign Minister had yet to take hold.

When Axworthy spoke at the 51st General Assembly of the United Nations in September 1996, what he called 'the new human security agenda' was indeed still new and its terminology was fluctuating. What had been 'individual security' before the UN Commission on Human Rights he now referred to as 'sustainable human security'. This linked sustainable development with human security directly, two ideas that had been seen as distinct four months before. The speech attempted to encapsulate such diverse issues as human rights, health, the rights of the child, and the recently added themes of education and food security under one unifying rubric. Changes in the lexicon and continuing adjustments to the meaning of human security suggest that, for Axworthy, it was still more idea than policy. The 'human security agenda', he said vaguely, would combine 'the need to husband natural resources, to generate growth and to ensure equity and peace'. The UN needed a 'new tool-kit . . . to respond to a variety of different situations' (Axworthy, 1996c).

To argue that the minister spoke or acted inconsistently in these early years is to ignore the innovation in his approach to foreign policy development. Axworthy himself had yet to determine how his vision could be translated into action and, instead of attempting to impose his still underdeveloped ideas, he used public addresses to generate dialogue and spark international interest. It was a process explicitly designed to make foreign policy more accessible, and involved Canadian publics in a way unheard of in the past.

In its preliminary stages, human security combined revolutionary high-minded idealism with pragmatic economic realism. Assuming, as Axworthy did, that the end of the Cold War could be equated with a dramatic decrease in transnational threats to world peace, the relative significance of traditional 'high' security issues (such as arms control and disarmament) could be reassessed. In this new environment, the nobler ideals of self-empowerment and self-sufficiency could and must be given greater attention. To make this happen, states ought to strive for economic prosperity by reducing expenditures on expensive instruments of high policy and refocusing available resources so they could best benefit individuals and communities.

Expansion in the use of the Internet and information technology in the mid-1990s gave Axworthy even greater confidence in his assessment of the state of international affairs. Individuals could exploit intelligence and resources previously available only to governments. Armed with this information, they were better able to insist that their concerns be heard. The combination of universal access to information and instruments of mass communication demanded a democratization of the foreign policy process (Axworthy, 1996a).

In such an interconnected and interdependent world, Axworthy told the National Forum on Foreign Policy in Winnipeg in December 1996, Canada was 'well placed to wield . . . "soft power" . . . the international influence that knowledge, information and an attractive set of values confer.' Canadian values were consistent with respect for individual rights, and 'the new international landscape', which assigned less importance to military strength, would make Canada's powers of moral suasion increasingly important. As he would say continuously over the next four months, Canada was a 'global power', a 'value-added nation', an 'honest broker', and a coalition-builder. It could use soft power to respond to pressing human security issues such as child labour and landmines, refugee flows, trade in illegal drugs, and the spread of disease (Axworthy, 1996a, 1997b).

With the introduction of 'soft power', Axworthy reassessed Canadian activism in international relations. In earlier speeches, he had spoken of leadership by example, and pledged to work in explicit partnership with the UN. Now, however, Canada planned to use its influence to play a more interventionist role outside of its borders, and references to the significance of the UN infrastructure had been reduced sharply. The meaning of 'human security'—no longer 'sustainable human security'—had also changed. Axworthy added landmine pollution and refugee flows to his list of concerns, two issues generating Canadian public concern. Food security, recently introduced, was now apparently abandoned (Axworthy, 1997b).

True to his commitment to increase public dialogue and global acceptance of human security, he titled his 1997 *International Journal* article 'Canada and Human Security: The Need for Leadership'. Drawing from a vision he had articulated in the *Liberal Foreign Policy Handbook*, Axworthy promoted a leadership role for Canada framed in morality and national values. He again proposed that the end of the Cold War had necessitated a reassessment of traditional approaches to the concept of security, the rights of individuals having increased in importance. This interpretation of security took on a variety of forms. It was keeping and building peace, banning anti-personnel landmines, assessing the value of international aid projects, and promoting the rights of children and economic development (Axworthy, 1997a: 185–90). It was everything but military influence.

As a middle power, Canada was suited perfectly to a world order that stressed human development over violence and favoured soft persuasion to hard coercion. Along with Norway and the Netherlands, two like-minded countries, it could use its disproportionate mediatory capabilities to leverage a leadership role in shaping the international agenda. Canadian specialties such as networking and coalition-building could have a greater impact in a foreign policy process that involved all members of civil society.

Axworthy's concept of leadership was being clarified. Canada would use its recognized ability in 'forging consensus' (ibid., 183) to minimize the need for the international community to resort to violent means of conflict management. Focusing intently on the proliferation of, and opportunities created by, information technology, he believed Canada could 'develop innovative foreign policy tools' to project influence abroad. Canada would not ignore the North Atlantic Treaty Organization (NATO), or the UN for that matter, but 'issue-based coalitions [would] become as important to the management of Canadian foreign policy as the alliance structure once was' (ibid., 193). Like-minded countries, whatever their traditional affiliations, and transnational actors from civil society could contribute to Canadian foreign policy in ways once reserved exclusively for aligned states. In this 'softer' system, Canada could play a role once filled only by great powers.

Axworthy's 1997 UN speech made the basis of human security as an international agenda item explicit: 'the breakdown of the old bipolar world affords new opportunities for civil society to influence multilateral diplomacy' (Axworthy, 1997e). There was also a 'growing feeling, coming from the grass roots of civil society, that the engines of war designed for the 20th century have no place in the 21st.' The initiative to eliminate landmines, an increasingly predominant Axworthy theme (Axworthy, 1997a, 1997b), was just one example of the strength of civil society. Because of this, argued the minister, 'the concept of human security . . . takes on a growing relevance.' Human security was clearly not new, it had simply become more germane and important.

For the first time, the Foreign Minister announced three distinct sets of human security priorities: confronting transnational issues such as landmines; addressing the root causes of conflict; and improving international responses to crises (Axworthy, 1997e). His organization of these issues under specific headings was novel, and reflected a more concrete understanding of the applications of human security.

Dejected by the slow progress of the UN's Conference on Disarmament and the accompanying Convention on Certain Conventional Weapons, Canada had joined a global coalition of state and non-state actors to ban anti-personnel landmines in January 1996. This thrust rejected the traditional means of international conflict resolution in favour of an ad hoc, inclusive, non-state-centred process. In October state representatives, NGOs, and other interested members of civil society were invited to a conference in Ottawa. At its conclusion, Axworthy issued a controversial proposal challenging the delegates of over 50 countries and 24 observer states to return to the Canadian capital in December 1997 with a treaty banning landmines in place. Canada was taking a leadership role in promoting the rights of individuals in war-affected countries through a broad association of actors. Success would prove that an international initiative could be undertaken and achieved without either great-power leadership or UN support.

After a series of meetings and multilateral consultations, in September 1997 the text of a treaty proposing a total ban on antipersonnel mines was adopted in Oslo, Norway. In December, it was signed in Ottawa.[3] The speed and results of the process were unexpected. Axworthy's vision of an innovative diplomatic order, one that incorporated government and civil society and was not dependent on great-power consent, had been given dramatic and concrete expression.

Along with DFAIT officer Sarah Taylor, the minister reported back to the academic community in a second *International Journal* article, published in the spring of 1998. Not only should the Ottawa Process be considered a victory in its own right, they argued, but it also proved that the nature of global politics had been transformed. Human security and the rights of the individual had triumphed; soft power had been used effectively; and a framework for international humanitarian law was demonstrably necessary (Axworthy and Taylor, 1998).

The Ottawa Process had been mentioned only briefly in Axworthy's 1997 address to the 52nd session of the UN General Assembly (Axworthy, 1997e). It had received similar treatment in the first *International Journal* article (1997a). Even at the Oslo NGO Forum on Banning Anti-Personnel Landmines in September 1997,

the minister had only been speaking of a beginning to his 'new foreign policy agenda' (1997f). In the Axworthy-Taylor article, however,
total victory was declared: 'The basic unit of analysis has shrunk from
the state to the community and even the individual. At the same time,
to tackle effectively problems that ignore state boundaries, the field
of action has expanded from the state to the region and even the
globe.' Human security, which privileged the needs of the individual
ahead of the state, had emerged as the unifying concept of the post-
Cold War order. Countries not generally known for their great-power
leadership were no longer 'simply acting as mediators; we were setting the agenda and providing international leadership' (Axworthy
and Taylor, 1998: 191, 193).

With the increasing importance of soft power, societies and
economies driven by military capabilities had lost some of their prestige. The success of traditionally less powerful international actors—
such as smaller powers and NGOs—in furthering their interests
through the Ottawa Process proved this. Canada's role was particularly influential. Balance-of-power realists were confronted head on
and were condemned for failing to accept the evidence of changes
to the international landscape. 'In a world where foreign ministers sit
down to discuss global warming, hate propaganda, and child labour,'
Axworthy wrote, 'it is clear that zero-sum applications of hard power
are not going to solve all the problems we face' (ibid., 202).

After two years of defining, theorizing, and promoting, Axworthy
had a palpable issue upon which to base his understanding of human
security, an idea that validated his analysis of the current state of
international relations and of Canada's proper role in the global community. With a real achievement to his credit, he had moved the
human security agenda from the theoretical level to the practical. In
a similar vein, he soon signed the Lysøen Declaration, committing
Canada and Norway to work together to promote human security and
good governance (DFAIT, 1998; Axworthy and Vollebaek, 1998).
Again, Canada worked outside of the UN and without explicit great-
power support. Human security had been one of many issues in
Axworthy's original addresses to the Canadian and international public. By 1998, it had become the dominant one.

Having been challenged so aggressively, it was inevitable that
those who disagreed with Axworthy's interpretation would respond.
In fact, there had been criticism well before the Ottawa Process
ended. In the fall of 1997, Axworthy defended the human security

agenda against charges of moral arrogance and naïve idealism. Canada, he argued, had 'never claimed to be the world's conscience. But we have come to be regarded internationally, on the basis of our record, as motivated by conscience as well as by interest.' The 'principled pragmatism' that shaped foreign policy met Canada's needs and reflected Canadian values (Axworthy, 1997c).

Axworthy had also rejected accusations that Canada responded to international violations of human rights selectively and inconsistently, choosing to act only when its political and economic interests would not be compromised. Humanitarian situations had to be considered individually, he explained, and Canadian responses varied accordingly. While these critiques might have placed the minister on the defensive, redemption had come through the Ottawa Process. The end of the Cold War created room for practical altruism. Human security was not a solution to all of the world's problems, but it was making tangible progress (Axworthy, 1997d, 1997g).

A second round of criticism would prove more challenging—and irritating. The flashy headline of an *Ottawa Citizen* article written by a prominent academic commentator described the Axworthy strategy as 'Foreign Policy for Wimps'. Kim Richard Nossal declared soft power a 'squishy notion', although admittedly 'great for the sloganeering that seems to be the mark of contemporary statecraft'. Axworthy was encouraging the notion that foreign policy could be done 'on the cheap' and implicitly justifying reductions in government expenditure on the foreign service, international development assistance, the armed forces, and intelligence services. 'After all, if soft power is the order of the day, who needs the expensive tools of traditional hard power.' But it was hard power that truly protected Canada's interests. Soft power could only be used successfully when others were already willing to be influenced (Nossal, 1998: A19).

The minister responded with his famous temper, more annoyed perhaps by the sensational charge of wimpishness because he was then being criticized in the military for insufficient attention to the hard end of the power equation. He accused Nossal and his fellow academics of losing touch with the changing nature of international relations and expressed pride in his defence of the national interest. By redefining international norms and improving international institutions, Canada was contributing positively and substantially to global peace and safety (Axworthy, 1998). Human security was more than just Canada's foreign policy agenda: it was Axworthy's own, and there was an air of wounded and improvised proprietorship about the reply. Nevertheless, it was surprising to find a fervent supporter of the democratization of the foreign policy process reacting so negatively to unfavourable comments, particularly when he had faced many of these same observations before. That his superiors had reduced his budget was indisputable; however, Nossal seemed to be hinting at a government strategy to present this reduction as beneficial to Canadians, with the minister appearing less a misguided idealist and more a stereotypically manipulative politician. By contrast, Axworthy saw himself as deeply and idealistically committed to doing the best he could with the resources available to him.

Foreign policy was a hot topic, by Axworthy's own design, and he was the most controversial minister in recent memory. A further charge was of blatant hypocrisy. How, asked journalist Mike Trickey (1998), could the country express a commitment to official development assistance while the federal government decreased its budget (as a percentage of GDP) for foreign aid?[4] To others, Axworthy's assessment of the international environment was simply wrong. Military power had not declined in importance, nor had interstate conflict subsided (Hampson and Oliver, 1998: 381–5). His policies, moreover, were condemned as ineffective, not least because his approach to world affairs often seemed a thinly veiled anti-Americanism in a world and on a continent where the United States was indispensable (Vincent, 2000). Analysts wondered, Trickey reported, 'why the federal government so often tweaks the Americans, be it on land-mines [or] Cuba' (Trickey, 1998).

Disappointed Canadians—and irate Americans—thus condemned an approach to foreign policy that apparently sought to minimize commitments while maximizing prestige. Axworthy was in the dock for moralizing arrogance. His concept of human security was so vague and broad that it covered virtually any foreign policy initiative, justifying Axworthy's triumphs and hiding his failures. The Foreign Minister was a poor relative of the Minister of Finance in a hard age, and there was simply no wallet to give meaning to the words. Axworthy practised a 'pulpit diplomacy' (Hampson and Oliver, 1998), a 'pinchpenny diplomacy' (Nossal, 1998–9) characterized by selectivity, conditionality, and opportunism (Rioux and Hay, 1998–9).

Axworthy did not change his approach. Canada chaired a 1998 conference aimed at the establishment of a world criminal court; the United States was one of seven holdout nations at the gathering

(*Economist*, 2000: 40). With Canada's election to a two-year term on the UN Security Council, Axworthy pledged that Canada would maintain its pursuit of the human security agenda there. The government would, for example, 'seek opportunities for the Council to draw more systematically on the views and insights of NGOs and other civil society actors with direct experience on the ground' (Axworthy, 1999c).

At the same time, Axworthy integrated many of the commentaries and criticisms into a revised platform. Substituting the concept of 'evolution' for 'change', he explained: 'The nature of threats to global security is evolving. Traditional military conflicts remain a concern. But the risks posed by others, often multifaceted and transnational, have sharpened.' No longer was the importance of the military downplayed: 'These new threats require that we see security increasingly in terms of human, rather than state, needs. This is not to say that traditional state-based security concerns are obsolete. Indeed, human security and national security are not mutually exclusive. On the contrary, they are opposite sides of the same global security coin.' Most significantly, in listing Canada's human security priorities, including a discussion of 'soft power' and 'new tools', he concluded: 'Finally, using robust action—when necessary. Let there be no mistake. Promoting human security can involve the use of strong measures including sanctions and military force' (ibid.).

When NATO moved against Slobodon Milosevic in Kosovo, therefore, Axworthy was ready with a rationale. Part of it was another rebuke to the UN, 'emasculated' by the veto possessed by every permanent member of the Security Council; Canada was forced to search for an international organization that could act as a 'functional equivalent' when there was no consensus of the great powers (Blanchfield, 1999: A10). But the heart of the argument, coming from a politician who had opposed Canadian participation in the Persian Gulf War, was the justification of military intervention on the grounds of human security imperatives. NATO's air campaign served to dispel the misconception that military force and the human security agenda were mutually exclusive. At Princeton's Woodrow Wilson School of Public and International Relations on 7 April 1999, Axworthy declared that the alliance's response to Milosevic's terror demonstrated 'how human security has become a force for global action. NATO is engaged in Kosovo to restore human security to the Kosovars' (Axworthy, 1999e). 'It's a robust Christianity you sometimes have to practise in politics', he mused soon after his retirement (Petrie, 2000).

Kosovo, moreover, symbolized for Axworthy how the world had turned his way, with human security having moved to the centre of the international community's attention and concern. The decision to fight was not motivated by a military threat to NATO territory but by 'an affront to Alliance values' and a conviction that individuals were paying the heaviest price from the rise in intrastate conflict and the failure of states, and from compact, readily available weapons of modern warfare. Axworthy even went so far as to align NATO's establishment 50 years before with the four freedoms of the World War II allies: the freedoms from want and fear, and the freedoms to worship and assemble peacefully. 'These are individual freedoms, not collective freedoms; their focus is on the rights of people, not states' (Axworthy, 1999e).

DFAIT continued its attempts to broaden the scope of the policy process by publishing the 1999 document, *Human Security: Safety for People in a Changing World*. The concept paper was developed 'to provide a definition of human security, to set out the rationale for a human security approach, and to clarify its relationship to national security and to human development'. It argued that, over the last two years, 'the concept of human security has increasingly centred on the human costs of violent conflict.' While consistent with Axworthy's most recent speeches, this statement demonstrated a marked change from Geneva in 1996. Human security was now 'like other security concepts—national security, economic security, food security', as opposed to including them. It was 'not synonymous with humanitarian action', although it certainly had been in the past. And this time there was a concrete means of differentiation: 'The litmus test for determining if it is useful to frame an issue in human security terms is the degree to which the safety of the people is at risk.'

The paper listed six specific foreign policy applications for human security, illustrating how much clearer the concept had become. Gone were 'soft power' and 'tool kits', and in their place 'freedom from fear and freedom from want' had come to represent the goals of Canadian foreign policy.

In May 1999, the minister was in Lysøen, Norway, for a meeting of what would become known as the Human Security Network. Representatives from the governments of Australia, Canada, Chile, Ireland, Jordan, the Netherlands, Slovenia, Switzerland, Thailand, and Norway (along with South Africa in the capacity of observer) met for two days and reaffirmed their commitment to 'a humane world where

people can live in security and dignity, free from poverty and despair
. . . [and where] every individual would be guaranteed freedom from
fear and freedom from want, with an equal opportunity to develop
their human potential' (Vollebaek, 1999).

The Network's agenda included a set of challenges and responses
to 10 specific issues: anti-personnel landmines; small arms; children
in armed conflict; international humanitarian and human rights law;
an international criminal court; the exploitation of children; the safety
of humanitarian personnel; conflict prevention; transnational organized crime; and resources for development. It aimed to function as
a unit promoting the work of international organizations, NGOs, and
civil society seeking to prevent threats to individuals around the
world. The pledge made a human security infrastructure available to
any state seeking to pursue a similar agenda, facilitating the future
integration of other great and small powers (ibid.; DFAIT, 1999a).[5]

By late spring of 1999, Axworthy had come to an all-but-final formulation:

> At its core, the human security agenda is an effort to construct a global soci-
> ety in which the safety of people is an international priority and a motivat-
> ing force for international action; where international humanitarian
> standards and the rule of law are advanced and woven into a coherent web
> protecting the individual; where those who violate these standards are held
> fully accountable; and where our global, regional and bilateral institutions
> are designed and equipped to enhance and enforce these standards.
> (Axworthy, 1999b)

Axworthyian human security was ending very differently from where
it began. DFAIT's *Freedom from Fear: Canada's Foreign Policy for
Human Security* (2000b), published as Axworthy was leaving office,
recognized the concept as central to Canadian foreign policy and
identified five policy priorities for its advancement: the protection of
civilians, peace support operations, conflict prevention measures, the
promotion of good governance and accountability, and the maintenance of public safety. While not tied to it exclusively, human security referred most commonly to non-military means of dealing with
the effects of violent conflict. State sovereignty was not eroding, but
it had no meaning if a state was not accountable to its citizens.

Human security had progressed from theoretical construct to 'new
norm of international behaviour'. It complemented national security

and had rid itself permanently of the phrase 'soft power'. Instead of a new world, there was a new approach to foreign policy. Rather than aiming to alter the meaning of security, humanist activists recommended a different emphasis. The state would be a partner, not an enemy. Change was best effected through a combination of intelligent negotiation and more forceful means of persuasion.

Axworthy had defined and redefined human security, but he never strayed from the tenets that governed a long political life. 'A man of principle' who 'stood for an active international conscience, and clung to a standard of international morality', one of the country's most prominent historians called him, and so he was (Bothwell, 2000). Less convincingly, Axworthy maintained that his stance remained consistent with the country's three declared foreign policy objectives—prosperity and employment, security within a stable global framework, and the propagation of Canadian values and culture abroad (DFAIT, 1995; Axworthy, 1996b, 1999c). The truth is that human security gradually overwhelmed Canadian policy until it seemed that nothing else mattered. At worst, Axworthy's preoccupation with a single theme deflected attention and inevitably resources from other issues that required detailed and thoughtful responses. At best, however, he gave a sense of unity and purpose to the fraying threads of a once proud tradition of liberal internationalism.[6]

Axworthyism was highly personal and intensely populist. In an address to Vermont's Middlebury College, where he briefly taught after leaving Princeton, he recalled a 1965 trip to a Martin Luther King demonstration that provided an early and crucial lesson in people's rights and government obligations. Authority, he concluded, was not absolute. It was 'conditional unless it is exercised properly by those who possess it. This experience demonstrated that when a government violates certain of its citizens' rights its legitimacy should be challenged' (Axworthy, 2000c).

Axworthy genuinely believed in a *people's* foreign policy. He liked to cite polls showing that 64 per cent of Canadians felt prouder of their country's international role in 1999 than five years before, and that 68 per cent rated human security as a top priority (Axworthy, 1999a). Human security was 'not a position that makes me popular with the striped crowd', he told the *New York Times*, 'but I think it has a resonance with the public' (DePalma, 1999). Like Pearson bristling at Pierre Trudeau's accusations that 1960s internationalism was somehow in conflict with the national interest, Axworthy stoutly defended his humanist activism as a 'Canadian approach' (Axworthy, 1999d), a 'Canadian response' (Axworthy, 1999a), an 'approach to the world that made sense to Canadians' (Axworthy, 2000d). Human security had turned Canada into a leader once more.[7]

A minister overflowing with ideas animated the most spirited foreign affairs debate in 30 years. He listened to criticism and demonstrated flexibility, disconcerting commentators who preferred a stationary target. Partnerships between government and the-public-as-civil-society democratized the policy process and propelled his issues forward (Gwyn, 2000). Taken together with the construction of an outwardly focused human security infrastructure, networks were established that will continue to create and raise expectations, suggesting a continuing prominence for Axworthy's concerns and initiatives on a wide variety of human and humane fronts.

Even though the place of human security in the future of Canadian government policy is unclear, Axworthyism cannot survive. While sounding some of the recently familar themes on humanitarian questions and weapons proliferation, Axworthy's successor as Foreign Minister, John Manley, instantly went out of his way to show that he will be a very different custodian of 125 Sussex Drive. The United States, and Canadian-American trade in particular, will be at the heart of policy, and a concerted effort will be made to rebuild a relationship Manley believes has been neglected, or worse (Barthos, 2001; Trickey, 2000b). The swashbuckling approach to public policy has disappeared with Axworthy, along with the search for the memorable, the effort to popularize, teach, and cajole, and perhaps some of the self-righteousness. 'Bland works', says Manley with a certain pride, implicitly signalling a return to the conventionally pragmatic in Canadian external affairs.[8]

NOTES

The authors thank the Social Sciences and Humanities Research Council of Canada for its support of the research in this paper, and for their advice Stephen Azzi, Erica Berman, Robert Bothwell, John English, Fen Hampson, Simon Heeney, Anne Hillmer, Stephen Hoogenraad, Jean-Noé Landry, Maureen Molot, Michael Pearson, Ryan Shackleton, and Denis Stairs.

1.   For a review of the development of human security before 1995, see Daudelin (1998).

2. A remark made at an international affairs conference, 'Activism and (Non)Alignment', Malmö, Sweden, 1–2 Dec. 2000.
3. For a detailed discussion of the Ottawa Process, see Cameron et al. (1998).
4. For an academic assessment, see Macdonald and Smith (1999–2000).
5. On the Lysøen Declaration and the Human Security Network, see Michael Small's article in McRae and Hubert (2001: 231–5).
6. See Andrew Cohen's excoriating examination of pre-Axworthy Liberal foreign policy: Cohen (1995).
7. See also Axworthy (2000a, 2000b, 2000c, 2000e), and his introduction to McRae and Hubert (2001: 8–9). For a critical analysis, see Chapnick (2000).
8. See Eayrs (1961: 153–5). The Manley quotation is from Barthos (2001).

REFERENCES

Axworthy, Lloyd. 1971. 'A Public Communication System: A study of the use of the new communications technology by government to enhance citizen participation and increase program effectiveness'. Winnipeg: Institute of Urban Studies.

———. 1993. *Liberal Foreign Policy Handbook*. May.

———. 1996a. 'Canadian Foreign Policy in a Changing World: Notes for an Address by the Honourable Lloyd Axworthy, Minister of Foreign Affairs, to a Meeting of the National Forum on Foreign Policy'. 96/57. Winnipeg, 13 Dec.

———. 1996b. 'Foreign Policy at a Crossroad: An Address by the Honourable Lloyd Axworthy, Minister of Foreign Affairs, to the Standing Committee on Foreign Affairs and International Trade'. 96/12. Ottawa, 16 Apr.

———. 1996c. 'Notes for an Address by the Honourable Lloyd Axworthy, Minister of Foreign Affairs, to the 51st General Assembly of the United Nations'. 96/37. New York, 24 Sept.

———. 1996d. 'Notes for an Address by the Honourable Lloyd Axworthy, Minister of Foreign Affairs, to the 52nd Session of the United Nations Commission on Human Rights'. 96/10. Geneva, 3 Apr.

———. 1997a. 'Canada and Human Security: the Need for Leadership', *International Journal* 52, 2 (Spring): 183–96.

———. 1997b. 'Canada and the United States in a Changing World: Notes for an Address by the Honourable Lloyd Axworthy, Minister of Foreign Affairs, to the World Affairs Council'. 97/14. Los Angeles, 14 Mar.

———. 1997c. 'Human Rights and Canadian Foreign Policy: Principled Pragmatism: Notes for an Address by the Honourable Lloyd Axworthy, Minister of Foreign Affairs, at McGill University'. 97/42. Montreal, 16 Oct.

———. 1997d. 'Notes for an Address by the Honourable Lloyd Axworthy, Minister of Foreign Affairs, at the Consultations with Non-Governmental Organizations in Preparation for the 53rd Session of the United Nations Commission on Human Rights'. 97/7. Ottawa, 5 Feb.

———. 1997e. 'Notes for an Address by the Honourable Lloyd Axworthy, Minister of Foreign Affairs, to the 52nd Session of the United Nations General Assembly'. 97/36. New York, 25 Sept.

————. 1997f. 'Notes for an Address by the Honourable Lloyd Axworthy, Minister of Foreign Affairs, to the Oslo NGO Forum on Banning Anti-Personnel Landmines'. 97/32. Oslo, 10 Sept.

————. 1997g. 'The University of Ottawa Gordon Henderson Distinguished Lecture: Notes for a Lecture by the Honourable Lloyd Axworthy, Minister of Foreign Affairs'. 97/49. Ottawa, 6 Nov.

————. 1998. 'Why "Soft Power" is the Right Policy for Canada', *Ottawa Citizen*, 25 Apr., B6.

————. 1999a. 'Notes for an Address by the Honourable Lloyd Axworthy, Minister of Foreign Affairs, to the Atlantic Forum'. 99/55. St John's, 5 Nov.

————. 1999b. 'Notes for an Address by the Honourable Lloyd Axworthy, Minister of Foreign Affairs, to the G-8 Foreign Ministers' Meeting'. 99/40. Cologne, Germany, 9 June.

————. 1999c. 'Notes for an Address by the Honourable Lloyd Axworthy, Minister of Foreign Affairs, to the National Forum'. 99/4. Montreal, 22 Jan.

————. 1999d. 'Notes for an Address by the Honourable Lloyd Axworthy, Minister of Foreign Affairs, to the Paasikivi Society'. 99/47. Finland, 1 Sept.

————. 1999e. 'Notes for an Address by the Honourable Lloyd Axworthy, Minister of Foreign Affairs, to the Woodrow Wilson School of Public and International Relations, Princeton University, "Kosovo and the Human Security Agenda" '. 99/28. Princeton, NJ, 7 Apr.

————. 2000a. 'Notes for an Address by the Honourable Lloyd Axworthy, Minister of Foreign Affairs, at the New York University School of Law—The Hauser Lecture on International Humanitarian Law: Humanitarian Interventions and Humanitarian Constraints'. 2000/5. New York, 10 Feb.

————. 2000b. 'Notes for an Address by the Honourable Lloyd Axworthy, Minister of Foreign Affairs, for "The Arthur Kroeger College Inaugural Lecture on Public Affairs and Civic Society" '. 2000/10. Ottawa, 22 Mar.

————. 2000c. 'Notes for an Address by the Honourable Lloyd Axworthy, Minister of Foreign Affairs, to the Middlebury College 200th Anniversary Symposium on International Affairs'. 2000/12. New York, 30 Mar.

————. 2000d. 'Notes for an Address by the Honourable Lloyd Axworthy, Minister of Foreign Affairs, to the University of Calgary Law School'. 2000/8. Calgary, 17 Feb.

————. 2000e. 'Notes for an Address by the Honourable Lloyd Axworthy, Minister of Foreign Affairs, to the Woodrow Wilson International Center for Scholars'. 2000/29. Washington, 16 June.

———— and Sarah Taylor. 1998. 'A Ban for All Seasons: The Landmines Convention and its Implications for Canadian Diplomacy', *International Journal* 53, 2 (Spring): 189–203.

———— and Knut Vollebaek. 1998. 'Now for a New Diplomacy to Fashion a Humane World', *International Herald Tribune*, 21 Oct. Cited from http://www.dfait-maeci.gc.ca/foreignp/HumanSecurity/Tribune-e.asp [4 Oct. 2000].

Barthos, Gordon. 2001. 'Ottawa's Bland Man Shows Spunk', *Toronto Star*, 5 Jan., A20.

Blanchfield, Mike. 1999. 'Axworthy Attacks "Emasculated" UN Security Council', *National Post*, 29 Mar., A10.

Bothwell, Robert. 2000. 'Lloyd Axworthy: Man of Principle', *National Post*, 19 Sept., A14.

Cameron, Maxwell A., Robert J. Lawson, and Brian W. Tomlin, eds. 1998. *To Walk Without Fear: The Global Movement to Ban Landmines*. Toronto: Oxford University Press.

Chapnick, Adam. 2000. 'The Canadian Middle Power Myth', *International Journal* 55, 2 (Spring): 188–206.

Cohen, Andrew. 1995. 'Canada in the World: The Return of the National Interest', Canadian Institute of International Affairs, *Behind the Headlines* (Summer).

Daudelin, Jean. 1998. 'Toward Human Security'. Ottawa: CIDA, Feb.

DePalma, Anthony. 1999. 'A Canadian Rousts Diplomacy (and Ruffles the US)', *New York Times*, 10 Jan.

Department of Foreign Affairs and International Trade (DFAIT). 1995. *Canada and the World*. Available at: http://www.dafit-maeci.gc.ca/english/foreignp/cnd-world/summary.htm

———. 1998. 'Canada and Norway Form New Partnership on Human Security', Press Release no. 117, 11 May.

———. 1999a. 'Axworthy Announces Progress on Human Security Agenda', Press Release no. 117, 20 May.

———. 1999b. *Human Security: Safety for People in a Changing World*. Apr.

———. 2000a. 'Axworthy to Attend Human Security Network Meeting', Press Release no. 99, 10 May.

———. 2000b. *Freedom from Fear: Canada's Foreign Policy for Human Security*. Cited from: http://www.dfait-maeci.gc.ca/foreignp/HumanSecurity/Human SecurityBooklet-e.asp [4 Oct. 2000].

Eayrs, James. 1961. *The Art of the Possible: Government and Foreign Policy in Canada*. Toronto: University of Toronto Press.

Economist. 2000. 'Shield or Ax', 6 May, 40.

Gwyn, Richard. 2000. 'Axworthy Made a Difference', *Toronto Star*, 20 Sept.

Hampson, Fen Osler, and Dean F. Oliver. 1998. 'Pulpit Diplomacy: A Critical Assessment of the Axworthy Doctrine', *International Journal* 53, 3 (Summer): 379–407.

Hillmer, Norman, and Dean F. Oliver. 2001. 'The NATO-United Nations Link: Canada and the Balkans, 1991–1995', in Gustav Schmidt, ed., *A History of NATO: The First Fifty Years*. London and New York: Macmillan.

Lee, Stephen. 2000. 'The Axworthy Years: Humanist Activism and Public Diplomacy', *Canadian Foreign Policy* 8, 1 (Fall): 1–10.

Macdonald, Douglas, and Heather A. Smith. 1999–2000. 'Promises Made, Promises Broken: Questioning Canada's Commitments to Climate Change', *International Journal* 55, 1 (Winter): 107–24.

McRae, Rob, and Don Hubert, eds. 2001. *Human Security and the New Diplomacy: Protecting People, Promoting Peace*. Montreal and Kingston: McGill-Queen's University Press.

Malone, David. 1999. 'The Global Issues Biz: What Gives?', in Fen Osler Hampson, Michael Hart, and Martin Rudner, eds, *Canada Among Nations 1999: A Big League Player?* Toronto: Oxford University Press.

Nossal, Kim Richard. 1998. 'Foreign Policy for Wimps', *Ottawa Citizen*, 23 Apr., A19.

———. 1998–9. 'Pinchpenny Diplomacy: The Decline of "Good International Citizenship" in Canadian Foreign Policy', *International Journal* 54, 1 (Winter): 88–105.

———. 2000. 'Mission Diplomacy and the "Cult of the Initiative" in Canadian Foreign Policy', in Andrew F. Cooper and Geoffrey Hayes, eds, *Worthwhile Initiatives? Canadian Mission-Oriented Diplomacy*. Toronto: Irwin.

Pearlstein, Steven. 1999. 'Canada's New Age of Diplomacy', *Washington Post*, 20 Feb., A13.

Petrie, Anne. 2000. Interview with Lloyd Axworthy, Canadian Broadcasting Corporation, *Moral Divide*, 17 Dec.

Rioux, Jean-François, and Robin Hay. 1998–9. 'Canadian Foreign Policy: From Internationalism to Isolationism?', *International Journal* 54, 1 (Winter): 57–75.

Trickey, Mike. 1998. 'Canada's Fall from Grace on World Scene', *Ottawa Citizen*, 8 July, A4.

———. 2000a. 'The Axworthy Doctrine', *Ottawa Citizen*, 5 Jan., A6.

———. 2000b. 'Manley's Mission: Fix Ties With US', *Ottawa Citizen*, 28 Dec. Available at: http://www.ottawacitizen.com/national/001228/5007713.html.

Vincent, Isabel. 2000. 'Axworthy Tilts at Foreign Policy Windmills', *National Post*, 16 Sept., A15.

Vollebaek, Knut. 1999. *A Perspective on Human Security: Chairman's Summary*. Lysøen, Norway, 20 May.

5

In the Liberal Tradition: Lloyd Axworthy and Canadian Foreign Policy

JOHN ENGLISH

In a Festschrift for the renowned historian Donald Creighton, a fierce critic of the Liberal Party and its foreign policy, his colleague Charles Stacey argued that there had been a Liberal tradition in foreign policy in the first half of the twentieth century. He asserted that there was remarkable continuity in Canadian foreign policy from Sir Wilfrid Laurier to Mackenzie King. When King and his adviser O.D. Skelton 'repudiated the Conservative readiness to participate in a common Commonwealth foreign policy based on consultation they were going back to Laurier—Laurier plus the new autonomy won during the war of 1914–1918.' While King knew that Canada would join a major war in which Britain was involved, 'he gave no hint of this to the public.' Such approaches recognized 'the need of preserving national unity, or preventing a division on racial lines'. As a result, in Skelton's description, most of their work was negative, but a negativism that was 'an essential stage in the development of Canadian nationality' (Stacey, 1970).

In 1914, when Canada had entered war without preparation, without a process of consultation with Britain, and without a peacetime Canadian contribution to the strengthening of the British, the irresponsibility of Laurier's foreign, military, and naval policies seemed self-evident to Canadian Conservatives, military leaders, and editorialists. British Prime Minister Asquith grumbled to King George V about the Canadians' 'continued default' on the eve of the war.[1] In 1939, when Canada once again entered war poorly prepared after many years during which Mackenzie King avoided debate about Canadian security policy, Canadian Conservatives, English-language commentators and editorialists, and military leaders complained angrily about the government's lack of realism about the choices it had faced. Privately, senior Department of External Affairs officers complained about their minister, Mackenzie King, and his prattle about values and his refusal to consider seriously the fact that Canada would go to war if Britain went to war. The government, in the view of its own diplomats Hume Wrong and Lester Pearson, was 'singularly stupid' in its refusal to confront the reality of the threats to Canadian security in Europe (Granatstein, 1982: 120–1).

War came, and the British imperial dream was one of its casualties. A foreign policy that had countered the allure of that dream was fundamental to the success of the King and Laurier governments, particularly in Quebec and western Canada. Whatever the view of Toronto editorialists and newspaper publishers, whatever the legitimate complaints of Donald Creighton and Hume Wrong about the trivialization of foreign policy by idealistic rhetoric, whatever the cogent arguments of military analysts about the failure to prepare, both Laurier and King responded that they maintained national unity. In Skelton's acid words, they had resisted those who possessed a 'greater share of wealth, influence, assurance and public position' and their calls to 'rally around'.[2]

With British decline and American ascendancy, Canadian foreign policy in the postwar era gained a new freedom. This was, it seemed, the age of the mandarins, of those remarkable diplomats whose efforts created a golden age for Canadian diplomacy. And yet the major policy document of the early postwar years, Louis St Laurent's Gray Lecture at the University of Toronto, asserted that 'national unity' was the pre-eminent concern for Canadian foreign policy-makers (MacKay, 1971: 388–99). In the Cold War's early light, national unity no longer appeared so fragile, and the close links with the United States bothered few until the 1960s when those on the left began to call for an 'independent foreign policy for Canada'.

Among those voices was a young Princeton student, Lloyd Axworthy, who bitterly dissented from the decision of Lester Pearson to accept nuclear weapons in 1963. Writing to Pearson shortly after the decision, Axworthy admitted that it was presumptuous for a student to tell a Nobel Peace Prize winner what Canada's role in foreign affairs should be. The circumstances, however, demanded candour. After two years at Princeton studying 'the role of the middle powers', Axworthy had come to understand that 'the only conceivable role for a country such as Canada is that of offsetting the great power arms race.' As for 'honouring' Canada's commitment to the North Atlantic Treaty Organization (NATO), 'may I remind you', Axworthy lectured, that NATO has not 'honoured its original commitments, as outlined in Article 2 of the treaty'. He further reminded the Liberal leader that Pearson himself had said that the way to meet the Communist challenge was not through a 'military response' but rather through activities in the 'economic, political, and diplomatic areas'. There was no need to rally around the pressures of 'Washington and the United States Air Force' because if we did so 'our past moral postures would be revealed as nothing more than hypocrisy.' In 1917 Skelton denounced the Tory jingoes and told Laurier that 'the voice of Toronto is not the voice of God.' In 1963 Axworthy implored Pearson, who had the support of the three Toronto papers, not to satisfy 'the paranoia of certain jingoistic groups'.[3]

Axworthy was less bitter in the winter of 1963 than Pierre Trudeau, who angrily denounced Pearson for selling out to 'les hipsters de Camelot', but both shared Liberal professor Stephen Clarkson's prescriptions for an independent foreign policy for Canada. This time independence meant not from Britain, as it had for Skelton, but from the United States. Nevertheless, the end was the same: a negativism towards the American Empire as 'an essential stage in the development of Canadian nationality'. When Trudeau and his adviser Ivan Head came to write the history of the foreign policy of the Trudeau governments, they entitled their study *The Canadian Way*. It argues, as did Clarkson in 1968, that an independent policy must involve the 'public' to counter the influence of those with 'a greater share of wealth, influence, assurance and public position' (Clarkson, 1968). Such a policy must also pay close attention to the particular circumstances of Quebec. Trudeau and Head explicitly rejected the 'realists', whom they equated with scholars, diplomats, and the military. Rejecting realist assumptions about the nature of power, 'the two of us believed that Canada's limited power and its vulnerable geographic position made the quest for community not only more necessary but more possible of success.' Moral principles mattered to them, their party, and to the identity of Canada (Head and Trudeau, 1995: 312ff.). The seeds of human security emerged from rich Liberal soil long before Lloyd Axworthy became Foreign Minister.

The critics of this tradition in Liberal foreign policy have been many, their critiques similar. The Ambassador to the United States complained to senior American officials that 'domestic' matters had influenced his minister's speech and that he did not share his nationalist views. The High Commissioner in London wrote that he hoped his minister would not be influenced so much by unreal majorities in the United Nations. The undersecretary of state for external affairs was totally unsympathetic with the weakness and moralism of his superiors. He complained that, in foreign policy, we need someone 'who has something other than holy water in his belly'. The Foreign Minister, the undersecretary wrote, was simply a 'brute', totally ambitious and dishonest and trusting too much in his own ability to settle matters by personal diplomacy. A former American Secretary of State denounced Canadian policy as moralistic, hypocritical, and harmful to Canada's long-term security interests (English, 1993: 60–1; Ritchie, 1981: 122; Bosher, 1999: 93–5; Acheson, 1966: 134–47). Holy water indeed!

These criticisms are not of Lloyd Axworthy but of Lester Pearson and, in one case—'the brute'—Paul Martin, his Foreign Minister from 1963–8. The Canadian Ambassador to Washington was Hume Wrong in 1951, not Raymond Chrétien in the 1990s. The High Commissioner was Charles Ritchie in 1956, not Roy MacLaren. The undersecretary was Marcel Cadieux in the mid-1960s, and the former American Secretary of State was Dean Acheson, not Madeleine Albright or Henry Kissinger. Although critics of Axworthy often argue that he does not reflect Pearson's more realistic approaches, Wrong, Cadieux, Acheson, and the Pearson and Axworthy journalistic critic Peter Worthington would almost certainly disagree. Just as Axworthy's opposition to American defence policies in the Bush-Mulroney years caught the attention of the US ambassador in the 1990s, an earlier ambassador, Livingston Merchant, complained in 1962 that Pearson 'has vacillated and equivocated outrageously on defense.' He preferred John Diefenbaker.[4] Surely Axworthy was not the subject of virulent attack that Pearson faced from Marcel Cadieux in the 1960s. Pearson, Cadieux wrote, 'has never understood the French-Canadians. Besides, he and his wife detest them, and it is in times of crisis like the one we are presently going through that his ignorance of the French presence in this country and his feebleness as the leader of the government does disservice to the vital interests of our country.' Weak on Vietnam, pathetic on France's De Gaulle, and too willing to sip holy water rather than firewater, Pearson did not understand the realities of power (Bosher: 1993: 94).[5]

Those who, like Norman Hillmer and Adam Chapnick in this volume, separate Pearson from Axworthy point to Pearson's strong support of NATO and of military expenditure in the early years of the Cold War. Pearson's rhetoric at the time of the Korean War was not so much different from that of Axworthy during the Kosovo War. Axworthy supported the war, but in foreign ministers' meetings he was a critic of the British and others who wanted to expand the war. Similarly, Pearson supported the Korean War but placed limits on the scale of war that others did not. Moreover, Pearson in the mid-1960s was the author of defence unification, the critic of Vietnam, and the doubter of the future of NATO. Cadieux, a strong advocate of the American effort in Vietnam and of NATO, was correct in his assumption that Pearson did not share his views. In *The Canadian Way*, Head and Trudeau identify two strains in Pearsonian internationalism. One reflected Pearson's close association with the conservative diplomats in External Affairs. In the early years of the Cold War, he tended to 'mute issues of moral principle' in the 'value structure of the collectivity'. For two decades, they write, 'Canada's interests were so coincident with those of the associations to which it belonged that the net benefit of membership far outweighed the occasional muffling of singular Canadian preferences.' But there was another Pearson, the author of *Partners in Development*, the US Vietnam critic at Temple University in 1965, the opponent of McCarthyism, the first Western Foreign Minister to visit the Soviet Union, and the sophisticated cosmopolitan (Head and Trudeau, 1995: 313). Significantly, they credit Pearson with building a domestic constituency for his

policies in the postwar era, although they point out that that particular constituency disintegrated in the 1960s.

Head and Trudeau, and of course Axworthy in his letter to
Pearson in 1963, place those years of close linkages between the professional diplomats and the government and of the tight Canadian-
American alliance during the early Cold War outside of the Liberal
tradition. In a sense, they argue that Pearson at those times moved
outside the mainstream because of the enormous challenge of the
Soviet Union, just as one might argue that King went to Britain's side
after years of hesitation because of the challenge of Hitler. They
moved away again when the threat receded. Similarly, despite the
nuclear weapons decision in 1963, Pearson clearly disappointed not
only the Americans but also the undersecretary during his prime ministerial tenure. One recalls Charles Ritchie's anecdote describing a
gathering of ambassadors in the mid-1960s with Lyndon Johnson.
After a few jibes at Ritchie for Pearson's Temple speech and Canada's
welcome for draft dodgers, President Johnson turned away and said
he now wanted to speak to a true and loyal friend, the ambassador
from Germany.

Johnson may have forgotten two world wars, but Axworthy in the
1980s and 1990s came to remember not the Pearson he attacked in
1963 but the UN activist and the 'man of peace' Pearson had come
to represent. The official publication of Foreign Affairs entitled its
commentary on Axworthy's resignation: 'Lloyd Axworthy: Man of
Peace'. Axworthy's ambition when he entered politics, he is reported
to have said, 'was to become Prime Minister; failing that, he wanted
to follow in the footsteps of Lester B. Pearson, who, in 1956, gave
the world the concept of UN peacekeeping missions.' He was, the
department publication declared, a 'worthy successor to Pearson',
because of his efforts to advance the cause of human security within
the UN system, especially during Canada's membership on the
Security Council in 1999–2000 (*Canada World View*, 2001: 14–15).

Canadian journalists have been more willing than academic critics to place Axworthy in a particular tradition, one that is populist,
nationalist, and idealist. Not surprising is the highly favourable 'year-
end' assessment of Axworthy in the populist, nationalist, and Liberal
Toronto Star (*Toronto Star,* 2000: A12). Axworthy, the *Star* editorialists wrote, 'brought idealism, energy and passion to the job. . . .
Axworthy ruffled feathers in Washington, but he made Canadians
proud.' More surprising was the 'year-end' assessment of the *Globe*

and Mail, which gave Axworthy an A, its highest cabinet minister ranking in 2000. 'Goes out amid talk he might have been Canada's best Foreign Affairs Minister since a guy named Lester Pearson. Bucked a conservative bureaucracy to earn himself respect around the globe' (*Globe and Mail,* 2000: A4).

In placing Axworthy within a Liberal tradition, one must identify those aspects of that tradition where the past has influenced him and where he himself has affected the future. Five particular areas merit discussion:

1.   the concept of independence;
2.   the role of Quebec;
3.   the Department of External Affairs;
4.   the relationship with the Department of National Defence;
5.   the place of non-governmental organizations and interest groups.

INDEPENDENCE

Carl Berger's classic study of Canadian imperialism argues that Canadian imperialists such as George Denison, Stephen Leacock, and G.R. Parkin were essentially Canadian nationalists, who expressed the hope that as Canada 'grew in strength and population the Empire would be transformed so as to accommodate her weight and influence.' Canada's future lay within its ever-increasing and ultimately dominant role within the greatest empire the world had yet seen. This dream was a nightmare for many French Canadians, but a mirage in the private view of Sir Wilfrid Laurier. His nationalism was of a different strain that looked forward to Canada as an autonomous nation, linked to Britain but in charge of its own destiny. Imperialists in the Liberal Party, such as John Willison, came to suspect that Laurier's vision was fundamentally different from their own, and they abandoned him in the election of 1911 when the Liberals supported free trade with the United States and opposed a direct contribution to the British Navy (Berger, 1970: 258).

Laurier lost the next election in 1917 when British-Canadian nationalism had its greatest and last triumph. After the war, autonomy and independence of decision became, as Stacey correctly argued, the central tenet of Liberal foreign policy. Do not commit, but insist on consultation. Do not arm, but never say that you will not fight for Britain. Autonomy meant the right to take one's own decision and the right not to go to war automatically, as Canada had in 1914. The imperialists like Leacock, Denison, and Parkin became Conservatives, and Toronto was the centre of imperialist sentiment in its private clubs, its university, and its newspaper editorials (with the significant exception of the *Toronto Star*). That left the broad centre for Liberal governments for most years from the end of World War I to the peace following World War II.

After the war, American power, British decline, and the Soviet threat combined to create a consensus that 'muted' the debate about independence. The Liberals, as Head and Trudeau note, created a strong domestic constituency for these policies. When that consensus dissolved in the divisive debates of the 1960s, however, independence once again gained powerful political appeal. Walter Gordon and several younger members of Parliament began to articulate a Canadian political nationalism defined against the United States. It was logical that this group combined to support Pierre Trudeau, who had attacked Pearson's embrace of 'John F. Kennedy's Camelot' in 1963 and who urged disengagement from NATO, North American Air Defence Command (NORAD), and other defence links with the United States.

The Liberals could do little to limit the economic ties with the United States, indeed, such ties had powerful appeal to Quebec, the Maritimes, and parts of Ontario that were supportive of the party. Foreign policy, thus, became a means of expressing political independence while accepting economic linkages such as the Auto Pact and defence production sharing with the United States. So often the response was symbolic, as it had been with King and Laurier in the days of the Empire. Trudeau's visit to Castro and King's visit to Hitler were symbols of the nationalism and independence that the Liberals of those different days wanted their party to represent. And yet the balance was essential. Donald Macdonald, one of the most aggressive spokespersons for independence and withdrawal from NATO in the late 1960s, later became the Royal Commission chair whose Liberal background gave legitimacy to free trade with the United States. There were certainly Liberals who stood outside the tradition, such as C.D. Howe, James Richardson, and Mitchell Sharp, who argued strongly against Gordon in the 1960s and Macdonald in the 1970s.

Lloyd Axworthy, however, left no doubt where he stood as the Liberals neared power in 1993. Writing in *Canadian Foreign Policy* as the Liberal Party's External Affairs critic, Axworthy deplored the evidence from a recent Angus Reid survey about attitudes to Canada in 15 other countries. The poll suggested that most thought 'that Canada basically follows the foreign policy dictates of the United States.' To Axworthy, the result was sad, especially since 'it interferes with the good qualities that others perceive Canada to have, such as our generosity in matters of foreign aid and our efforts to promote peace and human rights.' A Liberal foreign policy, therefore, must centre 'on how to develop a more independent role for Canada' and avoid 'the continentalist view of the [Mulroney] government'. Globalism, he argued, was a code word for a right-wing agenda, and Canada had to find an alternative agenda (Axworthy, 1992–3).

Axworthy did not become Foreign Minister in the new Liberal government. An opponent of NAFTA, one wonders what he argued in cabinet as the Foreign Minister, André Ouellet, and International Trade Minister, Roy MacLaren, urged Canada's adherence to the treaty. Nevertheless, much of the agenda Axworthy developed in opposition did find its place in the Senate-House of Commons review of Canada's foreign and trade policy. When he became minister, the balance tipped from trade to independence and a foreign policy in which 'the role of leadership . . . is to encourage the embrace of a global ethic. An ethic that abhors the present imbalance in the basic human condition—an imbalance in access to health care, to a nutritious diet, to shelter, to education, one that extends to all space and through all time.' Although this ethic reflects Axworthy's hopes in 1996, the actual words are those of Pierre Trudeau at Mansion House in London a generation earlier (Head and Trudeau, 1995: 317). When Winnipeg celebrated 25 years of public service by Lloyd Axworthy in 1998, the loudest applause was reserved for Pierre Trudeau's tribute, which ended with a sentence expressing the former Prime Minister's support for Axworthy's foreign policy, 'especially' his policy towards Cuba. It was a peculiar moment because other speakers had extolled international human rights, but the comment, of course, had much more to do with Washington than with Havana.

QUEBEC

With King and Laurier, foreign policy was inextricably linked with national unity. English Canada's emotional link with Britain was not shared by French Canadians or by many of the new ethnic groups that entered Canada in the twentieth century. Canada before 1945 had a British majority, but that majority lacked political coherence. When this majority was challenged, unity could be found, as in 1917 when the Liberals suffered their worst defeat in Canadian history and were reduced to a Quebec rump, or in 1942 when the conscription plebiscite indicated an overwhelming pro-war, pro-British majority as well as an even more overwhelming French-Canadian opposition. Studies of voting support revealed that the base for Liberal Party support in the postwar era was Francophones throughout Canada and newly arrived ethnic groups in Ontario and Quebec. If one was Anglican and British, the chances were that one's vote was Progressive Conservative. If one was Italian and Catholic, the odds were overwhelming (almost nine out of ten) that one's vote was Liberal (Clarke et al., 1979).

In the era of King and Laurier, the negativism towards the British Empire brought positive response from French and German Canadians. In the postwar era, the circumstances changed, and imperialism was no longer a meaningful vision or threat for most Canadians. The last inning of Liberal anti-imperial nationalism was the Suez crisis, when St Laurent attacked imperialism and Canada, for the first time in its history, did not support a British war. In Britain's defeat and Pearson's Nobel Prize lay the foundation for a new Canadian identity, one that Pearson as Liberal leader hoped would create a new sense of nationality. The flag, the creation of la Francophonie to parallel the Commonwealth, and the recognition that the language of Canadian foreign policy had been English were Pearson's attempt to reinvent the Liberal tradition to fit an age when the Empire was a distant memory and decolonization had created a new discourse of liberation. So long as a Liberal Prime Minister and Foreign Minister resisted the entreaties of Downing Street, Rosedale, and Westmount, it did not matter much that they spoke only English. After the Quiet Revolution, no longer could Canadian foreign policy or Canada's Prime Minister be unilingual.

The Department of External Affairs did not accept these changes easily. In his report for the Royal Commission on Bilingualism and Biculturalism, Gilles Lalande wrote: 'Not always without ill will, the authorities of the Department gave us numerous examples of their general distrust of outsiders, including researchers of good standing, who desire to consult the official records, even the least confidential ones, dealing with Canadian foreign policy' (Lalande, 1969: XIV). His report was a devastating indictment of a department that purported to represent Canada but most of whose senior officers could not speak the language of over one-quarter of the population.

Axworthy was not fluently bilingual, but he could respond to interviews and questions in French. DFAIT, of course, had responded exceptionally well to the critiques of Lalande and others and had become remarkable in its capacity to conduct Canadian foreign policy bilingually. Although Axworthy's deputies were Anglophones, Francophones such as Claude Laverdure, Gaetan Lavertu, and Philippe Kirsch were senior and central to his most important initiatives. He believed, with considerable justification, that Quebec opinion would find his human security agenda highly congenial. Axworthy's predecessor, André Ouellet, had been deeply immersed in Quebec politics and was notably skeptical of many non-governmental organizations (NGOs) in Quebec. He drastically reduced funding and garnered much criticism for his actions. Even though Axworthy could not restore funding, his message about the significance of NGOs and the importance of co-operation silenced some critics. These same critics became strong supporters of his landmine initiative and, in most cases, the International Criminal Court campaign. Neo-conservatism was a weaker strain in the Francophone press, and Axworthy's style and issues had greater resonance in Quebec. 'Il a donné', Serge Truffaut wrote in *Le Devoir*, 'un allant au Canada, qui faisait défaut avant lui' (Truffaut, 2000).

THE DEPARTMENT OF EXTERNAL AFFAIRS

As Gilles Lalande suggested, the Department of External Affairs only reluctantly embraced the new directions undertaken by the Pearson government. When Pierre Trudeau took office, the diplomats faced a whirlwind generated by a Prime Minister who deeply resented the department's failure to reflect Canada's bicultural and bilingual character. Moreover, he shared the complaints of Stephen Clarkson and other left Liberals that the department was conservative, if not archaic. Clarkson wrote in 1968: 'To change from a quiet to a more independent approach to our foreign policy will require a transformation of the values of the practitioners, the diplomats in the Department of External Affairs. So long as the personnel of External Affairs maintain a secretive, distrustful attitude towards the public, an independent foreign policy is doubly stymied.' Canadian diplomats were smug and conservative, and the undersecretary, Marcel Cadieux, apparently did not believe that 'the public has any greater part to play than to stand and wait, deferentially yet comprehendingly in the spectators' boxes.' We know now that Clarkson's suspicions were true (Clarkson, 1968: 264–5).

Trudeau and Lloyd Axworthy shared many of Clarkson's views. Both regarded the department as a conservative force that resisted a popular and populist foreign policy for Canada. Trudeau's foreign policy review tried to bring in outsiders and questioned the fundamental precepts of Canadian foreign policy. Axworthy also turned to academics, human rights specialists, and NGOs for advice, and more controversially. How difficult such exercises could be (Stairs, 2000).

Liberal foreign ministers frequently troubled the department because it believed that for them politics too often was the highest trump. Norman Robertson thought his minister, Mackenzie King, absolutely mediocre and second rate. Hume Wrong complained about Pearson's attention to matters of 'domestic consumption'. Charles Ritchie never felt close to Pearson after he turned to politics, a dirty trade. Cadieux was contemptuous of Martin: 'Encore une perle pour la collection' was Cadieux's usual introduction to another incident where Martin, in Cadieux's harsh view, was 'ambitious, ignorant, shallow, or dishonest' (Bosher, 1999: 94).[6] Axworthy had similar difficulties. At a *Canada Among Nations* workshop in the late 1990s, the strongest critics of Axworthy's foreign policy were, reportedly, members or former members of the department of which he was a minister.

Nevertheless, DFAIT under Axworthy had a voice in cabinet, a prestige domestically, and, perhaps, an influence internationally that it had lacked since Pierre Trudeau declared in the late 1960s that he would learn more from reading the *New York Times* than dispatches from Canadian diplomats. Part of the problem was surely Axworthy's style, which placed high demands on the department. One senior official compared Axworthy to a flint that produced dazzling sparks, but those sparks too often died and failed to ignite. Yet some did ignite most spectacularly and the brilliant glow illuminated Sussex Drive. The light shone upon some remarkable foreign service officers, such as Jill Sinclair and Kirsch, who had been taken up by the flood of human security issues and had been swept to international prominence. The voyage often seemed perilous, the crew weary, and the shoals near.

Having NGOs on board was not always easy. In a recent study of NGO consultation, Denis Stairs observes that NGO participants thought the bureaucrats were not responsive to their arguments but rather were too concerned with briefing the NGOs. He correctly notes that what NGOs wanted was not something that 'public officials can comfortably entertain'. They may report, but they do not have to 'do the politics' themselves (Stairs, 2000: 37). This tension made the times difficult for the department, but one should note that foreign ministries throughout the West faced similar problems. For a department whose morale was, astonishingly, the subject of a Royal Commission in the 1980s and that laboured under severe budgetary restraint in the first half of the 1990s, the Axworthy years interrupted a voyage too often recently bound in shallows and miseries. Better memories of the journey may come after the *mal de mer* fades.

THE DEPARTMENT OF NATIONAL DEFENCE

The Defence Department in peacetime has been a poor brother to External Affairs, its ministers unknown and its budget the first target of government restraint. In the era of Laurier and King, defence specialists recognized that Canada no longer faced direct attack from the United States but that thousands of Canadians could die in a European war. In this period, ties between the Canadian and British military were strong and, as Norman Hillmer has shown, their 'alliance' was distrusted by King and Skelton (Hillmer, 1978). The ethos of the Canadian military was Conservative, British, and rightly suspicious of King's intentions.

In the postwar era, the ties with the British atrophied but the linkages of the Canadian military with the United States grew through NATO and later through NORAD. After the 1950s, however, Canadians were ragged partners. Liberal governments unified the armed forces, cut defence budgets, reduced commitments to NATO and NORAD, and favoured UN peacekeeping commitments over those made to NATO. Occasionally, military historians compared the irresponsibility of Liberal governments of the 1970s and 1980s with those of the 1930s.

Lloyd Axworthy reminded Pearson in 1963 that he had once said that 'we prepare for war like precocious giants, and for peace like retarded pygmies.' Axworthy's recent biography in the official publication of the Department of Foreign Affairs places his sympathies clearly on the side of the pygmies. 'During his tenure', the biography declares, 'Mr. Axworthy tirelessly championed the cause of peace, and was nominated for the 1998 Nobel Peace Prize after the adoption of the Ottawa Convention' (*Canada World View*, 2000). That Convention, according to public opinion polls, received overwhelming support from Canadians, but defence strategists found the triumph hollow. A Canadian Press summary of foreign policy in 1997 described how the landmine campaign made Axworthy 'a regular on British and American TV news, delivering his all-Canadian message of a new world order and feel-good globalism'. The same story, however, quoted Fred Crickard, a retired admiral then at Dalhousie University's Centre for Foreign Policy Studies, who deplored the pathetic state of Canada's military and the 'abysmal, irresponsible' failure to buy new equipment. 'They're necessary infrastructure if we're to have any teeth in our foreign policy.' Similarly, Chris Sands, a 'Canada-watcher' at Washington's Center for Strategic and International Studies, said that Canada was 'jeopardizing its trump card in the international community: Peacekeeping'.[7] Canada, Sands concluded, was undermining its 'ability to be there, except as talkers'. Despite nearly universal approval in the Canadian press, a sharp attack on Axworthy's landmine campaign came from defence specialist David Lenarcic (Lenarcic, 1998).

In their elegant but critical assessment of the so-called Axworthy Doctrine, Fen Hampson and Dean Oliver argue the absent means, notably the hard power of military preparedness, commitment, and strength, vitiated the ends of the Axworthy Doctrine (Hampson and Oliver, 1998). More assertively, the *Ottawa Citizen* placed the headline 'Foreign Policy for Wimps' over a Kim Nossal article (Nossal, 1998) that summarized bluntly an attack by Nossal on Canada's 'Pinchpenny Diplomacy' (Nossal, 1998–9). As Hillmer and Chapnick note in Chapter 4, Axworthy's early musing about soft power and 'punching above our weight' internationally irritated the military and others who believed that such arguments could be employed to justify budget cuts and a weak military. Some remembered his hesitations about cruise missile testing in the 1980s and his doubts about the Gulf War in 1990–1. Lenarcic's study of the landmine initiative reflects the frustrations of a Defence Department that felt excluded from a debate about a military weapon. While Axworthy led a campaign to ban a military weapon and expanded humanitarian law into the security domain, Canada's military reeled from recent budget cuts and inadequate preparation for their tasks. The unease came not so much from the banning of landmines—indeed, many Canadian military officers publicly supported the ban—but from the sense that the military voice had been so faint.

Axworthy could argue correctly that he had supported funding for a military suitable to the new tasks the human security agenda proposed. Moreover, his relationship with Defence Minister Art Eggleton was good, and the two worked together effectively in advancing their departments' joint interest. The Defence Department actually did much better than Foreign Affairs in the cabinet budget discussions where, despite the acclaim for Axworthy's work, the human security agenda failed to gain much support. Axworthy, moreover, responded to the critics by sharpening his definition of human security and abandoning 'soft power', the term that so irritated his 'realist' critics.

Nevertheless, the critics of Axworthy echo earlier defence and security spokespersons who defined the Liberal approach to foreign policy as 'woolly', moralistic, and insufficiently attentive to security concerns and national interests. There was and is a moralistic and idealistic strain in the Liberal tradition, one that exists uneasily with military interests. Canadian Liberalism formed a part of what historian Robert Kelley termed the 'transatlantic persuasion', the most powerful advocate of which was nineteenth-century British Prime Minister William Ewart Gladstone, who cut military budgets and who stormed the country in his seventies denouncing the indifference his Conservative rival, Benjamin Disraeli, showed to the Bulgarian atrocities (Kelley, 1969). Gladstone's 1876 demands that Turks leave the province they had 'desolated and profaned' were scarcely different from Axworthy's arguments demanding that the Serbs leave Kosovo. Similarly, Mackenzie King identified war and warriors as part of the forces of 'blood and death' (Bercuson, 1973) and constantly turned to Morley's *Life of Gladstone* for guidance (Esberey, 1980: 141). Morley resigned from the cabinet when Britain entered World War I, and King never served in that war. Lester Pearson did, and he later took an active interest in security questions, yet he, like Gladstone and Axworthy, spoke incessantly of values as well as interests. He irritated Dean Acheson, the American realist, every bit as much as Lloyd Axworthy bothered Acheson's Washington heirs.

NON-GOVERNMENTAL ORGANIZATIONS

Axworthy celebrated the campaign to ban landmines as an example of the new diplomacy, one that combined the energy and skills of non-governmental organizations with the diplomatic resources of states frustrated by the rules of consensus and veto that obtained in many multilateral organizations. In this case, Axworthy reflected others who had noted the increasing role of NGOs. UN Secretary-General Boutros Boutros-Ghali, for example, wrote in 1996 that the 'notion that the chief executive of the United Nations would have taken [NGOs] seriously might have caused astonishment. The United Nations was considered to be a forum for sovereign states alone.' Now, he continued, 'nongovernmental organizations are . . . considered full participants in international life' (Boutros-Ghali, 1996: 7).

Axworthy's interest in the role of NGOs came early, along with his belief that they could break down encrusted bureaucratic approaches. He was active in the civil rights movement in the 1960s, a member of the United Church, which promoted social activism, and a supporter of the participatory democracy that Trudeau embraced in his first government. Although a remarkably effective Manitoba politician, he did not attribute his success to his traditional political skills that brought abundant new buildings and businesses to Winnipeg, but to the Core Area Initiative (CAI). This program to rebuild Winnipeg's core relied, in Axworthy's words, 'on the active involvement of inner-city residents and local agencies'. The result was 'a program that supported the creation of local, community-based organizations that could go on to apply for capital or operating funds to build health clinics or self-help employment centres, turn old garages into community theatre sites or initiate in-fill housing. This spawned a network of community-based organizations and gave rise to new leadership in the inner city.' The CAI, he later wrote, 'has already gained the recognition and approval of the Organization for Economic Co-operation and Development, the European Economic Community, the United Nations and the World Bank as a model for comprehensive community-level economic and social development' (Axworthy, 1990: 253–4).

Axworthy applied this same approach when he served as foreign policy critic in the early 1990s. He worked closely with academic specialists, human rights organizations, ethnic groups, and NGOs to develop Liberal foreign policy. In his 1992 summary of Liberal foreign policy, he recognized 'the need for promoting within Canada much stronger involvement of our non-government organizations, churches, universities, business organizations and aboriginal groups'. Foreign policy in Canada could no longer be 'treated either as a closed shop or as an opportunity for Prime Ministerial photo opportunities'. When Axworthy finally became Foreign Minister in 1996, his range of contacts and earlier experience became the ingredients for the closer involvement of NGOs in the pursuit of his initiatives. A foreign service officer has said that when Axworthy looks at Colombia he sees how it fits into the landmine initiative or the International Criminal Court campaign, while the department thinks of bilateral and regional economic and political relations. It is a distinction that is an important difference (Axworthy, 1992–3: 8, 14).

Allison Van Rooy has described in this book the impact of NGOs and outsiders on Canadian policy during the Axworthy years. Both the Canadian foreign service and Canada's military regard themselves as professionals, and the increasing intrusion of so-called 'non-professionals', without the same kind of credentials, has created uncertainty. These same challenges face politicians in other democracies, and few others have Axworthy's experience and skill in dealing with NGOs. Denis Stairs has warned that bureaucrats as well as politicians must keep in mind the constitutional principles upon which the institutions they inhabit are based (Stairs, 2000). Axworthy himself expressed impatience with NGOs when they made him a target during the controversy over the activities of Talisman, a Canadian energy company, in Sudan. There are dangers, but surely 'politics' is different now, and Axworthy's remarkable experience as Canada's Foreign Minister provided lessons and landmarks for future politicians and ministers.

CONCLUSION

Lloyd Axworthy may seem a revolutionary, but his manifesto and methods drew upon a bulging storehouse constructed from the Anglo-Canadian liberal and Liberal tradition. For him, as for Laurier and King, an independent policy was sometimes negative and often reflective of the fears as much as the hopes of Canadians. Nevertheless, such independence was, as O.D. Skelton wrote, 'an essential stage in the development of Canadian nationality'. His arguments for human security reflected Pierre Trudeau's belief that 'In the final decades of the twentieth century, social justice can no more be compartmentalized than can quality of life be isolated.' Like Lester Pearson before him, Axworthy knew that his position in the state gave him a status with non-state actors that he could use to promote domestic and foreign goals. His diplomacy was not so much new as a late twentieth-century revision of the text most familiar to Canadians in the last century. Like the title of the Donald Creighton Festschrift, his revolution was, profoundly, a matter of his character and Canada's circumstance.

NOTES

1. H.H. Asquith to George V, 11 Feb. 1914, National Archives of Canada (NAC), British Cabinet CAB 41, v. 35, reel A903.
2. NAC, Hume Wrong Papers, O.D. Skelton, 'Automatic Belligerency', n.d., v. 3.
3. NAC, MG 26 N2, v. 50, file 806–2, Pearson Papers, Axworthy to Pearson (no date, but probably early Feb. 1963).
4. National Archives, Washington, American Embassy, Ottawa, to Department of State, 8 May 1962, State Department Records 742.00/5–862 XR611.42.
5. The translation is by Bosher (1999), who examined Cadieux's papers in the National Archives. Cadieux wrote memoranda regularly on events of the day. This particular memorandum was written shortly after the De Gaulle incident in 1967. The papers are not yet open to other researchers, but Bosher's book indicates that Cadieux had contempt for both Pearson and Martin but enormous respect for Norman Robertson. Did he express such views to Robertson, and did Robertson agree? In his evaluation of Canadian foreign policy in 1967–8, Robertson expressed support for the status quo.
6. Martin, however, was lavish in praise for Cadieux in his memoirs and private interviews.
7. See www.canoe.ca/CNEWS1997/canabroad.html

REFERENCES

Acheson, Dean. 1966. 'Canada: "Stern Daughter of the Voice of God"', in Livingston Merchant, ed., *Neighbors Taken for Granted: Canada and the United States*. New York: Praeger.

Axworthy, Lloyd. 1990. 'Regional Development: Innovations in the West', in Thomas Axworthy and Pierre Trudeau, eds, *Towards a Just Society: The Trudeau Years*. Toronto: Penguin.

———. 1992–3. 'Canadian Foreign Policy: A Liberal Party Perspective', *Canadian Foreign Policy* 1, 1 (Winter): 7–16.

Bercuson, David. 1973. 'Introduction' to William Lyon Mackenzie King, *Industry and Humanity*. Toronto: University of Toronto Press.

Berger, Carl. 1970. *The Sense of Power: Studies in the Ideas of Canadian Imperialism 1867–1914*. Toronto: University of Toronto Press.

Bosher, John. 1999. *The Gaullist Attack on Canada 1967–1997*. Montreal and Kingston: McGill-Queen's University Press.

Boutros-Ghali, Boutros. 1996. 'Foreword', in Thomas Weiss and Leon Gordenker, eds, *NGOs, the UN, and Global Governance*. Boulder, Colo.: Lynne Rienner.

Canada World View. 2001. Issue 10.

Clarke, H., J. Jenson, L. LeDuc, and J. Pammett. 1979. *Political Choice in Canada*. Toronto: McGraw-Hill Ryerson.

Clarkson, Stephen, ed. 1968. *An Independent Foreign Policy for Canada*. Toronto: McClelland & Stewart.

English, John. 1993. *The Worldly Years: The Life of Lester Pearson 1949–1972*. Toronto: Knopf.

Esberey, Joy. 1980. *Knight of the Holy Spirit: A Study of William Lyon Mackenzie King*. Toronto: University of Toronto Press.

Globe and Mail. 2000. 'Liberals Who Made the Grade', 29 Dec., A4.

Granatstein, J.L. 1982. *The Ottawa Men: The Civil Service Mandarins 1935–1957*. Toronto: Oxford University Press.

Hampson, Fen Osler, and Dean F. Oliver. 1998. 'Pulpit Diplomacy: A Critical Assessment of the Axworthy Doctrine', *International Journal* 53, 3 (Summer): 379–407.

Head, Ivan, and Pierre Trudeau. 1995. *The Canadian Way: Shaping Canada's Foreign Policy, 1968–1984*. Toronto: McClelland & Stewart.

Hillmer, Norman. 1978. 'Defence and Ideology: The Anglo-Canadian Military "Alliance" in the Nineteen Thirties', *International Journal* 33, 3 (Summer): 588–612.

Kelley, Robert. 1969. *The Transatlantic Persuasion: The Liberal-Democratic Mind in the Age of Gladstone*. New York: Knopf.

Lalande, Gilles. 1969. *The Department of External Affairs and Biculturalism*. Ottawa: Information Canada.

Lenarcic, David. 1998. *Knight-errant: Canada and the Crusade to Ban Anti-personnel Land Mines*. Toronto: Irwin and Canadian Institute of International Affairs.

MacKay, R.A., ed. 1971. *Canadian Foreign Policy 1945–1954: Selected Speeches and Documents*. Toronto: McClelland & Stewart.

Nossal, Kim Richard. 1998. 'Foreign Policy for Wimps', *Ottawa Citizen*, 23 Apr., A19.

———. 1998–9. 'Pinchpenny Diplomacy: The Decline of "Good International Citizenship" in Canadian Foreign Policy', *International Journal* 54, 1 (Winter): 88–105.

Ritchie, Charles. 1981. *Diplomatic Passport: More Undiplomatic Diaries 1946–1952*. Toronto: Macmillan.

Stacey, Charles. 1970. 'Laurier, King, and External Affairs', in John Moir, ed., *Character and Circumstance: Essays in Honour of Donald Grant Creighton*. Toronto: Macmillan.

Stairs, Denis. 2000. *Foreign Policy Consultations in a Globalizing World: The Case of Canada, the WTO, and the Shenanigans in Seattle*. Montreal: Institute for Research on Public Policy.

Toronto Star. 2000. 'Laurels: A 2000 Treasury', 31 Dec., A12.

Truffaut, Serge. 2000. 'Les enjeux négligés: après l'idéaliste Axworthy', *Le Devoir*, 23 Nov.

6

An Assessment of the US Contribution to Global Human Security

EARL FRY

Lloyd Axworthy's emphasis on human security was both an effort to humanize some of the rough edges of globalization and a reminder to the G-7 and other Western governments that the conduct of foreign affairs must always take into account the needs and aspirations of the more than six billion people currently inhabiting the planet. This chapter will assess the US contribution to human security, concluding that the overall contribution during the Clinton years was greater than often appreciated, but that lower priority may be given to this agenda by the new Bush administration.

US FOREIGN POLICY AND HUMAN SECURITY: THE INSULAR LEGACY

President Bill Clinton was one of the first national leaders in the early post-Cold War period to give significant credence to the term 'globalization'. Indeed, he insisted that the United States would be the chief beneficiary of globalization if it could maintain a strong national economy and a pre-eminent position in the development of high technology, especially information technology.

In many respects, globalization was affecting mainstream American life even before Clinton defeated George Bush in the 1992 election. The US had already emerged as the world's largest importer and exporter, largest foreign direct investor and host nation for foreign direct investment, and largest international portfolio investor (along with Japan). By the end of the 1990s, US imports easily topped $1 trillion annually, and exports of goods and services were approaching $1 trillion. Cumulative foreign direct investment neared the $1 trillion plateau, with foreigners controlling over $8 trillion in total US assets. Almost 50 million foreigners were visiting the United States every year and spending about $80 billion during their visits. More than one-half million foreign students were also enrolled in US institutions of higher learning, and nearly 27 million foreign-born people were living in the United States on a permanent basis, representing almost 10 per cent of the total population, double the percentage of 1970. In all, 18 million American jobs were linked directly to international trade, investment, and tourism activity. Perhaps even more importantly, US businesses were beginning to recognize that in the vast American marketplace they were competing not just against other domestic companies but against foreign-owned businesses as well. This competitive dimension has been heightened even more dramatically in the Information Age, with the nearest competition for domestic firms now being less than a second away—the time needed for a signal in cyberspace to be sent from any part of the planet to the United States.

Bill Clinton entered the White House in January 1993 with little interest in foreign affairs, even though he had studied abroad and had travelled rather extensively. As governor of Arkansas for 12 years he had concentrated on domestic issues, with his main international focus being on Taiwan, which he visited on four separate occasions.

'It's the economy, stupid' had helped propel Clinton into the Oval Office and he pledged in 1993 to devote almost full time to the advancement of domestic issues, publicly disdaining pursuits in the international arena. In this respect, Clinton perhaps mirrored American society; and this perspective continues to represent one of the major challenges to productive US involvement in the advancement of human security issues worldwide. Most Americans favour US engagement internationally, but few know very much about international affairs, in spite of the proliferation of world news on cable news channels and through Internet information sources. In extensive polling on American public opinion towards foreign policy issues done by the Chicago Council on Foreign Relations in 1999, public perceptions of US vital interests being at stake actually declined in terms of bilateral relations with most countries. By 29 percentage points, the general public is less inclined than US 'leaders' to have the United States take an active part in world affairs. When asked to name two or three problems facing the nation at that time, foreign policy issues were far down the list; when asked to name two or three foreign policy problems requiring attention, the most frequently cited answer was 'don't know'. Fifty-four per cent of the general public perceive that 'globalization' is 'mostly good', and only 48 per cent believe that the United States should pay over $1 billion in back payments to the United Nations (Rielly, 1999).

The public's lack of interest in and awareness of international affairs, combined with tepid support for US engagement in the global arena, can be explained by a number of factors. First, there has been a long tradition of isolationism or semi-isolationism, starting with George Washington's famous farewell address in which he warned against entangling alliances with European nations, followed in the twentieth century by extreme reluctance to become involved in the two world wars, the Senate's refusal to join the League of Nations after World War I because national sovereignty could be jeopardized as a result of the League's collective security provision, and the Senate's support for membership in the United Nations after World War II, but only after the US had been provided with a veto power in the Security Council. During the 1990s, this wariness of international involvement was manifested in lukewarm public support for the World Bank, the International Monetary Fund (IMF), the creation of the North American Free Trade Agreement (NAFTA) and the World Trade Organization (WTO), the refusal of Congress to extend fast-track authority to President Clinton to negotiate new bilateral and regional trade agreements, and the failure of the Senate to ratify a number of international accords linked to the environment, the non-proliferation of weapons of mass destruction, a ban on testing nuclear weapons, and the creation of a permanent world criminal court.

POSITIVE CONTRIBUTIONS TO THE CAUSE OF HUMAN SECURITY

In spite of public wariness concerning the nature and extent of US engagement abroad, there are more than a dozen ways in which the United States has contributed to greater human security in the post-Cold War period, even though some were not intended specifically to address this cause.

Unprecedented domestic economic growth. Clinton's emphasis on improving the domestic economy and fostering technological development was very successful. During the period 1993–2000, the US economy grew by more than $3 trillion, an increase greater than the total annual gross domestic product (GDP) of any other nation on earth except for Japan. By the end of the year 2000, US unemployment stood near a 30-year low, 23 million net new jobs had been created over an eight-year period, the welfare and poverty rates were the lowest since 1965 and 1973 respectively, and there had been 117 consecutive months of economic expansion, the longest in American history. This had all occurred while the national economy was absorbing the impact of almost one million new immigrants per year. Robust economic growth averaging more than 4 per cent per year over President Clinton's last term in office also permitted several years of federal budget surpluses and allowed the government to pay down the accumulated debt by over $300 billion by the end of fiscal year 2001. In 1992, the US federal government had incurred a budget deficit of $290 billion, the largest nominal debt in history; in fiscal year 2000, the budget surplus was $237 billion, the largest nominal surplus in history.

This all added up to the federal government being able to spend more money on foreign and defence policy. Whereas the Department of State's budget had been trimmed by 30 per cent between fiscal years 1991 and 1997, it increased by 17 per cent between 1998 and 2001. The Pentagon also received billions of dollars for added spending after enduring major cuts in the early and mid-1990s. The government also forgave $500 million in African debt, and additional funds were allocated for medical treatment for AIDS victims in sub-Saharan Africa, two million micro-credit grants to residents of developing countries, and several other health-care, educational, and humanitarian programs, including $300 million for the Global Food for Education Initiative and $155 million for international basic education projects.

NAFTA. Clinton was often accused of governing by polls, but in the case of NAFTA he went against the wishes of many of his constituents and supported the creation of the largest free trade area in the world. Congress also approved the pact between the United States, Canada, and Mexico, even though a majority of Democrats in both the House of Representatives and the Senate voted against the accord. Arguably, NAFTA has been a great boost to all three member countries, helped contribute to unprecedented political change in Mexico, and may pave the way for the creation of a hemisphere-wide Free Trade Area of the Americas (FTAA).

World Trade Organization. The White House and Congress both supported the creation of the WTO, which was the successor organization to the General Agreement on Tariffs and Trade (GATT). The WTO should help to entrench globalization, in part through its attention to arenas either barely covered or completely ignored by GATT, including trade in services, intellectual property protection, liberalized direct investment activity, and more effective dispute-settlement mechanisms. Of course, some leaders in developing countries are not as positive about the WTO and the entrenchment of globalization, perceiving that both work in favour of the rich countries and against the overall interests of the poorer nations. Hopefully, growing interdependence will bring greater prosperity to almost all nations, with a renewed emphasis on sustainable development instead of simple GDP growth. Clinton recognized the challenge ahead when he asserted that it is no longer acceptable that 'part of the world lives in the information age' while the other 'has not even reached the clean water age' (Sanger, 2000). Nonetheless, he felt that signing over 300 bilateral and multilateral trade agreements during his eight years in office was a step forward in bringing greater economic security to many people around the world.

China's entry into the WTO. Both the executive and legislative branches in 2000 finally approved permanent normal trade relations (PNTR) with China, helping clear the way for China to join the WTO and to take upon itself international standards accepted by over 130 WTO member countries. Ideally, WTO membership will help persuade Chinese leaders to strengthen the rule of law within China and provide better treatment to religious, ethnic, and other persecuted groups.

Haiti. The United States played the lead role in the 1994 operation in Haiti that threw out an authoritarian regime and provided international support for the protection of the Haitian people and the implementation of a system based on the rule of law. There is no guarantee that this system will remain in place in a nation still marked by pervasive corruption and violence, but the effort was noteworthy.

Northern Ireland. Bill Clinton and former Maine Senator George Mitchell played instrumental roles in bringing about the Good Friday Peace Accord, which involved various actors from Northern Ireland, Ireland, and the United Kingdom. Tensions have certainly eased and people in Northern Ireland have recently enjoyed a much greater sense of security, in spite of sporadic incidents of violence. The new stability and tranquility in Ireland itself have also contributed to that island nation enjoying among the highest economic growth rates in the world.

Israel and the Palestinian Authority. President Clinton devoted huge amounts of his personal time and political capital in an effort to finalize a permanent peace accord between the Israeli government and the Palestinian political authority. Although his efforts did not result in a new accord, Clinton's laudable goal was to bring about the end of bloodshed and the restoration of human rights and security in a highly troubled region of the Middle East. A criticism of his quest might be his failure to include other prominent actors, whether national governments or international organizations, in his peace effort.

North Korea. By the end of his administration, Clinton's efforts over a six-year period to normalize relations with North Korea, establish a viable working relationship between North and South Korea and Japan, and defuse the volatile issue of weapons of mass destruction seemed to be working. A successful long-term agreement would result in greater regional security and help provide a higher quality of life for the residents of North Korea.

Kosovo. North Atlantic Treaty Organization (NATO) intervention in Kosovo in 1999, led by the United States, helped to end the tyrannical rule over Kosovo by the Serbian government, stopped the policy of ethnic cleansing, and paved the way for the ouster of Slobodan Milosevic and the restoration of democratic rule in Serbia itself. The post-intervention period, however, has not resolved the bitter differences between ethnic Serbians and the Albanian Kosovars, and much remains to be accomplished in bringing about political stability and the rule of law in Kosovo. US military power was put on display during the conflict, with US planes flying 38,000 sorties over the 78-day air campaign.

START II. The US Senate ratified this strategic arms reduction treaty in 1996, with the Russian parliament approving it four years later. This agreement, combined with other US accords with Russia and the former Soviet republics of Ukraine, Belarus, and Kazakhstan, has already resulted in the deactivation or dismantling of over 1,700 Soviet-era nuclear warheads, 425 missiles, and 300 missile launchers, and prospects remain fairly bright for future arms-reduction initiatives between Washington and Moscow. When completely implemented, START II would lead to a two-thirds cutback in long-range nuclear warheads from Cold War peaks.

Chemical Weapons Convention. This accord was signed by the first Bush administration but was not ratified by the Senate until 1997. In many respects, chemical weapons are just as lethal as nuclear ones and this accord should ease worries around the world concerning the use of such weapons in wartime situations or against innocent civilian populations. The Chemical Weapons Convention bans the development, production, acquisition, stockpiling, transfer, and use of any chemical weapons.

NATO enlargement. In 1996 Clinton called for the inclusion in NATO of the Czech Republic, Poland, and Hungary, and the organization invited these nations to join a year later. Understandably, the Kremlin was very upset, accusing NATO of surrounding Russia with potentially unfriendly member states. Nevertheless, all three former members of the Soviet bloc were eager to join NATO and safeguards were put in place to ease some of the concerns of the Russian leaders and the Russian people.

The peso crisis and other financial turmoil. Clinton acted decisively to help NAFTA partner Mexico when the peso crisis erupted at the end of 1994. Using the little known Exchange Stabilization Fund, Clinton provided $20 billion in funding to Mexico, with the IMF kicking in another $30 billion in available credit. The crisis ended relatively quickly, the US Treasury was repaid ahead of schedule with over $1 billion in additional interest payments, and Mexico returned to positive GDP growth in 1996.

The 'Asian flu' crisis of 1997, the Russian financial crisis of 1998, and the Brazilian crisis of 1999 were also contained with limited global damage, thanks in part to the actions of the US Treasury and Alan Greenspan's Federal Reserve Board. Conversely, little has been done to resolve the problem of 'hot money' entering and leaving national financial markets quickly, nor has much progress been made in creating a new financial architecture for an era of globalization.

AMERICAN FAILURES IN PROMOTING HUMAN SECURITY

Unfortunately, the US government during the 1990s missed out in several ways on opportunities to facilitate the promotion of human security globally.

Clinton's steep learning curve in the foreign policy arena. Clinton got off to a very slow start in the foreign policy arena, highlighted by his perplexing statement that he expected to put foreign policy on the back burner and concentrate almost exclusively on domestic affairs. In an age of globalization and the growing overlap of domestic and foreign policies, even a former governor from a landlocked state should have recognized that this course of action was ill-conceived. Later on, his unwillingness to spend time or political capital in pushing for the ratification of various treaties also tarnished his overall reputation in the foreign affairs arena.

Overreliance on governance by polls. Even though President Clinton showed great political courage in supporting NAFTA in the face of stiff opposition from organized labour and environmental groups, his constant eye on polling data may have had an adverse effect on some other foreign policy decisions linked to human security. The fixation on polls might have convinced him to reject intervention in Rwanda, to hesitate to intervene in Bosnia, Kosovo, and East Timor, and to state publicly that he would not carry out a land war in Kosovo, thus limiting military options and providing tactical advantages to the Serbian opposition. Furthermore, survey data may have muted his willingness to push vigorously for fast-track authority for the inclusion of Chile within NAFTA and for compromises that might have solicited eventual Senate support for the landmine and test-ban treaties.

Congressional parochialism and exaggerated partisanship. With the Republicans capturing control of both chambers of Congress in 1994, one should have expected much more in terms of their own international agenda. In particular, allowing Senator Jesse Helms to assume the chairmanship of the Senate Foreign Relations Committee, instead of assigning him to the chairmanship of a lower-profile committee, tainted the Senate Republican caucus with an indelible isolationist and unilateralist label. In addition, bitter acrimony would characterize Republican-Democratic relations within the Beltway just before, during, and after the impeachment phase of the Clinton presidency. Democrats on Capitol Hill did little to improve the situation, voting overwhelmingly against the implementation of NAFTA and pushing for conditions that made it nearly impossible for the Republican majority to grant President Clinton fast-track authority to negotiate Chile's entry into NAFTA.

Ironically, the most pragmatic vision on foreign affairs came from the nation's 50 governors, who strongly supported the passage of NAFTA, the granting of fast-track authority to President Clinton, and the continuation of vigorous discussions leading to the formation of the FTAA. As the chief executive officers of the states, most governors were able to see very clearly how globalization could positively affect their own constituents and thus were less prone to play the partisan and at time nonsensical games found on Capitol Hill.

Inadequate foreign aid and maldistribution of such aid. The United States is ranked last among major Western nations in the amount of money, as a percentage of GDP, devoted to foreign assistance. In addition, with almost half of official foreign assistance going to just two nations, Israel and Egypt, little has been left over for 170 developing countries, especially the poorest two dozen that are overwhelmingly concentrated in sub-Saharan Africa. Cutting the budget of the State Department during a period when the US was grappling for a new post-Cold War policy emphasis, and when about 20 new nations were being created after the breakup of the Soviet Union, Yugoslavia, and Czechoslovakia, was also a major mistake.

Rwanda. In his visit to Rwanda in 1998, President Clinton apologized for the failure of the United States and the international community to come to the assistance of the beleaguered Tutsi in 1994 (US Information Service, 1998). Tragically, the genocide that occurred in Rwanda may have cost the lives of one-half million Tutsi at the hands of the Hutu. Clinton's lack of action was undoubtedly linked to the lack of public support for such an intervention, the killing of American soldiers in Somalia in 1993, the US military's reluctance to become engaged in an area where supply and logistical problems would be magnified, and America's historical legacy of according Africa the very lowest priority among the regions of the world. On the other hand, the Rwandan massacre also poignantly showed the lack of resolve and preparedness on the part of other major Western nations to intervene energetically in this civil conflagration.

Helms-Burton, unilateral sanctions, and Cuba. Both Congress and Clinton are guilty of having passed and signed a piece of legislation that smacks of aggressive unilateralism, extraterritoriality, and disjointed foreign policy priorities. Following the tragic and unjustified shooting down by Cuban fighter jets of two US civilian airplanes that had violated Cuban airspace, the Helms-Burton Act was passed, allowing the US government to bar any foreign company from doing business in the United States if it operates facilities in Cuba on land previously confiscated from Americans. Moreover, executives of these companies and their families can be barred from entering the United States altogether.

Helms-Burton basically tells other nations, particularly close allies of the United States, that Washington wants the right to dictate how companies from those nations interact with Cuba, with a warning that if these companies defy US sanctions against Cuba they could be punished. This is an illegal and politically corrosive effort to extend US law to other sovereign nations. The law also reinforces the inefficacy of US unilateral sanctions, the political costs involved in applying such sanctions, and the incongruity between the harsh sanctions opposed against Cuba versus the active engagement policy towards another totalitarian government in China.

UN dues. Primarily through the efforts of the US Ambassador to the United Nations (UN), Richard C. Holbrooke, who helped arrange the visit of several members of Congress to the UN and, in turn, UN representatives to Capitol Hill, Jesse Helms finally dropped his opposition in January 2001 to making an instalment payment of $582 million in US back dues to the UN. In return, the UN membership agreed to lower the US share of UN administrative costs from 25 per cent to 22 per cent and its share of peacekeeping costs from 31 per cent to 26 per cent. Nevertheless, the United States still owes over $1 billion in delinquent payments, with the chief opposition to such payments concentrated in certain Republican circles on Capitol Hill. Without any doubt, the United Nations is guilty of cronyism, periodic corruption, and sporadic inefficiencies, but it is the international organization best equipped to handle many of the crises around the world. The failure of Congress to provide prompt payment of US dues during the 1990s was a setback for international co-operation and the cause of human security in general.

Environmental failures. The White House and Capitol Hill have performed erratically in helping people around the world address the challenges of environmental degradation. The failure to make adequate progress on global warming is a classic example. The United States singlehandedly accounts for over one-third of global warming emissions, but the fear that a few US businesses might lose their competitive edge prompted White House representatives to postpone the fulfilment of commitments made in the early 1990s in the Kyoto Protocol. Ozone deterioration, acid rain, deforestation, desertification, the loss of freshwater sources, declining fish stocks, and overall sustainable development are among the pressing issues facing North America and the world in general, but these concerns have received only token consideration by US officials.

Too much unilateralism. Aggressive unilateralism, accompanied by the lack of consultation and co-ordination with close allies, continues to characterize too many US actions in the foreign policy sphere. This has certainly been the case with US policy towards Cuba and, to a lesser extent, with Iraq, Iran, Israel, China, and North Korea. The US Senate was also mistaken when it failed in 1999 to ratify the Comprehensive Test Ban Treaty, an accord signed in 1996 by President Clinton and the leaders of more than 150 nations. In addition, Clinton should have endorsed the Landmines Convention, an agreement that went into effect without US participation and since 1997 has brought about the destruction of 20 million stockpiled mines (Axworthy, 2000). His worries about the safety of 38,000 US troops in South Korea were certainly justified, but reasonable safeguards could have been arranged to allow the United States to be a signatory to an agreement intended to keep thousands of innocent civilians from being killed or maimed annually by the explosion of landmines, some of which have been around since World War II, the Korean War, and the Vietnam War. During his last month in office, Clinton signed the accord creating the International Criminal Court, but he left the almost herculean task of garnering congressional support for the accord to George W. Bush. Clinton could have done much more to elicit US public support for the tribunal, and a change in attitude will also be required in the US Senate if the treaty is ever to receive two-thirds support for ratification. On a positive note, during the Clinton years the United States became the biggest financial contributor to the International Criminal Tribunals for the former Yugoslavia and Rwanda, and Clinton also appointed the first US Ambassador-at-Large for War Crimes Issues.

Too sanguine about consequences of proposed National Missile Defense (NMD) system. The United States has spent about $130 billion over the past two decades in research and testing related to the proposed Strategic Defense Initiative (SDI) and, more recently, the NMD system. Clinton signed the National Missile Defense Act of 1999 instead of sending it back to Congress for further study and deliberations. The NMD is intended to dissuade any rogue state from ever launching missiles against the United States, although one would think that the threat of being decimated by a US counterattack would be sufficient to deter any other nation from ever launching such a pre-emptive strike. In addition, the NMD plan is technically flawed, not taking into account various countermeasures that could be taken by an enemy to ensure that its missiles were not intercepted in the atmosphere or in space. The system might also cost hundreds of billions of dollars, and could spark an arms race with Russia and China and bring these nations closer together in a proposed Amity Pact. Indeed, the NMD would confirm the worst fears of Moscow and Beijing that the major threat to global security and their own national security is none other than the United States itself.

SPECIAL CHALLENGES FACING THE ADMINISTRATION OF GEORGE W. BUSH

It is difficult to define a 'Clinton Doctrine', although it is fair to say that Bill Clinton believed in a type of globalization that would expand the number of 'market democracies' around the world. Both democratic government and market systems that bring prosperity to the vast majority of a nation's inhabitants would qualify as bolstering the cause of human security worldwide. Freedom House has estimated that at the end of the year 2000, 120 countries had electoral democracies, up from 69 in 1989, and that nearly 41 per cent of the world's population was living in 'free' countries, a record percentage. Moreover, 'free' countries experienced economic growth over the past decade 70 per cent higher than those that were not free (Freedom House, 2000). In this respect, the United States' record in helping bring about international conditions conducive to the spread of democracy and open markets was perhaps somewhat better than some critics might admit.

Nevertheless, George W. Bush faces a host of major challenges that will sorely test the US contribution to global human security in the first decade of the twenty-first century. The *Encyclopedia of the Future* estimates that scientific information is doubling every 12 years and general information every two and one-half years (Marien, 1998: 23). Bill Gates predicts that more change will occur in the world's business community over the next decade than during the past half-century. He depicts this first decade of the new century as being characterized by velocity, and adds that 'the forces of digital information are creating a business environment of constant change. This is constant upheaval marked by brief respites—this is punctuated chaos' (Gates, 1998: xiii, 412). Potential chaos is also underlined in the *Global Trends 2015* report released in December 2000 by the US National Intelligence Council. The Council concludes that 'US global economic, technological, military, and diplomatic influence will be unparalleled among nations as well as regional and international organizations in 2015' (National Intelligence Council, 2000). The document then proceeds to outline traditional concerns about relations with Russia, China, the Middle East, and other nations and regions, but later focuses on newly emerging problems: 'Governments will have less and less control over flows of information, technology, diseases, migrants, arms, and financial transactions, whether licit or illicit.' Alliances will be built among powerful criminal organizations such as the Mafia and Chinese triads, and their 'income will come from narcotics trafficking; aliens smuggling; trafficking in women and children; smuggling toxic materials, hazardous wastes, illicit arms, military technologies, and other contraband; financial fraud; and racketeering.' Terrorism, such as that exemplified by Osama bin Laden's worldwide Al Qaeda movement, will threaten Americans and could disrupt the US infrastructure, which is increasingly dependent on information technology. The United States will also be increasingly vulnerable to chemical and biological attacks; as William Cohen, Clinton's Secretary of Defense, warned, under ideal temperature and wind conditions, anthrax contained in a five-pound sugar bag could wipe out 70 per cent of the people in Washington, DC (Cohen, 2000). The *Global Trends* report also highlights the growing risk from infectious diseases, stressing that at least 170,000 Americans annually will die from diseases that largely originate from overseas.

Global Trends 2015 concludes by offering four possible scenarios for the year 2015 and beyond. The first is referred to as 'inclusive globalization' and would lead to a 'virtuous circle' among 'technology, economic growth, demographic factors, and effective governance, which enables a majority of the world's people to benefit from globalization'. The second scenario, 'pernicious globalization', shows global élites thriving but the majority of humanity failing to benefit. The third is 'regional competition', whereby regional identities sharpen in Europe, Asia, and the Americas, resulting in intense competition, growing protectionism among the blocs, and rising concerns in areas of the world not included in the three major regional blocs. The final scenario is dubbed the 'post-polar world' and is the most bleak, with the US economy stagnating, the United States becoming more isolationist, US-European tensions heightening, national governance crises proliferating, and Chinese belligerence in Asia accelerating.

These are just some of the issues with which George W. Bush must grapple during his tenure as President. Bush entered the White House with a much greater appreciation for foreign affairs than his predecessor, even though both were governors of states sharing a common border in the US Southwest. Texas is the second most populous state in the United States and could be inserted among the top 10 nation-states in the world in terms of its annual production of goods and services. It also shares a very long border with Mexico and Governor Bush was well acquainted with cross-border issues. Moreover, his father devoted many years to foreign policy issues as the US liaison in China, as CIA director, and as Vice-President and President, and the younger Bush was the recipient of his father's tutelage on the subtleties and vagaries of foreign affairs.

President Bush will continue his predecessor's tradition of signing trade pacts and is an enthusiastic supporter of a Free Trade Area of the Americas and of China's entry into the WTO. On the other hand, he risks a further deterioration in relations with Moscow by pushing for the NMD, abrogating the 1972 Anti-Ballistic Missile (ABM) Treaty with Russia, and threatening to cut off financial assistance to Russia until progress is made by the Kremlin in eliminating corruption and implementing structural reforms. He has also called for a halt in 'vague, aimless, and endless deployments' overseas of US troops, hinting that he might cut back the US commitment in the Balkans. Currently, about 250,000 troops are stationed abroad, with 30,000 involved in peacekeeping-related functions. Bush has also supported an increase in the overall defence budget, even though the United States already spends more on defence than the next dozen nations combined and 22 times more than the combined spending of the so-called rogue states. On the positive side, the new President has asked for a comprehensive review of the entire defence system and has been reluctant to endorse costly new weapons requested by the various military branches. At the end of the year 2000, the United States possessed about 7,500 nuclear warheads on missiles, submarines, and bombers, while the Russians had about 6,500. It is widely anticipated that Bush would favour cutting these arsenals below the 2,000–2,500 levels discussed by American and Russian negotiators back in 1997 as part of a new round of strategic arms reduction talks (Myers, 2001).

Bush will be less inclined than Clinton to commit troops to combat genocide and other gross violations of human rights within individual nation-states. Indeed, both the President and his closest advisers spoke prior to the inauguration of returning to a foreign policy based on national interests instead of humanitarian interests or the interests of the 'international community' (Traub, 2001). The Powell doctrine, named after Bush's Secretary of State, Colin Powell, may also work against rapid intervention for humanitarian reasons. This doctrine states that the United States should only intervene if a clear national interest is threatened and then only with overwhelming force levels, a condition requiring weeks or even months of careful preparation. In addition, the new President's commitment to assisting developing areas, especially sub-Saharan Africa, may lag behind that of Clinton, one of the few presidents who actually took time to visit the region and observe first-hand problems linked to absolute poverty, environmental degradation, and endemic diseases such as malaria, cholera, and AIDS.

Bush's foreign policy team is very experienced and should provide him with an appropriate range of policy alternatives. Vice-President Dick Cheney served as President Gerald Ford's chief of staff and as the senior Bush's Secretary of Defense during the Gulf War; Colin Powell was President Reagan's national security adviser and the chair of the Joint Chiefs of Staff during the senior Bush's presidency; Secretary of Defense Donald Rumsfeld held the same post under President Ford, as well as serving as President Richard Nixon's ambassador to NATO and for a time as Ford's chief of staff, and National Security Adviser Condoleezza Rice was a highly respected political scientist at Stanford University with an academic emphasis on the former Soviet Union. Rice has already moved to reduce staffing on the National Security Council by one-third from the levels in the Clinton administration and has pledged to focus on defence strategy and international economic issues. What were once separate divisions for Europe, Russia, and the Balkans have been consolidated, and divisions handling environmental and health issues have been eliminated (De Young and Mufson, 2001). The major concern with Bush's senior foreign policy team is that all of them were experts on Cold War issues and may not yet appreciate the new set of challenges to be found in a post-Cold War era of globalization, growing interdependence, and rapid technological change. Their orientation towards the developing world is also limited, especially towards Africa and Latin America.

Neither the White House nor Congress should be expected to endorse wholeheartedly enhanced international co-operation, even though such co-operation seems imperative in an era of globalization and growing interdependence. The fact that both congressional chambers are almost evenly divided between Democrats and Republicans, with the Senate actually starting off 2001 with a 50–50 split, will complicate efforts to form working majorities on foreign policy issues. If the abrupt slowing in US economic expansion experienced in late 2000 and early 2001 were to continue, this would further muddle the outlook on foreign affairs, causing government leaders to focus even greater attention on domestic issues and prompting them to slash the relatively meagre budgets currently devoted to foreign aid and humanitarian assistance. A general reduction in foreign policy expenditures would become an even greater certainty if President Bush's proposed $1.6 trillion tax reduction package is ever implemented, especially during a period of slow economic growth.

However, the overall US record on human security issues need not be too gloomy over the next four to eight years. Ideally, President Bush will manifest his concern with global issues by resubmitting the Comprehensive Test Ban Treaty for Senate ratification. Certain safeguards can be put in place before submission, as recommended by a commission headed by John Shalikashvili, former chair of the Joint Chiefs of Staff. Although a long-shot proposition, the Ottawa Convention banning anti-personnel landmines might also be given renewed consideration, and in the interim the United States should definitely increase its funding to international agencies involved in defusing the millions of landmines scattered around the developing world. In spite of the chances being much less likely under Bush than if Al Gore had won the presidency, additional negotiations might also lead to eventual US ratification of the International Criminal Court, a step that would reinforce the US commitment to eliminate genocide and ethnic cleansing globally and to punish those responsible for such heinous acts. There is also a high probability that the United

States will pay all of its dues to the United Nations and co-operate more closely with UN agencies to improve the lives of people in the developing world. Improved relations within the Americas can also be bolstered through implementation of the FTAA by the middle of the decade, and Bush may even take the lead in promoting a new multilateral round of trade negotiations.

US 'foreign affairs' at the state and local levels can also contribute to strengthening human security in the first decade of the twenty-first century (Fry, 1998). Financially, US states and cities are in better shape than ever before, experiencing over $60 billion in budget surpluses in the year 2000. Most governors continue to support efforts that will foster greater international co-operation and eliminate protectionist barriers in the economic arena. Over 40 state governments now operate 180 offices abroad and half of the governors lead international trade and investment missions every year. Twelve hundred US cities have also entered into partnerships with 2,100 cities in 127 nations through Sister Cities International. One very successful local-to-local partnership has been between La Crosse, Wisconsin, and Dubna, Russia. The focus of this program is strengthening health-care services in Dubna and the efforts have borne significant fruit, with Dubna's health statistics being far better than Russia's statistics in almost every category (Wines, 2000). Such humanitarian co-operative programs can be repeated in scores of different ways with thousands of cities in developing countries, permitting many Americans to contribute directly to the well-being of their fellow citizens around the world via national and subnational governments as well as churches, civic groups, and other non-governmental agencies.

What is needed from the US government itself is a greater appreciation of what can be accomplished by acting in concert with other nations to enhance human security globally, an endeavour that Lloyd Axworthy consistently championed during his tenure as Canada's Minister of Foreign Affairs. In September 2000, 150 leaders from the 188 nations represented in the United Nations gathered in New York City to participate in the Millennium Summit. The principal theme of this historic conference was how globalization and rapid technological change could be combined to foster international co-operation and ease the plight of billions of people around the world. The summit concluded that by the year 2015 co-operation, appropriate technology transfer, and bilateral and multilateral assistance could cut in half the one billion people currently living on one dollar or less per day, reduce by half the one billion people who do not have access to clean water on a regular basis, ensure that all children receive at least a full primary school education, and halt the spread of AIDS. The UN members also agreed to set up a 'Net Corps' composed of volunteers who would travel to developing nations and help close the digital divide between the North and the South. These volunteers would train people to set up Internet networks and to use computer technology to improve local conditions in the fields of health, education, the environment, and small enterprises. Enthusiastic support from the Bush administration, combined with the allocation of significant US resources to this worthy cause, would do much to improve the overall performance of the US in the area of human security.

In conclusion, the United States remains too insular, too unilateral in its policy orientation, and too out of touch with the humanitarian challenges facing people around the globe. Nevertheless, its unparalleled military, diplomatic, and economic power base has contributed to regional stability in various parts of the world, helped expunge ethnic cleansing in the Balkans, and contributed to the defusing of tensions on the Korean Peninsula and the Formosa Strait, and in the Middle East, the Caribbean, and the British Isles. Its direct financial assistance to developing nations is far too low and the distribution of aid is skewed far too heavily towards the Middle East, thus failing to help those developing nations in greatest need. One remains skeptical whether George W. Bush can match Bill Clinton's record on human security, but, hopefully, the overall US contribution from the federal, state, and local government levels, as well as the non-governmental sector, will be more meaningful during the first decade of the twenty-first century than during the last decade of the twentieth century.

REFERENCES

Axworthy, Lloyd. 2000. 'Notes for an Address to the Woodrow Wilson International Center for Scholars', Washington, 16 June.

Cohen, William S. 2000. Speech to the Center for Strategic and International Studies, Washington, 2 Oct.

De Young, Karen, and Steven Mufson. 2001. 'Leaner, Less Visible NSC Taking Shape', *Washington Post*, 10 Feb., A1.

Freedom House. 2000. 'Global Democracy Continues Forward March'. Available at: <http://www.freedomhouse.org/media/pressrel/121900.htm>.

Fry, Earl H. 1998. *The Expanding Role of State and Local Governments in U.S. Foreign Affairs.* New York: Council on Foreign Relations Press.

Gates, Bill. 1999. *Business @ the Speed of Thought.* New York: Warner Books.

Marien, Michael. 1998. 'The Information Revolution May Not Benefit Society', in Paul A. Winters, ed., *The Information Revolution: Opposing Viewpoints.* San Diego: Greenhaven Press.

Myers, Steven Lee. 2001. 'Bush Takes First Step to Shrink Arsenal of Nuclear Warheads', *New York Times*, 9 Feb., A1, A10.

National Intelligence Council. 2000. *Global Trends 2015.* Available at: <http://www.cia.publications/globaltrends2015/index.html>.

Rielly, John E., ed. 1999. *American Public Opinion and U.S. Foreign Policy 1999.* Chicago: Chicago Council on Foreign Relations.

Sanger, David E. 2000. 'Economic Engines for Foreign Policy', *New York Times*, 28 Dec., A1.

Traub, James. 2001. 'W.'s World', *New York Times Magazine*, 14 Jan., 30.

US Information Service. 1998. 'Transcript: Clinton Meets with Rwandan Genocide Survivors', 25 Mar.

Wines, Michael. 2000. 'A Fit City Offers Russia a Self-Help Model', *New York Times*, 31 Dec. Available at: <http://www.nytimes.com/2000/12/31/world/31RUSS.html>.

7

Humanizing the UN Security Council

MICHAEL PEARSON

Canada's most recent tenure on the United Nations Security Council is just over. Was it worth it? The major diplomatic effort and expense to win accession; the constant pressures of participation; the struggle to advance a Canadian agenda within an 'old boys' club that frowned on change: did it make any difference? The critics will say probably not, although evaluation of diplomatic and political endeavour by a 'temporary' member in the Security Council—the most challenging of multilateral arenas—is admittedly an imperfect and subjective exercise, especially so soon after it is finished. Whether the critics are judging too quickly remains to be seen, but an initial review suggests an argument can be made that it did matter, that perhaps it was worth the trouble. As is so often the case in foreign relations, being at the right place at the right time with some of the right ideas and the right people—the right combination of 'fate and will', as political scientist James Eayrs (1967) put it—can result in the ability to make progress, achieve advances in thinking and decision-making, and make a mark.

The balance of forces in play while Canada served its two-year term on the Security Council (January 1999–December 2000) held the key to determining if progress was possible and the right combination was there. Some forces were specifically Canadian, some in the nature of the Council's work and the issues it was dealing with. This balance favoured Canada—a country well-regarded in UN circles with a track record of UN leadership, voted onto the Council first in its group and on the first ballot. It also had an experienced and wily ambassador, well-liked in New York, backed (and often fronted) by a purposeful Foreign Minister pushing a well-considered agenda. The Council in 1999 was obviously freed of the constraints of the Cold War, but it was still bedevilled by failures in Africa and weakened by the knowledge that UN commitments faced constant financial shortfalls. Sanctions policies against Iraq and Angola were not working, peacekeeping missions were struggling with changing dynamics and insufficient support, and global hotspots (the Balkans, Middle East, central and western Africa, Kashmir, East Timor) were getting hotter. More hopeful were the existence of an activist UN Secretary-General and relatively calm relations among the Council's five permanent members (the US, the UK, Russia, France, China— the P-5). Also convenient was the preordained opportunity offered the Canadian seat to hold the gavel of the Council—the monthly rotating presidency—on two occasions, the first only a month (February 1999) after joining. The presidency of the Security Council offers significant procedural authority; its wise use can do much to move preferred agendas.

All of these factors—strong personalities and clear agendas with some authority and credibility to wield in an institution bothered by past failure, pressing challenge, and no serious irritants—created a favourable balance, open to the potential of new approaches. This chapter will review how this potential played out and address whether and how the Canadian agenda for a revitalized Security Council had an effect on the Council's business and, by extension, the business of the United Nations. What was pursued? Did it move forward? Did it result in measurable change? Where do we go from here? These questions will be considered first by placing the Canadian approach to its Security Council role in the broader historical and political context—the place of the UN in Canadian foreign policy, including in the mind of a Foreign Minister who has generally been identified much more closely with Canada at the UN than the Prime Minister. The second context within which I will place Canada's role is the human security policy framework. The interests of Foreign Minister Lloyd Axworthy underlay his belief in the significance of human security as an organizing policy principle for both Canada and the UN. I will then review the Canadian preparations for Council membership, focusing on the substantive policy agenda constructed from Axworthy's human security 'world view', following that with a study of how those policy initiatives unfolded over the two-year period, with a particular focus on Canada's two Council presidencies (February 1999 and April 2000), where a clear push was made to promote the Canadian agenda. I will examine in various ways how the Canadian effort can be measured to determine evidence of progress or lack of progress. Based on this record, I will provide some preliminary assessments on Canada's relative achievements and look forward to where these might go post-Council membership.

CANADA AND THE UN: A FAVOURED CALLING

Any review of Canada's foreign policy priorities, past, present, or future, inevitably places relations with the United Nations near the top of the list. For five and a half decades, beginning with the role played in the negotiations leading up to the signing of the UN Charter in San Francisco in 1945, Canada's foreign relations have been characterized by the multilateral impulse, centred on the UN. Canadian leaders immediately after World War II highlighted support for the UN system as a necessary focal point of foreign policy. The advent of new personalities and parties in charge of the national government, along with the foreign policy reviews that often accompanied them, never resulted in any questioning of the importance of the UN in Canadian foreign policy, while other long-standing priorities were questioned, even changed. Such consistent and bipartisan federal government support for the UN, based in part on continued high levels of public support, was both a function of history and a practical understanding of Canada's security requirements in the last half of the twentieth century.

Postwar experience simply reinforced a UN focus in Canadian foreign policy. Notable milestones (among many) along the way included the instrumental contribution made by Canadian External Affairs Minister Lester B. Pearson to the establishment of the first major UN peacekeeping mission in the Suez in 1956, Prime Minister Pierre Trudeau's Strategy of Suffocation (of nuclear weapons) announced before the UN General Assembly in 1978, and the Mulroney government's insistence that US President George Bush (the elder) seek UN endorsement via a UN Security Council resolution[1] of a military action in the Persian Gulf to roll back Iraq's invasion of Kuwait in 1990.

Canada's enduring commitment to the UN has been matched by the expectations of the international community that Canada was and continues to be a major UN player. Initial leadership and ongoing participation in UN peacekeeping operations are an important reason for this reputation, as has been ongoing Canadian diplomatic excellence throughout the UN system. Another symbol has been participation in the Security Council, the highest-ranking decision-making body of the UN. Among the non-permanent members of the Security Council, Canada ranks among the highest repeaters, with the latest 1999–2000 term marking the sixth time since initial membership in 1948–9. To be a member of the Security Council any country must receive at least two-thirds voting support from the UN membership. In Canada's case, it has received this level of support on the first ballot of every election—an important indication of the degree of confidence and credibility Canada has earned from the international community.

Clearly, Canada was no stranger to UN activism when it assumed its Council seat on 1 January 1999 for the last two years of the twentieth century. Nor was it burdened by domestic doubts, uncertain support, or unconsidered policy priorities. In fact, the combination of historical commitment and reputation, a Foreign Minister with a well-developed foreign policy agenda, particularly in its global/multilateral character, and the specific nature of the successful campaign for a seat created significant expectations for a robust Canadian presence at the Council table. It could be argued that too heavy a weighting of Canada's role on the Security Council skews a proper assessment of Axworthy's approach to the UN. However, the opposite is argued here: Axworthy's Security Council agenda and activities most clearly defined the foreign policy priority of human security as pursued by Canada during his time as Foreign Minister, and therefore a study of that agenda and those actions allows for the most useful and encompassing assessment to be made.

DEVELOPING A HUMAN SECURITY AGENDA IN THE UN

When the Liberal Party won the 1993 election and took office after nine years in opposition, Lloyd Axworthy was not named Foreign Minister even though he had been the Liberal Party's foreign affairs critic since 1990 and had been the architect of the party's foreign policy platform.[2] However, as was evidenced in that platform and in other activities taken on as foreign affairs critic, including the organization of a public symposium on UN reform in 1992, Axworthy had clearly developed views on the UN's place in Canadian foreign policy. The man who did become Foreign Minister in 1993, André Ouellet (another former Trudeau cabinet minister who had been foreign affairs critic immediately preceding Axworthy under John Turner), was also a UN enthusiast. He was committed to the implementation of the Axworthy-inspired Liberal platform's UN reform agenda (including a more 'interactive' Security Council), using his first appearance before the annual fall UN General Assembly (UNGA) session in September 1994 to promote a number of Canadian suggestions for reform, including the strengthening of the UN's capacity to react quickly in establishing a peacekeeping presence in areas where international peace and security were threatened (Ouellet, 1994).[3] Subsequently, Ouellet released the February 1995 foreign policy statement, *Canada in the World*, that emphasized the central role of the UN in Canadian foreign policy. Notably, the statement also included a specific endorsement of the concept of 'shared human security', defined as 'focussing on the economic, social and political needs of the individual'. When he spoke again before the UNGA during its fiftieth session in the fall of 1995, Ouellet continued to put attention on reform, highlighted by the tabling of a Canadian study on the UN's rapid reaction capability (Ouellet, 1995).

The replacement of Ouellet as Foreign Minister by Lloyd Axworthy in January 1996 was thus not a dividing line separating different emphases on the importance of the UN in Canadian foreign policy. What Axworthy did bring to the position of Foreign Minister was a long-developed and well-considered agenda in foreign affairs, coupled with a sense of urgency. This resulted in an accelerated level of activism across many fronts, the UN included.

Axworthy's agenda took shape on two levels—policy initiatives and international consensus-building. Much has been said (and no doubt more will be) about Axworthy's high and varied number of policy initiatives, but less has been said about his basic approach to policy development and the 'selling' component of policy ideas, critically important in today's globalized and information-glutted human society. As the saying goes, an idea is never a good one until you convince someone else that it is. Axworthy had a keen understanding of the shifting nature of international affairs at the end of the twentieth century and also knew the importance of promoting consensus around new ideas and concepts. He read constantly and widely and was not in the least unwilling to borrow from suggestions articulated by academics and others, putting them to work in policy development and explanation. The idea of 'soft power' came from Joseph Nye (1990), while the minister's oft-recited description of the fundamentally changing international landscape as representative of the 'shifting tectonic plates of cultures and civilizations' creating 'convulsive change' came from the writings of Felipe Fernandez-Armesto (1995). Axworthy believed deeply that world politics were in a fundamental period of evolution and Canada was in an excellent position to affect that evolution. An ardent admirer of Lester Pearson's diplomacy, Axworthy saw his mentor and predecessor's commitment to the principles of internationalism *plus* the importance of consensus formation and coalition-building within international institutions as the model to follow. He envisaged that the path laid down by Pearson (and followed, eventually, by Pierre Trudeau as well as by Brian Mulroney and Joe Clark) of Canada as idea-generator and seller/promoter had continued, if not increased, relevance under his watch. He was determined to be in the same mould of seizing opportunity to advance causes in the role of 'value-added nation'.

What was the 'cause' in the winter of 1996? For the new Minister of Foreign Affairs, the issue defining the change in world politics was human security. Axworthy's belief in it was stated in his first speech as Foreign Minister three weeks after entering the world of diplomacy:

> My involvement at the World Summit for Social Development in Copenhagen last year brought home to me the need to define 'security' beyond a political or military concept. True security means progress on all

fronts—environmental, social and economic. If your drinking water is poisoned or you lack basic health care or education, how secure can you feel about today, let alone tomorrow? . . . From the Earth Summit in Rio to the Human Rights Conference in Vienna; from the Population Conference in Cairo to the Women's Conference in Beijing, the world is beginning to recognize the links. Canada must become a leading voice in the expression of this need for a broader definition of security. (Axworthy, 1996a)

Thus began an odyssey of activity and initiative to develop, promote, and implement an idea and a belief that led, notably, to the peacebuilding initiative, the anti-personnel landmines campaign, the push for the International Criminal Court, the Canadian international information strategy, the Arctic Council, the corporate social responsibility code, Kosovo as an exercise in human security, and the thrust for rights of the child.

The application of the concept of human security and Axworthy's approach to promoting it in the Canadian agenda for the UN were critical and enduring preoccupations for the minister. In that first speech as Foreign Minister, the indicators he mentioned as reference points for a broadening of the definition of security were all UN conferences. Axworthy clearly recognized the UN system, in its many manifestations, as a vital instrument for developing and implementing human security policies. The UN-related efforts of Lester Pearson and the recent work of Ouellet were also important antecedents. This is not to say he always took the UN route. The landmines campaign was an excellent example of bypassing the UN in favour of a process that would not be shackled by UN rules of consensus, and there are a number of other issues where the minister pursued avenues outside the world body to achieve his human security policy goals. However, this was not a deliberate strategy, but an exercise in practical diplomacy. Axworthy's instinct was always to work under UN auspices, but when that way was blocked, as it was in the case of landmines, he was quite willing to go another route. However, UN sanction was always important to the minister and he succeeded in ultimately getting it for the landmines treaty. The UN is the embodiment, above all other institutions, of the world community, and therefore the real success of human security was most importantly measured in its UN context. As will be explained further below, this is why he wanted the Security Council, the UN's 'cabinet', to be exposed to and involved in the concept.

The shape of human security that Axworthy wanted to fashion through the UN was revealed in his first speech to the General Assembly in September 1996. In it, he used the term 'sustainable human security', although the first word was dropped thereafter as superfluous. The speech illustrated the minister's broader approach to international affairs and how UN reform was defined through the human security prism:

> Changing times have set us a new and broader agenda, which includes focusing on the security needs of the individual—in other words, sustainable human security. Unfortunately, new times have not sufficiently been reflected by a rededication to the UN as an expression of the spirit of internationalism. . . . The need for recommitment to the UN is clear, and so, too, is the need for the renewal, restructuring and refocusing of the organization and its various bodies and agencies. . . . The road map is clear; we do not need to study it any further. Now is the time to move forward in a concerted, comprehensive way.

It also provided the first glimpse of the minister's thinking regarding the Security Council:

> Another priority is to strengthen the effectiveness of the Security Council by giving it greater accountability, representativeness, transparency and responsibility. Canada attaches particular importance to the need to ensure meaningful participation in decision-making by those members whose nationals—military or civilian—are in the crossfire of the conflicts over which the Council is deliberating. (Axworthy, 1996b)

APPLYING HUMAN SECURITY TO THE SECURITY COUNCIL

Having last served on the Council in 1989–90 and with a tradition of being on it once a decade, it was perhaps expected that Canada would have wanted to both run for and be successful in election to the Council in October 1998, regardless of who was in charge and what agenda was being promoted. There is no question that the notion of running for a Council seat was being actively considered by the Department of Foreign Affairs and International Trade (DFAIT) at least two years before the fall of 1998. This was hardly surprising, given the effort that must go into running a successful bid.

Although not the subject of this chapter, a whole book could be written on the intricacies of developing and executing a strategy for getting the two-thirds UN membership vote required to win a seat; it makes running a national election campaign seem simple by comparison.

What is particularly notable and relevant about the campaign for a Canadian seat was the nature of the agenda Canada promoted to attract votes. In past election campaigns for a Council seat, Canada emphasized in general its 'good UN membership' credentials. Early discussions on the nature of the latest campaign looked at it in the same way. However, Axworthy decided to take the 'talking points' to another level. His developing ideas regarding human security and its applications were, in his mind, easily transferable to the context of running for a Council seat. This meant articulating not just credentials and reputation, but an actual agenda of issues and ideas to be pursued as a Council member. Three major themes were agreed upon in the lead-up to the vote: greater *transparency* in the Council's work; applying concrete elements of *human security in Council debates and decisions (resolutions)*; and increasing *the credibility and effectiveness* of the Council.

Now it is one thing to actively pursue an agenda, especially one involving necessary change in the Council's way of doing business, after winning a seat. It is quite another to do so *before* an election. Voting for Council seats is by secret ballot, unlike many other UN votes. Oral, even written, promises to support candidacies cannot be treated as guarantees when it comes to the 'ballot box', as Australia had found to its consternation and grief when running for a seat a couple of years before Canada. To promote a substantive reform agenda in advance entailed a risk that some thought unnecessary and potentially dangerous. Canada was in a tough competition with the Netherlands and Greece for two seats, neither of which was promoting an agenda for change in the Council.[4]

Perhaps to the dismay of some Canadian officials, these factors did not overly concern Axworthy. The minister saw Council membership as a clear opportunity to promote human security in a powerful world body. If Canada was able to demonstrate it could be elected to the Council with a clearly defined and transparent agenda, laying out the tenets of human security in a framework of Council reform, so much the better—it could be used as an important source of legitimacy to be drawn on when the slogging got difficult. Besides,

Lloyd Axworthy was a true democrat. He liked the idea of being open, of being voted in based on a clear set of goals known to all.

The minister used his 1998 UNGA speech to set out the Canadian agenda and call for support from UN members:

> The Security Council remains at the centre of what the UN is all about. However, the Council's legitimacy is increasingly being questioned. To remain credible, the Council must re-examine the traditional interpretation of its mandate. The Council needs to broaden its horizons in addressing emerging threats that impact on our security. Thematic debates on these issues, where all member states can participate, are a good step. The addition of peacebuilding in the Council's range of responses to threats to peace and security is also welcome. . . . The way the Council does its work must be more open and transparent. Far from constraining the Council's efficiency, this will improve the decisions it takes and render its actions more effective. The trend for permanent members increasingly to assume more control over the Council's agenda, thereby marginalizing elected members, runs contrary to democratic principles which so inform our political institutions at the close of the 20th century. The distinction between permanent and elected members needs to be narrowed rather than widened. In sum, the Council we need for the next century must be more responsible, more accountable and less impenetrable. We hope you will support Canada to advance these aspirations. (Axworthy, 1998)

It sounded almost like a stump speech on the campaign hustings, and in a way it was. Axworthy laid out clearly the three themes mentioned earlier, but it is notable that he put more emphasis on the importance of transparency in the Council: this had been a key sore point for both UN member states and the interested public, who alike were often in the dark on how the Council made decisions. The repeated reference to 'elected' versus 'permanent' members (which would sound familiar to Canadians contemplating MPs and senators) was probably included just to make this point. To the wider membership of the UN, transparency sounded both necessary and clearly reasonable. In the end, the vote was a solid endorsement—Canada secured 131 of 177 votes on the first ballot, easily beating the two-thirds requirement and finishing ahead of the Dutch (to the surprise of many).

PURSUING THE REFORM AGENDA: THE FEBRUARY 1999
PRESIDENCY

Finding specific issues and opportunities to advance the causes of
transparency, a human security imprint, and Council credibility while
on the Council is easier said than done. Much of the Council's work
is responsive—reacting to a crisis, renewing peacekeeping mandates,
responding to reports of the Secretary-General and requests for issues
to be discussed. The time left to be proactive is precious little. Using
that time to try to do too much too soon would risk undermining the
entire enterprise barely before being out of the gate. Fortunately, the
luck of the alphabet had Canada assuming the presidency of the
Security Council only one month into its two-year term. The presidency provided an ideal position from which to advance agendas.

Increasing the Council's transparency was perhaps the easiest
agenda to advance, although not because of any standing rules. The
Council, some say as a result of P-5 obstinance, has never adopted
anything beyond provisional rules of procedure. This can make the
establishment of new procedural norms or the expansion of existing
practices difficult. For example, there is no tradition for the Council
to provide easily accessible public information on its meetings in
advance beyond basic references to the time of meeting. There are
no requirements to hold any Council sessions in public, and usually
there were no more than one or two a month. There was also little
tradition in the Council of briefing sessions with non-members on
current issues before it.

Canada used its position as president to try to change these
dynamics. Canada started providing a weekly breakdown of the
Council's program of work for public consumption (albeit on a
Canadian-generated Web site, not the official UN Web site). A number of open sessions were held and the president (who is usually the
ambassador to the UN, in this case Robert Fowler) regularly spoke to
the press after meetings, whether open or closed. He also regularly
briefed non-Council member states on the results of closed consultations and various resolutions and other Council decisions, in part
expanding on like-minded initiatives started by former Council members (the so-called Arias formula meetings, instigated by Venezuela,
involving meetings of Council and non-Council members).

Canada's second agenda—increasing the Council's credibility—
was pursued during its February presidency through the review of

UN sanctions against Angola. The civil war in Angola has been long and bloody, fuelled by the continuous availability of arms purchased through illegal diamond sales. UN efforts to stall the inflow of arms and prevent illegal sales through sanctions had not met with much success and a recent escalation in the violence threatened the future of the UN's peacekeeping presence in the country. The credibility of the sanctions effort was increasingly in question, raising the spectre of a total UN failure. Canada had agreed to assume the chair of the Angola sanctions committee when it joined the Council (turning down the opportunity to take on the Iraq sanctions committee chair, where progress remained totally stalemated) and used the dual position of committee chair and Council president to push for a new approach to the sanctions effort. This took the form of a proposal for an experts study on measures to address the complex interrelationship between the diamond (and oil) trade and the movement of illegal proceeds (dollars) from the trade into arms trafficking that continued to allow Angola's rebels (UNITA) to defy the Angola peace agreement.

The importance of the Council's endorsement of the recommendation to establish an expert panel (through Resolution 1229 of 26 February 1999) and subsequently to authorize the panel (Resolution 1237 of 7 May 1999) lay in its willingness to concentrate on a practical, but comprehensive, approach to address the weakness of the sanctions regime in Angola and to allow an entity outside of the UN Secretariat to take responsibility for conducting it. As we will see below, under the April 2000 Canadian presidency, this led to a set of recommendations for UN action that gave the sanctions effort the chance to achieve the goals set out for it.[5]

The third agenda—the human security imprint—was the area where Foreign Minister Axworthy took personal leadership. As president, Canada secured agreement from the Council to hold an open session on the thematic subject of civilians in armed conflict. Axworthy himself chaired the session. The debate was remarkable in several ways, not least of which was the participation of the heads of the International Committee of the Red Cross (ICRC, which had never before been invited to speak at the Council) and UNICEF. At the conclusion of the debate, Axworthy issued a presidential statement on behalf of the Council that expressed its direct responsibility to consider and act on the issue: 'The Security Council expresses its willingness to respond, in accordance with the Charter of the

United Nations, to situations in which civilians, as such, have been targeted or humanitarian assistance to civilians has been deliberately obstructed' (UNSC, 1999a). The statement went on to authorize the Secretary-General to prepare a report within eight months on means by which the UN could better ensure the protection of civilians in armed conflict, including through the use of Council resolutions. This was a first for the Council—to endorse specifically the possible use of UN authority not just to deal with the consequences of civilian attacks, but to intimate readiness to take measures against perpetrators.

Canada chaired a second Council session later in the month on the same theme, this time to allow UN member states not on the Council to address the issue, including suggestions for the Secretary-General to consider in his analysis and the expression of views on the interventions of the ICRC, UNICEF, and others. More than 20 member states took up the opportunity. The significance of these sessions is not to be underestimated. Not only was Canada able to bring a thematic issue to the Council's agenda, but it was able to do so in open session, with member states not on the Security Council participating in unprecedented fashion. It was able to secure clear supporting language from its fellow Council members (including China, Russia, and others that have traditionally been averse to endorsing a UN role in ways that might trespass on national sovereignty) and ensure proper follow-up through the requirement of a report from the Secretary-General. Furthermore, in a resolution passed by the Council later in February on the Eritrean–Ethiopia conflict (Resolution 1227 of 10 February 1999), wording was included that specifically cited the necessity of protecting civilians, human rights, and international humanitarian law. References to human rights and humanitarian law were not new for Council resolutions, but in the past they were sporadic and not coherently brought together. The combination of all three references in one resolution was notable.

In summary, the February 1999 presidency was a strong start for Canada in promoting its three-pronged reform agenda for the Security Council. However, success in getting the Security Council to be more transparent, more engaged in human security, and more prepared to acknowledge past failure and to consider different approaches takes more than a month of chairing meetings. The real question is whether others followed a trend in these directions. Subsequent presidencies of the Council after February suggest that indeed there was a positive trend towards open meetings, the inclusion of civilian protection references in resolutions, and practical decision-making. Canada benefited in its efforts to promote these trends from like-minded Council members such as the Netherlands and the UK, which under the Blair government had become much less conservative in its Council participation. Progress was such that the Council agreed to hold further thematic debates in 1999, including on the protection of children in armed conflict, small arms (which resulted in a detailed presidential statement [UNSC, 1999b]), and conflict prevention (with an emphasis in the resulting presidential statement on the intent of the Council to 'give special attention to the humanitarian consequences of armed conflicts and [build a] culture of prevention') (UNSC, 1999c). When the Secretary-General delivered his report to the Council in September 1999, Resolution 1265 of 17 September 17 1999 included 23 operative paragraphs, unusually long by Council standards, including the following:

> 10. *Expresses* its willingness to respond to situations of armed conflict where civilians are being targeted or humanitarian assistance to civilians is being deliberately obstructed, including through the consideration of appropriate measures at the Council's disposal in accordance with the Charter of the United Nations, and *notes*, in that regard, the relevant recommendations contained in the report of the Secretary-General;

> 11. *Expresses* its willingness to consider how peacekeeping mandates might better address the negative impact of armed conflict on civilians;

> 12. *Expresses* its support for the inclusion, where appropriate, in peace agreements and mandates of United Nations peacekeeping missions, of specific and adequate measures for the disarmament, demobilization and reintegration of ex-combatants, with special attention given to the demobilization and reintegration of child soldiers . . .;

> 13. *Notes* the importance of including in the mandates of peacemaking, peacekeeping and peace-building operations special protection and assistance provisions for groups requiring particular attention, including women and children . . . .

This was an important achievement for Canada. In less than a year on the Council, it had passed several significant milestones in all three of its areas of reform and was making real progress in getting other Council members to respond to and emulate Canadian efforts. When Axworthy addressed the UN's 54th General Assembly in September, he had reason to feel pleased with developments. However, there could be no resting on laurels, apparent or real. The minister put the issues at play in context:

> There are legitimate questions about the purposes, limits and standards for Council engagement for humanitarian ends, which also raise difficult contradictions with regard to the principle of non-interference. Clear and consistent criteria are needed against which the necessity, or not, of humanitarian intervention—including enforcement—can be judged and applied. These tests must be very demanding, based on fundamental breaches of international humanitarian and human rights law. The human dimension makes it imperative that the Council adapt the blunt instrument of sanctions into a targeted tool so they hurt where they are supposed to hurt. The Council also needs to show the resolve to implement sanctions once they are in place. This is Canada's objective as Chair of the Council's Angola Sanctions Committee—to develop tougher measures to constrain the trade in arms and diamonds, thereby making it more difficult for UNITA to wage war. . . . A human security agenda highlights the urgent need to face clearly the Council's representation and its decision-making processes—especially the inappropriate use and persistent threat of the veto—where it can compromise, complicate and slow down determined, urgent international action to protect people. The Council needs to come to grips with these challenges if it is to maintain its credibility in the eyes of the people it serves. Membership on the Council is a trust—and Council members need to demonstrate their capacity to maintain this trust. (Axworthy, 1999a)

Preachiness is an accusation that has often been levelled at Axworthy, and one could perceive this speech in this manner, but to do so would miss the point. The minister's view was a recognition of the importance of codifying Council practice to ensure it could address human security effectively and in timely fashion. The challenge for Axworthy, Robert Fowler, and the Canadian government was to cement this emergent practice in the short time left to Canada as a member of the international system's chief decision-making authority.

PURSUING THE REFORM AGENDA: THE APRIL 2000
PRESIDENCY

When Canada reassumed the presidency of the Security Council on
April Fool's Day of 2000 (the day fell on a Saturday when the Council
does not usually sit), it had completed 15 months of its 24-month
stay. The reform agenda it had been pursuing had been given time
to take root and grow. There was clear evidence of change in the
Council's methods of work and the nature of its substantive positions
on issues. The US, Council president in January 2000, chaired seven
open meetings, a record. The March president's statement detailing
the Council's concerns regarding the 'humanitarian aspects' of its
business was notable in its use of human security language. Even the
shadow of the NATO bombing campaign against Serbia for trans-
gressions in Kosovo the previous year, and Canada's inability (along
with other NATO members on the Council) to gain Council support
for NATO's action, was not seen as a step back or a threat to the further evolution of progress in the business on 1st Avenue and 44th
Street in New York City.[6] Consequently, Axworthy and his team felt
the time was ripe for a more ambitious set of goals during the second presidency. The minister decided to spend a significant part of
the month in New York, personally chairing Council sessions. In the
end he chaired six sessions, a record number to be chaired by a
Foreign Minister in a single month that, Wayne Gretzky-like, will
probably never be broken.

The issues Canada brought to the Council's agenda in April, in
addition to the normal workload, focused on a number of conflict
situations and themes, interweaving the agendas of transparency,
credibility, and human security. They included: the human rights
dimension of the Afghanistan conflict; the lessons of Rwanda; the
Angola sanctions regime; the broader issue of the effectiveness and
humanitarian impact of sanctions; and another go-around on the protection of civilians in armed conflict. In each case, Canada insisted
on open debates ('transparency in action'). Out of the discussions
came two resolutions, on the protection of civilians in armed conflict
and Angola sanctions, a presidential statement on Afghanistan, and
the creation of a working group to assess further the impact of sanctions on human security. In all cases, the Canadian chair sought to
focus the debate on the human security issues at stake and the necessity of addressing these issues in credible, practical ways. For exam-

ple, the Rwanda debate was not designed as yet another retrospec-
tive, but rather as a consideration of the lessons of Rwanda for future
Council action to protect civilians in armed conflict, with current
challenges in Sierra Leone and the Congo specifically cited. The
Afghanistan debate centred on the humanitarian situation rather than
the terrorist threat, while the general sanctions review, to which non-
Council UN members and others were invited to speak, was an effort
to place attention on how to make sanctions more effective and targeted, maximizing the pain intended to political leaderships and min-
imizing that forced on innocent publics.[7] The agreement by the
Council to sponsor an informal working group on sanctions policy,
to report back by the end of the year, was seen by observers as an
important breakthrough in dealing with an issue constantly overshadowed by the debate over the utility of sanctions against Iraq.

On Angola, the Canadian president sponsored and received the
unanimous support of the Council to adopt Resolution 1295 (18 April
2000) that incorporated a large majority of the recommendations
made by the expert panel group established under the previous
Canadian presidency in February 1999. The resolution was notable
in its specific naming of sanctions violators and authorizing punitive
action against them if necessary, as well as in its establishment of a
new monitoring mechanism for ensuring adherence to UN-authorized
sanctions. UN observers familiar with the sanctions issue saw this as
a key, if not the crucial, Canadian accomplishment of its presidency
because it brought the Council to another level of effectiveness in
utilizing what is often seen as the most blunt instrument of diplomacy
short of war. As for the protection of civilians, the April discussion
looked at means to reinforce the commitments made by the Council
in Resolution 1265 the previous September through the adoption of
a successor resolution (1296 of 19 April 2000). This was designed to
give the Council specific guidance on means to ensure that resolutions on specific conflicts and peacekeeping missions included clear
reference to the responsibilities expected and resources required to
protect civilians. Both Foreign Minister Axworthy and Secretary-
General Kofi Annan highlighted the fact that the Council had already
taken the requisite action through the adoption of appropriate language in its authorization of peace support operations in Congo,
Sierra Leone, and East Timor.

With success did come some failure. Axworthy attempted to have
the humanitarian impact of the civil war in Sudan, a particular pre-

occupation of the minister, discussed by the Council, but he was rebuffed. As mentioned earlier, the Council also refused to consider endorsement of the NATO air campaign against Serbia, although this occurred before Canada assumed the presidency of the Council. Overall, Canada's April 2000 presidency was an unparalleled success. Its accomplishments were of major consequence. It is too soon to tell whether there will be sustained commitment over time by Council and the wider UN membership to Canadian priorities and progress, but this cannot diminish Canada's effort and the measurable results it achieved.

ASSESSING THE EFFORT

Canada went into its two-year term on the Security Council with three major agenda elements: increasing the transparency of the Council's business, instilling a human security component into Council debates and decision-making, and raising the credibility of the Council's work and output—procedure, policy, and practice. Canada used its presidencies to advance these goals.

Did it work? Did it make a difference? The foregoing suggests a generally positive view. The interconnected nature of the three agendas helped significantly. It was easier to argue thematic debates should be more open and it was easier to promote resolutions with a human security focus when the credibility of the Council was at stake. In this regard, it seems Canada chose its issues wisely and did its work astutely. The vigorous support of like-minded Council members and the Secretary-General was also important, as was crucial backing from P-5 members, especially the UK. Let us take each agenda element in turn.

Transparency

When one is operating from the starting point of no clearly defined rules of procedure, measuring progress is not simple. Endeavours in past years, including that co-spearheaded by Canada to have the Council consult with troop-contributing countries before adopting peacekeeping resolutions, had unquestionably been spotty. However, there have been more open sessions of the Council, in part related to the increased number of thematic debates. Participation in Council debates by non-Council member states has clearly been on the general increase. Canada used its position as president of the Council to push for and hold open sessions and to give them a higher profile by having the Foreign Minister in the president's chair. Before 1999, the Council would hold open sessions (debating, as opposed to simple resolution adoption sessions, which are always open) rarely more than once a month. Now, it holds them three to six times a month, to the point where there seems to be a contest as to which president can call the most open meetings. In January 2001, Singapore scheduled five. For the first time, other than a very select few UN officials, non-governmental actors, both from UN-related agencies and from civil society NGOs, have addressed the Council. A publicly available program of work (Council business) is being posted and more public consultations and briefings have been taking place, such as the Arias-formula informal briefings/consultations under Council sponsorship for non-Council states and non-governmental organizations, an initiative begun in 1998. Canada took the initiative to produce weekly summaries of the Council's work that have been available on the Department of Foreign Affairs Web site. Also, new Council members are now allowed to sit in on Council deliberations in the month (December) immediately preceding their accession to the Council so they can start getting accustomed to how the Council works.

These are all favourable developments. However, as some UN observers have noted, charting progress is one thing; evidence of a trend-line indicating sustainability is another. It is too early to tell whether the trend towards more transparency will hold. But the signs are there.

Continued advocacy is essential. Canada was a champion of transparency as a Council member, and used that position, as did Argentina, Portugal, Venezuela, and others before it, to pursue this objective. New champions within the rotating non-permanent membership of the Council need to carry the torch to secure these advances and promote further ones. A P-5 champion would be even better. The UK was very supportive of Canada's approach and might well be expected to continue in a similar vein. The rest of the UN membership needs to advocate as well, as Canada no doubt will from the UN 'backbenches'. These efforts need to be co-ordinated with other member states, agencies, NGOs, and UN watchers.

Human Security
Reviewing the nature and content of the some of the Council's resolutions during the 1999–2000 period, one may measure the impact

of a human security agenda on Council business. Before the end of the year 2000, when Canada was required to vacate its seat (along with the Netherlands from its UN regional group, succeeded by Ireland and Norway), the Security Council had adopted a total of 49 resolutions, down from 64 in 1999.[8] Of the 49, seven could be classified as 'thematic' in nature, for a total of 10 thematic resolutions over the two years. There were also a number of other thematic debates that did not call for, or result in, a resolution. In the immediately preceding year (1998), the Council had been very busy (72 resolutions adopted), but only two could be considered thematic. In 1997 there were no thematic resolutions among the 53 adopted.

Numbers cannot tell a story or point to a conclusion on their own, but it is not unreasonable to suggest that Canada's efforts to promote thematic debates and resolutions clearly had an impact and discernible results. By definition, Security Council resolutions are considered to be of major international consequence, reflecting as they do the decisions of the world's most representative 'cabinet', and enforceable as they are under international law. In this sense, the Council's adoption of resolutions on civilians, women, and children in armed conflict as a result of ongoing Canadian agitation and leadership (to the point where one exasperated P-5 diplomat said: 'what's next—protecting pets in armed conflict?') is meaningful evidence of attention to the UN's responsibility to protect the innocent victims of war in a continued conflict environment. Specific conflict and peace support operation resolutions with components on civilian protection, child protection, human rights monitors, and similar commitments constitute concrete advances. In addition, the Secretary-General was of crucial help to Canada's effort. Kofi Annan's commitment to human security ideas has been as strong as Axworthy's; Annan's reports on civilians and children in armed conflict provided the additional impetus necessary to turn a thematic debate into a concrete commitment via resolution.[9]

Nonetheless, real questions remain. They are primarily related to the issue of continuity and the maintenance of momentum. Axworthy sponsored the creation of a multinational 'human security network' of approximately a dozen like-minded states, including Norway, Ireland, Chile, Mali, and Slovenia, that was intended to shepherd the human security agenda at the UN and elsewhere. Ireland and Norway are now on the Council, but will they deliver? Canada also announced earlier in 2000 its intention to create a 'group of friends' of the civilians in armed conflict to monitor and promote progress. This group remains to be formalized. Canada's own continued commitment under the tenure of the new Foreign Minister, John Manley, is also unknown; informal soundings within DFAIT indicate his interest in human security is 'somewhat less' than Axworthy's. This is not to say he or DFAIT officials in Ottawa, New York, or elsewhere will not continue to have an interest and a say in the deliberations of the Council, but without regular priority attached to the underlying agenda that guided Canada's actions while on the Council, it is inevitable that attention to that agenda will slip.

Credibility of the Council

The Angola sanctions review and follow-up; the expert panel process; the broader sanctions policy review and follow-up; the increased references to achievable and resourceable peace support operation mandates—these are all indications of the Council's recognition of and acting upon the need to adopt more credible resolutions and to focus on practical action. This commitment was reflected in the Millennium Summit Declaration (Resolution 1318 of 7 September 2000) approved by the heads of government of the 15 Council members. The Brahimi Report (Brahimi, 2000) on the future of peace support operations and the subsequent Council endorsement of most of the Report's recommendations through Resolution 1327 (13 November 2000) are further important steps in this direction.

However, one of the clearest and most needed indicators of the UN capacity to respond effectively to crisis and ensure credible action is a rapid deployment capability, which was promoted by Canada through Foreign Minister Ouellet in 1995. Annan himself, in speaking before the Council during its April 2000 debate on Resolution 1296 regarding the protection of civilians in armed conflict, emphasized the critical need for this capability. Unfortunately, Axworthy's active support for moving this agenda forward was notable in its absence. Other ministers in the Canadian government (Defence Minister Arthur Eggleton, in particular) have shown some interest, but significant follow-up by the Canadian government to the bold steps taken five years ago remain to be seen (Langille, 2000). Ironically, in the recent cases where rapid deployment occurred and clearly made a difference (East Timor and Sierra Leone), it was undertaken through the unilateral initiative of Australia and Britain, respectively, and only subsequently endorsed and reinforced through Council resolution. This is a disappointing reality, and Canada's lack of serious support is lamentable.

All this being said, it is reasonable to suggest that Canada made a huge effort to create and enhance new norms of Security Council action during its two-year term. The evidence suggests that this norm-building effort met with considerable success.

LOOKING AHEAD

Now that Canada has left the Security Council, a number of reviews and assessments will doubtless emerge, with varying perspectives on Axworthy's success or failure in achieving a goal of reform on the Council. There are some important questions that should be asked about the future of the Council. Canada benefited from a useful constellation of forces that accompanied its well-considered agenda for the Security Council. Such constellations by definition are not easily replicated. Where the politics of Security Council agenda-setting worked in Canada's favour in 1999–2000, those same politics could easily turn the tide in the other direction. The new Bush administration in Washington is not likely to support UN activism, even while it is apparently determined to stay out of global trouble spots.

This will have important implications for the implementation of the Brahimi Report, which should be a critical focus for Canadian UN policy in the months to come. Sixteen of the top 20 troop contributors to UN missions are countries from the developing world. Will the necessary reconciliation between their capacities and the needs of complex peace support operations, as outlined by Lakhdar Brahimi, be met, and will Canada try to play a leading role in making it so? Both ministers and officials have said Canada will do so, but the lack of effort on the rapid deployment front is cause for concern. There is also the question of following up the useful advances in policy thinking on sanctions. The new US Secretary of State, Colin Powell, has already come out in favour of continuing tough sanctions against Iraq and has not yet shown any sensitivity to the lessons of the past. This may be understandable given his personal history on Iraq, but it leaves many questions as yet unanswered. One can hope, though it is probably unlikely, that he will have on his reading list the useful analyses undertaken by the Council expert groups, let alone Canadian sources (see Drohan, 2000). The utilization (or not) of the expert groups by the Council will, in the minds of some UN observers, tell the tale.

The question of Foreign Minister Manley's commitment to human security at the UN or elsewhere has already been raised. The commitment of the Council and the broader UN membership will also bear watching. Axworthy left behind a Canadian-sponsored International Commission on Intervention and State Sovereignty[10] that is to report to the UN by October 2001 on how this difficult issue should be handled. The reaction of key players to the Commission's report will be instructive. The square peg and round hole will need to be reconciled, as Axworthy put it in his Princeton speech:

> the very same countries that argue against humanitarian intervention on the basis of sovereignty are the most anxious to join trade and commercial organizations, which, by their nature, involve ceding a certain amount of national control. It is hard to understand why it is acceptable to sacrifice sovereignty for economic interests, but not in the human interest. (Axworthy, 1999b)

A fair lament, but will people listen?

Finally, in looking ahead, one is struck by the singular lack of interest Canada has shown in promoting the expansion of the Security Council. Axworthy and others have not hesitated to comment on the importance of closing the gap between permanent and elected members of the Council, intimating that the legitimacy of the Council is being called into question the longer such a gap remains wide. There have been repeated calls to reduce the use (or threat of use) of the veto and to expand the elected membership of the Council at any given time. However, there seems little appetite in Ottawa for a campaign to promote this most fundamental and difficult reform of the Security Council, whose membership has remained practically unaltered in 55 years. There is no question many other UN countries seem similarly unable to take on this cause; even the pressures brought by Japan and Germany appear to have receded. However, in a situation where two-thirds of the UN membership have never served on the Security Council, Canada's promotion of greater democracy should perhaps be taken to a higher level than rhetoric.

NOTES

A significant portion of the research for this paper was conducted in the form of off-the-record interviews of Canadian officials and a number of other UN participants and observers in Ottawa and New York. Accordingly, they are not specifically cited in the text. The author would like to thank all those who generously shared their time and thoughts.

1. Notwithstanding the debate as to whether this was any more than a useful international legal/political cover to justify the American-dominated military offensive in January-February 1991, given that the Security Council did not participate in any way with regard to the nature or conduct of the offensive.

2. Instead he was appointed Minister of Human Resources Development Canada, a portfolio in which he served until he was appointed Minister of Foreign Affairs.

3. Ouellet's speech came only a few months after the horrific violence in Rwanda and reflected his deep disquiet over what happened there before the eyes of a helpless UN peacekeeping force led by Canadian Romeo Daillaire. In September 1995, the minister released the Canadian study promised in his 1994 speech: *Towards a Rapid Reaction Capability for the United Nations*. The study included 26 recommendations focused around the creation of a rapidly deployable mobile headquarters that would provide the UN Security Council an option for immediate action when faced with a breach of the peace.

4. Voting for the 10 non-permanent seats on the 15-member Security Council (five countries—the US, Russia, China, the UK, and France—have permanent membership acquired when the UN was formed in 1945 and they represented the largest powers on the 'winning side' of World War II) is done on a regional basis, with each region given a set number of seats. Canada is a member of the WEOG group (Western European and Other), which has two seats. As both Greece and the Netherlands are EU members, they were likely to be supported by most other European states, including those looking for a way into the EU. Canada was also more like the Netherlands in its foreign policy outlook and international wealth status, while Greece was a poorer 'cousin' that might elicit more support because of an interest in voting for different types of players.

5. It also became part of a larger effort spearheaded by Canada and others to reconsider the role and nature of sanctions as an instrument of affecting international behaviour, given experiences in Iraq, Angola, and elsewhere that were demonstrating the ineffectiveness of the instrument (including its negative impact on civilians).

6. An interesting defence by Axworthy of the Kosovo action as an exercise in human security can be seen in his speech in early April at his alma mater, Princeton University (Axworthy, 1999b).

7. Canada undertook to support this analysis with a major study, co-sponsored by the International Peace Academy in New York and supported by the UN Secretary-General on the impact of sanctions in the 1990s. The results of the study have been released by the IPA in a book entitled *The Sanctions Decade*.

8. In comparison, during Canada's last Council experience (1989–90), 20 (1989) and 36 (1990—including 13 on Iraq's invasion of Kuwait) resolutions were adopted.

9. See also Kofi Annan's Millennium Assembly Report, *We the Peoples: The Role of the United Nations in the Twenty-First Century*, for an excellent and compre-

hensive exposé of Annan's view that drove his support for many of Axworthy's initiatives on the Council, greatly assisting the minister in garnering support from a number of key countries in the less-developed world (Annan, 2000).

10. Axworthy announced the Commission in his last speech before the UNGA in September 2000. The co-chairs are Gareth Evans, Australia's former foreign minister, and Algerian Mohammed Sahnoun, who has long-time UN experience and is well known in Canadian circles, having been a member of the Board of Governors of the International Development Research Centre. DFAIT is acting as the secretariat to the Commission.

REFERENCES

Annan, Kofi. 2000. *We the Peoples: The Role of the United Nations in the Twenty-First Century*. Report of the Secretary-General. UN Doc. A/54/2000, 27 Mar.

Axworthy, Lloyd. 1996a. 'Address at the consultations with non-governmental organizations in preparation for the 52nd session of the United Nations Commission on Human Rights', Ottawa. 13 Feb.

————. 1996b. 'Address to the 51st Session of the United Nations General Assembly', New York, 24 Sept.

————. 1998. 'Address to the 53rd Session of the United Nations General Assembly', New York, 25 Sept.

————. 1999a. 'Address to the 54th Session of the United Nations General Assembly', New York, 23 Sept.

————. 1999b. 'Notes for an Address to Princeton University', Princeton, NJ, 7 Apr.

————. 2000. 'Address to the 55th Session of the United Nations General Assembly', New York, 14 Sept.

Brahimi, Lakhdar. 2000. *Report of the Panel on United Nations Peace Operations* (S/2000/809).

Drohan, Madelaine. 2000. 'Attention General Powell: Economic sanctions don't work', *Globe and Mail*, 27 Dec., B9.

Eayrs, James. 1967. *Fate and Will in Foreign Policy*. Toronto: CBC Publications.

Fernandez-Armesto, Felipe. 1995. *Millennium*. Toronto: Doubleday.

Langille, Peter. 2000. *Renewing Partnerships for the Prevention of Armed Conflict: Options to Enhance Rapid Deployment and Initiate a UN Standing Emergency Capability*. Ottawa: Canadian Centre for Foreign Policy Development, Spring.

Nye, Joseph S., Jr. 1990. *Bound to Lead: The Changing Nature of American Power*. New York: Basic Books.

Ouellet, André. 1994. 'Address to the 49th Session of the United Nations General Assembly', New York, 22 Sept.

————. 1995. 'Address to the 50th Session of the United Nations General Assembly', New York, 25 Sept.

United Nations Security Council. 1999a. Statement by the President of the Security Council, 12 Feb.

————. 1999b. Statement by the President of the Security Council, 24 Sept.

————. 1999c. Statement by the President of the Security Council, 30 Nov.

8

The Axworthy Years:
Canadian Foreign Policy in the Era of
Diminished Capacity

DARYL COPELAND

The Canadian government's reluctance to pay the price of principled commitment to either human or common security is reflected in its failure to provide itself with an appropriate military capacity as well as in its niggardly funding of international economic development and equity. . . . However the world has changed, preventing deadly conflict, especially involving nuclear or other weapons of mass destruction, must take precedence over other goals. (Oliver, 1999: 19, 23)

SETTING THE STAGE

Iraq . . . Bosnia . . . Somalia . . . Rwanda.

When Lloyd Axworthy succeeded André Ouellet as Canada's Minister of Foreign Affairs in January 1996, the euphoria of tumbling walls and Soviet collapse had worn off. Deprived of the disciplines imposed previously by East-West bipolarity, failing states unleashed the malevolent genies of identity politics, religious strife, ethnic war, and opportunistic plunder. It had become clear that the peace dividend would remain unpaid. Far from a golden age of broadly based development, civil society, and economic justice, the world was instead in the throes of profound change, much of it unexpected and more than a little unwelcome.

Canada was involved, to varying degrees, in a range of conflicts, which were symptomatic of tectonic movements in the underpinnings of international relations. North American free trade, integration in Central and Western Europe, and the dynamic rise of the Asia-Pacific, to name but a few of the major elements, when piled on top of the end of the Cold War and the eruption of intrastate violence, bring the magnitude of the realignment into sharper relief. The infrastructure of the international system was being recast, with globalization creating a new and sharper dichotomy between haves and have-nots, winners and losers, within and between states. These shifts carried profound implications for Canada's place in the world. Canadian foreign policy, however, remained in large part untransformed.

With Axworthy, that would change. But all change comes at a price. The debate over these issues, in terms of both foreign policy and the impact on the Department of Foreign Affairs and International Trade (DFAIT), is the subject of this assessment.

The 1995 policy statement, *Canada in the World* (DFAIT, 1995), tried to address the changing world. The analysis, which was predicated on an elaboration of *three pillars* of foreign policy—prosperity, security, and the promotion of Canadian culture and values—was longer on generalities than on more precise prescriptive direction. The first two pillars were sufficiently generic to support just about anything, and indeed have remained credible even as the nature of security continued to evolve. The third lacked substance and existed mainly in the realm of exhortation.

One way or another, many of the trends and forces reshaping the world were also reflected inside Canada, where the public environment was in transition and the relationship between the polity and its view of the world was at sea. The postwar consensus on Canada's role and place, rooted in notions of Pearsonian internationalism, middle-power diplomacy, and a vision of Canada as an 'honest broker', 'helpful fixer', and compassionate donor, was unravelling. The vestiges that remained were found mainly in off-the-shelf speeches, dated editorials, and in the minds of a diminishing flock of want-to-believers. Even here, the old truisms seem markedly less compelling than was the case in the era of doctrinal certitude and evil empires.

The rise of issue-driven advocacy, single-interest lobbies, job insecurity, generational change, and growing disquiet over pressing matters closer to home, including constitutional debates and the sharpening of the national unity question, all contributed to a fracturing of support for the familiar old model. Bottom line? The international policy community was dispersed and divided; support for Canadian foreign policy lacked both breadth and depth. Canadians, perhaps feeling adrift in a turbulent and confusing world, had redrawn the lines of their individual moral engagement closer to the front door. Notwithstanding the restoration of fiscal health and an improved economy, Canadians were looking inward just when they should have been looking out.

If Lloyd Axworthy was to leave his imprimatur on Canadian foreign policy, he would have to take full account of the changed environment. He needed to match the tools at his disposal with the opportunities available. He needed to know where Canada, and hence where he, could make a difference. As will be seen, as the human security agenda, which came to incorporate both soft power and niche diplomacy, ascended, there came to be room for little else. And by the end of the excursion, big-ticket items gathered dust on the policy option shelves. But he had a plan, he had the intellectual ability and experience to adapt it to evolving circumstances, and he had the time to see it through.

FOR SOMETHING COMPLETELY DIFFERENT

It was clear from the beginning that the minister doubted he could get the kind of new thinking and innovative policy advice he needed from the traditionally conservative DFAIT. So, from existing resources he set out to finance and cultivate his own networks. He greatly increased the number of political staff, centralized control of communications on key policy initiatives, appointed a ministerial advisory council of selected academics, met frequently with the representatives of international non-governmental organizations (NGOs), and co-opted and reprofiled the Canadian Centre for

Foreign Policy Development (CCFPD), which nurtured links with universities and international affairs interest groups across the country. This parallel structure was run directly from the minister's office.

It would be an overstatement to suggest that, stripped of its core policy advisory and development functions, the department was side-lined, reduced to organizing ministerial travel, orchestrating trade visits, rewriting briefing books, and delivering consular services, while other government departments—Environment, Natural Resources, Heritage, Industry, and others—were expanding the nature and scope of their international activities across the board. Yet there is more than a kernel of truth to this critique; many of these trends had been incubating for years, and most were exacerbated by cuts mandated by Program Review in the mid-nineties.

On the policy side, analysts have accorded Axworthy's tenure mixed reviews. The commentary has been diverse and has come from across the ideological spectrum. Certainly a closer inspection of the record is warranted. But it will first be necessary to examine exactly how and on what basis the former minister executed his striking foreign policy makeover, an exercise that left at least as many observers, both at home and abroad, convinced that Canada had never been more progressive, more committed, more activist, and more engaged in the world. The case is complex, but it matters. Fundamental Canadian interests—political, economic, humanitarian—were in play.

START WITH A DASH OF SOFT POWER

Much has been written of 'soft power' and how—or if—this theory can be applied in service to the human security foreign policy theme that dominated the later stages of the Axworthy mandate. Though slagged in the popular press, pilloried by academics, ravaged by the political right and by some academics, and destined to fall quickly into disfavour in high places, there is no question that the compelling *idea* of soft power informed much of what Axworthy was able to achieve. It deserves a closer look.

Joseph Nye, an American political theorist, popularized the idea of 'soft power' in his book, *Bound to Lead: The Changing Nature of American Power* (1990). He highlighted the global influence of American popular culture and challenged the conclusions of Paul

Kennedy and other pundits subscribing to the imperial-over-stretch/US-in-inevitable-decline school of thought.

Nye placed great emphasis on the potential for achieving desired outcomes through attraction rather than coercion, prevailing not through force but by convincing others to want what you want. His approach relies heavily on the power of ideas and information, on the horizontal management of issues rather than the vertical management of resources, and on the ability to shape an agenda in ways that influence preferences and behaviour. Though often overlooked by its detractors, Nye never imagined soft power as a substitute for or alternative to the harder variety, but instead as a useful and effective complement.

Soft-power savants view knowledge brokerage, media savvy, strategic alliances with the like-minded, partnerships with NGOs, and coalition-building with elements of civil society as germane. The battles are fought for minds and emotions using PR (public relations) ordnance. The highest authority is the court of public opinion, where image is everything. Less emphasis is placed on more conventional instruments such as development assistance, the military, the intelligence apparatus, and the foreign service; more on information, communication, technology.

Canada's soft-power practitioners have also sought to occupy the world's cerebral rather than its territorial space. In this country, where hard-power assets are stretched or limited, soft power has a special appeal. Globalization and reduced national resources have constrained the capacity of government and rendered many of the state's more traditional instruments less effective. Canadian adherents had little choice but to adapt Nye's doctrine, to refashion it around the contours of middle-power possibility, and to harness it in service of different objectives: the pursuit of what political scientist Andrew Cooper (1997) has termed 'niche diplomacy'.

Unlike soft power, variations of which have always been found in the 'public affairs' section of the foreign policy tool box, the decision to focus on particular 'niches'—landmines, small arms, an international criminal court, war-affected children—was a more radical departure from traditional Canadian policy. This series of shorter-term, media-friendly special projects, each with clearly demarcated purposes, beginnings, and ends, produced demonstrable results.

In the second half of the 1990s, the prevailing climate of reduction and restraint in Canadian public administration required that tough choices would have to be made. Though never publicly acknowledged, the new dedication to niches meant that a raft of longer-term, difficult, shoulder-to-the-wheel types of international enterprise, where progress is measured in small increments and often over decades, would in large part have to be given up. So it came to pass that certain familiar overarching themes and motifs—sustainable development, poverty eradication, arms control, follow-up on the environmental commitments made at the Rio Summit—were quietly shunted aside (see Chapter 11 by Smith).

Canada did much on the world stage in the second half of the nineties, but we no longer did that kind of diplomacy any more, at least not as seriously as had previously been the custom. Scarce resources—money and people, the measures of serious intention— had to be redeployed in service of the new priorities.

THEN ADD SOME HARD REALITY

For some, this metamorphosis reduced to all 'soft' and no 'power'. Critics have alluded to formlessness, drift, and a disconnect from essential Canadian interests related to humanitarian welfare, national security, and distributive justice. Professor Kim Nossal, for instance, slammed Canada's 'foreign policy on the cheap'. He lamented the lowered sights and greatly reduced capacity of the Canadian state, and accused the architects of 'pinchpenny diplomacy' of using soft power disingenuously and ineptly to cover something more profound—Canada's retreat from the global playing field (Nossal, 1998–9). Joining the debate, but in contrast to the realist critique, Irving Brecher (1997) argued that Canada has become narrowly preoccupied with mercantile concerns and regrettably unprincipled in most other areas of international affairs. Elizabeth May of the Sierra Club documented Canada's failing performance and turn away from global environmental leadership (Sierra Club, 1999).

Others have observed that Canada appears to have abandoned broad, interrelated foreign policy goals such as a wide-front human rights, democratic development, and good governance agenda in favour of narrow trade and investment opportunities and '*flavouritism*': the pursuit of a limited number of diverse objectives that tend like fashion to change from month to month, year to year. And a key promise in the government's 1995 foreign policy statement—to intensify efforts to project and promote Canadian culture and values (diversity, tolerance, compassion) abroad as the 'third pillar' of Canadian foreign policy (DFAIT, 1995)—is almost universally seen to have been neglected.

ET VOILA: THE HUMAN SECURITY APPROACH

Undaunted, Axworthy pressed ahead. Soft power and niche diplomacy were ultimately situated in the context of human security, a notion pioneered by the United Nations Development Program earlier in the decade. Great effort was expended on its definition, conceptualization, and operationalization. Human security is distinct from national security (internal stability and external defence), collective security (alliances), common security (against the threat of war, the shared enemy), and co-operative security (preventive diplomacy, regional arrangements, and informal, 'Track II' type initiatives). In the human security approach to foreign policy, the security of the person, in contrast to the security of the state, represents the greatest good and highest end in international diplomacy. Everyone is entitled to an adequate quality of life, the absence of extreme privation, and access to fundamental rights.

This conception is deeply rooted in the traditions of modern liberalism, wherein the rights of individuals are paramount, while concern with territories and countries is secondary. The human security approach emphasizes the safety and well-being of people and communities, appreciates the consequences of intrastate, more so than interstate, conflict, and is focused on reducing the toll exacted by modern conflict on non-combatants. It emphasizes the role of civil society and puts a premium on the development and implementation of remedial approaches to the spread of transnational challenges often associated with globalization—ethnic and religious fissures, refugees and mass migrations, environmental collapse, disease, terrorism, crime, and narcotics abuse. In later, tighter iterations, Canada would emphasize five specific areas in which it possessed particular comparative advantage: protection of civilians in armed conflict; peace support operations; conflict prevention; governance and accountability; and public safety.

On Axworthy's watch the combination of soft power/niche diplomacy/human security became the defining element of Canadian foreign policy. We have heard from the critics on the downside implications of this policy, especially regarding the charge that absent a commitment to poverty alleviation and basic needs, it will never be able to deliver. Yet advocates believe the minister did what he could—and more—with what he had to work with. Pursuing freedom from want would be prohibitively expensive; promoting freedom from fear seemed a much better fit. His strategy and approach were both appropriate to the prevailing resource environment and politically canny—Foreign Minister Axworthy's silver bullet, a new diplomacy for the cyber age. At minimum, the human security agenda served as a most versatile rubric upon which to construct a distinctively Canadian model of world order and permitted the retrofit of Axworthy's earlier initiatives into a more coherent and formidable package.

WHICH IS SUBJECT TO SPIN

Proponents claim that this reformulation of Canadian foreign policy made a virtue of necessity, allowing the strategic leveraging of scarce diplomatic capital by investing only in areas where Canada could make a difference. They cite as examples the impact of media interventions by Brian Tobin and Royce Frith in clinching the 1995 fish war 'victory' over Spain; Canadian leadership in forging coalitions with the like-minded during the (ultimately unnecessary) humanitarian intervention in Rwanda/Zaire in 1996 and in the campaign to establish the International Criminal Court in 1998; and, most ardently, the successful nurturing of partnerships with NGOs and similarly inclined states in the campaign leading to the signature of the Ottawa Convention banning landmines in 1997. Soft power directed within selected niches and wielded in service to human security, it is argued, has produced some amazing results. Unlike so many of those noble preoccupations that proved so resistant over time—disarmament, development, environmental advocacy—the supporters of human security assert that, quite simply, it works.

Analysts Fen Hampson and Dean Oliver (1998) dubbed this package the 'Axworthy Doctrine'. Working for ourselves was wed to working for the world, doing well to doing right. As a result of the shifts outlined above, a new balance, geographic and substantive, was introduced into the overall foreign policy mix.

There have also been putative gains on the home front. When the dust finally settled, the reductions mandated by the Program Review exercise imposed new disciplines, economies, and accountabilities.

Whatever the costs to DFAIT, through the efforts of Parliament's Standing Committee on Foreign and Defence Policy, through annual consultations between DFAIT and the NGO community on issues such as human rights and peacebuilding, through the establishment of the ministerial advisory committee, the advisory and policy-making process has been significantly opened. The series of National Forums on Canada's international relations, organized across the country by the CCFPD, provided Canadians with a direct line into the minister's office.

Set-piece exchanges have given way to more genuine interaction, and the bureaucracy has been ventilated by bringing those from the outside in and turning the inside out. At the crucial junction of process and substance the case is made that ground has been gained.

So, to the crux of the issue: do soft power and niche diplomacy harnessed in service of human security amount to doing more, doing it smarter, and doing it with less? Or just to doing less, to a retreat, or at least a tactical withdrawal, from Canadian internationalism? To what extent have the Axworthy years advanced core Canadian foreign policy interests? In the midst of conflicting evidence and equivocation is it possible to reconcile the opposing assessments? Or might one opt for the sophisticated alternative—the mature pleasure of living with paradox?

AND COUNTERSPIN

Canada is doing very different, if, in some respects, smaller, things in the world. But whether that is a clever, even dazzling, distraction covering an otherwise ignominious flight from our glorious Pearsonian past or a rational and intelligent adjustment to transformed national and global realities is mostly in the eyes of the beholder. Where you stand depends on where you sit. You can spin it either way.

The fact that public backlash has been muted suggests that contemporary foreign policy has served with exceptional effect to smooth the recalibration—measured in terms of the implications of diminished defence, development assistance, and foreign affairs budgets—of Canada's international capacity, which has been in relative but inexorable decline since the end of World War II. It stands to reason in the face of these realities that when policy resources are substantially downsized, so, too, is this country's place in the world; sooner or later practical objectives must be brought into line.

It is not difficult to see why Axworthy's priorities—children in conflict, circumpolar affairs, peacebuilding, Aboriginal partnerships— had more political appeal than global poverty reduction or international conflict resolution. The components of the human security agenda were emotionally appealing, media-friendly, inexpensive, and demonstrably responsive to Canadian entreaties. In short, the human security agenda, advanced as Canada's foreign policy for the twenty-first century, was an easy sell, with manageable risks and the prospect of substantial rewards.

It should also be stated—notwithstanding the popularity of the 'turning inwards' theme popular in speeches and symposia—that none of this is tantamount to isolationism. The change might more fairly be characterized as pragmatic, another typically Canadian quality. Moreover, with just minor surgery the existing formula might be reshaped to produce something of a foreign policy synthesis, one that avoids any excessive reliance or packaging or optics. But before we get to that we should deal first with the crucial issue of foreign policy resources.

IS THERE A CREDIBILITY GAP?

The Department of Foreign Affairs hosts annual peacebuilding consultations, which in recent years have been extremely well organized and widely attended, with hundreds of registrants drawn from the NGO community, academia, government, and private-sector consultants.

The presentations and discussions are structured along geographic (Indonesia, Sudan, Colombia, Sierra Leone), thematic (war-affected children, small arms, civilian deployment in peace support), and technical (evaluation methods, academic research) lines. There is ample time for exchange among the participants and panellists, and the content has varied in nature and quality from rigorous to rambling, searching to sectarian. As an exercise in bureaucratic outreach and the democratization of foreign policy development, these talks are certainly to be commended. Yet they have also given rise to a vague but unsettling sense of unease, a gnawing feeling that something is somehow amiss.

Looking back at the proceedings over several years, we can see the essential contours of the problem: Canada's international performance has become longer on conceptualization than it is on delivery. Our ambitious rhetoric is facing contradiction by the reality of what we are doing on the ground. We will sponsor high-toned initiatives—the International Commission on Intervention and State Sovereignty[1] is the latest example—but come up short in the capacity to follow through. If this trend continues, a credibility gap, with disturbing ramifications for Canada's international position, may well be the result.

There are rattling questions. Has Canada been coasting on an enviable international reputation it can no longer sustain, surfing a wave that is about to hit the beach? Is our place in the world the result mainly of circumstances that no longer obtain? In economic terms, the answer is probably yes—it is hard to imagine that Canada would be asked to join a group like the G-7 if it was reconstituted today. Yet the roots of our difficulties may be even more basic, and this could engender more elemental concerns.

THE ISSUE IS POLICY INTEGRITY

The showpiece achievements of the human security agenda may have made a difference, but even here there are troubling questions—how much of a difference, and to what? The landmine treaty has resulted in the partial destruction of stockpiles and much useful work in afflicted areas, but has yet to be adopted by many of the largest manufacturers and users of mines, including the US, Israel, China, and Russia. The Rome Statute, which provides the legal basis for the creation of the International Criminal Court, is not yet in force, but, if the experience of The Hague War Crimes Tribunal is any guide, it may be some time before we can expect to see major violators in the dock. The choice of child soldiers as a policy focus has been likened to the use of baby harp seals by Greenpeace in its early efforts to connect emotionally and attract world attention. And when Canada hit hard on human rights violators—Nigeria, Burma, Sierra Leone—it appeared to do so mainly in areas where Canadian interests were not exposed.

This is perhaps too harsh a judgement. Yet there is not much solace to be gained from a survey of Canadian macroeconomic and trade policy. Several observers have noted the irony of Canada's robust support for structural adjustment, policy conditionality, economic reform, and the whole neo-liberal agenda that is globalization. For others it has exacerbated polarization and encouraged distributive inequities and thus contributed to precisely the types of conflict and insecurity that our foreign policy has then attempted to address. Could we be stoking the fire while standing in the bucket brigade?

An especially instructive illustration of inherent strain and tension is the handling of the case of Canada's Talisman Oil and Gas and its investment, in concert with partners from Malaysia and China, in a hydrocarbon play in southern Sudan (see discussion in Chapter 10 by Brown). NGOs, churches, Sudanese refugees, and others have alleged that this enterprise is, at minimum, fuelling the long-running Sudanese civil war by providing the regime in Khartoum (depicted variously as corrupt, bloodthirsty, terrorist-sponsoring, fundamentalist, and undemocratic) with hard currency with which to pursue the war. Pointed accusations have placed Talisman in much closer proximity to the Sudanese government, by collaborating actively with local officials and according the Sudanese armed forces the use of company facilities and equipment.

In early 1999 Axworthy announced that he would dispatch a special envoy to inquire into the situation and, if the charges proved well founded, follow appropriate action. Yet when John Harker produced a report broadly substantiating the critics' allegations, nothing happened. Though there was every indication that the minister wanted to act, his inability to do so was attributed to concerns elsewhere in the government about the western vote in the November 2000 election and the possibility of sending mixed messages to the business community, which was otherwise being encouraged to promote trade with and investment in non-traditional markets. While he did manage to place the issue of corporate social responsibility back on the political agenda, if briefly, and opened a small diplomatic office in Khartoum to monitor events more closely, this impasse must nevertheless have hurt. With the end of his stewardship in sight, Foreign Minister Axworthy hosted the September 2000 Conference on War-Affected Children in Winnipeg, with some of the principal victims of the conflict in Sudan—the intended beneficiaries of his human security approach—in attendance.

This performance gap was highlighted during the conference proceedings. Departmental officials had done yeoman work in pulling
the human security action plan into tighter shape for the occasion.
Former UN Ambassador Stephen Lewis slammed the government for
alleged duplicity in a keynote speech, and NGO representatives complained bitterly that the Sudanese, among others, should never have
been invited to attend. These sorts of complications, in concert with
the concerns over the cost and the fact that the minister's pending
departure had taken the political wind from the event's sails, combined to cloud what might otherwise have been recorded as a crowning achievement. Venturing into the unfamiliar realm of trade and
investment policy, in the case of Sudan he had moved the goalposts
too far down the field.

Canadian participation in the bombing of Belgrade and the
destruction of the civil infrastructure throughout Serbia during the
Kosovo episode, if a bit of a stretch for the human security mantra,
nonetheless stands as a clear instance in which this country
matched words and deeds. Canada's position exposed some rich
ambiguities on the home front, where a generation of new
Canadians, recruited in large part from non-traditional sources,
found it difficult to share the enthusiasm of the government for military engagement in the Balkans. Why such unease? The immediate impact of the controversial intervention was to worsen the
carnage in Kosovo exponentially. By sidestepping the UN and failing to seek Security Council authorization, the North Atlantic Treaty
Organization's actions undermined the moral authority of the world
body. As an offensive, out-of-theatre operation, the bombing violated the NATO Charter and shattered claims to a purely defensive
alliance. It alienated Russia, whose co-operation is essential to
rebuilding Europe's security architecture. The bungling and failure
of intelligence that led to the bombing of the Chinese embassy
infuriated China, the world's fastest-growing power and the cornerstone of Asia-Pacific and world security.

Reservations were voiced from the beginning. But the arguments
in favour of 'humanitarian' intervention, in this case, the putative support of human rights through 'human security bombing', carried the
day. The government judged that appeasement would fail, that
European security was at risk, and that when our best friends and
closest partners were going to war, Canada was not to be left cheer-
leading on the sidelines. Whatever the merits—or demerits—of the

Kosovo case, it provided real insight into the power of alliance politics, historical association, and core allegiances.

AND OPPORTUNITY COSTS

It was earlier suggested that a number of large files had to be set aside to permit a concentration on the new priorities. While that is an important part of the story, also to be considered are the implications of the many roads not taken—and some that were—as Axworthy's years in office wore on.

For example, after a decade in place, the economic sanctions applied against Iraq have by almost all accounts made a significant contribution to human insecurity and suffering, particularly among the young and infirm, while achieving little by way of loosening the grip of Saddam Hussein. Although Canada produced a report and convinced the UN Security Council to study further the issues surrounding such sanctions, we were able neither to budge the US or UK nor to join France and others in championing the lifting of the embargo. Canada could have spoken out over Russia's brutal campaign of repression in Chechnya, a humanitarian and human rights disaster, but opted instead for silence, punctuated occasionally by expressions of understanding for Russia's need to act against the threat to its territorial integrity posed by terrorists and fundamentalists. Canada responded acrimoniously and froze relations with India and Pakistan after both carried out nuclear tests, but declined to pursue an initiative floated briefly with Germany in 1998 to reform NATO's Cold War era nuclear doctrine. And unlike some countries—Norway's initiative in the Middle East springs to mind—Canada did not attempt any kind of creative diplomacy in service of conflict resolution.

The possibility of incoherence, or at least inconsistency, at the heart of Canada's world vision could be related to a host of more palpable problems at the level of resource allocation and program delivery. If the invisibility of foreign policy in the November 2000 federal election, though hardly unprecedented, was troubling, then so, too, is the lack of concrete support for international policy initiatives in recent federal budgets, budgets notable for their support of the priorities of other government departments with significant new spending. In a town awash in new money, Canada's institutions of international policy have precious little to show.

LESS MEANS LESS

Measured in terms of the public administrative equivalent of fuel economy, Canada has in recent years eked a great deal of mileage out of very little gas. Some would argue that we are well into the reserve tank and the red light is flashing. If Canadian diplomacy has for years been running on fumes, it cannot run on empty.

The many high-profile successes of recent years, including not only those mentioned earlier but also Canada's re-election to the UN Security Council (see Chapter 7 by Pearson), leadership in efforts to curb illicit trafficking in the diamonds that fuel conflicts in western and southern Africa, and a plethora of less publicized accomplishments, are all the more exceptional in view of the harsh fiscal climate still prevailing on Sussex Drive. From underfunded missions abroad to foreign service officers picketing over undercompensation at home, the neglect is showing. Notwithstanding the repeated denials, difficulties in recruiting top candidates and retaining qualified personnel now threaten to foreclose on the department's future and to overcome the ability of its basic systems. When added to the significant reallocations required to deliver on Foreign Minister Axworthy's many commitments, the effect was to intensify a long-standing pattern of forcing demands down; workloads increased relentlessly while terms and conditions of service declined. Even if one were prepared to accept a more beaten-up and less adept or productive department, the status quo has nonetheless become difficult to sustain.

DFAIT has done more than its share to contribute to the unprecedented prosperity enjoyed by many Canadians. Why, then, is the general resource situation still so wrung out and dreary, with miserly thinking and hard-scrabble calculation very much the rule? The answer may lie in the department's chronic inability, at both the political and bureaucratic levels, to focus its attention on overcoming challenges and winning battles on the home front. This unfortunate combination has hurt.

One need look no further than the latest federal budgets, which have reinforced a disturbing trend towards the marginalization of foreign affairs (and national defence and development assistance) within the broader constellation of Canadian governance. The share of these departments expressed as a percentage of total expenditures has been in steady decline for over a decade.

The Departments of National Defence and Foreign Affairs have fared poorly in the annual resource auction—most recently for DFAIT a token $10 million per year over five years for the Human Security Agenda and modest 'program integrity' funding to help cover burn-out and rust-out. Canada's performance in terms of foreign aid has been even worse. Despite marginal increases, with robust economic growth Canada's total Overseas Development Assistance (ODA) expenditures have cratered to about .24 per cent of gross domestic product (GDP).

This ODA level places us near the bottom of the Organization for Economic Co-operation and Development (OECD), well below the comparative expenditures of our Western European and Nordic partners. It is substantially less than the .46 per cent of GDP reached in the early nineties and is nowhere near the long-term target of .7 per cent. It is unrealistic to expect to sustain Canada's reputation as a generous aid donor when our real expenditures have fallen by almost 50 per cent in less than a decade. And although innovation is always to be saluted—leveraging our expertise and influence by negotiating joint ventures with Japan and regional development banks, for example—we can only get so far with other people's money.

In terms of reputation and influence, not to mention the self-image of Canadians as compassionate, peacekeeping internationalists, much is at stake. If we are to maintain or enlarge Canada's global role, to continue to champion humanitarian causes, and to lead by example, more money will be needed. Our ability to remain an active and effective peacekeeper, a conscientious player capable of following through on commitments to human and global security, depends on it. In this era of interdependence and the world economy, and in the face of Canada's lofty exhortations and extensive multilateral commitments, the lack of increased investment in the instruments of our global capacity is vexing.

AND IT SHOWS

Inattention to financial and human resource needs and the emergence of a less capable department are the least visible, yet arguably the most damaging, aspects of the Axworthy years. No amount of creativity, soft power, or sanctimony can substitute for the demonstration of conviction through resource allocation, both in terms of seeing to the requirements of those on the front lines and in regard to support of various policy ventures. Yet the minister's apparent disinterest in administrative or institutional reform issues seemed almost complete.

The department proposed a major restructuring of the foreign service in the mid-1990s, which would have created a senior professional designation and would have addressed many of the fundamental problems that had for years plagued Canada's diplomats. But the political ground had not been prepared, and the initiative was rejected by Treasury Board. In 1997, with Axworthy's encouragement, the department proposed adoption of the Canadian International Information Strategy (CIIS), an avant-garde compendium that sought to bring a concerted, coherent approach to international communications using satellite television, radio, and, prophetically, the Internet and Web-based media. If implemented, the CIIS would have vaulted Canada way out in front of the competition, leveraged our advantages in technology and innovation, and provided soft-power practitioners with a substantial range of new tools and venues. It lost out to landmines and died unfunded.

Meanwhile, DFAIT was squeezed, relentlessly, and the juice ran out. The mid- to late 1990s were a time of few promotions, dwindling compensation, and proliferating demands. In some areas, one-half of the foreign service officers who had joined the department since 1990—a group crucial to the future well-being of the institution—have voted with their feet and left. Even senior officers, many of whom had ridden up the demographic escalator and, because the system worked so well for them, had great difficulty reconciling themselves to the dire straits now everywhere evident, started bailing out. Among those who remained, particularly at the working level, unhappiness, frustration, and an absence of motivation or incentive became commonplace.

How might these developments find expression in policy performance? Few outcomes in international affairs are less desirable than failing to deliver as advertised, or more odious than not being taken seriously, especially by those one seeks to influence, let alone lead. How close is Canada now to those abject precincts? Closer, possibly, than might widely be expected, and for reasons that extend well beyond the specific difficulties at DFAIT. Recall the case of Sudan, the minister's 'bridge too far', examined earlier. The hollow 'Third Pillar'—promotion of Canadian culture and values—remains on precarious display. The energy and enthusiasm that once characterized

Canada's commitment to bilateralism have ebbed as resources flowed elsewhere. The country that helped orchestrate the Rio Summit on Environment and Development less than a decade later was unable to cobble together a deal with industry and the provinces and arrived at the Kyoto conference on greenhouse gas emissions and climate change without a position (see Chapter 11 by Smith). At a follow-up session in The Hague, Canada arrived with a position, but was singled out for international rebuke as an impediment to progress. That meeting dissolved into acrimony. A third try in Ottawa ended similarly. These are not outcomes Canadians are accustomed to. It must be asked: what is the real value of championing international causes if you are seen to back away at the eleventh hour?

Axworthy seemed genuinely to believe that dealing with issues and problems in speeches was tantamount to addressing them substantially. That approach plays well in church basements, but it is not the best way to leverage your influence internationally. If the world is finally starting to notice that Canada has changed, some very quick footwork and repositioning may be required. If we elect to keep coasting on historical inertia, Canada will still face the very real risk of either failing very publicly or having to step—or be pulled—away from the podium because no one is listening. Unpalatable alternatives, all.

SYNTHESIS IS EVER ELUSIVE

Axworthy showed almost no interest in commercial or trade files, in international economic institutions, or in a variety of other tools that, if used, might have permitted the delivery of a broader agenda attuned to a wider spectrum of Canadian interests. His human security agenda, which required a high degree of coherence and consistency if it was to retain its credibility, was applied selectively and unevenly. His influence in cabinet was uncertain, and his years in power were characterized by what might be interpreted as a persistent ambiguity concerning the ultimate purpose of foreign policy, a blurring of the lines between the national and the personal. Yet in taking Canadian foreign policy off in new directions, Axworthy has made it difficult, if not impossible, to revert to a strategy of resting on our laurels and hoping to smooth over the bumps. Though he drew down the reserves, ignored crucial structural issues, and was able to do little by way of new investment, he also laid a new foundation upon which it should be possible to resume construction.

What lessons, if any, might be drawn from the analysis set out above? What, for instance, if the application of soft power were refined slightly and marshalled in support of a diplomacy defined in terms of a focus on areas and issues in which the interests of Canada and the world intersect? Under this formula, rather than risking what might appear as a quixotic dedication to remedying whatever needs fixing, or a bias towards addressing the preoccupations of single-interest groups, Canada's foreign policy and diplomatic engagement would remain global, but there would be a greater emphasis on objectives characterized by a mutuality of interest. If Canada were to deploy all of the tools in its soft-power shed on the nexus of shared interest—as distinct, for instance, from using them to excavate niches—the effect could be salutary.

Within this approach there is ample room for focus and shaping. By way of example, a host of political, environmental, and socio-economic issues fit the criterion: salvaging sovereignty in the age of globalization; bridging the digital divide; Canada's shifting strategic requirements and their relationship to democratization; air and water quality; the inclusion of minimum labour standards in multilateral trade agreements. So, too, would the ultimate national and global security issue, nuclear weapons. The treatment of this most fundamental foreign policy issue, perhaps as expressed in a more detailed policy response to the American plans to develop a National Missile Defense shield and thus abrogate the 1972 Anti-Ballistic Missile Treaty, could serve as an early litmus test for any broader repositioning.

A recasting of the basis for engagement could provide a relevance and appeal that would fire again the collective imagination of Canadians and rekindle their enthusiasm for enlarging this country's place in the world. After all, the revival of a broadly based constituency of support for Canada's traditionally robust internationalist role is itself a precondition for successful global activism.

The past few years have yielded for Canada a substantial catalogue of things done, and left undone, in the world. The record has shown that the pursuit of fundamental interests, and, even more so, balancing them against competing priorities and deeply held values, is enormously difficult.

Lloyd Axworthy demonstrated that a foreign policy based on soft power and niche diplomacy in a human security context can produce results and provide a certain focus and unity. His keen sense of political opportunity allowed him to capitalize on matters of climate and timing, and his bent for a very public style of diplomacy was turned to substantial advantage. By making strategic use of the press, the Internet, and communications technologies as instruments of foreign policy, he showed a supple understanding of one of Marshall McLuhan's most penetrating insights—that new technologies create a new environment, new relationships, new possibilities, that 'the vested interests of acquired knowledge and conventional wisdom have always been bypassed and engulfed by new media' (McLuhan, 1964). And while he may not have effected a full-fledged revival of the interest of Canadians in foreign policy, he captured a piece of the public's imagination with his appeal to altruism and, at minimum, stemmed the slide into irrelevance and international impotence. Measured by his own standards, and playing on the margins because that was the only place he felt that Canada could make a quick difference, he achieved success. All of that said, his achievements are not as easily reconciled against the hard realities of bureaucratic politics, international power, and global economic competition.

Half-empty or half-full? The debate promises to be long and rich and the room for interpretation and manoeuvre substantial. Though mentioned prominently in the Throne Speech of 30 January 2001, human security is widely expected to slip down the list of departmental priorities. Time will tell how Axworthy's legacy endures.

For DFAIT, improvements in public finance and the arrival of a new minister present a rare opportunity to reinsert itself into the policy development process and to make up lost ground on the resource front. There are wide open spaces to build on if the money is there. With recent changes in senior management and beefing up of the policy planning apparatus, there are signs that a move into this opening is under way.

Foreign policy is aptly likened to a delicate high-wire act, with the most versatile performers sliding skilfully along a never-ending continuum between idealism and realism. The see-saw between these two poles of creative tension is perhaps the defining element of international affairs. With Axworthy, Canadians were exposed to a lengthy period of tilt towards the former; now the latter will probably be more prominent.

Whatever the heading in these early days of a new century, this, at least, is clear: Canada would not want to find itself typecast in the role of pitchman at a carnival sideshow . . . threadbare, gaunt, hoarse but still standing, box of matches in one hand and garden hose in the other, talking the walk.

As the crowd moves on.

NOTES

The views expressed in this chapter are those of the author alone and do not represent the views or the policy of the government of Canada.

1. This Commission, led by Gareth Evans of the International Crisis Group and former Australian Foreign Minister and Lloyd Axworthy, is exploring the challenges of intervention in the twenty-first century.

REFERENCES

Brecher, Irving. 1997. 'Canadian Foreign Policy: Show Me the Money', *Behind the Headlines* 55, 1 (Autumn): 4–11.

Cooper, Andrew. 1997. *Niche Diplomacy: Middle Powers after the Cold War.* Basingstoke, UK: Macmillan.

Department of Foreign Affairs and International Trade (DFAIT). 1995. *Canada in the World.* Ottawa: Canada Communications Group.

Hampson, Fen Osler, and Dean F. Oliver. 1998. 'Pulpit Diplomacy: A Critical Assessment of the Axworthy Doctrine', *International Journal* 53, 3 (Summer): 379–407.

McLuhan, Marshall. 1964. *Understanding Media: The Extensions of Man.* New York: McGraw-Hill.

Nossal, Kim Richard. 1998–9. 'Pinchpenny Diplomacy: The Decline of "Good International Citizenship" in Canadian Foreign Policy', *International Journal* 54, 1 (Winter): 88–105.

Nye, Joseph, Jr. 1990. *Bound to Lead: The Changing Nature of American Power.* New York: Basic Books.

Oliver, Michael. 1999. 'Canada on the Security Council', *Behind the Headlines* 56, 3: 16–23.

Sierra Club of Canada. 1999. 'Earth Day 1999: Canadian Environmental Policies Stuck in a Time Warp', press release. Available at: <http://www.sierraclub.ca/national/media/earthday-warp.html>.

Part Two

After Axworthy: Emerging Issues in Canadian Foreign and Security Policy

9

US Leadership on Global Economic Issues: From Bill Clinton to George W. Bush

SUSAN ARIEL AARONSON

In 1995, America's premier advice columnist, Ann Landers, printed in her column two letters about trade.[1] One reader asked Ann why America's trade deficit was so big. Ann responded by writing 'Mickey Kantor, call your office.' Her answer chided the United States Trade Representative (USTR) for not addressing public concerns about trade. The second reader, wrote that 'we're supposed to "buy American," right?' and wondered why she/he could not find any American-made clothes. Ann again responded that she was not able to give a good answer and offered to print one from any government source. However, in the coming week, no government source replied (Landers, 1995).

The letters to Ann Landers, which were published nationwide, signalled public concern and confusion about trade policy, which came to a head during the Clinton years. This is ironic, because from 1993 to 2001 the global economy became increasingly integrated. Trade as a share of US gross domestic product (GDP) increased from 21.7 per cent in 1993 to 30.7 per cent in 1999, almost one-third of GDP (Council of Economic Advisors, 1994: 268–9; USTR, 2000a: 2). The US economy was at the core of this globalization phenomenon. The Clinton administration negotiated a record number of trade agreements (some 300), which had an amazing impact on the US and global economy. These agreements helped companies, US and foreign, meet global markets, producing enormous economics of scale and scope. Consumers benefited from a wider range of high-quality competitively priced goods.

But many American consumers were not aware of these benefits. Americans heard a great deal about the costs of the huge trade deficit, but they heard very little about how both imports and exports affected them in their daily lives.

Moreover, despite this record of accomplishment, the Clinton administration was unable to get new fast-track authority. Although the United States has moved forward on bilateral trade agreements, as well as on new agreements provided under the 1993 authority, Congress has not provided the assurance that if the President negotiates a trade agreement it will approve it without amendments.

The Clinton administration was not only unable to build an élite consensus in support of trade liberalization, it was also unable to build public support for its strategy to reconcile trade and social goals. Meanwhile, a wide range of opinion polls taken throughout the decade revealed that many Americans think that their nation's trading partners are unfair, that the only beneficiaries of trade are big business executives, and that trade agreements ignore or undermine other important public policy concerns, such as preserving the environment and promoting human rights.[2]

This chapter examines the Clinton administration legacy on trade and the agenda for the Bush administration. It discusses the eight years of trade accomplishments and the ironic failure of Clinton administration policy-makers to communicate effectively a fuller picture of what trade agreements do. It also criticizes the Clinton team for relying so much on trade policies to regulate global markets. Clinton administration policy-makers seemed to believe that trade liberalization could foment policy reform as well as market liberalization. But these trade agreements did little to help newly emerging nations find the right combination of government intervention and free markets to facilitate a rising standard and quality of life. Moreover, they did little to create greater global equity.

President Clinton and his advisers understood that it would be impossible to prod a wide range of nations to develop and finance a social compact—a strong system of laws protecting consumers, workers, and citizens. So he tried to make trade agreements achieve some social goals, such as protecting workers in developed economies from low-wage foreign competitors. He tried to achieve this goal by pressing to include social objectives in trade agreements—a laudable goal and an understandable strategy. But the strategy did not yield greater support for trade agreements. The President was well aware of the limitations of trade policy in ensuring that globalization benefits the many and not the few. In his farewell address, he warned, 'the expansion of trade hasn't fully closed the gap between those of us who live on the cutting edge . . . and the billions around the world who live on the knife's edge of survival. . . . Global poverty is a powder keg that could be ignited by our indifference' (Clinton, 2001). The only way to prevent that powder keg from exploding is for nations around the world to adopt social safety nets and other measures to limit economic volatility and compensate individuals hurt by market change. Yet, many nations do not have enough funds or adequate systems of governance to develop and implement such measures.

THE CLINTONIAN LEGACY

President Clinton began his term by making a broad-based effort to sell the North American Free Trade Agreement (NAFTA). NAFTA was the first modern trade agreement to acknowledge that non-trade policy goals would have to be enshrined within the agreement. Yet the public debate over NAFTA was essentially a food fight about the number of jobs NAFTA would create or destroy.

The Canada–US Free Trade Agreement and NAFTA taught Canadians, first, and, later, Americans about the impact of trade on the social compact. During the years of NAFTA negotiations (1991–3), non-governmental organizations forged a trinational movement that weighed issues of concern to social groups in all nations. In the United States, the NAFTA debate exposed divisions among these civic groups as to whether one could be pro-trade liberalization and pro-environment/democracy/human rights at the same time and whether incremental reform proposals, such as the side agreements to NAFTA, were useful. This division seemed to foster the belief among analysts and policy-makers that one was either pro-trade or protectionist, although the debate about trade policy had become so much more complex.

In the United States, progressives concerned about the impact of trade on regulatory policy goals, such as protecting the environment, consumers, and human rights, forged an alliance with economic nationalists, isolationists, and protectionists. Thus, consumer advocate Ralph Nader, business leader Ross Perot, and nationalist Pat Buchanan and their supporters forged a powerful lobby to block forward movement on trade. At the same time, some internationalist, environmental, and human rights groups, equally concerned about trade's impact on national systems of social and environmental regulations, began to see their counterparts—this informal alliance of left-wing and right-wing nationalists and protectionist groups—as obstructionist and often unnecessarily protectionist. They were willing to accept the approach of the side agreements in the recognition that public policy moves incrementally. The Clinton administration's strategy of horse-trading congressional votes for NAFTA with votes for other unrelated policies convinced many trade agreement critics that trade and other policy goals must be reconciled.

By 1992, many individuals of the left in the US and abroad had developed an overwhelmingly negative view of trade agreements. Although trade had done much to bring economic growth and improve living standards around the world, they could only see its costs. They had seen little progress on labour rights, and they perceived the proposals before the Uruguay Round talks of the General Agreement on Tariffs and Trade (GATT) as deregulatory. They saw the GATT as a secretive and undemocratic institution. Moreover, they viewed the tuna-dolphin case as evidence that trade regulation and social regulation could not be complementary. In the United States, 26 environmental and consumer groups called on Congress to reject the 1991 draft Final Act text of the Uruguay Round. The signatories included many environmental and consumer groups with a long commitment to internationalism.[3] Approximately 160 non-governmental organizations from 60 countries wrote to their heads of government to oppose the Uruguay Round. Concern about the draft text came not only from the left. Sir James Goldsmith of Great Britain, a Conservative member of the European Parliament, also lobbied to oppose the round. In Europe, he was joined by nationalists such as Jean-Marie Le Pen of France's National Front and the Movement for France. Vandana Shiva of India and Martin Khor Kok of Malaysia also urged their governments to reject the Uruguay Round (Lang and Hines, 1992: 48–9; Dunne, 1992: 5; Hines, 1998; *NAFTATHOUGHTS*, 1994: 9; Watkins, 1998; *Economist,* 1998).

CLINTON ROPES A TRADE ACCORD: THE ACHIEVEMENT OF THE WTO

This negative view of the GATT was not shared by President Clinton. Early on, Clinton won fast-track legislation extending the deadline for concluding the Uruguay Round to December 1993. This put pressure on other nations to emphasize their negotiating priorities and seemed to give the United States increased leverage. Japan and the European nations feared that Clinton could be more protectionist than his predecessors, and this fuelled their interest in compromising and completing the round (Destler, 1995: 219–21; Schott, 1994: 6–7; Lang and Hines, 1993: 47).

President Clinton did not use that leverage in ways that pleased many trade agreement critics of the left and right. First, he agreed to transform the informal GATT into a permanent umbrella institution, the World Trade Organization (WTO). The WTO charter provided legal authority for a secretariat, a director general, and a staff, and strengthened and unified the trade regime's system of dispute settlement. With agreement on this new structure, the Uruguay Round was finally completed in December 1993 and participants signed the Final Act in Marrakesh on 5 April 1994 (GATT Secretariat, 1993).[4] However, to trade agreement critics of the right and left, this new structure threatened to thwart national sovereignty. In 1994, the President submitted the results of the Uruguay Round to the Congress. But neither the President nor Congress moved rapidly in 1994 to gain approval. The President's top priority was health-care reform. Republicans and Democrats alike found many reasons to stall development of the implementing legislation (Aaronson, 1996: 145–6; President of the United States, 1994). During the delay, a wide range of groups and individuals came out against the Uruguay Round. Social activists were particularly disappointed. They saw the Clinton administration, a Democratic administration with a strong base of labour and environmental support, as unresponsive to their concerns and captured by international business.[5]

But the administration, however much it may have shared the objective of reconciling trade liberalization with social and environmental protections, was not able to convince most GATT contracting parties of the merits of this objective in 1993. Moreover, the administration seemed to presume that the potential economic benefits would persuade the American people and their representatives. The Clinton administration soon found that the GATT debate did not focus on numbers, as did NAFTA, but on issues of sovereignty. Because the Uruguay Round was so broad and so controversial, there were many hearings on various aspects during the 103rd Congress.[6] But the implications of changing the GATT to the WTO were never far from the debate. While proponents of the new, more formal global regime tried to focus the debate on its benefits and costs to the economy as a whole, much of the public and congressional debate focused on the WTO's potential impact on American sovereignty. The Senate Commerce, Senate Foreign Relations, and House Ways and Means Committees held specific hearings on the WTO and how this new institution might affect US law.[7] This focus was a small victory for these trade agreement critics; although they had not achieved their goals within the negotiations, they did set the terms of congressional debate.

The debate over GATT/WTO raised important real questions about whether or not American law and institutions should adapt to the global economy. Even supporters of strengthening the GATT infrastructure questioned the WTO's effects on sovereignty. Clyde Prestowitz, former trade negotiator and president of the Economic Strategy Institute, noted that 'the environmentalists . . . are correct when they express their concern for the potential reversal of US regulations via findings of the WTO' (Collins and Bosworth, 1994: 78–9). Almost one month after the mid-term congressional elections in November 1994, Congress overwhelmingly approved the GATT/WTO. Seventy-six per cent of both houses voted in favour of the Uruguay Round Implementing Act on 1 December. However, because the GATT was approved in lame-duck session, Pat Buchanan, Lori Wallach, and other trade agreement critics argued that it was rammed through the Congress.[8]

In the end, the WTO did not include labour standards and had done little to place environmental considerations on a par with trade. But trade agreement critics, in fact, had made considerable progress. They had greatly shaped both the élite and the public debates over trade agreements. No longer could people argue that food safety, labour standards, and other aspects of the social compact were not trade issues. What many trade agreement critics gleaned from the GATT debate, however, was that trade agreements were deregulatory. These individuals began to forge a global movement to oppose both globalization and specific trade agreements. They would argue that trade agreements should include social goals, but in truth many of these critics saw such trade agreements as subordinating social to trade policy goals. Nonetheless, the Clinton administration continued to pursue a strategy of using trade agreements to meet social and environmental policy goals.

THE RISE OF TRADE AGREEMENT CRITICS AND THE FAILURE TO RETHINK CLINTON ADMINISTRATION STRATEGY

In January 1994, however, some of these activists decided that they had tackled only part of the problem by criticizing trade agreements. Maude Barlow and Tony Clarke from Canada, Edward Goldsmith and Helena Norberg-Hodge from the United Kingdom, Vandana Shiva from India, Martin Khor from Malaysia, and Americans Lori Wallach, Jerry Mander, John Cavanagh, and Mark Ritchie, among others, met in San Francisco to convene a new international organization, the International Forum on Globalization. These individuals aimed to 'expose the multiple effects of economic globalization in order to stimulate debate' and 'to reverse the globalization process by encouraging ideas and activities which revitalize local economies'. They noted that the world needs new international agreements 'that place the needs of people, local economies and the natural world ahead of the interest of corporations'. With this organization, trade agreement critics could find common ground on how to speak out against the real problem, 'economic globalization'.[9] Moreover, they offered an alternative strategy, a sort of ecological nationalism.[10] This broader critique did not alter their strategy of thinking locally and acting globally. They remained determined to protect their national systems of consumer, environmental, and worker protections.

The Clinton administration seemed to continue to think it could still try to link social and trade objectives within trade agreements. However, business leaders did not concur with this strategy and made sure that many members of Congress would back them up. This would have important implications for obtaining fast-track authority from the Congress.

SOME PROGRESS, LESS DEMOCRATIZATION

In the years 1996–2000, trade policy moved two steps forward, two steps back. Negotiators achieved little progress in the Asia-Pacific Economic Co-operation forum (APEC), in the expansion of NAFTA to include Chile, or in moving ahead on the Free Trade Area of the Americas (FTAA). But the US did achieve permanent normal trade relations (formerly most-favoured-nation [MFN] status) for China, a landmark trade agreement with Vietnam, and legislation on trade with Africa and the Caribbean basin. The US, Canada, and many other WTO members also achieved a global high-tech agreement, eliminating tariffs on information technology goods, and a financial services agreement. These agreements were achieved without so-called fast-track authority. Moreover, these are important economic achievements for which the Clinton administration deserves credit.

However, the President tried and failed twice, in 1995 and 1997, to get new fast-track authority. He was not able to convince many Republicans that fast-track needed to include labour and environmental objectives. US Trade Representative Charlene Barshefsky began to proclaim boldly that she did not need fast-track to achieve progress on trade. But this sort of talk seemed undiplomatic. The US is unique in that the executive does not have sole authority to make trade agreements. Under the Constitution, the President has authority to negotiate treaties and agreements, but the Congress has the authority to regulate commerce and levy taxes. This sharing of powers provided the legal basis for a bifurcated trade policy. Yet, to achieve true progress the President and Congress must agree that trade liberalization is in the interest of the American people.

THE PRATTLE AFTER SEATTLE

But perhaps the most important failure was the decision to use the WTO ministerial in Seattle in December 1999 to build public understanding of what trade agreements do and to encourage further trade liberalization. The Clinton administration debated for years whether or not to host a ministerial. Once the US decided to host it, the next problem was to decide where. Rumour has it that the administration preferred Hawaii, but Hawaii would not bring with it a business constituency. The next most desirable venue was San Diego, but it, too, did not bring with it a large enough corporate constituency to finance the global meeting. Money was important because the administration was unwilling to go to Congress for funds to support the WTO ministerial and called on the private sector to raise most of these funds.

The Clinton administration had used this strategy before to finance the North Atlantic Treaty Organization (NATO) ministerial. But this strategy came with a significant downside. All previous ministerials or GATT rounds had been financed by the host government and the GATT/WTO. Many of the firms called on to support the ministerial were the same ones that might benefit from trade talks if such talks succeeded. But somehow the administration did not foresee that potential conflict of interest. Moreover, many observers saw the administration's negotiating priorities on agriculture and e-commerce as designed to benefit key political constituencies for the 'New Democrats'—the wing of the Democratic Party more oriented to a free-market ideology. This led to criticism that the fox was funding and guarding the chicken coop, leaving the people outside. It also furthered the impression that the only beneficiaries of trade liberalization were big business executives and their major shareholders. Thus, the Clinton administration strategy actually seemed to support the concerns of many trade agreement critics that trade regulation was being captured by big business interests and did not reflect the public interest. The ministerial was, in the American way, a business-dominated event. Yet the Seattle host committee did not raise the funds to cover the basic costs of the ministerial. Some saw this as evidence that business was not hungry enough to want a new round. At the same time, the costs for the ministerial were higher than anticipated, due to the increased policing costs as a result of the protests.

The Clinton administration had to proceed to Seattle without fast-track authorization. This, of course, meant nothing in regard to commencing the negotiations, but it did yield a public relations problem. American trading partners knew that there was no domestic consensus on what trade agreements should do. The Clinton administration did try to ascertain public views to some degree. Administration officials held several public hearings to discuss the concerns of the non-governmental/non-business community before Seattle. I attended several of these hearings, which were directed by Janet Hall, the counsellor to the US Trade Representative. Everyone talked and listened politely, but it was obvious that the administration and trade agreement critics were not listening to each other.

The ministerial was also a lost opportunity to focus on how to help developing countries raise their living standards and governance institutions. Policy-makers paid little attention as to how to help improve irrigation standards in Guatemala, for example, so that food exports from Guatemala to the US or Canada would not be tainted with pesticides or disease. Instead, the debate focused on whether labour issues were trade issues. Many developed countries were determined to use their power to thwart that agenda, which seemed so desperately demanded by the protestors in the streets.

The street protests gave an impression to many foreign officials that US officials somehow covertly encouraged the protests as a negotiating tactic, to add public pressure to the broad US agenda of reconciling trade and social policies. This was not true. Similar protests had occurred at other international meetings, such as the WTO fiftieth anniversary in Geneva in 1998 and meetings of the World Economic Forum in Davos. But to many foreign leaders, the US was an ill-prepared host. Not only did the US let the protestors disrupt the negotiations, but US officials also did not make adequate preparations to facilitate the negotiations. For example, some developing-country officials complained that the US did not bring enough staff to ensure a successful negotiation. They were livid about the 'green-room process', under which smaller groups of countries were brought into the so-called 'green room' to build a limited consensus. Some argued this process actually impeded consensus and created even greater anger at the negotiations, over the negotiating priorities, and probably at the United States.

But the final failure of the ministerial was the failure to communicate to the American people why their counterparts were so divided on trade and to give them the tools to make their own decisions about trade. Most Americans had little understanding as to why their fellow citizens had taken to the streets. US leaders made it clear that trade policy was their main tool for addressing globalization. But this strategy made it harder to find a way forward that addressed legitimate public concerns about the environmental, human rights, and health and safety costs of expanded trade.

THE FAILURE TO COMMUNICATE

There is one final irony of the Clinton years on trade. During this period, the Internet grew to be a major economic force. It also transformed how individuals communicated about trade. The Internet not only can help communicate policy, but also could help greater numbers of citizens to influence such policies. The US, however, has not effectively tapped that tool.

The USTR Web site (www.ustr.gov) was recently revamped, but this office uses its Web site to disseminate press releases and information about trade agreements, and the site is not interactive. Citizens (and other visitors) cannot ask questions of USTR staff. Yet the Internet is a cost-effective way to reach out to Americans. Other governments, such as Canada and Australia, have used their trade ministry Web pages much more effectively to provide information about trade and trade agreements, to reach out to their constituents, and to attempt to involve them in trade policy. In another example of more advanced uses of this technology, the European Union's Commissioner for Trade regularly engages in an interactive Internet dialogue with the interested public. Canada's Web site stresses, 'we want to hear from you' (www.dfait-maeci.gc.ca/hna-nac/consult-e.asp). It sends a message that the public's views on trade policy matter. The US can learn from these strategies.

UNFINISHED BUSINESS

As Ambassador Charlene Barshefsky turned out the lights in January 2001, she admitted there was much to do on trade. The agriculture sector in particular is eager for a new round of trade talks. Business now seems increasingly hungry to join a new round, as US market growth slows. The European Union (EU) and Japan seem to believe that a new round is necessary to address a potential economic slowdown. These nations will also have to monitor new members of the WTO to ensure they meet their obligations. Finally, the WTO has not been able to resolve effectively trade disputes on bananas, tax, and beef that bedevil EU/American trade relations.

Both the United States and Canada want to jump-start the stalled Free Trade Area of the Americas talks. However, some nations fear a North American focus on hemispheric trade could only undermine efforts at the global level (de Jonquieres, 2001). The US also wants to gain approval for trade agreements with Singapore and Jordan. The Singapore negotiations have not received the blessing of Congress. Moreover, some US business leaders are angry about the trade agreement developed with Jordan. This agreement was designed to reward Jordan for its support of the Middle East peace process—a laudable (but non-economic/trade) policy goal. Many influential Democrats tout this agreement as a model because of its labour and environmental provisions. Many Republicans and some business leaders fear this model for that very reason. It may have a troubled reception on Capital Hill (Barshefsky, 2000).

Although Ambassador Barshefsky occasionally bragged she did not need fast-track authority, the Bush administration will need fast-track to proceed with many of these negotiations. But to gain approval for trade agreements, any government will need a legislative/executive consensus.

Many observers believe fast-track convinces trading partners of US sincerity in the negotiations, yet the American executive has not had fast-track authority for some eight years. This stasis has not convinced the many bright and creative people on Capital Hill to develop alternative means with which Congress and the executive can share authority for trade. Instead, most proposals have focused on revamping fast-track or reforming it, rather than on coming up with something new. For example, Gary Hufbauer of the Institute for International Economics has proposed that Congress authorize the President to negotiate new agreements. Congress would then vote these 'up' or 'down' on a 'no amendments' basis within the life of the Congress (if submitted during its first session). Representative Phil English has proposed a 'narrow-track' idea that would permit the President to seek agreement on plurilateral or multilateral measures that would reinforce labour and environmental standards (Hufbauer, 1999). Congressman Sandor Levin, the ranking Democrat on the Ways and Means Trade Subcommittee, has long argued that fast-track is too narrow a policy tool to deal with the problems of globalization, especially in regard to US relations with developing nations. I.M. Destler, a leading American authority on trade policy, has argued that any request for renewal of fast-track authority should be accompanied by a presidential report certifying progress towards goals such as environmental protection.[11] These wide-ranging suggestions focus on both procedural and substantive reforms. But at bottom one must ask: is this the only and best way to provide authority to make trade policy? Moreover, does this strategy facilitate negotiation of the kind of trade barriers—norms, health and safety standards, competition policy—that are likely to be needed? In addition, reforming fast-track does not address the underlying problem of trade policy—the lack

of public support or understanding. Americans do not really understand their role in the global economy or why their government
wants to participate in trade talks.

The new administration has an opportunity to rethink this
dilemma. As of this writing, it did not get off to an auspicious start.
The USTR was among the last cabinet positions named by the
President-elect (which signalled to some Americans he did not see it
as a priority). Moreover, the Bush team went public with a debate
regarding the rank of the USTR—should it remain a cabinet-level position? This question deeply offended the ranking Democrat, Senator
Max Baucus, and the ranking Republican, Senator Charles Grassley,
on the Senate Finance Committee. Business leaders expressed fears
that downgrading the USTR office would signal that the Bush administration was less interested in trade. This, in turn, would make it
more difficult to negotiate trade, and too easy for trade policy to take
a back seat to national security considerations.[12] The issue was ultimately resolved—the US Trade Representative remained a cabinet-
level position. But the new administration raised doubts as to how
much it cared about trade policy.

IMPLICATIONS FOR CANADA

Canada (and every other nation) will only benefit if Americans
become more knowledgeable about trade. Without such support,
America's trade impasse will continue.

President Bush's second trip abroad was to Canada at the end of
April 2001 to seek to jump-start the long-stalled PTAA. (Symbolically
to some in Canada, the President's first trip outside the US was to
Mexico.) Canada continues to be the foremost export market for the
US and its single largest trading and investment partner. In general,
the relationship is good. Yet the United States still perceives a wide
range of barriers to trade at the federal and provincial levels. Some
of these disputes reflect different views about the appropriate role
of government in the economy, while others relate to federalism
(which policies are regulated at the provincial or the federal level).
In the end, most of these disputes in no way bedevil the close relationship.[13]

At the same time, the two nations have not always communicated
as clearly and effectively as they might have. It can be hoped that
President Bush will make it a priority to listen to and learn from

Canadian perspectives. One area where Canada has taken a leadership role is in asking its constituents for feedback on trade. Another area where Canada has led is in positing alternatives to trade policy as a tool to govern globalization.

CONCLUSION: THE TASK FOR THE BUSH ADMINISTRATION

Global economic interdependence is here to stay. Thus, it is up to political and business leaders to make a case for trade agreements. The only way to do that successfully is to relate trade to citizens' daily lives and their many roles as taxpayers, workers, producers, consumers, and friends of the earth. The people of the world will benefit if Americans gain a better understanding of trade and of global economic interdependence. This will require that talk about trade shifts from a sole emphasis on economics to include issues of governance. Markets are global and there is a need to develop global rules to govern global commerce.

Second, policy-makers must be honest about the costs and benefits of protectionism versus freer trade. Protectionism is a blunt policy tool that can create inequities among citizens; it favours certain interests and policy-makers find trade protection difficult to abandon once it has been granted. Trade agreements are built on this reality. They make global markets more equitable by regulating how entities may trade and how governments may protect. In this sense, they regulate the use of protection.

But US leaders must be truthful about the potential and limitations of trade agreements to regulate globalization. We ask too much of trade policy if we ask it to regulate all of the costs of global economic interdependence, from protecting consumers and the environment to promoting human rights and public health. Trade policy alone simply cannot do it all. We must find ways to reconcile trade liberalization with the achievement of other equally important social and environmental policy goals.

NOTES

1. This chapter contains material from other articles, including 'Trade is Everybody's Business', an unpublished article written with John Huenemann, formerly Assistant USTR for North America, now vice-president at GPC O'Neill; my columns on trade from <intellectualcapital.com>; and my book, *Taking*

Trade to the Streets: The Lost History of Public Efforts to Shape Globalization (Ann Arbor: University of Michigan Press, 2001).

2. See Immerwahr et al. (1991), and more recent data at <www.publicagenda.org/issues/red_flags.cfm?issue_type=economy>. According to the Program on International Policy Attitudes, 'a majority of Americans support the growth of international trade, especially when the removal of trade barriers is clearly reciprocal. However, Americans are lukewarm about the actual net benefits of trade. A strong majority feels trade has not grown in a way that adequately incorporates concerns for American workers, international labour standards and the environment.' Last year PIPA surveyed 1,826 Americans and found that some 88 per cent thought that increasing international trade should be balanced with other goals, such as protecting workers, the environment, and human rights, even if this means slowing the growth of trade and the economy. Americans do not want globalization to hamper the achievement of other important policy goals. 'Support for fast-track is low, apparently because it signifies the increase of trade without incorporating these concerns.' See 'Americans on Globalization' at <www.pipa.org/OnlineReports/Globalization/executive_summary.html>.

3. The letter urging representatives to reject the Dunkel draft included 17 environmental groups, 5 consumer groups, 9 labour groups, 5 citizens' groups, 6 farm groups, and 3 religious groups. Many of these same groups had expressed concerns about NAFTA. See Citizen Trade Watch Campaign (1992).

4. The information on the WTO is in GATT Secretariat (1993: Annex IV, 91).

5. Interviews with Lori Wallach, Public Citizen, 2 July 1998; Brent Blackwelder, Friends of the Earth, 3 Aug. 1998.

6. The 1994 hearings on the Uruguay Round included hearings held in January, February, and June by the House of Representatives Ways and Means Committee; March and April hearings by the House Agriculture Committee; and February, March, and June hearings by the House Foreign Affairs Committee. On the Senate side, the Finance Committee held hearings in February and March, the Commerce Committee in October and November, and the Foreign Relations Committee in June.

7. The Senate Foreign Relations Committee held hearings on the request of Senators Helms and Pressler. Senators Jesse Helms and Larry Pressler, letter to Senator Claiborne Pell, chair, Senate Foreign Relations Committee, 4 May 1994. Some of the Senate Commerce Committee hearings were held after the election, when Congress was in recess.

8. The Uruguay Round vote in the House was: 167 Democrats and 121 Republicans for (288), and 89 Democrats, 56 Republicans, and one independent against (146). In the Senate, 41 Democrats and 35 Republicans voted for, 14 Democrats and 10 Republicans voted against (Lamb, n.d.; Sanger, 1994: A1; Buchanan, 1995).

9. On the International Forum on Globalization, see 'History of the IFG' and IFG Associates at <www.ifg.org/about.html> and <www.ifg.org/assoc.html>.

10. Interviews with Victor Mennoti, International Forum on Globalization, 25 Aug. 1998; Lori Wallach, 9 Apr. 1999; Colin Hines, 23 Sept. 1998.

11. The views of Destler and other analysts are cited in Schott (1998: 10–25).

12. Aaronson discussion with Richard Chriss, Chief Trade Counsel, Senator Charles Grassley, Senate Finance Committee, 17 Jan. 2001; Pearlstein (2001).
13. USTR (2000b). The section on Canada begins on p. 37. Available at: <www.ustr.gov/regions/whemisphere/canada/trade.shtml>.

REFERENCES

Aaronson, Susan Ariel. 1996. *Trade and the American Dream: A Social History of Postwar U.S. Trade Policy*. Lexington: University of Kentucky Press.
Barshefsky, Charlene. 2000. 'Thoughts at a Moment of Transition', speech to Economic Strategy Institute, 19 Dec.
Blackwelder, Brent. 1998. Author interview, Friends of the Earth, 3 Aug.
Buchanan, Patrick. 1995. 'An American Economy for Americans', *Wall Street Journal*, 11 Sept.
Citizens' Trade Watch Campaign. 1992. 'Consumer and Environmental Briefing Packet on the 20 December 1991 Uruguay Round GATT Final Act Text'. Washington, Spring.
Clinton, William. 2001. Farewell Address, *Washington Post*, 18 Jan. Available at: <http://www.washingtonpost.com/wp-srv/onpolitics/elections/clinton-text010801.htm>.
Collins, Susan M., and Barry Bosworth, eds. 1994. *The New GATT: Implications for the United States*. Washington: Brookings Institution.
Council of Economic Advisors. 1994. *Economic Report of the President: Transmitted to the Congress February 1994*. Washington: Government Printing Office.
de Jonquieres, Guy. 2001. 'EU and Japan Lead Call for a New Trade Round', *Financial Times*, 23 Jan.
Destler, I.M. 1995. *American Trade Politics*, 3rd edn. Washington: Institute for International Economics.
Dunne, Nancy. 1992. 'Consumer Protest at World Trade Plan', *Financial Times*, 11 Dec., 5.
Economist. 1998. 'France's Right: An Utter Mess', 19 Aug.
General Agreement on Tariffs and Trade Secretariat. 1993. 'Final Act Embodying the Results of the Uruguay Round of Multilateral Trade Negotiations', 15 Dec.
Hines, Colin. 1998. Author interview, 23 Sept.
Hufbauer, Gary Clyde. 1999. 'World Trade after Seattle: Implications for the United States', International Economics Policy Briefs, Dec.
Immerwahr, John, Jean Johnson, and Adam Kernan-Schloss. 1991. 'Cross-Talk: The Public Experts and Competitiveness', A Research Report from the Business Higher Education Forum and the Public Agenda Foundation. Washington.
Lamb, Debbie. n.d. 'Congressional Votes on International Trade Bills', unpublished paper.
Landers, Ann. 1995. Syndicated column, *Washington Post*, 28 Sept., 15 Oct.
Lang, Tim, and Colin Hines. 1993. *The New Protectionism*. New York: New Press.
Mennoti, Victor. 1998. Author interview, International Forum on Globalization, 25 Aug.
NAFTATHOUGHTS. 1994. 'Citizens' Groups Raise Concerns about GATT', 4, 1 (Apr.).

Pearlstein, Steve. 2001. 'Trade Representative to Keep Rank: Business Opposition Defeats Plan to Make It Sub-Cabinet Job', *Washington Post*, 9 Jan., A21.

President of the United States. 1994. Message Transmitting the Uruguay Round Trade Agreements, Texts of Agreements Implementing Bill Statement of Administrative Action and Required Supporting Statements, 27 Aug.

Sanger, David E. 1994. 'Trade Agreement Ends Long Debate but Not Conflicts', *New York Times*, 4 Dec., A1.

Schott, Jeffrey. 1994. *The Uruguay Round: An Assessment*. Washington: Institute for International Economics.

———, ed. 1998. *Restarting Fast-track*. Washington: Institute for International Economics.

United States Trade Representative. 2000a. *Annual Report 1999*. Washington: Government Printing Office.

———. 2000b. *National Trade Report on Foreign Trade Barriers*. Washington.

Wallach, Lori. 1998. Author interview, Public Citizen, 2 July.

———. 1999. Author interview, 9 Apr.

Watkins, Kevin. 1998. Author interview, Oxfam, 24 Sept.

10

Africa in Canadian Foreign Policy 2000: The Human Security Agenda

CHRIS BROWN

As the year 2000 drew to a close, an unwed Nigerian teenage mother named Bariya Ibrahim Magazu became something of a *cause célèbre* throughout Canada.[1] The young woman, who was variously described as being as young as 13 or as old as 17, had fallen afoul of the strict application of the Islamic judicial code, *sharia*, in the northern Nigerian state of Zamfara. She was sentenced in September, while still pregnant, to 100 lashes for premarital sex and to a further 80 lashes for falsely charging that three associates of her father had forced her to have sex with them. Editorialists, church groups, human rights groups, and many others in Canada expressed outrage that such a harsh sentence could be imposed on someone so young; the outrage was only compounded by the widespread suspicion that she was in fact telling the truth and had been a victim of rape. A church group in British Columbia began raising funds in the hopes of bringing her to Canada as a refugee, while a spokesperson for the Canadian branch of Amnesty International stated that, if the full sentence were actually carried out, it could quite possibly prove fatal. Reacting to the widespread public concern, the Canadian government sent a formal note to Nigerian President Olesugun Obasanjo in December expressing shock at the sentence and asking that he do everything in his power to prevent it from being carried out. However, the Canadian protest was to no avail. The Nigerian teenager's baby was born in late December. In mid-January 2001 an appeal court struck down the 80 lashes for false accusation but affirmed the sentence of 100 lashes for premarital sex. In late January this sentence was carried out.

The saga of Bariya Ibrahim Magazu had a very different meaning in Nigeria than in Canada. For many Canadians this was a straightforward humanitarian issue, but for Nigerians it was simply another chapter in the long-running story of the religious and regional conflicts that have divided the country since independence in 1960. A large country with an estimated population over 110 million, Nigeria is roughly split between the Islamic north and the Christian and animist south. Much of the post-independence history of Nigeria can be told as the story of ongoing conflict between these two regions. President Obasanjo, who was elected in 1999 as part of a return to democratic civilian government after 27 years of often bloody military rule, is himself a Christian from the south, the first southerner ever to hold the office of president. He was elected, however, with widespread support in the north, an electoral base that he is keen to maintain. In recent years, northern politicians have called with increasing fervour for the imposition of *sharia*, which they see as an antidote to a rising tide of crime and immoral behaviour, especially among Nigeria's youth. In this call, they have widespread public support, at least in the north. The governor of Zamfara state, Ahmed Sani, made *sharia* a major plank in his election platform. When Zamfara became the first Nigerian state officially to adopt the code in January 2000, Sani could convincingly argue that he had a strong democratic mandate to do so.

If *sharia* is a vote-winner in northern Nigeria, it is seen in southern Nigeria as a potent symbol of northern domination and of religious discrimination against non-Muslims. Many people, including President Obasanjo himself, have argued that *sharia* is contrary to Nigeria's constitution, which makes Nigeria a secular state.

Nonetheless, given the precarious religious and regional balance in the country, and his own electoral calculations, Obasanjo has been reluctant to move decisively against northern governors who implement *sharia*. It is in this context that the saga of Ms. Magazu played itself out. While President Obasanjo did ask the state government to set aside the sentence, Governor Sani of Zamfara vowed not to bend to pressure from non-Muslims, essentially daring Obasanjo to a showdown over the issue. Judging perhaps that Nigeria's young democracy and fragile civil peace were more important than the punishment meted out to one teenage girl, Obasanjo did not push the issue.

The saga of Bariya Ibrahim Magazu is in many ways representative of Canada's foreign policy towards Africa. On the one hand, that Canadians should have been so affected by her story points to the laudable humanitarianism that underpins much of our approach to the world. Indeed, it is notable that, among Western states, the Magazu case became a *cause célèbre* only in Canada; in the United States and Western Europe it attracted only passing attention. Foreign Affairs Minister Lloyd Axworthy put humanitarianism at the centre of Canada's foreign policy with his human security agenda. As a continent where human security is manifestly at risk, Africa came to figure far more prominently in Canada's foreign policy during 2000 than a narrow examination of national interests might suggest. Especially through its seat on the United Nations (UN) Security Council (see Chapter 7 by Pearson in this volume), Canada became a leading advocate of measures to improve human security in Africa. On the other hand, the fact that Canada's protests ultimately proved futile in the Magazu case is also instructive, for the humanitarian response of the human security agenda frequently seemed inadequate in the face of complex African realities. It is difficult to point to concrete examples of Canadian success in promoting human security in Africa during the year. All too often, it appeared that Canada was unable to back up its rhetoric about human security with sufficient resources to achieve results. Equally, it was unable to convince its Western allies to follow its lead. The relatively poor performance in achieving its stated goals inevitably raises questions about the human security agenda itself.

The rest of this chapter presents these arguments in three sections. The first section looks at Africa in Canadian foreign policy, arguing that, due to the human security agenda, the continent assumed a far greater salience for Canadian foreign policy in 2000 than would otherwise have been expected. The second section then examines four major African conflicts that occupied much of the time of Canadian foreign policy-makers in 2000—those in Angola, the Democratic Republic of Congo (DRC), Sierra Leone, and Sudan. In each case, conflict rages on and human security has not meaningfully improved, despite the best efforts of Canada. Finally, the conclusion brings together all the arguments of this chapter in a reassessment of the concept of human security.

AFRICA IN CANADIAN FOREIGN POLICY

Any analysis of Canadian foreign policy towards Africa must start with the obvious point that Africa is peripheral to Canada's national interest, however that slippery concept may be defined. Canada was not formerly a colonial power in Africa, nor is it presently a global superpower with national interests at stake around the globe. Unlike the United States and our major European allies, therefore, Canada lacks the complex and contradictory relationship with African states that comes with long historical ties. Reflecting this lack of historical ties, there are no large and well-established African immigrant communities in Canada, similar to the immigrant communities from Europe or even Asia, that are capable of exerting a major influence over Canadian foreign policy towards their homeland. In the past decade or so there have been increased immigrant and refugee flows to Canada from Africa, especially from Somalia, but this has not yet led to the emergence of anything resembling a powerful 'Africa lobby' in Canadian politics.

Perhaps most importantly for this analysis, Canada's economic ties with Africa are minimal.[2] Canada's total exports to Africa in 1999 were approximately $1.1 billion, while imports were approximately $1.2 billion. This trade represented a significant increase over the mid-1990s, but even so it accounted for less than one-half of 1 per cent of total Canadian trade in 1999. To put the same figures in a different light, the Department of Foreign Affairs and International Trade (DFAIT) has estimated that, in 1997, Canadian merchandise exports to Africa created or sustained 7,008 Canadian jobs, a mere drop in the bucket of the overall Canadian economy. Investment figures tell a similar story. Canadian direct investment in Africa nearly doubled from $400 million in 1993 to $777 million in 1997, with Canadian companies particularly active in mining and related activities. Nonetheless, this still represented less than one-half of 1 per cent of total Canadian direct foreign investment. Given these figures, it is not surprising that aid still looms large in the Canada–Africa relationship. Indeed, Africa was allocated $807 million of Canadian aid in 2000, approximately one-third of the total aid budget. As one consequence of the continued predominance of aid in Canada's economic relations with Africa, non-governmental organizations (NGOs) in the development or human rights sectors are often the strongest domestic Canadian voice on issues related to Africa.

By any standard of measurement—historical, social, or economic—Canada's ties to Africa are therefore minor. One implication of this is that Canadian policy-makers enjoy an unusual degree of latitude with respect to their Africa policy. With so few vested interests at stake, they are remarkably free to shape policy as they wish. They can, if they so choose, rest their policy on a strong moral or ethical foundation. This was certainly the case during the late 1980s, the one other period in recent decades when Africa featured prominently in Canadian foreign policy. At that time, with relatively few economic ties to South Africa, Canada was able to assume a lead role in the international sanctions movement against the apartheid regime. In 2000, a similar logic allowed Canada, with Axworthy in the lead, to place humanitarianism at the forefront of Canada's Africa policy.

One might expect that Africa would occupy at best a marginal place in Canadian foreign policy given the lack of extensive ties between Canada and Africa. In 2000, however, just the opposite seemed to be the case. It frequently appeared that Canadian foreign policy was dominated by African concerns. When Canada assumed the rotating presidency of the UN Security Council in April 2000, for instance, Axworthy outlined a five-point agenda that Canada intended to promote. Two of these agenda items referred exclusively to Africa (sanctions against the UNITA [Union for the Total Independence of Angola] rebel movement in Angola and a report on the UN's role in Rwanda) and a further two were general global issues with an important African dimension (the protection of civilians in armed conflict and the effectiveness of sanctions). Only one (humanitarian dimensions of the conflict in Afghanistan) was unconnected to Africa. How did Africa come to occupy such a central place in Canadian foreign policy? The answer is the human security agenda.

Human security is not a new idea, nor is it one promoted only by Canada. Nonetheless, under Lloyd Axworthy the concept of human security was put at the centre of Canadian foreign policy and Canada became perhaps the leading advocate of human security on the world stage. According to a DFAIT policy document, the concept of human security 'represents an important progression in the global lexicon' because it recognizes that 'the protection of people is at least as important as the sovereignty of states.'[3] Canada's human security agenda 'means building a world where universal humanitarian standards and the rule of law effectively protect all people; where those who violate these standards and laws are held accountable; and where our global, regional and bilateral institutions are equipped to defend and enforce these standards.' Specifically, the document highlights 'five foreign policy priorities for advancing human security': protection of civilians, peace support operations, conflict prevention, governance and accountability, and public safety. In 2000, this agenda dominated Canadian foreign policy or, as Axworthy put it in his introduction to the DFAIT policy document, 'this perspective informs Canadian foreign policy today.'

In this context, it is perhaps easier to understand why Africa loomed so large in Canadian foreign policy in 2000, for Africa is manifestly a continent where human security is at risk. Of the five continents, Africa has the lowest per capita income and the lowest life expectancy. It also has the highest number of ongoing conflicts. According to one source, 20 of Africa's 53 states were involved in wars of one kind or another in 2000 (Johnson, 2000: A18). These conflicts have generated millions of refugees and placed the personal security of millions of others at risk. According to the same source, '15 African states are suffering serious food shortages, often as a result of the ravages of war.' These include Eritrea, where 500,000 people are affected; Rwanda, where 900,000 need food assistance; Somalia, where 1.6 million people are starving; Sudan, where 2 million are reliant on food aid; and the DRC, where a staggering 10 million people are short of food. These sorts of figures cried out for a humanitarian response from sympathetic countries such as Canada, and this is precisely what happened. With the latitude to do so and the human security agenda as his rationale, Foreign Minister Axworthy pushed African issues to the forefront of Canada's foreign policy in 2000.

Canada promoted its Africa-related human security agenda most forcefully through its seat on the United Nations Security Council. As noted above, it used its presidency of the Council in April 2000 to highlight a number of Africa-related issues. Throughout the year, it was actively involved in all the major African issues to come before the Security Council. These included the effort to curb the illegal diamond trade that finances rebel groups in Angola and Sierra Leone; the broader question of the effectiveness of international sanctions; the re-examination of peacekeeping operations in light of a major report on the UN's failure to prevent the 1994 genocide in Rwanda; and proposed or actual UN peacekeeping missions to the Central African Republic, the DRC, Eritrea and Ethiopia, and Sierra Leone. Canada also sponsored a major international conference on war-affected children and continued to provide leadership in the implementation of the 1997 Ottawa Mine Ban Convention. Outside the UN framework, Canada promoted its African human security agenda through multilateral institutions such as the Commonwealth and la Francophonie and bilaterally in its relations with individual African states. Perhaps the highest-profile example of the latter concerned Canada's relations with Sudan, where Talisman Energy Corporation, Canada's largest independent oil and gas producer, was involved in a controversial oil development project. This listing, extensive as it is, provides only a partial accounting of the many Africa-related initiatives taken by Canada in 2000 under the rubric of the human security agenda. Obviously, it is not possible to discuss all these initiatives within the confines of one chapter. Instead, the next section examines in detail four major African conflicts—those in Angola, the DRC, Sierra Leone, and Sudan—and Canada's role in them in 2000.

FOUR AFRICAN CONFLICTS

Angola

Angola achieved independence from Portugal in 1975 amid civil war among three rival liberation movements. One of them eventually faded away, but the other two continue their war to this day—the People's Movement for the Liberation of Angola (known by its Portuguese acronym as the MPLA) and the Union for the Total Independence of Angola (UNITA in the Portuguese acronym). Angola was long Africa's major Cold War battleground, with the Soviet Union backing the MPLA, while the United States and South Africa supported UNITA. With the assistance of 40,000 Cuban troops, the MPLA controlled the capital, Luanda, and formed the government; significantly, it also controlled Angola's large oil reserves in the Cabinda enclave in the northwest, giving it a secure source of funding for its war effort. UNITA, meanwhile, with ongoing support from South African troops based in neighbouring Namibia, waged a guerrilla war against the MPLA from its bases in the south and east of the country.

The end of the Cold War seemed to offer hope for the resolution of the conflict in Angola. For one thing, Namibia, Angola's neighbour to the south, achieved its independence in 1990 under a successful UN peace plan. As part of this plan, all the Cuban troops were withdrawn from Angola while South African troops were withdrawn from Namibia. Later, with the collapse of the Soviet Union and the end of apartheid in South Africa, both the MPLA and UNITA lost their major foreign source of support. Under strong international pressure to end the war, the two movements agreed to enter into peace talks. These culminated in the Bicesse Accords of 1991, which called for an interim government of national unity leading up to general elections in 1992. Unlike Namibia, where the international community mounted a large-scale operation to help ensure a successful transition to independence and democracy, the international presence during the Angolan election of 1992 was relatively modest. Partly as a result, the election campaign was characterized by increasing violence and intimidation on both sides. When it was announced that the MPLA had narrowly won the election, UNITA leader Jonas Savimbi withdrew from the government of national unity (in which he had never fully participated in the first place) and resumed the war. His actions caught the MPLA off guard, nearly allowing him to achieve by the gun what he had failed to accomplish through the ballot box. In the end, however, the MPLA was able to regroup and restore the military status quo ante.

As a result of his refusal to accept the outcome of democratic elections, Savimbi quickly became a pariah in the West and around the world. He was condemned as a gross violator of human rights by the very same American government that had previously provided him with military and financial support. Declaring that Savimbi was responsible for the resumption of the war, the UN imposed a fuel and arms embargo on UNITA in 1993. Many observers thought that, without official South African support and in the face of international sanctions, UNITA would be unable to continue to prosecute the war. During the 1980s it had funded its war in part by slaughtering the elephant herds of Angola for their ivory. As this source of cash was depleted, UNITA came increasingly to rely for funds on diamond sales from mines in the areas it controlled. It easily circumvented the UN embargo by buying weapons and fuel on the international black market and smuggling them into Angola through neighbouring Zaire. Much to the surprise of the international community and the chagrin of the MPLA, therefore, UNITA did not fade away after 1993, but, instead, consolidated its position and even managed to step up the military pressure on the MPLA. Recognizing the importance of diamonds, the UN imposed an embargo on diamond purchases from UNITA-controlled areas in 1998. The fall of the Mobutu regime in Zaire in the previous year, and the transformation of that country into the Democratic Republic of Congo, seemed to offer the prospect that UNITA's supply lines could be cut and the embargo made to work. As the year 2000 approached, however, there was little evidence that this was happening.

It was in this context that Canada began playing an active role in Angolan affairs in 1999 and 2000. Certainly, the civil war was a humanitarian disaster. According to the UN, the war had cost the lives of approximately 500,000 people during the 1990s alone, while displacing four million others. Once it assumed its seat on the Security Council, Canada began demanding more forceful measures to make the sanctions against UNITA work. It took over the chairmanship of the Angola sanctions committee and managed to convince the Security Council to appoint a committee of experts to investigate why the sanctions were not working and to recommend measures to make them work. In March 2000, Canada's UN ambassador, Robert Fowler, presented the report of the committee of experts to the Security Council.

The Fowler Report, as it became known, found that UNITA had managed to sell $4 billion worth of illicit diamonds since the original 1993 sanctions, making its financial position more secure during the 1990s than it had been in previous decades when UNITA relied on American and South African financial aid. It also found that UNITA had diversified its supply lines since the fall of Mobutu, using its diamond money to purchase favours. Unusually for a UN document, the report pulled no punches as it described how UNITA managed to sell its diamonds and buy guns and fuel in return. The diamonds were sold in Antwerp, Belgium, site of the world's largest diamond exchange, where allegedly 'lax controls' allowed UNITA diamonds to go undetected. Weapons and fuel were purchased from the proceeds, primarily from Eastern European countries, especially

Bulgaria. To smuggle the diamonds out of Angola and bring in the weapons and fuel, Savimbi had purchased co-operation in a number of African countries. The report named Presidents Blaise Compoare of Burkina Faso and Gnassingbe Eyadema of Togo as two heads of state whose assistance had been purchased by Savimbi. In addition, the report charged that UNITA had smuggling operations in Congo, Côte d'Ivoire, the DRC, Gabon, Namibia, Rwanda, South Africa, and Zambia, though not always with government knowledge and support. The report recommended 39 measures that could be taken to tighten the sanctions, mostly involving monitoring and enforcement designed to make it more difficult for UNITA to continue its smuggling activities. The most controversial recommendation, however, was that the UN should impose secondary sanctions on countries found to be knowingly violating the primary sanctions against UNITA.

The Fowler Report was championed by Canada as a major example of its human security agenda in action. Here was concrete action to support peace, prevent future conflict, and protect civilians, all key human security objectives. Certainly, there is no doubt that the Fowler Report stands out in the annals of UN official reports for its blunt language and willingness to 'name and shame'. It caused a stir in the UN and beyond, where those named were quick to condemn the report and defend their sullied reputations. Representatives of the Antwerp diamond exchange argued that the report was outdated, because it did not take into account improved controls that had been instituted over the previous year. Similarly, De Beers, the South African diamond giant, claimed that it had long since ceased purchasing suspect diamonds and had taken measures to certify the origin of all the diamonds it did purchase. As for the African countries named in the report, they all stoutly denied their complicity in smuggling.

When the Security Council debated the Fowler Report, it adopted most of its recommendations, albeit with a six-month grace period to allow those named in the report to respond to the accusations and change their practices. Significantly, however, the proposal for secondary sanctions was quietly dropped, thus stripping the agreed resolution of the one recommendation in the report with real teeth. As the year ended, the furor over the report died down and the agreed recommendations were officially being implemented. Perhaps over time the improved monitoring and enforcement of the sanctions, together with improved certification by De Beers and the Antwerp diamond exchange, will slowly starve UNITA of funds and squeeze its supply lines. This is certainly the hope. On past evidence, however, it is at least as likely that as long as UNITA has diamonds to sell, it will be able to find a willing buyer. With the money it earns, it will then be able to buy the weapons and fuel it needs, opening new smuggling routes even as old ones are exposed and shut down. Certainly, at the end of 2000 the Angolan civil war continued unabated, with no early resolution in sight. Canada, inspired by the human security agenda, had led an attempt at the Security Council to end the war through tightening existing sanctions against UNITA. Its efforts were only partially successful.

The Democratic Republic of Congo

Blessed with extensive copper, gold, diamond, and other mineral resources, the DRC is potentially one of Africa's richest countries. In reality, as a result of colonial neglect and over four decades of dictatorship and civil strife, its people remain among the poorest on the continent. In 1965, with American backing, Colonel Joseph Mobutu seized power in a military coup. Changing the name of the country to Zaire and restyling himself Mobutu Sese Seko, he established a personal dictatorship that set new lows for incompetence and venality, even by Africa's sorry standards. Systematically looting the national treasury for his personal gain, Mobutu amassed a personal fortune estimated at over $10 billion, making him one of the richest men in the world. Meanwhile, the country's infrastructure, such as it was, was falling apart because of a lack of new investment and the poor maintenance of existing infrastructure. Gradually, the state itself crumbled, leaving ordinary people to fend for the most basic amenities. Academic specialists labelled Mobutu's rule a 'kleptocracy' and commented on the 'decline and fall' of the Zairean state. Throughout it all, Mobutu seemed immune to serious criticism by Western governments, especially the United States, because of his hostility to communism and his willingness to allow Zaire to be used as a base of support for UNITA.

In the late 1990s, the end finally came for Mobutu. As one consequence of the Rwandan genocide and its aftermath, hundreds of thousands of Hutu refugees arrived in eastern Zaire in 1994. Many of these refugees had blood on their hands; among them were members of the *interahamwe*, the Hutu militia responsible for organizing the genocide. The new Tutsi-dominated government of Rwanda saw these refugees as a security threat and, together with its Ugandan allies, invaded eastern Zaire in 1996 in an attempt to push the refugees back from the border. To give their actions greater credibility, they also allied themselves with Laurent Kabila, an obscure Zairean rebel who had been waging a desultory guerrilla struggle against the Mobutu regime since the 1960s. So great was the decay of the Zairean state that Mobutu's army simply collapsed in the face of these attackers. What had started out as a limited operation in the border areas quickly became a full-scale invasion, as huge swaths of territory were conquered without opposition and large numbers of government troops deserted to the invaders' side. In early 1997 Kabila entered the capital, Kinshasa, and declared himself President of the newly rechristened Democratic Republic of Congo (DRC). Mobutu fled the country with his family and retainers, only to die of prostate cancer a few months later in exile.

If the Congolese people expected a new era of democracy and prosperity under Kabila, their hopes were dashed. Although he initially promised elections, Kabila soon moved to muzzle the press and ban all opposition parties. His economic policy consisted primarily of selling the concession rights to the DRC's mineral resources to the highest foreign bidder. Fatefully, he fell out with his Rwandan and Ugandan backers in 1998, and armed conflict resumed in eastern DRC. On the premise that 'the enemy of my enemy is my friend', he allied himself with the Hutu militias, thereby earning himself suspicion and enmity in the international community. When the military tide seemed to be going against him, he appealed for support from neighbouring African countries. Angola, Chad, Namibia, and Zimbabwe all sent troops, while Zambia supplied logistical support. This unprecedented level of intervention by African states in an African civil war led some observers to label the conflict Africa's 'First World War'. By 1999 an uneasy military stalemate had emerged, with Rwanda, Uganda, and various anti-Kabila rebel groups controlling much of eastern and northern DRC, including the main gold mines, while the Kabila regime held on to Kinshasa in the west, and the copper and diamond mines in the south, only with the aid of its African allies.

Under pressure from their allies and the international community, the various parties to the conflict agreed to seek a negotiated solution. The result was the Lusaka Accord of July 1999, which was signed by all the main domestic and foreign parties. The Accord called for a joint military council, the disarming of all rebel factions, the withdrawal of all foreign troops, and the establishment of an intra-Congolese dialogue leading to national reconciliation. A weakness of the Accord was that it had been negotiated in the absence of an explicit UN resolution promising the necessary support. After repeated violations of the Accord, the UN Security Council finally passed a resolution in February 2000 to establish a peacekeeping force in the DRC, to be known by its French acronym, the United Nations Organization Mission in the Congo (MONUC). The resolution reiterated the terms of the Lusaka Accord and pledged a UN force of 5,537 to monitor the process.

Canada was in fact a reluctant supporter of MONUC. While it strongly supported the DRC peace process, it argued that the proposed UN force was too small to do the job. As UN ambassador Fowler noted, the DRC is roughly 32 times larger than Sierra Leone and has approximately 10 times the population, yet the UN peacekeeping force sent to Sierra Leone around the same time was twice as large as the proposed DRC force. Nonetheless, he justified Canada's ultimate decision to vote in favour of the mission in human security terms: 'There are few places in the world where civilians are more in need of protection. . . . In situations such as this, there is an imperative to act and to do what is possible to relieve the suffering' (Knox, 2000: A7). Canada pledged $2.5 million for the peace process and offered to assist with logistics, communications, and transportation. It made no concrete offer of personnel, but Fowler made it clear that any Canadian contribution would be small, probably less than 200 peacekeepers in total.

As it turned out, MONUC was never deployed and the conflict continues unabated. Much of the blame rests with the parties to the dispute, who repeatedly violated the Lusaka Accord and seemed more interested in retaining control over mineral revenues than in seeking a peace settlement. Rwanda and Uganda, in particular, were quite content to retain their de facto occupation of over half of the DRC, as this gave them access to significant mineral revenues and allowed them to keep the Hutu *interahamwe* at bay. President Kabila, for his part, refused to co-operate when the UN sent advance teams to the DRC, insisting that only the rebel groups needed to disarm. In early 2001 Kabila was assassinated by his own troops. This seemed to make little difference to the prospects for peace. He was quickly replaced by his son, who promised to continue the policies of his father.

Part of the responsibility for the failure of MONUC, however, rests with the UN, where Canada played an active role through its seat on the Security Council. As part of the human security agenda, and in response to the earlier peacekeeping failures in Rwanda and elsewhere, Canada argued that future UN peacekeeping missions need to be more robust. They required both the troops and equipment to do the job and a mandate to use all necessary force. Persuasive as these arguments were in the abstract, they carried little weight in the specific case of MONUC. No Western power offered troops for the mission; the mandate to use force was highly restrictive; and, as Fowler's comments make clear, all those involved knew that the proposed force was simply too small for a country as large as the DRC. Canada itself was prepared to offer only limited support for the mission and was unable to convince its Western allies to do more. Looking at the record, it is hard not to conclude that the human security agenda counted for little, while cold calculations of national interest counted for a great deal more, especially when it came time to put money and personnel on the line in the DRC.

Sierra Leone

The current conflict in Sierra Leone dates from 1991, when the Revolutionary United Front (RUF) under Foday Sankoh launched a guerrilla war against the government. The RUF is notable for the brutality of its methods and the vagueness of its political objectives. Its standard modus operandi is to terrorize civilian populations in areas it controls by hacking off people's arms or legs with a machete. It also routinely coerces children to join its ranks. As for its political platform, the RUF has never articulated one. From its actions, it is clear that the RUF wants to continue to control the diamond-mining areas of Sierra Leone, but it has never stated why it wants to overthrow the government or what type of regime it would create should it ever seize power. However vague the RUF's goals may be, it is clear that its war has been a humanitarian disaster for Sierra Leone. In a country with a total population of approximately 4.5 million, 30,000 people have amputated limbs, 100,000 people have died, and a further 2 million have been displaced. The economy has collapsed and life expectancy at birth is among the lowest in the world.

The war has directly contributed to extreme government instability in Sierra Leone. There were three military coups during the 1990s. The third of these coups, led by Major Johnny Paul Koroma in September 1997, overthrew the democratically elected government of President Ahmad Kabbah. With the assistance of a mainly Nigerian peacekeeping force known as ECOMOG, Kabbah was restored to power in April 1998 and Koroma launched his own bush war against the government. In January 1999, the RUF invaded and briefly occupied most of the capital, Freetown, before being pushed back by ECOMOG. Subsequently, all sides agreed to peace talks and in July 1999 the Lomé Accord apparently brought the Sierra Leone conflict to an end. Under the terms of the Accord, amnesty was granted to all rebels, Sankoh and Koroma were given senior cabinet positions, and the RUF was given effective control over the diamond mines. In exchange for all these concessions, the rebels agreed to disarm and to function as normal political parties.

Later, however, the rebels were reluctant to hand over their arms to ECOMOG, against whom they had so recently been fighting. It was therefore agreed that ECOMOG would be replaced by a UN peacekeeping force, known as UNAMSIL, which was already in existence but would now be bolstered significantly in order to take on its new role. The total projected strength of UNAMSIL was 11,000 troops. The first UNAMSIL contingent arrived in January 2000 and by May, when the last ECOMOG troops departed, its strength was 8,700. As it turned out, the RUF forces were not willing to hand over their guns to the UN either, for hostilities broke out again when the UN troops tried disarming the RUF. The renewed conflict quickly enveloped the entire country, with Koroma's forces now fighting on the side of the government against the RUF. In an unprecedented embarrassment for the UN, the RUF captured and disarmed approximately 500 peacekeepers, most of whom came from Kenya and India, holding them hostage in the interior. In response to the deepening crisis, Great Britain sent 1,600 paratroopers in mid-May to secure the airport at Freetown and facilitate the evacuation of foreign nationals. Eventually, the UN hostages were released and the crisis eased. By the end of 2000 the government claimed that it was making progress against the RUF, but no final resolution to the conflict was yet in sight.

Canada was a leading advocate at the UN of a strong peacekeeping force for Sierra Leone. Reports of child soldiers and children with amputated limbs shocked Canadians. Many commentators suggested that Sierra Leone was the place where the lessons learned in Rwanda needed to be applied; a robust peacekeeping force should be deployed to prevent the RUF from committing further atrocities. As Foreign Minister Axworthy put it, 'here is a place to make a stand' (Gee, 2000: A15). These strong words, however, were not matched by strong action. Canada refused to commit soldiers to UNAMSIL, despite an explicit request from Nigerian President Obasanjo that it contribute a battalion of 700 troops. Instead, it contributed an Airbus to help ferry troops from Bangladesh, India, and Jordan to Sierra Leone; 30 cargo specialists to help them move; and 1,700 fragmentation vests and 1,700 helmets to bolster their equipment. Justifying this 'small but effective' contribution, Defence Minister Art Eggleton stated that Canada could do no more because it was 'overstretched, overextended in terms of our troop deployments throughout the world' (Sallot, 2000: A9). At the same time, Canadian officials expressed frustration with their inability to convince the United States to do more in Sierra Leone.

Just as in the DRC, there was a yawning gap here between Canada's rhetoric in terms of the human security agenda and its willingness and ability to back up the rhetoric with concrete action. Despite calling for a robust peacekeeping force and stating that Sierra Leone was a place where the UN must make a stand, Canada refused to contribute troops to UNAMSIL. Instead, it contented itself with providing logistical support for peacekeepers from less-developed countries. Equally, Canada failed to convince its Western allies to commit troops to UNAMSIL. Only when its own nationals appeared threatened did Great Britain send soldiers in; even then, they operated outside the UN mandate and with the limited objective of evacuating British and other foreign citizens.

Sudan

Africa's largest country by area, Sudan is situated along the same religious fault line as Nigeria. The north is primarily Arab and Islamic, while the south is primarily black and Christian or animist. The correlation between ethnicity and religion is not perfect, as many blacks, especially the black minority in the north, are Muslims. As a result, according to official government statistics, the Sudanese population is only 40 per cent Arab, but 70 per cent Islamic. Historically, the north, which contains approximately two-thirds of the population, has dominated the political and economic affairs of the country. Over the years, a succession of southern-based political movements have fought for greater regional autonomy or even outright independence. The first armed rebellion in the south began in 1955, a year before independence. The Addis Ababa Accord of 1972 granted significant autonomy to the south and ended the war. The war resumed in 1983 when a new government attempted to impose Islamic *sharia* law; it has continued to this day. The main southern rebel group is currently the Sudanese People's Liberation Army (SPLA), led by John Garang.

Sudan has had a succession of military and civilian governments over the years, all dominated by Arab Muslims from the north. The enduring issue of Sudanese politics has been the place of Islam in national life. Previous regimes, seeking to appease the south and end the war, have attempted to make Sudan a secular state. The present government of Omar al-Bashir, dominated by the fundamentalist National Islamic Front (NIF), has sought to make Sudan an Islamic state. To this end, it has imposed a strict version of *sharia* law and has adopted a policy of military confrontation with the SPLA. Internationally, Sudan has become something of a pariah state; it has been condemned by Amnesty International for widespread human rights abuses and by the United States government for harbouring terrorist movements. The United States imposed unilateral trade and investment sanctions on Sudan in 1998 and has urged its allies, including Canada, to do the same. There is widespread human suffering in Sudan, especially in the south, as a result of the endless civil war and recurrent drought. By one estimate, one-fifth of the total population of 35 million has been displaced by the war and 2 million people are dependent on food aid.

There is no UN peace process currently under way in Sudan, though a regional African grouping, the Inter Governmental Authority on Development (IGAD), has been attempting to foster dialogue between the SPLA and the government. In 2000, Canada contributed money to the IGAD secretariat and attempted to promote intra-Sudanese dialogue in other ways. Sudan also figured prominently in the conference sponsored by Canada on war-affected children. Canada's major involvement in Sudanese affairs in 2000, however, came through the controversy surrounding Talisman Energy. In 1998, this company entered into a consortium with state oil companies from China and Malaysia to develop and exploit newly discovered oil fields in southern Sudan. Talisman's stake was $800 million, or 25 per cent of the total investment in the project.

From the moment the project was announced, Talisman became the target of criticism by Canadian churches and developmental and human rights groups, all of whom demanded that it withdraw from Sudan. The critics charged that Talisman was contributing to gross human rights violations both directly, in that force was used to clear local people from the area of the oil fields, and indirectly, in that the oil revenues, once they started to flow, would allow the cash-strapped Sudanese government to step up its war against the SPLA. Talisman responded that the specific allegations about clearing the oil fields were simply untrue and that its investments allowed it to be a voice for positive change in Sudan. Furthermore, it argued, it would be futile to abandon its investments, because less scrupulous Chinese and Malaysian partners would jump in to fill the void.

The case of Talisman Energy put the government in an awkward spot. On the one hand, Canada had long condemned Sudan for its human rights abuses and was a supporter of the IGAD dialogue process. Ignoring the critics would make a mockery of Canada's professed commitment to the human security agenda. On the other hand, Talisman had done nothing illegal under Canadian law. Acting against it might seem unfair, especially in Alberta, Talisman's home base. The response of the government, therefore, was to appoint in October 1999 a special representative, John Harker, to look into the allegations against Talisman. At the time, Foreign Affairs Minister Axworthy stated: 'if it becomes evident that oil extraction is exacerbating the conflict in Sudan, or resulting in violations of human rights or humanitarian law, the government of Canada may consider, if required, economic and trade restrictions' (Trickey, 2000: A1).

In early January 2000 the Harker report was submitted to the government. It accused the government of Sudan of widespread human rights abuses. While it found no direct link to Talisman, it did conclude that oil development was fuelling the war in the south. Furthermore, it agreed that the future oil revenues would assist the government in its war effort. After a month of internal debate and intense lobbying, the government publicly released the report, and its response to it, in February. Axworthy rather sheepishly announced that while the government accepted the findings of the Harker report, it would impose no sanctions on Talisman. Instead, in a reversal of his earlier position, Axworthy declared that Talisman was a positive force for change in Sudan. He also pointed out that the government lacked a legal basis to force Talisman to withdraw from Sudan, as the existing legislation dealt only with trade, not investment. To prevent a similar situation from arising in the future, he also announced his government's intention to amend existing legislation to cover overseas investment. Predictably, Talisman was pleased with this decision—and its share price rose dramatically—while its critics were outraged. The United States also blasted Canada, comparing its two-year-old trade and investment sanctions against Sudan with Canada's refusal to act.

What happened? It appears that Axworthy simply lost the debate in cabinet. Intense corporate lobbying seems to have convinced cabinet that sanctions against Talisman would place a major Canadian oil corporation at financial risk, all to no good purpose. In other words, when the human security agenda ran up against powerful economic interests, the economic interests won.

CONCLUSION

This analysis is not meant to present a uniformly negative picture of Canada's foreign policy towards Africa in 2000. By promoting the human security agenda, such as in its sponsorship of the conference on war-affected children, Canada brought attention to the plight of many the world's most marginalized people. Equally, many of the actions discussed above did have positive consequences, for instance, in improving the monitoring and enforcement of international sanctions regimes. Furthermore, many positive actions taken by Canada are not discussed here. For example, Canada participated (albeit in a minor role) in the successful peacekeeping mission that ended in 2000 in the Central African Republic and is providing 400 soldiers for what appears likely to be a successful peacekeeping mission on the border between Ethiopia and Eritrea. As well, in countless small ways, including through seed funds and special emissaries, Canada contributed to the advancement of human security in many countries throughout Africa.

Even so, the Canadian record in Angola, the DRC, Sierra Leone, and Sudan does give pause for concern. Each conflict received considerable personal attention from the Minister of Foreign Affairs. In each case Canadian policy was informed by the human security agenda, and in each case serious questions need to be asked about the ultimate impact and effectiveness of the policy. In Angola, Canada led the effort to tighten an existing international sanctions regime. At the end of the day, many useful improvements were made, but the strongest measures advocated by Canada were not adopted and the sanctions have not yet achieved their intended purpose. In the DRC and Sierra Leone, Canada advocated robust peacekeeping forces to support a peace process. In both cases, however, Canada's own contributions to peacekeeping were minor if not minuscule. Furthermore, Canada was unable to convince its Western allies to make significant contributions, essentially leaving UN peacekeeping in Africa to frequently poorly equipped and poorly trained troops from developing countries. Finally, in Sudan, Canada agreed that oil development was contributing to human rights abuses and fuelling the war, but in the end did nothing to halt investment of a major Canadian energy company. Overall, perhaps the greatest condemnation of the human security agenda is that in all four African cases examined, and despite all the rhetoric and all the actions of Canada and others in the international community, the conflicts continue unabated with no end in sight. If a foreign policy meant to promote human security has had no discernible impact in ending conflict, then perhaps some fundamental questions need to be asked about the policy itself.

First, and most obviously, a human security agenda is meaningless without the will and resources to back it up. Obviously, Canada is only one actor on the global stage, so all the ills of the world cannot be laid at its door. At the same time, however, what is most striking is how few resources Canada was willing and able to commit to the pursuit of its human security agenda in Africa. There have been successful UN peacekeeping missions in Africa in the past, most notably in Namibia. The Namibian operation, however, involved a massive commitment of international resources, to which Canada made a significant contribution. Nothing like a proportionate response from Canada to Africa's peacekeeping needs was evident in 2000. Second, Canada should more forthrightly acknowledge the limits to the human security agenda and the ways in which other considerations may override it. The decision over Talisman was not necessarily wrong. But it made Canada appear hypocritical because the whole issue was framed in the context of the human security agenda. Finally, one needs to ask how the human security agenda portrays Africa and Africans. It is founded on laudable humanitarian principles. Yet, an essentially humanitarian approach to Africa risks perpetuating the unfortunate stereotype of Africa as victim. If 20 out of

53 states in Africa were involved in some way or another in armed conflict in 2000, 33 were not. By focusing on the minority of African states experiencing violent conflict, there is a danger of ignoring the majority that do not. By focusing on war, there is a danger of ignoring the many states now consolidating democratic governance institutions. By focusing on humanitarian disasters, there is a danger of ignoring those states that are successfully building a market economy. It is unfortunate indeed if the ultimate legacy of the human security agenda is to blind Canadians to these and other positive developments in Africa.

NOTES

I would like to thank Jill Zmud for her research assistance in preparing this chapter. The chapter discusses sub-Saharan Africa only; it therefore excludes North Africa and the Middle East. Throughout, 'Africa' should be read to mean 'sub-Saharan Africa'.

1. For a good background on the Magazu case, see 'Islam in Nigeria: A child-mother caught in a storm', *Daily Mail and Guardian Online*, 12 Jan. 2001. Available at: <www.mg.co.za>.
2. These economic statistics are all from two government of Canada Web sites: <www.infoexport.gc.ca> and <www.dfait-maeci.gc.ca>.
3. 'Freedom from fear: Canada's foreign policy for human security', available on the DFAIT Web site (note 2).

REFERENCES

Gee, Marcus. 2000. 'A place to make a stand', *Globe and Mail*, 10 May, A15.

Johnson, R.W. 2000. 'The Problem-child continent', *National Post*, 25 Jan., A18.

Knox, Paul. 2000. 'Canada criticizes UN mission to Congo', *Globe and Mail*, 25 Feb., A7.

Sallot, Jeff. 2000. 'Canada offers cargo handlers to UN', *Globe and Mail*, 17 May, A9.

Trickey, Mike. 2000. 'Axworthy targets Canadian firms operating abroad', *National Post*, 20 May, A1.

11

Chicken Defence Lines Needed: Canadian Foreign Policy and Global Environmental Issues

HEATHER A. SMITH

In the summer of 2000, Canadian newspapers commented with concern about the northward migration of West Nile disease. The disease, carried by birds and mosquitoes, seemed on the verge of ignoring the Canada–US border. In response, chicken defence lines were established. If the chickens got sick, we would know that West Nile disease had infiltrated Canada. Sick and dead chickens would equal certainty. Action would be required.

The kind of certainty offered by the chicken defence lines is rare when one ponders global environmental issues. In contrast to the intangible nature of most global environmental issues, a sick chicken is a stark symbol of our own vulnerability to the changing environment. It is this sense of vulnerability that often impels us to act quickly. The norm, however, is to approach environmental issues in a cautious and incremental manner.

In contrast to the effusive rhetoric frequently associated with Canadian foreign policy, Canada's behaviour on global environmental issues, such as biosafety and climate change, seems to be guided by some sort of realist script. Global environmental alliances are built. States square off in international meetings. The environment is lost in the power plays. In the meantime, we construct chicken defence lines to serve a purpose similar to the Distant Early Warning (DEW) system—they provide us with early warning. But, one must wonder, if the DEW line indicated that Russian missiles were en route to Canada and the US, would this really be early warning or would we be beyond the point of no return? Do the chicken defence lines function in a similar manner? Do we act assertively only when threatened? Will the behaviour of Canada on international environmental issues result, in the long term, in more chicken defence lines?

To offer an understanding of Canadian activities in the global environmental arena, this chapter begins with a brief discussion 'global environmental issues'. Various issues that fall under the umbrella of global environmental issues are then identified. The section ends by linking global environmental issues to Canadian foreign policy and identifying the various actors that affect policy development. The third section of the chapter focuses on biosafety and climate change. These cases offer us a means by which to draw some conclusions about Canada's behaviour in international environmental negotiations.

A series of observations are offered in the fourth section of the chapter. The first centres on the theme of leadership. In the late 1980s and early 1990s Canada was heralded as a leader on global environmental issues. This does not appear to be the case any longer. This shift from leader to laggard in a coalition of laggards is explained by a variety of factors that are addressed in the concluding section. Of particular importance, however, is the fact that real costs are associated with implementation that are not associated with agenda-setting and norm-building, foreign policy activities at which Canada excels. Second, Canada is functioning in a dependent manner. Third, governments, including the Canadian government, use science to serve their own ends. Fourth, the cost of environmental measures is defined in terms of impacts on competitiveness and the Canadian economy generally, yet there are costs involved in our delaying behaviour and the kinds of costs we deem important render the environment marginal. Ultimately, national interest is defined very narrowly. Finally, some areas of possible reform are considered. While the government has been taking action on international environmental issues, it is necessary that it find the political will to take more assertive steps. This may be difficult given the political, economic, and fiscal constraints the government faces, but there are alternatives to the present route taken by the government of Canada. Ultimately, long-term and concerted efforts are required to alter the social, economic, and political inequalities that cause environmental degradation. At the present pace, prospects for long-term change are limited. By the time we decide to act decisively, the chickens will be dead.

DEFINING TERMS AND SETTING CONTEXTS

If asked to define 'global environmental issues' some might deem the phrase a rather innocent one that signifies problems such as climate change or ozone depletion. However, we need to challenge any assumptions about the unproblematic nature of this phrase. Global issues are not simply global, they are also local. The problems are often caused by the everyday activities of everyday people, and many of the problems we are facing currently stem from the everyday activities of individuals living in industrialized countries. The local and the global fuse. The notion of 'global' does suggest something bigger than us, but we must also remember that it is all of us (see Elliott, 1998: 3).

We must also use care when we attempt to categorize the issues under examination as 'environmental'. Indeed, a central element in the following discussion is the natural environment, but it is difficult, if not impossible, to separate the environmental from the social, political, and economic. Environmental issues cannot be considered in isolation from these other sets of power relations because the causes of environmental degradation are situated in those relationships (ibid., 245). Furthermore, the means by which to counter environmental degradation are also found, or potentially found, in the realm of the political, social, and economic.

In addition, we need to ponder the labelling of environmental degradation as an 'issue'. We need to ask how the issue is framed— is it about the environment, trade, agriculture, competitiveness, or, perhaps, security? Each of these starting points comes with implications in terms of including and excluding certain views, legitimizing arguments, or rendering marginal other views. It is also necessary to ask for whom is the environment an issue. There are numerous answers to this question, each dependent on the perspective one takes or the actors one examines. This question is important because it reminds us that what we construct as an issue from a Canadian perspective may be far less an issue from a Chinese perspective or from the perspective of a woman who must somehow find safe drinking water for her children. We must try to avoid the assumption that our concerns are universal.

The theoretical complexity of the term 'global environmental relations' is a reflection of the complexity of the issues the term encompasses. We are faced with a host of issues, each vying for our attention. If the statistics below, courtesy of the World Resources Institute (2000), are any indication, the scope of the problems we are facing is staggering. For example, if we continue to function in a business-as-usual fashion it is predicted that by 2010 global energy consumption, and with it annual carbon dioxide emissions, will rise by approximately 50 per cent from 1993 levels. The use of chlorofluorocarbons (CFCs) that cause ozone depletion has dropped by 70 per cent since 1987 and undoubtedly this is a success story in which Canada played a significant part. There are now, however, threats arising from the growth of a CFC black market. The total global forested area continues to decline, thus affecting biological diversity, climate, and watershed management. Water resources are predicted to be a very important issue in this century, especially as population grows, and today 1.4 billion people are without safe drinking water. Freshwater ecosystems are severely threatened by industrial and agricultural activities, overfishing, and water diversion. Bioinvasions, that is, the arrival of non-native species that disrupt ecosystems, now rank second to habitat loss as the major threat to biodiversity. Predicted impacts of climate change include rising sea levels, the northward migration of infectious diseases such as the West Nile virus, increased desertification, crop shifts, and glacial melting. The implications for Canada's North in this regard are worrisome, as the Arctic is deemed extremely vulnerable to climate change. Potential impacts include change to sea ice and snow cover, alteration of permafrost patterns, and adverse effects on wildlife as a result of decreases in the sea ice (Natural Resources Canada, 2000b: 1). Meanwhile, the population continues to grow and that growth portends further environmental stress.

Not only are the problems complex, but so is their management. Minister of Foreign Affairs Lloyd Axworthy's use of the term 'human security', which includes an ecological component, may lead one to think that the issues above are the stuff of foreign policy. For two reasons, this observation is only partially accurate. First, the environment never was a central part of human security as conceived by Axworthy. Recent government publications on human security that emphasize peacebuilding, democratization, and global governance support this point. Second, global environmental issues defy the foreign-domestic boundary and do not fit neatly into either provincial or federal jurisdiction. These issues cross the mandates of federal departments and all are subject to industry and environmental group pressures. They are not foreign policy as traditionally understood.

In the area of climate change, for example, the Department of Foreign Affairs and International Trade (DFAIT), in tandem with Environment Canada, tends to lead the international negotiating teams with the Minister of Environment delivering the Canadian country statements. Natural Resources Canada is the primary department responsible for domestic implementation, which is shared by the provinces because of their jurisdiction over natural resources. Biosafety includes the participation of the following federal departments: Health Canada, Environment Canada, Agriculture and Agri-Food Canada, Industry Canada, Foreign Affairs and International Trade, the Canadian Food Inspection Agency, Natural Resources Canada, and the Department of Fisheries and Oceans. The provinces are also crucial players in areas such as biodiversity, fisheries, and forestry. In the areas of both climate change and biodiversity, the federal government and the provinces have worked together to implement international conventions, as is required when an international convention affects an area of provincial jurisdiction. The intergovernmental implementation has sometimes met with limited success. On climate change, for example, the federal-provincial relations have often been divisive. Beyond the provinces one must consider the roles of industry and sectoral interest groups. Biosafety regulations can potentially have a huge impact on agricultural production and the export of Canadian products. Thus one finds actors such as the Western Canadian Wheat Growers Association actively involved in lobbying the federal government on biosafety. Climate change is of keen interest to the oil and gas industry, which is concerned about potential detrimental impacts arising from new regulations aimed at reducing greenhouse gas emissions. The insurance industry, for fear of costs related to damage arising from shifting weather patterns caused by climate change, has lobbied the government to be more proactive. Then there are the environmental groups, such as Greenpeace, Friends of the Earth, and the World Wildlife Fund, which have been active lobbyists on a variety of environmental fronts.

Indeed, DFAIT always presents the 'Canadian' face internationally, but there is disinclination, in part because of the functional divisions, to claim that the international dimensions of environmental issues are foreign policy. The label does not fit with the reality of Canadian bureaucratic and constitutional practice. Responsibility and authority are far more diffused than may be initially expected. The disinclination may also be explained by the fact that international environmental issues are simply not a priority for the government or the Minister of Foreign Affairs. During Axworthy's tenure the priorities were norm-building and issues such as landmines. For an ambitious minister environmental issues were no-win situations. The complexity and intractability of environmental issues, the lack of federal government support for the environment generally, and the dominance of the US on these matters all left little room for DFAIT to manoeuvre.

SNAPSHOTS OF CANADA AND GLOBAL ENVIRONMENTAL ISSUES

In the late 1980s and early 1990s Canada saw itself, and was seen by others, as a leader in global environmental relations. In the areas of climate change and stratospheric ozone, for example, Canada had considerable technical, scientific, and diplomatic expertise. The decision to hold the ozone negotiations in Montreal in 1987 was recognition of Canada's contribution. A conference held in Toronto in 1988 on the changing atmosphere has been recognized as integral to the agenda-setting phase of the climate change issue. Canadian Maurice Strong chaired the 1972 United Nations Conference on the Human Environment (UNCHE) and the 1992 United Nations Conference on Environment and Development (UNCED). He was also the first director of the United Nations Environment Program, a position filled by another Canadian, Elizabeth Dowdeswell, after UNCED in recognition of, among other things, the vital role she played in the negotiation of the Framework Convention on Climate Change (FCCC). At least at a rhetorical level, the Conservative government of Brian Mulroney offered a vision of a new environmental ethic—a vision that was never really put to the test after their defeat in 1993. Nonetheless, this rhetorical ethic and sense of leadership underpinned Canadian activities at UNCED. As American President George Bush was jeered by crowds in Rio, Prime Minister Mulroney called on states to 'force the pace and stretch the limits of international cooperation' (Vincent and Rusk, 1992: A8) and championed the Convention on Biodiversity (CBD) in the face of fierce US opposition.

This time of leadership is an important starting point for the present analysis because it offers a sense of where we came from. UNCED saw the negotiation of both the CBD that houses the Biosafety Protocol and the Framework Convention on Climate Change, the precursor to the negotiations at The Hague in late 2000. In addition, the leadership of the past gives us the means by which to measure present behaviour.

In contrast to past leadership, the cases below reveal the activities of a state strongly committed to the aims of coalitions of which it is part. In both cases Canada was part of negotiating coalitions. In the case of climate change, Canada was and is an integral member of a US-dominated coalition originally called JUSCANZ (Japan, United States, Canada, Australia, and New Zealand) and now called the Umbrella Group. On biosafety Canada acted as the leader of the Miami Group of agricultural exporting states. This group again included the US, in spite of the fact that the US is an observer rather than a signatory to the Biodiversity Convention. Practically, this coalition commitment is important for understanding the cases discussed below because coalition positions broadly reflect the Canadian positions.

Another element that will become apparent is that the Canadian positions are largely driven by concerns about economic competitiveness and Canadian economic growth. Economic competitiveness translates into attempts to avoid adverse impacts on Canadian agricultural and biotechnical industry. Agrotechnology and biotechnology more generally are highly concentrated and lucrative industries. In Canada alone, the biotech industry had revenues of $1.1 billion in 1997 'with the agri-food sector responsible for 44 per cent of that' (Environment Canada, 2000a). In the case of climate change, the government seems to be acting to ensure that the oil and gas industries are not adversely affected. 'In 1998, Canadian oil and gas production contributed some $26 billion to Canada's gross domestic product (GDP). Oil and gas exports added more than $13.2 billion to Canada's balance of payments' (Natural Resources Canada, 2000a: 2). These trends become more apparent as we examine the cases. We begin with the negotiation of the Biosafety Protocol.

The Convention on Biological Diversity was adopted on 22 May 1992 and entered into force on 29 December 1993. The United States has not ratified the Convention. Canada was one of the first countries to sign the CBD and has since ratified it. The Biosafety Protocol finds its international legal home in the Convention on Biodiversity, which provides for the negotiation of a protocol to address living modified organisms (LMOs) that may have an adverse affect on biodiversity. At the heart of this issue are various LMOs, many of which are used in agriculture. On the one hand, the Canadian-led Miami Group composed of the dominant agriculture exporters—Argentina, Australia, Canada, Chile, the United States, and Uruguay—believes that the LMOs they have developed are safe. They want an open and unfettered market for their products and are leery of labelling requirements. For Canada, labelling requirements pose a problem because many Canadian crops are mixed LMO and non-LMO. For this group it is a matter of trade. On the other hand, the European Union (EU) has concerns over food safety and regards the use of LMOs as a health issue. The EU is in part driven by a strong consumer concern. It has adopted regulations regarding LMOs that are viewed by some as protectionist. These regulations have resulted in almost a complete moratorium on the import of LMOs, an action that has essentially closed European markets to Canadian canola, which is often genetically modified. Add to this the concerns of developing states for food safety, biological diversity, and the potential of becoming testing grounds for unapproved LMOs and one has a hint of the complexity behind this issue.

Beginning in 1996, states met to draft a framework to address biosafety. At the final session, held in Cartagena de India, Colombia, delegates were unable to come to consensus. After three sets of informal consultations, a protocol was finally negotiated in Montreal in January 2000.

Over the course of the negotiations, five negotiating blocks formed. Those blocks were the Central and Eastern European countries, the Miami Group, the European Union, the Like-Minded Group (most developing states), and the Compromise Group (Japan, Mexico, Norway, South Korea, and Switzerland).

The points of division at the Cartagena meeting were numerous, but underlying almost all of them were the commercial interests of LMO-producing countries—the Miami Group—and the environmental and health concerns of LMO-importing states, especially the European Union (see Falkner, 1999). During the course of the meeting the EU demanded labelling of LMO products. The Like-Minded Group of developing states pressed for a clause to cover liability stemming from LMOs. The Miami Group rejected these demands, the first because it would interfere with trade and the second because of the inherent difficulty in assigning liability. Another serious point of difference was the relationship of the proposed protocol to the World Trade Organization (WTO). The Like-Minded Group wanted to ensure that the Biosafety Protocol was not subordinated to the WTO. The EU wanted the right to use the precautionary principle,[1] which would allow regulatory action in spite of a lack of full scientific certainty, to evaluate risks associated with LMOs. The Miami Group, in particular the United States, felt that 'this precaution would be used as a justification for arbitrary and what it saw as non-science based import restrictive actions' (Gupta, 2000: 3). Another point of contention was the process by which LMOs would be transported and how the threat to importers would be assessed and regulated.

Two issues that stymied the Cartagena negotiations were what items would be covered by a proposed strict regulatory process and, in particular, whether or not grains would be included. The Miami Group viewed agricultural products (in particular LMOs destined for food, feed, or processing) as dead and therefore as posing no threat to the importers. It was further argued that the products were designed for consumption and therefore would not affect biodiversity. They were, simply put, safe. The EU countered that there were threats arising from the co-mingling of LMO and non-LMO products. The Like-Minded Group argued that testing in the US, for example, did not ensure safety elsewhere. Moreover, one delegate pointed out, 'our farmers don't know or care about the intended use of an exporter. If they see a grain, they want to grow it' (Dawkins, 1999: 3). In response to the issues surrounding grains, one American delegate is said to have exclaimed 'the future of a multi-billion-dollar industry is at stake!' (ibid.). A consensus could not be reached.

Some degree of momentum was maintained through the vehicle of informal consultations, and ultimately the Protocol was negotiated in Montreal in January 2000. In the end, the Protocol addressed many of the contentious issues noted above—some were resolved and some were wrapped in such suitably vague language that the provisions are open to multiple provisions. On the matter of LMOs for food, feed, and processing, the Miami Group continued to insist that they be exempt while members of the Like-Minded Group continued to disagree. Ultimately, only a limited number of LMOs were subject to rigorous transport and import regulations through what is called the Advanced Informed Agreement. In regard to labelling, the compromise came in the use of the language 'may contain LMOs'. Parties have agreed to a process, two years after the Protocol comes into entry, that will determine if further information will be required on documentation. On the precautionary principle, 'the final agreement in Montreal retains the reference in the objectives, but also explicitly spells out the right of parties to take import restrictive actions in operative articles of the text dealing with decisionmaking on commodities and LMOs for planting' (Gupta, 2000: 6). Finally, on the relationship of the WTO to the Protocol, three statements in the preamble appear quite contradictory but are viewed as an attempt to balance the two regimes (ibid., 5) and thus avoid a statement that implied hierarchy.

Canada's position on the Protocol can be gleaned from the positions of the Miami Group that Canada led. Canada is keenly interested in promoting and protecting the interests of its agro-tech industry. Not surprisingly, statements by the Minister of Environment, David Anderson, upon the completion of Biosafety Protocol diplomatically gloss over the rivalries. For example, he stated that 'Canada recognizes the right of every country to restrict the imports of LMOs that would harm its biodiversity. That is why Canada supports the precautionary approach which allows nations to take action even in the absence of full scientific certainty' (Environment Canada, 2000c: 1). He further stressed that the agreement would not have been possible without flexibility by all parties.

For a more direct explanation of Canada's involvement in the negotiations and its commitment to the Protocol we can consider the government's Biosafety Consultation document (Environment Canada, 2000e), which was published after the Montreal meeting to provide information to Canadians on Canada's position on the issue of biosafety. First, Canada has neither signed nor ratified the Protocol. It will not do so until appropriate domestic consultations have taken place. This move is open to many interpretations. It may be a delaying tactic or a recognition of a need for genuine public consultation. It may also be a route by which to give the government leverage in the event of non-signature. Second, conflict over biosafety and regulations limiting export of LMOs already exists. It is not merely a potential issue projected into the future and therefore subject to a wait-and-see approach. It is expected that Canadian exporters will have to adjust to some new regulatory requirements whether or not Canada signs and ratifies the Protocol. Thus, it is in Canada's interest to be at the table crafting rules that cause the least pain for Canadian exporters, as was the case with labelling and provisions adopted for grains. On the matter of the precautionary principle, the Canadian interpretation is quite loose. It is based on the assumption that our science deems LMOs safe. The Protocol allows importers to invoke the precautionary principle, but to do so they will have to make the case that the science is uncertain. For developing states, with limited scientific capacity, this may prove difficult. The consultation document on this principle indicates that, while precautionary measures must be based on some scientific information, at the same time 'a lack of scientific certainty shall not prevent the taking of import decisions as appropriate' (Environment Canada, 2000e: 7). Finally, regarding the relationship of the Protocol to the WTO, Canada apparently accepts that there is no hierarchy of international agreements. Many remedies are available, however, including dispute settlement under the WTO on trade-related matters. The question then hinges on what is interpreted as a trade matter and what is seen as one of biodiversity. Further reflection on this set of negotiations follows a description of Canada's involvement in the international negotiations on climate change.

The Framework Convention on Climate Change included a voluntary emissions reduction target to stabilize greenhouse gas emissions at 1990 levels by the year 2000. The FCCC came into force in March 1994. In early 1995 the first Conference of Parties (COP) was held in Berlin, the main objective of which was to review progress on the commitments made under the FCCC. It became obvious at this meeting that, largely because of perceived economic costs, emissions reductions had proven difficult to achieve for many states, including the US, most of the members of the EU, and Canada. Progress was seen to be inadequate and therefore parties to the Convention adopted the Berlin Mandate, which called on states to aim for a legally binding protocol by the third COP in Kyoto, Japan, in 1997. The Berlin Mandate did not demand commitments on the part of developing states.

By the time of COP III in Kyoto, Canada was an integral part of the JUSCANZ coalition and was in no position to meet the FCCC stabilization commitment. Just prior to the Kyoto meetings the Minister of the Environment, Christine Stewart, announced that Canada's position at Kyoto would be for industrialized states to seek a 3 per cent reduction of greenhouse gas (GHG) emissions to 1990 levels by 2010 with further reductions of 5 per cent by 2015. This position broke from a national consensus crafted with the provinces (see Macdonald and Smith, 2000).

At Kyoto the EU, frequently in tandem with developing states, faced off against Canada, the United States, and their partners in JUSCANZ (now including Switzerland, Norway, and Iceland at times). The division was initially over emissions reduction commitments. The EU aimed for more ambitious targets than the JUSCANZ coalition, and the EU was willing to hold out until the JUSCANZ targets appeared to improve (International Institute for Sustainable Development, 1997: 41). To break this deadlock the chairman of the Kyoto conference proposed differentiated targets for industrialized states. These targets were acceptable to Canada and the United States only if they had 'maximum flexibility' in implementation. An attempt was made to bind developing states (non-Annex I parties) to some sort of voluntary commitment, even a promise of binding emissions reductions in the future. New Zealand was supported in this intervention by the US, Canada, Australia, Japan, Poland, and Slovenia. This position was rejected by the EU and vehemently rejected by the G-77, China, and a host of other developing states.

Ultimately, differentiated reductions for Annex I states were adopted. For Canada this meant accepting a reductions target of 6 per cent of greenhouse gas emissions from 1990 levels by 2008–12. Market-based mechanisms (also known as flexibility mechanisms), such as joint implementation and emissions trading, in addition to a new mechanism called the Clean Development Mechanism (CDM), were included in the Kyoto Protocol. These potentially provided for the flexibility in emissions reductions required by the American-led coalition. The CDM, for example, was intended 'for the purposes of assisting developing countries in achieving sustainable development and helping Annex I parties meet their emissions limitation and reduction obligations' (Ott, 1998: 42). Provisions were also made for the inclusion of carbon sinks, associated with forestry, into the calculations of emissions reductions. The inclusion of sinks was a highly desired element of the Protocol for Canadian negotiators because Canada has huge tracts of forest that can act as carbon sinks. No conditions imposed voluntary commitments for developing states.

The fourth Conference of Parties was held in Buenos Aires in November 1998 and the fifth in Bonn in November 1999. From these meetings several themes emerge. First, the United States eagerly seeks voluntary commitments from developing states, in part because it needs these commitments if the Protocol is ever to get through the US Senate. Second, there is an emphasis on the flexibility mechanisms since Canada, the United States, and their allies have a strong interest in moving quickly on the definition of the mechanisms that they view as crucial to their reduction plans. At Buenos Aires, a significant debate developed over the issue of whether or not the proportion of emissions reductions a country can count from the flexibility mechanisms should be capped. The EU and developing states insisted on a cap while the Umbrella Group, Canada included, 'steadfastly opposed it, stressing the need for maximum flexibility in meeting targets' (Kellett and Carpenter, 1998: 2). At Bonn, carbon sinks were also discussed, although delegations await further research on this area. Finally, at Bonn the COP decided to convene its next meeting in November 2000 and to accelerate the work program during the intersessional period.

Following numerous formal and informal meetings, the sixth Conference of Parties was held at The Hague in November 2000. While issues such as the structure of the compliance regime and finance were left unresolved, the meeting ultimately crumbled under the issues of sinks and supplementarity.

On the matter of the flexibility mechanisms, such as joint implementation and the Clean Development Mechanism, the EU was concerned that these could be used as a means by which to avoid significant domestic actions. The EU wanted limits on the use of the mechanisms. The Umbrella Group remained resistant to such caps. The Europeans seemed prepared to move some on this matter when they showed a willingness to accept the notion of qualitative limits on the mechanisms. Canada was prepared to accept this compromise 'as long as it felt that it had room to meet much of its target through credits from carbon sinks' (International Institute for Sustainable Development, 2000: 2). The US refused to accept that European proposal. The American-led Umbrella Group also wanted to include sinks as activities acceptable under the mechanisms and pushed for simple procedures to define those mechanisms. Such efforts were viewed as loopholes. The inclusion of sinks in the CDM, in particular, was a sticking point between the Umbrella Group and the EU. Similarly, the Umbrella Group wanted to include additional activities, such as land use, under the sinks provisions of the Protocol. The EU was opposed. 'Countries such as the US and Canada believe it is in their best interest to include as many carbon sinks as possible to enable them to meet their Kyoto targets without drastic emissions cuts. They therefore sought a broad interpretation of the sinks provision as a precondition for ratifying the Protocol' (ibid.). There was some movement on sinks over the course of the meeting, but ultimately disagreement prevailed. Canada initially wanted the right to gain credit for selling nuclear power to developing states through the CDM, but towards the end of the meeting it indicated a willingness to remove this demand. The talks, however, ultimately collapsed with the aim of resumption in May 2001.

In an effort to restore some sense of hope, the EU and Umbrella Group met in Ottawa on 7 December 2000 to continue discussions regarding international climate change negotiations. Environment Minister Anderson noted Canada's facilitation role in these meetings and also commented on Canada's activities at The Hague: 'Canada was instrumental in presenting constructive solutions and was ready to accommodate the concerns expressed by other parties. Canada championed a comprehensive approach that would ensure the environmental integrity of the Kyoto Protocol' (Environment Canada, 2000d: 1).

That Canada played a constructive role in The Hague negotiations is open to question given its position in the Umbrella Group that was seen as consistently blocking consensus. However, these interpretive questions can be left for the next section. Here, we need to explain Canada's positions in the climate change negotiations. While one could craft any number of explanations, the driving force behind Canada's behaviour is economics. Canada is fundamentally concerned about the impact of domestic emissions reductions on the Canadian economy, in particular, on the oil and gas sector. Canada has consistently taken positions that it deems cost-effective and efficient and that will not undermine the integrity of the Canadian economy.

Concern for the economic implications of emission reductions stems from projected impacts on Canada's GDP. The Canada Country Study, for example, offers a fair assessment of the debate surrounding costs. The study recognizes that many incalculable costs are related to unanticipated impacts, adaptation, and catastrophic events. The 'best guess cost estimate' suggested that the 'impact of climate change on Canada could be $8-$16 billion annually, based on a 1995 Canadian GDP of $776 billion' (Environment Canada, The Canada Country Study: 7). This assessment, however, can be contested, especially when one poses questions about the type of valuation involved in the assessment.

Canada's behaviour in international negotiations is directly related to concern about economic competitiveness. The alliance with the United States reflects the dependence of the Canadian economy on the United States. We do not want to be out of step with our largest trading partner. The promotion of the flexibility mechanisms is an effort to reduce global emissions levels, but these mechanisms may also be seen as a way of relieving the pressure for domestic emissions reductions. Canada is committed to some reductions at home, but the mechanisms are necessary if Canada is to achieve, through various systems of assigning credit, its emissions reductions target, which is, in effect, a 26 per cent reduction from the business-as-usual scenario.

ANALYSIS AND CONCLUSIONS

The two cases described in this chapter lend themselves to some generalizations about the roles played by Canada in international environmental negotiations. It was noted earlier that in the late 1980s and early 1990s Canada played a leadership role in agenda-setting and in the promotion of a new global ethic. Without a doubt, leadership is a subjective term, open to many interpretations, and some may suggest that by protecting and promoting the interests of Canada, the government has shown leadership. It may also be suggested that by speaking for the Miami Group and being steadfast in positions that protect the interests of the coalitions, Canada showed leadership. The view here, however, is that we are no longer playing a leadership role. Leadership, in this context, involves building norms and implementing policies that protect the environment, or at the very least recognize how inextricably the environment is intertwined with the economy. Economic interests, in the cases examined here, have been placed ahead of environmental considerations, a course that can hardly be called leadership. But how do we understand this change over time, this shift from rhetorical leadership to laggard among a coalition of laggards?

It is difficult in limited space to explain the shift fully, but some key points can be raised. First, in the case of climate change the provinces became very active in the issue after the departure of the Mulroney government. This constrained the actions of the Chrétien administration because of the need to co-operate on implementation. Second, in both cases addressed here, the issues were at the point in their life cycle where tangible and costly actions had to be made to support earlier commitments. There is a big difference between championing an issue such as biodiversity and implementing policies that will inevitably have an effect on some sector of the national economy. In other words, norm-building is cheap and implementation is not. Finally, we must recognize that international environmental policies are nested in the broader orientation of the government. As noted in the discussion of DFAIT and the environment, environmental issues simply are not a priority for the Liberal government. Of all the departments, Environment Canada was one of the hardest hit by budget cutbacks.

In spite of the assertion that Canada is not a leader, what role we are playing remains open to interpretation. One might suggest that the behaviour of the present government is consistent with a middle-power approach. Canada is behaving in a pragmatic manner, participating in the management of global affairs, guided by its own interest and some concern for global well-being. Certainly, the statements made by the minister at the time of the Montreal negotiations and the statement from the 7 December 2000 climate meeting in Ottawa suggest that the Canadian government is interested in flexibility and in seeking compromises from all parties. For example, at the 7 December meeting of the Umbrella Group and the EU, Environment Minister Anderson stated that 'Canada is pleased to play a role in facilitating these discussions', and he emphasized that at The Hague meetings 'Canada was instrumental in presenting constructive solutions and was ready to accommodate the concerns of other parties' (Environment Canada, 2000d: 1).

The middle-power explanation, however, blinds us to some of the harsher realities of the cases and could function to legitimize Canada's behaviour. We need to step away from the rhetoric of compromise and flexibility and focus on the very self-interested nature of Canada's behaviour. Expecting that Canada should get significant credits for its geography as a prerequisite of its ratification of the Kyoto Protocol is akin to searching for loopholes to avoid action. On biosafety, Canada is acting because Canadian exporters will be affected regardless, so crafting the best and most efficient tools only makes sense. Both sets of negotiations are ultimately about protecting billion-dollar industries.

In both cases—biosafety and climate change—we would be well served by reconsidering the satellite/dependency literature and combining it with the insights of critical theory. Canada's behaviour is largely consistent with American objectives. This is not to suggest that Canada is a mere lackey of the United States. That argument undermines Canadian agency. Choices are made regularly by the Canadian government and those who govern must be held accountable. This said, we must not underestimate the role of the US. Our geography blessed us with lots of carbon sinks, but also determined we were north of the world's largest economy.

The role of science is another theme that transcends both cases. While scientists may seek the truth they are generally willing to accept that there are 'incalculable feedbacks'. Yet, science is manipulated by governments, and in this Canada is not unique. Science is used to support one position or to refute another. Such is the case with biosafety, where it is assumed that the science informing the Miami Group's position is somehow more credible and certain. That science is Western in its lens and may not be appropriate for developing states. Furthermore, the EU's desire to invoke the precautionary principle, after experiences with mad cow disease for example, is viewed as justification for trade barriers while the Miami Group's science is not viewed as an excuse for trade liberalization. The science of carbon sinks is uncertain and yet in this instance the uncertainty is acceptable because it supports the Canadian position.

The one body of knowledge that does not seem subject to significant reflection by the government is economics. There is a general acceptance of the models that tell us that Canadian competitiveness will be undermined if we must reduce carbon dioxide emissions. Yet, competing views of competitiveness suggest that rather than protecting and subsidizing the oil and gas industry, we need to focus more intensely on alternative energy sources and increased energy efficiency. The economics need to be questioned because many of the calculations of competitiveness and economic well-being do not include any valuation of the inherent beauty of a tree, or the need for biological diversity or clean air. To some, this may seem unrealistic and naïve, but one only has to ask the people of Walkerton, Ontario, about the cost of polluted water. The cost, in that instance, translated into lives.

The reality is that there are no easy solutions. Costs are going to be involved regardless of the actions taken. The government is indeed constrained both by the influence of the US and by such domestic factors as industry and provincial jurisdiction over various aspects of the environment. It must be made clear, however, that the federal government has taken some action. For example, it has committed funds to combat climate change. The 2000 budget included $60 million to establish the Canadian Foundation for Climate and Atmospheric Sciences (Environment Canada, 2000c: 1) and another $500 million was committed to activities related to climate change prior to The Hague meeting. This is to be applauded. Similarly, continued support for public education and awareness through the Climate Change Action Fund must be recognized as a positive contribution to the fight against climate change. Efforts to raise awareness and consult on the matter of biosafety are also noteworthy. But there is a long way to go. Canada is ranked poorly in terms of its position on climate change and has received failing grades from the World Wildlife Fund for its policies on biodiversity.

Practically speaking, one of the most important things the federal government can do is to ensure that Environment Canada is not hobbled by a small budget. We have the expertise to propose creative solutions for these issues and that creativity can be found in Environment Canada, but the department must be allowed to do its job. Increased funding for research is worthwhile, but so is staffing the negotiating teams in numbers that represent a genuine commitment to the issues. Our negotiators, both at Environment Canada and DFAIT, are overworked and undersupported. Monies must be made available not just to send huge delegations of observers to meetings but also to support the research and efforts of the negotiating team. For example, if Canada is truly committed to joint implementation, then there must be increased staffing in the joint implementation office in DFAIT, thus allowing the government greater ability to work with industry and non-governmental organizations involved in the various issues. In addition, to avoid being caught looking confused, Canada must endeavour to develop its own policies based on its own interests, not those of the United States. This is likely easier said than done. Also, the interprovincial dimension must be examined. This, however, is a very difficult issue. Short of constitutional change, co-operation will remain necessary. The federal government must be mindful of the need to take leadership on international environmental issues at home, thus setting an example for the provinces. The government must also do more work in the area of citizen awareness. Both biosafety and climate change are the concerns of select industry and environmental groups. Attempting genuinely to engage the public means that the government can then sense if, for example, there is consumer fear about genetically modified foods. Surely that would affect decision-making at the federal level.

Finally, the government must accept that there are alternative ways of viewing the world. Part of the reason the government complains of constraints is because it holds the idea that there is no alternative. This is incorrect. Work from the Suzuki Foundation, the World Wildlife Fund, and Friends of the Earth shows us that there are alternative visions. We need to factor in the environment. If we do this, maybe we will realize that we need to stop waiting for proof of environmental degradation. There is little doubt that the environment is under stress, and chicken defence lines, constructed in the future, will not halt global warming or protect extinct species. We have the opportunity now to change, but we will have to shoulder some costs. We either pay now or we pay later.

NOTE

1. The precautionary principle encourages states and other actors to take action on an issue in spite of a lack of full scientific certainty. In this instance, the Europeans want to use it as a means by which to limit LMOs that might harm human health. Canada and other Miami Group states interpret it to mean that trade can occur in spite of a lack of full scientific certainty.

REFERENCES

Dawkins, Kirstin. 1999. 'Unsafe in Any Seed: US Obstructionism Defeats Adoption of an International Biotechnology Saftety Agreement', *Multinational Monitor* (Mar.): 1–6 (proquest database).

Depledge, Joanna. 1999. 'Coming of Age at Buenos Aires', *Environment* (Sept.).

Elliott, Lorraine. 1998. *The Global Politics of the Environment*. New York: New York University Press.

Environment Canada. 2000a. 'Biosafety Protocol Negotiations—Montreal Canada', 24–8 Jan. Available at: <http://www.bco.ec.gc/ProjectsBiosafe05-e.cfm>.

———. 2000b. 'Statement by the Hon. David Anderson, Minister of Environment, Government of Canada, at the Conclusion of Negotiations of the Biosafety Protocol, 29 January'. Available at: <wysiwyg://225/http://www.ec.gc.ca/minister/speeches/bio2_s_e.htm>.

———. 2000c. 'Budget 2000: Enhancing Climate and Atmospheric Research', Feb. Available at: <http://www.ec.gc.ca/budget/cc3_htm>.

———. 2000d. 'Statement by Environment Minister David Anderson: Climate Change Officials Make Progress', 7 Dec., 1.

———. 2000e. 'Cartagena Protocol on Biosafety—Consultation Document'. Available at: <http://www.bco.ec.gc.ca/protocol/EN/protocol.cfm>.

———. The Canada Country Study—National Summary for Policy Makers. Available at: <http://www.ec.gc.ca/climate/ccs/policysummary_e.html>.

Falkner, Robert. 1999. 'Frankenstein or Benign?', *The World Today* 55, 7 (July): 24–6.

Gupta, Aarti. 2000. 'Governing Trade in Genetically Modified Organisms: The Cartegena Protocol on Biosafety', *Environment* (May): 1–12 (proquest database).

International Institute for Sustainable Development. 1997. *Earth Negotiations Bulletin* 12, 76 (Dec.). Available at: <http://www.iisd.ca/linkages/download/asc/end127e.txt>.

———. 2000. 'Climate Canada: A Canadian Lens on Global Climate Change', 5 Dec.

Kellett, Victoria, and Chad Carpenter. 1998. 'Inching Forward at Buenos Aires', International Institute for Sustainable Development Web site: <http://www.iisd.ca>.

Macdonald, Douglas, and Heather A. Smith. 1999–2000. 'Promises Made, Promises Broken: Questioning Canada's Commitments to Climate Change', *International Journal* 55, 1 (Winter): 107–24.

Natural Resources Canada. 2000a. 'Notes for Remarks by the Honourable Ralph Goodale, Minister of Natural Resources Canada, to the World Petroleum Congress', 12 June. Available at: <http:///www.NRCan.gc.ca/css/imb/hqlib/200050e.htm>.

———. 2000b. Press Release: Backgrounder, 'Government of Canada Action Plan 2000 on Climate Change: Canada's North', 6 Oct.

Ott, Hermann. 1998. 'The Kyoto Protocol: Unfinished Business', *Environment* 40, 6 (July-Aug.).

Strauss, Mark. 2000. 'When Malthus Meets Mendel', *Foreign Policy* (Summer): 105–12.

Vincent, Isabel, and James Rusk. 1992. 'Bush Summit Speech Greeted by Jeers, Hoots', *Globe and Mail*, 13 June, A8.

World Resources Institute. 2000. Sustainable Development Information Service: Global Trends. Available at: <http://www.wri.org/trends>.

12

National Missile Defense, Homeland Defense, and Outer Space: Policy Dilemmas in the Canada–US Relationship

JAMES FERGUSSON

In the spring of 2000 the issue of Canadian participation in a future operational United States National Missile Defense (NMD) system emerged from the shadows into the limelight. Editorial pieces appeared in major Canadian newspapers that ran from full-scale condemnation to the call for immediate, full-scale Canadian support and participation. The Standing Committee on National Defence and Veterans Affairs also took up the issue. Senior officials from Foreign Affairs and International Trade (DFAIT) and National Defence (DND), the Deputy Commander-in-Chief of the North American Aerospace Defence Command (NORAD), academics, and other representatives from the attentive public testified on the merits and demerits of NMD and Canadian participation. In June, the Standing Committee (2000) issued a report on the topic. Although it failed to recommend a specific policy option for the government, it did tentatively lean towards a positive response if, or when, the US issued an invitation to Canada. Regardless, the report clearly echoed the government's policy: in the absence of a deployment decision and a formal invitation from the US, it was premature for Canada to make a decision.

Almost as quickly as NMD emerged, it retreated back into the shadows, only to reappear with Russian President Vladimir Putin's visit to Ottawa in mid-December and the January 2001 inauguration of President George W. Bush. Not only was Putin firmly opposed to NMD, but the new American President was strongly committed to it, having made the issue one of the cornerstones of his foreign and defence policies in the election campaign.

It is difficult to predict exactly when Canada will be forced to make a decision about NMD. Nonetheless, it is a decision that the government cannot avoid. In order to shed some light on the dilemmas that Canadian policy-makers face, the first part of this chapter examines the current status of the NMD program. In so doing, it goes beyond the public debate on NMD to situate this program within the much broader context of Homeland Defense. The next section focuses on the Canadian policy dilemma and suggests that Canadian policy-makers will try to avoid making tough choices by agreeing 'to participate without participating'. Even so, the final outcome is difficult to foresee, not the least because a Russian–American agreement on the ABM Treaty would enable policy-makers to avoid choosing whether to support or oppose NMD.

In the third part the issue of outer space is examined. Other things being equal, the NMD debate will be replayed on this issue. Currently, the outer space dimension is only seen as a factor directly related to the NMD decision, either in terms of fears that it is a return to President Reagan's Star Wars initiative of the 1980s or in terms of its implications for Canada's military strategy on space. However, more important issues, largely independent of NMD, concerning the military use of outer space are rapidly maturing in the US national security debate. The NMD debate will be replayed in Canada unless a dramatic shift in favour of NMD occurs in Canadian policy.

NMD AND HOMELAND DEFENSE

With the Clinton administration's decision to pass the NMD deployment issue on to the next administration, some hoped that the US debate on NMD was over for the time being. This belief, at best, was wishful thinking. President Bush and his new Defense Secretary, Donald Rumsfeld, are long-standing supporters of missile defence. The key issue that will emerge is whether the current NMD architecture should be adjusted, expanded, and/or significantly changed.[1] The balance of forces in Congress is such that the Republicans still hold a majority, albeit slim, in the House of Representatives, and are tied with the Democrats in the Senate. While a tie in the Senate may produce some interesting outcomes, the 1999 Missile Defense Act passed with overwhelming bipartisan support in both houses. The political issue now is not whether but when the executive and/or Congress will certify technological feasibility and Congress subsequently will appropriate the funding for deployment.[2] The decision to deploy NMD is inevitable, and its timing will most likely hinge on the results of successful testing.

Beyond the testing or technological feasibility criterion, the inevitability of deployment, in whatever form, is also a function of the contemporary security environment as influenced by the Gulf War. Iraqi Scud attacks against Israel and Saudi Arabia during the Gulf War, which were met with Patriot defences, dramatized the necessity of ballistic missile defence in the minds of many US policy-makers. The Gulf War and Saddam Hussein's secret program to build missiles and acquire nuclear weapons helped to raise the proliferation of weapons of mass destruction and long-range missile delivery capabilities to the top of the security agenda. The acquisition of ballistic missiles capable of striking the US by so-called 'states of concern' (formerly 'rogue states') became a prime rationale for NMD deployment. On 20 January 1999, Secretary of Defense William Cohen announced that the rate of proliferation had reached the point at which an NMD deployment decision should be made, assuming that the other three criteria also justified such a decision.[3]

The threat criterion, as it came to be understood, focused directly on when 'states of concern' acquired or would acquire intercontinental ballistic missiles (ICBMs) capable of striking at the US. Drawing especially on the Rumsfeld Commission Report (1998), NMD proponents asserted that North Korea, Iraq, or another 'state of concern' could acquire this capability more quickly than previously estimated in the 1995 National Intelligence Estimate, and that US intelligence assets could fail to provide sufficient warning.[4] Critics, however, argued that the rate of missile proliferation was significantly overstated and was driven by regional concerns. They also doubted that any state would launch a missile attack against US territory, knowing full well that the US would retaliate.

However, whether such states actually acquire an operational ICBM capability, as well as the associated concern about accidental or unintentional launches, may be less important than the domestic politics of this issue in the US. At the most basic level, no President or Congress can accept a situation in which deployed military forces and regional allies can be defended from a missile attack but the continental US cannot. In the absence of an ability to defend the US against missile threats, real or imagined, the willingness, if not the ability, of the US to remain engaged internationally and multilaterally is jeopardized. In fact, US engagement overseas in somewhat peripheral conflict zones has also created a broader US defence strategy of 'Homeland Defense' of which NMD is but one component.

Homeland Defense, which includes NMD, is a core element of US engagement and may be understood as part of a response to the underlying fear of a return to isolationism. Isolationism in this context does not mean the complete US withdrawal from international security politics outside of North America. Rather, the issue, and hence the fear of US allies, including Canada, is that the US would either withdraw from the existing security architecture and/or act unilaterally. Freed from the constraints imposed by the Cold War, the US could readily shed itself of entangling alliance commitments and act unilaterally to defend what are perceived to be its vital national security interests.

For US policy analysts, the linkage between engagement and military superiority has led to concerns that existing and/or potential adversaries will respond asymmetrically. Rather than confronting the US on a conventional battlefield, such states will employ different means to deter US intervention and, if necessary, fight the US. Asymmetric responses, in turn, are seen as the acquisition of means, such as nuclear-armed ballistic missiles, by 'states of concern' that can threaten the US directly.

The strategy of Homeland Defense is premised on the need to respond to or deter a range of potential asymmetric threats to the US. Alongside the fear of these states acquiring a long-range ballistic missile capability and weapons of mass destruction, the strategy is also premised on the threats posed by cruise missiles and terrorism, as well as a range of unconventional means of weapons employment. With regard to cruise missiles, which are seen as a relatively mature and available technology, emphasis has been placed on the possibility that US adversaries will use different platforms, especially sea-based, in close proximity to US territory. Cruise missiles are extremely difficult to detect. In contrast to the Cold War strategy to intercept Soviet bombers in the Far North before they released their cruise missiles, sea-based launch platforms dictate the need for a capacity to intercept the missiles themselves. Problematic for an effective defence is not just predicting likely launch points around North America and thus providing ample warning time. It is also the difficulty of detecting the missiles themselves on radar. Thus, alongside NMD early warning requirements for ballistic missile attacks vital to cue battle management and command, control, and communications (BMC^3) for the missile interceptors, attention is also being directed to early warning and cueing requirements for cruise missile defence (CMD). Whereas ballistic missiles can be detected and tracked but not yet intercepted, cruise missiles can be readily intercepted but are often difficult to detect and track.

Alongside NMD and CMD, Homeland Defense also focuses on a range of threats to population centres and critical infrastructure by either state-sponsored terrorist movements and/or independent terrorist groups that act in response to US actions overseas. Such groups may employ a range of methods, including the unconventional delivery of biological, chemical, radiological, and conventional ordnance and attacks against critical infrastructure and information or computer networks. Responses to these types of asymmetric threats take several forms, including passive civil defence arrangements and preventive measures. They also demand significant co-ordination among a range of government departments and agencies (Hart-Rudman, 2001). Central to preventive measures, and of special importance to Canada and its security relationship with the US, is the issue of border controls.

As well as the importance of intelligence co-operation and co-ordination between the US and Canada, these threats raise issues concerning a common or harmonized set of procedures on the flow of people and goods into North America, and subsequently the open movement of both across the borders between Canada and the US. The most prominent case was the arrest of a suspected terrorist at the British Columbia border carrying explosives reportedly to blow up the Seattle Space Needle. Also relevant is the earlier congressional legislation to strengthen US border controls. Although directed primarily at the southern border, the legislation threatened to affect dramatically the movement of people and goods across the Canada–US border. As a result, Canada was exempted from the legislation. Nonetheless, this may be a harbinger of the future, depending on the degree of co-operation between Canada and the US with regard to asymmetric threats. Finally, it is vital to recognize, as in the border case, that Canadian and American critical infrastructure is deeply intertwined. Striking at a power system or computer network in Canada amounts also to a strike against the US.

Like NMD, these other elements of Homeland Defense are being debated in terms of the reality and probability of such threats. It would be a mistake, however, to dismiss the domestic political implications of these threat perceptions simply because they may appear unrealistic and improbable. Homeland Defense is simultaneously a practical response to potential options adopted by the weak in light of US military superiority and a psychological response designed to reassure the American public.

Canadian policy has long been predicated on US engagement, and US engagement has long been central to the Canadian multilateralist preference. What is at issue for Canada in the NMD debate is much deeper than is currently supposed. The implications of NMD and Homeland Defense for Canadian foreign policy run deeper than simply arms control and disarmament and Canada's long-standing commitment to both. Canada's reputation and the future bilateral defence relationship are also at stake. Unfortunately, these particular dimensions of policy too often are overlooked by the public and the media.

There is some danger in believing that Canada's bilateral defence relationship will be immune to a Canadian decision not to participate in NMD. Canadian co-operation with regard to the non-NMD elements of Homeland Defense is important to the US. However, it is not as important as it was during the Cold War, when Canadian geography provided a significant degree of leverage and influence for Canada on US policy. Canada was able to negotiate an ABM exclusion clause in the 1968 NORAD renewal, which was subsequently dropped in the 1981 renewal as a function of the existence of the ABM Treaty. Similarly, the Mulroney government could sidestep official Canadian participation in Star Wars, the Strategic Defense Initiative (SDI). However, Canada's geographic importance has largely diminished with the end of the Cold War. Certainly, Canadian support and participation in co-operation with the US on Homeland Defense would be useful to the United States, but it is not essential, as most of the elements of NMD could be deployed without having to use Canadian geographical assets at all.

Canadian policy-makers may believe that saying no to NMD will not endanger Canada's security and defence relationship with the United States, because of our close ties on other dimensions such as trade and investment. However, how Canada responds to NMD will likely be interpreted as an indicator of overall Canadian co-operation on other components of Homeland Defense. If Canada is unco-operative, US policy-makers may come to question the utility of conceptualizing US security in continental rather than national terms. More dangerous may be the emergence of a belief that Canada is a security liability. Even worse, the US may impose elements on Canada in areas deemed critical. Nevertheless, as momentum on Homeland Defense builds in the US under the new administration, it is increasingly likely that the NMD issue will become a litmus test of the overall Canada–US security relationship.

THE NMD POLICY DILEMMA

Timing, of course, is critical for Canadian policy-makers. There has, as yet, been no US decision to deploy and no US invitation to participate, and thus there is nothing to decide. Moreover, a US decision to deploy and appropriate the necessary funds, already authorized in the 1999 and 2000 defence budgets, does not necessarily mean that the US will extend an immediate invitation to Canada. It will take roughly five years from when the decision to deploy is made before a system becomes operational. Although Canadian policy-makers do not have to respond immediately when a deployment decision is made, they will not have the luxury of being able to wait the full five years.

The emphasis on the deployment decision/invitation has obscured the implications for Canada of ongoing decisions with regard to NMD architecture and operational strategy. Planning, modelling, and simulation have been under way for a significant period of time. As a result, decisions about BMC^3 strategies, procedures, and employment are already well advanced.[5] As these develop further, software will be built on a certain set of assumptions that will be made without Canadian involvement and, more importantly, without

Canadian input. Thus, the longer Canadian decision-makers delay, the more likely the system will be constructed to the neglect of specifically Canadian interests and requirements in continental defence. In short, the longer Canada delays a formal involvement decision, the less Canada can influence key aspects of the NMD system.

More importantly, the idea that the US will extend a formal invitation, either privately or publicly, may be somewhat misleading. The key will be the open or hidden signals Canada sends to the US and how they are received. Given the historical nature of the relationship, an actual US invitation is likely to occur only if Canada signals that it is favourably inclined to participate in NMD. Even if we did, there remains the possibility that the US would still not reciprocate.

The current policy mantra and the inability of Canada to decide underscore an ongoing policy dilemma facing the Canadian government. This dilemma is neither new nor is it based on the opposition to NMD expressed by Lloyd Axworthy during his tenure as Foreign Minister. Rather, it reflects a much deeper division, if not contradiction, in Canadian policy that successive governments have sought to manage for decades. It reflects the tension between the two pillars of Canadian security policy: arms control/disarmament and Canada–US defence co-operation.

This division also manifests itself between DFAIT and DND about the most appropriate approach to Canadian security—a division that has only surfaced clearly once in the past, during the interdepartmental nuclear weapons debate in the 1960s Diefenbaker government. The Department of External Affairs (DEA) led by its minister, Howard Green, fundamentally opposed Canada's acquisition of nuclear weapons required for new delivery systems—the Bomarc-B surface-to-air missile, the Genie air-to-air missile, and the Honest John artillery rocket. The acquisition of these systems was considered to conflict with Canada's policy on nuclear disarmament. DND, led by Douglas Harkness, believed that Canada's standing as a faithful ally in continental defence required their acquisition, albeit under US control (in a *dual key* arrangement), not least of all because the Bomarc-B missile was designed to carry a nuclear warhead. Even though the Pearson government would decide the issue in favour of defence, the legacy of this debate would continue to be reflected in the debates on missile defence up to and including today.

In the ABM and SDI missile defence debates of the 1960s and 1980s, respectively, DEA and DND squared off on the same grounds. DEA emphasized the threat posed to arms control and disarmament prospects (the Non-Proliferation Treaty in 1967 and strategic arms reductions in general in 1985), whereas DND officials concentrated on the importance of the bilateral defence relationship in terms of Canadian national interests. In the ABM case, the issue was resolved through the negotiation of the ABM exclusion clause as part of the process leading to the renewal of NORAD in 1968. In the case of SDI, it was resolved by taking the issue out of the hands of the departments, which could not agree on a joint memorandum to cabinet, and placing it in the hands of a third party. Out of four options identified, the government chose the minimalist one of permitting industry involvement without official government involvement.

Of course, other political factors also played a role in these debates. In the case of the ABM, the Liberal government was acutely aware of US Secretary of Defense Robert McNamara's opposition to the ABM. It also had to deal with the wave of Canadian nationalism directed against the US, not least of all a result of the war in Vietnam. In the case of SDI, the Conservative government was also influenced by the evolution of the US policy position on allied participation in SDI research, following Secretary of Defense Casper Weinberger's invitation to the allies to participate.[6] Months before the final policy announcement on 7 September 1985, American officials accepted the minimalist response. In fact, Prime Minister Brian Mulroney had already communicated Canada's basic position on SDI at a meeting with Vice-President George Bush (the elder) and Secretary of State George Schultz on the occasion of the funeral of the Soviet President Chernenko in Moscow in March 1985.

Above all else, the political-strategic context of the Cold War enabled Canada to manage its policy dilemma. Specifically, Canada stayed out of both the ABM and SDI without significantly damaging the bilateral defence relations with the US and without compromising its stance on arms control and disarmament. One key was the strategic importance of Canadian territory for North American defence from the bomber threat of the late sixties and the cruise missile threat of the eighties. Another was a shift in the arms control context. In the case of the ABM, this was signalled by the adoption under President Richard Nixon of a so-called 'point defence' for one of its land-based ACBM fields (Grand Forks, North Dakota) and the subsequent negotiation of the ABM Treaty. In the case of SDI, it was possible because of Reagan's acceptance of British Prime Minister Margaret Thatcher's position on deployment—a position that required negotiations with the Soviet Union—and the reality of SDI as a research program, notwithstanding its image in the popular press.

These factors are absent in the current case of NMD. The Cold War is over and Canadian territory is no longer strategically critical, even though Canadian territory would be of value for NMD and CMD, as would Canadian co-operation in other elements of Homeland Defense. Hence, the ABM/SDI strategic context, which enabled Canada to sidestep direct involvement without significantly damaging the defence relationship, is absent.

In terms of the other pillar, NMD is a violation of the letter of the ABM Treaty, and this has been central to Russian opposition as well as to some allied concerns. The new Bush administration will likely withdraw from the treaty, as legally permitted by Article XV, unless it is amended to permit NMD deployment. In this context, DFAIT has consistently portrayed the ABM Treaty as *the* cornerstone of strategic stability and as essential for nuclear disarmament and the future of the arms control and non-proliferation regime. In effect, the Canadian government now faces a situation that most governments seek to avoid: having to make a clear choice between arms control and defence with a broad range of political implications one way or the other. It is in this sense that the NMD issue is arguably the most important strategic issue facing Canadian policy-makers today.

Of course, the need to choose may simply disappear. Given the reality that NMD will go ahead under President Bush, the Russian government may realize that an amended ABM Treaty is preferable to no treaty at all, not least of all to ensure that some constraints remain on future US missile defence plans. Even China may eventually seek an alternative policy path rather than outright opposition (Eckholm, 2001). As a result, NMD may go ahead with the ABM Treaty preserved in some form and with relatively good relations between the US and Russia and China. Canadian policy-makers will be able to signal a positive response, and the end result may be some form of Canadian participation. This outcome, in fact, has been clearly enunciated as the preferred alternative by the new Foreign Minister, John Manley.

In the absence of such an outcome, the only other option available outside of making a choice between the two pillars is an attempt to replicate the past, that is, for Canada *to participate without participating*. This policy option reflects the role of Canada with regard to US strategic retaliatory forces. In the past, Canadian decision-makers had no role in a decision to release US strategic forces. However, the vital early warning or integrated tactical warning/attack assessment function was assigned to NORAD, and Canadian personnel were fully integrated. In the case of a nuclear attack against North America, it was possible that an attack assessment rendered by a Canadian would have set in motion a US-only decision to release its retaliatory forces. Even in the case of the ABM, NORAD would have provided the same assessment to US Continental Air Defence Command for Safeguard during its brief operational life.[7]

However, the likelihood in the NMD case for Canada *to participate without participating* is extremely low. It is highly unlikely that the United States would find this acceptable, not least of all if one of the US motives for Canadian participation is to gain a measure of international legitimacy. It will also be extremely difficult to compartmentalize Canadians within the NORAD Cheyenne Mountain Operational Centre given the ongoing systems integration. Canadians would no longer be able to undertake certain essential roles, such as Command Director. Instead, NORAD, and thus Canada, would be relegated to the periphery of air defence/sovereignty functions, with a range of potential additional costs that could bring the utility of NORAD into question. Finally, it is also unlikely that the Canadian government would be willing to undertake such an option for domestic political reasons. Thus, Canadian policy-makers, through their failure to develop a national policy on NMD, have put themselves on the horns of a dilemma—a dilemma time alone will not resolve.

THE LOOMING ISSUE OF OUTER SPACE

The relationship of outer space to the debate on NMD and Canadian participation has taken two basic forms. First, critics make pejorative reference to NMD as the 'son of Star Wars' (Kenna, 2000; Robinson, 1997). They portray NMD as the first step in the future development of a layered missile defence architecture that will include space-based weapons. In response, proponents argue that there is no evidence to sustain this viewpoint. The current system is purposely designed to be a limited ground-based one, initially consisting of 20 interceptors, growing to 100, at a single site in Alaska, with additional contingency plans to add another 100 interceptors at a second site, if so warranted. Moreover, even the most vehement US supporters of missile defence are not advocating a space-based interceptor system (Commission on Missile Defense, 1999). Certainly, some consideration is given to a space-based weapons capability.[8] Nonetheless, the desire to increase investment in space capabilities is directed to the new generation of space-based sensors, especially the Space-Based Infra-Red System in low earth orbit, for warhead tracking in space, target discrimination, and the cueing of the ground-based x-band radar. They also suggest the possible utility of either replacing or augmenting the current architecture with a sea-based system by employing the Navy's Theater Missile Defense in a national role.[9]

The second form concerns the implications of a Canadian decision for the current National Defence space strategy. It hinges on limited, selective investments into, and in co-operation with, US military space programs. For example, National Defence is contributing $250 million to the US to add capability to its advanced military communication system in return for assured access, a program known as CANMILSATCOM.[10] In addition, the Joint Space Project represents a planned $599 million investment in co-operation with the US in the areas of intelligence, environmental observation, space surveillance, surveillance from space, and early warning. Currently, only the definition phase of a ground-based optical sensor system for the surveillance of space has been funded ($7 million), with $63 million earmarked for a larger contribution to the US Space Surveillance Network.[11]

While some have portrayed this contribution to the Space Surveillance Network as a potential asymmetric Canadian contribution to NMD, presuming that the government participates, Canadian security interests underpinning the Joint Space Project are independent of NMD. As outlined in official policy:

> Canada's defence interests in space concern Canadian and allied assets, any objects which pass over or can observe Canadian territory and areas of Canadian interest, and the unhampered legitimate exploitation of space by Canada. A comprehensive space capability is fundamental to effective force projection in regional crises, rapid response under conditions of uncertainty and instability, high mobility with minimized forward presence, and maximum efficiency through the use of space in support of operations. (DND, 1998: 2)

With the high costs of space exploitation and the fiscal constraints facing DND, limited and selective investment in US programs is arguably the only option.[12] However, unless Canada participates in NMD, the viability of this option may collapse. If the NMD mission is assigned to Space Command, NORAD will likely be relegated to an air defence/sovereignty role only. Canadian involvement in space and missile operations almost certainly will become highly restricted. The ultimate outcome could possibly lead to the collapse of Canada's space strategy (Fergusson, 1999).

Both elements of space in the NMD debate should not be ignored. However, as recognized in current space policy, the importance of space goes well beyond the missile defence issue. Indeed, developments over the last several years in the US clearly signal the increasing significance of space for its national security. This significance has both military and civilian components, and raises the spectre of an emerging debate on the weaponization of space in the near future. The outcome of this debate, in turn, will have significance for Canadian policy, not dissimilar to the significance of the NMD issue today.

While the military importance of space has a long pedigree (see Burrows, 1998; McDougall, 1997; Stares, 1985), its increasing significance is a function of military and civilian technological developments and applications over the last decade. The Gulf War is recognized by some as the first space war, in the sense that the US military relied heavily on a range of space-based assets, such as the Global Positioning System. In conjunction with the ideas and concepts embraced within the 'revolution in military affairs', space-based assets are increasingly being seen as key to US military superiority. Central to the 'revolution in military affairs' is the acquisition of real-time battlefield awareness or transparency as the key to information dominance. Space is recognized as the ideal medium to facilitate this transparency because it permits unrestricted observation of any region or country. Space is also the ultimate high ground, which could provide a venue for the application of force against terrestrial targets, a capability that has been labelled as global engagement and is predicted to be technologically available by 2020 (US Space Command, 1998).

Alongside the military exploitation of space, its economic importance is also increasing. Currently, space activities employ roughly 800,000 people and generate approximately US$90 billion in revenues. More importantly, more than 50 per cent of the active pay-loads in space are commercially operated. It is estimated that 70 per cent of 1,700 satellite launches over the next 10 years will be com-mercially funded and US$60 billion in private investment is expected over the next five years (James and Fergusson, 2000: A5–6). Private information services already depend significantly on space, and fur-ther payoffs are expected in the future from telecommunications, remote-sensing, and end-user value-added products. Thus, space is sometimes portrayed as the future economic centre of gravity for the West, especially when the costs of space access are reduced with the future, cost-effective reusable single-stage-to-orbit space planes.[13] In addition, significant investment is taking place in improving the capa-bility and reducing the costs of satellites, which includes research into micro-satellites.

The independent military and economic importance of space is not alone in generating attention. Increasingly, countries are depend-ing on access to commercial communication and data acquisition sys-tems for military purposes, and military systems such as Global Positioning now have private and commercial application and impor-tance. The inherent and growing dual-use nature of space assets raises a number of security issues. Most prominent has been the issue of shutter control on commercial remote-sensing, which has military utility. For example, during the Gulf War, Iraq reportedly obtained imagery initially from a commercial French system, but this ended as a result of US–French co-operation. More recently, the issue of shutter control on RADARSAT II, whose imagery will be commer-cially vested in RADARSAT International (RSI), was resolved through negotiations between Canada and the US, after it was initially raised by DND in discussions with the Canadian Space Agency. Shutter con-trol is a denial measure, a component of the much larger concept of space control that is receiving increased attention in the US. Based on the belief that space is becoming a military and economic centre of gravity for US national security, the requirements for a space con-trol capacity are under consideration. Alongside the importance of space surveillance, this capacity entails the ability to deny adversar-ial access to space assets and/or data and to defend one's own access. Both can be achieved through a range of passive and active measures. The former include electronic measures and countermea-sures, such as imposed signal degradation, export controls, interna-tional agreements for denial purposes, encryption and frequency-hopping, stealth, satellite hardening, and enhanced satellite manoeuvrability for defence. Active measures include the use of anti-satellite systems for denial and defence and a range of counter-space capabilities, such as the ability to destroy (and defend) ground stations and intercept ballistic missiles targeted against space systems.

For Canadian policy-makers in the future, the key issue is not future developments of enhanced passive measures but the range of active measures centred on the possibility of the deployment of weapons in outer space. Currently, there is no legal prohibition on the deployment of weapons in outer space, except for weapons of mass destruction as embedded in the 1967 Outer Space Treaty.[14] Canadian policy is currently directed towards expanding the Outer Space Treaty to prohibit the deployment or stationing of weapons in space (DFAIT, 2000). With a primary focus within the Conference on Disarmament, Canada, among others, has been seeking since 1994 to resurrect the Ad Hoc Committee on the Prevention of an Arms Race in Outer Space. However, current US policy has blocked discussions on the basis that there is no arms race and thus nothing to talk about.[15]

This does not mean that the issue of weaponization has been decided in the US. Even within the US Air Force community, a debate exists on the merits of space as a sanctuary from weapons (DeBlois, 1998). At the same time, however, discussion has begun on the notion of the Air Force transitioning first to an *air and space* force, and then to a *space and air* one. More recently, the congressionally mandated Commission on National Security Space Management and Organization, chaired by recently appointed Secretary of Defense Rumsfeld, released its report. Among its recommendations are direct references to weaponization:

> Evident national security and guidance and defense policy is needed to direct development of doctrine, concepts of operations and capabilities for space, including weapons systems that operate in space and that can defend assets in orbit and augment air, land, and sea forces. This requires a deterrence strategy for space, which in turn must be supported by a broader range of space capabilities.[16] (Rumsfeld Commission, 2001: 16)

The various arguments surrounding the issues of space control and weaponization are too complicated to address fully here. Nonetheless, the broad categories of the forthcoming debate are almost identical to those currently surrounding NMD. On one hand, there are the concerns surrounding their implications for international security, strategic stability, arms races, and arms control, non-proliferation, and disarmament—the DFAIT agenda. On the other, there are the implications for continental defence and the Canada–US bilateral defence relationship—the DND agenda. Crosscutting both are Canada's independent interests in space from a commercial and military perspective that also bring into play a host of other considerations, represented in some ways by the agenda of the Canadian Space Agency relative to DFAIT and DND. Whereas the Canadian debate on NMD has largely been a clash between DND and DFAIT, space will entail the involvement of the Space Agency within a triangle of competing and complementary interests.

To date, as witnessed in the RADARSAT II saga, little if any consideration has been given to the political, economic, and strategic elements necessary for Canada to exploit outer space. Rather, Canadian policy remains largely ad hoc and issue-specific, with the last co-ordinated effort having occurred in 1964 with the Chapman Report. This report rejected a space launch capability for Canada and emphasized the peaceful exploitation of space as the cornerstone of Canadian policy. What the report did not foresee were the significant changes—technological, strategic, and political—involving the exploitation of space. As a result, the inherent dual-use nature of space assets and data and the commercial-security nexus have raised the importance not just of revisiting Canadian policy, but also of closely examining the co-ordination and integration of policy relative to the key agencies or departments.

More importantly, the US debate is at the preliminary stages, not least because the technologies to exploit space fully in military terms remain in the distant future (US Space Command, 1998). In addition, the debate has not yet extended into the wider public domain. If Canadian policy-makers want to influence the emerging security issues surrounding outer space, rather than simply react, as they have on NMD, the time for engagement is today. Unfortunately, the past record, no more evident than in the NMD case, indicates that policy-makers are more likely to avoid the issue until it is forced upon them. As in NMD, the result is likely to be a Canadian debate held long after a decision has been made elsewhere. The US NMD debate can be traced back to the passing of the 1991 National Missile Defense Act. Canada engaged in debate in 2000, long after the US debate on whether to develop had ended and had been replaced by the debate on when to deploy.

CONCLUSION

In the wake of the end of the Cold War, a resounding chorus cutting across the political spectrum called for a fundamental rethinking of security policy. While one can debate the extent to which this has occurred and led to new policy over the past decade, such rethinking in the context of NMD and outer space is largely absent. Instead, the parameters of Cold War debates remain firmly entrenched.

Nowhere is this more evident than in the constant reference, from proponents and opponents alike, to the implications of NMD for strategic stability. Yet strategic stability as embedded in the debate remains deeply bound to the Cold War logic in which it emerged. Simply put, strategic stability, defined as the preservation of an invulnerable, assured second-strike or retaliatory capability, was premised on the adversarial relationship between the US and Soviet Union, in which the probability of war was relatively high. It only made and makes sense within the context of a Cold War-style adversarial relationship. But, the Cold War is over. The US and Russia may not be the best of friends, but neither are they hostile adversaries. Their relationship today exhibits what may be understood as a normal mix of co-operative, competitive, and conflictual relations. Concerns about the relationship between NMD and strategic stability must begin with an explanation of the political conditions that would lead to a replication of the Cold War relationship. In the absence of such an explanation, strategic stability exists as a technical issue, devoid of politics.

This example of Cold War logic is illustrative of a much more fundamental question for Canada as it continues to adjust to the new political-security environment. As discussed above, the Cold War environment enabled Canadian policy-makers to manage significant tensions in the elements of foreign and defence policy. It permitted them to compartmentalize and pick and choose under the broader umbrella of internationalism. However, internationalism emerged as a policy response to the lessons of interwar policy failures and as a guide to the Cold War. Today, it is treated as a set of policy principles that transcend time, space, and political-strategic environments. In other words, Canada has avoided re-examining its own policy and its relevance in a new environment.

In effect, the underlying or deeper issues are largely hidden in the NMD debate. The ultimate decision or choice, whether made directly as a result of NMD or avoided by virtue of a Russia–US deal on the ABM Treaty and therefore deferred to the future, is really about setting the foundations for future policy directions. Internationalism will remain part of the rhetoric, but its actual policy meaning will likely be defined quite differently from how it was during the Cold War. This alone speaks to the NMD/Homeland Defense/outer space nexus as the most important strategic issue facing Canada. Decades from now, historians likely will come to see this nexus as a watershed in Canadian policy, not dissimilar from World War II and the initial years of the Cold War. Unfortunately, the activist role of policy-makers in the 1940s that defined internationalism appears to be absent today, and with this absence no strategic assessment of Canadian interests has been forthcoming.

NOTES

1. The current architecture consists of 100 interceptors deployed around Fort Griely, Alaska, an x-band radar at Shemya, upgraded early warning radars, and centralized BMC^3 in NORAD or Space Command Headquarters in Colorado.
2. In fact, Congress could do both independent of the President, and force the Pentagon to proceed. In an earlier case, even though the administration, the Pentagon, and the Marines did not want the V-22 tilt-rotor aircraft (Osprey), Congress forced it upon them, and this was upheld in a court decision.
3. The other criteria are cost, feasibility, and international security/allies. Notwithstanding the inclusion of deployment funds in the last two defence budgets, the passing of the 1999 Missile Defense Act has made technical feasibility the only operative criterion.
4. The subsequent failure of US intelligence to provide adequate warning of the North Korean three-stage missile test in August 1998 and the Indian and Pakistani nuclear tests in early 1999 politically validated the warning of the Rumsfeld Commission.
5. Apparently, the current strategy entails using up to five interceptors per incoming warhead to raise the probability of kill well above the 95 per cent level. With a planned deployment, known as Capability-Prime, of 100 interceptors, the system will be essentially optimized to engage 20 warheads and thus protect 20 targets in North America.
6. On 26 February 1985 at the NATO Nuclear Planning Group meeting in Luxembourg, Secretary of Defense Weinberger, apparently without the full knowledge of the administration, invited all the allies to participate in SDI research.
7. This role was only operational for the brief life of the Safeguard ABM system from the spring of 1975 until the fall of the same year.

8. Research and development into a space-based laser capability does continue at comparatively low investment levels. The first space-based test is currently planned for 2013.

9. There are two naval programs in the R&D phase: the Naval Lower Tier or Area Wide will employ the Standard Missile-2, Block IVB, and the Upper Tier or Theater Program that will employ the Standard Missile-3. Both programs are designated for the Aegis class cruiser and/or destroyer. The former uses a conventional intercept within the atmosphere and is targeted for operational deployment in 2001–2. The latter employs a kinetic kill outside the atmosphere and should be operational sometime between 2007 and 2010. It is the latter that is seen as potentially valuable for a national defence role. Of course, its employment in such a role would violate Article V of the ABM Treaty.

10. This is the Canadian Military Satellite Communications program, and the Canadian contribution represents 4 per cent of the total cost. A further $229 million is earmarked for end-user equipment.

11. The Joint Space Project is led by the Directorate of Space Development, which is currently examining a range of options for a space-based Canadian contribution to the Space Surveillance Network, including a deep-space sensor.

12. The high costs of space exploitation are perhaps best demonstrated by current launch costs on the order of US$25,000 per kilogram (James and Fergusson, 2000: A9).

13. For example, NASA is currently funding the Lockheed Martin X-33, with an experimental demonstrator scheduled for testing shortly. The X-33 is to be the basis for a commercial follow-on known as VentureStar. Besides this program, 17 others are also under way (James and Fergusson, 2000: A10).

14. Space is legally defined in terms of an object completing a single orbit, not the transition point to the vacuum of space. Although weapons of mass destruction are legally prohibited, there is no legal prohibition on the detonation of any weapons in outer space. The only prohibition is on the testing of nuclear weapons, as invested originally in the 1963 Limited Test Ban Treaty.

15. Consensus is required in the Conference on Disarmament in order to establish an ad hoc committee as part of adopting the annual agenda of work.

16. In an earlier speech, Rumsfeld made direct reference to a report on the Chinese development of a parasitic anti-satellite system that connects itself to a satellite, waiting to destroy it when necessary (Gafney, 2001).

REFERENCES

Burrows, W.E. 1998. *This New Ocean: The Story of the First Space Age*. New York: Random House.

Commission on Missile Defense. 1999. *Defending America: A Plan to Meet the Urgent Missile Threat*. Washington: Heritage Foundation.

DeBlois, Lt. Col. Bruce. 1998. 'Space Sanctuary: A Viable National Strategy', *Airpower Journal* (Winter).

Department of Foreign Affairs and International Trade (DFAIT). 2000. The Non-weaponization of Outer Space. Available at: <http://www.dfait-maeci.gc.ca/arms/outer3-e.asp>.

Department of National Defence (DND).1998. *Space Policy*. Ottawa: National Defence Headquarters.

Eckholm, Erik. 2001. 'China and US Explore Options on Missile Shield', *International Herald Tribune*, 29 Jan.

Fergusson, James. 1999. *Déjà vu: Canada, NORAD, and Ballistic Missile Defence*. Occasional Paper #39. Winnipeg: Centre for Defence and Security Studies.

Gafney, Fred. 2001. 'Time for countdown on U.S. space defense', *Washington Times*, 8 Jan.

Hart-Rudman Commission. 2001. United States Commission on National Security/21st Century. *Final Report*. Washington.

James, Steve, and James Fergusson. 2000. *Space Appreciation 2000*. Ottawa: Directorate of Space Development, DND.

Kenna, Kathleen. 2000. 'Son of Star Wars heats up', *Toronto Star*, 21 May.

McDougall,W.A. 1997. *The Heavens and the Earth: A Political History of the Space Age*. Baltimore: Johns Hopkins University Press.

Robinson, Bill. 1997. 'Return of SDI', *Ploughshares Monitor* (Dec.).

Rumsfeld Commission. 1998. *Report of the Commission to Assess the Ballistic Missile Threat to the United States*. Unclassified Executive Summary. Washington: US Congress, 15 July.

———. 2001. *Commission on National Security Space Management and Organization*. Washington: US Congress, 11 Jan.

Standing Committee on National Defence and Veterans Affairs. 2000. *National Missile Defence: An Overview*. Ottawa: House of Commons.

Stares, P.B. 1985. *The Militarization of Outer Space*. Ithaca, NY: Cornell University Press.

US Space Command. 1998. *Long Range Plan: Implementing USSPACECOM Vision 2020*. Colorado Springs.

13

Civil Society and the Axworthy Touch

ALISON VAN ROOY

One can no longer relegate NGOs to simple advisory or advocacy roles in this process. They are now part of the way decisions have to be made. They have been the voice saying that government belongs to the people, and must respond to the people's hopes, demands and ideals. (Axworthy, 1997)

The last decade has seen remarkable changes inside the Pearson Building. Non-governmental organizations (NGOs), once rarely invited past the foyer, now make regular visits to desk officers and assistant deputy ministers alike, sit on delegations, co-author treaties. Their views on human rights had been sought since the 1970s, but today the issues that involve civil society organizations in a substantive way are legion: peacemaking in the Sudan, democracy in Nigeria, trade policy in Brazil. How did this happen?

Much credit (or blame, depending on one's point of view) for this new degree of involvement—indeed, of democratizing foreign policy—is laid at the feet of Lloyd Axworthy. The peak of Axworthy's non-governmental profile, of course, came with the 1997 Mine Ban Convention, but he brought NGOs to the table in other instances as well: the International Criminal Court, the expansion of the human rights process, the campaign at the Security Council (see Chapter 7 by Pearson in this volume), and the campaigns against child soldiers and the proliferation of small arms, among others.

Much of this openness comes from Axworthy's personal convictions—the 'Axworthy touch'—but many unexamined factors shaped what he could, would, and did do, and what remains afterwards. This chapter looks at some of those factors. Bustled along by an activist Foreign Minister, Canada has made changes in its inclusive practices at home and has made a difference by its example abroad, and we should be proud of that. However, while Axworthy's efforts have been real and sincere, some of those changes may have been cosmetic, and still take place in a foreign policy culture unconvinced of the value of non-governmental inclusion but forced to accept it nonetheless.

THE GRAND SUCCESSES

It might be useful to begin with a brief review of two of the successes of Lloyd Axworthy's tenure as Foreign Minister most interwoven with civil society activism: the Convention banning landmines and the establishment of the International Criminal Court.

The Landmines Convention

The signing in Ottawa by 122 countries in December 1997 of the Convention on the Prohibition of the Use, Stockpiling, and Production and Transfer of Anti-Personnel Mines and on Their Destruction was the apex of Axworthy's most important venture, and the one he owes most to close co-operation with NGOs. Of course, while Axworthy had the domestic limelight, he acknowledges that he joined a civil society bandwagon, not vice versa, casting his lot in with the International Campaign to Ban Landmines (awarded the Nobel Peace Prize) and the International Committee of the Red Cross. Starting in 1996, the incredibly quick 14-month Convention-building process is probably a diplomatic record. Axworthy wrote that 'those of us in government must recognize that civil society has earned a place at the table' (Axworthy, 1998: 1).

Not only was Axworthy's inclusion of NGOs important in the success of the venture, it set a precedent for a different kind of foreign policy-making:

> The Ottawa Process [in the campaign to ban landmines] *democratized foreign policy* within the framework of existing representative institutions by using a partnership with civil society to expose policy to the test of publicity. . . . The public democracy practised in the Ottawa Process compelled policy-makers to provide public reasons for their actions and exposed them to criticism from civil society by bringing an NGO coalition into the policy process, both as domestic partners and international allies. (Cameron, 1998: 441, 443; emphasis added)

The International Criminal Court (ICC)

A less spectacular but equally daunting achievement was the 1998 establishment of the International Criminal Court (ICC) to try crimes against humanity. The stakes were high: Axworthy's commitment to a human security agenda meant that a number of institutions needed to be strengthened or created to assure that both sticks and carrots could be held over international miscreants. While there had been temporary courts in Yugoslavia and Rwanda, as well as their post-World War II predecessors in Nuremburg and Tokyo, no permanent and overarching authority had sufficient reach.

As in the case of the Landmines Convention, Canada joined what had begun as a United Nations (UN) and NGO campaign, chairing the like-minded group, urging members to identify shared cornerstone positions and to co-ordinate on strategy.[1] The battles to push through the Rome Convention were myriad: France wanted to limit the powers of the prosecutor and maintain a high-threshold definition of 'war crimes'; Japan was concerned that retroactive accusations would overturn existing negotiations over compensation to the 'comfort women' abused in World War II; and the US remained opposed to any court that might supersede its own judicial system, particularly fearing retaliatory acts against its own peacekeepers (Almeida, 1999).

Against that wall of opposition, Axworthy showed strong leadership. Canada was among the first to ratify the Convention and to put forward implementing legislation as well as a host of promotional activities, including funding for further research, debate, and out-reach by civil society organizations like the NGO Coalition for an ICC, Rights and Democracy, and the International Centre for Criminal Law Reform and Criminal Justice Policy. Today, relationships with these groups and those who are part of the Canadian peacebuilding com-munity continue to be strong, collaborative, and a backbone of Axworthy's human security policy, discussed below (Durno, n.d.).

MAKING IT DIFFICULT: WHY INCLUDING NGOS IS NOT AN EASY SELL

These well-known examples, however, are even more noteworthy when one considers what a very hard sell it has been to include NGOs into the active work of (some parts of) the Department of Foreign Affairs and International Trade (DFAIT). A number of bureaucratic and personal reasons help to explain this difficulty, and thus highlight the success of Axworthy and DFAIT officials.

An Insular Culture
The most important factor is the department's infamously insular cul-ture: foreign policy is to be the realm of professionals, not amateurs (Stairs, 2000; see also Chapter 5 by English in this volume). That spe-cialist culture arises from a host of elements, including the origins of our foreign service as part of the British cadre and its one-time small size as a department, but today it is reinforced by highly specialized recruitment practices. The benefits of the system are obvious in its population of intelligent career officers; the curse of this system is seen in the closed-door attitudes it has historically maintained in the face of outside activists.

Indeed, at the beginning of the last decade, when the Canadian International Development Agency (CIDA) was celebrating over 20 years of active engagement with development NGOs, Environment Canada regularly engaged with environmental groups, and Heritage Canada enjoyed active policy conversations with the multicultural community, DFAIT had a pretty minimal record of civil society involvement. There was really only one example that could easily be categorized under the heading of 'public consultation', the annual Human Rights Consultations, held every year before Canada went to Geneva for the meeting of the Commission on Human Rights.[2]

Although the record began to change in the 1990s, as we shall see, it is a small and recent evolution.[3] In opposition, Axworthy himself called the department a 'closed shop' (Nossal, 1995: 34).

Criticism about such closed-door practices has long been voiced. In 1986, the Special Joint Committee of the Senate and of the House of Commons on Canada's International Relations complained that 'ultimately a foreign policy concocted in isolation in Ottawa poses inherent political risks. . . . Canadians are knocking on the door of this country's foreign policy with more messages to deliver: they want in' (cited in Lee, 1998: 56).

Growing Activism and Antagonism

In the 1970s and 1980s, 'wanting in' focused on the anti-apartheid campaign and efforts to get the Canadian government to change its policies on Guatemala, El Salvador, and Nicaragua (Matthews and Pratt, 1982; Kirton and Dimock, 1993–4; Dobell, 1972). In this decade, as described below, attention has focused much more on international trade issues. The problem, however, is that the new activism has contributed to departmental resistance in opening the doors any further. 'Wanting in' has not always made things easier for officials, professionally or personally.

FREE TRADE AGREEMENTS

The debates over Canada's accession to the Canada–US Free Trade Agreement in the late 1980s and the North American Free Trade Agreement (NAFTA, ratified over 1993–4) were bitter. For officials working the trade side of DFAIT, nearly daily confrontations with solidarity groups and unions—most significantly with a coalition called Common Frontiers—made openness to friendly engagement difficult. Activists engaged in high-profile media and protest work related to NAFTA, as early as 1990 and after its ratification, continued with attention-getting reviews of the agreement's impact, often confrontationally (Foster, 1999).

As negotiations continue over the Free Trade Area for the Americas (including during the April 2001 Summit of the Americas in Quebec City), the temperature rose still higher. As trade and globalization have become the primary focus of activism, engaging a part of DFAIT that has fewer experiences of engagement than those involved in human rights issues, antagonisms have mounted.

ASIA-PACIFIC ECONOMIC CO-OPERATION FORUM

A similar source of antagonism carried over to meetings and events surrounding the APEC meeting in Vancouver in 1997. Canada was host of the forum that year, a club of largely Asian countries that has met annually since 1993 to discuss economic and trade goals. Among their numbers, and invited to Vancouver, was Indonesian President Suharto. While most Canadians know APEC only by the pepper-spray incident (when non-violent protestors against the Suharto regime were sprayed by overreacting RCMP), those closer to the action were further scarred by the vitriol spent by many activists over the forum's trade liberalization efforts in a region just then suffering a colossal economic collapse. Canadian anti-trade and anti-globalization activists met with officials in a round of increasingly frustrating and unpleasant encounters. Over APEC, too, officials' desire for further 'public engagement' waned.[4]

MULTILATERAL AGREEMENT ON INVESTMENT

Little more than a year later, another incident was added to dampen the enthusiasm. The well-orchestrated 1998 campaign to puncture the Multilateral Agreement on Investment (MAI) was hailed in the non-governmental world (led by the Council of Canadians, but joined by hundreds of other groups in other parts of the world) as a spectacular success. The story began when a copy of the Organization for Economic Co-operation and Development (OECD) draft treaty (under discussion in one form or another since 1993) fell into the hands of the Council in 1997. A campaign of teach-ins, community meetings, newspaper advertisements, and petitions was organized, increasingly through the use of the Internet. A growing international coalition followed the negotiations, legal opinions were sought, provincial and municipal governments lobbied, and critiques were published. These activities may have contributed to uncertainties that already existed within the negotiating group, and the deal fell apart (see Dymond, 1999, for a fuller story).

The International Trade Minister, Sergio Marchi, admitted that part of the problem was not involving NGOs in the first place, and reportedly said that the lesson he learned 'is that "civil society"—meaning public interests groups—should be engaged much sooner in a negotiating process, instead of governments trying to negotiate around them' (Perlas, n.d.). It was a big lesson for the department, but also a source of dismay for officials on the trade side, who felt that the agreement would have been a positive contribution to Canada's trade regime. Angered that an international process could be so easily derailed (leaving aside for a moment the likelihood it probably would have failed without NGO intervention), many officials demanded to know 'just who voted for these people anyway?'[5]

PROTESTS IN SEATTLE, WASHINGTON, WINDSOR, PRAGUE, AND BEYOND

That question was again repeated when the pictures were broadcast from the protests at the World Trade Organization meeting in Seattle in December 1999, in Washington at the World Bank meeting the following April, in Windsor at the Organization of American States (OAS) meetings in June and in September, and when further protest erupted in Prague over the annual meeting between the World Bank and the International Monetary Fund. By the time this book is published, more pictures will have appeared from Quebec City, where the Summit of the Americas took place in April 2001.

These events have reinforced a defensive stance for many officials, many of whom have been personally affected by antagonism even when broad consultations were conducted, as was the case prior to Seattle (Stairs, 2000). While it is now seen to be necessary to 'engage' as a strategy to defuse future nasty events, as well as to obtain public input (increased resources and staff have been mobilized for that work within DFAIT), the attitude is not one of happy interaction by a democratizing foreign service.

TALISMAN IN SUDAN

A final example comes particularly close to damaging Lloyd Axworthy's success with his human security strategy. Calgary-based Talisman Energy is the country's biggest international oil producer, with a 25 per cent stake in Sudan's southern Heglig oil fields. In 1999, Axworthy, US Secretary of State Madeleine Albright, church groups, and others expressed fears that Sudan's Islamist government might be using oil revenues to fund its war effort against rebels in the mainly Christian and animist south. Those accusations were confirmed in a report by Axworthy envoy John Harker, sent to the region in October 1999; Harker said Axworthy had asked him whether Talisman could be a force for peace and progress in Sudan (Ljunggren, 2000).

In the end, however, Axworthy's decision not to interfere in the company's investments was fiercely condemned.

> All the Canadian government has done about Talisman is to warn the company about the dangers its personnel may face by working in a war zone. . . . What is lacking is political will. . . . The weight of evidence suggests that Talisman is effectively complicit in crimes against humanity in Sudan, and presents the Government of Canada, and all shareholders in Talisman, with a clear moral imperative: act now to prevent Talisman from aggravating an already too costly civil war. (Inter-Church Coalition on Africa, 1999)

Axworthy's reputation was decidedly tarnished. The perception was that the chief proponent of the human security agenda should be accepting the costs incurred—including a loss of revenue to a Canadian company—as well as the plaudits earned.

EXPLAINING WHAT HAPPENED

If a closed-door culture and a whole decade of unpleasant interactions explain why DFAIT has not taken keenly to 'civil society engagement', then how was Lloyd Axworthy simultaneously able to win such success in partnership with non-governmental activists? In all cases, of course, he needed the support and active engagement of his own departmental staff in carrying that work through consultation mechanisms and by reporting to the public. How was that possible?

The following paragraphs present one explanation of the forces that pushed the engagement agenda over the crest of what was, and is, tangible reluctance. While Axworthy's personal drive was important, he was riding a much larger wave.

The Non-Governmental Explosion

At the top of the list of factors is the worldwide explosion of organizations engaged in international policy issues, including aid, trade, finance, human rights, peace/disarmament, and international governance. While the published numbers are notoriously impressionistic, data indicate a remarkable swell in organizational enthusiasm at the international level. In 1968 there were 741 registered NGOs active in more than one country. By 1986 this number exceeded 21,000, and a decade later more than 38,000 registered NGOs were working in more than one country, nearly double the number of a decade earlier (Figure 13.1). Global figures for national and local NGOs are more of a guess: some estimate 800 registered organizations in Ghana,

Figure 13.1

Numbers of International Organizations

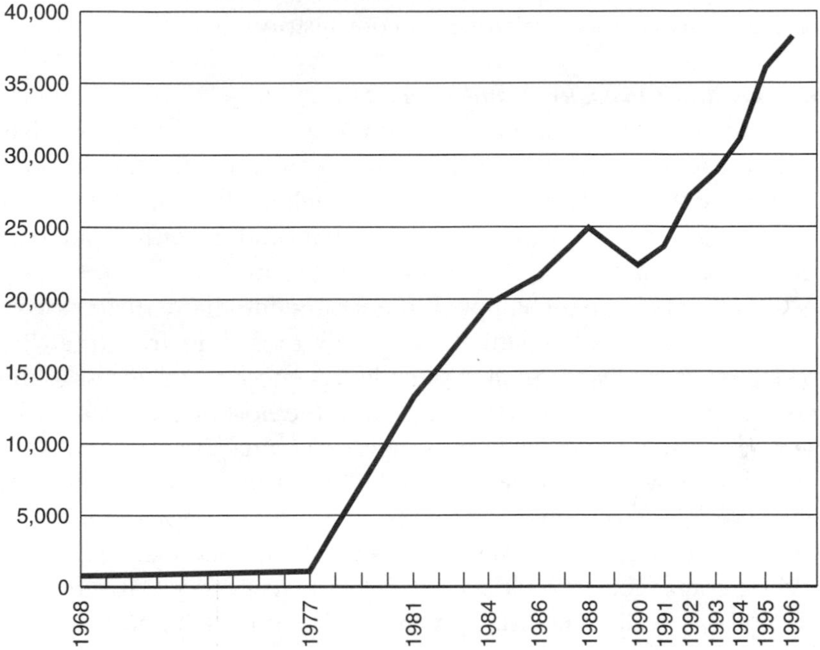

Source: Data from Union of International Organizations <www.uia.org>.

11,000 in Thailand, more than 17,500 in Egypt, and at least 2 million in India (Anheier and Salamon, 1998). In Canada, there are some 175,000 registered not-for-profit organizations.

Easier to numerate are the organizations rallying around specific meetings and intergovernmental bodies. Figures from the 1990s round of UN conferences show big numbers: the standard-setting 1992 Earth Summit in Rio de Janeiro saw 1,200 NGOs and an estimated 15,000 people at the parallel event; at Vienna's 1993 Human Rights conference, 7,000 participants from 800 NGOs attended; the 1995 Copenhagen Social Summit saw 4,500 people at the parallel event; and the Istanbul Habitat meeting in 1996 hosted 8,000 people from 2,400 NGOs (Anand, 1999: 90, 92, 96, 101). Moreover, some 37 per cent of World Bank projects involve NGOs (a cumulative total of some 752 since 1973; see World Bank, n.d.); and the International Monetary Fund (IMF) has some 900 NGOs on its mailing list. The

November 1999 demonstrations over the World Trade Organization (WTO) meetings in Seattle saw more than 700 organizations and between 40,000 and 60,000 men and women take part, the biggest rattling of civil society swords in recent history.

International Pressures and Precedent

That growth of international organizations, and their activism, has already had large effects on the practice of international relations (Foster and Anand, 1999; Weiss and Gordenker, 1996). It is no longer possible to exclude NGOs from international meetings, in part because of Canada's own international activism.

Canada has been a champion in encouraging the participation of NGOs in multilateral organizations. Springboarding from the 'Rio model' set at the Earth Summit, Canada has encouraged access to the OAS, the World Bank, the WTO, APEC, and the host of UN conferences over the past decade on human rights (Vienna 1993), population (Cairo 1994), women (Beijing 1995), habitat (Istanbul 1996), children (New York 1990), and social development (Copenhagen 1995). Known as a dependable ally in pursuit of international social and environmental goals, Canada has earned the respect of NGOs in other countries as well. While its consultative record at home has been under question, its behaviour abroad has been remarkably consistent and successful.

New Policy, New Partners

The demands of Axworthy's human security policy (see Chapter 4 by Hillmer and Chapnick) were another factor in opening the door to civil society engagement. By promoting an idea that extends the reach of international authority beyond the nation's borders—to reach the security of the human being, especially when threatened by her or his own government—the doctrine involves some serious rethinking of the whole concept of sovereignty.

Elements of concern have included the trade in small arms, the exercise of autocratic rule, the violation of human rights, the exploitation of children, the proliferation of nuclear weapons, the destruction of the environment, and the protection of civilians in wartime. Dealing with these challenges—many of which go beyond traditional statecraft—requires more and more varied alliances: other governments must act in coalition; international organizations must lend their sanction and logistical support; and, of course, NGOs and the media need to provide information, supply humanitarian services, and lobby their own governments to act. Foreign policy must involve more than foreign policy experts. As Stairs (1998: 47) notes, Axworthy has made 'much use of the NGO community as a political buttress for advancing his own priorities'.

A further pull towards engagement is not only the role of NGOs in providing human security services (most notably in humanitarian intervention and lobbying), but also their role as funnels for new sources of money. DFAIT has almost no money to implement its human security agenda and must look elsewhere. Tug-of-wars with CIDA over that agency's annual budget of almost $2 billion have gained some success—$100 million for landmines eradication and over $8 million for the International Conference on War-Affected Children, for example—but the dollars do not come close to matching the agenda. However, non-governmental bodies, funded through campaigns at home and matching dollars from CIDA (and its counterparts elsewhere in the OECD), add both human and financial resources to the endeavour.

Party Policy

A further underlying factor was the orientation of the Liberal Party itself, long a proponent of liberal pluralism (Stairs, 1998). It is not surprising, therefore, that engaging with civil society and 'democratizing foreign policy' were also part of party policy when the Liberals were in opposition in the early 1990s. The new government came to power in 1993 waving the Red Book, the party's platform and promises for its new mandate. On that list of promises, elaborated in the *Foreign Policy Handbook* (much of it penned by Axworthy), was the commitment to an annual public forum on Canada's place in the world, the establishment of a Centre for Foreign Policy Development, and a major review of foreign policy. Coupled with evident prime ministerial enthusiasm, the department was certainly in for a change.

The Foreign Policy Review of 1994 was met with a great deal of enthusiasm among the churches, unions, ethnic associations, solidarity groups, and development organizations that were keen watchers of Canada's policies abroad. The process began with several open debates in the House of Commons on specific issues (such as peacekeeping in Bosnia) and in the new National Forum on Canada's International Relations. A Special Parliamentary Committee was set up to pull those debates together with a series of cross-Canada consultations. That massive tour-de-table spoke with 500 people in over 70 meetings, and received more than 550 briefs (half from development NGOs). While encumbered by a short deadline, poor co-ordination, and the usual intercommittee infighting, the Review strongly endorsed the Red Book's democratization-of-foreign-policy agenda.

The first forum was held in March 1994, and on the invitation list of some 130 names were broadly representative constituencies: business (not many), academics, NGOs (many), and indigenous organizations, as well as 100 observers. While there were problems with the process (participation was considered by the Committee to be too narrow and there were too many issues on the table to be discussed thoroughly), the forum held great promise for opening the insular policy process at the Pearson Building.[6]

Another Red Book idea, elaborated by the Special Committee, was to set up a centre to promote dialogue among government, business, academics, professionals, Parliament, and non-governmental organizations through the year. Established in 1996, the Canadian Centre for Foreign Policy Development sits inside the Pearson Building but outside the foreign service, serving as a direct source of advice to the minister on topics of the minister's choosing. Enabled by a small source of funding (the John Holmes Fund) for non-governmental and academic round tables, the Centre's small staff has worked as a funnel on selected issues to the minister's office.[7]

The Consultative Imperative

These new promises and institutions brought in by the Liberal Party did not germinate on dry ground, however. There had already been significant moves by earlier governments to open up the process to public participation. In the early 1990s, the Conservative government's Public Service 2000 task force was set up to examine how the federal public service was meeting public needs (by and large, it concluded, poorly), and it distributed a set of consultation guidelines for managers throughout the civil service. (That set of guidelines, since amplified by individual departments, is now being updated by the Privy Council Office.) One reason to increase DFAIT's consultative process, therefore, was precedent and pressure from the broader public service.

Another reason stemmed from the will of previous ministers who, like Lloyd Axworthy, felt that the public ought to be more involved in deliberations on foreign policy. In the late 1960s, Trudeau's government undertook public reviews of foreign policy under the rubric of 'participatory democracy'. In the 1980s, Foreign Minister Joe Clark's group of Conservative populists seemed particularly keen to meet with public interest groups on foreign policy. Both Prime Minister Brian Mulroney and his External Affairs Minister, Barbara McDougall, spoke on enhancing the transparency of government decision-making and increasing consultations with the public, and held forums on South Africa, Central America, the Tiananmen Square crackdown in China, and the Gulf War (Nossal, 1995: 32–3).[8] Mulroney, in particular, had encouraged NGO involvement in preparations leading to the Earth Summit (in part because environmental concerns topped the list of Canadians' priorities at the time).

By the time the Liberals took office in 1993, there was already a groundswell of interest—and practice—in engaging the public in foreign policy discussions. The public service was pushing reform and some senior ministers (including prime ministers) had been taking an interest. Axworthy was able to take off with a head start.

Axworthy's Personal Preferences

At the end of the list of reasons to explain Lloyd Axworthy's civil society successes, despite real obstacles, is the strength of his own convictions. Chapter 5 by English and Chapter 4 by Hillmer and Chapnick in this volume argue that the origin of those convictions lies in his early activism, his Christian faith, and his leadership in community development in his home of Winnipeg, both in his earlier career as an academic and a provincial politician and, later, as an MP. As Stairs notes, 'once in office, Axworthy moved much more vigorously to support open consultation than a mere obeisance to his party's formal commitment would have required' (Stairs, 1998: 44). In his practice as Foreign Minister, it seems he did believe that civil society's involvement is important for democracy, accountability, and better policy. In a speech in Mexico in January 1999, he said:

> Advancing human security requires not only that we look at what issues we address but how we address them. To this end, the time has come to further redefine the interaction between governments and non-state actors, through dialogue, consultation and participation to meet emerging challenges and threats. Strengthening civil society is not only a key element in the consolidation of democracy. It promotes accountability, and contributes to the formulation of better policy by taking into account the concerns, pre-

occupations and expertise held by citizens. (Canadian Council for International Cooperation, n.d.)

Of course, these powerful convictions, however much buttressed by other forces, could not create some ideal system of civil-professional policy engagement. As Hillmer and Chapnick argue, trouble came when the going got rough: there was the Talisman crisis, as well as heavy controversy over cuts to official development assistance in 1995 and later and over the bombings in Kosovo in 1999. Some critics went so far as to accuse Axworthy of 'pulpit diplomacy' (Hampson and Oliver, 1998) and to argue that he was not applying the same principles when the costs were heavier. None of these currents undermine for one minute the role that Axworthy has played in raising the profile and legitimacy of civic involvement in foreign policy. Yet, they suggest that 'the Axworthy touch' has depended on a host of sometimes countervailing pressures: historical, personal, bureaucratic, global, and idiosyncratic.

CONCLUSION

At the end of the day, for those concerned about an overly inflated role for NGOs in today's foreign policy, do not worry. While DFAIT's doors have opened, in large part due to Axworthy's enthusiasm, the level of resistance to outside intervention is still high. While there are positive signs (the government's support of the Voluntary Sector Initiative, for example, and the recent hiring of new foreign service officers more open to engagement), there is no obvious future. My guess is now that Lloyd Axworthy has left, the pressure to consult may well taper off, leading to a more decorative, pro forma practice.

The repercussions of such a downgrading may be remarkable. A strange notion persists within DFAIT that Canadians are ambivalent about their international role and that foreign policy ought rightly to be clutched to the bosom of the professional. Yet, a key finding from an April 1998 Compas poll showed that 'Canadians are passionate about world affairs, interventionist, and more united than one might have predicted. Far from being parochial or isolationist, Canadians appear to have convictions, often devoutly democratic, about almost everything in the international arena' (cited in Gwyn, 1999). As Canadians are becoming more vocal both as individual citizens and as members of organized groups, one wonders what new demands will surely be made of our foreign policy-makers.

NOTES

Alison Van Rooy is a Research Associate with the North-South Institute in Ottawa and the Senior Social Policy Adviser at the Canadian International Development Agency. The views expressed in this paper are, however, personal views and do not represent the views of her employers.

1. For more, see <http://209.217.98/79/english/08_canadaICC_e/08_canadaICC_e. htm#2>.

2. True, there were a couple of invitation-only 'consultations' through the Industry Trade Advisory Committee and the Sectoral Advisory Groups on International Trade, but aside from a small number of labour and environmentalist members, they included only industry representatives. Now and again, round tables would be held—such as on the Tiananmen massacre—but the episodes were intermittent. Indeed, the only other engagement of note was the consultative process set up in 1990 to prepare for the 1992 Earth Summit: along with CIDA and Environment Canada, DFAIT organized working groups with NGOs over a range of environment and development issues.

3. This point of view, of course, is not shared by all. See Curtis (2000) for an argument about the opening of the process.

4. These assessments are drawn from confidential interviews conducted with officials and activists at the time.

5. 'Who voted for these people anyway?' is a common question, but it gets at the right issue in the wrong way. As NGOs gain in influence over public opinion, and occasionally over public policy, it is important to ask questions about legitimacy. However, elections are not the only or most important source of public legitimacy. For more on this topic, see The North-South Institute's ongoing series on *Voices: Nongovernmental Voices in Multilateral Organizations*, at <www.nsi-ins.ca/ensi/research/voices>.

6. Sadly, the record from then on was largely downhill. Subsequent forums (and associated workshops) have welcomed a similarly handpicked crowd, largely from the business world and big universities, with many fewer from the non-governmental realm.

7. Unfortunately, this effort has also come to something less than its promise. While purposely designed to be outside the bureaucracy (ostensibly to shield the Centre from old-fashioned diplomatic prejudices), the Centre has been sidelined. Advice, recommendations, and events generated there deflect off policy practitioners, irritated to have their professional advice to the minister leapfrogged by non-professionals. The Centre has also not won too many friends in the outside community, in part because it deals almost entirely with issues in which the minister is already interested, but not necessarily those that Canadians want to bring to the minister. As a resource for funnelling (select) non-governmental and academic advice, the Centre has been very successful. As a tool for democratizing foreign policy? Far less so.

8. Note, however, that McDougall's approach was much more cautious than Axworthy's ever was: she wrote that 'the influence of pin-striped diplomats is being displaced by high-profile pressure from a variety of disconnected interests' (in Stairs, 1998: 34). However, while Axworthy complained that the Progressive Conservative government seemed 'unwilling to carry on a serious dialogue with the public or Parliament on important foreign policy decisions' (in Nossal, 1995: 32), he had obviously forgotten the debates that were indeed held during the Mulroney era.

REFERENCES

Almeida, Iris. 1999. 'Civil Society and the Establishment of the International Criminal Court', in *Civil Society Engaging Multilateral Institutions: At the Crossroads*, Montreal International Forum 1, 1 (Fall).

Anand, Anita. 1999. 'Global Meeting Place: United Nations' World Conferences and Civil Society', in Foster and Anand (1999).

Anheier, Helmut, and Lester Salamon. 1998. *The Nonprofit Sector in the Developing World: A Comparative Analysis*, Johns Hopkins Nonprofit Sector Series 5. Manchester: Manchester University Press.

Axworthy, Lloyd. 1997. 'Notes for an Address by the Honourable Lloyd Axworthy, Minister of Foreign Affairs, to the Oslo NGO Forum on Banning Anti-Personnel Landmines', DFAIT Statement, Oslo, 10 Sept.

———. 1998. 'Lessons from the Ottawa Process', *Canadian Foreign Policy* 5, 3 (Spring): 1–2.

——— and Sarah Taylor. 1998. 'A Ban for All Seasons', *International Journal* 53, 2 (Spring): 189–203.

Cameron, Maxwell. 1998. 'Democratization of Foreign Policy: The Ottawa Process as a Model', in M.A. Cameron, R.J. Lawson, and B.W. Tomlin, eds, *To Walk Without Fear: The Global Movement to Ban Landmines*. Toronto: Oxford University Press.

Canadian Council for International Co-operation. n.d. 'Linking Globalization to Human Development in the Americas', CCIC Americas Policy Group Brief on the Free Trade Area of the Americas. Available at: <http://fly.web.net/ccic/devpol/APG2_FTAA_Brief.htm>.

Curtis, John M. 2000. 'Involving NGOs in Trade Policy Negotiations', *Optimum, The Journal of Public Management* 30, 2.

Dobell, Peter C. 1972. *Canada's Search for New Roles: Foreign Policy in the Trudeau Era*. Toronto: Oxford University Press for the Royal Institute of International Affairs.

Durno, Janet, Co-ordinator of the Canadian Peacebuilding Co-ordinating Committee. n.d. 'Partnerships for Peacebuilding: Canadian NGO-Government Relations'. Available at: <http://www.sgi.org/quarterly/0001/feature-3.html>.

Dymond, William A. 1999. 'The MAI: A Sad and Melancholy Tale', in Fen Osler Hampson, Michael Hart, and Martin Rudner, eds, *Canada Among Nations 1999: A Big League Player?* Toronto: Oxford University Press.

Foster, John. 1999. 'Confronting the "Global Economic Constitution" ', in Alison Van Rooy, ed., *Canadian Development Report 1999: Civil Society and Global Change*. Ottawa: North-South Institute.

———— and Anita Anand, eds. 1999. *Whose World Is It Anyway? Civil Society, the United Nations and the Multilateral Future*. Ottawa: United Nations Association of Canada.

Gwyn, Richard. 1999. 'Lloyd Axworthy Makes Pearsonianism Permanent', *Policy Options* (Dec.): 13–16.

Hampson, Fen Osler, and Dean F. Oliver. 1998. 'Pulpit Diplomacy: A Critical Assessment of the Axworthy Doctrine', *International Journal* 53, 3 (Summer): 379–407.

Inter-Church Coalition on Africa. 1999. *Urgent Action Bulletin*, 1999/#3, 20 Sept.

Kirton, John, and Blair Dimock. 1983–4. 'Domestic Access to Government in the Canadian Foreign Policy Process, 1968–1982', *International Journal* 39, 1 (Winter): 68–99.

Lee, Steven. 1998. 'Beyond Consultations: Public Contributions to Making Foreign Policy', in Fen Osler Hampson and Maureen Appel Molot, eds, *Canada Among Nations 1998: Leadership and Dialogue*. Toronto: Oxford University Press.

Liberal Party of Canada. 1993. *Creating Opportunity: The Liberal Plan for Canada* (Red Book). Ottawa. (The *Foreign Policy Handbook* is an annex.)

Ljunggren, David. 2000. 'Canada oil probe says Sudan rights abuses widespread', Reuters newswire, 26 Jan.

Matthews, Robert, and Cranford Pratt. 1982. *Church and State: The Christian Churches and Canadian Foreign Policy*. Toronto: Canadian Institute of International Affairs.

North-South Institute. *Voices: Nongovernmental Voices in Multilateral Organizations*. Available at: <www.nsi-ins.ca/ensi/research/voices>.

Nossal, Kim Richard. 1995. 'The Democratization of Foreign Policy: The Elusive Ideal', in Maxwell W. Cameron and Maureen Appel Molot, eds, *Canada Among Nations 1995: Democracy and Canadian Foreign Policy*. Ottawa: Carleton University Press.

Perlas, Nicanor. 'Civil Society and the Collapse of the WTO Agenda in Seattle', *Info3-das Monatsmagazin für Spiritualität und Zeitfragen*. Available at: <http://www.info3.de/English/e-0100perlas.html>.

Stairs, Denis. 1998. 'The Policy Process and Dialogues with Demos: Liberal Pluralism with a Transnational Twist', in Fen Osler Hampson and Maureen Appel Molot, eds, *Canada Among Nations 1998: Leadership and Dialogue*. Toronto: Oxford University Press.

————. 1999. 'The Axworthy View and Its Dilemmas', *Policy Options* (Dec.): 7–12.

————. 2000. *Foreign Policy Consultations in a Globalizing World*. Montreal: Institute for Research on Public Policy.

Weiss, Thomas, and L. Gordenker. 1996. *NGOs, the UN and Global Governance*. Boulder, Colo.: Lynne Rienner.

World Bank. n.d. 'Frequently Asked Questions'. Available at: <http://wbln0018.world bank.org/essd/essd.nsf/NGOs/home>.

14

Mexico under Vicente Fox: What Can Canada Expect?

JUDITH TEICHMAN

Since the signing of the North American Free Trade Agreement (NAFTA), trade and investment between Canada and Mexico have increased dramatically. With total Canada–Mexico trade in 1998 at $11 billion (Cdn), Mexico is Canada's most important trading partner in Latin America. Canadian investment in Mexico has increased by 324 per cent since 1993, raising Canada from ninth to fourth place among foreign investors in Mexico (DFAIT, 2001a: 1–3). But Canadian interest in Mexico is now much more than economic. Growth in economic relations has produced expanding Canadian interest in political developments in Mexico, manifested in Canadian concerns about the progress and quality of democracy, human rights, and the war in Chiapas. The last two Mexican national elections (1994 and 2000) were watched closely by Canadians, with the Canadian government sending an unprecedented number of observers to watch the electoral process first-hand. The most recent national elections in July 2000 saw the victory of the 'Alianza por Cambio' and presidential candidate Vicente Fox, who succeeded in wresting power from the Institutional Revolutionary Party (PRI), which had ruled Mexico for more than 70 years. For most observers, domestic and international, Fox's win opened a new era in Mexican politics; his victory signalled the coming to power of a democratically elected, market-friendly government that would encourage trade and investment while respecting democratic practices. However, a close examination of the Mexican political scene, in general, and Vicente Fox, in particular, suggests that Mexico's transition to democracy may not be a smooth one and that the spectre of political crisis may loom on the horizon if pressing political issues such as poverty and corruption are not adequately addressed. The reality of Mexico's enormous political challenges may make Canada's relationship with its Latin NAFTA partner an increasingly uneasy one, precisely because Canada's involvement with Mexico has come to encompass a broadened concern for political and social issues.

Canada's objectives regarding Mexico evolved from a narrow business goal of increasing trade and investment to a concern for improvements in democracy and human rights. The government of Prime Minister Brian Mulroney, the administration in power when the North American Free Trade Agreement was negotiated, resisted pressures from opposition parties and human rights activists for a link between human rights and trade and instead gave primacy to pragmatic and business considerations. Throughout the NAFTA negotiations, Canada took the position that alleged human rights violations in Mexico ought not to get in the way of negotiating an economic agreement (Schmitz, 1994). Our position at the time was that market liberalization policy in Mexico and further opening as a consequence of NAFTA would facilitate changes in the direction of democracy and improvements in human rights. It is likely that the stiff resistance, indeed, the hostility of the Mexican government of then President Carlos Salinas to what it regarded as outside interference in Mexican domestic affairs played an important role in the Canadian government's decision not to involve democratization and human rights in the negotiation process.

The growth of political violence in Mexico, particularly in the southern state of Chiapas where the Zapatistas launched their rebellion on the day the North American Free Trade Agreement went into effect, focused the attention of international and Canadian human rights organizations on Mexico and increased the pressure to link commercial policy with human rights, social justice, and indigenous issues. In a 1996 address to non-governmental organizations, the Minister of Foreign Affairs, Lloyd Axworthy, signalled an important departure from the previous Canadian administration's reluctance to link trade with broader political and social issues. He advanced the notion that trade could provide Canada with openings to 'promote the human rights and democratic development agenda'. He made an explicit link between human security and alleviating poverty, noting that people could not feel secure in a situation in which drinking water, health care, and education are lacking. Canada must, he stated, 'become a leading voice in the expression of this need for a broader definition of security' (Axworthy, 1996: 2). The changes in Canada–Mexico relations that emerged after 1994 reflected the minister's vision and echoed the mounting demands from the leaders of a wide cross-section of Canadian societal organizations. While the conflict in Chiapas has been of special concern to Native leaders and human rights organizations, labour and environmental activists have seen Mexico's cheap and vulnerable labour force and the country's failure to enforce environmental legislation as ultimately undermining the quality of Canadian life.[1]

Hence, Canadian relations with Mexico have deepened and expanded into a wide variety of arenas—a development reflected in the proliferation of meetings at all levels. Not only did Prime Minister Jean Chrétien and President Ernesto Zedillo meet frequently between 1995 and 1999, but the foreign and trade ministers also met often, as did diverse members of the cabinets of both countries (DFAIT, 2001b: 1). Canada currently has 50 bilateral agreements in place with Mexico—over 40 of which have been signed since 1990 (DFAIT, 1999a: 1). Discussions and co-operative agreements and arrangements have covered efforts to promote democracy and human rights, indigenous rights, health, education, protection of the environment, and labour rights. There has been increasingly close co-operation between the Canadian and Mexican electoral commissions and Canada has been promoting closer ties between Canadian parliamentarians and members of the Mexican Congress (DFAIT, 1999a: 1). In 1995, the human rights commissions of the two countries signed a bilateral co-operation agreement, while in 1996 alone Canada supported 12 human rights-related projects in Mexico (Axworthy, 1996:

3). In 1998, the government sent a parliamentary delegation in partnership with representatives of the Assembly of First Nations to
observe the human rights situation and state and local elections in
Chiapas first-hand (DFAIT, 1999b, 1998a: 1). In response to concerns
expressed by the First Nations leaders in this delegation, a fund for
the socio-economic development of indigenous communities, admin-
istered by the Canadian embassy in Mexico, was established and initiatives were taken to promote government-to-government
co-operation and dialogue on indigenous issues and to promote
exchange and co-operation between the indigenous communities of
the two countries (DFAIT, 1999b).[2] At the same time, many Canadian
non-governmental organizations (NGOs) funded by the Canadian
International Development Agency (CIDA) are active in Mexico. In
1996–7, Canada contributed almost $1.3 million through Canadian
NGOs for projects on community health, education, and private-sector development in Mexico (DFAIT, 1998b: 2). Moreover, the Joint
Report on the 1999 Joint Ministerial Committee meeting indicates that
further co-operation and exchange are anticipated in such areas as
social and labour market development programs, the decentralization
of social programs, and human capital development, and agreement
has been reached to collaborate on a variety of environmental issues
(DFAIT, 1999c: 2–5).

It is indeed true, however, that the expansion of trade and investment has remained an important priority. Clearly, Canada has assid-
uously pushed for the expansion of business opportunities in Mexico:
it has pressed for the continued reduction of tariff and other trade
barriers and for the lifting of investment restrictions in areas such as
financial services and in sectors such as hydroelectric power stations
and the transmission of natural gas, from which private, especially
foreign, investment had been excluded (DFAIT, 1999a: 2). The most
important effort mounted to expand trade and investment in Mexico
was the 1999 Team Canada mission, which involved not only the
Prime Minister and federal cabinet ministers but also provincial premiers and approximately 300 Canadian companies. A record 91 commercial deals, worth $230 million (Cdn), were signed (ibid., 1). But,
even here, the concerns and accomplishments were not just business
ones. Six new bilateral agreements were signed in development co-
operation, the model forest program, anti-narcotics, telecommunications, education, and health. Moreover, Sergio Marchi, the Minister
for International Trade at the time, and the premiers raised a num-

ber of non-business matters with President Zedillo, including Canada's concern about the situation in Chiapas. Further, Canada took the opportunity to contribute $60,000 to the state of Chiapas regional office of the Mexican Red Cross to provide humanitarian assistance to people displaced by violence in that state. The presence of Canadian Aboriginal leaders in the Team Canada delegation made possible the signing of a Memorandum of Understanding between the Saskatchewan Federated College and the Autonomous University of Chiapas to establish a joint program in indigenous studies and capacity-building (DFAIT, 1999b).

Those Canadians concerned with political developments in Mexico recognize that although Mexican elections are now free of the flagrant violations of the past, much still remains to be done, especially in the area of human rights. Non-governmental organizations concerned with such issues as human rights and the environment saw the election of Vicente Fox as an unprecedented opportunity to push for continued improvements. They grasped this opportunity during the August 2000 visit of President-elect Vicente Fox to Canada to call on him to expand both democracy and the protection of human rights. Indeed, NGOs met with the incoming President to discuss their concerns about the political situation in Mexico. Moreover, in a press conference, the spokesman for Amnesty International urged Prime Minister Chrétien to contribute to the achievement of real improvements in Mexico by placing the human rights issue at the forefront of Canada's relations with Mexico (Publiservice, 2000b). The Prime Minister's response showed how much the Canadian government had moved on the issue of Canadian involvement in Mexico's domestic political developments since the early 1990s: the Prime Minister, having raised the human rights issue during his discussions with Fox, declared it to be an important part of Canada's foreign policy agenda. For his part, Fox responded with a strong public commitment to the protection of human rights in Mexico and promised that NGOs would be welcome to operate in Mexico—thereby rejecting past Mexican government practice of resisting NGO human rights and social justice endeavours and expelling a number of them for 'political involvement' (Publiservice, 2000a).[3] Fox, in fact, spoke warmly about his willingness to work with NGOs to improve the human rights situation in Mexico and to advance democratization.

The issue of trade and investment was another important aspect of the Fox agenda on this visit, even though these discussions took a somewhat lower profile. In his conversations with the Prime Minister and, more importantly, in his meeting with Canadian business leaders, Fox pressed for the expansion of trade and investment between the two countries (ibid.). Fox's discussions with Prime Minister Chrétien also involved advocacy for the development of NAFTA along the lines of the European Union—it is widely believed that his initial proposal was for a currency union, a proposal that was firmly rejected by both Prime Minister Chrétien and the Canadian business community.[4]

What do these new Fox initiatives—a greater openness to pressures for democratization from Canada, combined with a desire to tighten trade and investment ties while developing a regional common market along the European model—mean for Canada's future relationship with Mexico? And what do they mean now that the Canadian government has adopted democratization and human rights issues as major foreign policy concerns for Mexico? On the surface, especially as a consequence of Fox's August 2000 visit to Canada, it might appear that closer, more friendly relations are in the offing—certainly, NGOs were encouraged by Fox's statements. And the Canadian private sector, which has already expanded into the Mexican market since the signing of NAFTA, was positively impressed by Fox's encouragement to Canadian trade and investment opportunities (ibid.). The only tension in the meeting appears to have revolved around Fox's vision for NAFTA, since the Prime Minister rejected development of NAFTA along the lines of the European Union.

Fox not only has raised international expectations about what he can accomplish, but he has also risen to power on the crest of very high Mexican public expectations, which he encouraged through a stream of policy pronouncements between his election in July and his inauguration on 1 December 2000. To ascertain the implications of Fox's election for Canada, two areas of inquiry need to be pursued: first, it is essential to sort out what policies Fox is likely to regard as top priority, and second, it is important to identify where Canada is likely to fit into Fox's vision for Mexico and for North America. The argument presented here is that Fox's vision for Mexico is not likely to alleviate his country's most glaring social problems, thereby raising the possibility of political unrest and continued difficulties in areas such as human rights. It is important to note that Fox's democratic credentials have been questioned by political observers inside Mexico. Fox sees the expansion of trade and investment under NAFTA and the agreement's revision as the panacea for Mexico's widespread social and development problems. Indeed, Fox's willingness to allow outsiders to monitor democracy and human rights issues is tied to the willingness of NAFTA partners to contribute to arrangements perceived as necessary to elevate Mexico into developed-country status. The Achilles heel of Fox's plan is found in the inadequacy of his domestic economic strategy, which shows a glaring lack of social justice content, a failure that has the potential to erode democratic institutions and undermine their legitimacy. Should this occur, the co-operative relations that his country is building with Canada in non-economic areas will surely unravel.

Although the most cursory glance at Fox's background can tell us a great deal about him, his electoral team suggested a desire to include a broad cross-section of opinion among his advisers.[5] As we will see, however, his recent cabinet appointments (executives from the private sector and old technocratic members of the PRI) suggest an administration whose priority concern is macroeconomic stability and a highly receptive business climate, law and order, and, only secondarily, concern for social justice. As the following section will show, the problems inherited by Fox's administration are enormous: severe inequality, concentrated wealth and massive poverty, violent political insurgency, powerful drug cartels, and widespread corruption. If the past 15 years in Mexico are any indication, it is unlikely that these immense problems will be solved by Fox's major policy remedy, the magic of the market.

THE CHALLENGES FACING MEXICO: ECONOMIC, SOCIAL, AND POLITICAL

Since the late 1980s Mexico has undergone a process of economic transformation that has involved trade liberalization, deregulation, and privatization. By the mid-1990s it was clear that the beneficiaries of this process were a relatively small number of domestic conglomerates. The biggest firms benefited from export incentives (Heredia, 1996), and the major shareholders in these firms bought up public companies. Indeed, by 1992 the country's most important financial, industrial, and service activities were in the hands of four conglomerates (Teichman, 1995: 187). Mexico's privatization process under President Salinas (1988–94) was permeated with cronyism: the close personal ties between Mexico's political leaders and the purchasers of public companies became common knowledge, contributing to a concentration of wealth and political power that is still legion.[6] The personal links between private-sector interests and the policy élite continued into the administration of President Zedillo (1995–2000) and were reflected in the bank rescue program in which the highly personalized access of bank owners to the policy élite produced a rescue operation favouring the biggest PRI contributors (López Obrador, 1999: 60).

The corollary of this concentration in economic power has been a tightening of the links between the country's top political leaders and the most powerful businessmen. Powerful business interests were behind the presidential electoral campaigns of both Salinas and Zedillo. Enormous contributions were sought by the PRI from its powerful business supporters and they usually complied. The most notorious example occurred in 1993 when the country's top business leaders were each invited to pledge $25 million (US) to the PRI's 1994 election campaign; public outcry resulted in a reduction of contributions to a third of a million each. Close and personal links between the heads of conglomerates and the President and political leaders in charge of the major economic ministries developed throughout the 1990s.[7] In fact, the involvement of the private sector in economic policy was even greater under President Zedillo than it had been under the previous administration (Teichman, 2001).

Another important feature of the last decade was the expansion of the drug trade in Mexico resulting in the growth in corruption at all levels, from state governors, judges, the police, and the military to highly placed federal government officials. Indeed, individuals close to former President Salinas, including four generals and Salinas's own brother, are believed to be linked directly to the drug trade.[8] In addition, US officials believe that former President Zedillo's private secretary, José Liébano Sáenz, was involved in drug trafficking (*Mexico & NAFTA Report,* 8 June 1999: 6). By the late 1990s, five major drug cartels were operating in Mexico; the Juarez Cartel, responsible for one-half of the cocaine entering the US, was reportedly most successful at corrupting Mexican government officials. As a consequence of the crackdown against the Colombian cartels, the

Mexican cartels, more violent than their Colombian counterparts and now regarded as a greater threat by US drug enforcement authorities, had taken over drug trafficking into the US market.

While political corruption ran rampant and wealth and political power became increasingly concentrated during the 1990s, social inequality and poverty increased, particularly following the peso crisis of 1995. In 1995 the Mexican economy contracted by 6.2 per cent in real terms, the biggest decline since 1932 (González Gómez, 1998: 52), and an enormous financial rescue operation was launched to pull the country out of the crisis. An emergency economic program called for sharp cuts in government expenditures along with price and tax increases. In 1995 alone, private consumption declined by 9.5 per cent and more than a million jobs were lost in the formal sector (Lustig, 1998: 210). Real industrial wages that had begun to creep up in the early 1990s dropped sharply after 1995 (ILO, 2000), while the percentage of the population classified as 'poor' increased from 36 to 43 per cent and the percentage of 'extremely poor' rose from 12 to 16 per cent between 1994 and 1996 (Cepal, n.d.). By the year 2000, there were 43 million people living in poverty in Mexico and 18 million in extreme poverty.[9]

The rural areas of Mexico have been especially disadvantaged by the current economic model. Between 1989 and 1994, when extreme and moderate poverty fell in the urban areas, poverty rose in the mining and agricultural sectors. Indeed, southern Mexico has been left out of the new market model altogether: between 1989 and 1994 poverty in the southeast of Mexico (the states of Chiapas, Guerrero, Oaxaca) rose to a level that was five times higher than in northeast Mexico and 40 times higher than in the federal district (Lustig, 1998: 204). These are regions with large indigenous populations and they are precisely the areas where political violence, including the activities of a variety of guerrilla groups, particularly the Zapatista Liberation Army (EZLN), has been on the rise. While decline in the international prices for the exports of these states—coffee, cocoa— is part of the explanation for their declining prosperity, neo-liberal policy changes involving increases in interest rates, cuts in subsidies, and elimination of support agencies, such as marketing boards that supported the co-operative *ejido*[10] arrangements, have also been important contributing factors.

Along with economic crisis, economic reform, and the failure to alleviate poverty, the country has also undergone important political changes, particularly over the last decade. Under pressure for democratization not only from the opposition parties but also from within the PRI, the Salinas administration adopted a controlled political liberalization strategy, ceding victories to the opposition Popular Action Party (PAN) in state elections. By 1995 there were four opposition PAN governorships. Meanwhile, a variety of political reforms creating a much fairer electoral process resulted in the 1994 federal election being widely regarded as the cleanest federal election ever.

The peso crisis of 1995 marked the beginning of a new political phase in Mexico, one characterized by more electoral reform and unprecedented gains by opposition parties. With the economic crisis, the government was confronted with widespread unrest from trade unions, the opposition leftist Party of the Democratic Revolution (PRD), and critics within the PRI itself who were demanding a fundamental change in the direction of economic policy, if not outright rejection of the free-market model. The political leadership was forced to allow the electoral process to provide institutionalized channels for opposition demands. Following further political reforms in 1996, the PRI experienced its greatest defeat ever. In 1997, the PRD won the governorship of the Federal District (Mexico City) and control of its legislature, along with control of the legislatures in the states of Mexico, Michoacán, and Morelos. Most important, the PRI lost control of the national House of Deputies. This electoral change led to revisions in economic policy legislation (in government budgets, in the bank rescue operation) and blocked others (privatizations in electricity and PEMEX petrochemical plants), events unprecedented in Mexican history at the time. The decision of the PRI to hold primary elections for the selection of its presidential candidate in December 1999, abandoning the traditional *dedazo* whereby the incumbent PRI President personally chose the candidate, reflected further progress in the direction of democratization. But, above all, the defeat of PRI presidential candidate Francisco Labastida and the election of Vicente Fox in the 2000 elections marked a momentous step forward in the Mexican political transition.

Nevertheless, the Mexican regime transition of the 1990s is not easy to categorize. Alongside important progress in electoral democracy, vestiges remain of old practices, and a marked increase has occurred in the level of political violence both by insurgent groups and by the state. Under President Zedillo, PROGRESA, a program targeting the very poor, replaced PRONASOL as the most important social program. Despite its claims to political neutrality, PROGRESA is widely believed to have been an important clientelistic mechanism used to pressure poor voters in rural Mexico to vote for the PRI in the 2000 election (Global Exchange/Alianza Civica, 2000: 10). At the same time, the efforts to combat the drug trade have contributed enormously to the level of political violence (Camp, 1999: 131). Critics have argued that the use of the state coercive apparatus to deal with drug traffickers is related to its use against insurgents and dissidents. In 1995, a civilian umbrella security agency, the National Security Council (COSENA), was established to bring together all law enforcement agencies under the control of the President. COSENA was given a full range of surveillance powers and empowered to create a special security force, while the public security budget was increased by 26 per cent in 1997 (*Latin American Weekly Report*, 29 Apr. 1997: 195).

Indeed, human rights violations are especially widespread in the Mexican countryside, especially in poor states such as Chiapas, Guerrero, and Oaxaca, where guerrilla insurgency is present (Handleman, 1997: 110). According to a 1997 report there was, by that year, a guerrilla presence in 17 of 32 states (*Latin American Weekly Report*, 9 Dec. 1997: 582). Amnesty International's 1999 report claims that over the previous five years there was 'a serious deterioration in the human rights situation in Mexico' involving the use of torture, 'disappearances', and extrajudicial executions by members of the military and security forces (Amnesty International, 1999: 1, 11, 17). Reports of the killing of peasants in Guerrero, Chiapas, and other states sullied the democratic credentials of the Zedillo administration, events made even worse by investigations linking such outrages to police or to paramilitaries trained by the military and to attempts by high-ranking government officials to cover up such misdeeds (ISLA, Aug. 1995: 11, 19). While the state military/security apparatus has been largely deployed against violent insurgents and drug dealers, opposition party members did not escape violent repression. In the first nine months of the Zedillo administration, 68 PRD members were assassinated (*Mexico & NAFTA Report*, 12 Oct. 1995: 4), the number reaching 150 by the end of the second year of his administration (*Latin American Weekly Report*, 5 Dec. 1996: 564). By 1997, Mexico had achieved the number-two spot after Colombia in the death toll of journalists (ibid., 30 Sept. 1997: 467).

By the summer election of 2000, Mexicans were ready for political change. Presidential candidate Vicente Fox's campaign statement that the choice was now between dictatorship (continued PRI rule) and democracy (election of his opposition coalition) caught on. Much of the Mexican public bought into Fox's characterization of the election of his coalition as a government of 'democratic transition'. Indeed, according to an exit poll carried out by *Time* magazine and the Mexican newspaper *Reforma*, 70 per cent of those who cited change as the main reason for their decision voted for Fox (ISLA, July 2000: 16). But, as we will see below, Fox has promised that his government will do considerably more than simply oversee a political transition.

VICENTE FOX AND THE POPULAR ACTION PARTY: A LOOK TO THE FUTURE?

It is not easy to ascertain what Vicente Fox stands for—his public statements are far from clear and often contradictory. Between his election on 2 July and his inauguration on 1 December, Fox issued a relentless stream of policy statements that included proposals to do the following: eradicate corruption, revive the economy, reform the police force, end the Chiapas rebellion, reduce poverty, create more than a million jobs a year, reform the tax system, open the energy sector to foreign investment, improve salaries, develop rural communities and the agricultural sector, support small and medium industry, and establish new programs to attract foreign investment. There was no attempt to indicate which of these would most occupy his attention. Fox appeared to be all things to all people; but the reality is that he will have to establish priorities and make hard choices.

Hence, what happens in Mexico over the next six years depends on Fox's personal policy predispositions as well as on what and how pressures are brought to bear on him. We can glean a few things from the track record of his party, the Popular Action Party (PAN). A party of the Catholic right, the PAN has formed the governorship of six Mexican states and controlled 285 of 2,400 municipalities. Its record in office has been less than glowing. In the case of the governorship of Baja California, for example, where it has ruled continuously since 1989, it has provided more efficient government than did the PRI, but corruption in the police and court system has continued (including links to drug traffickers), while the crime rate has risen (ISLA, June 2000: 16). And although independent state electoral institutions and fraud-proof voter credentials count among the accomplishments of the PAN, there are charges that free-market policies, such as steep hikes in water fees, have contributed to an increase in the level of poverty in the state.

Fox, however, has distanced himself from PAN traditionalists, denying opposition to abortion and homosexuality, and pledging that he will not use the state to impose lifestyle or codes of behaviour or to alter the status quo of secular education (ISLA, July 2000: 5). Meanwhile, in *caudillo* (strong-man) fashion, Fox has cultivated his own basis of support outside of his party. A civic movement, not tied to the PAN, known as the 'Amigos de Fox' reportedly has three million members, 10 times more than PAN membership (ISLA, Apr. 2000: 4). In addition, other separate organizations led by Fox are the National Unity Movement, with one million members, and the 40,000-member Migrants for Change, based in Los Angeles (ibid.). Indeed, Fox's electoral base of support is more heterogeneous than his right-wing Catholic party might suggest. Traditionally weak in rural areas, the PAN-dominated Alianza por Cambio increased its share of the rural vote from 15 to 31 per cent between 1994 and 2000 and was able to garner 70 per cent of the vote in poor urban areas where free milk was handed out (*Mexico & NAFTA Report*, 15 Aug. 2000: 3). Although it maintained and even expanded its strength in central and northern Mexico, the Alianza captured a significant proportion of the vote even in the south. But along with this expansion of electoral support from the rural and urban poor there will also be expectations from these groups about what benefits his administration should bring.

Meanwhile, Fox has surrounded himself with powerful members of the private sector and PRISTA technocrats who played a key role in market reform under President Salinas. Fox's chief economic adviser during the election campaign was economist Luis Ernesto Derbez, a 14-year veteran of the World Bank and a close associate of Rosario Green, Minister of Foreign Relations under Zedillo.[11] Derbez, a neo-liberal fiscal conservative whose major objective is to keep interest rates at 5 per cent and establish a stable framework for monetary policy (ibid., 7), has been appointed Minister of Economy. Eduardo Sojo, an economist with a degree from the Instituto Technologico de Estudios Superiores de Monterrey and a Ph.D. from the University of Pennsylvania, was a senior official in the Finance Ministry under the previous PRI government and served as Fox's chief political adviser during the election campaign (ibid., 11 July 2000: 12). Sojo has since been appointed to the Fox cabinet as the co-ordinator of public policy advisers. The powerful position of Minister of Finance has gone to Francisco Gil Diaz, a former official in the central bank and Ministry of Finance under the PRI presidencies of Miguel de la Madrid Hurtado and Carlos Salinas and probably the most important figure in Mexico's 1985–8 trade liberalization program (Teichman, 2001).

Moreover, the private sector is overwhelmingly represented among those closest to Fox and as a whole reflects the new administration's firm commitment to continued market liberalization. Roberto Hernández, the main shareholder in the country's largest bank, BANAMEX, and Justino Campéan, a senior executive in the media giant Televisa, are leading members of the 'Amigos de Fox' movement. An unprecedented number of cabinet appointments (nine) have gone to individuals with experience in the private sector, suggesting the continuation of a close relationship between the political leadership and powerful members of the private sector that characterized past regimes. Pedro Cerisola y Weber, formerly the head of TELMEX (the giant privatized telecommunications company) in the federal district, ran Fox's electoral campaign and was appointed Minister of Communications and Transport. Ernesto Martens Rebelledo, a strong proponent of private investment in the energy sector and a former executive of Union Carbide, is Minister of Energy, while the incoming Minister of Agriculture, formerly Minister of Agriculture under Fox when he was governor of Guanajuato, is owner of an agricultural export company. The new director of the state petroleum company, PEMEX, is a former executive of Du Pont and a member of the board of directors of a variety of important private companies (*Reforma* <www.reforma.com/ flashes/nacional/gabinete_fox/>).

Initially, Fox drew a number of advisers from the intellectual left and claimed that he would continue to do so. Jorge Castañeda and Adolfo Aguilar Zinser, the latter an adviser to leftist presidential candidate Cuauhtémoc Cardenas in the 1994 national election, served as Fox's advisers on international relations during the election campaign. But it is probably important to note the roots of these links. Fox, along with Castañeda and Zinser, are members of the Mangabeira Group, an organization of Latin American politicians and intellectuals co-founded by Castañeda and Brazilian Harvard professor Roberto Mangabeira Unger. The group is calling for revisions to neo-liberalism. An examination of Mangabeira's ideas sheds light on the possible ways in which the Mexican left and market reformers can attempt to reconcile their distinct concerns. The Mangabeira Group does not stray far from the neo-liberal path: it calls for an increase in domestic savings, increased lending to micro, small, and medium enterprises, the construction of a smaller but more efficient state, the promotion of regional trading groups, and a reduction in inequality through increased targeted social spending supported by increases in tax revenues. It also supports the breakup of monopolies but explicitly rejects the Asian model of state-directed industrial policy. Moreover, the group has taken a page from old-style market reformers, advocating that political leaders exploit their powers to drive through their policies and avoid getting bogged down with legislative negotiations, suggesting the use of American-style fast-track approval and referendums (*NAFTA & Mexico Report*, 11 July 2000: 1, 3).

Fox's track record as governor of the state of Guanajuato (he was elected governor in 1995, the same year he jointed the Mangabeira Group) suggests that he has already adopted some of the key ideas of the Group. He established a state bank to provide credit to micro enterprises (ISLA, Apr. 2000: 11), increased government spending on technical education to create a better-educated labour pool, and devoted most of his time to trips abroad to flog Guanajuato to foreign investors (ISLA, Aug. 2000: 64). As governor he was faced with the same situation he faces as president: he did not have control of Congress. His critics have compared him to Peru's former authoritarian market-oriented president, Alberto Fujimori, accusing Fox of a similar predisposition to try to bypass democratic deliberative mechanisms during his stint as governor (ISLA, May 2000: 7). This skepticism regarding Fox's democratic leanings is reinforced by his highly personalistic and charismatic leadership style and by the fact that he has built up a mass popular base independent of his own party. Furthermore, Fox's chameleon nature, reflected in his policy pronouncements, makes it difficult to believe in his sincerity. He praised the country's bankers when speaking to them, criticized the Catholic Church when speaking to Protestants (ISLA, Apr. 2000: 7), promised the poor he would fight poverty (ISLA, July 2000: 5), described himself as centre-left on some issues (ISLA, May 2000: 8), praised the student uprising of 1968 (ISLA, July 2000: 5), and sought conciliation with the leftist PRD party and with homosexuals (ISLA, Aug. 2000: 6).

Certainly, much of the Mexican left has doubts about Fox's reformist pronouncements. Only one leftist, Jorge Castañeda, who was appointed Minister of Foreign Relations, sits in Fox's new cabinet. Other leftists, in particular leading members of the PRD invited by Fox to lead the Ministry of Social Development, the Office of Budget Control, and the Ministry of the Environment, turned him down. Instead, the PRD has called for negotiation and dialogue to establish the government's agenda, leaving open the issue of future cabinet appointments (*Reforma* <www.reforma.com/nacional/articulo/048725>). The PRD's rejection of participation in the new government stemmed from its concern that neither the Fox government nor its program was substantially distinguishable from that of the former PRI government. The PRD has been highly critical of Fox's cabinet as reflecting too close collaboration with what has been termed 'the neo-liberal technocratic project' (*Reforma* <www.reforma.com/nacional/articulo/051334>).

Fox's solution to Mexico's devastating social problems revolves largely around the market. He has declared that to reduce poverty there must be one million jobs created annually and for this the economy must grow (his 7 per cent per year target was later reduced to a more realistic 4.5 per cent) (ISLA, Apr. 2000: 3). In Fox's vision of things, attracting foreign investment is key to achieving this growth: he plans to double foreign investment in Mexico to $2 billion (US) annually (ISLA, Aug. 2000: 30–1). To attract this investment a 'disciplined economic model', one that will produce a fiscal surplus by Fox's fourth year of office, is essential, as are measures to bring inflation down (from 9 to 3 per cent), enhance Central Bank autonomy, and privatize more public companies (ISLA, Apr. 2000: 3). While in early 1998 Fox had said that he would privatize PEMEX, characterized as obsolete and incompetent, public outcry caused him to back off and he has since pledged that it would not be privatized (ISLA, June 2000: 43). He nevertheless has promised the opening of the electricity sector to foreign investment and the privatization of PEMEX petrochemical plants—both measures blocked by the leftist PRD, trade unions, and restive PRI congressmen in the last administration (ibid.). Hence, foreign investment from Mexico's NAFTA partners is crucial to his vision of how economic growth and prosperity are to come to Mexico.

Fox's faith in the ability of the Mexican economy alone to solve the country's problems of poverty and unemployment remains weak. It is here that Fox's support for a North American common market modelled after the European Union—an idea pushed by his leftist advisers, Castañeda and Aguilar Zinser—enters the picture. The objective of the revised union would be to reduce the gigantic gap between Mexico and its two other NAFTA partners. Hence, under the slogan of 'open borders, compensatory funds, and a common market', Fox's proposal includes free mobility of labour, making it possible for Mexicans to move freely to jobs in the rest of North America. In addition, along the European Union model, Fox envisions the establishment of regional development funds to provide funding for infrastructure and to alleviate inequality through investment in human capital in the poor areas of Mexico (ISLA, Aug. 2000: 41).[12] In return, Fox would pledge the enforcement of Mexican labour law and workers would be guaranteed independent unions and free collective bargaining. The plan would also see the modification of the NAFTA side accord to include real sanctions if workers are denied the right to organize and bargain collectively (ibid., 43). The proposal to revise NAFTA is important to Fox's view of how Mexico's very serious problems are to be addressed, since, as we will see below, Mexico faces formidable difficulties in confronting those problems on its own.

Increased social spending, even targeted spending, requires an increase in the country's tax base. Fox has promised to double spending on education and to continue the previous administration's program to channel money to the extremely poor (*Mexico & NAFTA Report*, July 2000: 11). Thus far, the Fox team has fielded a number of ideas to increase government revenue. One of these, an increase in wealth or property taxes, was mentioned and quickly dropped.[13] Powerful private-sector resistance to increased taxation has been a persistent theme in state/private-sector relations (Teichman, 1988: 51). Another proposal, to end the sales tax exemptions for food and medicines, was dropped when it met with strong public criticism from opposition parties, trade unions, and even PAN traditionalists. Indeed, Fox has acknowledged that his most difficult task will be fiscal reform, an essential component of expanding social programs (ISLA, Aug. 2000: 30). Privatizations could bring in funds for social programs as they have in past administrations, but privatizations in the sacrosanct areas of electricity and petroleum are contingent on overcoming the opposition that blocked such measures in the previous administration. It is of crucial importance, therefore, for Fox that he obtains Canadian and American co-operation in his efforts to alleviate poverty, not only through increased investment in Mexico, but also in the form of arrangements that would see regional organizations providing development funding to stimulate Mexican economic growth. While in August 2000 Prime Minister Chrétien promised to help Mexico to 'improve the lives of its people', he rejected a major revision of NAFTA along the lines envisioned by Fox (Publiservice, 2000a).

In the interim between his election and inauguration, Fox's position on indigenous issues, especially the conflict in Chiapas, moved from an initial position denying them as national issues of critical importance requiring careful and skilled negotiation (best exemplified by his comment that he would solve Chiapas 'in fifteen minutes') to a much more conciliatory stance. He now claims that ending violence in Chiapas is a top priority (ISLA, Aug. 2000: 29). In fact, the day after his inauguration, Fox announced that he would send a bill to Congress, based on the earlier agreement reached with the Zapatistas, to end the conflict in that state. He also promised a 10-point program that includes the establishment of a National Commission for the Development of Indigenous People (ISLA, July 2000: 43) and of a 'Transparency Commission', responsible to Congress, to probe human rights violations and corruption scandals (ISLA, Aug. 2000: 21). The defeat of the PRI by the 'Alianza por Chiapas', an alliance of parties that includes the PAN and the PRD, in the August 2000 gubernatorial election in Chiapas opened the opportunity for renewed negotiations with the new governor of that state mediating between the Zapatistas and the federal government. Fox has raised expectations that a solution to the Chiapas conflict is imminent and he has opened the process to further pressure from the international community—Canadian NGOs and the Canadian government can be expected to watch this process closely. Indeed, the march of the Zapatistas into Mexico city to secure congressional approval of the 1996 agreement focused world attention on the Chiapas conflict. While Fox's public stance has been conciliatory, his refusal to meet Zapatista demands for a show of good faith by withdrawing seven (of 252) military contingents from that state, and the hostility of Panistas and some Pristas in Congress to the Zapatista demands, suggests that a peaceful resolution of the conflict is by no means assured. The costs, in terms of domestic and international credibility, will be enormous if Fox is unable to reach agreement with insurgents and such a development would impact negatively on Canadian–Mexican relations.

Like his NAFTA proposals, Fox's strategy to combat crime, particularly the drug trade, was developed on the advice of his leftist advisers. Fox has called for the termination of the US certification program, whereby Latin American countries are 'certified' every year by the US Congress as to their efforts in support of US anti-drug trafficking programs. Instead, he advocates a multilateral enforcement and co-operation agreement that includes the participation of the Organization of American States (OAS) and the United Nations (ISLA, June 2000: 5). The position of his administration is that the US has not done enough to stem the flow or the consumption of illegal drugs and that US anti-drug policies involving US aid to fight drug production and trafficking in producer countries exacerbate corruption and violence while securing only the relocation of drug production and trafficking rather than its elimination (ISLA, July 2000: 29). Especially with the Republican win in the 2000 American presidential election, Mexico can expect substantial resistance from the US on this issue, while the new Mexican administration may well press Canada to support the Mexican position.

Fox has characterized the fight against corruption, not the reduction of poverty and inequality, as a central focus of his desire to expand democracy. He places a strong emphasis on a variety of institutional reforms, claiming, for example, that his government will replace the PRI-controlled state institutions with 'free and representative' institutions (ISLA, June 2000: 38). He argues that the establishment of US-style checks and balances in Mexican government will help curb corruption (ISLA, July 2000: 28). In particular, he has promised to clean out the Interior Ministry, accused of spying on the citizenry and of covering up government crimes (ibid.), and he has said that he will reform his country's corrupt police and judiciary and create a new Federal Prosecutor's Office that will be autonomous from the presidency (ISLA, Aug. 2000: 4). All of these initiatives are positive signs. They are measures that will receive strong support from the Canadian government. While necessary and important, however, such initiatives do not address the country's social problems—problems also officially recognized as important by Canadian authorities in recent years.

CONCLUSION

A survey of incoming President Fox's election campaign promises and the various pronouncements he has made since his election suggests a politician promising to solve all of Mexico's major problems in the space of one presidential term—certainly an impossible task. Which pressing issues get addressed by the Fox administration will be key to the country's political stability. Fox's newly appointed cabinet suggests a strong commitment to the free-market model. His most powerful cabinet members are former PRI technocrats and leading business executives. In this sense his administration is the direct descendant of the previous PRI administrations he has so vehemently maligned. Fox's technocratic and private-sector advisers will guide the direction of domestic economic policy, and there is relatively little place in it for expanded social policy. Fox's remedy for Mexico's massive poverty is expanded trade, investment, and changes in the original NAFTA arrangements. He is unlikely to look for, or to find, the resources to solve Mexico's massive social problems from within, so he is searching for help from an alteration and deepening of arrangements among NAFTA partners.

While there is ample evidence that Vicente Fox is not likely to place the interests of Mexico's poor, indigenous, and labouring people at the top of his agenda (improvement in their lives is to come largely as a consequence of market-oriented policies), many poor and working Mexicans voted for Fox because a vote for him was perceived as the best and only way to remove the PRI from power. Nevertheless, the expectations of all Mexicans of what the Fox administration can accomplish are high. If the administration fails to alleviate the deplorable social conditions faced by those citizens who have placed such high hopes on democracy, there is the danger that the legitimacy of the country's electoral and political process will be undermined. Certainly, the political violence in the southern states cannot be resolved simply by a renewal of negotiations, but must also involve an alleviation of the conditions at the root of the unrest—poverty and inequality. Over the last 15 years, the expansion of trade and investment has not proved effective in solving Mexico's searing social problems. However, the solution of these problems is crucial to the stability of Mexico's incipient democracy and to the trade and investment opportunities the country has to offer its NAFTA partners.

The consequence for Canada is a NAFTA partner whose long-term political stability and democratization remain problematic. This is true despite the fact that there have been promising signs: Vicente Fox has pledged to improve democracy, support the expansion of human rights, and find a solution to the conflict in Chiapas. He has welcomed human rights organizations and other NGOs into Mexico to help in these endeavours. Meanwhile, officially, Canada has demonstrated the will to help expand democracy and human rights in Mexico. Moreover, NGOs that were allowed to influence the policy process while Lloyd Axworthy was Minister of Foreign Affairs will press for the maintenance of the Canadian government's expanded role in the areas of democratization, human rights, and social and indigenous issues. But political unrest will not abate for long if the new Mexican administration fails to address the root social causes of those political difficulties, especially in states like Chiapas. Despite his rhetorical commitment to democracy, Fox's democratic track record is far from impeccable. There is a good chance that he could lose patience with political opponents and have recourse to the repressive and authoritarian practices of past administrations. Hence, Canadian observers may find themselves with much to criticize in Mexico on both the social and political fronts.

Furthermore, as long as Jorge Castañeda is Minister of Foreign Relations, Mexico can be expected to press its positions on the revision of the original NAFTA agreement and on how the war on drugs should be handled. These Mexican demands are unlikely to receive much encouragement from Canada. The issue of revisions to the NAFTA agreement is especially problematic. The spectre of the free mobility of labour and a monetary union would be strongly opposed by both the Canadian business and labour communities, and there is little likelihood that the Canadian taxpayer could ever be convinced of the efficacy of transfer payments to Mexico's poor southern states. It would indeed be surprising if Canadian observers did not, at some point, raise some serious questions about the efficacy of a regional social pact, such as the one proposed by Castañeda, where NAFTA partners are brought on board to help alleviate Mexico's severe social problems while Mexican policy-makers relegate social policy to the bottom of their list of domestic priorities. However, Castañeda may be replaced by an appointee who is a closer fit with the rest of the Fox cabinet. Should this occur, programs to alleviate Mexico's devastating poverty will slide further down the government's list of priorities, and with them, the long-term prospects for expanding democracy and the protection of human rights.

NOTES

1. This is so, they maintain, because the relentless pursuit of multinationals to lower their costs puts downward pressure on Canadian labour and environmental standards (Kreklewich, 1993: 265–6).
2. In addition, Ovide Mercredi, at the time National Chief of the Assembly of First Nations and a member of the Canadian delegation, called for an explicit link between trade and human rights and for a trilateral independent human rights monitoring agency (Schmitz, 1994).
3. A 1998 incident that had caused tension in Canadian–Mexican relations was Mexico's expulsion of two Canadians working with a human rights organization from Chiapas on the grounds that they had violated article 33 of the Mexican constitution, which prohibits foreigners from engaging in domestic political activities. Foreign Affairs Minister Axworthy raised the issue of the free movement of human rights organizations with his Mexican counterpart (DFAIT, 1998c).
4. Fox's specific proposals for changes in NAFTA will be discussed later in the chapter. US President Bill Clinton also rejected Fox's proposals for changes in NAFTA.
5. Most notably, well-known Mexican leftists, Adolfo Zinser and Jorge Castañeda, became advisers to Fox during his election campaign.
6. The case of TELMEX, which at sale provided for monopoly control of the country's telecommunications industry until 1997 to President Salinas's close confidant, Carlos Slim, is the most notorious example. Another is the privatization of the state copper companies, which resulted in one man, Jorge Larrea, obtaining control of 90 per cent of the nation's copper production (Teichman, 1995: 153).
7. Claudio X. Gonzalez, for example, a shareholder and member of the boards of directors of three of the country's biggest conglomerates, was a personal friend of Salinas, arranging his meetings with other conglomerate heads, acting as his adviser on foreign investment issues, and accompanying both Commerce Minister Jaime Serra Puche and José Córdoba, the president's top adviser, on official trips abroad (*Proceso* 974, 3 July 1995: 39). President Zedillo integrated top businessmen into his policy team, such as the son of powerful businessman Claudio X. Gonzalez, who became head of Special Projects in the President's office (*Proceso* 1972, 18 May 1997: 9).
8. A Swiss investigation revealed that Raúl Salinas, brother of Carlos, had laundered very large amounts of drug money through Swiss bank accounts and had, through his brother Carlos, protected big Mexican drug cartels, allowing shipments of cocaine to get into the US.
9. Persons living in poverty are those with incomes below about US $60 per person per month. Persons living on less than US $30 per month are deemed to be living in extreme poverty.

10. *Ejido* refers to a co-operative form of agricultural organization designed to combine economies of scale with traditional communal practices.
11. At the World Bank, Derbez worked on Chile between 1986 and 1989, a period during which tough structural adjustment was implemented, as well as on structural adjustment programs in Francophone Africa between 1993 and 1994 (*Mexico & NAFTA Report*, Aug. 2000: 6).
12. Castañeda points out that the European Union set aside $35 billion (US) to help its poorest members (ISLA, Aug. 2000: 45).
13. In Mexico, wealth and property taxes bring in only the equivalent of 0.3 per cent of GDP, versus 3.2 per cent in the US (*Mexico & NAFTA Report*, Aug. 2000: 8).

REFERENCES

Amnesty International. 1999. *Mexico: Under the Shadow of Impunity*. London.

Axworthy, Lloyd. 1996. 'Notes for an Address by the Honourable Lloyd Axworthy, Minister of Foreign Affairs, at the Consultations with Non-governmental Organizations in Preparations for the 52nd Session of the United Nations Commission on Human Rights'. Available at: <www.dfait-maeci.gc.ca/english/news/statements/96_state/003e.htm>.

Camp, Roderic. 1999. *Politics in Mexico*. New York: Oxford University Press.

Cepal. 'América Latina, Magnitud de la Pobreza y la Indigencia', Cuadro 16. Available at: <www.eclac.cl/español/estadisticas>.

Department of Foreign Affairs and International Trade (DFAIT). 1998a. 'Axworthy, Marleau Announce New Initiatives for Chiapas'. Available at: <www.dfait-maeci. gc.ca/english/news/press_releases/98_147e.htm>.

———. 1998b. 'Canada–Mexico Relations'. Available at: <www.dfait-maeci.gc.ca/mexico/relation1-e.asp>.

———. 1998c. 'Canadian Embassy in Mexico Outlines Role in Recent Consular Case'. Available at: <www.dfait-maeci.gc.ca/english/news/press_releases/98_0903. htm>.

———. 1999a. 'Canada–Mexico Bilateral Relations'. Available at: <www.dfait-maeci. gc.ca/mexico/relatios-e.asp>.

———. 1999b. 'Canada–Mexico Indigenous Cooperation'. Available at: <www.dfait. gc.ca/mexico/aborigin-e.asp>.

———. 1999c. 'Summary Report of the 13th Canada–Mexico Joint Ministerial Committee Meeting'. Available at: <www.dfait.maeci.gc.ca/mexico/meeting-e.asp>.

———. 2001a. 'Stats Summary—Canada–Mexico Trade'. Available at: <www.dfait-maeci-gc.ca/geo/html_documents/81420-e.htm>.

———. 2001b. 'New Directions: Canada–Mexico 1999 Declaration of Objectives and Action Plan'. Available at: <www.dfait.maeci.gc.ca/mexicofinald-e.asp>.

Global Exchange/Alianza Civica International Delegation. 2000. *Pre-electoral Conditions in Mexico 2000*. San Francisco: Global Exchange.

González Gómez, Mauricio A. 1998. 'Crisis and Economic Change in Mexico', in Susan Kaufman Purcell and Luis Rubio, eds, *Mexico Under Zedillo*. Boulder, Colo.: Lynne Rienner.

Handleman, Howard. 1997. *Mexican Politics: The Dynamics of Change.* New York: St Martin's Press.

Heredia, Blanca. 1996. 'Contested State: The Politics of Trade Liberalization in Mexico', Ph.D.thesis, Columbia University.

International Labour Organization (ILO). 2000. Oficina Regional para América Latina y el Caribe, 'Panorama Laboral '99, Anexo Estadistico'. Available at: <www. ilolim.pe/>.

Information Services on Latin America (ISLA). Various dates. Oakland, Calif.

Kreklewich, Robert. 1993. 'North American Integration and Industrial Relations: Neoconservativism and Neo-Fordism', in Ricardo Grinspun and Maxwell A. Cameron, eds, *The Political Economy of North American Free Trade.* New York: St Martin's Press.

Latin American Weekly Report. Various dates.

López Obrador, Andrés Manuel. 1999. *Fobaproa: Expediente Abierto. Reseña y archivo.* Mexico City: Editorial Grijalbo S.A.

Lustig, Nora. 1998. *Mexico: The Remaking of an Economy,* 2nd edn. Washington: Brookings Institution.

Mexico & NAFTA Report. Various dates.

Proceso (Mexico City). Various dates.

Reforma (Mexico City). Available at: <www.reforma.com/national/>.

Publiservice, News Room Archives. 2000a. 'Prime Minister Jean Chrétien meets with Mexican President-elect Vicente Fox to discuss relations between the two countries', 23 Aug. Available at: <http://a-v.publiservice.gc.ca/archivesaug2000_e. asp>.

———. 2000b. 'Amnesty International and the Sierra Club of Canada raise concerns with Prime Minister Chrétien and President-elect Vicente Fox regarding the detention and torture of two Mexican environmental activists', 22 Aug. Available at: <http://a-v.publiservice.gc.ca/archivesaug2000_e.asp>.

Schmitz, Gerald. 1994. 'The Mexican Crisis and Implications for Canada', Parliamentary Research Branch, Feb. Available at: <www.parl.gr.ca/36/ref-mat/library/PRBpubs/bp384-e.htm>.

Teichman, Judith A. 1995. *Privatization and Political Change in Mexico.* Pittsburgh: University of Pittsburgh Press.

———. 1998. *Policymaking in Mexico: From Boom to Crisis.* Boston: Allen and Unwin.

———. 2001. *The Politics of Freeing Markets in Latin America: Chile, Argentina and Mexico.* Chapel Hill: University of North Carolina Press, forthcoming.

15

In Support of Peace: Canada, the Brahimi Report, and Human Security

GRANT DAWSON

This chapter examines Canada's role in peacekeeping and peace-building in 2000. It argues that the latter activity was more important to Canada for two reasons. First, peacebuilding fit very well with the cornerstone of Canadian foreign policy, human security, and could be used to advance that agenda. Second, this activity was less likely to be constrained by the country's limited military capacity, and it did not require considerable resources to be pursued. Peacekeeping remained important, but most of Canada's deployable troops remained locked into the Bosnia operation. As a result, Canada's efforts in 2000 were focused on short deployments—to Kosovo, East Timor, and Ethiopia/Eritrea—and on supporting rapid reaction and reforming operational mandates. The year 2000 demonstrated how the peacekeeping agenda had widened to encompass a broader range of tasks that aim to build sustainable peace and why, because of its foreign policy focus and its resources limitations, Canada preferred to concentrate on the non-military side of peacekeeping.

Canada's strong interest in the scope and complexity of contemporary missions was shared by the Panel on United Nations Peace Operations. Convened in March 2000 by United Nations Secretary-General Kofi Annan, with Lakhdar Brahimi as the chair, the panel was asked to assess the UN's ability to conduct peace operations and to provide 'frank, specific and realistic recommendations' on how it could improve in the future (Brahimi, 2000: viii). The panel was assembled in response to the alarming conclusions reached by a Secretariat report on the UN failure in Srebrenica and an Independent Inquiry's report on its similar lack of success in Rwanda (Annan, 2000a: 1). These documents, released in November and December 1999 respectively, highlighted a number of serious problems affecting the UN's field performance. In particular, they argued that the UN's failures in peacekeeping stemmed from a lack of political will, inadequate mandates and resources, and poor doctrinal and institutional judgements. Both reports encouraged member states to engage in a process of analysis and reflection to address the mistakes of peacekeeping, in order 'to clarify and to improve the capacity of the United Nations to respond to various forms of conflict' (Annan, 1999a: 111; see also Carlsson, 1999: sect. 19). But, ultimately, the Secretary-General decided that a more complete review was necessary. The expert 10-member panel he convened published its findings, known as the Brahimi Report, in August 2000.

The panellists examined peace operations and not simply peacekeeping. The former is a broader approach because it involves efforts to build the foundations of lasting peace. It comprises four interconnected, mutually reinforcing activities: peacemaking, conflict prevention, peacebuilding, and peacekeeping. The panellists agreed that the UN does not wage war—peace enforcement was something it should generally not attempt (Brahimi, 2000: 10). Underpinning all of these components was an awareness that the meaning of 'security' had changed. Since the Cold War, when it was synonymous with the defence of territory, the requirements of security had evolved to include the protection of communities and individuals from internal violence (Annan, 2000b: 43). This, in turn, required the deployment of more complex, integrated missions capable of keeping the peace, rebuilding institutions, and encouraging the parties to reconcile and settle future disputes through political means. In the 1990s, the UN had often failed to meet this challenge, but it was a 'fundamental premise' of the panellists that it must learn how to do so. They believed that three conditions were most important for success: the political support of member states, rapid deployment, and a sound peacebuilding strategy (Brahimi, 2000: 9, 1). Political will had to come from the member states, but the panel was able to offer numerous recommendations for reform of the other two conditions and much else, in areas ranging from decision-making and strategy to operations and the UN organizational structure.

Canada fully supported the Brahimi Report because it complemented the government's own beliefs about security and peace operations, and because it attached considerable importance to UN reform. Foreign Affairs Minister Lloyd Axworthy said that it 'provides a blueprint for action. It is a comprehensive strategy for strengthening the UN's capacity to help people. . . . We will be its strongest advocate' (Axworthy, 2000a). The report was welcomed because its call for comprehensive and robust peace operations, with particular attention to human rights and other peacebuilding issues, fitted well with Axworthy's human security agenda. In addition, reform along the lines recommended in the Brahimi Report, especially after the damning reports of the previous year, was considered critical to the future credibility and relevance of the UN. 'For our part,' said Ambassador Paul Heinbecker, Canada's Permanent Representative to the UN from late 2000 on,'we fear that if Brahimi fails, the UN will fail too.' He told the General Assembly's 5th Committee (Administrative and Budgetary) in November that the 'UN's reputation is at stake here and quite possibly its future as well. . . . [Its] recent failures and near failures—Rwanda, Srebrenica and Sierra Leone—dwarf its successes at least in the public mind' (Heinbecker, 2000a).

'PEACE OPERATIONS' AND THE BRAHIMI REPORT

The Brahimi Report divided peace operations into peacemaking, conflict prevention, peacebuilding, and peacekeeping, discussed how they work together, and made recommendations on how each could be improved. It also stressed that reform would not proceed without firm political backing. The UN would not become a credible force for peace, the panellists cautioned, unless UN member states provided the necessary political, financial, and operational support (Brahimi, 2000: viii). The report was founded on the awareness that the requirements of peace operations have changed. Previously, the UN had been asked to monitor ceasefires or force separations, but now most contemporary missions were being deployed to consolidate and build peace.

The least-discussed term in the Brahimi Report is 'peacemaking'. For the panellists, peacemaking involves UN diplomats, national representatives, or private individuals attempting to bring about a negotiated end to a crisis. Peacemaking was not a major focus for the Brahimi panellists because questions such as whether and how to initiate negotiations are typically ad hoc political decisions.

Conflict prevention is also a political activity, but here the report's focus is on short- and long-term efforts to fortify the foundations of peace. Short-term prevention could involve a fact-finding mission or another initiative by the Secretary-General. However, to be successful, the host state's concerns about any compromise to its sovereignty would have to be addressed, and member states, in general, would have to provide the requisite financial and political support. Long-term prevention seeks to constrain or end an ongoing conflict, for example, by improving the effectiveness of multilateral sanctions. It also involves such problems as underdevelopment, undemocratic governance, and environmental degradation, which could lead to violence if left unchecked and, because of globalization, are potentially threatening no matter where they occur. As the Secretary-General noted in the implementation plan for the Brahimi Report, recent long-term initiatives have reflected 'our collective realisation that, in order to be effective, preventative strategies must address the root causes of violent conflict and the environments that support it' (Annan, 2000c: 4–5).

This realization also extends to peacebuilders, who address many of the same human security issues, although they concentrate on reconciliation and the construction of a self-sustaining peace. Peacebuilders can be given an extremely varied range of tasks, but their major objective is to strengthen governance institutions. This may involve the use of UN civilian police to reform, train, and monitor the local police, and perhaps also to enforce whatever law is in place, or it may mean supporting the local civil society or conducting elections. In extreme circumstances, it can involve the actual running of government and the creation of institutions *de novo*, as in both Kosovo and East Timor. The Brahimi Report argues that an especially critical task is to disarm, demobilize, and reintegrate former combatants back into civilian society. The panellists admit that this is a difficult process, but, if successful, it would contribute considerably to peace by making a return to violence less likely.

Peacebuilders will also be required to co-operate extensively with peacekeepers in complex operations. This type of collaboration should be built into the 'entry strategy' of every mission. 'History', the Brahimi Report argues, 'has taught that peacekeepers and peacebuilders are inseparable partners in complex operations' (Brahimi, 2000: 5). Peacekeepers are deployed to ward off the lingering effects of war, but their departure depends on the success of the peacebuilders. The latter must address a variety of human security issues to build lasting peace, but they require the protection provided by peacekeepers to do so. The panellists also recommend that the UN needs improved procedures to support the rapid and effective deployment of peacekeepers and peacebuilders. This includes the establishment of on-call lists of military and police officers who are ready to leave at short notice, because the first 6–12 weeks after a political settlement are often the critical ones when it comes to the rebuilding of peace.

When deployed, the Brahimi Report argues, peacekeepers should continue to respect traditional principles—consent of the local parties, impartiality, and non-threatening behaviour—but not at the expense of standing aside while gross human rights violations take place. Impartiality is central to the humanitarian principles of the UN Charter, meaning that if peacekeepers see civilians being attacked within their area of operations, 'they should be presumed to be authorised to stop it' (ibid., x). To operate in dangerous environments, where they may be compelled to deter an attacker, peacekeepers require clear, specific, and achievable mandates that specify the operation's authority to use force. Equally important is the provision of sufficiently robust rules of engagement so that the force will not be compelled to cede the initiative to 'spoilers'—that is, groups that might seek to undermine the peacebuilding effort. In line with this, the Brahimi Report argues, the UN must learn to plan for worst-case scenarios, not the best case as it had done in the past. All of this means that peacekeeping forces should be larger, 'better equipped and more costly, but able to pose a credible threat, in contrast to the symbolic and non-threatening presence that characterizes traditional peacekeeping' (ibid., 9). For the more complex UN missions, the panellists believed that robust forces would be needed to build the peace and prevent future violence.

CANADA AND PEACEBUILDING

The Brahimi Report demonstrated how peacebuilders and peace-keepers needed to work as partners in contemporary peace operations in order to meet the challenge of creating sustainable peace. In complex missions peacekeepers can be military or civilian and they can have a role in reconstructing societies torn apart by civil war. However, for the most part, activities that aim 'to reassemble the foundations of peace and provide the tools for building on those foundations' fall under the category of peacebuilding (ibid., 3). According to the Brahimi Report, peacebuilding tasks include strengthening the rule of law, investigating human rights abuses, promoting resolution and reconciliation techniques, and reintegrating former combatants into civilian society.

In 2000, Canada participated in civilian policing, which included providing support for investigations by the International Criminal Tribunal for the former Yugoslavia (ICTY), launched various local-level human security projects focused on promoting dialogue or reconciliation, and financially contributed to programs related to the disarmament, demobilization, and reintegration of former soldiers. Although Canada's military was used to support peacebuilding in Bosnia during 2000, and in East Timor and Kosovo for the first half of the year, for the most part the government concentrated its attention and resources on non-military peacebuilding activities. The tendency to favour civilian policing and humanitarian assistance programs in 2000 is not surprising. As Hillmer and Chapnick point out in Chapter 4, while Axworthy's formulation of human security in 1999 did not ignore the importance of military power to the achievement of security, it tended to emphasize non-military ways of reaching this goal. Axworthy made this clear in a January 2000 press release, which reported on Canada's work at the halfway point of its term on the UN Security Council. Canada would, Axworthy said, continuously push 'for the Council to broaden its concept of security to include conflict prevention, peacebuilding, human rights and humanitarian issues' (DFAIT, 2000a).

Civilian policing advanced Axworthy's human security agenda. It also suited 'harder' Canadian security interests. In July 2000, Canada had up to 202 civilian police in the field, including roughly 130 in Kosovo, 30 in Bosnia-Herzegovina, 16 in Haiti, and 15 in East Timor (RCMP, 2000: 15). At the same time, there were 7,416 total UN civilian police (UN, 2000a: 51). Canadian police trained and evaluated local police forces to ensure they were respecting human rights, and also assisted 'training the trainer' programs. As a part of the UN Interim Administration Mission in Kosovo (UNMIK) and the UN Transitional Administration in East Timor (UNTAET), both of which are peace operations tasked with temporarily administering their respective territories, Canada's civilian police helped enforce law and order and recruit, train, and organize the new national police forces. Civilian policing was a good fit with Canada's human security policies because it could contribute to social justice by punishing human rights violators and restoring citizens' confidence in their institutions and the guardians of public order. Justice was also the principal goal behind the participation of the RCMP and Canadian scientists in UN forensic investigative teams. Canadian specialists were deployed to Kosovo during March–October 2000 in support of the International Criminal Tribunal for the former Yugoslavia (two other teams had been sent in 1999), while a small group of Canadians helped UNTAET to look into possible human rights abuses in March–May 2000. According to Ambassador Heinbecker, Canada strongly supported these inquiries because there 'can be no lasting peace without reconciliation and no reconciliation without justice' (Heinbecker, 2000b).

Policing was important to Canadian national interests of a more traditional variety. Globalization, propelled forward by developments in technology, communications, and trade, has created new vulnerabilities. A variety of non-traditional security threats could flourish in disordered post-conflict environments. In particular, Canadian security is threatened by the growth of Eastern European transnational criminal organizations working in Bosnia-Herzegovina and Kosovo. Some of these groups have extensive contacts with their counterparts in North America (RCMP, 1999). Peacebuilding is in Canada's interests because by re-establishing public policing, the rule of law, and firm border controls, illegal activities such as drug trafficking and the smuggling of people are becoming more difficult. In addition, Canadian law enforcement agencies are able to acquire experience that could be put to use within Canada in combatting transnational crime.

The government argues that policing, humanitarianism, and other civilian peacebuilding activities are areas where Canadian expertise is needed most. This was made clear in a November 1999 press release, which announced a new $100 million package of initiatives in support of the rehabilitation of the Balkans, including $12 million over five years for policing in the form of a Canadian Regional Training and Support Project. According to the press release, Canada 'will focus on internationally recognized areas of Canadian expertise', such as human rights, humanitarian aid, mine action, peacekeeping training, and civilian police training to fight organized crime—but not military peacekeeping (DFAIT, 1999). The government believed that these areas, which could mostly be handled through financial programs tailored to its budget, were critical to personal and civil security. It doubted that the UN would be able to accomplish these tasks unless Canada, along with other states, stepped forward to offer assistance. In the face of increasingly complex and demanding operations, Canada argued, the UN's ability to plan and fund them has 'eroded' (DFAIT, 2000b). One of the government's main goals was to carve out a few a niches within UN peacebuilding where it could help build up the UN's capacity and be seen to be making a useful contribution to the overall effort of conflict resolution.

Canada's role in Kosovo, Bosnia, Africa, and East Timor illustrates how it tried to bolster the international community's peacebuilding efforts with financial programs and the deployment of personnel, although the vast majority of the people contributed went to the Balkans. Canadian support to Kosovo in 1999–2000 included a large civilian police contingent as well as human rights and demining experts, corrections officials, and police trainers. Axworthy commented that all of these people were being sent to help the UN 'address the continuing public security challenge' and to 'facilitate the establishment of a safe, democratic and multi-ethnic Kosovo' (Axworthy, 2000b). The government sought as well to advance the process of reconciliation, and, in accordance with its foreign policy priorities, one of the key areas in 2000 was to reintegrate war-affected children back into society. Through the Canadian International Development Agency (CIDA), Canada provided $10 million for an education project to train teachers and to reform the Kosovo education system. Programs such as this, Axworthy said, were 'aimed at improving the delivery of health and education services in Kosovo.

. . . They are advancing efforts to promote peaceful coexistence and reconciliation' (DFAIT, 2000c).

Canada also contributed monies and civilian and military personnel to assist with peacebuilding in Bosnia. Since 1995, Canada has committed over $93 million to the international community's peacebuilding efforts in Bosnia (DFAIT, 2000d). In support of the UN, Canada provided civilian police to the UN Mission in Bosnia-Herzegovina (UNMIBH). Canadian civilian police served with the International Police Task Force, which is one of the main responsibilities of the UN in Bosnia, the other being to monitor and assess the functioning of the country's judiciary. As mentioned above, in 2000 Canada continued to support stability programs covering the entire Balkan region, but it was also active at the local level. Some of its financial support went into small-scale programs designed to enhance local stability in the areas where Canadian troops were operating. Most of these peacebuilding initiatives, called Civil-Military Co-operation projects, were initiated and managed by the Canadian Forces and funded in whole or in part by CIDA. In 2000, for example, CIDA provided 45,000 Deutschmarks of the total 85,000 DM cost for the construction of a medical centre by the Canadian Forces in the town of Krnjeusa (DFAIT, 2000d; Potvin, 2000).

Canada's peacebuilding role in Africa was confined, for the most part, to financial support of programs that enhanced the awareness of human rights and the need for human security (see Chapter 10 by Chris Brown). In Africa, Canada concentrated on promoting dialogue concerning issues like the protection of children and women in war. To assist with the UN Mission in Sierra Leone (UNAMSIL), $180,000 was granted to support programs such as human rights training for Sierra Leone's police and training for human rights field monitors (DFAIT, 2000e). In addition, Sierra Leone received $12 million for several initiatives, including the establishment of a Truth and Reconciliation Commission and the development of radio programming aimed at reducing conflict and encouraging reconciliation; and $9 million more was given to the Cease-Fire Monitoring Group of the Economic Community of West African States (ECOMOG) for a program dealing with the disarmament, demobilization, and reintegration of child soldiers in Sierra Leone (DFAIT, 2000a; 2000f).

In the Democratic Republic of Congo (DRC), Canada was also active in peacebuilding, but again chiefly in terms of financial contributions. Canada sought to complement its effort to reform the UN

Security Council, so that it incorporated human security into its approach to conflict, with concrete measures to assist the UN in tackling these problems on the ground. According to Axworthy, Canadians were 'contributing strongly to the momentum' that was putting people at the forefront of peacebuilding and conflict resolution (Axworthy, 2000c). Canada provided $500,000 to the DRC for a Joint Military Commission, which was expected to work with the UN in implementing the Lusaka peace agreement, $1 million to help fund inter-Congolese dialogue, and a further $1 million for disarmament, demobilization, and reintegration programs, with part of that sum going to the DRC National Commission on Child Soldiers (Axworthy, 2000d). The government believed that support for the reconciliation process was the most valuable contribution that Canada could make towards the achievement of lasting peace in the Congo. As Axworthy noted in January 2000, in addition to encouraging the UN, 'we believe that our most useful contribution is in supporting inter-Congolese dialogue as well as the institutional development of the DRC' (ibid., 2000d). But considering the size and scope of the continuing problems, both in the DRC and in Sierra Leone, it is questionable what real impact Canada's programs can or will have.

Canada's peacebuilding effort in support of UNTAET was different from the African pattern because it involved 15 RCMP officers and, for six months beginning in September–October 1999, approximately 650 Canadian Forces members. Sailors from HMCS *Protecteur* and the RCMP co-operated to refurbish a building in Dili, East Timor's capital, which the new country's national police will use as their training academy (Henderson, 2000). However, because of the cost of deploying military units and the limited forces that Canada has available, the government did not want the military in East Timor for long-term peacebuilding. Two of the three C-130 Hercules aircraft that left in December 1999 and the subsequent ship and army contingents had returned home by the end of March 2000. Only five Canadian Forces officers remained with UNTAET headquarters staff during the remainder of the year. From March onward, Canada focused on civilian policing and on political and financial assistance to the peacekeeping and peacebuilding process. As UN Ambassador Robert Fowler noted in February 2000, 'the bulk of Canada's future contribution is likely to take the form of humanitarian assistance. Since last April, Canada has provided almost $7 million in support of the United

Nations consultation process, humanitarian assistance and reconciliation efforts in East Timor' (Fowler, 2000a).

CANADA AND PEACEKEEPING

The Brahimi Report was very clear in its discussion of the challenges that peacekeepers faced in the 1990s and likely will continue to face. Peacekeepers have been deployed in conflict zones where no clear victor has emerged or where at least one party is not committed to ending the fighting. The concept no longer means just monitoring force separations or ceasefires, as it did during the Cold War. In the contemporary context, the Brahimi Report argued, UN peace operations generally 'do not deploy into post-conflict situations so much as they deploy to create such situations' (Brahimi, 2000: 4; Hillmer, 2000).

Canada was aware that the UN had repeatedly failed to meet this challenge during the 1990s. The government welcomed the Brahimi Report's frank investigation into the failures of peacekeeping because many of its recommendations were similar to Canada's own reform priorities. According to Ambassador Michel Duval, Canada's Deputy Permanent Representative to the UN since September 1997, the report echoed many of the long-standing concerns of his government, including 'the need for clear and achievable mandates, matching mandates with appropriate human and financial resources, and rapid deployment' (Duval, 2000: 2). While the bulk of Canada's energies were expended on prevention and peacebuilding in 2000, the government also called for reform of peacekeeping operations. It sought to improve rapid reaction by pushing, unsuccessfully, for greater acceptance of its Rapidly Deployable Mission Headquarters (RDMHQ) initiative. Canada also worked to make peacekeeping mandates more responsive to human security concerns, especially the protection of civilians and children in conflict. Canada's largest operational commitments were to Bosnia-Herzegovina, Kosovo, East Timor, and Ethiopia/Eritrea. Except for Bosnia, these were or are intended to be short-term deployments.

During its time on the Security Council in 1999–2000, especially on the two occasions when it assumed the presidency of the Council, Canada sought to adapt Security Council mandates to reflect human security concerns and the humanitarian costs of conflict. Canada's objective was to protect the credibility of collective action under the

UN, which it feared could be undermined if the UN neglected the security of civilians when planning and managing field operations. By working to reform peacekeeping mandates to 'reflect the new realities of global peace which increasingly turn on matters of human security', Axworthy said, Canada sought 'to build a Council for the new century, not the last' (Axworthy, 2000e).

Canada's efforts to include human security in peacekeeping mandates resulted in several notable successes. At its 'insistence', several new missions were authorized to protect refugees, civilians, and groups with special vulnerabilities, such as children, women, and the elderly. In 1999, the mandates authorizing the deployment of the Australian-led peace enforcement coalition known as the International Force in East Timor (INTERFET) and the UN's transitional administration mission that followed INTERFET into East Timor included human security provisions. In 2000, the expansion of the UN Mission in Sierra Leone to 11,100 military personnel, its further adaptation permitting it to use force to save civilians threatened within its area of operations, and the expansion of the UN Organization Mission in the Democratic Republic of the Congo (MONUC) incorporated human security concepts and were collectively, Axworthy proudly proclaimed, 'a first for the UN' (Axworthy, 2000e).[1]

A related issue is whether these reforms really matter in an operational sense. When UNAMSIL was expanded in February 2000, Ambassador Fowler commented that 'the Mission will have the benefit of a strong mandate that provides for the protection of civilians, and personnel levels that are equal to the task. Canada believes this is a sign that we are learning from past mistakes' (Fowler, 2000b). But in the first week of May, UNAMSIL was attacked by elements of Foday Sankoh's Revolutionary United Front (RUF), a rebel movement that had committed grievous human rights abuses—including subjecting thousands of civilians to forced amputations—as a part of its campaign against the government of Sierra Leone. This resulted in hundreds of peacekeepers being taken hostage and the seizure of weapons, armoured personnel carriers, and other mission equipment. Other peacekeepers fled the attacks. Part of the reason for this humiliating setback was the quality of troops sent by member states. The soldiers in question were badly equipped, easily intimidated, and poorly trained, with some not even following basic military procedures such as securing the perimeters of their bases (Perlez and

Wren, 2000: A6). The peacekeepers were so frightened by the RUF forces that they did not stop serious human security violations, such as rapes, murders, and abductions, from occurring (Perlez, 2000: A10). Clearly, incorporating human security language in mandates means little if member states fail to provide what is needed. In July 2000, Fowler argued that the events of May reflected 'the pitfalls of under-resourcing peace operations' and how Security Council decision-making was driven 'by outside political and financial considerations rather than *realistic* operational imperatives' (Fowler, 2000c). This problem—certainly not a new one in the context of peacekeeping—suggests that despite Canada's success in reforming mandates, the Council remains unwilling to support human security in Africa when the financial and human costs associated with doing so seem prohibitively high.

Criticism can also be levelled at Canada, because it did not commit many troops to Africa's complex emergencies during 2000. In August, there were five Canadian military observers and no civilian police (out of a UN force of 12,447 military and 34 civilian police) serving with UNAMSIL. At the same time, Canada's contribution to MONUC was two officers (out of 264 military in total) (DFAIT, 2000g; Dubois, 2000; UN, 2000b: 2). This level of participation was unchanged as of February 2001, although 10 Canadian officers were also participating in an International Military Assistance Training Team in Sierra Leone by that time (DND, 2001). Canada supported these operations through financial assistance for peacebuilding programs and diplomatic pressure for mandates that reflected human security concerns. But Canada was unwilling to send its own troops into the field, except for the occasional observer mission. Canadian military skills in areas like communications, argues David Malone, a former Deputy Permanent Representative to the UN, are still vitally needed: 'there aren't many others that can provide them. It's just that we don't anymore. Signals would still be extremely valuable—we could have been extremely useful in Sierra Leone providing signals, we just weren't there' (Malone, 2000).[2]

The government's decision not to send a larger ground contingent to Sierra Leone was related to the episodic nature of its Africa policy and, perhaps, to its unease about direct involvement in the continent's complex civil wars. For the most part, Canada does not have major trading or other national interests at stake in Africa, and so its attention to the political crises and conflicts on the continent is sporadic and occasioned by specific circumstances such as a humanitarian emergency or conflict. In the case of Sierra Leone and the Democratic Republic of Congo, Canada's involvement, limited as it was, was driven by its interest to support certain long-held foreign policy values associated with the UN and Canada, including human rights, good governance, and the rule of law. The fact that human security concerns are not central to national interests seems to have contributed to the government's decision to avoid a ground role. Its decision not to deploy a larger military force to UNAMSIL and MONUC may also reflect a certain level of unease about military engagements in Africa. As Malone has argued, 'our willingness to deploy is less than it was. Particularly to Africa. Now we did deploy in the Central African Republic, which nobody else much besides France from the West was willing to do, but I think that the general leeriness about Africa that [other] Western countries have is shared in Canada' (Malone, 2000).

The government did deploy significant forces elsewhere in the world. Most important were the new missions to Kosovo in June 1999, East Timor in September–October 1999, and Ethiopia/Eritrea in November 2000. Canada also continued its large commitment to Bosnia throughout 2000. Canada had at least 4,500 Canadian Forces members overseas at all times during 1999, amounting to 5 per cent of its troops, or 3 per cent more than most other countries. The peak was at around 4,700, which was reached in late 1999, but as National Defence Minister Arthur Eggleton admitted, the military's personnel limitations acted as a powerful constraint on what Canada could do (DND, 2000a, 2000b; Leach, 1999). The Canadian Forces can sustain only about 2,000–3,000 deployed troops without considerable pressure being put on the soldiers and their families. When the military exceeds that limit, Eggleton said in November 1999, 'we need to do some of those missions on an emergency, surge basis, and [then] pull them back' (McIlroy and Fraser, 1999: A6).

It was not hard for the military to experience such strain in 2000, especially in the first half of the year when it had large contingents in East Timor, Kosovo, and Bosnia. A considerable number of the forces that Canada had available—about 1,350 in the spring and 1,650 by the fall—were stationed in Bosnia, serving with the NATO Stabilization Force (SFOR). They will also be there for the foreseeable future, owing to an April 1998 cabinet decision that Canada's military presence in Bosnia 'will be of an indefinite duration' (Pugliese, 1999: A2). Eggleton repeated this in February 2001, when he commented that 'We're there now, and I don't see any move out in the short run' (Geddes, 2001: 26). The deployments to Kosovo and East Timor, involving roughly 1,375 and 650 troops and beginning in mid- and late 1999 respectively, used what resources the Canadian Forces had left. In the fall of 1999, the government recognized that the military's commitments were unsustainable. The East Timor mission was planned as a short-term deployment, and in November the government announced that by necessity Kosovo would be as well. Prime Minister Jean Chrétien made it plain, in a letter to Eggleton, that Canada was withdrawing from the latter operation because of 'the costs involved and the lack of capability to respond to new peace and security challenges' (McIlroy and Fraser, 1999: A6). The East Timor and Kosovo deployments, which were fully withdrawn by March and June 2000 after spending six and twelve months overseas respectively, were 'surge' missions that Canada withdrew from as soon as it could.

Owing to these pressures, Canada in 2000 concentrated on Bosnia, while politically it worked to improve the UN's rapid reaction capability, in part because it believed this was the most efficient way to rebuild peace. In the summer of 2000, Canada withdrew from Kosovo, but at the same time it expanded its contribution to SFOR to 1,650. It also accepted an expanded area of operations within SFOR as part of a general NATO plan to rationalize the size of allied forces in Bosnia and Kosovo. Canada's peacekeepers continued to be responsible for the maintenance of a safe and secure environment in the area assigned to them. Within the limits of their resources, they also assisted peacebuilding by providing civilian agencies, such as the Organization for Security and Co-operation in Europe, with communications and logistical support to help with its election supervision task (DND, 2000c). Canadians also took on senior leadership responsibilities within SFOR. On 18 September 2000, Major-General Rick J. Hillier assumed command of NATO's 4,000-strong Multinational Division Southwest, a first for Canada. This position will rotate annually among the division's main contributors, the Netherlands, the Czech Republic, the United Kingdom, and Canada. Hillier commented that one of his priorities will be to assist peacebuilding by seeking to bring indicted war criminals to justice before the ICTY (DND, 2000d: 12).

Canada sought to generate support for its RDMHQ initiative because it saw rapid reaction as the most cost-effective way to restore lasting peace. As Duval pointed out in March 1999, the 'speed with which a peacekeeping operation can be planned and deployed . . . directly affects the efforts and cost the international community will ultimately expend' (Duval, 1999). The RDMHQ concept was a key recommendation from the Canadian report, *Towards a Rapid Reaction Capability for the United Nations* (September 1995). 'The need for disarmament, demobilization, and reintegration', Ambassador Fowler argued in March 2000, 'is felt most keenly in peace processes built on the tenuous trust of weary combatants. It is an ephemeral opportunity that offers few second chances' (Fowler, 2000d).

Without improvements in rapid reaction and the establishment of an RDMHQ, the government believes that the international community will continue to look elsewhere for timely responses to crisis and the UN would become less relevant. For Axworthy, 1999 and 2000 highlighted the UN's incapacity to deploy peacekeepers and peacebuilders quickly enough for complex peace operations in places like Kosovo, East Timor, and Sierra Leone. Not only had the UN been shut out of its normal role as the central military peacekeeper in both of the first two cases, but, he noted with concern, the UN was also having considerable trouble deploying the civilian experts and police needed to fulfil its peacebuilding responsibilities in those territories (DFAIT, 2000a). In Sierra Leone, the UN's deficiencies were made clear when, in May 2000, an intervention by the United Kingdom was needed to bolster UNAMSIL after it had been attacked. Although expanded to 11,000 personnel in February, UNAMSIL still had not reached full strength by May. An attempt by Secretary-General Annan to mount a rapid reaction deployment once the situation started to deteriorate was not supported by any of the Western powers (Perlez, 2000: A10). Axworthy believed that the growing tendency to rely on non-UN help, as in all three of these emergencies, made the UN's rapid reaction capacity even more critical. 'Enhancing the UN's stand-by arrangements, including a Rapidly Deployable Mission HQ capacity,' he argued, 'is vital to reversing this trend.' Despite the importance Canada attached to rapid reaction, he said, 'efforts to implement these forward-looking approaches are, quite frankly, left to languish' (Axworthy, 2000f).

In 2000, Canada sought to generate political support for the RDMHQ, but UN member states, particularly those from the developing world, were unwilling to provide the necessary political momentum. This concerned Axworthy because he saw a trend in the

Kosovo, East Timor, and Sierra Leone crises: the international community was ignoring the need for faster deployments in favour of just getting by with ad hoc 'coalitions of the willing and paying'. This tendency, Axworthy argued, had to be arrested, because the 'voluntary approach places undue burdens on those able to pay, and erodes the principle of universal participation in collective security enshrined in the Charter' (Axworthy, 2000a). Nevertheless, many developing states continued to be unenthusiastic about rapid reaction. Malaysia, for example, questioned the commitment of rich nations to peacekeeping and improved rapid reaction when the developing states were providing the majority of the troops (UN, 2000c).[3] In a discussion of the Brahimi Report's recommendations, Cuba also questioned whether it was in the security interests of developing states to give the Security Council and UN headquarters structures more powers to speed reaction, to the detriment of the General Assembly (UN, 2000d).

RDMHQ did not generate the political momentum it needed to come into real effect in 2000, and as a result, in October the UN General Assembly decided to set it aside for further review. Duval noted in March 1999 that only two full-time positions existed within the Department of Peacekeeping Operations for the RDMHQ, and both of these had been created in 1998 just to get the concept established in an embryonic form (Duval, 1999). Some progress on these matters was evident in March 2000 when, in the Secretary-General's report on the support account for peacekeeping operations covering the 2000–1 UN fiscal year (A/54/800), a revised concept for the RDMHQ was proposed involving the creation of a Rapidly Deployable Management Unit (RDMU). This four-person unit would include the existing RDMHQ positions as well as two new posts. The General Assembly's Advisory Committee on Administrative and Budgetary Questions, in its report on the peacekeeping support account for 2000–1, chose to reject this proposal because the RDMU had not yet been reviewed by the Special Committee on Peacekeeping Operations or the General Assembly (UN, 2000e: para. 24). In response, the 5th Committee of the General Assembly declined the funding request for the additional posts for the RDMU. These developments also made it clear that the RDMU/RDMHQ concepts were still under review and potentially a long way from realization; for this reason, the two RDMHQ posts that had been approved in 1998 were redeployed as humanitarian officers (UN, 2000a: 51). For the time being, the RDMHQ ceased to be a part of the organizational structure of the Department of Peacekeeping Operations.

Although Canada's RDMHQ initiative was not successful, November 2000 saw the first deployment of another rapid reaction initiative, the Multinational Stand-by Forces High Readiness Brigade (SHIRBRIG), to Ethiopia/Eritrea. In theory, SHIRBRIG is meant to comprise a multinational brigade of roughly 4,000–5,000 drawn from the UN Stand-by Arrangements System, which would rapidly deploy a mobile headquarters as well as several battalions and other units into the field. SHIRBRIG is a 'first in, first out' strategy in that it would deploy quickly and stay in theatre for a period of no more than six months, at which point it would be relieved by longer-term UN staff. It is also intended to be used only for 'traditional' peacekeeping missions—that is, operations mounted under Chapter VI of the UN Charter, which do not have the authority to use force and are normally deployed to help facilitate the implementation of a pre-existing peace agreement. Devised by Denmark and the Netherlands, the concept had long been supported by Canada because it believed it could complement its own RDMHQ initiative (DND, 2000e).

The deployment in support of the UN Mission in Ethiopia/Eritrea (UNMEE) involved contributions from Canada and the Netherlands, and in its first test SHIRBRIG seems to have had a positive impact, particularly in terms of the speed with which the mission headquarters was established. Resolution 1320, which authorized UNMEE, was approved on 15 September 2000. The bulk of the Canadian contingent of 450 arrived in December, where they met with their Dutch counterparts and completed mission-specific training. This gap between authorization and deployment does not at first glance seem 'rapid'. Nevertheless, it was considered timely by the standards of senior UN administrators (Mansfield, 2001).[4] The key point is that SHIRBRIG quickly established a functioning mission headquarters for the UN Force Commander, which has permitted UNMEE to make more progress by this point than it could have without it (Mansfield, 2001). Participation in this operation brought Canada's total deployed personnel to just over 3,000, in other words, to the outer edge of the number that the Canadian Forces can sustain comfortably. The embarrassment the government felt over its failure to engage in the DRC and Sierra Leone likely caused it to join in the 'stampede' for a role in UNMEE, a relatively safe 'classical' mission, David Malone has argued (Malone, 2001). For Canada, the role also made sense because it long had been a supporter of rapid deployment and UNMEE was an occasion where words could be put into action, and if all went well, the effectiveness of rapid deployments could be demonstrated.

CONCLUSION

The Brahimi Report is historically significant as a comprehensive statement of the state of the art of peace operations in 2000. It highlighted how the peacekeeping agenda has widened since the end of the Cold War to include a variety of tasks related to the reconstruction of war-ravaged societies. The panellists argued that the way the UN mounted missions also has to change: they have to become larger and more robust. Brahimi identified three conditions that are critical for the success of peace operations: political will, rapid reaction, and peacebuilding strategies. These arguments found favour with Canada's leaders, and realizing the Brahimi Report's recommendations was a key objective for Canada throughout 2000.

Canadian peacebuilding mostly involved civilian policing, contributions to international investigations into human rights abuses in East Timor and Kosovo, and financial support for a broad range of humanitarian projects. Civilian policing advanced Axworthy's human security agenda because it contributed to the re-establishment of public security and justice. In the Balkans, policing also impeded the activities of transnational criminals, who pose a potential threat to Canada. The government also believed it had something to offer and that it could support the UN's peacebuilding functions. The manner in which Canada involved itself in UN peacekeeping operations— concentrating on Europe, where Canada has considerable traditional interests, and largely ignoring direct involvement in the complex African emergencies—illustrated how, when the rhetoric is swept away, direct interests in Europe mattered more to Canada than the Democratic Republic of Congo and Sierra Leone.

Canadian long-term peacekeeping and peacebuilding efforts on the ground were focused on the Balkans in 2000. Here Canada has made a significant contribution, but by 'locking' a considerable number of its available troops into these missions it has limited its ability to respond to new emergencies. Despite this limitation, Canada participated for six and twelve months in the peacekeeping missions to East Timor and Kosovo and it also deployed to Ethiopia/Eritrea. Except for this last mission, none of these operations were under direct UN control, unhappily so from the Canadian standpoint. This further underscores the importance of improving the UN's rapid reaction capability.

Canada's wariness about peacekeeping in Africa demonstrates that the issues or values driving the human security agenda—humanitarianism, the rule of law, good governance, and others—are too vague and generic to justify high-cost, high-risk troop deployments. Clearly, while Axworthy's rhetoric called attention to the importance of human security, Canada's participation in peacebuilding and peacekeeping in 2000 fell well short of what was needed to make a difference on the ground.

In terms of peacekeeping mandates, Axworthy and Fowler successfully incorporated human security into a number of UN Security Council mission authorizations. The UN and non-UN operations in East Timor and the UN's missions to Sierra Leone and the DRC all included human security concerns, such as the need to protect civilians, in their mandates. However, the hostage-taking incident in Sierra Leone in May 2000 raised questions about whether this matters much if UN member states are unwilling to provide the necessary resources or will to operationalize the robust language in these mandates.

Another priority for Canada in 2000 was the improvement of the UN's capability for rapid response, but here, too, it had only limited success. Canada sought to generate support behind its own initiative, the RDMHQ. It believed that by reacting rapidly, the international community would minimize the costs it would ultimately have to pay to restore peace. In addition, a faster, more effective UN would be better able to play a major role in new emergencies, instead of losing its position as the primary military peacekeeper as it had in Kosovo and East Timor. However, because of the unbending resistance of many UN member states, especially from the developing world, the RDMHQ initiative was defeated and has been eliminated from the organizational structure of the Department of Peacekeeping Operations. On the other hand, SHIRBRIG deployed for the first time in November 2000. Canada participated, with a small contingent, because it wanted to back up its previous statements in support of rapid reaction with action.

The government strongly supported the Brahimi Report's recommendations—particularly rapid reaction, peacebuilding, and the need for greater political support of the UN—because they suited its political perspective and the military constraints that governed its response to conflict throughout 2000. The panellists consulted with the government during their comprehensive review, and the Canadian rapid reaction study of September 1995, which is in the report's bibliography, was also of some use to the panel (DFAIT, 2000h). Canada praised the report because its recommendations complemented the human security agenda of its activist Foreign Minister, Lloyd Axworthy. In addition, the stress placed on a wider view and understanding of the challenges of peacekeeping, one that encompassed peacebuilding, was also seen as positive. The government of Canada has come to view peacebuilding primarily as a political and civilian activity, meaning that it can be pursued independently from peacekeeping where Canada's capabilities are limited and declining.

NOTES

1. The relevant resolutions and their dates are: INTERFET: Resolution 1265 (15 Sept. 1999); UNTAET: Resolution 1272 (25 Oct. 1999); UNAMSIL: Resolution 1289 (7 Feb. 2000) and Resolution 1313 (4 Aug. 2000); MONUC: Resolution 1291 (24 Feb. 2000).

2. David Malone was Deputy Permanent Representative from September 1992 to August 1994. He is currently president of the International Peace Academy in New York.

3. Developing nations were providing 77 per cent of the 37,733 UN peacekeepers as of mid-January 2001. See 'In Brief: Around the World', *Globe and Mail*, 17 Jan. 2001. Cited from: <http://www.globeandmail.com/>.

4. Major Jeremy Mansfield was the desk officer at National Defence Headquarters responsible for Operation Eclipse, Canada's UNMEE (SHIRBRIG) contribution. This and the following citation are his personal opinion, and do not necessarily reflect the official DND viewpoint.

REFERENCES

Annan, Kofi. 1999a. *Report of the Secretary-General Pursuant to General Assembly Resolution 53/35: The Fall of Srebrenica*. A/54/549. 15 Nov.
———. 2000a. *Report of the Secretary-General on the Work of the Organization: 2000*. New York: UN, 2000.
———. 2000b. *'We the Peoples': The Role of the United Nations in the 21st Century. Millennium Report*. New York: UN, 2000.
———. 2000c. *Report of the Secretary-General on the Implementation of the Report of the Panel on United Nations Peace Operations*. A/55/502. 20 Oct.

Axworthy, Lloyd. 2000a. 'Address to the 55th UN General Assembly', 00/31. New York, 14 Sept.

———. 2000b. 'Address to the North Atlantic Council Meeting', 00/25. Florence, 24 May.

———. 2000c. 'Address to the NGO Peacebuilding Consultations', 00/9. Ottawa, 29 Feb.

———. 2000d. 'Statement to the United Nations Security Council Session on the Democratic Republic of the Congo', New York, 24 Jan. Cited from: <http://www.un.int/canada>.

———. 2000e. 'Address Accepting the McGill International Review Award of Distinction', 00/02. Montreal, 27 Jan.

———. 2000f. 'Address to the United Nations Security Council Session on Rwanda', 00/16. New York, 14 Apr.

Brahimi, Lakhdar. 2000. *Report of the Panel on United Nations Peace Operations.* A/55/305-S/2000/809. 21 Aug.

Carlsson, Ingvar, et al. 1999. *Report of the Independent Inquiry into the Actions of the United Nations During the 1994 Genocide in Rwanda.* S/1999/1257. 15 Dec.

Department of Foreign Affairs and International Trade (DFAIT). 1999. 'Canada Announces $100 Million in New Initiatives for Kosovo and the Balkans', Press Release, no. 237, 1 Nov.

———. 2000a. 'Canada on the United Nations Security Council: First Year Report', Press Release, no. 13, 27 Jan.

———. 2000b. *Freedom from Fear: Canada's Foreign Policy for Human Security,* 4 Oct. Cited from: <http://www.dfait-maeci.gc.ca/foreignp/humansecurity/ HumanSecurityBooklet-e.asp>.

———. 2000c. 'Canada Announces $10-Million Teacher-Training Program in Kosovo', Press Release, no. 222, 11 Sept.

———. 2000d. 'High Representative Wolfgang Petritsch to Visit Canada', Press Release, no. 92, 4 May.

———. 2000e. 'Canada Announces Over $2 Million in Additional Assistance for Sierra Leone', Press Release, no. 90, 1 May.

———. 2000f. 'Axworthy to Visit Sierra Leone and Attend Commonwealth Meeting in London', Press Release, no. 87, 28 Apr.

———. 2000g. 'Canada Supports Creation of Special Court for Sierra Leone', Press Release, no. 201, 14 Aug.

———. 2000h. 'Canada Welcomes Recommendations of Peacekeeping Review', Press Release, no. 205, 23 Aug.

Department of National Defence (DND). 2000a. 'Defence: Background Facts and Figures', *Budget 2000 and the Department of National Defence.* Feb. Cited from: <http:// www.dnd.ca/menu/budget/bkgfacts_e.htm>.

———. 2000b. 'Minister Eggleton's Reaction to Budget 2000', *Budget 2000 and the Department of National Defence.* Feb. Cited from: <http://www.dnd.ca/menu/ budget/ min_reaction_e.htm>.

———. 2000c. 'Backgrounder—Operation Palladium: Canadian Forces Participation to NATO-Led Stabilization Force in Bosnia and Herzegovina'. Cited from: <http://www.dnd.ca/menu/Operations/palladium/html/op_e.htm>.

———. 2000d. 'Canada Takes the Lead', *The Maple Leaf* 3, 35 (10 Oct.): 12.

————. 2000e. 'Backgrounder: The Origins and Status of SHIRBRIG', 20 Sept. Cited from: <http://www.dnd.ca/eng/archive/2000/sept00/21shirbrig_b_e.htm>.

————. 2001. 'Current Operations', 5 Feb. Cited from: <http://www.dnd.ca/menu/Operations/index_e.htm#currentops>.

Dubois, Aline. 2000. 'Phase two of UN mission in Congo imminent', 20 July. Cited from:
<http://www.dnd.ca/menu/Operations/Crocodile/html/ml3_27_05_e.htm>.

Duval, Michel. 1999. 'Statement Before the Special Committee on Peacekeeping Operations', New York, 24 Mar. Cited from <http://www.un.int/canada>.

————. 2000. 'Statement to the 4th Committee of the General Assembly on Agenda Item 86: Comprehensive Review of the whole Question of Peacekeeping Operations in all their aspects', New York, 8 Nov.

Fowler, Robert. 2000a. 'Statement to the United Nations Security Council on the Situation in East Timor', New York, 3 Feb. Cited from <http://www.un.int/canada>.

————. 2000b. 'Statement to the United Nations Security Council on the Situation in Sierra Leone', New York, 7 Feb. Cited from <http://www.un.int/canada>.

————. 2000c. 'Statement to the United Nations Security Council on the Role of the Security Council in the Prevention of Armed Conflicts', New York, 20 July. Cited from <http://www.un.int/canada>.

————. 2000d. 'Statement on Maintenance of Peace and Security: The Role of the United Nations in Disarmament, Demobilisation and Reintegration', New York, 23 Mar. Cited from <http://www.un.int/canada>.

Geddes, John. 2001. 'The Price of Peacekeeping', *Maclean's* 114, 7 (12 Feb.): 26–7.

Heinbecker, Paul. 2000a. 'Statement to the 5th Committee of the General Assembly', New York, 27 Nov. Cited from: <http://www.un.int/canada>.

————. 2000b. 'Statement to the United Nations Security Council on the United Nations Interim Administration in Kosovo', New York, 16 Nov. Cited from: <http://www.un.int/canada>.

Henderson, Chris. 2000. 'RCMP and Navy Join Forces at the Dili Police Academy'. Cited from: <http://www.rcmp-grc.gc.ca/html/peace-etimor-e.htm>.

Hillmer, Norman, 2000. 'Mike Was Right: The Pearson Impulse in Canadian Peacekeeping', Briefing Paper of the Lester B. Pearson Canadian International Peacekeeping Training Centre, presented to Public Fora in Halifax, Montreal, Ottawa, Toronto, Winnipeg, Calgary, and Victoria, Sept.–Oct.

Leach, William. 1999. 'Talking Points for Chief of the Land Staff, Speaking on Behalf of the Chief of the Defence Staff at the 1999 Atlantic Canada Diplomatic Forum', St John's, 5 Nov. Cited from: <http://www.dnd.ca/eng/archive/speeches/05nov Leach2_s_e.htm>.

McIlroy, Anne, and Graham Fraser. 1999. 'Pulling Troops from Kosovo Will Ease Strain', *Globe and Mail*, 13 Nov., A6.

Malone, David. 2000. 'Interview with David M. Malone at the International Peace Academy', New York, 26 June.

————. 2001. 'Interview with David M. Malone', 6 Feb.

Mansfield, Jeremy. 2001. 'Interview with Major Jeremy G. Mansfield of the Canadian Forces', 31 Jan.

Perlez, Jane. 2000. 'A Doomed Peace: Missteps and a Weak Plan Marred Effort for Sierra Leone', *New York Times*, 10 May, A10.

Potvin, Marc. 2000. 'Soldiers Leave Legacy of Health Care'. Cited from: <http://www.dnd.ca/menu/Operations/palladium/html/ml3_21_10_e.htm>.

Pugliese, David. 1999. 'Chrétien Orders Troops Out of Kosovo', *Ottawa Citizen*, 12 Nov., A1–2.

Royal Canadian Mounted Police (RCMP). 1999. 'Canada Announces $100 Million in New Initiatives for Kosovo and the Balkans', Press Release, 1 Nov.

————. 2000. *Annual Review: Peacekeeping 1999–2000*. July.

United Nations. 2000a. General Assembly. 'Resource Requirements for Implementation of the Report of the Panel on United Nations Peace Operations: Report of the Secretary-General: Addendum'. A/55/507/Add.1. 27 Oct.

————. 2000b. Department of Public Information. 'Background Note: United Nations Peacekeeping Operations'. DPI/1634/Rev.16. 1 Aug.

————. 2000c. 'Lack of Participation by Developed Countries in UN Peacekeeping Missions Raised in Fourth Committee'. GA/SPD/199. Press Release, 8 Nov.

————. 2000d. 'Security Council's Expanded Role, "Double Standards" Among Issues Raised as Fourth Committee Concludes Discussion of Peacekeeping Operations'. GA/SPD/202. Press Release, 10 Nov.

————. 2000e. 'Support Account for Peacekeeping Operations: Report of the Advisory Committee on Administrative and Budgetary Questions. A/54/832. 5 Apr.

Wren, Christopher S., and Jane Perlez. 2000. 'U.N. Reports Rebels Now Hold 300 of Its Troops in Sierra Leone', *New York Times*, 6 May, A1, A6.

The Canada Among Nations Series

Canada Among Nations 1998: Leadership and Dialogue, edited by
Fen Osler Hampson and Maureen Appel Molot
0-19-541406-3

Canada Among Nations 1999: A Big League Player?, edited by Fen
Osler Hampson, Michael Hart, and Martin Rudner
0-19-541458-6

Canada Among Nations 2000: Vanishing Borders, edited by Maureen
Appel Molot and Fen Osler Hampson
0-19-541540-X

Canada Among Nations 2001: The Axworthy Legacy, edited by Fen
Osler Hampson, Norman Hillmer, and Maureen Appel Molot
0-19-541667-8

Date Due

JAN 5 '78			
FEB 23 '78			

PRAEGER WORLD OF ART SERIES

Ancient Arts of the Americas

Ancient Arts of the
Americas

G. H. S. Bushnell

FREDERICK A. PRAEGER, Publishers

NEW YORK · WASHINGTON

BOOKS THAT MATTER

PUBLISHED IN THE UNITED STATES OF AMERICA IN 1965
BY FREDERICK A. PRAEGER, INC., PUBLISHERS
111 FOURTH AVENUE, NEW YORK, N.Y. 10003
This revised edition 1967

Contents

Introduction

The Pre-Columbian art of America has left its most conspicuous remains in the areas where the ancient civilizations reached their highest levels, namely Mexico with its southern neighbours, for which I shall use the name Mesoamerica, and Peru. Some branches of it, particularly architecture, have for various reasons left few traces outside these regions, though others, especially pottery and metalwork, were notably successful in parts of Central America and the northern Andes. Of the two main areas, Mesoamerica is superior to Peru in some ways, and notably so in the amount and vigour of its stone sculpture. On the other hand the dry climate of the coast of Peru has allowed the preservation of perishable materials, especially textiles, of which our knowledge in other places is almost entirely dependent on indirect evidence such as carving on stone.

Apart from two isolated instances of uncertain age in Mexico, there is nothing in the New World to compare with the rich Pleistocene art of the Old. These instances are a dog-like animal head carved from the sacrum of an extinct llama found over 80 years ago at Tequixquiac, about 40 miles north of Mexico City, and some confused scratches on a small piece of mammoth bone which are thought to include outlines of a bison, a tapir and some mammoths or mastodons, from Valsequillo, Puebla.

Artistic development in Mexico cannot be said to begin until after the establishment of settled agricultural villages round about 1500 B C. In Peru, sophisticated designs are found on textiles and on some small carved objects in coastal settlements which may date from 500 to 1,000 years earlier. On the coast of Ecuador, well-made monochrome pottery, decorated in various ways, appeared well before 2500 B C, and it was soon followed by a curious type of hand-modelled female figurine.

7

In both Mexico and Peru there was a great step forward when the earliest great religious centres supported by dependent cultivators were developed early in the first millennium B C. It used to be thought that this led up in both areas to an intellectual and artistic climax or period of florescence named the Classic Period, within the first millenium A D. What went before, starting with the first permanent villages in Mexico and with the earliest pottery in Peru, about 1800 B C, has been named the Pre-Classic or Formative Period, and what followed, up to the Spanish Conquest, has been named the Post-Classic Period. This general scheme is still convenient and will be used in this book as a chronological framework for these areas, but it is neither so significant nor of such wide application as we used to believe. It fits the Maya civilization of south-east Mexico and the adjacent areas well, since this had its climax from about A D 300 to 900, but developments which took place in the lowlands of Tabasco on the Gulf Coast roughly a millenium earlier cannot reasonably be called anything but Classic in character. A climax was reached in Peru at about the same time as that of the Maya, say from A D 250 to 750, but it differed considerably in character, and it can justly be claimed that what the art gained at this time in technical perfection it lost in vigour in comparison with an earlier period. In some places, such as western Mexico, it is not possible so far to detect a corresponding Classic stage, and elsewhere, for example in Ecuador and Colombia, different systems of chronology are more suitable.

The production of works of art was distinguished throughout by great manual skill with few mechanical aids. Stone carving, from the great sculptures of Mesoamerica to the most delicate jades, was done with stone and bone tools and abrasives, and hollows and perforations were made with tubular drills of bone or wood and sand. Metal was unknown in Mesoamerica until Post-Classic times, and its introduction had no effect on stone working, but it may have been used for this to some extent in Peru, where hardened copper was known long before. The wheel was, for practical purposes, unknown in any form, and all pottery was made by coiling, hand-modelling, paddle and anvil, or casting in moulds. This did not diminish its quality, but it meant that there was an absence of essentially wheel-made shapes. Textiles of surpassing excellence were made and many examples from the dry Peruvian coast survive in good condition, but the looms were of the simplest, and many processes could have been carried out only by hand.

CHAPTER ONE

Mexico

It has already been said that artistic development in Mexico does not begin until after the establishment of permanent villages, but it is not always possible from the archaeological record to tell whether a village was settled throughout the year or occupied only at certain seasons. The earliest permanent village which we know of in Mexico, at Chiapa de Corzo, Chiapas, was settled between 1500 and 1000 B C, but some sites near Tehuacán in Puebla may prove to be rather earlier. Solid hand-modelled figurines have been found at Chiapa de Corzo, also well-made white and red-and-white pottery bowls and storage jars, but these are rather the forerunners of the art of the Formative Period than works of art in their own right. Somewhat similar assemblages are found at villages such as El Arbolillo and Zacatenco near the great lake which used to fill much of the Valley of Mexico where Mexico City now stands, but these are now thought by some to be rather later in date, from 1000 B C onwards. The figurines found here are of many types, but all are handmade and most of their features are formed by applied fillets of clay, including the 'coffee bean' eyes found on some. They represent women, who may have an elaborate head-dress but no other clothes, and are very numerous. They are thought to have been used in a fertility cult.

OLMEC

The first well-developed art style is found in the lowland region of swamps and tropical jungles on the Gulf Coast, at the southern-most limits of the Bay of Campeche where Tabasco joins Vera-cruz. The name Olmec has come to be applied to both the civi-lization and the art style, although it properly belongs to a people of much later date. The main centre so far known, which may indeed have been the principal shrine, was on a low island surrounded

1 Mask, thought to represent a highly stylized jaguar face, of serpentine blocks, coloured sands and clays. La Venta, Tabasco

by swamps at La Venta. The nucleus of this site is about half a mile long, and there are some outlying ruins which extend it to about 1 ½ miles. The central area, which has been partly excavated, is aligned along an axis about 8 degrees west of true north. It contains a large pyramid measuring 420 by 240 feet and 100 feet in height, north of which is an elongated court enclosed by low platforms and bounded to the north by a mound. North of this again is another court bounded by low platforms each crowned by a closely-set palisade of natural basaltic columns. Unlike the later stone-faced structures, pyramid and platforms are built of brightly-coloured clays, red, yellow and purple.

This site, with its orderly grouping of great masses of material, gives the keynote to all ancient American architecture, which was always concerned more with external lay-out and the enclosure of space than with the interiors of buildings. If the great pyramid at La Venta and its other mounds or pyramids ever supported any buildings, they must have been of perishable materials and they have left no trace, but even the temples which crowned the most majestic Maya pyramids had small and dark interiors, and not until Post-Classic times were large areas sometimes roofed.

La Venta appears to have been occupied from about 800 to 400 B C, during which time there were four rather extensive reconstructions, perhaps at 104-year intervals to mark the ends of double calendar cycles of 52 years, because such 52-year cycles were important to many of the later peoples and their endings were marked by the reconstruction and enlargement of their monuments. Among the features associated with the reconstructions at La Venta were the burial of enormous quantities of small serpentine blocks; a deep square or rectangular pit was dug and filled up by layer upon layer of pavement composed of these greenish stones, and in three cases a mosaic mask, believed to represent a stylized jaguar, made of serpentine blocks with the openings filled with coloured sands, was laid on top *(Ill. 1)*. Almost

2 Altar 5, La Venta, Tabasco, showing adults with typical Olmec faces holding baby were-jaguars with cleft heads

3 Colossal stone head with typical Olmec features, from La Venta. Now at Villahermosa, Tabasco

immediately this was buried and hidden from sight until the archaeologists found it over 2,000 years later. One such offering, for such they must have been, contained some 1,200 tons of serpentine, and the total weight of it found on the site was estimated to be about 5,000 tons. Its source was 112 miles away as the crow flies and some 350 miles by water. Similarly, the basaltic columns used on the site were brought 240 miles. Other things found were four colossal basalt heads with loose-lipped puffy faces, the largest over 8 feet high *(Ill. 3)*, also several stelae and massive basalt blocks, generally called altars *(Ill. 2)*, bearing carved figures

4   Offering 4, La Venta. Sixteen Olmec figurines and six celts forming a ceremonial group. The jade celts make a background, and one figurine, of conglomerate, leans against them. The other figurines are of serpentine ·or jade

and groups in high or low relief, many of them with similar loose-lipped 'baby faces'. Similar heads from San Lorenzo, another Olmec site, show signs of having been coated with plaster and painted. There were also caches which include jade and serpentine celts, also figurines representing curious sexless individuals with baby faces like those on the large monuments. The most remarkable of these consisted of sixteen figurines grouped in front of a row of six slender jade celts as though taking part in a ceremony *(Ill. 4)*. Study of Olmec art from this and other centres has shown that there is a series grading from baby faces at one end to jaguar ones at the other, and a mutilated carving at Potrero Nuevo, another Olmec site, which appears to show a jaguar copulating with a woman, has suggested that the baby-faced or jaguar-faced monstrosities were thought to be the result of such a union. They have been given the name of were-jaguars. Many of them are shown with notched or cleft skulls, and it may be that certain infants having this deformity were regarded as examples *(Ill. 5)*. On some carvings they are shown as squalling babies *(Ill. 6)* and on others they are elaborately dressed and float in the air holding clubs. It has been shown that the faces may have developed into those of the rain gods in later cultures, hence it is thought that the were-jaguars may have been celestial rain spirits. Some stelae and other monuments bear carvings in low relief showing richly adorned personages with aquiline noses wearing elaborate head-dresses, which may have a sort of chin-strap *(Ill. 7)*. In some cases they seem to be bearded, and all have such strong individuality that they are thought to be portraits. They may be accompanied by baby-faced dwarfs, as on a stela from Alvarado, Veracruz, and possibly on some of the La Venta monuments, which shows that they are contemporary and part of the same Olmec heritage. One example appears on Monument 19 at La Venta in the curve of a serpent, who may

5   Jade celt representing an Olmec figure, combining delicate engraving ▶
with heavy carving. The eyebrow fringes are very characteristic

16

well be the forerunner of the plumed serpent god, Quetzalcóatl, who has such a prominent place in the religion and art of Classic and Post-Classic times *(Ill. 7)*.

La Venta was a remote island site, far from the maize patches [of t]he peasants who supported it, and this may have been a reason [for c]hoosing it as a holy place. It is believed that its resident [popula]tion could not have been more than about 150, composed [of a p]riestly ruling class, their attendants and master craftsmen. [For its] support and the building work of the sanctuary, it is t[hought tha]t there would have been a widely scattered population of [18,]000 people. It would be difficult to exaggerate the stren.gth of the drive, and of the control exercised by a few men over a multitude, which caused these enormous structures to be erected, these vast quantities of stone to be carried so far, and so much time, energy and skill to be expended on these great carvings, all for non-material ends. La Venta, which could in many aspects be regarded as a typically Classic site, seems to have been abandoned and many of its monuments defaced about 400 B C, several centuries before the Classic Period proper began.

6   Reclining infantile Olmec figurine

7 Monument 19, from La Venta, showing figure with aguar head-
dress overshadowed by a plumed rattlesnake.   Now at Villahermosa

8 Dark green jade Olmec carving, unique in showing two superposed faces. The hands, breech-clout and other details are delicately engraved. Only two and a half inches high, its massive effect is notable in spite of its small size. Provenance unknown

Olmec art is essentially naturalistic and not abstract, in spite of the mythical character of the were-jaguar which is the most frequent subject depicted in some form or other. The abstract character of the jaguar mask mosaics at La Venta is a rare exception, although faces engraved on jades are occasionally shown similarly by means of a vertical bar for the nose, a pair of circles for the eyes and another pair of circles for the mouth. The V-shaped depression in the top of the head links these masks with the more usual were-jaguar baby with its cleft head. In contrast, the famous bearded wrestler now known to come from the hamlet of Antonio Plaza on the Uxpanapa river in southern Veracruz is a splendid realistic example which may well be a portrait of an actual person *(Ill. 9)*. Olmec objects, celts, masks and even figurines, generally have rectangular or trapezoidal outlines with rounded corners and slightly convex sides, which gives an effect of massiveness and strength even to the smallest examples, an effect which is shared alike by the gigantic heads and the small jade figurines *(Ill. 8)*.

9 Basalt Olmec figure of a realistic type, known as 'The Wrestler,' from Antonio Plaza, Veracruz

A frequent feature is a combination of carving in relief and very delicate engraving on a single object, particularly on the masks, figurines and celts of the dark grey-green jade which is so characteristic of the style *(Ills. 5,8)*. Reliefs on stelae fill the spaces they occupy in a satisfying manner like well-drawn heraldic charges, but they do not sprawl all over the background in the way that Maya designs do. The figures in reliefs are generally shown in profile with the feet pointing in the same direction, as in the early stages of Maya art.

The greatest concentration of Olmec remains is found in the limited tropical Gulf Coast area where La Venta lies, and this was doubtless the homeland of the art style, but signs of its presence are known from a far wider area. Rock carvings, which could not be transported and hence prove the presence of Olmec artists, are found as far away as Chalchuapa, El Salvador, where two figures, probably warriors, have typical Olmec profiles and were-jaguar faces. A masked figure at San Isidro Piedra Parada, Guatemala, is more akin to the presumed portrait reliefs of the home area on the Gulf Coast. Nearer home, there are examples at Chalcatcingo, Morelos, which include a group of three elaborately helmeted warriors brandishing war clubs, two of whom wear bird masks and threaten a naked bearded prisoner. These again relate rather to the portrait reliefs of La Venta than to the were-jaguars, and like the other two examples they have been thought to show that the Olmec presence in the outlying areas consisted of invading warriors.

More frequent and widespread are small portable objects such as jade figurines, and plaques and celts with incised designs. Many are unprovenanced, but a number come from Puebla, Morelos and the Valley of Mexico, with a notable concentration in Guerrero. This suggested to Covarrubias, the noted Mexican artist and one of the pioneers in Olmec studies, that Guerrero was the original Olmec homeland, but the knowledge now available about the Gulf Coast area has shown that this view cannot reasonably be sustained. From Guerrero comes the one surviving wooden Olmec object, a mask encrusted with pieces of jade *(Ill. 10)*. The

10 The only surviving wooden Olmec object, a mask inlaid with jade from Cañon de la Mano, Iguala, Guerrero

11 White-slipped hollow Olmec pottery figurine from Tlatilco, on the outskirts of Mexico City

Valley of Mexico seems to be the northern limit of the style, but portable Olmec objects are found thinly scattered far to the south, the remotest being two jade figurines with bat-like wings from Costa Rica.

Two hollow pottery figurines which, from their fragility, suggest local manufacture, were found at Gualupita, Morelos, but the most remarkable example of Olmec influence is at Tlatilco, a Formative Period village of unique character near Mexico City. Among many objects of local types, a small proportion of distinctively Olmec pottery figurines have been found (Ill. 11), as well as a few jade ones, and Olmec influence is also seen in the jaguar claws which are engraved on some pottery vessels.

12 Two columns of carved glyphs, Monte Albán I. Monte Albán, Oaxaca. They have not been read, but must, from later analogies, be calendrical

13 *Danzante* with glyph near the mouth. Monte Albán I. Monte Albán, Oaxaca

The effects of Olmec influence were not confined to the spread of carvings and portable objects in pure Olmec style, and other signs of it in the shape of Olmec-derived styles can be detected both in its own time span and later. The first of these is exemplified in Oaxaca by the Monte Albán I stage, beginning about 700 B C. Within the great Zapotec centre of Monte Albán (*Ill. 74*) can be seen a number of stone slabs bearing incised figures of naked men, probably corpses, in loose-limbed, floppy, tumbling postures, called *Los Danzantes* ('The Dancers'), which were set in a stone-faced platform hidden under later buildings (*Ill. 13*). They lack many specifically Olmec features, but the mouths of some are Olmec in character and the overall effect points strongly to Olmec influence. Unlike true Olmec monuments they are accompanied by definite glyphs, carved on the figures themselves and on separate slabs *(Ill. 12)*. Monte Albán I pottery, found at Monte Albán itself and the neighbouring site of Monte Negro, includes incense burners which are decorated with strongly Olmecoid faces *(Ill. 14)* and pots with narrow spouts at the side, a type which survived into later periods. Like most of the later Zapotec pottery in the same area, it is a monochrome grey ware.

14 Face urn of grey pottery, with Olmecoid mouth. Monte Albán I. Monte Negro, Oaxaca

15 Grey pottery jar, Monte Albán I, from Nochistlán, Oaxaca. This type, with lateral spout, carries over into the subsequent stage

Tres Zapotes is a site some 100 miles north-west of La Venta which has given plenty of evidence of occupation during the period when the latter flourished, including a colossal basalt head, but it continued after La Venta's destruction. To the later stage belongs Stela C, a slab bearing a date which, in the Maya bar-and-dot system, corresponds to 31 B C. This is earlier than any known Maya inscription, and if the systems are the same, as they surely must be, it is the earliest dated monument in the New World. On the other side of it is a highly stylized were-jaguar type of face, showing Olmec inspiration but not itself Olmec.

There are many other monuments at Tres Zapotes, but they point more forward to the Classic Period than backward to the Olmec. They belong to a style which is found also on a stela at

El Mesón, central Veracruz, as well on a number of monuments far away on the tropical Pacific coastal plain at Izapa, Chiapas, near the Guatemalan border, at Kaminaljuyú on the outskirts of Guatemala City, and at other places. The style has been named Izapa, but this does not imply that it necessarily originated there and it may well have started on the Gulf Coast. Thorough studies of Izapa, is which a large and important site, have not yet been published, but it is known that the monuments are placed within groups of courts like those normally found in Mesoamerican ceremonial centres and that the earthen mounds surrounding the courts are in some cases faced with cobble stones. Stelae bearing figures and complex groups are found at these sites *(Ill. 16)*, and like the later Maya ones many of them are accompanied by an 'altar' which may, in their case, take the form of a giant toad, a rain symbol *(Ill. 17)*. Human figures and gods are shown with the legs in profile as though walking, but with the body partly turned towards the viewer and the head again in profile like early Maya ones. The chief god has a trunk-like upper lip, apparently an exaggeration of the loose lip of the Olmec were-jaguar, and is a forerunner of the long-nosed Maya rain god. In contrast with the Olmec style, scrolls and appendages begin to sprawl over backgrounds in the manner adopted by the Maya. Monument C at Tres Zapotes shows armed figures floating in the air, and these are thought to be a florid version of the sort of scene shown on some Olmec carvings, such as Stela 3 at La Venta. At El Baúl, Guatemala, there is a stela carved in the Izapa style which bears a date corresponding to A D 36, a little later than the Tres Zapotes date already referred to, on the assumption, which is entirely reasonable, that they are both written in the system normally associated with the Maya at a later date. Covarrubias suggested long ago that the monuments of the Izapa style were permeated in general by the Olmec spirit, but in many other respects it is not difficult to see features in common with early Maya work. The Izapa style is regarded, with reason, as a connecting link in time and space between the Olmec civilization and the Classic Maya which came after.

16 Stela 5, Izapa, Chiapas, showing a complex scene

17 Stela 3, with toadlike Altar 2 at Izapa. The stela is one of a group which ▶
are framed above and below but not at the sides. It appears to depict
a figure accompanied by a feathered serpent

28

THE VALLEY OF MEXICO : *Formative and Classic*

The figurines which were the first feelers towards art at the villages
round the great lake have already been mentioned, and so have
the Olmec influences at Tlatilco. This was an exceptional place
in other respects also, and in an attempt to explain the differences
between it and its neighbours it has been described as an aristo-
cratic village in the midst of ones of lower class. Olmec influences
have also been held responsible for the differences, but Olmec
objects amount to only a small minority of the material, and
there may also have been influences from some other direction,
at present unknown. The chief differences were the greater rich-
ness of the burials and the presence of special types of pottery
and figurines. Brown, black, red and white pottery is found,
with a limited amount of painted decoration in red and white
or yellow *(Ill. 22)*, and there are many forms of bowl and jar,
but the outstanding examples are vessels modelled to represent
fish, birds, animals and gourds in a very accomplished manner,
the best being in polished black ware *(Ills. 20, 21)*. Among the

30

18 *(far left)* Head of a pottery figurine from the Valley of Mexico

19 *(above left)* Female figurine of the Formative Period, Valley of Mexico, modelled in a non-Tlatilco style

20, 21 *(right)* Two polished black-ware vessels representing a fish and a dog. Part of the fish bowl has an unpolished surface, originally tinted red with haematite. Tlatilco

22 Bowl showing diamonds and stripes in brown to brownish grey, the colour of the ware, against a ground of red to dark red paint, the variations being due to firing differences. The designs are outlined by incision. Tlatilco

peculiar forms is a bottle with a spout in the shape of a stirrup, in which two branches rise from the top of the closed vessel and join to form a single tubular opening above. This type becomes most common in Peru at a later date, and there is reason to believe that it was one of several elements carried there from Mexico early in the first millennium B C. One remarkable vessel has the form of a rapidly tapering screw. The chief forms of surface decoration are produced by roughening or otherwise differentiating certain zones, which are limited by broad incised lines, and several processes are used. The zones may simply be left unpolished, or they may be recessed by scraping, or covered with stabbed dots or with rocker stamping, a series of zig-zag lines produced by rocking a curved object like the edge of a mollusc shell over the surface. Recessed areas may be tinted red by rubbing in haematite powder after firing. These processes are used to depict hands, jaguar claws and snakes, as well as geometrical forms.

23, 24   Male figurine wearing helmet and two-headed female pottery figurine with traces of black painting on yellow. Both from Tlatilco

Also of pottery are remarkable figurines *(Ills. 23, 24)*, which are much superior to those of the neighbouring sites *(Ills. 18, 19)*. Many are of women, young or old, naked or wearing a short skirt, and some are painted with lines and patches in black, red and yellow, perhaps applied in life with pottery roller stamps, of which many have been found here. Many are very graceful, some have rattles on the legs and appear to be dancing, some hold a child, and one is playing with a dog. Some have two heads, and some a Siamese twin double head, in which each is complete apart from sharing a central eye. There are men with masks, probably shamans, and others with helmets, also hunchbacks, dwarfs, acrobats, musicians playing drums, and even the first known player of the ball-game, which was played right up to the Spanish conquest, shown with protection on right hand, knee and ankle, but otherwise wearing only a loin-cloth. There are pottery masks, showing human or animal faces, natural or grotesque, the most remarkable of which is divided vertically into half a face with protruding

33

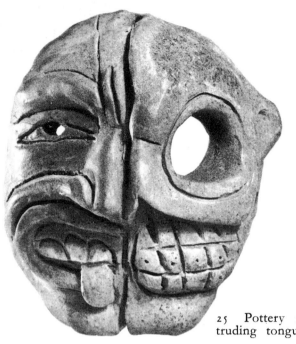

25 Pottery mask, half face with protruding tongue, and half skull. Tlatilco

tongue and half a skull, presumably symbolizing life and death (*Ill.* 25). Dualism of this kind is found also in Chavín culture masks of much the same age in Peru, whither it is thought to have travelled with other things from Mexico. Tlatilco is thought to have been first settled about 800 B C.

After Tlatilco there were no artistic developments of any importance in the Valley before the beginning of the Classic Period. That the idea of the ceremonial centre was present there in late Formative times, the last three centuries B C and the first two or three A D, is shown by the massive tiered conical platform at Cuicuilco on the outskirts of Mexico City. This differs from most later pyramids in having a round rather than a square or rectangular plan, and in having two great ramps rather than stairways for its ascent. It was built of layers of clay and rubble faced with volcanic rock, and it seems to have been raised in stages. It supported successively three superimposed elliptical clay altars covered with a coating of brilliant red cinnabar.

The last century B C saw the rise of Teotihuacán some 30 miles to the north-east, but it was not until the second stage here

34

26 Earlier stage of the main pyramid in the Ciudadela at Teotihuacán, showing feathered serpents with rattlesnake tails and rain god masks. Note also the sea shells indicating contact with the coast

that the Classic Period really began. This great centre, in size and influence probably the most important of all Classic sites, is grouped about a great avenue running at least two miles on a line 17 degrees east of north. At its north end is a great stone-faced pyramid now called the Pyramid of the Moon and near by and to the east of the avenue is a greater one called the Pyramid of the Sun, facing at right angles to the avenue towards the sunset on the day the sun is at its zenith. It was sadly mutilated by injudicious restoration many years ago. On either side of the avenue are the remains of smaller pyramids, platforms, courts and palaces, few of which have been excavated and restored although work on them is now proceeding actively and scientifically. The grouping is orderly but does not attempt to be symmetrical. Unlike most Classic centres Teotihuacán was a city, that is to say the ceremonial nucleus was surrounded by the dwellings of the people, a development which was not possible in the forests in which the great Maya centres were built, and in other cases was prevented by the topography.

Religious architecture at Teotihuacán is based on the principle of the slope and panel, that is to say the pyramids and platforms, made of adobe (mud brick) with stone facings, are composed of steps, each of which consists of a recessed vertical panel with a plain frame of rectangular section, standing on a much lower slope, which is overshadowed by the frame of the panel (*Ill. 27*). In the court known as the Ciudadela the chief pyramid shows an earlier stage in which the panels are filled with monumental sculpture, showing feathered rattlesnakes which meander along them with their heads alternating with the stylized bespectacled faces of the rain god (*Ill. 26*). Sea shells accompany the serpents' bodies, and serpents also adorn the supporting slopes and the balustrades of the great stairway. Like so many Mesoamerican monuments, this was hidden by a later and larger pyramid, whose slopes and panels are plain though they may at one time have been plastered and painted (*Ill. 27*).

The 'palace' groups, thought to have been the residences of the élite, are arranged round rectangular courts. They have open

27 Main pyramid in the Ciudadela at Teotihuacán which illustrates a slope-and-panel profile. The earlier stage is seen in the background

fronts, with the roofs supported by square or rectangular columns, which may be carved with stiff figures in low relief. They are crowned with battlement-like crestings, in which the merlons may bear motifs such as the mouth of the rain god.

Apart from the carvings already mentioned, little monumental sculpture attributable to Teotihuacán has survived. The chief example is the great basalt figure, said to be a water goddess, which looks like a support for an architectural feature. Its outline is squat and is built up chiefly of squares and rectangles, and even the face is almost rectangular, although it tapers very slightly downwards. The figure is clothed in the skirt and *huipil*, a sort of blouse, which are still widely used by Mexican women, and there are large circular ear ornaments. The head supports a rectangular block. It is typical of the severe rectilinear character of high-

28   Stone mask of Teotihuacán style, found at Cholula

land Classic sculpture.   A somewhat similar statue, from Coatlichán,
near Texcoco, now stands outside the National Museum of Anthropology in Mexico City.   On a small scale, the same style is exemplified by the alabaster ocelot-bowl in the British Museum, and by
a jaguar from recent excavations at Teotihuacán *(Ill. 29)*.   Of the
other small sculptures, the most characteristic are the stone masks
(Ill. 28), at least some of which could have been used as false
faces for mummy bundles.   They are softer in outline than the
giant figures and the animals, but the widely-set oval eyes, the
straight or gently curved top, and the delicately-shaped slightly
open mouth give a highly characteristic appearance of great serenity.
The eyes are recessed, apparently to receive a coloured inlay, and
it has been suggested that the form of the top was intended to fit
under a head-dress of soft materials.

29 Jaguar of alabaster found during the recent work at Teotihuacán. A somewhat similar object, a bowl said to represent an ocelot, is in the British Museum

Chronological stages at Teotihuacán are marked by different styles of figurine (*Ill. 31*). The earliest, which precede the building of the great pyramids, share some characteristics with those of the simpler villages by the lake. They have markedly prognathous faces, and the mouths and eyes are formed by applied strips of clay. In both first and second stages broad headgear is similarly shown, and the rare complete ones are dressed in capes and skirts in some cases. In the second period, when the pyramids were being built, the figurines were more delicately modelled, there is less prognathism, the nose is deftly pinched out to a fine point, and the eyes and mouth formed by cuts. It has been suggested that the rectilinear style of sculpture belongs to this stage. In the third stage modelling is much more accomplished, and the faces resemble those of the stone masks. Some examples were made in moulds. They are sometimes described as the portrait type, with little justification since their outstanding feature is standardization. They generally wear only a loin-cloth, and some already have articulated arms and legs, originally attached to the trunk by cords. A few gods accompany the human figures, notably the fire god with his wrinkled face. In both stages two and three there may be a depression or notch in the top of the head, which may be an inheritance from the cleavage of the heads of the Olmec were-jaguar babies. Stage four is marked by a great outburst of decorative detail and a great variety of types, which accompany the invariable use of moulds. Most are elaborately dressed, with accessories like great feathered head-dresses, and some are stylized into squat conical shapes. The ringed eyes of the rain god are of frequent occurrence (*Ill. 30*), and it is probable that most of the figures depict gods of some kind, in contrast with the predominance of human beings at earlier stages. This stage is believed to date from after the destruction of Teotihuacán, which took place about A D 600 according to recent studies, and most of the figurines belonging to it come from Atzcapotzalco and other sites where the civilization lingered on.

Pottery shapes are highly characteristic, particularly a flat-based tripod with straight or slightly concave sides, vertical or

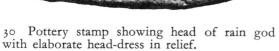

30 Pottery stamp showing head of rain god with elaborate head-dress in relief.

31 Series of figurine heads : *a* first stage; *b* second stage; *c-d* third stage; *e* fourth stage Teotihuacán

sloping gently outwards, and small nubbin feet, made in brown ware *(Ill. 32)*. Some such tripods have cylindrical or slab-shaped feet, which may be hollow. They may have incised designs, or part of the surface may be cut away and rubbed with red haematite, forming champlevé decoration, and the finest are covered with stucco, with mythological designs, gods or priests, formed by inlaying patches of different colours, red, blue-green, black, yellow and white *(Ill. 33)*. This decoration, which is generally called paint cloisonné, cannot by any stretch of the imagination be called a potter's technique, and is very fragile so that few examples have survived intact, but the effect is gorgeous indeed. Some vessels of this shape have a conical, fitting lid with a knob at the top, which may take the form of a head, often that of a bird. Other forms include flat-based jars with a globular or high-shouldered body surmounted by a flaring neck. A variety of this, called a *florero* or flower vase, has a small body and a trumpet-shaped neck of exaggerated height, flaring out to a diameter greater than that of the body. This type, like several others *(Ill. 34)*, is generally made in grey or brown ware.

33 Jar covered with polychrome stucco, the decoration including a rain god face with elaborate headdress. Teotihuacán

32, 34 Two tripod vessels in brown ware with nubbin feet. Teotihuacán. One *(far left)* has applied mask and negatively painted brown dots on black, the other *(left)* has simple decoration made by burnishing part of the surface

An art which was extensively practised at Teotihuacán was mural painting, probably in true fresco, of which some of the most striking examples have been found in outlying 'palace' groups, probably the dwellings of the élite ; some have perished since their discovery but are known from copies. Alongside the avenue is a buried platform, known from its position to be early in date, which has the panels painted with interlaced scrolls, related to Classic carvings of the Gulf Coast, with green roundels on a red ground on the frames. Similarly simple paintings are to be seen on the so-called Temple of the Quetzal Bird-Butterfly, discovered recently near the Pyramid of the Moon. Here the rooms have delicate frets and step designs in white on a rose-red ground, framed by a line from which a row of hooks projects inwards, all in white. Part of the red ground is powdered with dark discs originally of shining brown mica. Among many figure designs, also near the nucleus of the site, are an elaborately dressed warrior in profile with shield and blunt arrows, and a sun disc on an altar flanked by even more richly-dressed priests. Priests and warrior have what must be speech scrolls emerging from the mouth, although they do not bear anything resembling a glyph. A painting which has perished shows a scene in which stiffly-drawn seated or standing figures in profile make offerings to a pair of massive statues recalling the great stone water goddess, before which stand great spider-like pyres. The whole rests on a wavy base representing water. At Atetelco, an outlying group, are jaguars and coyotes in profile, framed by an interlacing border made up of parts of the same animals. At another outlying site, Tetitla, is a pair of stiff, squat full-face rain gods, with vast plumed head-dresses bearing an owl-like rain god mask *(Ill. 35)*, within a frame of interlaced serpents. In the same group is a striking painting, part of which has been removed and is now in the Bliss collection in the United States. It shows a priest disguised as a jaguar, wearing an enormous plume of feathers on his head and carrying a shield and a plumed sceptre-like rattle, approaching a temple along a path marked by footprints. He wears a net costume on which his disguise is mounted, a characteristic of the priests of the Aztec

35 Wall painting, Tetitla, Teotihuacán. Rain god with blue scrolls representing water, and other objects, flowing from his hands

rain god Tlaloc in later times, and the background consists of thin cusped diagonal bands of blue-grey and green on a rose-red ground, from which depend deep fringes composed of long thin triangles of darker red, which has been interpreted as a rain symbol. This painting as a whole is in two shades of red, green, blue-grey and yellow, a very usual Teotihuacán combination, to which black and white may be added and bright blue take the place of the blue-grey. Throughout the whole series there is a predominant interest in water and the rain god *(Ill. 36)*, which may betray a growing shortage as the population increased and more woods were cut down to supply fuel to burn lime for the vast amount of plaster needed in the buildings. The same interest is shown in a painting at Tepantitla, another of the outlying groups, in a style

which contrasts with the static character of the others and must surely be the latest in the series *(Ill. 37).* It shows lively little human figures with speech scrolls, dressed only in loin-cloths, dancing, swimming, chasing butterflies and monkeys, waving branches, picking flowers or resting, in well-watered tropical surroundings, done in blue, green, yellow and pink on the usual dark red ground. Above it are the remains of a rain god, exceptionally florid even for Teotihuacán, standing on bands of complex scrolls denoting water, in which are starfish and peculiar swimming creatures. Drops fall from his hands, and priests attend him on either side. The scene is thought to represent the rain god's paradise, where the souls of those who please him are in bliss.

About A D 600 Teotihuacán was destroyed, but as I have said the culture lingered on elsewhere. During the next two centuries some of the people returned to the ruins as treasure hunters, and a great pit in the court of the Temple of the Quetzal Bird-Butterfly testifies to their activities. That they were related to the original users of the site is demonstrated by the potsherds they left behind.

37 *(opposite)* Partly reconstructed wall painting, Tepantitla, Teotihuacán, show- ▶
ing figures disporting themselves in the rain god's paradise, over which he
presides. He is separated from the scene below by a band of interlacing serpents,
among which is a small rain god

The great Classic centres of Mesoamerica are thought to have been ruled by a priestly class. Their most important buildings were religious, and they have no signs of fortifications, indeed most of them were sited in places incapable of defence. There are no indications of any but local fighting, and no evidence for a ruling warrior class. The centres had widespread contacts with one another and influenced each other, but did not build empires. Although it came to an end some three centuries before most of the others, Teotihuacán was in its prime extremely influential, and may well have been the most influential of them all. Signs of its contacts with the Gulf Coast can be seen in some of the figurines and other pottery of Remojadas in Veracruz, and Gulf Coast scrolls can be seen on Teotihuacán pottery as well as on the mural already cited. Many of the best stone masks of Teotihuacán style come from Guerrero. Much further away, at Kaminaljuyú, on the outskirts of Guatemala City, is a pyramid which shares many specific features with the Pyramid of the Moon, and there are many nearly cylindrical covered tripod pots of pure Teotihuacán shape, decorated with Maya designs in the Teotihuacán 'paint cloisonné' stucco technique. In this case the relationships are so intimate that they can reasonably be explained only by the presence of artificers from Teotihuacán, and probably of those who directed them. Besides widespread evidence of trading contacts in the intermediate areas, such as Teotihuacán pottery on Maya sites and Maya jades in Teotihuacán, there is increasing evidence for the sharing of ideas, such as is shown by the recent discovery of a rain god of Teotihuacán form and style carved on a slab at the great Maya site of Tikal. Some more general resemblances, such as that of the faces on the Classic Zapotec funerary urns of Monte Albán to the stone masks of Teotihuacán, and features like the wide distribution of forbears of the later Mixtec year sign, a rectangle interlaced with an inverted V, in Teotihuacán, Oaxaca and Maya sites, may point to a common cultural ancestor, perhaps in the Olmec civilization.

Teotihuacán is the best known of the highland Classic sites of central Mexico, but it is not the only one. An early building period in the great pyramid at Cholula in Puebla for example, shows the use of the slope and panel in much the same form as that of Teotihuacán. Cholula has had a very long occupation, from late Formative times until the present, when a Colonial church crowns a considerable hill, the weathered remains of the largest pyramid in the Americas.

THE VALLEY OF MEXICO: *Post-Classic*

The fall of Teotihuacán marked the beginning of a period of obscurity, which probably reflects a real confusion in the affairs of the Valley of Mexico. Paradoxically, the surviving documents, the oldest of which were written in late pre-Conquest times, reach back at the earliest to about this period. To the south arose the sanctuary of Xochicalco in Morelos, a hill-top site of complex plan culminating in an ornate platform crowned by a temple, both of slope-and-panel outline. This differs from the Teotihuacán type in that the slope is much higher than the panel, which is crowned by an overhanging chamfered cornice. This reduces the strong horizontal emphasis given by the heavily-framed panels of Teotihuacán, and gives a larger field for sculpture on the amplified slope. There is a facing of carved andesite slabs, having wavy feathered serpents on the lower slope with glyphs and seated dignitaries in the waves, and similar seated figures and glyphs in the panels and on the slope of the temple wall. The decoration shows strong Maya influence, and there is a ball-court elsewhere on the site with the sloping walls found at some Classic Maya centres like Copán and Piedras Negras. This is the earliest known ball-court in Central Mexico. The main buildings at Xochicalco are believed to date from late Classic times and to have continued in occupation into the Post-Classic, which in Mesoamerica was marked by the rise of a ruling military class and the increasing prominence of warfare and human sacrifice. Xochicalco, standing on its terraced hill-top, was fortified with walls and moats, and some of the figures carved on its platform have been identified as warriors. Its civilization is thought to have been one of the strands from which the subsequent Toltec one was spun.

The Toltecs exemplify the early Post-Classic Period in central Mexico. They seem to have been a mixture of peoples from various sources, the chief of whom were originally barbarians from the north-west, but more civilized elements from the Gulf Coast, Puebla and Xochicalco also played their part. Their most important remains are at Tula, Hidalgo, some 40 miles north-west of Mexico City, which was their capital, at any rate in their heyday from about the mid-tenth century to the mid-twelfth (A D 968—1168 in the opinion of some historians, but some would prolong it into the thirteenth century). Along with the settled agricultural life, the barbarians quickly adopted many of the features of the civilization of their predecessors and associates, including imposing ceremonial buildings. The rapidity with which the civilizing process occurred calls for a brief remark, since the same happened to subsequent barbarian immigrants from the same quarter. Many of the original inhabitants of the Valley must still have lived there, and doubtless greatly outnumbered their conquerors, who can for their part have had little in the way of a cultural and artistic heritage of their own. It would therefore be natural to expect the newcomers to absorb much of what they found, though they might well make profound changes in its content. The great change to be seen at Tula is an abundance of signs of a preoccupation with war, and it came to a violent end. After its overthrow it was so thoroughly destroyed that few believed that it could have been the Toltec capital, until excavation revealed its size.

The pyramid which has been most fully studied is faced with stone, and over this was laid an outer facing of carved slabs secured by tenons. It has five stages, with yet another variety of the old slope-and-panel facing, a lower plain slope and a 'panel' divided into two, the upper division being roughly equal in height to the slope and the lower slightly greater. The upper division has a row of passant jaguars and coyotes framed above and below with a plain square moulding, and the lower has pairs of eagles eating human hearts, similarly framed, with a recessed panel between each pair bearing a composite crouching monster crowned with feathers, which is identified as the feathered serpent god

38 Tula. Remains of facing on east side of north pyramid, showing two sets of friezes of jaguars, coyotes, eagles and monsters

called by the Aztecs Quetzalcóatl, in the guise of the morning star *(Ill. 38)*. The whole was formerly plastered and painted. The jaguars and eagles are thought to be the insignia of orders of warriors, the predecessors of the well-known Aztec orders, but the arrangement of the jaguars also resembles the older painted frieze at Atetelco, Teotihuacán. The pyramid was crowned by a temple of which little remains but four great standing figures, 15 feet high *(Ill. 39)*, and four square piers bearing carving in low relief, which must have supported the roof. Each consists of four separate stones tenoned together, which had been thrown down and scattered. The figures are grim warriors carrying spears and spear-throwers, and every detail of their dress and insignia is carefully carved on their massive columnar bodies, down to the knots which tie their garters. Several features connect them with the feathered serpent. The piers are covered with rather

51

39 Tula. Warrior figure and two square columns of basalt. Top of north pyramid

40 Tula. North pyramid with remains of vestibule and colonnade below

stiff, wiry carvings representing Toltec warriors in rather a shamb-
ling attitude, with legs and head in profile and body in three-
quarter view like the much older early Classic Maya figures, alternating with bundles of arrows. Generally, the style of carving
recalls that on the composite piers in the Temple of the Quetzal
Bird-Butterfly at Teotihuacán. A new feature here is a large
vestibule at the foot of the pyramid stairway (*Ill. 40*), which had
three rows of square piers supporting the roof. Behind the
pyramid is a wall about 8 feet 6 inches high called the serpent
wall, carved with rattlesnakes eating human skeletons and crowned
with a cresting of scrolls inspired by sections of conch shells, a
symbol of Quetzalcóatl. Gone are the lively little figures of the
rain god's paradise at Teotihuacán, gone is the exaggerated floridity
of the later paintings of the god himself, everywhere are signs of
that obsession with war and death which was to reach such a
climax in Aztec times.

The god who is most prominent in the art of Tula is the feathered
serpent, Quetzalcóatl, and at that site at least the rain god suffers
something of an eclipse. Confusion has been caused by the adoption

53

of the name by the ruler who founded the city, called in full Ce Acatl Topiltzin Quetzalcóatl (Ce Acatl, One Reed, being the day of his birth), around whom many legends have gathered, some concerning the god and some the prince. He is described as being at enmity with a more warlike god, Tezcatlipoca, the smoking mirror, named from an obsidian or haematite mirror which replaces his right foot, and it appears that shortly before A D 1000 a rival faction of this god's devotees expelled Quetzalcóatl and his followers. They wandered away to the south-east and disappeared overseas, prophesying their return, a story which had its consequences when Montezuma thought that Cortés and his followers were they. It is more than a coincidence that carvings virtually identical with those at Tula appeared on a whole series of new buildings dating from the end of the first millennium at the old Maya site of Chichén Itzá in Yucatán, and that a Mexican ruler named Kukulcán, meaning feathered serpent in Maya, is reputed in Maya legend to have appeared there in A D 987. At Tula itself, it is curious that there are many carvings alluding to Quetzalcóatl but none to Tezcatlipoca.

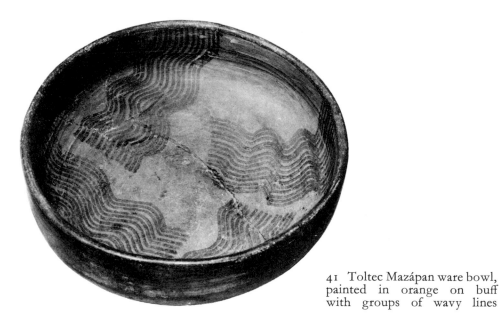

41 Toltec Mazápan ware bowl, painted in orange on buff with groups of wavy lines

Apart from the carvings at Tula, many of which have been mentioned, little remains of Toltec art, apart from some characteristic pottery styles. The chief of these, of local manufacture, is Mazápan ware (*Ill. 41*), orange to buff in colour, generally in the form of bowls which are decorated inside with groups of parallel wavy lines painted with a composite brush. Less important is a red-on-cream ware named Matlatzinca (*Ill. 43*). A trade ware which had a wide distribution at this time was Plumbate (*Ill. 42*), named from its appearance but not its composition, which is ascribed to the west coast near the Guatemalan frontier. Sherds of it are found in the Toltec refuse at Tula. It takes many forms, some of them human or animal effigy vessels, and is grey or brown in colour. It is extremely hard, has a vitreous lustre, and is properly described as a glazed ware. Glazing is almost unknown in ancient America, except in parts of the south-west of the U.S.A. where a dark lead glaze paint may be used for linear decoration but not for covering a surface. In the case of Plumbate ware, there is no lead in the glaze, which is thought to owe its existence to the physical properties of the clay. Pottery figurines continued to be made in moulds at this time, but there is nothing remarkable about them.

The end of Tula was brought about by the arrival of further waves of nomads from the north-west, called collectively the Chichimecs, who do not appear to have differed materially from the nomadic component of the Toltecs. They belonged to various tribes which, with one exception, had a common language, Nahuatl, and as they settled down and acquired some of the features of the civilization of the surviving Toltecs and other inhabitants of the Valley, they set up a number of small states which were constantly fighting among themselves. One group settled in 1224 at Tenayuca, a short distance to the north of Mexico City. Here they rebuilt a pyramid first constructed in Toltec times, which has been carefully excavated to show the eight reconstructions that it has undergone. It carried twin temples on the top, like the great pyramid at Tenochtitlán, the Aztec capital where Mexico City now stands, and it was surrounded by a ring of stone snakes, whose carved heads and tails were united by a body made of small stones in a matrix of lime

◄ 42 *(opposite)* Plumbate ware pot in form of animal with inlaid shell eyes. Trade ware of Toltec age

43 *(above)* Toltec Matlatzinca ware tripod bowl

mortar. They were originally plastered and painted, some green with black scales, and some with red bellies and black backs marked with white circles.

The Chichimecs of Tenayuca were followed by several other tribes, Acolhuas, Tepanecs and Otomís, and there was a great deal of fighting between them, ending with the emergence of the Aztecs as the predominant group in the fifteenth century. This is not the place to say more of the history and social institutions of the Aztecs than is necessary to the understanding of their art. They were great warriors, probably the fiercest of all in Mexico. Their tribal god was Huitzilopochtli, a war god who came to be identified with the sun. He had an unquenchable thirst for human blood and especially for human hearts, to sustain him in his struggles with his jealous elder sister the moon, and brothers the stars, who were gods of the night, born before him of the earth goddess, Coatlicué. Each morning he had to overcome them, in order to rise and pursue his journey through the sky. Above all he needed the hearts of warriors taken in battle, and this accentuated the ferocity of the Aztec warriors. As the latest comers to a well-populated land they constantly had to be ejected from territories claimed by others, and this increased the unpopularity engendered by their barbarity. They eventually settled on an island adjoining the unpromising swampy land on the western shore of the great lake, and there founded Tenochtitlán about 1350. They thought of themselves as the chosen People of the Sun, destined to collaborate with the gods and, by feeding the sun, to prevent the world from coming to an end. They would be better able to do this and to obtain more prisoners if they dominated the other peoples of the world, and it was this more than anything which caused them to embark on their career of conquest in the fifteenth century. At the final dedication of the great temple at Tenochtitlán in 1488, with its twin shrines of Tlaloc, the rain god, and Huitzilopochtli, it is confidently stated that 20,000 prisoners were sacrificed by cutting out their hearts. It would have been remarkable enough if there had been only 200!

It is difficult to point to much that is indigenous in Aztec art, beyond a primitive brutality which is seen particularly in their

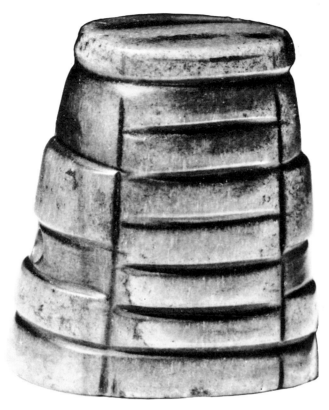

44 Jade showing extreme stylization of a sacrificial temple pyramid. Aztec

monumental sculpture, and which can easily be understood from
what has already been said.   Examples can be seen in the colossal
statue of the earth goddess, Coatlicué, which was found in Mexico
City on the site of the ceremonial centre of Tenochtitlán, and
another from Coxcatlán, Puebla.   The first is a block of nearly
rectangular outline when seen from the front, with two fanged
rattlesnake heads where the human head should be, a necklace of
hearts and hands with a skull as the central ornament hanging over
the pendant breasts, and a skirt of snakes *(Ill. 46)*.   The other has a
death's-head instead of the two snakes heads and lacks the necklace,
but the grinning skull, the over-large raised hands and the serpent

45 Basalt mask showing the skin from face of a sacrificed victim as worn by priests of the god Xipe

46 *(opposite)* Colossal statue of the Aztec earth goddess Coatlicué ▶

skirt give an equally grim effect. In a more realistic but similarly horrific vein are some much smaller sculptures, such as the statuette showing a devotee or priest of Xipe, the flayed god, dressed in the skin of a sacrificed victim, and that showing a goddess giving birth, both in the Bliss Collection at Dumbarton Oaks. In the British Museum are the famous crystal skull and the stone Xipe masks (*Ill. 45*). These and many others, and the innumerable rattlesnakes of all sizes (*Ill. 49*), show a preoccupation with horror and death which is entirely in keeping with the character of the Aztecs.

47   The stone of Tizoc, with historical scenes influenced by Mixtec manuscripts

There were other strains in Aztec sculpture. One of them seems to show the influence of the painted manuscripts of the Mixtecs of Oaxaca, and among these a fine example is the great stone of Tizoc found in the centre of Tenochtitlán *(Ill. 47)*. This is a low cylindrical drum, whose circumference bears scenes showing the conquests of Tizoc, fifth king of the Aztecs, who died in 1486. Few sculptures of this style have survived, and they are divided between historical scenes like those cited, and purely religious or mythological subjects like the well-known calendar stone from the same area. Another group consists of very attractive realistic carvings of animal or vegetable forms such as the giant red grasshopper, some 18 inches long *(Ill. 48)*, the green stone pumpkin, and the basalt cactus, which were seen in Europe in the exhibition of Mexican art in 1952-53. These appear to be purely representational, but in view of the religious character of the equally naturalistic rattlesnakes, a similar religious function cannot be excluded.

48 Naturalistic red stone giant grasshopper, with wings folded and legs drawn under the body. Aztec

49 Miniature Aztec rattlesnake of black stone veined with white, with a human head between its jaws

63

The art of the Aztecs owes a great deal to what is called Mixteca-Puebla art, which belongs to the Mixtec people who lived mainly in Oaxaca, and especially to developments of it originating in the important and already ancient centre of Cholula in Puebla which must at this time have been within their sphere of influence. It is by no means devoid of brutality, for instance there are pictures of human sacrifice in the manuscripts; indeed this and many other features of Aztec religion, such as the gods Xipe, Quetzalcóatl and Tlaloc, had their origins far back in the past, but it is the exaggeration of barbarity which differentiates their religion and was reflected in their art.

The surviving Aztec wood-carvings are a few drums, gongs and spear-throwers, the latter embellished in some cases with gold leaf. They are all strongly under Mixtec influence and there is little to distinguish Mixtec from Aztec work, beyond an observation by Covarrubias that 'Mixtec *teponaztli* (horizontal cylindrical gongs) differ from the Aztec ones in that in the Mixtec gongs the sides are carved with small intricate designs in low relief *(Ill. 50)*, while Aztec ones tend to adapt the gong to the form of an animal or a human being' *(Ills. 51, 52)*. The great war drums, such as that from Malinalco, bear carvings which include eagles of the quality of the best medieval European heraldry.

50 Mixtec *teponaztli* (two-tongued drum), with intricate carved designs. Note the Mixtec year sign on bottom right-hand corner

51, 52 Two wooden Aztec (*teponaztli*). With owl carved on side *(above)*
and in the form of a curly-haired animal *(below)*

53 *(right)* Aztec sacrificial knife, with chalcedony blade and wooden handle encrusted with malachite, turquoise, red and white shell mosaic, pyrites and jet, representing an eagle warrior

54 *(below)* Head-dress given by Montezuma to Cortés as a gift for his sovereign. Mainly of green quetzal feathers, but blue, crimson, brown and white feathers were also used, as well as gold ornaments

Of jewellery and other minor works in metals and semi-precious stones there is nothing to say, since all seem to have been brought from Mixtec territory or made by Mixtec artists. Even the mosaic objects in turquoise, red and white shell, pyrites and jet, such as the handle of a sacrificial stone knife which represents an eagle knight *(Ill. 53)*, and the mask whose base is the face of a human skull, have both, along with others also in the British Museum, been claimed as Mixtec work, but they are surely Aztec in spirit. No pre-Conquest Aztec manuscript paintings have survived but there are several which date from the first years after the Conquest (e.g. Codices Borbonicus and Magliabecchi), as well as some rather later ones when European influence had become fairly strong (e.g. Codex Florentino). The first group includes calendrical matters, genealogies and tribute rolls, and comparisons with surviving pre-Conquest Mixtec manuscripts suggest that their style had changed very little. There are only rather minor differences between them and the Mixtec ones, which will be mentioned in their place. A minor art which can be considered a variety of painting, or even of mosaic, is the feather work in which two

layers of feathers, a lower one of medium-sized feathers and a top one of carefully selected small ones, were glued to a base of soft cloth. A few examples still exist, among them a round shield showing a blue coyote outlined with gold on a pink ground, said to be the name glyph of King Ahuizotl. Rather a different technique, in which the feathers were woven or sewn into the backing, was used for some objects, including Montezuma's magnificent tiara of green quetzal feathers *(Ill. 54)*. Both these examples were given by Montezuma to Cortés and sent by him to Charles V. They are now in the Museum für Völkerkunde, Vienna, where there is also a splendid feather-work mitre, one of a number which prove the survival of the craft after the Conquest.

The chief indigenous Aztec pottery is a thin, delicately made orange ware, decorated with fine cursive designs in grey or grey-black. Even this probably came from Puebla at an earlier date, when it was adopted by the Chichimecs of Tenayuca from whom it came to the Aztecs. The designs are mostly found on the insides of open bowls, many of them tripods on slender feet *(Ill. 55)*, and they go through a series of developments in detail. Four stages have been recognized and wrongly labelled Aztec I to IV, but in fact Stage II belongs to Tenayuca and only III and IV are Aztec. The first designs are stylized serpent heads within borders of concentric lines, scrolls, dots, etc., but by Stage III the central part of the design is generally abstract, though it may take other forms, for example a heraldic-looking eagle, and at Stage IV attractive naturalistic drawings of birds, fish, butterflies or insects may appear. This continued after the Conquest, and a remarkable fragment exists showing part of an Imperial double eagle with a crown over the heads. To Stage IV also belongs a fine glossy red ware bearing somewhat heavier but still delicate designs in black, typically running scrolls *(Ill. 56)*, or in some cases sections through conch shells, which were possibly a symbol of Quetzalcóatl. An imported ware was a remarkable, highly polished, glossy polychrome in red, black, yellow or orange, blue-grey and white, brought by trade or as tribute from Cholula *(Ill. 81)*. It has complex designs such as plumes, skulls and stone knives, which indicate a connexion with the religious cult.

56 Black-on-red cup supposed to be for drinking pulque. Aztec IV. Pulque is an intoxicating drink, made from the maguey plant, an aloe

57 *(left)* Black pottery spindle whorl. Aztec
58 *(centre)* Red pottery figurine perhaps representing Tonantzin, the Aztec
goddess of motherhood
59 *(right)* Red pottery stamp showing a monkey. Aztec

Among smaller pottery products of local origin are mould-made
figurines in dull monochrome ware in the form of gods, temples on
pyramids, and human beings, but they have a mass-produced appearance and are lacking in inspiration *(Ill. 58)*.   They contrast remarkably with the finer things, and they were probably made for use
in humble households. More attractive are spindle whorls in
black or grey ware *(Ill. 57)*, with designs engraved or in relief,
and stamps showing a lively monkey *(Ill. 59)*. This and some
eagles in relief on a spindle whorl are practically identical with
contemporary examples from the Huastec region on the Gulf
Coast *(Ill. 72)*.

Aztec art as a whole, whether indigenous or derived in varying
degrees from outside, is full of strength and vigour. It pulsates
with life, even though much of it is obsessed with death.

THE GULF COAST
The Classic and Post-Classic art of the Gulf Coast had a character
of its own, although it both received influences from the highlands,
especially Teotihuacán, and gave them to it. The key-notes of

highland art are angularity, order and a certain stiffness and severity, whereas the Gulf Coast is distinguished by softer modelling and a great development of curvilinear scrolls. Covarrubias has observed that both of them reflect the character of the modern Indians, the highlanders being suspicious and reserved, and the coast people extrovert and gay. The focus of the coastal plain shifted northwards from the Olmec area to north and central Veracruz, but some stone sculpture, particularly the early Classic stelae of Cerro de las Mesas in south-central Veracruz, can be related to the Izapa style and through it to the Olmec. The area as a whole is rich in sites and in the quality of its art, but few detailed studies have been made and it is not yet possible to relate all its aspects to one another.

What is now called the Classic Veracruz civilization can be exemplified by the important site of El Tajín in the north. It is an extensive ceremonial centre which is far from being completely excavated, but it has the usual features of temple pyramids, platforms and courts, besides at least seven ball-courts, suggesting that the ball-game was particularly important there. In some form or other this was played from Formative times (evidence for it at Tlatilco has been given) to the Spanish Conquest. A heavy rubber ball was propelled to and fro in a stone-walled rectangular court with transverse extensions at either end, so that it resembled a letter H with an exaggerated crosspiece. The game had a religious character, and the courts were closely associated with temples. In some cases it involved the sacrifice of the leader of the losing side, and courts at El Tajín have stone reliefs depicting the game, one of which shows the sacrifice of a ball-player by others who are about to cut out his heart under the eye of the death god (*Ill. 60*). These scenes are framed and entangled in a maze of curvilinear scrolls which are yet subordinate to a general rectangular arrangement. Similar 'inhabited scrolls', to borrow an analogy from Europe, are found on stone discs used as the backs of pyrite mirrors, which occur both locally and as far away as Kaminaljuyú in Guatemala, and unaccompanied scrolls of similar character are carved on stone vases from the Ulua Valley in Honduras (*Ill. 63*).

60 Relief from ball-court, showing sacrifice of ball-player. Classic Veracruz style. El Tajín, Veracruz.

The number of players in the game, if it can be called one, varied widely; three a side was a usual figure among the Classic Maya, but the singles shown in sixteenth century codices and the teams of seven carved on the great Toltec Maya court at Chichén Itzá also spring to mind. They could strike the ball only with elbows, knees or thighs, and sometimes received serious injuries. Those in the codices are shown wearing only a loin-cloth, but earlier sculptured representations are heavily armoured. This protection sometimes took the form of a padded U-shaped leather belt with a separate upright piece in front, particularly on the Gulf Coast where it is shown on clay figurines *(Ill. 61)* as well as on the scenes mentioned

62 Graceful pale buff pottery head, the eyes decorated with pitch. Classic Veracruz style

61 White pottery figurine with some details picked out in black pitch, showing ball-player wearing yoke and *palma*. Classic Veracruz style. San José de Acatenco, Puebla

63 Marble vase carved with scrolls of similar character to those seen in *Ill. 60*. Ulua Valley, Honduras

64 Finely-carved stone *hacha* showing head with dolphin crest.
Diorite, probably originally inlaid. Classic Veracruz style

65 Stone yoke in Classic Veracruz style, representing a stylized toad seen from above, covered with scrollwork patterns. Classic to Late Classic Period

above. The importance of this for our purpose is that some of the finest portable stone carvings from the area are considered to represent these things, those called yokes the belts *(Ill. 65)*, and those called *palmas* or palmate stones the uprights, while a third type, called from its shape *hacha* or axe *(Ill. 64)*, may depict an object attached to the back of the yoke. The carvings are crisp and very competent, and they may be exceedingly elaborate. Yokes have such subjects as a serpent head at either end and a human one in the middle, joined by the characteristic scrolls; *palmas* may have figures or scenes inhabiting a mass of scrolls (a well known

75

example shows a sacrificed man with a gash in the chest, and another has interlace which is almost Anglo-Saxon in character); *hachas* frequently show heads, animals or birds.

A notable feature of El Tajín is the Pyramid of the Niches, which has six stages supporting a temple reached by one steep stairway. Each stage is faced with a row of stucco-covered square stone niches under an overhanging cornice, giving the pyramid a character unparalleled in any other area, and the stairway is broken at intervals by triplets of similar niches and confined by balustrades adorned by step frets. Like pyramids elsewhere, it was enlarged at some time and has an older one of similar type inside it. The main building activity here was in the late Classic Period, but the site seems to have survived the disturbances which marked the end of the period elsewhere, and flourished until about 1200. There are various features of Post-Classic character, such as representations of Eagle Knights, besides the death gods and scenes of human sacrifice, which may date from the later centuries of the occupation.

66 (*left*) Classic Veracruz hollow pale buff figurine of woman wearing skirt and *quexquemitl*, the eyes and ear ornaments painted with black pitch

67 (*above*) Classic Veracruz buff pottery 'laughing head'

68 Large hollow pottery figure of seated woman, wearing lip plug, with the eyes and nipples painted with black pitch. There was formerly a large pendant hanging from the necklace. From El Salto, Ignacio de la Llave, Veracruz. One of a number of remarkable recent discoveries near the boundary between Oaxaca and Veracruz, it shows a mixture of the Remojadas and Zapotec styles

Central Veracruz, near the city of that name, is known for the pottery figurines which abound at Remojadas and neighbouring sites. Starting in the Pre-Classic with entirely handmade ones, the art developed great exuberance in the Classic with the production of much more elaborate hollow figures, of which the faces alone may be mould-made. Among many varieties are women dressed in a modern Mexican fashion in skirt and *quexquemitl*, a pointed blouse *(Ill. 66)*, and they may have features such as the eyes or cheeks picked out with black pitch *(Ill.62,66,68)*. The well-known 'laughing heads' with filed teeth *(Ill. 67)*, which show an expressiveness unique in America, are another product of the Classic in this area. They have broad, flattened heads and wear elaborate head-dresses, and the recent discovery of complete figures shows that they were dancing boys and girls wearing little but an abbreviated loin-cloth and narrow brassière. Gods such as Xipe, the flayed god, the death god and the wind god may be represented in a similar style, with some use of pitch to pick out details.

69 Black-on-cream 'teapot' vessel.
Huastec. Post-Classic

Later pottery styles have been ascribed to the forbears of the
modern Totonacs. They include a striking ware with designs in
red and black, outlined by fine incised lines on an orange background, and a painted type showing leaping animals and other
designs in orange on a black ground *(Ill. 70)*.

The Huastec zone lies to the north of those already dealt with,
and includes the oil-producing region of Tampico. It is a Maya-
speaking area, but is separated by a long distance and great differences in material culture from the main Maya country, so the two
are believed to have been parted at a very remote time. A long
succession going back beyond Formative times has been established
but many of the most striking works of art belong to the Post-
Classic stages, when strong influences were moving between Toltecs, Mixtecs and Huastecs. One result of this is the importance of
Quetzalcóatl, a sign of which is the frequency of circular temples on
conical 'pyramids', in which he was worshipped in his character
of the wind god. A more particular instance is a remarkable red
painted frieze at Tamuín, showing a procession of richly-dressed
priests or gods in a strongly Mixtec-influenced style, which recalls
in a general way the painted lintels at Mitla in Oaxaca although

78

the composition is more crowded. On the other hand, there is a highly characteristic local pottery style, a soft cream ware decorated with bold patterns in black, which is best represented by the 'teapot' vessels with an upturned spout emerging from one side *(Ill. 69)*. Carving in stone and shell flourished in the Huasteca, and Quetzalcóatl was frequently depicted in reliefs and shell plaques. Rather stiff standing limestone figures, partly covered with intricate patterns in low relief representing tattooing or textiles, are found here. Their head-dresses may end in a spike and are surrounded by a great semicircular halo, and some figures have a skull or a complete skeleton carved on the back. Of the same style is the well known 'adolescent', from Consuelo, near Tamuín, San Luis Potosí, a naked youth with about half his body painted or tattooed, a dwarf figure slung on his back, and pierced enlarged ear-lobes, which is generally recognized as one of the finest sculptures of the area *(Ill. 71)*. At the very end of the story comes strong Aztec influence, shown by such things as clay stamps with Aztec monkey designs, and by the birds of prey depicted on finely-designed spindle whorls *(Ill. 72)*.

70 Bowl showing orange leaping animals on black ground. Central Veracruz. Post-Classic

71 'The Adolescent'. Huastec statue with the body partly painted or tattooed, carrying an infant said to represent the sun on his back. Consuelo, near Tamuín, San Luis Potosí

72 Spindle whorl of cream-coloured pottery showing two birds of prey in relief

OAXACA

Oaxaca was occupied in Classic and Post-Classic times, and probably before, by the Zapotecs and Mixtecs. The Zapotecs lived chiefly in the middle of the State around the Valley of Oaxaca, and the Mixtecs in the hilly country to the north-west, whence they spread and took control of the Zapotec area in Post-Classic times.

Zapotec culture is known chiefly from the great hill-top centre of Monte Albán near the city of Oaxaca *(Ill. 74)*, which has already been mentioned in connexion with the Olmecoid *Danzante* carvings *(Ill. 13)*. This forms a great court, oriented approximately north-south and enclosed by pyramids and platforms, with a separate group of them in the middle. There is a great stairway at the north end, leading to a platform bearing the remains of two rows of circular columns, with a smaller sunken courtyard beyond. A stairway and buildings at the south end have not been fully excavated. Adjoining the north-east corner of the great court is a ball-court with sloping walls. All these buildings belong to the height of the Classic Period, called Monte Albán Stage III, dating from about A D I to 900. There is also an older spear-head shaped building oriented N E-S W, thought to be an observatory, near the central axis of the court towards the south end, which is ascribed to the late Formative Stage II, about 300 B C to A D I, and before this come the *Danzante* slabs (Stage I, about 700 to 300 B C), incorporated in a later group on the west side. From Stage II onwards there is continuity leading to a Classic florescence in Stage III, followed by decadence and abandonment of Monte Albán, except as a burial place, at the end of that stage. On the other hand, there is a break at the end of Stage I, which is ascribed to the arrival of new people bringing new features, perhaps as conquerors. The 'observatory' is faced partly with re-used *Danzante* slabs, and partly with slabs of its own date bearing incised glyphs, thought to denote places, each supported by an inverted head, perhaps to indicate its fall.

The pyramid and platform façades of Stage III are based on a variety of the 'slope-and-panel' type found at Teotihuacán, in which the slope is relatively much taller than it is there and the panel attempts to retain its importance by a heavy projecting frame enclosing its top and sides. A number of important stone-lined tombs have been found on the sides of the hill and generally under minor courts on the top. From being simple rectangular boxes in Stage I, they become chambers reached by stone stairways with small rectangular niches in side and back walls in Stages II and III, and in some cases the niches grow into transepts to produce a cruciform plan. They are roofed either with flat slabs, or with two sloping rows of slabs leaning against one another to form a ridge. Some are painted, a good example being Tomb 104. At the far end of this is a life-size face, possibly the maize god, opposite which on the side walls are two priests with the attributes of the maize god and possibly Xipe, accompanied by a macaw with a maize seed in its beak perched on a chest, heads probably glyphs, and numerals, painted in red, blue, yellow, black and grey. The tomb was sealed with a slab, carved on the inner side with an intricate pattern which appears to consist mainly of glyphs. The style of the carving resembles that of the paintings, and is distinguished by rather stiffly curvilinear scrolls, rounded forms and boldly drawn detail, which contrasts with the delicate and sometimes angular detail in the Classic paintings of Teotihuacán. There are other painted tombs, also carved stelae and other slabs showing one or more figures accompanied by glyphs, a frieze of warriors, and similar subjects, all in the same bold style.

Little indigenous work in jade has been recognized, and what there is is not of the first quality, but a number of fine objects which are thought to have been brought from the Olmec, Teotihuacán and Maya regions have been found. Among those tentatively

73 Mosaic mask of jade, with eyes and teeth of shell. Monte Albán II ▶

74 General view of Monte Albán, looking across the great plaza from the north

ascribed to the Olmec area is a splendid mosaic mask representing the bat god *(Ill. 73)*, made of 25 pieces of jade with eyes and teeth of white shell, which was found with a mask of pure Olmec style and many beads in a tomb of Stage II.

Zapotec pottery has some elements derived from the *Danzante* stage, a few Formative types of figurine, face urns, deep bowls with a vertical spout at the side, and above all the use of a monochrome grey clay, but many forms are new. Some of these show relationships to the Maya, but more to Teotihuacán, for example low flat-based bowls which may have tripod feet, and *floreros*, but peculiarly Zapotec are spool-shaped pot stands and, above all, funerary urns for placing in tombs or at their entrances. These

84

urns begin in Stage II as elaborate face jars, which may be a development from those of Stage I, in which a beautifully modelled head with a rich head-dress is applied to a cylindrical jar. Some of these must be portraits and some must represent gods. Finely modelled standing figures without urns may be found in the same tombs, but neither are common. In Stage III the head grows into a complete seated cross-legged figure with the hands resting on the knees, which covers the front of the urn entirely, and the head-dress and ornaments are greatly elaborated. Where the face is human it is standardized to a form which reveals a likeness to Teotihuacán figurines, showing that the individual has been submerged in his rank or office. The urns which represent gods, or

75 Funerary urn of grey pottery, representing Cocijo, the Zapotec rain god

men with god masks, most commonly show the attributes of Cocijo, the local rain god, with a forked serpent tongue and scrolls round the eyes *(Ill. 75)*. Others have their faces covered with a flayed face to represent Xipe, and others wear a head-dress made of a serpent face with its snout turned up and a great bush of quetzal feathers above to depict the maize god. Some of these are painted in rather soft and fugitive colours, such as red, green, blue and yellow, perhaps after firing. These urns become abundant at this stage, and the earlier ones are still finely modelled by hand, with some details cut out on the damp clay with a knife, but the later ones tend to be mass-produced in moulds.

76 Late Zapotec grey pottery vessel in form of eagle's claw. Monte Albán IV

Monte Albán was abandoned about A D 900, but whether this was connected with the Mixtec invasion is uncertain, because the known Mixtec sites in the area seem to be later. At any rate, the abandonment was followed by a stage of Zapotec decadence (Monte Albán IV), during which urns and other grey pottery were still made, a characteristic form being a small vase shaped like an eagle's claw *(Ill. 76)*. Little is known of the early stages of Mixtec archaeology, although their painted books, dating from the fourteenth to the sixteenth century, contain genealogies from *c.* A D 600. There are many Mixtec sites in central Oaxaca, among which are Zaachila and above all the famous site of Mitla, some 25 miles east of the city of Oaxaca. ˙There are five main groups of buildings at Mitla, of which the southernmost, consisting of a court with a pyramid on the east side and platforms on the others, all in very bad condition, is of Classic Zapotec date, but the remainder were built later, either by Mixtecs or by Zapotecs under Mixtec control. One of them, also in bad condition, is like the southern group in plan, though unquestionably later, but no details can be seen. The others are of the 'palace' type (dwellings of chiefs or priests), and some were still occupied when the Spaniards came. They have some features in common with those of Monte Albán, such as panels heavily framed at top and sides, but their general aspect is different. The Group of the Columns consists of two courts touching at one corner. The main one has buildings on three sides and is open to the south, and the other is similarly arranged but is open to the west. All the buildings are long and low, and the effect is accentuated by the elongated panels of stone mosaic with which they are decorated. These mosaics are highly characteristic of the Mixtec stage, each panel having a motif in relief in which zig-zag lines are prominent, such as a stepped hollow square or one of several varieties of step fret, many times repeated *(Ill. 78)*. The main building of this group is on the north side of the north court, and consists of a large hall, with a row of plain columns along its long axis, which originally supported the roof beams. It leads into a small court behind, surrounded by rooms which are lavishly decorated with mosaics like those outside; the roof of one room has been restored with the aid of sixteenth century descriptions, and this brings home to us how dark they must have been. The south court is chiefly remarkable for two large cruciform stone-lined graves centrally placed beneath the north and east buildings and reached by stairways from the floor of the court. In both these courts the buildings are raised on low platforms and do not touch at the corners, which are therefore open. In the other two groups of buildings, there are no platforms and the buildings touch at the corners, so closing them, and it has been suggested that these two features may indicate a slightly later date. The better preserved of these groups consists of three courts joining one another along a north-south line, the southernmost containing the Colonial church, to erect which some of the buildings were destroyed. It is known as the Church Group. The lintels of some of the doorways are delicately painted with figure subjects in red in styles resembling those of the Mixtec painted books.

77 Mixtec stone figurines. Oaxaca

78 The stone mosaics in the hall adjacent to the court behind the Building of the Columns, Mitla

It has already been mentioned that there was an important centre of Mixtec art in Puebla, whence it is sometimes called Mixteca-Puebla, and that the influence of this extended far beyond its own area and was responsible for some of the best in Aztec art. The Mixtecs showed great skill in minor decorative arts, such as metalwork and other jewellery, small carvings of bone *(Ill. 86)* and hard stone *(Ill. 77)*, mosaic, and painting on walls, manuscripts and pottery. Large Mixtec sculptures are practically unknown, although signs of Mixtec influence on Aztec sculpture are evident as has been mentioned.

79 Drawing of Mixtec polychrome tripod pot, compared with interlocking head design on a Chimú textile from Peru

Most of the best surviving pre-Columbian manuscripts are of Mixtec origin *(Ill. 83)*, and like others they take the form of screenfolded strips of gesso-coated deerskin, painted on both sides and protected by wooden covers. One group is concerned with genealogies, marriages, conquests, episodes in the lives of notables, and the like, which are depicted by scenes after the manner of cartoons showing richly-attired and brightly-painted figures in profile, according to standardized conventions, accompanied by a wealth of symbols, from which Professor Alfonso Caso and others have extracted a vast amount of historical information. The chief colours are yellow, brown, red, blue, green, grey and black. An important feature which distinguishes Mixtec manuscripts is the use of a sign like an A interlaced with a rectangle or oblong to denote the 365-day year, although it will be remembered that a very similar sign was used architecturally at Teotihuacán and elsewhere in the Classic Period. Individuals are identified by their name glyphs, denoting the day of their birth in the 260-day calendar cycle. A good example is given by the record of the life of a chief called 8-Deer, which has been pieced together from several books, where he is accompanied by a deer's head, the day sign Deer, and eight dots. He is shown performing sacrifices, conquering towns, capturing prisoners, marrying, having his nose pierced to receive a turquoise ornament denoting chieftainship, and finally being captured and sacrificed. The other group shows gods, associated calendrical matters, divination and mythological scenes. Mixtec wall paintings are of similar styles, but surviving examples are rare. The red-painted ones of Mitla have been mentioned, and there are polychrome ones at Tizatlán, Tlaxcala, which are comparable to the second group of books. A similar style is used for polychrome painting on pottery, and the colours are similar, except that the blues and greens are replaced by blue-grey, and orange is widely used. Among many beautiful examples in this style is a bowl from Zaachila, Oaxaca, with a bird perched on the lip *(Ill. 82)*. In addition to gods and figures like those on the manuscripts, there are symbols such as the section of a conch shell which denotes Quetzalcóatl, and angular patterns possibly derived from textiles, some of which are so like the interlocking head patterns of Peru

80   White Mixtec tripod bowl

81, 82 Two vessels of the Mixtec pottery generally called Cholula Polychrome. The one, from Cholula, Puebla *(above)*, has feathers, stone knives (in upper row), skulls (in bottom row) and other symbols. The other, from Zaachila, Oaxaca *(below)* has a humming bird on the rim

83 *(opposite)* Page from the Mixtec Codex ▶ Nuttall, showing scenes from the life of the Lady Three-Flint, who had previously given birth. Starting at top right, she offers various sacrifices, and ends at top left sitting with her husband the Lord Five-Flower in a house of government

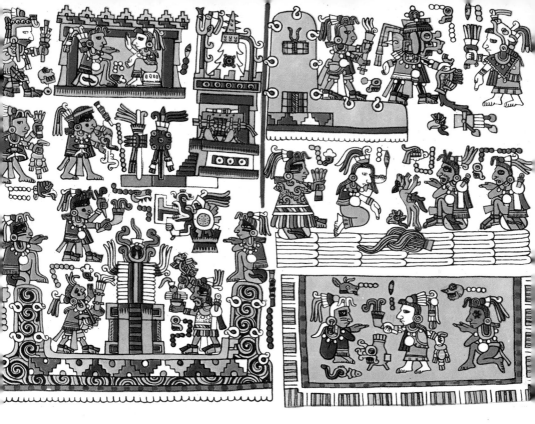

as to suggest direct copying *(Ill. 79)*. (It would have been easy for Peruvian textiles to have been carried to Mexico, in spite of the lack of contacts between the peoples as a whole.) This ware, which has a high polish and is sometimes described as lacquered, is called Cholula Polychrome, after the great centre in Puebla where at least some of it was made. Very typical shapes are spheroidal bowls, standing on a fairly low pedestal base *(Ill. 82)* or pointed tripod feet, and they generally have a collar which is vertical or expands upwards. It is this ware which is often found also in Aztec contexts. Similar tripods are found in monochrome white pottery *(Ill. 80)*, and there is a plain grey ware in the Zapotec tradition, in which a typical form is a flat-based open bowl with tall tripod feet ending in eagle or snake heads. The Mixtec stage in Oaxaca is called Monte Albán V, although there was little use of that site except for burial.

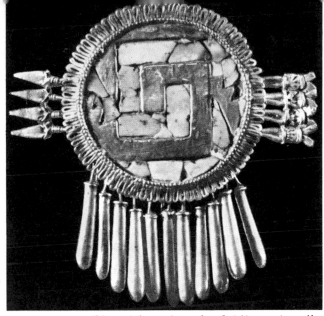

84 Mixtec jewel of gold and turquoise. Yanhuitlán, Oaxaca

The richest hoard of Mixtec jewellery known was found by Caso in Zapotec Tomb 7 at Monte Albán, which had been re-used for a Mixtec burial. It contained jade, turquoise, rock-crystal, shell, bone, gold, silver and copper, beautifully worked. A gold pendant 4 ¹/₂ inches high, shows a head with a rich head-dress, issuing from a pair of plaques bearing two Mixtec year symbols and the glyphs of the Mixtec year 11 House, its Zapotec equivalent 10 Wind, and the day 2 Knife. Another consists of 4 plaques hanging from one another by rings, with danglers and 4 bells below *(Ill. 85)*; the top plaque shows a ball-court with two players and a skull between, the second is a solar disc, the third has a moon glyph and the fourth an earth symbol. There was also a thick gold mask of the god Xipe, 3 ¼ inches high. This elaborate work was done by the cire-perdue process, still skilfully practised in Oaxaca. A famous Mixtec jewel *(Ill. 84)*, from Yanhuitlán, takes the form of a round gold shield with four arrows placed horizontally behind it and little bells hanging below, which bears a gold step fret set off by a similar form interlocking with it in turquoise mosaic. A replica of this was presented by the Mexican Government to H. M. the Queen as a wedding present. Returning to Tomb 7, other treasures which it contained were gold rings and nose ornaments, bead necklaces of shell, turquoise and large

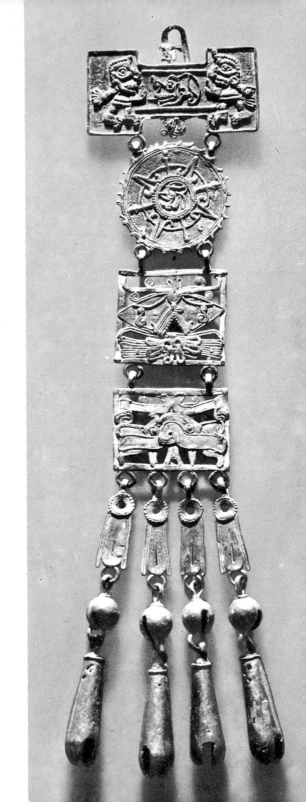

85 Mixtec gold pendant.
Tomb 7, Monte Albán

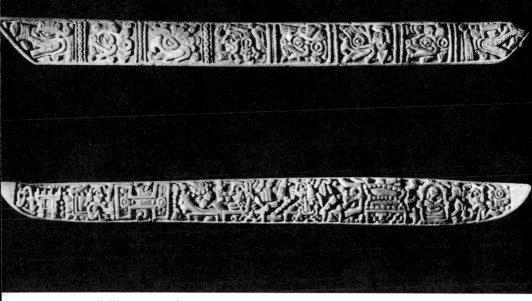

86 Two out of about 30 carved jaguar bones showing calendrical and other subjects. Mixtec. Tomb 7, Monte Albán

pearls, a crystal cup, and above all over 30 delicately carved bones *(Ill. 86)* showing the birth of a chief, animal heads, calendar signs in Mixtec style and other subjects, some of them set off by a background of turquoise mosaic. Among many other things were the remains of a human skull covered with turquoise mosaic, which supports the suggestion made in connexion with the Aztecs, that the famous 'Aztec' mosaics in the British Museum and elsewhere were Mixtec work.

THE WEST

Western Mexico is a large area with many facets; it lacks great ceremonial centres and stone monuments, and the chronology is little known in detail, but it is doubtful if the framework of Formative, Classic and Post-Classic has much meaning there, since work of Formative aspect may well have persisted through Classic times elsewhere. The chief artistic expressions in this area were

96

87 Bowls with red and black decoration on cream slip. Late Formative.
Chupícuaro, Guanajuato

in pottery and small stone carvings, the latter particularly in Guerrero. The potters were concerned more with daily life than with
the religions of other parts of Mexico, and we look in vain for
the feathered serpent, Tlaloc, Xipe, Huitzilopochtli and the rest.

On the northern threshold of the area, at Chupícuaro, Guanajuato, a cemetery of late Formative date has produced a striking
pottery style (*Ill. 87*), mainly bowls of various forms which
may have pedestal or tripod feet, decorated with geometrical
designs in red and black on cream. Stepped or zig-zag forms
are characteristic. There are large hollow figurines similarly painted,
as well as a small, well-modelled, solid type ('pretty ladies'), with
large heads and applied details which include exaggerated slanting
eyes (*Ill. 88*). They may have a touch of red or white paint here
and there.

Further west is Michoacán, which in late post-Classic times
was the home of the Tarascans, whose name has been mistakenly

97

88 Solid figurine, of red pottery, with touches of red and white paint. Late Formative. Chupícuaro, Guanajuato

89 *(centre)* Highly stylized face of dark green stone. Mescala or Guerrero style

90 *(right)* Olmecoid red pottery head from Iguala, Guerrero

given to much west Mexican art. At the time of the Conquest they were known as skilled metal-workers and jewellers, who produced such things as gold and copper bells, needles and fish hooks, and obsidian ear-plugs encrusted with turquoise mosaic of great delicacy. The local variety of pyramid was T-shaped in plan, with a central stairway on the cross bar and a round platform at the foot of the upright, on which was a circular shrine.

Guerrero is an area abounding in hard rocks, where communications are difficult and little is known about the archaeology. It has produced many small carvings in hard stones of many colours, including serpentine and jade, in the form of heads, masks, figurines, animals and temples, at least some of which are of Pre-Classic date. Details are shown by means of grooves or slits in preference to drilled holes, though these are not absent. The result is a highly characteristic local style with a marked abstract effect *(Ill. 89)*, which is sometimes called Mescala after a place near which many examples have been found, but Guerrero is preferable because it fits their range better. The masks and figurines may approach stone celts of various forms in outline, and some indeed are modified

98

celts. In addition to those of the local style, there are figurines and masks of Olmec and Teotihuacán styles, and some hybrids which have been called Guerrero-Olmec or Guerrero-Teotihuacán, in many of which the local element quite overshadows any outside one. The true Olmec and Teotihuacán ones have given rise to much speculation as to whether Guerrero was the place of origin of these styles, but it is now thought more likely that the local specialist stone-carvers copied them from models perhaps of pottery, provided by outside clients. Indigenous pottery figurines with some Olmecoid features have been found (Ill. 90), but they are not really typical of that style.

The chief remaining areas in the west are the states of Nayarít, Jalisco and Colima, which can for our purposes be considered as a whole, although each has its special features. All are noted for their large hollow pottery figurines, which are vigorously hand-modelled and spontaneous in character. Those of Nayarít have an element of rugged caricature, with massive features and thin arms. There are individual figures and scenes of everyday life, such as a woman giving a man a drink, and there are groups of solid figures of smaller size, one of them showing a ball-game watched by an informal-looking audience. Into this class fall a number of examples of a man, in some cases highly stylized, lying on a bed and apparently bound to it *(Ill. 92)*. From this area also come some attractive pottery vessels modelled to represent vegetable forms *(Ill. 93)*. The figures of Colima *(Ill. 96)* are also concerned with daily life, but are softer and more rounded in contour than the rugged ones of Nayarít. They are smoothly finished and some have a red slip. Subjects include men and women sitting on the ground or on stools, standing, and drinking, also hunchbacks, warriors and prisoners. Most famous are the fat, hairless Colima dogs *(Ill. 94)*, which may be shown in a variety of natural attitudes, but some wear a mask and there is a pair dancing together, one fat and the other with the backbone showing and the ribs indicated by incised lines to give an effect of emaciation. Some of these dogs are jars, and they and some other jars have a narrow spout which emerges at a slant but is cut off horizontally. As in Nayarít, there are solid single figurines *(Ill. 95)* and groups, one of which has a ring of women dancing round three

91 Large red-slipped tripod jar, in the shape of a gourd, the feet in the form of birds, probably parrots. Colima

92 Man bound
to a bed. Red
on yellow slip.
Nayarít

93 Red-slipped pot in the form
of a flattened gourd. Nayarít

94 Jar in the form of a fat hairless
dog of red ware. Colima

seated male musicians. There are large bowls with constricted mouths surrounded by flaring lips, and even the plain spherical ones give an effect of elegance, but many are modelled to represent fruits, snails, heads and other forms in a very attractive way *(Ill. 91)*. Jalisco is intermediate both in position and character. Good examples of the figure-modelling are given by armoured warriors brandishing a club or an arrow with an effect of purpose which draws the eye away from such details as the incompetent handling of the feet—a defect shared by many other figures in this region. All in all, the modelled work of these three states can justly be described as folk art.

95 *(above)* Solid figurine of buff pottery. Colima

96 *(right)* Large hollow pottery figure of man blowing conch shell trumpet. Colima

CHAPTER TWO

The Maya

Formative and Classic

It is difficult to speak of Classic Maya art without some use of superlatives because it includes so much work of surpassing excellence. It is chiefly seen in a large number of ceremonial centres of different degrees of influence and importance, containing the usual elements of platforms, temple pyramids, palaces (probably the dwellings of rulers and priests), and ball-courts *(Ills. 98, 99)*, ranged around open spaces, with the addition of corbelled vaults *(Ill. 97)* as a roofing method and a large number of stelae, which are rectangular columns or slabs of stone. As in other areas, the emphasis is on the outsides of buildings and their disposition in space, for temples and rooms were small, dark and cramped in comparison with the volume of masonry used in their construction. The centres are distributed over a wide area, from north-west Honduras, through the lowland forests of Campeche and the Guatemalan Petén region, to the open plains of Yucatán, and they differ greatly in detail while sharing many features in common, just as their builders spoke several dialects of one language. There is reason to believe that each of the more important centres had its own sphere of influence which included a number of smaller ones, but that they themselves were independent of one another. Their rulers are thought to have been high priests, in friendly contact with one another and with Teotihuacán and other great centres, for reasons already given in the chapter on the Valley of Mexico. In addition they probably collaborated among themselves in devising and correcting their calendar, which was a great feature of Maya culture. It shared a 52-year cycle with other Mesoamerican civilizations, but added further terms and cycles which were used by no one else, including a count of days from a beginning far back in time. Many stelae were erected to mark period endings in this count, and the dates in it and in cycles moving

97 Copán, Honduras. Corbelled vault from the temple on the side of the ball-court.   Classic Maya

concurrently with it were recorded on them in hieroglyphic inscriptions of great complexity, which formed an important part of the decoration.   The writing is not alphabetic, and insofar as it has been deciphered it can best be described as a form of pictorial rebus writing.

Maya art reflects the Maya character, and is serene, formal and impersonal.   From its beginnings to the end of Classic times it was based on a stable culture, which was undisturbed by wars against peoples of similar status.   There were constant rebuildings, involving enlargements and the burial of old pyramids under new, as in other Mesoamerican cultures, and there were changes in style.   Nevertheless, there was a high degree of continuity. Stone sculpture was one of the chief media of expression, and the quantity which remains makes it particularly suitable as an index of stylistic development.   It is seen typically on the stelae, on which the chief feature is a single figure of immense dignity, heavily loaded with ornament (*Ill. 100*).   Whether these are gods,

98 *(above)* Copán, Honduras. Looking across the ball-court to the main plaza, with the Hieroglyphic Stairway in right foreground. Classic Maya. Note sloping walls of court

99 *(below)* Chichén Itzá, Yucatán. Post-Classic Maya ball-court. Note vertical walls

priests impersonating them, or rulers is uncertain, but most examples give the impression that the office mattered more than the man. Although the majority were erected to mark steps in the calendar, some stelae are now thought to have been put up at significant points in the life of a ruler. There is little impression of action and groups are rare, although minor figures on a smaller scale, such as attendants or prisoners, may accompany the principal one. Motifs and symbols are comparatively constant, changes occur slowly, there are few signs of individual artists' mannerisms and many of conformity to a rigid system. On the other hand, there are many differences between the various centres, thus the figures may be shown in very low flat relief, as on some thin, tombstone-like stelae at Tikal, and at the other extreme they may be in such high relief as to stand nearly clear of the stela, as in some at Copán. Some plain stelae may have been plastered and painted, and the intricacies of some of the later carved ones may well have been clarified by polychrome painting.

The length of the Classic Maya period was originally defined by the calendar cycles during which dated monuments were known to have been erected, namely from A D 317 to 889 in our calendar. Its beginning is further marked by the introduction of polychrome pottery and the corbelled vault as a roof structure, so there is reason to retain this date, although an earlier stela dated A D 292 and substantial ceremonial buildings several centuries older have been found at Tikal in the Petén. A notable Pre-Classic stone pyramid thickly coated with stucco was found within a later pyramid at Uaxactún, also in the Petén, and this was decorated with large stucco masks of Olmec affinities, which supports the idea already mentioned that Maya art was at least partly rooted in the Olmec.

Maya sculpture has been the subject of an important study by Miss Tatiana Proskouriakoff, to which any discussion is bound to owe much. She shows that the earliest stelae are related to other styles, like Izapa, and have the main figure with head and feet in profile and the body partly turned towards the viewer, an attitude seen also in miniature on the famous jade plaque, the

100 Stela D, Quiriguá, Guatemala. Showing majestic figure of a god or ruler. Late Classic Maya, probably erected A D 766 ▶

Leiden plate. Early in the Classic, in the fifth century, the same attitude persists but the dress and ornaments become more specifically Maya, and attributes like the serpent bar, a kind of sceptre supported on both arms, are developed. There was a gap from 534 to 593 when scarcely any dated stelae were dedicated, after which there was an increasing interest in detail at the expense of the main subject. The figure stands with his body facing the viewer, with both feet splayed out, but his head is generally in profile at first. Elaboration of detail continued to increase, but the subject remained static until about 750, after which for another 60 years came what is called the Dynamic Phase, in which an effect of movement is produced on some carvings largely by means of asymmetrical poses, accompanied by increasingly large feathered head-dresses and other appendages. After 810, decadence set in and was marked by excessive flamboyance—sandals with great sprouting tassels which would make it impossible to walk, and so on. This continued until the abandonment of many of the great centres by the end of the ninth century.

Each of the greater centres excelled in some feature of architecture or sculpture, and in Yucatán and Campeche are architectural styles which extend over a considerable area. Tikal, which is the largest of them all, is known for the great height of its pyramids, the towering, intricately carved roof combs of the temples which crown them, and the carved wooden lintels over the temple doors. The fine series of high relief stelae for which Copán in Honduras is distinguished has already been mentioned, and at Quiriguá in Guatemala, not far away, the figures are constrained within the rectangular shape of the column, from which the head looks out like the face on a mummy case *(Ill. 100)*. Here is the tallest stela of all (35 feet high), and there are four great boulders whose whole surface is covered with elaborate carving thought to represent a sky monster, with a richly-dressed human figure sitting between its jaws. Piedras Negras, also in Guatemala, is outstanding for the beauty of its carving both on stelae and on glyph-bordered wall panels, one of which shows a ruler on his throne surrounded by attendants. Palenque is beautifully placed on rising ground

101 Temple of the Sun, Palenque, Chiapas, with the Temple of the Inscriptions in the background, showing elaborate roof comb and remains of stucco relief decoration. Late Classic Maya, probably dedicated A D 692

against a background of tree-covered hills, looking out north-wards over the plain of Chiapas (*Ill. 101*). Its low relief limestone panels and its stucco reliefs are unsurpassed in dignity of form and delicacy of execution (*Ills. 102-104*). The late Classic buildings of the Puuc, the hilly region of south-western Yucatán and part of Campeche, will serve as an example of a regional style. The buildings are of lime concrete veneered with thin, well-cut stone slabs, sometimes forming an ornate mosaic, and there are more palace-type buildings in proportion to the number of temple pyramids than there are in the Petén.

102, 103 Full fi-
gure numerical
glyphs, part of
an inscription
from the Palacio
at Palenque, Chia-
pas. This type,
which is rare,
shows a time-
period or day on
the right, support-
ed by a number
on the left. Both
are regarded as
gods. Limestone.
Late Classic Maya

104 (opposite)
Low relief lime-
stone carving
from a slab co-
vering the coffin
in the tomb under
the Temple of the
Inscriptions,
Palenque, Chia-
pas. It shows a
reclining figure
from which
sprouts a tree or
plant. Late Clas-
sic Maya.

◀ 105 *(opposite)* House of the Turtles at Uxmal, Yucatán. Plain façade pierced by three doorways : columned frieze below a row of small turtles. Lime concrete veneered with thin stone slabs. Late Classic Maya
106 *(above)* Palace of the Governor, Uxmal, Yucatán. Façade with heavy decorated frieze pierced by two tall corbelled ' arches '. Late Classic Maya, Puuc style

Uxmal is among the foremost examples of this style. It is noted for its long façades, in which a comparatively low plain wall, broken by a series of doorways, is crowned by a higher frieze covered with intricate mosaic decoration. These are well seen in the 'Nunnery' court, and in the fine Palace of the Governor *(Ill. 106)*, also known for two exceptionally tall corbelled 'arches' which break the long line of the façade. Contrasting with these is the plain-looking House of the Turtles *(Ill. 105)*, with a frieze adorned only with vertical columns, above which is a row of small turtles. Part of the decoration of the ' Nunnery ' court consists of masks of the long-nosed rain god, similar to those which are seen in profusion both on late Classic and Post-Classic buildings at the great centre of Chichén Itzá in northern Yucatán.

The Maya were adepts at the use of stucco, which was widely used for floors and the decoration of buildings. At Palenque, where it reached its highest level, there are fine panels in relief showing figures or groups on the temples, and a procession of richly-dressed priests adorns the secret tomb which was found buried beneath the Temple of the Inscriptions. The same tomb contained two magnificent stucco heads modelled in the round and decorated with red paint (*Ill. 107*), with the typical long Maya noses and retreating foreheads and plumed head-dresses. Traces of paint are often found on modelled stucco, and much of the decoration on buildings was probably coloured; for example, polychrome stucco masks have recently been found on late Pre-Classic buildings at Tikal.

From painted modelled plaster it is but a step to mural paintings. Traces of polychrome paintings have been found in many places —Uaxactún, Palenque, Tikal and others—but the most remarkable come from three corbelled vaulted rooms making up a building at Bonampak in Chiapas (*Ill. 110*). The paintings are obscured by a coating of stalactite and we owe our knowledge of them to careful copies made by two artists under great difficulties. Opinions differ as to whether they were painted on dry plaster or in true fresco. They form a sequence showing a great ceremony; the robing of the priests and an orchestra, a raid on an inferior tribe to get prisoners (not a war between equals), their arraignment and sacrifice, and finally a dance and blood-letting ceremony by the high priest and his family. They show a wide range of colours, blue, green, black, white and a number of shades of red, brown and yellow. Although they were done about A D 800, during the Dynamic Phase of sculpture, their liveliness and realism far exceed anything which was attempted in stone. Even the attitudes and facial expressions of the participants reflect the scene they appear in; they are fierce in the fighting, and dignified and unmoved at the sacrifice, the collapse of the dead prisoner is vividly shown, the next in turn raises his hands in supplication and the rest squat helplessly below. It is to their outlines that these paintings owe most of their expressiveness, and it has been well said that they are best regarded as coloured drawings. The artists worked within certain conventions : thus heads are always shown in profile, which occasionally results in such anatomical absurdities as twisting the neck through 180°, and the feet are nearly always in the stiff splayed or sideways positions of the stelae. There is no interest in any life forms except human ones, and depth is shown only by partial superpositions, sometimes at different levels.

107 Head of a young man wearing an elaborate plumed head-dress. Stucco with traces of red paint. Late Classic Maya. Burial chamber under the Temple of the Inscriptions, Palenque, Chiapas ▶

108 Bowl decorated with marine monsters and stylized glyphs. Orange and black on buff slip. Late Classic Maya. Caracol, British Honduras

109 Design from a vase showing priests and dignitaries in full costume. Red, yellow and black paint on buff slip. Late Classic Maya. Chama, Guatemala

110 Wall painting *(copy)* depicting a raid on a inferior tribe to get prisoners. Polychrome paint on plaster (perhaps true fresco). Maya, *c.* A D 800. Bonampak, Chiapas

111 Polychrome vase showing kneeling figures with headdresses above a band of glyphs.   Classic Maya

In contrast are the faces already mentioned and above all the hands, which show a multitude of gestures and almost seem to speak.   All in all these paintings are among the greatest works of art in ancient America, and can, in their own way, bear comparison with wall paintings anywhere.

Pottery is another medium for polychrome painting (*Ills. 108, 109*); reds, browns and yellows predominate, with the addition of black and sometimes blue, the same as that of the Bonampak paintings, of which the exact nature still baffles investigators.   Painting is found on vessels of many shapes, mostly some form of plate or bowl.   There are open bowls, which may have a flange low down on the outside, vertical-sided tripod bowls with slab feet like those of Teotihuacán, shallow open tripods, deep cylinders, pear-shaped jars which may have a ring base, and many others (*Ill. 111*). Some basal-flanged bowls and some Teotihuacán-type tripods have

112 Tripod bowl of thin black ware with incised designs, including a bird which is also modelled on the cover. Early Classic Maya. From the painted tomb at Tikal, Guatemala, A D 457

low conical lids topped by a bird or animal *(Ill. 112)*. Painted scenes include processions, scenes of offering and other ceremonies, accompanied by glyphs which in many cases appear to be merely decorative and without meaning. Some of these shapes, including the Teotihuacán-type tripods, may be covered with painted stucco, the 'paint cloisonné' decoration already described for Teotihuacán itself, or may be made in polished black ware with delicate incised designs. Most of the decoration is Maya in character, but some instances recently found at Tikal show strong Teotihuacán influence. These are some of the more notable decorated pottery types, but there are many others, and figurines were also made. Solid handmade ones, some of them crude but others well-fashioned and already showing Maya facial characteristics, belong to the late Formative Period *(Ill. 114)*. The other main group dates from the late Classic and comes largely from the Mexican states of

113 Whistle figurine in the form of a seated man wearing elaborate plumed head-dress. Grey pottery, mould-made, the necklace painted blue. Late Classic Maya. Jaina

114 *(right)* Red pottery female figurine, wearing large necklace and ear-spools. Hand-modelled with touches of red and white paint and applied details. Late Formative Maya

Campeche and Tabasco. These are mould-made, many of them hollow, and of fine quality. Notable examples come from Jonuta, the island of Jaina, and Palenque. Some of these figures are also whistles *(Ill. 113)*.

The Classic Maya showed great skill in a number of minor arts. The nature of their textiles and feather work can be deduced only indirectly because none have survived, but judging from sculptural representations they wove elaborate patterns. They also engraved complicated scenes with great delicacy on bones, of which a great deal has been learnt from recent finds at Tikal. Most important was jade, the most precious material known to the Maya. To judge from grave offerings and sculptures, a dignitary was loaded with it. Elaborate bead collars with pendants, large ear ornaments, belt ornaments, anklets and beaded kilts were all used. Jade is a hard intractable material to shape with stone tools and abrasives, but the Maya worked it with great skill. The Leiden plate, with its delicate incised decoration, is an early example. Heads and masks used as pendants, figurines, beads and ear ornaments were carved in the round, and many plaques with heads or groups in low relief were made *(Ill. 115)*. A prominent part of an ear ornament was a funnel-shaped flare, whose neck passed through the lobe and was held by a backing plate; some were adorned with a tassel in the middle and some formed the seating of a cylindrical bead. Such flares had other uses, and one of the finest examples *(Ill. 116)*, from Pomona,

15 Seated dignitary or god wearing elaborate headdress. Pale green jade plaque, carved and drilled in low relief and highly polished. Classic Maya. Unprovenanced

16 Large annular ware; glyphs on a plain surface. Earpool shape, but perhaps belt ornament. Dark green jade, engraved and highly polished. Proto-Classic Maya (Late Formative). Pomona, British Honduras

British Honduras, which is 7 inches in diameter, may have been a belt ornament. It has incised glyphs, so far not read. It is curious that some finely worked low relief plaques are asymmetrical or even irregular in outline, as though the makers were only interested in the surface.

Finally, great dexterity was shown in the shaping of flint. Caches of flint objects are found buried under Maya monuments, and these take the form of finely shaped blades, crescents, discs and curious irregular objects, some of which are thought to have been heads of ceremonial staves. The outlines of some of these incorporate human profiles *(Ill. 117)*.

117 Eccentric flint flaked to incorporate human profiles. Perhaps the head of a ceremonial staff. Maya. Unprovenanced

118 El Castillo at Chichén Itzá, Yucatán. General view of the pyramid crowned with a temple. Post-Classic Maya

Post-Classic

Beginning with Copán early in the ninth century, the Maya ceased to erect dated stelae at one centre after another during the next 75 years or so, and the hierarchy at least abandoned them to the forest, though in some cases the peasants remained in the neighbourhood. Some sites in Yucatán, notably Chichén Itzá, were reoccupied in the tenth century after a short interval, and at others such as Uxmal it is difficult to draw a line between Classic and Post-Classic. At Chichén Itzá itself some late Classic buildings were modified in the Post-Classic, and many new ones were built. There were still pyramids crowned with temples (El Castillo at Chichén is a splendid example, *Ill. 118*) and ball-courts, but the character of the wall-painting and sculpture changed and spacious colonnaded buildings of a new type were set up. The sculpture in particular was very closely related to that of Tula, as has already been hinted. There is a new preoccupation with violence and death, seen in reliefs showing rows of skulls on poles *(Ill. 119)*

119 Relief showing human skulls on poles. Shallow carving on the *tzompantli* or skull rack. Post-Classic Maya. Chichén Itzá, Yucatán

and eagles and jaguars eating human hearts. The worship of the feathered serpent is seen in his representation as a square column of Toltec type, with his head on the ground and his rattlesnake tail in the air, where it was used to support a lintel *(Ill. 120)*. Of the same Toltec origin are the Chac Mools, reclining stone figures bearing a stone bowl on the stomach. The great ball-court, with its painted temples, has new features such as vertical sides in each of which is a stone ring, and if a team was lucky or skilful enough to propel the ball through it, the result was an outright win. The consequences can be guessed from a series of stone reliefs on the walls of the court at ground level, in which two heavily armoured teams of seven players are seen facing one another. The leader of one has dropped on one knee, and from his neck sprouts a luxuriant plant surrounded by six snakes; the leader of the other holds a stone knife in one hand and his opponent's head in the other. The scene is repeated six times. It has been inferred that the game was a fertility rite in which the victim's blood fertilized the ground.

Notable wall paintings have been found here, although few details now survive in a recognizable condition. They do not approach those of Bonampak in dignity and composition, but are

120 Pillar in the form of a feathered serpent, its rattle snake tail formerly supporting the lintel of the temple entrance. Post-Classic Maya. Temple of the Warriors, Chichén Itzá, Yucatán

121 Wall painting of a waterside village *(copy)* showing various activities and canoes carrying warriors. Polychrome on plaster. Post-Classic Maya. Temple of the Warriors, Chichen Itzá, Yucatán

full of ethnographic interest. There is a waterside village with people sitting or moving among the houses and canoes carrying warriors in front (*Ill. 121*), and an attack on a Maya village by Toltecs, in which a large area is covered with little warriors fighting in great confusion.

For the first time metal comes into the picture. Water is found on the dry plateau of Yucatán only in deep holes called *cenotes*, formed by underground solution of the limestone, and the Great Cenote at Chichén, which is a deep pool surrounded by vertical cliffs 65 feet high, was a place of sacrifice into which people and valuable things were thrown. Dredging of this has yielded, among many other things, several finely-embossed gold discs showing war between Toltecs and Mayas, culminating in one on which a victim is killed by the Mexican method of cutting out the heart. The gold came from Panama, but the workmanship is Mexican.

Chichén Itzá ruled Yucatán for about 200 years, after which it was displaced by Mayapán, some miles to the west. Like many Post-Classic centres this was a walled town, and the ceremonial nucleus was a very pale reflection of the older ones. Toltec influence had faded away and the Maya emerged again as rulers of their own people, but they retained militaristic habits and did not recover their artistic skill. Excavation of Mayapán has revealed a sorry state of affairs—building of poor quality with ill-fitting stones and the defects made good with plaster, little decorated pottery except mass-produced incense burners varied only by paint and minor applied details, and a dearth of jade and other beautiful objects. The best masonry was found not in religious buildings but in chiefs' houses outside the nucleus. Mayapán was sacked in a revolt in about 1450, but the warring states which succeeded it did nothing to arrest the artistic decline.

CHAPTER THREE

A Glance to the North

The art of the ancient inhabitants of North America suffers by comparison with that of Mesoamerica because it lacks monumental sculpture and had comparatively little which can be regarded as architecture. This is not to say that the peoples of the area had no artistic ability, for in some areas they produced fine examples of small carvings, pottery and even metalwork, though this came exclusively from naturally occurring metals and not from ores. A few examples will give some idea of what was achieved.

Temple pyramids surely inspired by Mexico were built more or less regularly round courts in the region of the middle Mississippi Valley after about A D 1000, but they are of earth and have weathered to nondescript shapes. To the north, mainly in Wisconsin, Minnesota, Illinois and Iowa, there are large earthworks in the shape of animals and birds, apparently dating from the second half of the first millennium A D. Some of the great 'apartment houses' in the southwest (mostly Arizona, Colorado and New Mexico), dating from about A D 1000-1300, with their numerous rectangular rooms and sacred circular *kivas*, have an impressiveness derived either from their setting beneath or clinging to the sides of great towering cliffs, or in the open from their size and regular lay-out. Wall paintings have been found in some of the *kivas*, showing gods and ceremonies, many of which can be interpreted in the light of surviving practices, largely concerned with weather control. They are painted in a wide range of mineral colours on mud plaster, and show angular schematized figures like modern Katchina dolls from the same area, animals, fish, jars with rain pouring out, arrows denoting lightning, and so on. They were not meant to last, and the fragmentary state of many is due not only to age but to frequent replastering and to deliberate destruction when a ceremony was finished.

122 Five ornamental geometrical forms, including scrolls and a swastika. Native copper, beaten, cut and annealed. Hopewell Culture. Ohio

Many minor arts are best illustrated by the Hopewell Culture (about 300 B C to A D 300), which has richly furnished burials under large mounds, chiefly in Wisconsin, Illinois, and especially Ohio. The grave goods include copper, stone, pottery and mica. Native copper was cut, beaten and annealed to form head-dresses with antlers, ear-spools, and plaques in the form of animals, fish, birds, crescents, swastikas and complex geometrical forms, some of them for sewing to robes *(Ill. 122)*. Sheets of mica were cut into silhouettes of bear or bird claws, hands and headless human beings *(Ills. 124, 125)*. There are finely-carved stone pipes, in which the bowl is a naturalistic figure, usually a bird or animal *(Ill. 123)*. Delicately-flaked obsidian knives and spear-heads, too large and fragile for use, were also deposited in the graves.

123 Three tobacco pipes with bowls in the form of marmot, frog, and snake. The front views show smoke channel. Steatite, carved, with some shell inlay. Hopewell Culture. Ohio

124 *(opposite)* Two silhouettes showing mutilated human figures. Cut ▶ from a thin sheet of mica. Hopewell Culture. Ohio

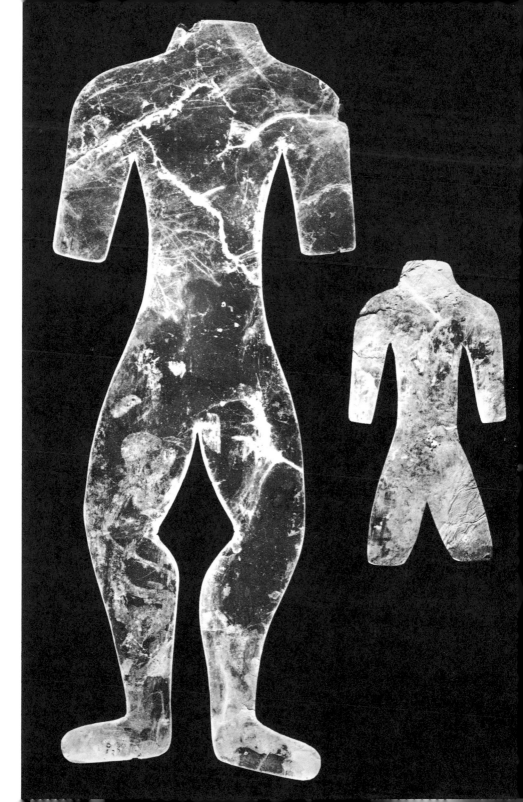

125 Two silhouettes of a human hand and an eagle's claw. Cut from a thin sheet of mica. Hopewell Culture, Ohio

Further south and later in date, in the Mississippi Valley and the South-East, are engraved or pierced shell discs, and pierced and embossed copper ones, bearing designs such as faces with weeping eyes, crosses, and eagle warriors carrying trophy heads, which, like the pyramid-building cultures with which they are connected, show Mexican influence, probably from the Huastec region, despite the great distance and the lack of connecting links.

Many works of art in carved wood were undoubtedly made, but few have been preserved. The best evidence about them comes from a find of late prehistoric date at Key Marco on the Gulf Coast of Florida *(Ill. 126)*, where the wood had been preserved by continuous immersion in water, but unfortunately it was found before the invention of modern methods of preservation and most of the objects have shrivelled up. Many of them were painted. There were beautiful animal and bird heads, masks, spear-throwers and other weapons, boxes and panels painted with animals and birds.

126 Deer-head mask, with large leather-hinged ears. Carved wood, originally painted. Late Prehistoric. Key Marco, Florida

127 Pottery bottle with swirl design, painted red and white. Middle Mississippi Period, after AD 1000.

128 Bottle with concentric linear designs. Potter with burnished black slip, incised after firing. Middl Mississippi Period, after AD 1000. Caddo

129 Black-on-white bowl, showing contrast between the areas of solid colour and hatching. Pueblo III, c. 1050-1300. Mesa Verde, Colorado

130 Coiled burden basket with geometrical designs, in red and black on natural ground. Basketmaker III, AD 500-700, Canyon del Muerto, Arizona

Attractive pottery was made in many places. Most wares are in one colour, with decoration by incision *(Ill. 128)*, stamping and the like, and occasionally modelling. Painting is confined to a few areas; it is sometimes found in the Mississippi area *(Ill. 127)*, but it can best be exemplified by the Southwest. In both these areas the idea but not the designs may have come from Mexico. In a large part of the Southwest, white-slipped jars, bowls and handled mugs decorated with a great variety of intricate, mainly angular, geometrical designs in black, were made between about AD 700 and 1300 *(Ill. 129)*. At the same time, and even earlier, similar designs were worked in basketry *(Ill. 130)*. Between 1000 and 1200, a particularly striking variety of black-on-white pottery

131 Bowl, stylized turtle within a geometrical border. Pottery, black paint on white slip. A hole has been punched in the centre, ceremonially 'killing' the dish for burial with the dead. AD 1000-1200, New Mexico

132 Sikyatki Polychrome bowl, incomplete, painted in black and red on yellow. Ruin 4, Horn House, Moki Reservation, Arizona

133 Vase with geometrical and scroll designs in compartments. Black and red paint on buff slip. *c.* AD 1300–1450. Chihuahua, Mexico

was made in the Mimbres Valley of New Mexico *(Ill. 131)*, which is marked by great delicacy in drawing and the introduction of life forms. Men, groups, animals, fish and insects are placed in the middle of a bowl, which may also have a geometrical border of great intricacy. The central design is all too often marred by the habit of 'killing' the bowl by punching out a disc when it was buried with the dead. Between about 1300 and 1450 another distinctive type was made in the Mexican state of Chihuahua *(Ill. 133)*. This is decorated in black and red on buff, mainly in geometrical designs, and the delicacy of the drawing suggests a Mimbres strain in its ancestry, but many of the vessel shapes, including effigy jars, are different. Back in Arizona and New

Mexico, the black-on-white gave place after 1300 to other types and colours. Black-on-red varieties already existed in the area, and white was added to these, and in some parts matt black was replaced by a black to brownish-green glaze paint unique in America. Yellow and orange backgrounds were also used. Among many varieties is a beautiful ware, Sikyatki Polychrome *(Ill. 132)*, in which conventionalised animal designs are painted in sweeping curves of black and red on large yellow bowls and jars.

CHAPTER FOUR

Peru

As a centre of high civilization in the New World Mesoamerica was rivalled only by Peru, which with highland Bolivia forms a unit sometimes called the Central Andes. The whole area has many cultural features in common, and at two periods, and to a lesser extent a third, it was united artistically by the spread of what is called a horizon style, but at other times there was a good deal of variety in different districts, which is seen particularly in pottery styles, and this was to a considerable extent the result of broken and complex topography. The area falls into three zones, of which one, the forested lowlands east of the Andes, can be ignored here because it has produced no artistic developments of any consequence; indeed there were no civilizations which would be likely to support any. Of the other two, the coastal plain is a narrow strip of rocky and sandy desert, where it seldom rains in some parts and never in others. It is crossed from east to west by a series of irrigated valleys running from mountains to sea, which were the cradles of many Peruvian cultures; the deserts separating them were formidable barriers, but some of the more powerful coastal states were, at different times, able to group several of them under their rule. To the east of the coastal plain lies the zone of the high Andes, with its snow-covered peaks, bleak plateaux, high passes and deeply-cut valleys, constituting obstacles to communication which led to much diversity in art styles. It is convenient to break both coast and highlands down into northern, central and southern sections. The central coast extends from just south of the Casma Valley to just south of Lima, with the northern and southern sections on either flank. Owing to lack of knowledge the corresponding highland sections are less well defined; the boundary between north and central sections is at about the same latitude as the coastal one, but that between the central and southern highlands is roughly 2 degrees south of the coastal boundary, between Pucára, some distance north-west of Lake Titicaca, and Cuzco, and the southern section extends far further south to cover the Bolivian highlands.

The chronology of the Peruvian area was briefly mentioned in the introduction, and it must now be amplified. For our purposes the sequence begins about 2500 B C during a Pre-Ceramic Period, long before anything deserving the name of art was known in Mesoamerica. A remarkable art style is expressed at this time chiefly in the unpromising medium of twined cotton textiles, found in such a faded and tattered condition that years of patient work have been necessary to reveal the patterns. Their makers lived on the coast, and about forty of their settlements have been found, some of them in places which now appear very dry but which yielded sufficient water for their limited needs. They lived largely on sea lions, shell-fish and fish, and cultivated a few plants, including the cotton used in their textiles. The beginning of the Formative is hard to define satisfactorily, but it may be put arbitrarily at about 1800 B C when the first pottery is known in the north highlands, although important temples were present earlier. There was little change in the life of the coast people until the arrival about 800 B C from Mesoamerica of new influences and possibly new people, bringing jaguar worship and a more productive form of maize. The art style connected with this marks the Chavín horizon, which spread widely through the coast and into the north highlands. This is the limited horizon style mentioned above. The Formative Period lasted until about A D 250, when it gave place to what it is convenient to call the Classic Period, although its character is very different from that of the Mesoamerican Classic. It was, for instance, a time at which fortresses were built and the importance of war and warriors is clearly shown in the art, and is deducible from the archaeological record. As has been said in the introduction, art lost in vigour what it gained in technical perfection at this time. The Classic Period was brought to an end between about 750 and 950 by the expansion of influence from Tiahuanaco in the south highlands.

138

It is thought that this first affected the important site of Huari in the Mantaro Basin, and then spread over all the coast, perhaps backed by military force in its later stages. It was first detected by the replacement of local art styles on the coast by new ones which were influenced to a greater or less degree by that of Tiahuanaco, and this has since been supported by the discovery of changes in coastal building plans and burial customs. This is one of the main horizons, demonstrated by their art styles, to which reference has been made. The other, coming at the end of the Post-Classic Period and of aboriginal history, is the Inca horizon, which began its expansion in 1438 and finished with the Conquest. Between them was a period when Tiahuanaco influence was dying away, and local states, each with its own pottery style, were emerging in the north, central and south sections of the coast.

Similar chronological frameworks have been outlined for Mesoamerica and the Central Andes, and the dates attached to the various sub-divisions are not very different in the two areas, but it must be emphasized that there was little direct connexion between them, and that the word Classic is simply being used for a technological and artistic climax, without implying similar political conditions. The one period at which there is evidence for direct contact between the areas is at the beginning of the Chavín horizon about the ninth century B C, when the introduction of the jaguar cult and certain ceramic features point strongly to Mesoamerica, and particularly to Tlatilco in the Valley of Mexico. The route is uncertain, but it seems most likely at present that the contact was by sea. From this time onwards direct contacts ceased, and Peru followed its own lines of development.

In some respects it is difficult to compare the art of Peru with that of Mesoamerica, owing to differences in materials and in the degree of preservation. In architecture, many of the Peruvian sites which must have been most impressive are on the coast, where the usual building material is some form of adobe, or mud brick. Weathering may destroy the form of buildings in this material beyond recovery, whereas the stone buildings of Mesoamerica provide evidence, in their fallen stones, for reconstructions, many of which have been successfully carried out. Textiles, an outstanding feature of Peruvian art, are well preserved on the dry coast but are virtually non-existent in Mesoamerica. Metals, which did not appear in Mesoamerica until the Post-Classic Period, began to be used for ornaments something like 1,500 years earlier in Peru.

When all allowances have been made, Peruvian art as a whole does not rise to the levels reached by the chief Mesoamerican cultures. In craftsmanship it is unsurpassed, but it has the limitations of the craftsman's art, and as A. L. Kroeber said long ago, the craftsman's feet were mired down in technology and he felt with his hands rather than with his emotions. There is a marked difference between the two areas in the Post-Classic Period, when some elements of Peruvian art are singularly lacking in inspiration, in contrast to the vigour which is evident in Central Mexico until the end. This is particularly seen in the mould-made black pottery of the Chimú State on the north coast, where dullness and mass production go hand in hand. The quality of awe, which is so prominent in many Mesoamerican works of art, is most nearly approached in Peru in the stone carving of the Chavín horizon of the Formative Period, and this quality is present to some extent in the pottery and textiles of the Formative and Classic of the south coast, and the pottery and stone carving of the south highland Classic. The Classic of the north coast is distinguished for the realistic modelling and lively silhouette painting of the Mochica pottery, showing a competence and sureness of touch which is worthy of admiration. At all times some objects of great interest and considerable charm were produced, such as textiles, metal or inlaid work in wood, stone and shell.

PRECERAMIC PERIOD

When the first refuse deposit of the Preceramic Period was excavated in 1946 at the Huaca Prieta, at the mouth of the Chicama river on the north coast, the only finds which suggested the existence of any form of art were two small carved gourds in an extremely decayed condition. One of these gourds has four

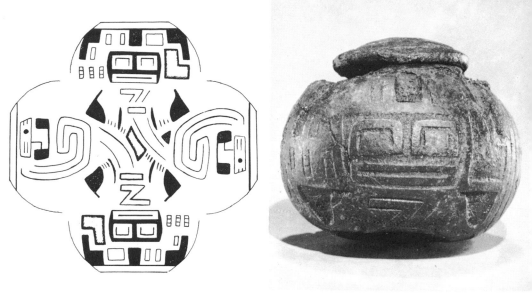

134, 135 Carved gourd vessel with cover found in an extremely fragile and decayed condition. *(left)* Drawing of the extended pattern seen on the gourd. Preceramic Period, *c.* 2000 B C. Huaca Prieta, Chicama Valley, North Coast.

highly schematic faces, skilfully and symmetrically placed, which can be regarded as some form of cat. The other bears what have been interpreted as two human figures interlocking across the bottom of the gourd, alternating with what look like two snakes in profile, and on the lid are two bird heads sharing a neck and forming a curvilinear Z-shaped figure *(Ills. 134, 135)*. They date from about 2000 B C. A great many plain gourds were found on this site, and it is remarkable that these were the only decorated ones. Carving, engraving and allied techniques are, indeed, very rare on any site at this period, and about the only examples which can be cited are a stone spindle whorl with a snake, a bird and a quadruped crudely engraved on it, and a bone pendant or spatula decorated by means of pricked dots with stars on one side and a pair of standing monkeys holding unidentified objects, perhaps blowpipes, on the other, both from Asia on the southern part of the coast.

To find anything related to the Huaca Prieta gourds, or indeed anything of any characteristic style, we must go to the textiles,

141

of which there are more. The extremely fragmentary, decayed and faded condition of these has made their study very slow and difficult. They are distinguished from later ones by having been made exclusively by a variety of manual methods, without the aid of a heddle loom, and of these twining was that most frequently used. The fibres were spun cotton and a wild bast, probably milkweed. Colours were obtained by using natural white and brown cottons, by red, blue, yellow and orange dyes, and by rubbing dry red powder into the yarn, but none of these has been easy to detect. Feather work was made by knotting the ends of the feathers into half-hitch looped fabrics, and this must have provided brightly coloured garments but nothing is known of any pattern. There are a number of ingenious ways of producing patterns in twined fabrics, a highly characteristic one being based on warp transposition. The warps were set up in pairs of two different colours, for example each pair may consist of a red and a blue warp. By transposing these in opposite directions, say red to the right and blue to the left in one pick and back again in the next, a patch of red colour can be held to one face and one of blue to the other, and they can be reversed elsewhere in

136, 137 Fragment of twined cotton fabric *(left)* which had lost all traces of dy
The original design, a male condor with a snake in its stomach, was determined

the same fabric. In this sort of way, complicated designs were woven—distorted rectangular birds recognizable by their powerful hooked beaks, snakes with a head at each end, combined figures such as a double-headed snake with two rock crabs appended, and even a pair of fantastic human beings. The latter are associated with a pair of bird heads at either end of a common neck, a clear link with the gourd lid mentioned above. Where the colour has disappeared, as it generally has, the design has been recovered by noting the directions of displacement of the warps with the aid of a microscope and laboriously plotting them out *(Ills. 136,137)*. Darning was used to a limited extent to produce plain weaves like those woven on a loom, but it is combined with twining in such a way as to exclude the possibility of using a heddle, and on cloths of this sort similar designs were made by means of warp floats. Designs were also made by forming holes of larger size than the normal in openwork looped fabrics, for instance a snake pattern found at Asia, and gauze appears to have been used elsewhere to produce interlocking fish heads. Although these designs are based on nature, the idea of combining two creatures, the double heads, and the way in which they are shown are highly sophisticated.

the analysis of every yarn movement. The photograph could thus be retouched to show how the piece originally looked *(right)*. Preceramic Period. Chicama Valley

It is true that the limitations of textile techniques must have imposed the general angularity of the designs, as they did right through Peruvian prehistory, but this is not all. The makers of these textiles were preceded by people who lacked cotton but buried their dead wrapped in twined rush mats, so the main technique was there, but at some time they began to apply it in very ingenious ways to the depiction in strange fashions of themselves and some of the creatures they saw around them. Where the stimulus came from we do not know, and the rarity of suitable conditions for preservation may mean that we shall never know. Twining as a way of making textiles ceased with the arrival of the heddle loom about 1200 B C, but double-headed, angular, interlocking creatures persisted until the Spaniards brought the ancient civilizations of Peru to an end.

Until recently, nothing was known of art in the highlands before Chavín, but a series of pre-Chavín stages is now known from Kotosh on the Huallaga river. The earliest, before 1800 B C, which appears to be Preceramic, has a rectangular stone temple on a high platform, adorned inside with plaster reliefs showing crossed hands.

THE CHAVIN HORIZON

The next episode in the art of the coast was the appearance of the Chavín horizon in the ninth century, but in the highlands decorated grey pottery appeared about 1800 B C at Kotosh. This has incised geometrical designs, painted after firing with red and rarely yellow and white. Chavínoid features appeared about 1000 B C, accompanied by some remarkable red pottery with broad-line incised designs which include human faces, painted on it with graphite after firing. Pure Chavín pottery is found shortly after. Chavín itself is an important temple some 10,000 feet up on the eastern slope of the Andes, in a small valley which ultimately flows into the Marañón, and it lies east of that upper part of the Santa Valley called the Callejón de Huaylas. Although it is not necessarily the centre of the style in Peru, its importance is unquestionable. Other highland sites are known but little inform-

138 Annular vessel of yellowish-grey ware with stirrup spout. On the rim are two human heads and two heads combining bird (probably owl) and feline features. Late Cupisnique (Coast Chavin) style. North Coast

139 Upper part of the Great Image, a monolith of white granite representing a human figure with feline fangs and snakes as hair. Double feline faces sharing a single jaw are shown on the projection above the head and elsewhere on the figure. Probably ninth century B C. From the oldest part of the temple at Chavín de Huántar

140 Part of symmetrical frieze of birds decorated with feline jaws and eyes, and snake heads. Lintel of the black and white portal in the temple at Chavín de Huántar

ation about them is available. Sites of the same period are found in coastal valleys, namely Cerro Sechín and Moxeke in the Casma Valley, and Punkurí and Cerro Blanco in the Nepeña Valley. There are rather close stylistic links between Chavín and Cerro Blanco, Moxeke and Punkurí are linked to one another and to Chavín, but Sechín is peculiar although it has features which connect it with Moxeke. The Chavín style is expressed chiefly by a notable pottery type at other coastal sites in the north *(Ills. 145, 146, 147)*, and its influence is seen in the southern coastal pottery style of Paracas, and in textiles from the central and south coast. The Chavín style is marked architecturally by massive terraced pyramidal platforms, of stone at Chavín itself, and of conical adobes or rubble set in mud mortar on the coast. Chavín art has recently been the subject of an important study by J. H. Rowe, and frequent reference will be made to it.

At Chavín itself, Rowe has distinguished several building stages, all similarly faced with regular courses of stone slabs, some of them thicker than the others. The interior is traversed by a connected series of galleries and chambers on two or three levels, efficiently ventilated by means of stone shafts. A row of human and feline heads was tenoned into the outside wall, and higher up was a projecting cornice of squared slabs with carvings on the under side and in some cases on the outer side also. The oldest part is a U-shaped block, open to the east, in the depths of which, in a dark passage, is what is called the *Lanzón* or the Great Image *(Ill. 139)*, nearly 15 feet high, of white granite, roughly prismatic in shape with a thinner projection at the top, carved in low relief to form a human figure with feline fangs. Rowe says that it has, in its setting, 'an awe-inspiring quality which can be felt even by a present-

day unbeliever'. Additions were made on either side of this block of buildings, and later on the south side alone, thus forming a great rectangular mass and changing the centre of gravity of the plan, a change which coincided, it is suggested, with a transfer of worship to a new image within it which can no longer be found. Access to the new southern block is through a portal, the north half of black limestone and the south of white granite, the doorway being flanked by a pair of grey andesite columns supporting a lintel on top of which was a striking frieze of standing birds, much of which still exists *(Ill. 140)*. Each column bears a composite figure in flat relief, having a human body and bird head, wings and claws, all liberally decorated with feline eyes and fangs. In front of the entrance is a sunken court flanked by buildings.

Other carvings at Chavín come from the cornice slabs, of which a notable example shows a jaguar, whose tail emerges from a fanged face and whose body is sprinkled with eyes, while snake heads sprout from the margin. Another slab shows a standing figure with cat face and hair composed of snakes, holding a conch and a spondylus shell in his hands, another shows a bat, and another a bird with a staring feline face on its body. Rowe suggests that, since these exterior carvings were part of the architectural decoration, they were not themselves objects of worship, though they may in some cases depict supernatural beings. On the other hand, there are two carvings which, like the Great Image, are more likely from their form and careful finish to have been cult objects. One is a long rectangular shaft called the Tello obelisk (after its discoverer, the Peruvian archaeologist Dr Tello), which bears carved alligators accompanied by lesser beings and decorated with the usual eyes and fangs. The other is the famous Raimondi stela now in Lima, a great rectangular slab over 6 feet high, showing a standing figure with feline face and claws, holding a staff in each hand, crowned with a great superstructure consisting of a series of grotesque upward-looking faces armed with fangs and surrounded by an aureole of snakes and scrolls. Rowe has suggested that this was a visible representation of the god hidden and worshipped in the newer southern block of the temple.

The commonest Chavín carvings are birds, which Rowe gives reasons to identify as eagles and hawks, not the condors they have generally been called, whereas cats (mainly jaguars) are less frequent, but almost all, whether birds, cats or others, are immensely complicated by the addition of what at first sight appear to be decorative features, especially feline fangs or faces, eyes or snake heads. It is clear that they are more than this and Rowe has suggested that they were supposed to have definite meanings, the feline features for instance indicating divinity and the snakes, hair. Whether this is accepted or not, the almost universal presence of jaguar attributes points to the importance of his cult.

Much Chavín carving is in flat relief, in which details are shown on flat surfaces by engraving or by cutting away the background, in fact a sort of champlevé, but the tenoned heads show that carving in the round was also practised, as do the small objects like mortars found at various sites. Other features of the style are a tendency to bilateral symmetry and to repetition, both of which can be illustrated by the bands of faces with feline jaws on the projection above the head of the Great Image and on its belt. These, although in profile, have an eye and a nostril on either side of the mouth, which is thus shared by two faces. There is also a tendency to reduce anatomical features to straight lines and simple curves, and to subordinate the drawing of a figure to a framework of straight bands as though following ruled guide-lines. Zig-zag bands within a frame representing jaws with teeth, and a multitude of fangs may be carved in what appears to be rather an aimless fashion on bodies or wings, as on the figures decorating the columns of the black and white portal, and these and the sharp points formed when two curves meet give a prickly appearance

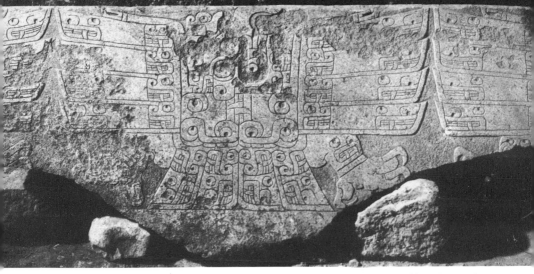

141 Low relief carving of bird decorated with feline heads in profile. Just below the damaged bird head are two feline faces sharing one jaw. Temple at Chavín de Huántar

to the surface of many Chavín reliefs. There is a general effect of massive angularity about Chavín carvings, which becomes more marked after the earliest stage, and this may be due in part to the influence of textile patterns which have not survived.

The Chavín style must have lasted a considerable time, perhaps about 500 years. Comparisons with the Paracas pottery style in the south show that its influence in that quarter had faded by about 300 B C. In the north, its influence was inherited by the much later Mochica pottery, and it may in remote areas have overlapped that style to some extent, but it is unlikely that the Chavínoid ceremonial centres survived much longer than the influence in the south of the style associated with them. During the life of the style, there were changes in detail, and Rowe has worked out a succession. It must suffice here to say that the Great Image in the oldest part of the Chavín temple appears to be one of the earliest carvings, and the Raimondi stela one of the latest, with the Tello obelisk followed by the carvings surrounding the black and white portal occupying intermediate positions.

Turning to the coastal sites, Cerro Blanco in the Nepeña Valley has not been very fully described, but it certainly includes courts on different levels enclosed by low rubble walls faced with clay plaster, modelled in pure Chavín style to show faces, eyes and fangs, painted brick red and greenish-yellow. It is possible that some jaguar masks in an imperfect state are made up of a pair of profile bird masks, and it has been suggested that the whole complex was meant to represent a bird in plan. Punkurí, in the same valley, is a terraced platform with a stairway on which stands a bizarre jaguar head and front paws, modelled in the round from mud and rubble and painted, with the grave of a sacrificed woman at its feet. Higher up the structure are walls of conical adobes, plastered with clay and decorated with incised designs of Chavín character, which Tello, the discoverer, considered to belong to a slightly later building stage. Of the sites in the Casma Valley, Moxeke is a terraced platform or pyramid which appears to have been partly faced with a mosaic of irregular stones. The upper part is much destroyed, but there appear to have been two high platforms side by side, rising from the back of a broad terrace which was partly occupied by a slightly sunken court, a feature which has been noted at other sites of the same age. Moxeke is known chiefly for a remarkable series of four clay plastered demi-figures and two heads, made of conical adobes, mud and stones, modelled in the round and painted black, white, red, blue and green, standing in niches separated by sections bearing figures in low relief. All are much damaged, but the best two of the demi-figures wear a sort of pleated kilt and a short cape, one of which is adorned with pendants in the form of four snakes almost identical with the stone ones of Chavín. Cerro Sechín was a temple of complex plan on a raised platform, but it is chiefly remarkable for what seems to have been the retaining wall of the platform, on either side of the stairway. It is composed of upright flat stones of irregular outline, alternating with smaller stones set above one another in pairs or threes. All bear strange incised designs, those on the uprights mostly standing men wearing loin cloths and truncated conical hats and carrying staves or clubs, but some appear to be conquered enemies because they lack weapons and have a limp appearance, while one appears to have been cut in half and one is a corpse without legs (*Ill. 142*). This group sometimes has the sort of pleated kilt seen on the

142 Two engraved slabs. A human figure with severed legs *(left)*, and a trophy head *(right)*. Chavín Period. Part of retaining wall of temple platform at Cerro Sechín, Casma Valley

Moxeke figures, and this forms a link with them.   Apart from the figures, one upright has six pairs of faces piled up on top of one another, and some are non-representational.   The smaller stones have severed heads in profile, the earliest known example of the head-hunter's trophy in Peruvian art.   The style of the carvings as a whole is quite unlike that of Chavín, but in addition to the link with Moxeke already mentioned some small objects from various parts of the coast bear designs which are common to the two styles. The dissimilarity is probably partly due to age differences, and writers have disagreed as to which is the older, but Collier and Thompson, who have worked most recently in Casma, regard Moxeke and Cerro Sechín as derivative from Chavín rather than as its prototype, though the stage at Chavín to which the influence belongs is not yet known.   Resemblances have been claimed to exist between the men on the stones at Cerro Sechín and the

143 Circular gold, repoussé plaque. Feline face with snake head appendages, within guilloche border. Late Chavín style. Possibly from Chavín de Huántar

Danzantes (Ill. 13) at Monte Albán in Oaxaca, Mexico, but it is doubtful if this amounts to more than that both are incised figures on flat stones.

Among the smaller stone carvings of Chavín style are mortars, bowls, plates and mace-heads. Prominent among these is a mortar in the form of a jaguar *(Ill. 144)*, probably from Chavín, now in the University Museum at Philadelphia, which Rowe ascribes to the earliest stage of the Chavín style. In spite of its comparatively small size—it is 13 inches long—it gives an impression of massive strength appropriate to a much larger object. Its jaguar markings have been stylized into L shapes and crosses. Two other animal mortars, from Pacopampa, the northernmost of the known Chavín sites, both show feline fangs, but one of them has a beak also, and this has been taken to show a combination of feline and owl. The other has the upper lip split in the middle, and from each half of it rises a volute enclosing the nostril. Both mortars have pestles with a feline head at the end of the handle, and both have the nostrils shown by the same convention as that of the second mortar, which is worth mentioning because a similar figure is transferred to form a sort of eyebrow on feline owl heads on a pot which will be described later. The under side of a plate from the north coast shows a relief carving of a quadruped with two feline heads, a combination

152

of the Chavín feline with the Preceramic heritage of two-headed figures. A cylindrical vessel in the Bliss Collection shows two grotesque dancing figures connected by a scroll or rope, each of them with a prolonged dentate jaw band with two pairs of fangs and one at the end. Many examples of the same sort could be given, in bone and shell as well as stone. The mace heads are graceful and doubtless effective objects with projecting flanges and points.

Gold, worked by hammering, welding and soldering, first appears on the Chavín horizon. Examples are a repoussé standing figure with fanged mouth holding two staves on a rectangular plaque, and another on a cylindrical crown, both from the Lambayeque Valley. Ear-spools with snake head and bird head designs are known from the same area, and in the Bliss Collection is a

144 Mortar in the shape of a jaguar, with stylized markings. Stone carved in the round and incised. The eyes were originally inlaid. Chavín Culture

145 Monochrome dark coloured bottle, with incised feline-inspired designs surrounded by rocker stamping. Cupisnique style

circular plaque, possibly from Chavín, with a feline face with snake head appendages in the middle, surrounded by a guilloche whose angularity betokens a late stage in the style *(Ill. 143)*.

The Chavín pottery of the coast is named Cupisnique, after the valley where it was first found. Typically it is a hard, monochrome ware, black, grey or buff in colour, decorated by modelling, incision, or some way of roughening the surface such as punctation or rocker stamping *(Ill. 145)*, a feature already seen at Tlatilco in Mexico (see page 32). There is only a limited amount of painting, chiefly in black and red, confined to the latter part of the period. The most typical shape is a closed vessel with a flat base and a stirrup spout, which consists of an arched tube with the spout emerging from the highest point *(Ill. 146)*. The stirrup spout is a form which is found on the north coast, with some interruptions, until the end of Pre-Columbian times, and these early examples are typically heavy in outline, with a relatively small opening under the stirrup and a low concave-sided spout, though some lighter forms are present and may be ascribed to the later stages. (Some which

146 Stirrup-spouted early Cupisnique jar of dark monochrome pottery, with rough surface perhaps suggested by a spondylus shell

have been claimed as Cupisnique, largely on grounds of colour, may belong to the later Mochica Culture.) Another common form is a jar with a narrow concave-sided neck, the upper part of which resembles the top of the stirrup spout. The bodies of these vessels may be spheroidal apart from the flat base, and decorated by incision with designs which in many cases include feline faces or fangs, and these may be emphasized by covering the background with punctation or rocker stamping *(Ill. 145)*. More typical are forms modelled in the round or in high relief to represent a wide variety of subjects, such as animal or human forms, houses, mollusc shells and vegetables. One remarkable vessel shows a nursing mother *(Ill. 147)*, one an aged wrinkled face, and a third is a hollow ring bearing two human heads and two heads which are combined feline and bird, probably owl *(Ill. 138)*. One feline owl has open eyes and the other has stylized ones in Chavín style, and one human face has open eyes and the other closed ones, possibly meant to show a contrast in each case between life and death. This is the vessel on which the double volutes into which the nostrils developed on the stone pestles and mortars have been moved up to form a sort of eyebrow on the feline owl faces. These pots are the earliest examples of the north coast tradition of realistic modelling, which reached its climax in the Classic Mochica Culture and was revived in an inferior form in the Post-Classic Chimú.

On the central coast, objects of pottery, wood and bone in Chavín style have been reported from a cemetery at Ancón, and three very curious instances of bird-feline heads, showing both beaks and fangs, in patches of cotton tapestry forming part of a loosely-woven plain weave cloth, were found in Professor Willey's excavations at Supe in the same area.

Far to the south in the Nasca and Ica valleys are graves belonging to the Paracas stage of the middle and later Formative. The early stages of this were deeply influenced by Chavín, and this is seen not only in incised and resin-painted depictions of fanged feline jaws on jars of local shapes but also in feline faces with extra

147 Modelled stirrup-spouted Cupisnique jar of dark pottery, representing a woman suckling her child

fangs and snake head appendages in pure Chavín style on painted cotton cloths. As has been said already, direct Chavín influence on the art of this area faded by about 300 B C, giving place to local developments.

The Later Formative and Classic Periods

After the Chavín horizon, different traditions developed in various parts of the country, and existing differences were accentuated. The main known areas of importance at this time are the north coast, the north highlands, the south coast and the south highlands. Artistically the central coast was unimportant, and the central highlands are virtually unknown.

THE NORTH COAST

During the later centuries B C the pure Chavín tradition died away, and a decorated pottery style of rather a different character called Salinar is found in graves in the Chicama Valley and to a lesser extent in the Virú Valley just to the south. This is its general position, but it is not clear to what extent it overlapped its predecessor and its successor. It was not accompanied by other artistic features of note.

It is distinguished by oxidized firing which produced red and brown colours, and sometimes has simple decoration such as lines, dots, triangles and steps in thin white paint. Vessel forms include (i) a modified form of stirrup-spouted jar, (ii) a spout and bridge jar in which a sloping spout was balanced by a figure, head or some other object, and joined to it by a thin bridge handle, and (iii) a bottle with a narrow vertical neck and loop handle. The first and third may be modelled or carry a modelled figure on the top, but the modelling is less accomplished than that of Cupisnique, though sometimes more lively (*Ill. 148*). Among the modelled forms are birds, animals, heads, houses, and little naked human beings or pairs of them which may be in erotic attitudes. The first Peruvian whistling jars are found among the spout and bridge forms, in which the figure is shown blowing a spherical whistle, which will sound when water is put into the jar and swung to and fro. In

157

148 Stirrup-spouted vessel of reddish-brown ware, in the form of a modelled monkey standing on an annular base. Salinar Culture, later centuries BC. Chicama Valley

later styles the whistle is hidden inside the figure. The style as a whole may show influence from the south, since the spout and bridge is essentially a south coast form, and white-on-red decoration may originate from the central coast. It is sometimes regarded as representing a white-on-red horizon of rather limited distribution.

A pottery style particularly characteristic of the Virú Valley, which is thought to begin after Salinar and to persist while the early stages of the Classic Mochica developed in the Chicama Valley, is called Virú or Gallinazo *(Ills. 149, 150)*. It includes stirrup spouts, spout and bridge pots with single or double containers, and wide-mouthed jars, with modelling if anything less realistic than that of Salinar, but its chief characteristic is negative or resist painting, in which designs in the colour of the vessel, generally red, appear against a black background. This is done by covering the areas to remain free of black with a resist such as wax or clay after firing.

149 Red spout and bridge jar with simple linear negative painting in black. Virú or Gallinazo style. Late Formative or Early Classic. Probably from Virú Valley

150 Spout and bridge jar representing a warrior carrying club and shield on a reed raft, with negative painting. Virú or Gallinazo style. Early Classic

The vessel is then smoked, or dipped in black stain and perhaps heated to fix it, after which the resist is removed. In the central and north coast this style follows the white-on-red and a negative horizon has been postulated on the strength of it, but when a larger area is considered it appears that this form of decoration started in this region on the south coast and spread northwards, reaching the north highlands in the Classic Period.

There is little to say about architecture in the northern valleys at this stage. Large terraced pyramids were built in Virú in the Gallinazo Period, using rectangular adobes marked by the cane moulds in which they were made, and some structures of this kind were built on steep spurs commanding the valley and were associated with platforms and rooms, all enclosed within a rock wall. These fortified sanctuaries derive a certain grandeur from their situation even in their decay. At a site on the valley floor a sunken court associated with such a pyramid had a retaining wall with two horizontal bands of geometrical decoration made by setting a row of mould-made adobe blocks with inset crosses above a row in the form of steps, with the background deeply recessed in each case. These blocks were painted green, red and yellow, with the recesses black, and the rest of the wall was white.

The Classic Period is marked by the development of the Mochica Culture, which originated in the Chicama and Moche Valleys and later spread south by conquest of the Virú Valley and beyond. It is distinguished by its well-known funerary pottery, of which the stirrup spout is the commonest form, but there are many others, including bell-shaped bowls with ring bases, flasks with flaring collars, double whistling jars and approximately hemispherical bowls. There are three forms of decoration—modelling in the round, modelling in low relief, and painting. The first is a continuation, and the acme, of the realistic modelling tradition of the area, but is more closely related to the Cupisnique variety than to Salinar or Gallinazo. Unlike Mexico, Peru has comparatively few figurines in comparison with its modelled pots at this period, or at any other time. A great deal of stress has been laid on Mochica realism, but it is only realistic within limits, and

151 Pottery bowl with fish alternating with decorative panels. With pressed relief, painted in red and white. Mochica

what the potters did was to stress a salient feature, such as the head of a figure with an elaborate head-dress, which they would represent with great fidelity, so catching the observer's attention that he does not notice that they have paid little attention to some other parts such as the lower limbs. Many modelled pots were made in moulds, themselves of pottery, and the same applies to those decorated in low relief, generally called pressed relief *(Ill. 151)*, but minor differences are introduced during the finishing process, so exact replicas are less frequent than might be expected. Most of the pots are painted in white and red, and the introduction of a little black and orange is a sign of a late stage in the period. This restraint in colour is characteristic of the north coast, and not only at this period. Some vessels lack modelled decoration and are skilfully painted with a wide variety of subjects in profile, including elaborate scenes, in red on a white ground *(Ill. 154)*. Unlike the modelled figures which appear static, many of them are designed to give an effect of movement which is accentuated in the later

161

stages, particularly when elaborately dressed figures appear to chase one another round a pot. The various modes of decoration are not mutually exclusive, and an example may be quoted which has a deer resting on the top of the pot and a deer hunt painted on the body *(Ill. 155)*. Five chronological stages, based on changes in the form of the stirrup spout and the nature of the decoration, have been distinguished, but the pottery is thin and well made throughout the period. Early Mochica stirrup spouts have much in common with Cupisnique ones *(Ills. 146,153)*, but stirrups later become larger, lighter and finally somewhat angular, and the spout loses its rim, becomes longer, passes through a tendency to have concave sides and may develop a slight taper. Painted scenes are introduced in the middle stages, and later become more complex and restless.

The subjects of the decoration on Mochica pots are extremely varied, and give valuable information about the life of the people. Plants, animals and birds are shown, and in some cases the species can be identified. There are naked prisoners, people with amputated

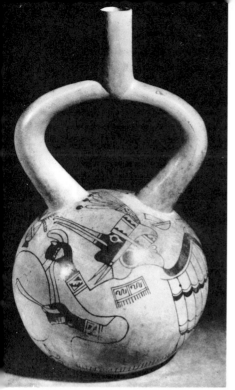

152-155 Four stirrup-spouted Mochica vessels. The first *(opposite left)* in the form of a house, painted in red and white. The second *(opposite right)* in the form of a seated man. Highly polished red slip. Early Mochica. The third *(above left)*, painted in red and white, shows a drummer wearing a humming bird mask and wings. Late Mochica. The fourth *(above right)* is decorated with a warrior chasing a spotted deer. A three-dimensional figure of a deer tops the vessel. Modelled and painted in red and white

156 Bone spatula handle with the engraved figure of a warrior dressed as a bird, and inset turquoise and pyrite nodules. Mochica. Santa Valley

157 Wooden head, inlaid with shell and turquoise, of a ceremonial digging stick. It shows a tusked figure holding a digging stick and accompanied by a boy. Mochica. Found in the grave of an old man and boy similarly dressed, at Huaca de la Cruz, Virú Valley

limbs or identifiable diseases, warriors, weapons, buildings *(Ill. 152)*, enthroned rulers, portraits *(Ills. 158, 159)* and gods. The well-known erotic scenes form but a small proportion of the whole (a figure of 2 % has been quoted). Painting and pressed relief include such diverse subjects as a procession of skeletons playing pan-pipes and a textile workshop. All bear witness to a complex, specialized, theocratic society, in which fighting played an important part.

Monumental architecture shows little that is new. It may be exemplified by the two enormous terraced pyramidal masses of unbonded adobes which make up the pyramids of the Sun and Moon in the Moche Valley between Virú and Chicama. Although they are rarely preserved, parts of buildings of this age were adorned with wall paintings of much the same character as the vase paintings, but without the colour restriction, as many as seven (black, white, red, grey, yellow, brown and blue) being noted on one example. The subjects were outlined by incision on the plaster, and patches of colour then painted in. A famous example at Moche showed personified weapons in battle with human beings, and getting the best of it. Another, discovered a few years ago at Pañamarca in the Nepeña Valley, shows a procession taking prisoners to sacrifice, illustrating a characteristic of this sort of painting, that the importance of a person was in proportion to his size.

Sculpture on a large scale is virtually unknown, but small objects were carved in various materials such as stone, bone *(Ill. 156)*, wood and shell. A good example is the contents of the grave of an old warrior priest of late Mochica date found in the Virú Valley. Among many other things, this contained three wooden staves. One of them is a copper-shod ceremonial digging stick, at the top of which is carved, and decorated with multi-coloured shell inlay, the figure of a tusked god (carrying his own digging stick), whom the old man himself was accoutred to impersonate *(Ill. 157)*. The second was an old war-club, with a pear-shaped head carved with a battle scene in low relief. The third was surmounted by an owl. Such carvings in general have much in common with the pottery modelling; they share its limited realism, and they gain interest from inlays of shell or turquoise.

158 Mochica portrait vase, a particularly fine example, painted in white and red

159 Mochica portrait vase with stirrup spout of a man wearing a decorated cap painted in red and white

Metalwork was well developed at this time, and gold, silver, copper and their alloys were worked and used for ornaments thoughout the coast. The north coast was exceptional in using copper for tools and weapons as well, and furnishes the best examples of metalwork in general. Particularly pleasing are small and delicate Mochica objects in which gold is combined with other materials, such as a pair of ear ornaments in the form of mosaic discs representing warriors in turquoise, shell and gold framed by a circular beaded gold rim, or a lunate nose-ornament of turquoise with a small gold mask in the middle and fringed with turquoise beads. A magnificent and unique object of unknown use, in the Mugica Gallo Collection, is a sheet-gold puma skin with the hollow head ingeniously modelled in the round. The body is made of two thicknesses of gold, each with a different form of repoussé decoration *(Ill. 160)*.

Remains which have been found in this area are enough to show a wide range of textile techniques, but they are rarely well preserved, and it is better to speak of this art in connexion with the south coast, where it was outstanding.

THE NORTH HIGHLANDS

Less is known about the north highlands than about the coast, but the chief artistic developments are found in two areas.

The first of these is the upper part of the Santa Valley and its environs, known as the Callejón de Huaylas. Here arose a notable pottery style called Recuay, which is thought to have developed out of a variety of the negative painted style of Virú found in the lower reaches of the Santa Valley itself. It flourished during Classic times. The vessels are of many shapes, very typical being flat-based globular jars with a constricted neck which may open out sharply into a wide flange round the mouth, or flare out gently. Most have some modelling on the body, generally in the form of a head, which may have a subsidiary tube spout emerging sideways from the mouth or the head-dress *(Ill. 161)*. Some more elaborate forms have the neck rising from one side of the body, the top of which is flattened to form a step where a group of modelled

160 Gold puma skin with three-dimensional head. On the animal's tongue a human face appears, and on its body a design of double two-headed serpents. The belly in two thicknesses forms a pouch. Gold repoussé work and wire. Mochica ▶

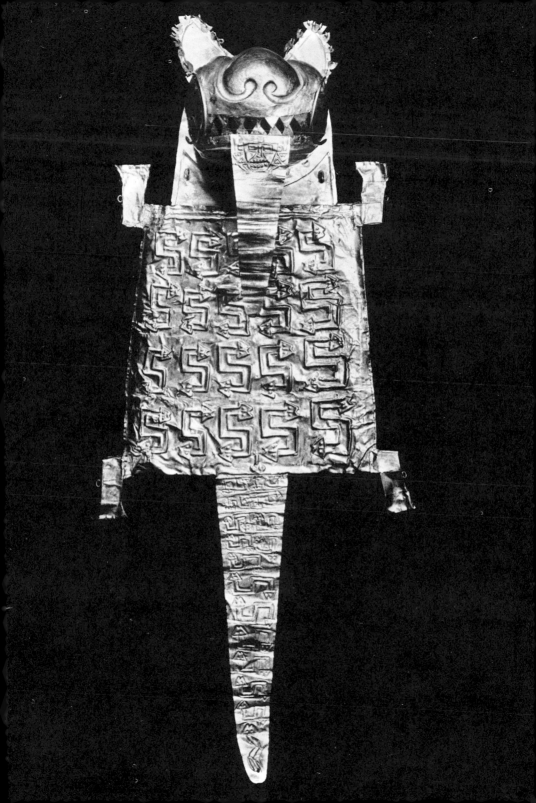

161 Jar with flange mouth and lateral spout emerging above a modelled human head between two animals. Decorated with black negative painting over white and red, showing a crested jaguar and other features. Recuay style. Callejón de Huaylas, North Highlands

figures may stand. Among forms of which several varieties are known is a modelled one showing a man leading a llama. Highly characteristic of Recuay pottery is black negative painting over a red and white ground, and many vessels have one or more examples of a jaguar with a large crest in this technique, and also steps, circles or dots. Ideas travelled between here and the Mochica area, and the modelling shows Mochica influence though it is far stiffer and more stylized. In the other direction is the rare occurrence of the flange mouth and lateral spout on Mochica jars.

No notable buildings have been ascribed to the Classic period in the Callejón, and the pottery comes from stone-lined subterranean galleries and box-like graves. Numbers of stone statues have been found; they are a metre or less high, of pillar-like or roughly conical form, showing no competence in carving in the round but a certain amount of ability in indicating surface detail. The brows and nose are shown as a T-shaped figure, the eyes are round and in relief, and the neck is hollowed out to throw the pointed chin into relief, but the other detail is very shallow. Squatting women and warriors can be distinguished among the subjects, the latter having decorated shields and wearing head trophies. There are also slabs showing felines and men in low relief, and these have features which link them to the statues and to Recuay pottery. The stone work does not approach its Chavín predecessors in quality.

The second highland area is round Cajamarca. Here an independent pottery style developed through later Formative and Classic times *(Ill. 162)*. It is called Cursive, from its lightly painted running scroll-like designs in brownish black or red on a white or cream ground. Small, highly stylized animals or heads may appear among the cursive scrolls, which are mostly found on the interiors of open bowls on low ring bases.

162 Bowl and two sherds, painted with cursive scroll pattern, including stylized faces and animals. Colours vary from red-brown to black, with some grey on the bowl, on a cream ground. Cajamarca, North Highlands

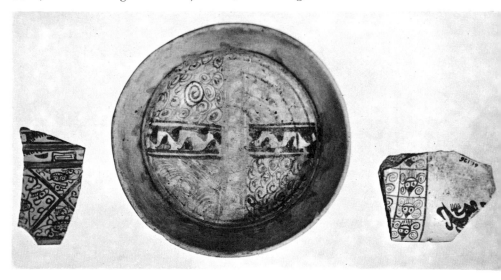

This area is of less artistic interest than its neighbours, although it contains prominent ceremonial centres in the form of clusters of pyramidal platforms built of rectangular adobes. Maranga, near Lima, is an example, and the earliest ruins of the important shrine of Pachacámac in the Lurín Valley are another. Here is a platform of many low terraces, each about 3 feet high, with polychrome paintings of plants and animals, surrounded by many later buildings.

The Classic pottery style of the area is called Interlocking, from the way in which angular designs derived from textile patterns interlock with one another. They are painted in rather dingy black, white and red colours on simple vessels such as bowls, beakers and jars, and the commonest of them are snakes and fish, or their heads.

THE SOUTH COAST

The earliest known Formative stage of any artistic significance is estimated to be rather later than the beginning of Chavín, and it gave rise to a different tradition, which we know largely from the very prominent cult of the dead. A large number of rich burials have been found; they are in a crouched position, unlike those of the north which are generally extended. One type, found in groups in deep, dome-shaped, rock-cut tombs, includes many individuals with skulls which have been trepanned, in some cases repeatedly, and another type, found in large numbers in rectangular pits, have highly deformed skulls. They are wrapped in many layers of specially-made textiles in mint condition, the making of which must have occupied many workers for a prodigious amount of time and involved far more effort than the grave deposits of the north, the chief constituent of which is pottery.

In pottery the south coast tradition is expressed by successive phases in the Formative Paracas style and the Classic Nasca style, upon which the chronological succession is based. It is distinguished by emphasis on colour, as many as eight colours appearing on some Classic pots, with no great skill in representational model-

163 Dark grey-brown spout and bridge vessel, the spout balanced by a stylized bird's head. The surface is burnished except for the bird's head and a large feline face incised at one end, some details of which are picked out in red paint applied after firing. Paracas style, Formative Period. South Coast

ling *(Ill. 165)*, as against the naturalistic modelling and restraint in colour of the north, and such life forms as are painted on pots are highly stylized. There is no interest in the realistic depiction of people and scenes in everyday surroundings, but rather in macabre features such as fantastic demons and a profusion of severed human heads, which is in accord with the exaggerated interest shown in the dead. Vessels have rounded bases, open bowls are very common, and the jar with spouts connected by a bridge, in which one spout may be replaced by a bird or human head, takes the place of the stirrup spout of the north. Beakers became common in the Nasca style *(Ill. 168)*.

Paracas pottery is decorated by incision, which may outline designs in vivid resinous colours painted after firing *(Ill. 164)*. The colours of these paints include red, yellow, orange, white, dark blue, dark green, black and brown, and are characteristic of the Paracas stage. The designs are feline faces *(Ill. 163)*, guilloches or geometrical forms such as circles or steps. Negative decoration,

164 Buff double spout and bridge vessel, with incised decoration suggesting matting on body and bridge. Parts of this are picked out in red,
yellow, black and white resinous paint applied after firing. Paracas style,
Formative Period. South Coast

consisting mainly of dots on a smudged background, was also
used, and together they were the first experimental attempts at
pottery decoration in the area. The earliest known Paracas phase
is thought have begun about 700 B C, and was strongly influenced
by the Chavín style, an influence seen particularly in the feline
faces. By about 300 B C the direct Chavín influence had died away
and a local style prevailed, even in feline designs *(Ill. 166)*. There
were minor changes in existing forms and new ones, including
doll-like effigy jars, were introduced, as was a new form of decoration consisting of fine line designs produced by burnishing
on black ware. Finally, in what is called the Early or Proto-Nasca
stage, about A D 100, the resinous colours were replaced by normal
pigments applied before firing, while the incised outlines were
retained. The dropping of the incision, perhaps a century later,
is held to mark the beginning of the Classic Nasca style.

165 Spout and bridge effigy jar modelled to represent a woman, and painted in black, white, dark red, yellow and orange. Nasca style, Classic Period. South Coast

166 Burnished black spout and bridge vessel representing a jaguar. The markings are incised, and most of the surface was probably originally covered with resinous post-fired colours, of which some red, yellow, grey and white remain. Paracas style, Formative Period. South Coast

167 Double spout and bridge vessel decorated with two rows of crabs. Red, orange, and dark grey paint over dark red slip. Early Classic Nasca

Classic Nasca can be divided into many stages, but it is convenient to group them into two main ones. In the first of these, the background slip is either a sombre red or white, and in the second it is generally white. Over these the designs are painted in three to eight colours, of which shades of red, black, white, brown, yellow, grey and violet are the most usual. The designs fall into two main groups, the first consisting of recognizable but stylized birds, fish *(Ill. 167)* or plants and the second of religious or mythological themes, such as the demons or trophy heads already mentioned, which become more frequent in the later stages at the expense of the first group. In the first stage the designs are fairly compact, whereas later they become more florid and tend to sprawl all over the background. Rowe has recently pointed out that the more recognizable natural forms come in the middle of the Paracas-Nasca sequence as a whole, early in Classic Nasca, with the more extravagant and stylized forms before and after. This is contrary to the common assumption, on which the original seriation of the Nasca style was based, that natural forms invariably come earliest in such a sequence. Within the limited range to

168 Beaker painted in red, purplish red, grey, yellow and black on a white ground, showing a demon between inner bands of geometrical design and outer ones of trophy heads. Late Nasca, Classic Period. South Coast

which it was applied, this seriation gave the right results, but it need not have done so.

The other great artistic medium in the south was textile production, and this is not due merely to better conditions of preservation than those in the north. Early in the Paracas succession such normal weaving techniques as gauze, brocade and double cloth in combinations of alpaca wool and cotton were in use, but the most notable feature of the phase is embroidery. This became fashionable later and persisted to some extent into the Nasca phase, but was used very little afterwards. The finest examples have come from the mummy bundles in the rectangular graves at Paracas, and consist of mantles, shirts, loin-cloths, turbans and other garments, embroidered in vivid reds, blues, yellows, greens, browns and other colours, all derived from combinations of red, yellow and indigo dyes with the colours of the natural cotton and wool. The designs include grotesque winged and masked humans, combined human and animal monsters holding trophy heads, animals, fish and birds, with little attempt at naturalism. Individual figures are small in scale, but they may be

169 *(left)* Part of the border of a mantle, covered with solid alpaca wool embroidery, showing outlines of small cats within larger ones, in rose red, yellow and dark blue. Paracas

170 *(below)* Rare type of tapestry in rose pink, light blue and yellow with a design showing a stylized monster worked in small shell beads strung on the warp. Nasca

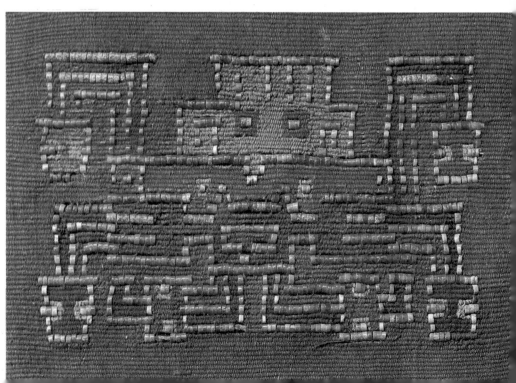

171 Lay figure dressed in richly embroidered mantle, turban and undergarments, from a Paracas mummy

powdered over the surface of a garment in different colour combinations with gorgeous effect. Complete garments survive, and the figures dressed in them in the National Museum at Lima are a splendid sight *(Ill. 171)*. Other noteworthy techniques were designs formed by plain weave against a background of gauze, and painting on cloth showing a much surer touch than later examples.

There are two strains in Paracas textile design, a curvilinear and a rectilinear one, which seem to reflect the passage of time to some extent. None but rectilinear designs are found in the early stages, and they were encouraged by the use of true textile techniques. A tendency to outline them gives a transparent effect, which may be accentuated by outline figures in a contrasting colour inside them, for example birds or miniature cats may be shown within large cats *(Ill. 169)*. Embroidery encouraged curvilinear designs built up in solid patches of colour, although rectilinear ones were far from being excluded, and there was a tendency at later stages towards floridity and the development of appendages and space-fillers, recalling the evolution of painting on Nasca pots. With the coming of Classic Nasca, tapestry and other textile techniques increased *(Ill. 170)* and embroidery diminished in importance.

About architecture there is little to say. As in other areas, ceremonial centres were based on stepped pyramids. One of the largest centres, of the Nasca phase, is a group of at least six, each accompanied by courts, but they are natural hills, terraced and faced with conical adobes. Even so, they do not approach the entirely artificial pyramids of the north in size.

An ability to delineate outline figures on a vast scale is demonstrated by the markings seen from the air on the desolate pampas round the Nasca Valley *(Ill. 172)*. There is an immense number of long, straight lines, also rectangles, triangles, spirals, zig-zags and occasional birds and fish, formed by removing the dark brown pebbles which cover the yellow, sandy surface. The animal forms recall some painted on Nasca pots, and a radiocarbon date of about A D 500, measured on a post associated with them, connects them with the Nasca phase. Their use is uncertain—astronomical

172 Markings on the barren plateau above the Nasca Valley. Linear patterns have been formed by removing surface pebbles to expose the yellow sandy soil. Nasca Culture

observations have been suggested—but it must surely have been a ceremonial one.

The end of Classic times is heralded by changes in the Nasca pottery style, which began about the eighth century, mainly by degeneration but partly by the appearance of new influences. Drawing becomes slovenly, background colours dull, there is a tendency to geometrical decoration, and modelled forms of birds, animals and human beings, previously very rare, become more frequent.

THE SOUTH HIGHLANDS

Important remains of the later Formative and Classic periods have been found in three places, Tiahuanaco, Pucára and Chiripa, and isolated examples of stone carving are scattered throughout the region.

At Chiripa, on the Bolivian side of Lake Titicaca, a group of double-walled rectangular adobe houses was found ranged round a court, and they were accompanied by thick-walled pottery painted with steps and similar geometrical designs in yellow on a red slip, which suggests the beginning of painted decoration like the white-on-red of the coast. Most examples are flat-based bowls with vertical sides. The site is dated to the first six centuries B C.

Much more important are the other two sites. The famous site of Tiahuanaco, also on the Bolivian side of the lake, had a long life, from well back in the Late Formative Period until after the Classic. The extent of its influence on the whole region in early Post-Classic times is one of the most notable features of American archaeology. Little has been published about the earliest stages, but it is known that there was incised and painted pottery, possibly related to Paracas. The oldest stone structures seem to date from the last centuries B C and to be contemporary with the pottery generally called Early Tiahuanaco. This includes a polychrome ware decorated in shiny black, white, red, orange and brown, directly on the micaceous brown clay or on a slip of the same colour, with interlocking geometrical designs such as triangles, or strange highly stylized animal forms. The vessels are flat-bottomed, and typical shapes are an open bowl with slightly diverging sides and wavy rim, bearing a modelled feline head and tail *(Ill. 173)*, the 'spittoon', and a tall-necked bottle. The feline heads already show the eye divided vertically into black and white halves, which is highly characteristic of the art style of the area. Similar shapes, apart from the spittoon, continued into the Classic Period. There are concave-sided bowls with feline heads and tails, but the head is more realistic though it issues from a square flange. There are similar bowls with plain rims which may have a pair of ring handles on the sides, but the most typical of all is a new form, a tall, graceful, concave-sided beaker, the *kero (Ill. 174)*, which may have a raised cordon round the middle. Vessels generally have a red slip, which gives them rather a sombre appear-

173 Bowl with feline head and tail and wavy rim, painted in red, black, white, orange and brown on pale brown ware. Note the divided eyes. Early Tiahuanaco, Formative Period. South Highlands

174 Beaker *(kero)* with upper band of stylized heads, lower of stylized felines, all in profile. Note vertically divided eyes. Polychrome paint on red slip. Classic Tiahuanaco

ance, over which they are painted in yellow, grey or brown, black and white, or some of these colours. The ware is fine and well polished, but the design colours, originally bright, may weather rather faint. The most usual designs are felines and condors in profile with divided eyes, and geometrical figures such as steps, triangles and the combined angular scroll and step called the step fret. The felines show a stylized nostril looking like a ring balanced on the snout. After the Classic Period the pottery passed into a decadent stage which lasted for an unknown time. Designs were carelessly painted, geometrical ones became more frequent, and animal forms broke down so that eyes or heads appeared repeatedly instead of whole figures. Shapes also changed, and in particular the *kero* became less graceful, some examples having a very small base, a feature which may have spread from the Cochabamba district where it appeared in Classic times.

Tiahuanaco is primarily known for its masonry and stone carving. Already in the Late Formative there was a rectangular platform with a retaining wall of massive dressed uprights alternating with a filling of smaller rectangular blocks, but most of the other surviving structures, which are greatly damaged by the looting of stone, are probably of Classic date. Their relationships are somewhat haphazard, and the site does not compare in its planning with the great Mesoamerican ones. There is a large rectangular stepped pyramid with smaller ones projecting from it on opposite sides, made by improving and facing a natural hill, and this was crowned with a reservoir as well as buildings. There is a semi-subterranean rectangular building with carved heads tenoned into the walls, and there are a number of remarkable large stone blocks, carved with great accuracy and skill, some of which have doorways, rectilinear niches, and such figures as stepped squares and rectangles, recessed or in relief. Some of these may have been assembled to form chambers with monolithic walls, and some to form larger buildings. Some stones were held together by accurately cut notches, and some by straight or T-shaped copper cramps recessed into the stones, and it has been suggested that tools of hardened copper must have been

175 Central figure from monolithic doorway, holding
staves thought to represent a
spear-thrower, and a quiver
of darts. Probably and important god. Classic Period.
Tiahuanaco, Bolivia

used to shape at least the notched ones, although most Andean
masonry was worked with stone tools. Perhaps the most notable
feature of the site is the great monolithic doorway, cut from a
block of lava about 12 feet by 10 feet, bearing a central figure
carved in low relief, flanked by three rows of attendants, with a
border at the bottom bearing complex frets ending in condor
heads and enclosing heads like those of the central figure *(Ill. 175)*.
This figure stands facing the front and holding a staff in each
hand. The hands have only three fingers and the thumb. The
staves, which may represent a spear-thrower and a quiver with
two darts, have a condor head at the lower end, and one has a
condor at the top to represent the hook of the spear-thrower,
whereas the other bifurcates and both halves end in a condor head.
The trapezoidal head is surrounded by radiating appendages,
some of which end in feline heads, each with the ring-like nostril

176 Kneeling me
statue of limeston
Probably Late Fo
mative. Pokot
near Tiahuanac
Bolivia

which appears on the pottery, and the remainder end simply in rings. The face has round staring eyes from which depend bands bearing circles, which suggest tears. Condor and feline heads are repeated on the body, and from the belt hangs a row of faces, perhaps trophy heads. The attendants, who face in towards the central figure, have heads like his, but in profile, or condor heads, and are dressed in winged cloaks bearing numerous condor head appendages. They also carry staves. The weeping eyes, the standing figure himself, the condor and the feline, represented so differently from the felines of Chavín, are features which recur constantly wherever the influence of Tiahuanaco is felt and must lie at the heart of its religion.

Massive statues have been found in and around Tiahuanaco, the largest being 24 feet in total height. They resemble pillars bearing relief designs rather than true sculpture in the round; clothing is shown in flat relief like the subsidiary figures on the great doorway, and the figures may carry beakers or unidentified objects. The flat relief carvings on statues and doorway may reasonably be supposed to have been derived from textile patterns, and although no highland Tiahuanaco textiles have been preserved, similar designs appear on coastal ones under Tiahuanaco influence. Classic Tiahuanaco pottery lacks some designs found on the stonework, such as the full-face standing figure, which appear on coastal pottery and textiles, and it is thought that textiles were the main vehicle for the transference of Tiahuanaco designs to the coast. Apart from the pillar-like statues there are slabs with relief designs and tenoned heads for insertion into walls at Tiahuanaco. Some of the slabs and a few statues show carving in rather a different style, sub-angular or heavily rounded rather than angular, which resembles Late Formative examples at Pucára, so it probably precedes the typical Tiahuanaco style. Kneeling statues by the churchyard at Tiahuanaco and at Pokotia are examples *(Ill. 176)*.

Tiahuanaco art, then, is stiff and formal with a limited repertory. Even living creatures are heavy and squat, and in the Classic Period all show a strong tendency to rectilinear forms. The sculptures and probably the buildings themselves were originally painted

177 Stone statue showing a man carrying a human head. Late Formative. Pucára, South Highlands, Peru

and some details appear to have been sheathed with gold plates, but this may well have accentuated the impression of massive severity which is given even by the scattered remnants of the ceremonial site.

Pucára is some way north-west of Lake Titicaca, and dates from the end of the Late Formative between about 250 B C and A D 100. The chief sanctuary here consisted of a horseshoe-shaped enclosure, bounded by at least two concentric walls composed of short, straight lengths with red sandstone foundations. The outer one enclosed small chambers containing one or two altar-like slabs in its thickness. Within the enclosure was a slightly sunken terrace surrounding a square sunken court bounded by white sandstone slabs. The masonry is not so well fitted as that of Tiahuanaco, and chinks may be filled with adobe or pieces of stone. The buildings themselves have vanished, but are thought to have been of adobe with thatched roofs.

The sculptures consist of statues and flat standing slabs. The typical statues are squat, heavy men wearing a cap and a loin-cloth with side flaps, and they may also carry a human head *(Ill. 177)*. Their sub-angular contours have already been mentioned. Many of the slabs have a notch cut out of one side at the top, and are carved in low relief with geometrical figures made up of checkers, stepped crosses, sharp zig-zags, diamonds and chevrons, with curvilinear patterns whose flow is interrupted by zig-zags, or with stylized fresh-water fish or lizards.

The decorated pottery, which is known only from fragments, is made of a reddish-buff micaceous clay, and designs are painted in red and black on the natural colour, or in black and rather fugitive yellow over a red slip *(Ill. 178)*. A characteristic feature is that the outlines of the colours are incised. Designs include felines in profile with the head shown full face in relief, human, feline and condor heads in profile, and geometrical figures such as stepped lines. As at Tiahuanaco, eyes are divided vertically, but the natural buff of the ware may replace the white used there,

178 Potsherd representing feline head with vertically divided eyes. Design in low relief, incised and painted in black and red. Late Formative. Pucára, South Highlands, Peru

and nostrils may be shown as rings balanced on the snout. Known shapes are a flat-bottomed bowl with flaring sides and a bowl with a low ring base, and what appears to be part of a trumpet. By the time that Tiahuanaco had reached its full flowering, Pucára seems to have been abandoned.

Early Post-Classic : The Tiahuanaco Spread

The end of Classic times is thought to have been marked by general unrest, during which the Tiahuanaco ceremonial pottery style appeared among the native ones in the Mantaro basin, and notably at the extensive site of Huari, which lacks important buildings. It was transmitted thence to the coast, probably in the tenth century, where it is found at Nasca and Pachacámac. The best examples come from Pacheco in the Nasca Valley, where a great dump of broken ceremonial pottery was found. Among the forms reconstructed are large inverted bell-shaped urns with flattened bases, painted in polychrome with full-face standing figures with divided eyes, closely resembling the central figure on the Tiahuanaco doorway. There are also large boldly-painted human effigy jars, and others in the form of a llama. A common feature here and on the central coast was a band of painted chevrons, forming a border or decorating the bridge of a double-spouted jar.

To begin with, the style was everywhere strongly Tiahuanacoid in character and comparatively uniform, with a similar range of colours to the highland style but brighter in tone. Some features of highland sculpture, especially the full-face standing figure, his face alone, and the attendant figures, appear on coastal pottery but not on that of Tiahuanaco itself. The same designs are found on coastal tapestries, but stone sculpture is totally lacking there. There are differences in detail between the two areas, for instance feline heads may replace condor ones, and the 'tear' bands on the face may be shown ending in trophy heads, but there is no doubt as to the identity of the figures. Pottery shapes also differ, but two are common to coast and highlands, the *kero* and a cup of more squat proportions, though the coastal *kero* was straight-sided and less graceful.

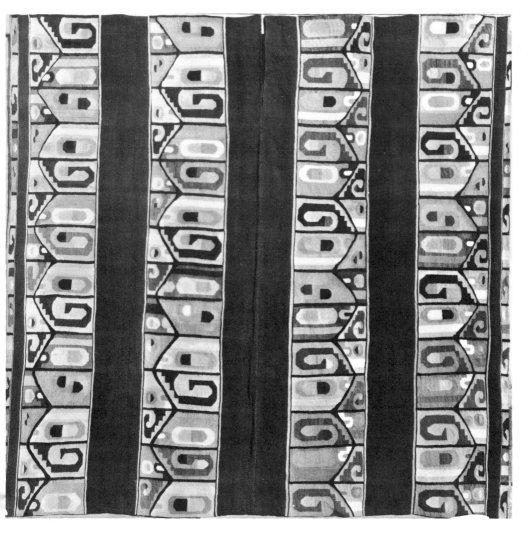

179 Poncho shirt, with vertical bands of tapestry bearing abstract designs. The vertically divided eyes show the derivation from Tiahuanaco. Coast Tiahuanaco, Early Post-Classic Period

180 Process of stylization from one of the falcon-headed, staff-bearing attendant figures on the monolithic gateway, Tiahuanaco *(left)*, to textile designs. This process can be more easily understood if the figure

After a comparatively short time, perhaps half a century, each of the three main centres, Huari, Pachacámac and Nasca, developed its own variety of Tiahuanaco-influenced pottery which spread through its own area. (The Pachacámac variety, which spread south to Ica, favoured the depiction of birds of prey.) The old artistic traditions were obliterated, and the Nasca and Interlocking styles vanished for ever. Tiahuanacoid influence spread far to the north, and the Mochica style also disappeared, though it reappeared later in a degenerate form, which suggests that it may have lingered on in remote northern regions as yet unexplored. After this the Tiahuanaco style gradually faded away, and this was shown on the pottery by a breakdown of Tiahuanaco designs and a reduction in the number of shapes and colours.

This, then, was the general sequence of events. The reasons for them are not certain, but the earliest contacts between highlands and coast, involving the transfer of religious symbols, can best be explained as a religious movement. The next stage, with its obliteration of the older art styles throughout the coast and the introduction of new building plans and the southern custom of burial in cloth-wrapped bundles to the Mochica area, strongly suggests military force emanating from Huari or the central coast. The north highlands were also affected, but by contact rather than conquest, except for a possible brief intrusion into the Callejón de Huaylas. Then came the gradual fading of Tiahuanaco influence,

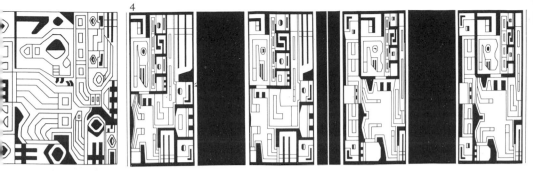

is regarded as a series of vertical zones which can be extended, contracted, or even transposed at will. The most contracted form can be seen on the right (4). Coast Tiahuanaco Culture.

perhaps by the absorption of the invaders, over a period of two to three centuries, followed by the emergence of three new coastal states. A few significant features of coastal Tiahuanaco art can now be discussed.

Textile production flourished. Tapestries bearing designs closely similar to those of the highland stonework have already been mentioned, but there are others in which the designs appear to be abstract, although most of them retain obvious Tiahuanaco motifs, such as divided eyes, executed in various colours. They belong to poncho-like shirts, on which the designs appear on a varying number of broad vertical bands symmetrically disposed about the central line, and it has been ingeniously suggested that they may have been a kind of uniform for officials, the grade denoted by the number and width of the ornamental bands *(Ill. 179)*. The designs are executed mostly in yellows, oranges and light browns, with a limited use of blue, green, red and pink, and, to take an example, steps in stylization have been traced from a close copy of one of the attendant figures on the Tiahuanaco doorway to an unrecognizable abstraction *(Ill. 180)*. If the figure is thought of as a series of vertical zones, some may be widened, some compressed, and some even transposed. In certain instances the process has gone so far that not even eyes remain, and the design's units may consist of some such pattern as a square with a pair of step frets balancing about a diagonal. Another interesting technique

191

181 Square cap of knotted wool pile cloth, with geometrical decoration in red, turquoise, blue, buff, brown and white. Coast Tiahuanaco, Early Post-Classic Period

was knotted pile cloth, used to make square caps *(Ill. 181)*, some of which were decorated with Tiahuanacoid figures with divided eyes. Similar caps were made in feather-work. Tie-dyeing *(plangi)* was used to produce rows of irregular hollow circles of the colour of the undyed cloth against a dyed background, and a patchwork of pieces of different colours is sometimes found.

Apart from the *keros* and cups already mentioned, common forms of painted pottery are double spout and bridge jars with rather long tapering spouts, which diverge much more sharply than Nasca ones *(Ill. 182)*, and jars with a modelled face on the neck. Painted designs, at first of clear Tiahuanaco character, break down in time and the end product is geometrical decoration in black, white and red *(Ill. 183)*, which in some cases can be seen to be the final degeneration of faces or figures. Monochrome black, grey or red wares decorated in relief by casting in pottery moulds (pressed relief) are common. The designs may take such forms as step frets or running scrolls, or sunken pictorial panels with such features as cats or men holding staves in low relief against a stippled background. Shapes are very varied and include canteen-shaped

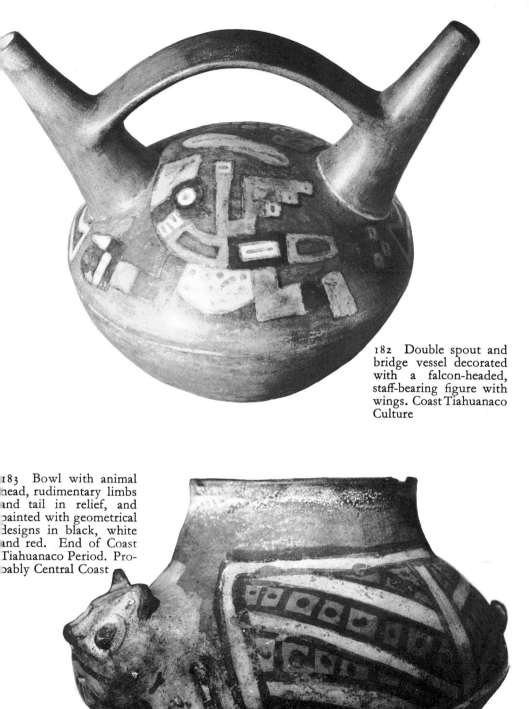

182 Double spout and bridge vessel decorated with a falcon-headed, staff-bearing figure with wings. Coast Tiahuanaco Culture

183 Bowl with animal head, rudimentary limbs and tail in relief, and painted with geometrical designs in black, white and red. End of Coast Tiahuanaco Period. Probably Central Coast

bottles, double vessels and double spout and bridge jars. Some of these designs and shapes carry over into the later Chimú black ware. Characteristic of a late stage, especially in the north, is a red to buff coloured face-collar jar, painted in very washy black, white and orange, which may have pressed relief designs on the body *(Ill. 184).*

A good many small objects in wood, shell, stone, bone or metal have been found in Coast Tiahuanaco graves or show characteristics of the period, but some would be hard to distinguish from those of the next stage. Many of them have multi-coloured inlays, showing great skill in the handling of the materials, and it is this, rather than any great artistic merit, which gives them their chief interest. There is little to say about coastal architecture, except that the southern invasion of the Virú Valley on the north coast was accompanied by the introduction of large rectangular adobe-walled compounds without interior divisions, as well as smaller ones enclosing groups of dwellings, which may foreshadow the urbanization of the following period.

The situation in the north highlands was different. Pottery belonging to a middle Coast Tiahuanaco stage is found with local wares in stone-lined graves in the Callejón de Huaylas, in probable association with some stone buildings, which are the only reason for drawing attention to the area. The most elaborate of these, now sadly decayed, is at Wilkawain. It has three storeys, each with seven rooms with ventilation shafts; it is of split but undressed stone, in alternating thick and thin courses, with the interstices filled with small stones. It is crowned with a projecting course of slabs, with a recessed one beneath it, below which was a row of tenoned cat heads, none of which are now in place. This is local masonry, with a remote resemblance to Chavín but none to Tiahuanaco, and the presence of the Coast Tiahuanaco pottery cannot mean more than a brief intrusion at the most.

Further north, in the highlands east of the Chicama Valley, is a great fortified hill-top group called Marca Huamachuco, which owes nothing to Tiahuanaco. It is skilfully built of irregular coursed rubble, with long-and-short quoins like those of late

194

184 Face-collar jar. On neck, head of man wearing hat and ear-spools; on body, felines in pressed relief. Painted in washy black, white and orange on buff ground. Late North Coast Tiahuanaco style

Saxon work in England, and some buildings had two or three storeys. The usual building unit was a long narrow gallery, with the upper floors normally supported on corbels, and some of these were arranged round courts and some placed irregularly. The outer wall of the main group is double, and itself forms a gallery round the perimeter. There was some ornamental stonework, including stylized feline heads with zig-zag crests, which might be a reminiscence of Recuay, tenoned for insertion into walls, and some small slabs with step frets in low relief. The main building period here is associated with painted pottery of Cursive style, related to that of Cajamarca in the same region.

Cajamarca itself was slow to be affected by Tiahuanaco. Pottery of north coast Tiahuanaco styles has been found there, but the local cursive manner of painting on white or cream paste continued and only the designs gradually changed under Tiahuanaco influence until there came to be a majority of carelessly drawn feline heads and circles, possibly representing eyes or jaguar markings. The original Cursive tradition remained strong enough to influence a north coast pottery style at the beginning of the next period.

The Later Post-Classic

Tiahuanaco influence on the art of the south coast died out by about A D 1100, though it may have lasted longer in the north, but by the thirteenth or the beginning of the fourteenth century new states were established on the coast, and each had its own pottery style, although there were few obvious differences in metalwork and textiles.

In the north was the kingdom of Chimú or Chimor, with its capital at Chan Chan near Trujillo; it is thought that there was an older independent state to the north of it, with its centre in the Lambayeque Valley, but this was absorbed by the Chimú in the fifteenth century. Insofar as they are known, its architecture and pottery were similar to those of Chimú—in fact this may be the one area where the north coast modelling tradition survived the Tiahuanaco spread. Chan Chan contained ten great compounds surrounded by walls, in some cases double, with few openings, of rectangular adobe bricks or cast adobe *(tapia)* up to 50 feet high, separated by irrigated areas, cemeteries and minor buildings. Each compound was carefully planned, and might include small pyramids, rows of houses and store-rooms, gardens sunk to the water-table, and stone-lined reservoirs. Some also contained imposing buildings with walls covered with designs in moulded clay plaster *(Ill. 185)* believed to be the dwellings of the nobility, who had concentrated their retainers in the com-

185 Relief on a wall in Chan Chan. Bands of birds, fish, and fantastic animals, and of scrolls and step-ornament. Moulded clay plaster. Chimú Culture. Later Post-Classic Period

pounds in order to control them. The designs vary a good deal; they include bands of step frets and scrolls, trellises, and comparatively realistic birds, fish and animals, as well as highly stylized bird designs like some of the Chimú textile patterns. Other important towns were similarly laid out. Large pyramids do not appear to have been built in this period, and those associated with some towns, *e.g.* Pacatnamú in the Jequetepeque Valley, are probably older. The question is complicated by the weathered state of the ruins, but the absence of imposing religious structures in important towns is in any case an indication of increased secularization. At the southern limit of Chimú, in the Fortaleza Valley, is a great terraced structure of rectangular adobes crowning a hill, which is believed to have been a frontier fortress.

186 Hammered silver double spout and bridge ceremonial vessel with ornamental band on body, openwork crest on bridge and freestanding elements in the form of two monkeys and four heads. Chimú. Lambayeque Valley

187 Drinking vessel *(paccha)* in the form of a man fishing from a reed raft. Black ware. Chimú

188 Black ware canteen, with pressed relief showing a jaguar on body, and two small handles. Chimú

189 Stirrup-spouted vessel with monkey on spout and a man holding a child, model-led in the round, on a cubical base. Black ware. Against a background of a contemporary buff textile with brocaded fish and pelican designs. Chimú

Chimú is known for its polished black modelled pottery, which has been likened to tarnished silver *(Ill. 189)*, and some well known pottery shapes are occasionally found in silver *(Ill. 186)* or gold, to which they seem well suited. The stirrup-spouted jar is a common form, but the spout differs from Mochica and older forms in that the loop tends to have a rectangular section, its sides may have a row of birds in pressed relief, and a small animal, usually a monkey, is perched on the junction between this and the upright. The body of the pot may be of a simple form, commonly spheroidal, in some cases with panels in pressed relief, *(Ill. 188)*, or it may be modelled to represent a wide variety of forms such as human and animal figures, heads, limbs, vegetables, houses or rafts *(Ill. 187)*. There are many other shapes, such as canteens, double spout and bridge jars or similar ones with one spout replaced by a head or figure, and double jars which may whistle, but in spite of the variety of subjects there is much standardization and a depressing lifelessness about the modelling, which is much inferior to most Mochica work. Pottery, metalwork, textiles and other products are thought to have been made under conditions something like mass production, and this is supported by the finding near Chan Chan of a workshop containing vast numbers of shell fragments at all stages in the production of inlay for wooden carvings *(Ill. 192)*. Although black pottery predominates, red ware in similar forms is also found, and Kubler has suggested that the modelled forms as well as the pressed relief were selected under the influence of metal-working, comparing the red ware to copper as he did the black to tarnished silver. There are smaller quantities of some painted wares, in dull red on white, and black or black and red on a dull reddish buff. The first two differ only in colour from the black ware, and the third, nearly all spout and figure jars, has black cursive decoration divided into zones by thin red bands. The painting points to influence from Cajamarca and some of the modelling may even point, at a long remove, to Recuay.

A good deal of the surviving metalwork is thought to be Chimú, but some of it cannot be located either in place or time so this brief

190 Repoussé gold beaker decorated with a standing male figure with plumed head-dress and ear-spools, holding staffs. The head-dress and the ear-spools are inlaid with turquoise. Chimú. Lambayeque Valley

summary must cover a wider range. There are graceful *Kero*-shaped beakers with repoussé designs *(Ill. 190)*, narrow nearly cylindrical ones of surpassing ugliness with a beaky face on one side, diadems, attractive little cast ear-scoops with a bird or animal on the top, knives, mace-heads, open-work crescentic-shaped nose-ornaments, model litters and a host of other things in gold, silver, copper and their alloys *(Ill. 193)*. Bronze probably dates from the Inca period. Silver objects may be inlaid with gold, copper

191 Gold funerary mask with stone eyes and traces of red and green pain[t]
Chimú. Lambayeque Valley

ones with silver and bronze ones with copper and silver. There
are wooden figurines inlaid with gold and shell, and wooden
spear-throwers sheathed in gold. Thin plaques and sequins were
made for sewing to garments, and ear ornaments, pectorals and
even mummy masks had danglers attached to catch the light.
The effect in some cases, particularly when the metal is very thin,
verges on the tawdry. Some of the most elaborate and flamboyant
objects come from the far north *(Ill. 191)*, and among them are
large gold ceremonial knives with semicircular blades from the
Lambayeque area. A good example has a plain handle with
danglers at the top, surmounted by the hollow figure of a deer
(Ill. 194). A type of which several are known has a handle consisting of a hollow dumpy figure with a large semicircular head-
dress, which must represent a god or ruler. His eyes, ears and

202

192 Ear-spool with a reversible design of two birds with a common body. Wood, with crenellated and polished edge, inlaid with coloured shell. Chimú

193 Thin silver, repoussé ear-spools showing a central head with head-dress, surrounded by ten similar heads. Chimú

194 Ceremonial knife. The blade has a semicircular tip and is surmounted by the hollow figure of a deer, and danglers. Blade of base metal with gold overlay, ornamentation in gold. Chimú. Lambayeque Valley

195 Painted plain weave cotton textile. Designs are in brown on a buff ground, originally white. Chimú. Painted designs of this time show far less sureness of touch than woven ones (cf. *Ills. 196, 197*)

clothing may be inlaid with turquoise and his face painted red with cinnabar.

Some of the pleasantest products of the period are textiles, but even here there is a tendency to standardization *(Ills. 195-8)*. A great variety of techniques was known, but gauzes, brocades and double cloth were particularly common, and tapestry, formerly so popular, was confined to small areas such as corners and narrow borders. The products of different parts of the coast can be distinguished by specialists, but there is an overall similarity and what is said here about Chimú can be applied to other areas. Birds, especially pelicans, fish and animals, were stylized in an almost uniform and very competent fashion, and arranged in horizontal or diagonal rows, or in the contrasting colour on squares or diamonds of two alternating colours, a type of design to which double cloth is particularly suited. Step frets were commonly used for borders. Featherwork was very popular; feathers of different colours were sewn to plain weave cloth to produce a sort of mosaic, making designs such as scrolls, birds, animals and fish. It was used on poncho shirts, and to make diadems, and similar mosaic designs are also found on the ends of wooden ear-plugs.

196 Double cloth with pelican designs in brown and white (*below*). The border of tapestry is worked on gauze with pelicans within scrolled lozenges. Chimú

197 Doll representing fisherman and net. Slit tapestry face, and warp-striped plain weave shirt, in pink, white, black, buff, yellow, green and pale lavender. Chancay Valley, Central Coast

198 How to draw a cat. Warp-striped textile with brocaded cats in blue, yellow and brown on dirty white. Chimú

On the central coast was a state called Cuismancu, much smaller than Chimú, which occupied the Chancay, Ancón, Rimac and Lurín Valleys. It is chiefly distinguished by its pottery style, which takes its name from Chancay (*Ill. 199*). It is a dull red or cream ware with a crumbly white slip over which simple designs such as stripes, wavy lines, cross-hatching, chevrons, dot-sprinkled

199 Large ovoid jar with black-on-white decoration. Chancay style, Later Post-Classic. Central Coast

triangles or small animals are painted in black. It grew out of a black-white-red style *(Ill. 183)*, or degenerated from it, and some examples retain red bands. Typical shapes are large ovoid jars with a flaring or cup-like collar and a pair of loop handles, and effigy jars of much the same shape, with rudimentary limbs and a curious flat face with a pointed chin on the collar. There are also bowls of various shapes and double jars with a spout, bridge and figure on the top. Although this is ceramically and artistically a degenerate style, it has become fashionable among collectors.

The architecture of Cuismancu is less known than that of Chimú, but it seems to have been similar, since Cajamarquilla and Armatambo, both in the Rimac Valley, were large cities with walled compounds. Some of the walls have relief decoration, and some are crowned with battlements.

On the south coast another state called Chincha covered the valleys of Ica, Nasca, Pisco and Chincha, with its capital in the Ica Valley. About A D 1100 a distinctive pottery style arose out of the disintegrated late Tiahuanaco variety sometimes called Epigonal, and it continued to develop up to the Inca conquest about 1475, and after it into early Colonial times. It covered the whole area but there were some minor variants in Chincha. The painted decoration, in black, white and red, was based on the repetition of small geometrical units, such as steps, crosses, squares, lozenges and zig-zags, or extremely stylized birds or fish which gave much the same effect. The patterns are clearly inspired by textiles. A common form is a bowl with a gently rounded base forming the maximum diameter, above which it slopes inwards to a somewhat constricted mouth encircled by a thickened and chamfered lip, which is highly characteristic *(Ill. 200)*.

200 Three bowls, painted with textile-inspired patterns in black, white and red. Note the thickened, chamfered lips of the outer bowls. Ica style, Later Post-Classic. South Coast

There is another form with much lower walls and no thickening of the lip, which gives a metallic impression. There are also numerous ovate jars with low necks and flaring lips, besides some with taller necks and a loop handle, and barrel-shaped canteens. The style shows much greater competence in design, material and colour than that of Chancay, and compares favourably with that of Chimú in being a new and vigorous style rather than a poor reflection of an older one.

Of the Post-Classic architectural remains in the southern valleys few are in good enough condition to show specific features and it is difficult to place them in the time sequence, apart from some of Inca style. The Tambo (guest-house) de Mora in the Chincha Valley, which may be of this age, had a large habitation area surrounding a ceremonial centre consisting of a court from which stairs led up to terraces, the whole flanked by two large pyramids. Tambo Colorado in Pisco is of uncertain date, though its good preservation shows that it must be late, and the trapezoidal doorways suggest that it may be Inca. There are long ranges of low adobe buildings, built with stone foundations on terraces on gently rising ground. They are plastered and painted red, yellow and white, and have doubly recessed niches of contrasting colours and openwork balustrades formed by setting adobes diagonally to form triangular openings. The site is probably the administrative centre of a small city.

Some buildings in the central and south highlands are worthy of mention. At many places in the Province of Canta, east of Lima, there are single-storey cylindrical towers of random masonry. They are apparently pre-Inca but are so well preserved that they are unlikely to be much older. The walls thicken upwards and are corbelled out both inwards and outwards, so the exterior expands somewhat towards the top, and a square central column, which also expands upwards, helps to support the slab roof. The chamber is generally empty, but mummy bundles may be buried beneath the floor. In the west of the same province, at Chipprak and other sites, there are rectangular towers of similar masonry which have one or more large trapezoidal niches extending the whole height of the façade, within which are small doorways of similar form. A small structure of similar form may be annexed to the main one. These buildings have subterranean chambers, some of them containing mummies, and the main chambers may have niches in the walls, which thicken upwards like those of the type previously described. These niches may contain crude pottery, and there may also be a fireplace with a chimney built in the thickness of the wall.

In the Titicaca Basin are the best-known *chullpas* or burial towers, of which the finest are at Sillustani. They may be round or square, faced with fine, dressed masonry or built entirely of random masonry. Most have the burial chamber inside them, but some of the rougher ones are solid and have the chamber underneath. They are believed to have been built by the Aymara people both before and after the Inca conquered them, and are associated with various crude pottery types which are thought to have developed out of the final stages of the Decadent Tiahuanaco style. The best *chullpas*, which show some resemblance to Inca masonry, have a plain projecting cornice and a corbelled vault.

THE INCAS

Although the Incas are believed to have settled at Cuzco at least as early as A D 1200, there was nothing notable about their art until they began to build up their empire in the middle of the fifteenth century.

All the known examples of the famous Inca masonry date from the Imperial period, and the idea of a rectangular urban lay-out, which was attempted at Cuzco itself, may well have been learnt from the Chimú after they were conquered between 1460 and 1470. Differences in the type of masonry are an indication of differences in function and possibly in origin, but not in age. The 'megalithic' type, made of large, perfectly fitted, polygonal blocks, is used for the retaining walls of terraces and for large enclosures, and there is a variety called cellular, of small polygonal blocks, which may also be used for buildings. It has been suggested that these were derived from rough stone walling, with the stones set in mud. The coursed ashlar type, built of rectangular blocks which generally have a somewhat convex surface with sunken joints, is used for buildings, and may have been derived from the turf construction which is still used for poor houses and field walls. Smooth ashlar, which was used for a few important buildings, was a refinement of this type. There are various intermediate varieties, and rectangular masonry can sometimes be seen surrounding a doorway in a cellular wall. Even the hardest stones, such as granite and syenite, are thought to have been pecked into shape with stone mauls.

The best example of 'megalithic' masonry is the great triple zig-zag rampart of the fortress of Saccsaihuamán, which crowns the hill overlooking Cuzco (Ill. 202). It is made of hard limestone and some of the stones in the lowest rampart are over 8 metres high. The finest ashlar is found in important temples, such as that of Viracocha, the sun and other gods, whose remains form part of the Dominican friary in Cuzco, where some of the stones were faced with gold plates. Even this had an essentially domestic plan, consisting of rectangular rooms set about a court within an enclosure. It has been described as a house of the gods made in the likeness of the houses of men. Buildings had little in the way of architectural ornament, although the thatched roofs are recorded to have been finely worked into patterns. They had trapezoidal niches, mostly in interior walls, and doorways of the same shape. They were usually long and low, some had two or rarely more storeys, but the upper one was in most cases a loft under the gabled roof. Most of the surviving remains derive their effect chiefly from their fine finish.

Machu Picchu, a town in the Urubamba Valley, contains a number of small ceremonial buildings of various forms, finely situated amid innumerable agricultural terraces on a saddle which falls steeply on either side to the river some 1,500 feet below. A striking feature of it is a low semicircular tower of the finest masonry which seems to grow out of the rock which it partly encloses (Ill. 201). Near by is a series of small stone basins

212

201 Machu Picchu. General view showing low semicircular tower of the finest masonry. Inca, after 1450

connected by drains, arranged one above the other up a steep hillside, a feature which recurs at other sites in the same area. Although they were not designed for effect, magnificent series of stone-faced agricultural terraces form some of the finest features

213

202 Lowest wall of zig-zag rampart of the fortress of Saccsaihuamán above
Cuzco. Irregular 'megalithic' masonry. Inca, mid-fifteenth century

of this steep-sided valley in several places, and there are many similar instances elsewhere. In the head of a tributary of the Urubamba at Moray in the same neighbourhood are three large artificial circular depressions about 500 feet across. They are lined with concentric stone-faced terraces and make a most impressive sight. A circular group of five rooms facing onto a central court is recorded at Runcu Raccay in the same region, but the finest circular building of all was probably the tower reservoir, whose foundations alone survive, on top of the hill at Saccsaihuamán.

The same rather standardized type of building is found wherever the Inca conquests reached, from Ecuador to Chile and north-west Argentina. Stone was the material normally used for important buildings in the highlands, and on the coast adobe took its place, but the same trapezoidal niches and doorways are found there. Many of the coastal buildings were put up to dominate older sites like the sanctuary of Pachacámac, where a great terraced platform towers above the remains of the older shrine.

Although sculpture on a large scale does not survive, and indeed there may not have been any, many small stone objects were made and some are very pleasing. Miniature alpacas, with a hole in the back for offerings, are the commonest, and some of these are executed with a most competent economy of line *(Ill. 203)*. Low, flat-bottomed stone bowls are also found, and many of them have snakes in relief on the outer wall and a pair of loop handles, which may be replaced by animal-head lugs.

203 Hard black stone statuette of an alpaca with hole in its back. Similar models of pottery are still used for ceremonies to promote the fertility of the alpacas. Inca

Inca pottery was hard, well made and polished, and was produced in a few standard shapes. The painted ware has a number of minor variants, but all can be grouped under the name of Cuzco Polychrome. The usual colours are red, white, black and yellow, with orange sometimes added, especially in a variety found near Lake Titicaca. Designs are in most cases geometrical, for example diamonds, checkers, cross-hatching and rows of triangles, generally grouped in zones. A stylized plant design rather like a fish's backbone is sometimes present, and some attractive vessels are powdered with little animals, birds or insects *(Ill. 204)*. The most typical shape is a jar with a low conical base, domed body and tall, flaring neck called the aryballus *(Ill. 207)*. Originally a water or beer jar, it was carried on the back by a rope passing through two vertical strap handles low on the sides and over a nubbin high up between them, which was sometimes modelled to represent an animal head. It came to be made in smaller sizes down to about 6 inches high. Another painted form is a shallow platter with a bird's head or loop as a handle and a pair of minute projections on the opposite side of the rim. There were also jars of several shapes with wide strap handles.

204 Polychrome jar with lugs in the form of jaguars. A good Inca shape with somewhat unusual decoration which includes painted snakes. Inca, after 1450. Region of Cuzco

205 Provincial Inca aryballus, with stylized plant design in black on white, the base red. Chile

206 Provincial Inca aryballus in black ware with a pressed relief. Chimu-Inca style, after the Inca Conquest (*c.* 1470). North Coast

207 Cuzco polychrome aryballus decorated with geometrical patterns. Inca, after 1450

These shapes are found throughout the Empire, and modified forms of them were made in local wares, for instances a short-necked aryballus with pressed relief panels was made in Chimú black ware *(Ill. 206)*, and this and other Chimú-Inca forms tended to spread through the coast in the years before the Spaniards arrived. Another variant of the aryballus, with the conical base truncated, was made in polychrome ware in Chile *(Ill. 205)*. It is often possible to detect Inca influence in the shapes of necks and strap handles on other provincial vessels, like a fascinating hybrid from the Ica region in which both these features are present on a jar shaped like an Ica bowl with thickened rim passing up into a fluted dome *(Ill. 208)*. The course of events in the Ica Valley is particularly interesting, because the Inca conquest introduced an Inca pottery style, which took the place of the local one in important graves until the arrival of the Spaniards in 1534, when the local one regained its importance. This continued for 26 years before the effective occupation of the valley, during which interval the inhabitants felt that they had been liberated from the Inca yoke.

208 Hybrid Inca-Ica vessel painted black, white and orange. After the Inca conquest *(c.* 1480). Ica Valley, South Coast

209 Polychrome vicuña wool tapestry poncho shirt. Inca. From an island in Lake Titicaca

Inca textiles, like those of older periods, were made by many processes. There was a revival of the use of tapestry for the best work, which was of fine quality but still had a tendency to standardization. Typical Inca poncho shirts have a V-shaped area round the neck, which is treated differently from the rest *(Ill. 209)*; the main part may consist of a checker pattern, with the squares plain or adorned with geometrical figures, or it may have a repeating design like rows of feathers, and the V-shaped area may be bordered with small squares and powdered with small devices or left plain. Similar ponchos, distinguished only by the introduction of European foliage designs, were made after the Spanish Conquest.

210 Silver llama with gold appliqué. The red inlay of the saddle blanket has been restored. Inca

The most characteristic Inca metal objects which survive are small figures of silver, gold or combinations of them, representing llamas, alpacas or little naked men and women. These may be solid or hollow, and the human figures are more curious than beautiful though the animals may be very expressively rendered. *(Ill. 210)*. Some bronze knives inlaid with silver and copper and adorned with cast heads or figures have also been found on Inca sites. Apart from these things, it is difficult to point to much that is specifically Inca; doubtless this is partly due to the destruction which has occurred since the Conquest, but it may partly be ascribed to an original paucity of indigenous Inca work, because it is known that the Incas brought Chimú artisans to Cuzco after subduing their country. In this, as in other matters, the Incas learnt much from the conquered peoples of the coast.

CHAPTER FIVE

A Glimpse of the South:
North-west Argentina and North Chile

These areas were finally incorporated in the Inca Empire, but previously they were what has been justly described as a melting-pot, in which influences from various quarters were fused to produce some strongly individual results. Art is chiefly expressed in pottery, metal and wood. There were forts and villages, largely of dry stone walling, which scarcely deserve the title of architecture. Stone sculpture is reported, but too little is accessibly published to allow any comment beyond a note that cylindrical drinking vessels, with feline and human figures competently carved in relief, are present in the Aguada Culture of what used to be called the Diaguite region in the Argentine provinces of Catamarca and La Rioja.

There are many indigenous pottery styles dating from about 200 B C onwards, but the important ones for our purposes are after A D 700. The most notable, dating from A D 700 to 1000, belongs to the same Aguada culture, formerly called Draconian from the 'dragons' shown on the pottery. These are really derivatives of the widespread Peruvian feline, mostly in a form which suggests Recuay more than any other style, and there are two main types, painted and incised. The first is oxidized and the colours are black-purple-yellow, black-red-white, or simply black-on-yellow. The second is reduced, grey or black, with the motifs simply outlined, or outlined and hatched, or with the backgrounds hatched giving a negative effect. Besides felines, there are birds, frogs and human beings, some with axes and trophy heads. Painted designs are generally shown with extreme liquidity, but the presence of zig-zag lines in crestings and jaws gives an effect of angularity to the incised ones even when the figures are composed largely of curved lines. The pottery of the later Argentine cultures, after

211 Santa Maria urn, used for child burial, painted in black and red on cream slip. The design on the neck is a stylized face. Late Period, after AD 1000. Catamarca and neighbouring provinces, N. W. Argentina

AD 1000, is chiefly known for the funerary urns of Santa María and Belén in the same region. Santa María urns *(Ill. 211)* have an ovoid body with a pair of horizontal strap handles and a very tall flaring neck, and are decorated with striking geometrical designs in black on yellow or red on cream, mostly incorporating a highly stylized face recognizable from the eyes and the great arched brows meeting in a V, the only relief feature on the urn. Belén urns are similar but smaller, the neck is less exaggerated, and the painting is simpler and in black on red.

To the same late horizon belongs one of the most attractive pottery styles of Chile, which is found in the area immediately west of the home of the Argentine styles mentioned above, and is generally called Chilean Diaguite *(Ill. 212)*. The commonest form is a rather thick-walled bowl with rounded base and straight or slightly concave vertical sides, but there are also more complex forms such as jars with a head connected to a wide opening by a bridge. The painted decoration is in white, red and grey, and consists mainly of delicately-drawn step frets, checkers or hatched triangles, but there are some very simplified white rectangular faces sprinkled with grey dots with the mouth slightly raised. Relief is always at a minimum and confined to such features as mouths, noses or beaks. Finally there are some variants of Inca pottery of considerable charm which show their local origin in minor modifications of the standard shapes and in the style of painting. The aryballus *(Ill. 205)* mentioned in the chapter on Peru is a good example.

212 Chilean Diaguite bowl, painted in white, red and grey. Late Period, after AD 1000. North Chilean Coast, near Coquimbo

213 *(top)* Four carved wooden tablets and two tubes for taking snuff. Human and animal motifs, some of which show Tiahuanaco influence. Atacameño region, Rio Loa area, North Chilean Coast

214 *(below)* Cast copper plaque showing human figure between two felines. Aguada Culture, AD 700-1000, N.W. Argentina

Wood carvings are best preserved in the arid coastal Atacameño region of Chile, which lies north of the Diaguite area and adjoins the Peruvian border. Apart from undecorated utilitarian objects, the best examples are miniature trays and tubes for taking snuff, which have handles formed by cats, birds and human beings carved in the round *(Ill. 213)*, besides incised designs of Classic Tiahuanaco character and shell inlay. This is a southward extension of the Peruvian area, which not only marks the southern limit of direct Tiahuanaco influence but shows it in an unusually pure form.

North-west Argentina was a notable centre for metalwork, especially in copper, and was remarkable for the early appearance of bronze between A D 700 and 1000. The Aguada Culture has ceremonial copper axes with the head and the handle in one piece and the butt expanded into a crested feline head, a series of radiating spikes or some similar feature. Some fine and curious cast plaques, showing felines and human beings in relief, appear to belong to the same culture *(Ill. 214)*. Large copper discs with faces and other designs outlined by raised lines, in a manner much inferior to the plaques, probably belong to the later stage, after A D 1000.

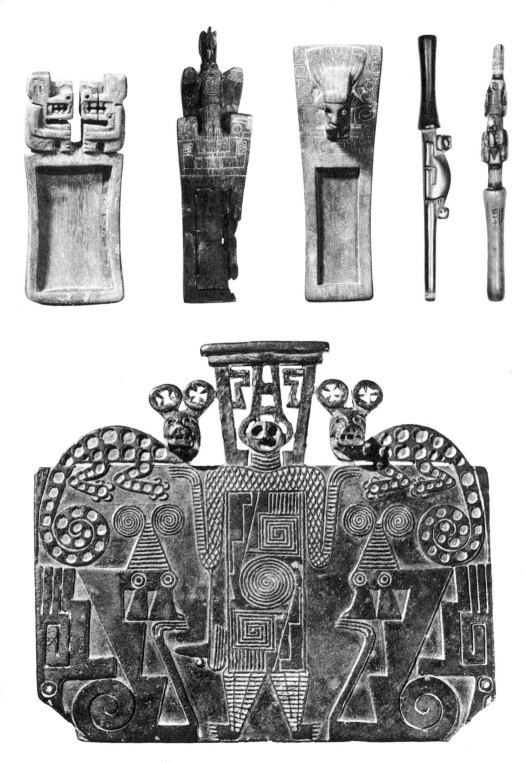

CHAPTER SIX

Central America and the Northern Andes

The organization of this, the intermediate area between Meso-america and Peru, was simpler politically than theirs and it has even been suggested that it remained on a Formative level. Most of it consisted of comparatively small units ruled by despotic chiefs, and only in the case of the Chibcha in highland Colombia are these units known to have formed a confederation. In the later stages the people normally lived in large villages with temples, but most of these were of perishable materials. More permanent structures existed and examples will be given, but there was nothing to compare in elaboration with the great ceremonial centres of the nuclear areas. On the other hand there was a notable mastery of metalwork, which developed long before that of Mexico.

CENTRAL AMERICA

The area from the southern limit of intense Maya influence south to the isthmus of Panama, now covered by the republics of Nicaragua, Costa Rica and Panama, can be broadly treated as a unit, within which the chief artistic developments took place after A D 500. In many ways it belongs more to South than to Mesoamerica, but influences from the north are never lacking.

There is nothing very notable in the way of architecture, although earth and stone mounds are sometimes ranged round courts, and alignments of stone columns or statues are sometimes found. Large stone carvings occur sporadically. In south-west Nicaragua there were tall statues of a man weighed down by a large animal on his back, or else showing in a curious way his face looking out from the animal's mouth, but we depend for our knowledge of these on drawings made by early explorers. Columns carved rather rudely with human figures in low relief are reported from

◀ 215 Lava figure of a man blowing a trumpet. Highland Costa Rica

Coclé Province, Panama. Smaller carvings are much better known. Finely carved stone club-heads, showing bird and crocodile heads among other designs, come from the Pacific coast of Costa Rica. From highland Costa Rica come standing or seated human figures, some showing a considerable degree of realism *(Ill. 215)*, but some, from the south highlands, are little more than a celt-shaped stone slab with a head and three slots separating the arms from the body and the legs from one another. Also from highland Costa Rica come thin rectangular slabs bordered at the sides with little figures in low relief and at the top with similar ones of monkeys or birds in the round; these were probably grave markers. Throughout Costa Rica and Panama there are beautifully carved *metates* or grinding slabs, standing on three or four slender legs or a complex support, some of which have a jaguar head and tail emerging from the ends *(Ill. 216)*. Of similar character are small circular objects like a miniature stool, on three legs or a central support, from highland Costa Rica and Chiriquí, Panama *(Ill. 217)*. Similar objects of wood and pottery have been found.

216 Stone grinding slab or *metate*. Costa Rica

217 Miniature stone stool, Province of Chiriquí, Panama

On a miniature scale are large numbers of finely-worked objects of jade from Costa Rica and mainly of other stones such as agate from Panama. Highly typical of the jades are celt or knife-like objects with a human figure in low relief occupying the butt half of the blade *(Ill. 218)*, but there are also angular figurines, coiled snakes, magnificent cylindrical beads and many other forms. The angularity of the carving is a clear response to the way of working this very hard material by sawing and drilling. From Coclé, Panama, come many agate pendants representing skilfully stylized animals, especially monkeys with arched tails, and also plain bar-shaped pendants which rely for their effect on the colour and banding of the stone.

The most individual metalworking centres in the region were in Coclé and Veraguas, Panama; other centres in Chiriquí, Panama, and Costa Rica appear to derive from them, and they themselves have much in common with Colombia. Hemispherical gold helmets are known from both Colombia and Panama, and a notable example from Coclé is covered with intricate embossed designs showing the local crocodile god, which also appears on gold discs. The commonest technique is cire perdue casting, and a large

218 Grey-green jade celt with a human figure forming the butt. Nicoya, Costa Rica

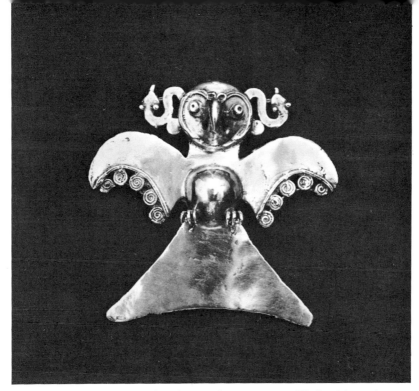

219 Gold pendant cast by cire perdue process. Bird with snake appendages. Veraguas Province, Panama

number of intricately decorated animals, monsters, bells, earspools and nose-clips were made in gold and the gold-copper alloys called *tumbaga*, which may be gilded by the mise en couleur process in which copper is leached from the surface with acid and the remaining gold burnished. Some of the most pleasing objects are of other materials combined with gold, such as earrods of agate, serpentine or opal with gold ends, and pendants made of a whale tooth with gold head and feet representing a bat or crocodile god. The most characteristic features of the Veraguas style are hollow castings with smooth, rounded contours spreading out at some points into sheets. Good examples are eagle pendants with great flat wings and tail *(Ill. 219)*, and frog pendants with large flat sub-rectangular hind feet. Men or gods stand on a rectangular flange, and have head-dresses of similar form. Most of these are gilded *tumbaga*, but some are gold.

220 Nicoya Polychrome tripod bowl with animal heads as feet. Pacific coast of Costa Rica

Only a few examples of the many pottery styles can be given. Among the most attractive are some types collectively called Nicoya Polychrome, from the Pacific coast of Costa Rica *(Ills. 220, 224, 225)*. Typical of this is an egg-shaped vessel with bulbous tripod feet *(Ill. 225)* or a ring base, decorated in black, red, orange, and rarely blue or purple, over a white to yellow slip. Some have a modelled head emerging from the side, generally a turkey, macaw or armadillo, other details of which may be shown in low relief or more usually in paint. Common painted designs show varieties of jaguar or plumed serpent, clearly derived from Mesoamerica, and some are shown in a pseudo-negative manner in the colour of the slip against a black ground. Other vehicles for such designs are figurines and bowls of various shapes, a common type being a shallow one with flaring sides and large animal heads forming

221 Globular jar with animal-head lugs, painted with two-headed alligator, in black, white and red. Alligator Ware, Chiriquí, Panama

222 Globular jar of Lost Colour Ware, with decoration in black negative painting over white and red. Chiriquí, Panama

tripod feet *(Ill. 220)*. Slightly different types of polychrome are found in the interior highlands *(Ill. 223)*, but they form a much smaller proportion of the pottery than on the Pacific coast. Among a profusion of one and two-coloured wares, whose distribution in time is only beginning to be worked out, are monochrome bowls standing on very tall tripod feet, generally in the form of an animal or fish, a type which extends into Chiriquí. Other notable Chiriquí wares, which are known to be of late pre-conquest date, are Lost Colour Ware and a polychrome called Alligator Ware. The first of these is decorated with simple negative designs such as dots and lines in rather fugitive black over a white or red slip or a combination of the two *(Ill. 222)*. It is used mainly for small objects such as jars and miniature double bowls. Alligator Ware is painted in black, white and red, and gets its name from the predominance of alligators and motifs connected with them *(Ill. 221)*.

One of the most remarkable pottery styles in a continent of remarkable styles comes from Coclé, Panama. It is found in the rich graves of that province and seems to have lasted, with minor variations, from at least the fourteenth century to the Conquest. There are plates, bowls and various types of jar decorated in white, red and black, to which may be added brown and purple, a rare colour on American pottery. The designs comprise scrolls, chevrons, birds, crocodiles, serpents, turtles and so on, frequently confined within zones or panels and drawn with a remarkable combination of sweeping boldness and delicacy of detail *(Ills. 226, 227)*.

223 Quadrangular tripod bowl with animal head and tail painted in black, white and red. Highland Polychrome. Costa Rica

224 Pottery figure of squatting woman wearing brassière, painted in black, white and red. Nicoya Polychrome. Pacific coast of Costa Rica

225 Ovoid tripod vase with applied animal head on side, the forelegs forming two of the vessel feet. Painted in black, white and red. Nicoya Polychrome, Pacific coast of Costa Rica

226 Pedestal dish, painted with crocodile heads and characteristic pointed hooks in red, black and purple on white. Coclé, Panama

227 Polychrome bottle, painted in black, red and purple on cream. Coclé, Panama

228 Coarse stone statue of a fanged human figure wearing a cap and loin-cloth, and carrying a staff and shield. San Agustín, Colombia

COLOMBIA

Colombia offers little in the way of architecture or stone sculpture. A group of sites round San Agustín, in the highland Department of Huila, forms an exception which has attracted much attention. They have small rectangular temples built of roughly-shaped stone slabs, enclosed in mounds rather like European megalithic tombs. Each contains a principal statue and several lesser ones, and the narrow open side forming the entrance may be flanked by caryatid figures. There are also subterranean galleries and tombs of similar construction. The statues are of various styles, which probably cover a considerable time-span. All are squat and some extremely so, some are carved in the round *(Ill. 228)*, some are slabs with details in low relief, and some are intermediate. Some have simple round eyes, in some they are a segment of a circle with the curve uppermost, and in some they are more realistically finished. Most have extremely wide nostrils, and large interlocking canine teeth like so many pseudo-feline faces in Peru and elsewhere.

They may hold a child, a snake, two staves, or other objects. Carvings are not necessarily moveable and rock outcrops, including a stream bed at Lavapatas, show figures, animals, snakes and many other forms. There is a single radiocarbon date of about 500 B C, but what point in the development of San Augustín it corresponds to is unknown. There has been much speculation about relations between this and other cultures from Nicaragua to Peru, and in some cases there is little but the trait of stone carving to connect them, but more precise dating may enable reliable conclusions to be drawn.

Colombia is a country of deep shaft graves, and the Tierradentro region in the Department of Cauca, north of San Agustín, contains some which are remarkable for their decoration *(Ill. 229)*. They are generally oval or round, some have columns left to support the roof, and some have niches. The shafts for access may have stairs cut in the rock. The chambers are covered with elaborate designs carved in relief or painted black, white, red and sometimes yellow; most are geometrical, but animal and human faces and figures also occur. Their age is not known, nor is their relation to statues and other carvings of San Agustín styles in the neighbourhood.

Colombia is renowned mainly for its metalwork, but little is known about the chronology of this or even of the most typical pottery styles. Great strides have been made recently in building up a cultural succession, but most of the metal comes from casual finds and grave-robbing, and much of the best pottery from unstratified, single-period sites. As in Central America, copper and *tumbaga* objects are as common as gold, and the same processes were used in working them. A number of regional styles have been distinguished, but some types, such as beads and ear-spools, were doubtless shared between more than one area, and the differences are blurred by trade. Perhaps the most distinguished style is the Quimbaya, of the Middle Cauca valley, known for the massive cire perdue gold castings in the British Museum and Madrid *(Ill. 231)*. There are graceful flasks, and figures of men and women with slit-like eyes, besides hemispherical helmets with embossed designs

229 View of interior of a shaft grave. Stone walls painted in several colours. Tierradentro region, Cauca, Colombia

in similar style. The finding of Quimbaya objects in Coclé, Panama, suggests a date within two or three centuries of the Conquest. Another attractive style is that of Calima, to the south-west of the Quimbaya and related to it. Typical of this are large kidney-shaped breast ornaments, with an embossed head in the middle having a large H-shaped nose ornament and ear-discs dangling from it. There are also masks, said to be for idols, diadems, elaborate crescent-shaped nose-ornaments with danglers, and cire perdue pins of *tumbaga* with little figures full of detail on the head. The general effect is one of rather barbaric profusion. On the strength of certain details it has been suggested that this style was contemporary with some San Agustín statues, but this needs substantiation. In the extreme north, towards Panama, the Darién style is distinguished by a most peculiar type of cire perdue casting of a semi-human figure with wide, plain, flat legs separated by a slit, contrasting with bat-like head and wings with intricate detail, in some cases so highly stylized as to be unrecognizable. The Province of Tolima, over the hills east of the Cauca Valley, has its own style. The characteristic feature is a gold or *tumbaga* pendant, flat except for the details of a face which appear to consist of applied strips but are actually cast by cire perdue. The flat body may have wings if it represents a bat, or angular limbs if a man or animal, and it generally ends below in a crescent with rounded ends. The bats have the body pierced with rows of slits and the edges cut into tatters. East of this area, around Bogotá, is the Chibcha or Muisca country, and this again has its own style, which has the least claim of all to artistic merit *(Ill. 230)*. Typical are flat or nearly flat plaques of gold or *tumbaga,* called *tunjos,* with a head and elongated triangular or quadrilateral body, with features, spidery limbs and insignia resembling applied wire, although cast by cire perdue. Groups of figures, pins, model spear-throwers and other objects were made in the same way. The impression they give is extremely crude, but some hollow human figures, conch shells and flat pendants with figures in relief are far superior in finish. Objects in Muisca style were being made at the time of the Conquest.

230 Gold figurine *(tunjo)*. A flat, human figure with wiry details wearing head-dress, carrying staff and shield, cast by cire perdue process. Chibcha, Colombia

231 Three objects of precious metal; a bell-shaped piece of uncertain use, decorated with a row of faces, a gourd-shaped flask, and a seated female figurine. Outer objects of *tumbaga* (gold-copper alloy), central one of gold. Quimbaya. Cauca Valley, Colombia

A few pottery styles deserve mention, mostly from the Quimbaya region. The first has negative painting in black over red *(Ill. 232)* or red and white, like that of the Lost Colour Ware of Panama, and it is doubtless related to styles showing the same technique in southern Colombia and Ecuador and, at a further remove, to Recuay in Peru. It is used not only on vessels but also on some examples of a curious, rather flat type of hollow figurine with a large, sometimes square head and spindly limbs, which generally squats or sits on a stool. Double vessels, spout and bridge and double spout and bridge jars are found in the same area; some are modelled in animal shapes, some are whistling jars and some are painted in red and white. These features point to the coast of Peru, but only generally because the details are very different, and in particular the form of loop-like bridge which unites the double spouts is found only here and in the neighbouring Calima district. Another unusual Quimbaya form of decoration is generally called champlevé; in it certain areas are differentiated by the deep excision of rows of small triangles or quadrilaterals *(Ill. 233)*.

Chibcha pottery does not reach a very high level, but it is worth mentioning because the use of applied strips of clay to show facial features and ornaments and spindly limbs in figure modelling, are recognizably connected with the type of decoration on the metal *tunjos*. This modelling is found on effigy vessels and hollow figurines, which are further decorated by incised lines and rows of circular reed impressions *(Ills. 234, 235)*. Much of the pottery is plain white, but some red painting on orange, buff or white is also found.

232 Bowl with black negative painting over red. Quimbaya, Colombia

233 *(above)* Red ware bowl with parts of the surface cut away after the manner of chip-carving, generally called champlevé. Quimbaya

234, 235 Two pottery heads, fragments of figurines, with applied, stamped and incised details. Chibcha, Colombia

The population of Ecuador is and was concentrated chiefly in the highlands, a series of basins between the east and west chains of the Andes, and on the broad coastal plain to the west. The rise from the coast to the highlands is extremely sharp, and conditions in the two areas are so different that cultural expressions differ a great deal. Work done since 1954 has given a clear picture of developments on much of the coast, but the study of this region suffers in comparison with that of Peru because perishable objects are seldom preserved owing to wetter conditions.

Pottery appeared on the Ecuadorean coast at a surprisingly early date, between 3000 and 2500 B C, well before its beginning in Peru, and this is taken to mark the beginning of the Formative Period. No cultural remains of an earlier date are known in this zone. Three Formative sub-divisions, each thought to have been started by an invasion, have been recognized, and the third of these brought Mesoamerican elements, including some features found at Tlatilco. Like the Chavín style in Peru, these probably came by sea, because nothing like them has been found in the intermediate area and nothing is seen here of the feline cult which accompanies similar elements in Chavín. The next stage is called the Regional Developmental Period from the variety of intense developments which were reached in different sections, one of which, the Bahía Phase in Manabí Province, is judged to have attained a Classic level; this lasted from about 500 B C to A D 500. The final period, which lasted to the Conquest, has been called the Integration Period. It is marked by a simplification resulting in the establishment of three cultural types or phases covering the whole coast. More than three tribes were living there at the Conquest period so these types did not correspond to political units, although some of the tribes may have been closely related. Coastal Ecuador was exceptional in the Intermediate Area in having large towns in the more fertile parts.

Architectural remains are rare on the coast. The Bahía Phase has rectangular stone-faced platforms near the port of Manta, and there are earth mounds arranged in a U-shape round a court,

236 Standing male stone statue. Manteño Phase, Integration Period. La Pila, Manabí, coast of Ecuador

237 Stone (dolerite) bat. Manteño Phase, Integration Period. La Libertad, Guayas, coast of Ecuador

which may have formed a ceremonial centre, at La Tolita in Esmeraldas further north, an area under strong Mexican influence. In the latest period, the Milagro Phase in the inland Guayas Basin has numerous large earth mounds to support buildings in a flood-prone area and for burial purposes, but this is hardly architecture. Manabí Province was a centre of stone sculpture. There are stone slabs carved in low relief to show monsters, women accompanied by monkeys and men with birds, which are probably associated with the platforms of the Bahía Phase. In the latest period, the Manteño Phase has the famous U-shaped stone seats, carved in one piece with a crouching man or jaguar which supports them. Free-standing stone statues, most of which represent men wearing only a close-fitting head-dress with a flat or rounded top and either a breech clout or a narrow belt with two pendant strips down the thighs, belong to the same phase (*Ill. 236*). These figures are much generalized; some have exaggeratedly square shoulders and the legs may be much too short or have squared outlines. Miniature versions are also found. These statues have been compared with those of San Agustín in Colombia, but they are very much more recent and the resemblances are too vague to inspire confidence. Statues which share some features with these, particicularly the head-dresses, but with a peg base for setting in the

238 Two carinated bowls, pale brown to black and highly polished. The larger has pairs of faint pinkish iridescent paint running down the body, and the smaller has the outside of the rim painted red and dots of faint iridescent paint on the body. Formative Period. La Libertad, Guayas, coast of Ecuador

ground, are ascribed to a hill-top near Guayaquil, further south, but have all been moved. To the same Manteño Phase belong two remarkable wooden posts found in the area. The better of these, now in Guayaquil, has nine tiers of human figures, normally each of two men and two women with prominent genitals, alternating horizontally and vertically, but somewhat disturbed near the top by the insertion of two alligators. Some stone animal carvings have been found in the same neighbourhood. There is a crouching monkey of almost gorilla size at Chongón near Guayaquil, which is still an object of superstitious regard to the inhabitants, and a miniature bat, from La Libertad on the Pacific shore, shown with considerable skill by a minimum of shaping on a lump of dolerite *(Ill. 237)*.

There is a great variety in Formative pottery on the coast, but taking it as a whole it depends for its interest on form and types of decoration such as application, incision and polishing rather than on colour, although there is a limited use of red and black painting and a peculiar inconspicuous iridescent paint is occasionally used for simple dots and stripes in a way which sometimes recalls negative painting. Some thin-walled, highly polished types were never rivalled in these respects, and in some cases the lustre seems to have been accentuated with iridescent paint

247

239 Three painted sherds, Guangala Phase, Regional Development Period, Province of Guayas, coast of Ecuador. One *(top left)* is from Guangala. Another *(top right)*, with stylized pelicans, is from La Libertad, as is the small sherd *(below)*

(Ill. 238). In the Regional Developmental Period, white-on-red and negative wares are found everywhere. The Bahía Phase, already mentioned, has polychrome wares and also painting done after firing which recalls the late Formative Paracas pottery of Peru, and its survival is remarkable in the wet climate of Manabí. The Guangala Phase of the Pacific coastal strip adjacent to Bahía on the south is distinguished by a thin, hard polychrome in black and red on yellow, showing pelicans and geometrical designs often derived from them. *(Ill. 239)*. This ware may be replaced locally by an equally fine two-colour chocolate on yellow, and there is a yellow type with bizarre faces and snakes in red outlined by engraved lines. Guangala also has a unique form of polypod bowl in unslipped red ware, with five or more pointed feet modelled to represent a human figure or face. Bahía is outstanding for the variety and interest of its figurines showing human beings and animals, some of them of Mexican derivation *(Ill. 241)*. It also has objects of very restricted distribution, such as head-rests, house models with swept-up ridge ends and certain figurines, which have been ascribed with some reason to the influence of a boatload of Asiatics who may have arrived about 200 B C. Guangala also has figurines;

248

they show far less variety than those of Bahía, though they are of related types, but they are generally superior in taste and finish. Among them is a hollow male figure wearing a domed cap and carrying a baby, which contains two whistles *(Ill. 242)*. The Integration Period is marked by a fashion for sombre coloured pottery, grey or brown, with incised, appliqué or pattern-burnished decoration *(Ill. 243)*. This is a curious parallel to the Chimú black ware of Peru and may be due to the development of mass production in both areas, but the expression is very different. The Milagro Phase in the Guayas Basin has a variety of fantastic bowls and jars with a profusion of appliqué figures of snakes, birds, lizards, frogs and human beings, probably for ritual purposes, which have been called 'witches' cauldrons'. Figurines continued to be made, especially in the Manteño Phase, but they are rather poor slab-like productions made in one-piece moulds *(Ill. 240)*. Face jars are common in the same phase *(Ill. 243)*.

240 *(left)* Slab-like grey pottery figurine of standing man with ear-spools and nose-ring. Manteño Phase, Integration Period. La Libertad, Guayas

241 *(below)* Hollow stone-coloured pottery figurine of standing woman with domed cap. Bahía Phase, Regional Development Period. Esmeraldas

242 *(far right)* Hollow whistle figurine of standing man wearing a swept-back domed cap and holding a child. Red-brown pottery largely smoked to dark grey. Guangala Phase, Regional Development Period

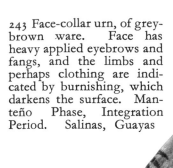

243 Face-collar urn, of grey-brown ware. Face has heavy applied eyebrows and fangs, and the limbs and perhaps clothing are indicated by burnishing, which darkens the surface. Manteño Phase, Integration Period. Salinas, Guayas

Metal was first worked in the Regional Development Period, but the bulk of the spectacular finds are of the Integration Period. Gold, silver and copper were worked, and Esmeraldas was remarkable for the working of platinum, which was combined with gold in some objects, for example it forms the eyes in some masks. Infusible at the available temperatures, grains of platinum were forged into a mass by repeated heating with a little gold dust, to produce an alloy of lower melting point, and hammering. The predominant decorative techniques were repoussé and the use of wire, and cire perdue was far less common than in Colombia and Central America. There are gold and silver bowls, helmets and collars all with repoussé decoration, and a multitude of smaller objects such as bracelets, beads, ear ornaments and nose ornaments, many of the latter composed of exceedingly elaborate arrangements

250

of flat wire spirals. Turquoise discs were sometimes set in gold objects. Copper, sometimes gilded, was used for ornaments in the simpler burials.

A burial of the end of the Milagro Phase in the Guayas Basin was very rich in metal, and to this we owe evidence of the skill of the ancient Ecuadorians in making textiles, many of which were preserved by the copper salts. Few details are available, but the mention of warp and weft floats and fine *ikats* suggest that they were comparable in skill with the Peruvians.

It has not yet been possible to correlate the highlands with the coast except to some extent in the south, but they were on much the same artistic level. Apart from some Inca masonry in the south and older mounds in other parts, some for burial and some as sub-structures, there is nothing to show on the surface.

244 Pottery figurine head wearing high domed cap, ear-spools and nose-ring. Bahía Phase, Regional Development Period. Said to be from Es-meraldas, but probably from Manabí, coast of Ecuador

245 Bowl on low ring base, with black negative decoration showing outlines of two animals over cream and red. Tuncahuán style, El Angel, Province of Carchi, North Highlands of Ecuador

There are many pottery styles, among which that called Tuncahuán, with animal silhouettes and geometrical forms in black negative paint over red and cream *(Ill. 245)*, is related to Colombian negative styles. Rich finds of gold and copper, repoussé discs, nose ornaments, ceremonial gold axes, and so on, have been made, chiefly in the southern province of Azuay, but most of the gold has been melted down.

CHAPTER SEVEN

Venezuela, the West Indies and Brazil

Art in Venezuela is virtually confined to the west and centre of the country, the areas where maize agriculture early displaced manioc cultivation. Its main expression is in pottery styles, dating between 1000 BC and the Conquest, which include figurines, but there are also stone figurines and pendants. Nowhere are there great ceremonial centres, and such ceremonial expressions as exist—shaft graves and shrines in caves—are in the west.

Among the various pottery styles a number of features recur. There are tripod bowls with the legs swollen near the top and prolonged upwards beyond the vessel rim, tetrapod bowls with modelled features representing animals, tripods or tetrapods with the feet united by a ring, vessels with ring bases pierced with holes, effigy jars with applied details, and black-on-white curvilinear painting. The Los Barrancos style, which is found in the centre and the east, where it seems to be an intrusive exception to the lack of artistic expression, has red or buff bowls with heavily flanged rims of triangular section, bearing deeply incised lines which may end in dots, and grotesquely modelled and incised head-lugs.

Most characteristic of Venezuela are vigorously modelled figurines, with more than a hint of the fantastic about them *(Ill. 247)*. The most usual subject is a woman with a head of enormously exaggerated width with curved or squared top, the latter representing a head-dress. They have applied coffee-bean eyes, breasts are rarely more than applied buttons, and the buttocks and lower limbs are excessively fat. Some are painted, generally with groups of parallel lines, in black and sometimes red on a white slip, especially in the west. Male figures without the excessive widening of the head and generally seated on a stool are also found.

246 (*opposite*) Polished stone figurine with top-knot. State of Trujillo, Venezuela

247 Pottery female figurine of characteristic Venezuelan type. State of Trujillo

There are also sexless stone figurines, some of which have excessively wide heads surmounted by a narrower top-knot, with the features and limbs ingeniously indicated by grooves and cuts. These may have a pleasing smooth convex surface (*Ill. 246*). They are found in the west, as are wide flat sub-rectangular or V-shaped pendants of schistose material.

The West Indies seem to have been populated chiefly from Venezuela, though there are features which point in other directions. The first pottery-making, manioc-growing people spread out from the Orinoco through Trinidad and the Lesser Antilles to Puerto Rico about A D 200, carrying with them thin, well-made pottery of a pre-Barrancoid style decorated with simple white-on-red painting and incised cross-hatching, but not of great artistic interest. The Los Barrancos style followed in Trinidad and Tobago in the second half of the first millennium. Apart from this there

255

248 Three-pointed stone depicting a *zemi*. Puerto Rico or Eastern Santo Domingo

is little to say about the Lesser Antilles. The pottery styles of the Greater Antilles are artistically unimportant, but of greater significance are objects of stone, shell and hardwood connected with the Arawak worship of *zemis*, deities which were shown on carvings in human or animal form. One Arawak group, which lived in Puerto Rico and Hispaniola at the time of Columbus, also had a form of ceremonial centre, a rectangular or oval area bordered with rough stone slabs which may bear reliefs of *zemis*, with perishable temples for *zemi* worship at the ends. These areas were used as ball-courts, and large portable stone rings, with figure-carving perhaps representing *zemis*, are found in some. These suggest the stone yokes of the Gulf Coast of Mexico, whence the idea of both them and the game may have come. *Zemis* are also depicted on ceremonial stone celts, generally in a simple way by abrading grooves on the surface, and more elaborately on three-pointed stones which were probably a local development *(Ill. 248)*. *Zemis* were also worshipped in caves, and to this we owe the preservation of some wooden objects, not only from

249 Wooden *zemi*, polished and with shell inlay, representing a male divinity with grooved cheeks. The bark cloth loin-cloth is probably a subsequent addition

250 Wooden stool with gold inlay on eyes, teeth and shoulders, probably representing a *zemi*. Hispaniola (Haiti or more probably Santo Domingo)

Hispaniola and Puerto Rico but also from Jamaica, which like Cuba lacked the ball-courts. From Jamaica comes a male figure with inlaid eyes and teeth of mother-of-pearl, naked except for indications of ligatures on the limbs *(Ill. 249)*, and another with a mixture of human and bird features. These and another were found in the eighteenth century and are in the British Museum, where another example, a bird with incised circles on the wings standing on a turtle, is described as from the Greater Antilles. There is

258

also a characteristic form of narrow four-legged stool used by chiefs as a sign of rank; this dips down a little from the front which bears an animal head, probably a *zemi*, and sweeps up again to a greater height at the back. Examples are known from Jamaica, the Bahamas and Hispaniola, the last inlaid with gold. *(Ill. 250)*. Forked snuff tubes, with animal or bird heads carved on them, are known from the same contexts, and it is reported that priests used them to snuff tobacco or other narcotics from the heads of *zemis*.

BRAZIL

Little of artistic importance is known from the vast territory of Brazil; much of the area consists of lowland tropical forests which proved unsuitable for the development of high aboriginal civilizations, and those parts in the east which might be expected to be more favourable were remote and difficult of access from the main centres.

Several sites in north-east Brazil have noteworthy pottery styles, and there is another group on the Tapajós River, a tributary on the right bank of the Amazon some 300 miles from the mouth. Of the first, the most important is the Marajoara style of Marajó Island at the mouth of the Amazon, which dates from the last few centuries before the Conquest. It arrived on the island fully developed, probably from eastern Colombia or Ecuador, and declined thereafter. It is known for large burial urns, many of which are modelled in highly stylized human form, triangular female pubic coverings, and cylindrical stools, but there are many forms of bowl and jar as well. The decorative techniques are spectacular, and entire surfaces are covered with elaborate and characteristic scroll patterns. They may be painted in red or black or both on a white slip, incised on white with or without red retouching *(Ill. 252)*, scraped through a red slip showing a white one underneath *(sgraffito)*, or excised on a red-slipped vessel, the background cut away and roughened leaving the design in relief *(Ill. 251)*.

At other sites near the mouth of the Amazon, on the Maracá river, are burial urns which are much inferior in execution but

251 Two pottery vases, with brown or red slip, which has been cut away (excised) to leave the design in relief. The roughened background shows remains of whitening. Crocodile design on left example, and sub-angular scrolls on the right. Marajó Island, Brazil. These are relatively small examples

deserve mention as curiosities. They take the form of a human figure sitting on a bench, with the body and limbs cylindrical and the head formed by a truncated conical lid with the features applied. The presence of glass beads with some of them shows that they were being made at the time of the Conquest.

From the Tapajós river comes the style generally known as Santarém, which was being made between AD 1000 and 1500, though its full duration is unknown and the floral decoration on some tobacco pipes indicates that these at least were made under European influence. It is distinguished by its exuberant modelling and has little painting apart from the occasional use of red. Typical are jars on a flaring ring base, with the body covered with a profusion of applied detail modelled in the round with subsidiary low relief, showing animals and bird heads. They have a bulging collar which may have a human face on it, above which are one or more flanges with a short tapering spout at the top. Another characteristically extravagant form is a bowl with low vertical sides covered with modelled animal life, and supported by three or four squat

260

human figures standing on a spool-shaped base. The eyes of both men and animals are round and bulging, and may be surrounded by a single or double raised ring. Men have mouths with swollen lips, which in the smaller instances are shown as a 'coffee bean'. On some bird heads the bulging may be so exaggerated that the eyes are on stalks, and the complexity may be increased by the placing of a knob or a head on the beak, which in many cases is curved down like the trunk of an elephant. There are also bowls covered with frogs, snakes and other details in low relief, which appear sober by comparison, although they somewhat resemble the 'witch's cauldrons' of the Milagro Phase of Ecuador, which are themselves remarkable for their exuberance. It has been suggested that the style is related to one called Arauquín in Venezuela, and that both derived elements from a common source in eastern Colombia, but, however this may be, nothing like the more elaborate types is known elsewhere and their extravagance is doubtless a local development.

252 Deep bowl with white slip, incised and retouched with red, to produce an angular S-pattern. Marajó Island, Brazil

It has only been possible to touch on the main features of the chief areas of artistic interest in ancient America, and some peoples such as the Eskimos have had to be omitted altogether, but it is hoped that enough has been said to show that art was not confined to the areas of high civilization, and that many others excelled, each in its own way. It is worth saying once again that mechanical aids were of the simplest, and that the many fine things which were made, as well as some which are more curious than beautiful, owed everything to the hand and eye of the American Indian.

Chronology

Bibliography

List of Illustrations

Maps

Index

Simplified chronological table showing the chief cultures and artistic styles mentioned in the book

MESOAMERICA	CENTRAL MEXICO	OAXACA	GULF COAST	MAYA
1500 ↑				
POST-CLASSIC	Aztec	↑ Mixtec	↑	Post-Classic Maya
	Chichimec		Huastec	
		Monte Albán IV		
	Toltec			↑ Toltec Maya ↓
1000				
↓	— Xochicalco —		Classic Veracruz	
CLASSIC ↑				Classic Maya
↓		Monte Albán III		
	— Teotihuacán —			
AD / BC	Cuicuilco		↓	Proto-Classic and Formative Maya
↑		Monte Albán II	Izapa style	
PRE-CLASSIC		Monte Albán I	Olmec (La Venta)	
	Tlatilco			
	Zacatenco			
	El Arbolillo			
1000				
1500 ↓				

THE CENTRAL ANDES	PERU					ECUADOR	N. W. ARGENTINA
	COAST			HIGHLANDS		COAST	N. CHILE
	NORTH	CENTRAL	SOUTH	NORTH	SOUTH		
1500	◄———— The Inca Conquests ————————————————————►						Santa María Belén
POST-CLASSIC	Chimú	Chancay	Ica				
						INTEGRATION	Chilean Diaguite
					Decadent Tiahuanaco	Manteño	
1000	◄——— The Tiahuanaco Spread ———►					Milagro etc.	
							Aguada
CLASSIC	Mochica	Interlocking	Nasca	Recuay	Tiahuanaco		
	Virú						
AD **BC**						REGIONAL DEVELOPMENTS	
				Pucára			
	Salinar		Paracas		Chiripa	Bahía	
	Chavín (Cupisnique)	Chavín		Chavín		Guangala, etc.	
FORMATIVE **1000**							
						FORMATIVE	
PRECERAMIC	Preceramic	Preceramic	Preceramic				
3000							

Short Bibliography

This bibliography is selective and incomplete, because the area is very unequally covered by published work, and for large sections the only material is in the form of papers in specialist journals or privately printed. Much of this is not easily accessible and is omitted, as are books known to be out of print.

General

KELEMEN, P. *Medieval American Art.* New York, 1956

KUBLER, G. *The Art and Architecture of Ancient America.* Harmondsworth, 1962
The dating system differs in many respects from that accepted in this book

LOTHROP, S.K. *Treasures of Ancient America.* Cleveland, Ohio and London, 1964

LOTHROP, S.K., FOSHAG, W.F. and MAHLER, J. *Pre-Columbian Art : Robert Woods Bliss Collection.* New York, 1957

Mexico

CASO, A. *The Aztecs, People of the Sun.* Norman, Oklahoma, 1958

COE, M.D. *Mexico.* London, [1962]

COVARRUBIAS, M. *Indian Art of Mexico and Central America.* New York, 1957

LINNÉ, S. *Treasures of Mexican Art.* Stockholm, 1956

MARQUINA, A. *Arquitectura Prehispánica.* Mexico, 1951

Maya

COE, M.D. *The Maya.* London, 1966

MORLEY, S.G. and BRAINERD G.W. *The Ancient Maya.* Stanford, California, 1956

PROSKOURIAKOFF, T. *A Study of Classic Maya Sculpture.* Washington, 1950

RUPPERT, K., THOMPSON, J.E.S. and PROSKOURIAKOFF, T. *Bonampak, Chiapas, Mexico.* Washington, 1955

THOMPSON, J.E.S. *The Rise and Fall of Maya Civilization.* Norman, Oklahoma, 1954 and London, 1956

USA

DOCKSTADER, F.J. *Indian Art in America.* London, [1961]
This deals mainly with modern objects, but illustrates some Pre-Columbian ones

DUTTON, B.P. *Sun Father's Way: The Kiva Murals of Kuaua.* Albuquerque, 1963

MARTIN, P.S., QUIMBY, G.I. and COLLIER, D. *Indians before Columbus.* Chicago, 1947

Peru, Argentina, Chile and Ecuador

BENNET, W.C. and BIRD, J.B. *Andean Culture History,* New York, 1960

BIRD, J.B. and BELLINGER, L. *Paracas Fabrics and Nazca Needlework.* Washington, 1954

BUSHNELL, G.H.S. *Peru.* London, 1963

MASON, J. ALDEN *The Ancient Civilizations of Peru.* Harmondsworth, 1957

ROWE, J.H., *Chavín Art.* New York, 1962

SAWYER, A.R. *Tiahuanaco Tapestry Design.* New York, 1963

STRONG, W.D. and EVANS JR., C. *Cultural Stratigraphy in the Virú Valley.* New York, 1952

Articles in *Handbook of South American Indians*, Vol. 2. Washington, 1946
A good deal of this is out of date, but more recent material is inaccessible

Peruvian Gold. London, 1964. The catalogue of the Arts Council exhibition of part of Sr Mujica Gallo's collection

Central America, Colombia

REICHEL-DOLMATOFF, G. and A. *Colombia.* London, 1965

Articles in *Handbook of South American Indians*, Vols. 2, 4. Washington, 1946-1948

Venezuela and the West Indies

ROUSE, I. and CRUXENT, J.M. *Venezuelan Archaeology.* New Haven, 1963

Articles in *Handbook of South American Indians*, Vol. 4. Washington, 1948

Brazil

Articles in *Handbook of South American Indians*, Vol. 3. Washington, 1948
When this was written, little was known of the chronology of the area. A later, work, which is concerned less with the artistic aspect than the chronology, is Meggers, B.J. and Evans C. *Archaeological Investigations at the Mouth of the Amazon.* Washington, 1957

List of Illustrations

The author and publishers are grateful to the many official bodies, institutions and individuals mentioned below for their assistance in supplying original illustration material. Abbreviations used are as follows : A M N H — American Museum of Natural History, New York; C M A E — University Museum of Archaeology and Ethnology, Cambridge; C N H M — Chicago Natural History Museum; I N A H — Instituto Nacional de Antropología, Mexico; M N A M — Museo Nacional de Antropología, Mexico; N G S — National Geographic Society. Metric measurements are given in brackets.

1 Pavement; stylized jaguar mask. Polished green serpentine slabs, coloured sands and clays. Olmec Culture, Middle Formative Period (800-400 BC). La Venta, Tabasco. About 15 ft × 25 ft (4.6× 7.6 m.). NGS. Photo Robert F. Heizer

2 Relief; figures holding were-jaguar infants. Carving on north end of Altar 5, La Venta, Tabasco. Basalt. Olmec Culture. *h.* of altar-stone 5 ft 1 in. (1.55 m.). NGS. Photo Matthew W. Stirling

3 Colossal head of basalt; man wearing helmet with side-flaps. Olmec Culture, Middle Formative Period. Formerly Monument 1 at La Venta, Tabasco, now in Villahermosa Park, Tabasco. *h.* about 8 ft (2.4 m.). Photo GHS Bushnell

4 Ceremonial group; sixteen figurines of jade and serpentine, one of conglomerate, and six jade celts, grouped possibly to show a sacrifice. Olmec Culture. Offering 4 at La Venta, Tabasco. *h.* of figurines between 6 5/16 in. and 7 5/16 in. (16 and 18.5). NGS. Photo Robert F. Heizer

5 Celt; figure combining delicate engraving with heavy carving. Grey-green. Olmec Culture. *h. c.* 1 ft (30.5). British Museum. Photo John Webb

6 Reclining infantile figurine with grimacing face; dark jade carved and drilled. Olmec Culture. Guerrero Province. AMNH

7 Carved monolith; figure with jaguar head-dress seated in the curve of a plumed rattlesnake. Basalt. Olmec Culture, Middle Formative Period (800-400 BC). Monument 19 at La Venta, Tabasco. Now at Villahermosa. Photo GHS Bushnell

8 Figurine; stylized figure with two superposed heads. Dark jade, carved and engraved. Olmec Culture, Middle Formative Period (800-400 BC). Provenance unknown *h.* 2 1/2 in. (6.5). Photo CMAE

9 Statue; squatting male figure, ('The Wrestler'). Basalt. Olmec Culture, Middle Formative Period. Antonio Plaza, Uxpanapa, Veracruz. *h.* 2 ft 2 in. (66). Private Collection. Photo Irmgard Groth-Kimball

10 Mask; human face with closed eyes and pierced ear-lobes. Wood, inlaid with jade. Olmec Culture. Said to come from a cave in the Cañon de la Mano, Iguala, Guerrero. *h.* 4 3/4 in. (12). AMNH

11 Figure; seated infant. White-slipped, hollow, pottery. Olmec Culture. Tlatilco, outskirts of Mexico City. *h.* 14 3/8 in. (36.6). Private Collection. Photo Irmgard Groth-Kimball

12 Two columns of carved glyphs; probably calendrical. Stone, low relief. Monte Albán I, Monte Albán, Oaxaca. Photo GHS Bushnell

13 Relief; *Danzante*; crouching human figure, with glyph near the mouth, probably a corpse. Shallow carving on sandstone revetment slab, found under later buildings. Monte Albán I, Middle to Late Formative Period. Monte Albán, Oaxaca. Photo Michael D. Coe

14 Face urn; human face with Olmecoid mouth. Polished monochrome grey ware. Monte Albán I, Middle to Late Formative Period. Monte Negro, Oaxaca. *h.* 6 1/8 in. (15.7). MNAM. Photo Irmgard Groth-Kimball

15 Grey pottery jar; this form with lateral spout survived into later periods. Monte Albán I. Nochistlán, Oaxaca. *h.* 3 1/8 in. (8). CMAE

16 Stela; shallow relief on stone showing complex scene. Stela 5, Izapa, Chiapas. Izapa Culture. Photo Brigham Young University — New World Archaeological Foundation

17 Stela and altar; shallow relief showing figure and other designs on Stela 3, Izapa, Chiapas, beneath which stands Altar 2, carved in the form of a giant toad. Izapa Culture. Photo as above

18 Head; with head-dress (fragment of pottery figurine). Modelled with incised areas and applied strips. Formative Period. Valley of Mexico. *h.* 3 1/8 in. (8). CMAE

19 Female figurine; Formative Period. Valley of Mexico. *h.* 2 3/4 in. (7). British Museum. Photo John Webb

20 Vessel; in the form of a fish. Black ware, with roughened areas originally tinted red. Formative Period. Tlatilco, Valley of Mexico. *h.* 5 1/4 in. (13.3). MNAM. Photo INAH

21 Vessel; in the form of a dog seated on its haunches. Polished black ware. Formative Period. Tlatilco, Valley of Mexico. MNAM. Photo INAH

22 Bowl; simple geometrical design. Diamonds and stripes in brown to brownish-grey, the colour of the ware, against a ground of red to dark red paint. Designs outlined by incision. Formative Period. Tlatilco, Valley of Mexico. h. 3 1/8 in. (18). CMAE

23 Figurine; male wearing helmet and loin-cloth. Painted pottery. Formative Period. Tlatilco, Valley of Mexico. Private Collection. Photo Irmgard Groth-Kimball

24 Figurine; female with two heads. Painted pottery with traces of black on yellow ground. Formative Period. Tlatilco, Valley of Mexico. h. 4 1/8 in. (10.5). Private Collection. Photo Irmgard Groth-Kimball

25 Mask; half a face, with protruding tongue, and half a skull. Light polished pottery. Formative Period. Tlatilco, Valley of Mexico. h. 3 1/8 in. (8). Private Collection. Photo Irmgard Groth-Kimball

26 Detail of the earlier stage of the main pyramid in the Ciudadela at Teotihuacán, Valley of Mexico. Alternating masks of the rain god and feathered serpents with rattlesnake tails and also marine shells. Teotihuacán Culture. Photo Irmgard Groth-Kimball

27 Main pyramid in the Ciudadela at Teotihuacán, Valley of Mexico, which illustrates a slope-and-panel profile. Earlier stage in background, Teotihuacán Culture. Photo INAH

28 Mask; dark slate, carved and engraved. Teotihuacán Culture. Cholula. h. 7 5/8 in. (19.3). Private Collection. Photo Irmgard Groth-Kimball

29 Statuette; a stylized jaguar. Alabaster, carved in the round and with engraved decoration. Teotihuacán Culture. Teotihuacán, Valley of Mexico. h. 7 7/8 in. (20). MNAM. Photo INAH

30 Pottery stamp; mask and head-dress of the rain god. Teotihuacán I. Valley of Mexico. w. 1 3/8 in. (3.7). CMAE

31 Five pottery figurine heads. Heads (a) and (b) modelled, with applied elements; (c) and (d) modelled; (e) mould-made. Teotihuacán I (a) II (b) III (c and d) and IV (e). Teotihuacán region, Valley of Mexico. h. of (e) head 2 3/4 in. (7). CMAE

32 Tripod bowl; mask applied on the side. Negatively painted brown dots on black.

Teotihuacán, Valley of Mexico. h. 3 3/4 in. (9.7). CMAE

33 Jar; decorated with head of rain god, and other designs in polychrome stucco. Teotihuacán, Valley of Mexico. h. 6 1/4 in. (16). MNAM. Photo INAH.

34 Wide-mouthed vase; geometrical design produced by burnishing. Period II. Teotihuacán, Valley of Mexico. h. 4 1/2 in. (11.5). CMAE

35 Wall painting; the rain god with blue scrolls representing water, and other objects, flowing from his hands. Polychrome paint on plaster. Teotihuacán Culture. Tetitla. Photo Eugen Kusch

36 Wall painting; the rain god Tlaloc sowing, with speech scrolls emerging from his mouth. Polychrome paint on plaster. Teotihuacán Culture. MNAM. Photo GHS Bushnell

37 Wall painting; figures disporting themselves in paradise of the rain god over which he presides. Polychrome paint on plaster (partly reconstructed). Teotihuacán Culture. Painted palace at Tepantitla, Teotihuacán, Valley of Mexico.

38 Low relief; remains of facing on east side of north pyramid at Tula, showing two sets of friezes of jaguars, coyotes, eagles and monsters, separated by a slope. Formerly plastered and painted. Toltec. Tula, Hidalgo. h. 15 ft (4.6 m). Photo Michael D. Coe

39 Columns; square in section, with low relief carving of human figures in profile and other motifs, one carved in the round in the form of a warrior. Basalt. Toltec. Summit of north pyramid, Tula, Hidalgo. h. 15 ft (4.6 m.). Photo Michael D. Coe

40 Tula, Hidalgo; north Pyramid with remains of vestibule and colonnade below. Toltec. Photo GHS Bushnell

41 Bowl; Mazápan ware painted orange with composite brush on buff ground with wavy lines. Toltec. diam. 7 1/4 in. (18.5). CMAE

42 Vessel; in form of animal, its legs serving as supports. Plumbate with ware shell inlay. h. 5 3/4 in. (14.8). CMAE

43 Tripod bowl; Matlatzinca ware; red paint on cream slip. Toltec. h. 4 1/4 in. (10.8). CMAE

44 Extremely stylized model of a temple pyramid (teocalli) in carved jade. Aztec. Valley of Mexico. h. 1 3/4 in. (4.3). CMAE

45 Mask; the flayed god, Xipe. On the back the god is shown in the skin of a sacrificial victim. Basalt. Aztec, late 15th C. Probably Tenochtitlán, Valley of Mexico. *h.* 9 in. (22.8). British Museum. Photo Edwin Smith

46 Colossal statue; the earth goddess, Coatlicué, her head replaced by two snake heads, wearing a skirt of snakes and necklace of human hearts and hands. Andesite. Aztec, late 15th C. Main plaza at Tenochtitlán, Valley of Mexico. *h.* 8 ft 3 in. (2.60 m). MNAM. Photo INAH

47 Carved stone; commemorating the victories of King Tizoc (1481-6) by showing him dressed as a god and seizing a series of captives, below glyphs naming the conquered regions. Influenced by Mixtec manuscript style. Low relief on cylindrical stone. Aztec. Main temple enclosure at Tenochtitlán, Valley of Mexico. *diam.* 8 ft 8 1/2 in. (2.75 m). MNAM. Photo INAH

48 Giant grasshopper; red stone. Aztec. Tenochtitlán, Valley of Mexico. *l.* 18 in. (45.8). MNAM. Photo INAH

49 Pendant; miniature rattlesnake, with human head in its mouth. Hard black stone veined with white. Aztec. *h.* 4 1/4 in. (11). CMAE

50 Two-tongued slit drum *(teponaztli)*; hollowed out log. Figures and glyphs intricately carved, back plain. Mixtec. Unprovenanced. *l.* 1 ft (30.5). British Museum. Photo John Webb

51 Two-tongued slit drum *(teponaztli)*; hollowed out log, carved with an owl face. Aztec. Unprovenanced. *l.* 19 in. (48). Photo Courtesy Trustees of the British Museum

52 Two-tongued slit drum *(teponaztli)*; hollowed out log, in the shape of a curly-haired animal, with dog teeth inserted. Aztec. Unprovenanced. *l.* 3 ft (91.5). MNAM. Photo INAH

53 Sacrificial knife; chalcedony blade and handle of carved wood inlaid with turquoise, malachite, red and white shell, pyrites and jet in the form of a crouching eagle warrior. Aztec. Tenochtitlán, Valley of Mexico. *l.* 13 3/8n. (34). Photo Courtesy Trustees of the British Museum

54 Head-dress; given by Montezuma II to Cortés. Mainly of green feathers woven and sewn onto a backing with gold ornaments. Aztec. Tenochtitlán, Valley of Mexico. *h.* over 4 ft (1.24 m). Museum für Völkerkunde, Vienna

55 Tripod bowl; with design of eagle in centre. Grey paint on orange ground. Aztec III. Mexico City. *diam.* 8 in. (20.5). CMAE

56 Biconical cup; perhaps for drinking *pulque*, fermented maguey juice. Glossy red ware with black scroll pattern. Aztec. *h.* 5 in. (12.7). CMAE

57 Spindle whorl; with engraved geometrical designs. Black pottery. Aztec. *diam.* 1 5/8 in. (4.2). CMAE

58 Figurine; perhaps goddess holding a child. Polished red pottery, mould-made. Aztec. *h.* 5 in. (12.7). Photo Courtesy Trustees of the British Museum

59 Stamp; monkey design, used for decorating textiles or the body. Red pottery. Aztec. *h.* 1 7/8 in. (4.7). CMAE

60 Relief; sacrifice of a ball-player, within a scroll frame. Classic Veracruz style. Panel of 4 stone slabs in south ball-court, El Tajín, Veracruz. Photo Michael D. Coe

61 Figurine; man dressed for the ball-game, with helmet, yoke, and *palma*. White pottery with some details picked out in black pitch. Gulf Coast. *h.* 5 in. (12.8). CMAE

62 Figurine head; pale buff pottery, eyes decorated with pitch. Classic Veracruz style. Gulf Coast. *Max. w.* 3 5/8 in. (9.2). CMAE

63 Vase; carved scroll ornament, lugs in the shape of animals. Marble. *l.* 11 in. (28). Ulua Valley, Honduras. Photo Courtesy Trustees of the British Museum.

64 *Hacha;* male head with dolphin crest. Diorite, probably, originally inlaid. Classic Veracruz culture. El Tajín, Veracruz. *h.* 11 in. (28). Private Collection. Photo Irmgard Groth-Kimball

65 Yoke, representing a stylized toad seen from above. Stone. Classic Veracruz style. Unprovenanced. *l.* about 18 in. (45.5). AMNH

66 Figurine; standing female wearing skirt and *quexquemitl*. Pale buff pottery. Eyes and other details touched in with black pitch. Classic Gulf Coast Culture. *h.* 9 in. (23). CMAE

67 'Laughing head' ; with filed teeth, wearing head-dress (fragment of a figurine). Classic Veracruz buff pottery. Gulf Coast. Max. *w.* 5 1/2 in. (14). CMAE

68 Pottery figure; seated woman wearing lip-plug with eyes and nipples painted with black pitch. A large pendant formerly hung from the necklace. *h.* 26 in. (66). From El Salto, Ignacio de la Llave, Veracruz. MNAM. Photo GHS Bushnell

69 'Teapot' vessel; animal head and forefeet at spout end, human head at the other, transverse handle. Black-on-cream ware. Huastec. *h.* 8 in. (20.5). British Museum. Photo John Webb

70 Bowl; inside, design of leaping animal in orange on a black ground. Post-Classic, Central Veracruz. *diam.* 7 3/4 in. (19.8). CMAE

71 Statue ('The Adolescent'); with distended ear-lobes and body partly tattooed . Carrying on his back an infant said to represent the sun. Sandstone. Huastec. Consuelo, near Tamuín, San Luis Potosí. *h.* 4 ft 4 in. (1.3 m). MNAM. Photo INAH

72 Spindle whorl; decorated in relief with two birds of prey. Cream-coloured pottery. Huastec. *diam.* 1 1/2 in. (3.9). CMAE

73 Mosaic mask; seven interlocking pieces of dark green jade, three pendants (beard) of slate, eyes and teeth of inlaid shell. Monte Albán II. Monte Albán, Oaxaca. *h.* without pendants 6 1/8 in. (15.5). MNAM. Photo INAH

74 Monte Albán, Oaxaca; general view, looking south. Site is an artificially levelled hilltop. Zapotec, Classic Period. Photo GHS Bushnell

75 Funerary urn; in the form of Cocijo, the rain god. Grey pottery. Zapotec. Monte Albán, Oaxaca. *h.* 14 1/8 in. (36). CMAE

76 Vessel; in the form of an eagle's claw. Dark grey ware. Zapotec. Monte Albán IV. Monte Albán, Oaxaca. *h.* 3 1/2 in. (9). CMAE

77 Five figurines; angular carving in jade and other hard stones. Mixtec. Some from Mitla, others unprovenanced. *h.* of tallest 1 7/8 in. (4.8). CMAE

78 Stone mosaic; in the hall adjacent to the court behind the Building of the Columns, Mitla. Mixtec. Photo GHS Bushnell

79 Woven textile; interlocking head pattern. Chimu. Peru. CMAE. Tripod vessel; interlocking head pattern, with other designs in polychrome. Mixtec. After Covarrubias

80 Tripod vessel; pottery, with white slip. Mixtec. *h.* 5 3/4 in. (14.8). CMAE

81 Vessel; Cholula Polychrome. Decorated with feathers, stone knives (in upper row) and skulls (in bottom row) and other symbols. Cholula, Puebla. *h.* 7 1/2 in. (19.2). CMAE

82 Vessel; Cholula Polychrome with a humming bird on rim. Zaachila *h.* 3 1/8 in. (8). MNAM. Photo INAH

83 Manuscript; Codex Zouche-Nuttall; part of the story of Lady Three-Flint. Pictographs painted in several colours on deerskin. Mixtec, after 1350. *h.* of page 8 in. (20.3). Facsimile; original in British Museum

84 Jewel; round shield, with step fret design and small pendant bells; behind it, four horizontal arrows. Gold, with inlay of turquoise mosaic. Mixtec. Yanhuitlán, Oaxaca. MNAM. Photo INAH

85 Pendant; four plaques in low relief and four dangling bells. Scenes on plaques are, from top to bottom; a ball game played between two gods, the solar disc, a stylized butterfly, and the Earth Monster. Gold, cast by cire perdue process. Mixtec. Tomb 7, Monte Albán, Oaxaca. *l.* 8 1/2 in. (21.6). MNAM. Photo INAH

86 Two carved spatulas; human scenes and calendar signs. Low relief on jaguar bone. Mixtec. Tomb 7, Monte Albán, Oaxaca. *l.* 7 in. (17.8).

87 Two bowls, one with tripod feet; geometrical step and chevron designs. Red and black on cream slip. Late Formative, Chupícuaro, Guanajuato. *h.* of large bowl 6 in. (15.2). CMAE

88 Figurine; solid, red pottery, with touches of red and white paints. Late Formative, Chupícuaro, Guanajuato. *h.* 4 in. (10). CMAE

89 Head; highly stylized face. Hard, dark green stone, flecked with black. Mescala or Guerrero style. *h.* 4 1/2 in. (11.7). CMAE

90 Head; face with Olmecoid features. Red pottery. Iguala, Guerrero. *h.* 2 in. (5). CMAE

91 Tripod vessel; gourd shape with narrow neck and flaring lip, feet in the form of parrots. Smoothly finished, with red slip. Colima. MNAM. Photo INAH

92 Figurine; man bound to bed. Red on yellow slip. Nayarít. *l.* 4 1/4 in. (11). CMAE

93 Vessel; gourd shape with narrow flared mouth Red slip. Nayarít. *h.* 4 3/4 in. (12). CMAE

94 Vessel; in the form of a seated hairless dog. Pottery, with red slip. Colima. *h.* 12 1/8 in. (31.1). British Museum. Photo John Webb

95 Figurine; solid buff pottery, modelled, with applied details. Colima. *h.* 6 1/2 in. (16.5). CMAE

272

96 Figure; man blowing conch shell. Hollow pottery, modelled, slipped. Colima. *h.* 16 in. (40.7). Arensberg Collection, Philadelphia Museum of Art

97 Corbelled vault from temple at side of ball-court. Copán, Honduras. Classic Maya. Photo GHS Bushnell

98 Ball-court at Copán, Honduras. Sloping stone sides. Classic Maya. Photo GHS Bushnell

99 Ball-court at Chichén Itzá, Yucatán. Vertical stone walls. Post-Classic Maya. Photo GHS Bushnell

100 Stela; human figure in elaborate costume and head-dress. Maya. AD 766. Stela D. Quiriguá, Guatemala. *h.* 35 ft (10.7 m.). Photo Courtesy Trustees of the British Museum, Maudslay Collection

101 Temple of the Sun at Palenque, Chiapas. General view, showing elaborate roofcomb, and façade originally covered with painted stucco. Late Classic Maya, probably dedicated in AD 692. Photo GHS Bushnell

102/3 Full-figure numerical glyphs; Part of a glyph series. Each pair of glyphs shows an era, in the form of a fantastic animal or figure, borne on the back of a number god. Low relief on limestone tablet. Late Classic Maya. Palenque, Chiapas. Photo Irmgard Groth-Kimball

104 Relief; detail of slab on the tomb under the Temple of the Inscriptions. Reclining human figure. Low relief on limestone. Late Classic Maya. Palenque, Chiapas. Photo Eugen Kusch

105 House of the Turtles, Uxmal, Yucatán. Plain façade pierced with three doorways; fluted frieze, below, a row of small turtles. Lime concrete veneered with thin stone slabs. Late Classic Maya. Photo Eugen Kusch

106 Palace of the Governor, Uxmal, Yucatán. Façade with heavy decorated frieze pierced by two large corbelled 'arches'. Late Classic Maya, Puuc style. Photo GHS Bushnell

107 Head; young man wearing elaborate plumed head-dress. Stucco with traces of red paint. Late Classic Maya. Burial chamber under the Temple of the Inscriptions, Palenque, Chiapas, (i.e. the same chamber as *Ill. 104*). *h.* 15 3/8 in. (39). MNAM. Photo Irmgard Groth-Kimball

108 Bowl; marine monsters and stylized glyphs. Orange and black on buff slip. Late Classic Maya. Caracol, British Honduras. *h.* 3 1/2 in. (9). CMAE

109 Design on vase; scene with priests and dignitaries in full costume. Red, yellow and black paint on buff slip. Late Classic Maya. Chama, Guatemala. *h.* about 9 in. (23). Cary Collection, The University Museum, Philadelphia. Painting by M. Louise Baker

110 Wall painting; raid on an inferior tribe to get prisoners. Polychrome paint on plaster (perhaps true fresco). Maya, *c.* AD 800. Bonampak, Chiapas. Copy by Antonio Tejeda. The Peabody Museum, Harvard University

111 Vase; kneeling figures with head-dresses, above a band of glyphs. Polychrome. Classic Maya. AMNH

112 Tripod bowl with cover; incised designs, including bird which is also modelled on the cover. Early Classic Maya, from the painted tomb at Tikal, Guatemala. AD 457. The University Museum, Philadelphia

113 Whistle figurine; seated man wearing elaborate plumed head-dress. Grey pottery, mould-made, the necklace painted blue. Late Classic Maya. Jaina, Campeche. CMAE

114 Figurine; female wearing ear-spools and necklace. Red ware with touches of red and white, modelled. with applied details. Formative Maya. *h.* 7 in, (18). CMAE

115 Plaque; seated dignitary or god wearing elaborate head-dress. Pale green jade, carved and drilled in low relief and highly polished. Classic Maya. Unprovenanced. *l.* 3 in. (7.7). British Museum. Photo John Webb

116 Large annular flare; four glyphs on plain surface. Ear-spool shape, but perhaps a belt ornament. Dark green jade, engraved and highly polished. Proto-Classic Maya (Late Formative). Pomona, Bristish Honduras. *diam.* 7 in. (17.8). British Museum. Photo Eileen Tweedy

117 Eccentric flint; flaked to incorporate human profiles. Perhaps head of ceremonial staff. Maya. Unprovenanced. *l.* 10 in. (25.4). Photo Courtesy Trustees of the British Museum

118 El Castillo, Chichén Itzá, Yucatán. General view of pyramid crowned with a temple. Post-Classic Maya. Photo Eugen Kusch

119 Relief; human skulls on poles. Shallow relief on the *tzompantli* or skull rack. Post-Classic Maya. Chichén Itzá, Yucatán. Photo GHS Bushnell

120 Pillar; in the form of a feathered serpent, its rattlesnake tail formerly supporting lintel of the temple entrance. Post-Classic Maya. Temple of the

Warriors, Chichén Itzá, Yucatán. Photo GHS Bushnell

121 Wall painting; a waterside village (copy), showing various activities and canoes carrying warriors. Polychrome on plaster. Post-Classic Maya, 12th C. Temple of the Warriors, Chichén Itzá, Yucatán *h*. 9 ft × 12 1/2 ft (2.75 m. × 3.83 m.). Copy by A. Axtell Morris, courtesy The Peabody Museum, Harvard University

122 Five ornaments; geometrical forms, including scrolls and a swastika. Native copper, cut, beaten and annealed. Hopewell Culture, Ohio. CNHM

123 Three tobacco pipes; bowls in the form of marmot, frog, and snake; front views show smoke channel. Steatite, carved, with some shell inlay. Hopewell Culture, Ohio. *l.* of frog pipe, 3 3/8 in. (9.2). Photo Courtesy Trustees of the British Museum

124 Two silhouettes; mutilated human figures. Thin sheet of mica. Hopewell Culture, Ohio

125 Two silhouettes; human hand and eagle claw. Thin sheet of mica. *l.* of eagle claw *c.* 10 in. (25.4). Hopewell Culture, Ohio. CNHM

126 Mask; deer head, with large leather-hinged ears. Carved wood, originally painted. Late Prehistoric. Key Marco, Florida. *l.* 10 3/4 in. (27.5). University Museum, Philadelphia.

127 Bottle; swirl design. Pottery, painted red and white. Middle Mississippi Period, after AD 1000. Child's grave at Halcombs Mounds, Arkansas. Peabody Museum, Harvard University

128 Bottle; concentric linear designs. Pottery with burnished black slip, incised after firing; traces of red paint in incisions. Caddo. Middle Mississippi Period, after AD 1000. Lafayette County, Arkansas. Museum of the American Indian, Heye Foundation

129 Bowl; black on white, showing contrast between areas of solid colour and hatching. Pueblo III, *c.* AD 1050-1300. Mesa Verde, Colorado. *diam.* 10 in. (25.4). British Museum. Photo Edwin Smith

130 Coiled burden basket; geometrical design in red and black on natural ground. Basketmaker III Period AD 500-700, Canyon del Muerto, Arizona. *diam.* 32 in. (82). University of Colorado Museum.

131 Bowl; stylized turtle within geometrical border. Black paint on white slip. A hole has been punched in the centre, ceremonially 'killing' the bowl for burial with the dead. AD 1000-1200. Swarts Ranch, Mimbres Valley, New Mexico. *diam.* 10 1/2 in. (27). Peabody Museum, Harvard University

132 Fragment of bowl; Sikyatki Polychrome. Painted in black and red on yellow. Ruin 4, Horn House, Moki Reservation, Arizona. Peabody Museum, Harvard University

133 Vase; geometrical and scroll designs in compartments. Black and red paint on buff slip. *c.* AD 1300-1450. Chihuahua, Mexico. *h.* 8 in. (20.5). CMAE

134 Design; extended pattern on carved gourd *(Ill. 135)*. Preceramic Period. Huaca Prieta, Chicama Valley, Peru. Drawing Courtesy the AMNH, New York

135 Carved gourd vessel with cover; Preceramic Period, *c.* 2000 BC. Huaca Prieta, Chicama Valley. *diam. c.* 2 3/8 in. (6). AMNH

136 Twined textile; design indicated only by direction of warp displacement. Cotton. Preceramic Period. Chicama Valley. *l.* 8 1/2 in. (21.5). By kind permission of AMNH

137 Twined textile; condor with snake in its stomach. *(Ill. 136)* after analysis with design plotted and superposed. By kind permission of AMNH

138 Annular vessel with stirrup spout; on ring, two human heads and two heads combining bird (probably owl)) and feline features yellowish-grey ware. Cupisnique (Coast Chavín) style. North Coast. *h.* 8 in. (20.5). Royal Scottish Museum

139 Carved monolith; upper section of the Great Image. Human figure with feline fangs and snakes as hair. White granite. Chavín Culture, probably 9th C. BC. Old temple block, Chavín de Huántar. Total height nearly 15 ft (4.58 m.). Rubbing by Fred D. Ayres, courtesy the Museum of Primitive Art, New York

140 Frieze; stylized birds with feline jaws and eyes and snake heads. Chavín Culture. Lintel of the black and white portal, temple at Chavín de Huántar. Rubbing. Photo Abraham Guillén

141 Low relief; bird decorated with feline heads in profile. Chavín Culture. Temple at Chavín de Huántar. Photo Abraham Guillén

142 Two engraved slabs; left, human figure with severed legs; right, trophy head. Chavín Period. Part of retaining wall of temple platform at Cerro Sechín, Casma Valley. Photo Hans Mann

143 Circular gold repoussé plaque; feline face with snake head appendages, within guilloche border. Late Chavín style. Possibly from Chavín de Huántar. *diam.* 4 13/16 in. (12.2). Bliss Collection, Dumbarton Oaks (Trustees for Harvard University)

144 Mortar; in the shape of a jaguar, with stylized markings. Stone, carved in the round and incised. Eyes originally inlaid. Chavín Culture. *l.* 13 in. (33). The University Museum, Philadalphia

145 Bottle; monochrome, dark-coloured, with incised feline-inspired designs surrounded by rocker stamping. Cupisnique style. Courtesy Rafael Larco Hoyle

146 Stirrup-spouted jar; dark monochrome pottery, with rough surface perhaps suggested by a spondylus shell. Early Cupisnique style. Courtesy Rafael Larco Hoyle

147 Stirrup-spouted jar; in the form of a woman suckling a child. Dark pottery. Cupisnique style. Courtesy Rafael Larco Hoyle

148 Stirrup-spouted vessel; in the form of a modelled monkey standing on annular base. Reddish-brown ware. Salinar Culture, later centuries BC. Chicama Valley. Courtesy Rafael Larco Hoyle

149 Spout and bridge vessel; spout balanced by human head with closed eyes, wearing cap. Modelled with simple, black linear negative painting on red ground. Gallinazo (Virú) style. Virú Valley. *b.* 6 in. (15). CMAE

150 Spout and bridge vessel; warrior carrying club and shield on reed raft. Negative painting. Gallinazo (Virú) style. Early Classic. Virú Valley. Courtesy Rafael Larco Hoyle

151 Bowl; fish alternating with decorative panels. Pottery, with pressed relief, painted in red and white. Mochica. *b.* 4 3/4 in. (12). CMAE

152 Stirrup-spouted pottery vessel; in the shape of a house with open porch. Painted in red and white. Mochica. Linden-Museum, Stuttgart

153 Effigy vessel with stirrup spout; in the form of a seated man wearing a cap. Highly burnished red slip. Early Mochica. *b.* 6 3/4 in. (17.1). Photo Courtesy Trustees of the British Museum

154 Stirrup-spouted jar; drummer wearing bird mask and wings. Painted in red and white. Late Mochica. *b.* 11 3/4 in. (29.9). British Museum. Photo John Webb

155 Stirrup-spouted jar; a warrior and his dog chase a spotted deer with a club, with the three-dimensional figure of a deer on top of the vessel. Modelled and painted in red and white. Mochica. *b.* 9 1/2 in. (24.2). British Museum. Photo John Webb

156 Spatula handle; in the form of an arm, with engraved figure of a warrior dressed as a bird, and inset turquoise and pyrite nodules. The blade is plain. Mochica. Santa Valley. *l.* 8 1/4 in. (21). British Museum. Photo John Webb

157 Wooden head of copper-shod ceremonial digging-stick; shell and turquoise inlay. Shows a tusked figure holding a digging-stick and accompanied by a boy. Found in the grave of an old man and a boy similarly dressed, at Huaca de la Cruz, Virú Valley. Mochica. After WD Strong

158 Portrait vase; head of a man with painted face wearing cap and ear-spools. White and red. Mochica. *b.* 6 1/4 in. (16). Collection Dr MGM Pryor

159 Portrait vase with stirrup spout; head of a man with painted face wearing a decorated cap. Painted in red and white. Mochica. *b.* 11 5/8 in. (29.6). British Museum. Photo John Webb

160 Gold puma skin with three-dimensional head; on the animal's tongue a human face appears and on its body a design of two-headed serpents. The belly in two thicknesses forms a pouch. Gold repoussé work and wire. Mochica. *l.* 24 5/8 in. (62.5). M. Mugica Gallo Collection. Photo John Webb

161 Jar; with flange mouth, and lateral spout above a modelled human head between two animals. Decorated with black negative painting over white and red, illustrating a crested jaguar and other features. Recuay style, Callejón de Huaylas, North Highlands. *b.* 7 1/8 in. (20). CMAE

162 Bowl and two sherds; cursive scroll pattern, including stylized faces and animals. Colours vary from red-brown to black, with some grey, on cream ground. Cajamarca, North Highlands. *diam.* of dish 4 3/4 in. (12.5). CMAE

163 Spout and bridge vessel; spout balanced by stylized bird's head. Surface burnished except for head and large feline face at one end. Some details picked out in red after firing. Paracas style, Formative Period. South Coast. *b.* 7 1/4 in. (18). CMAE

164 Double spout and bridge vessel; buff with incised decoration suggesting matting on body and bridge. Parts picked out in red, yellow, black and white resinous paint, applied after firing. Paracas style, Formative Period. South Coast. *b.* 5 1/2 in. (14). CMAE

165 Spout and bridge effigy jar; modelled to represent a woman and painted in black, white, dark red, yellow and orange. Nasca style, Classic Period. South Coast. *b.* 6 1/4 in. (16). CMAE

275

166 Spout and bridge vessel; represents a jaguar. Burnished black. The markings are incised and most of the surface was probably originally covered with resinous post-fired colours of which some red, yellow, grey and white remains. Paracas style, Formative Period. South Coast. *h.* 5 7/8 in. (15). CMAE

167 Double spout and bridge vessel; two rows of crabs. Red, orange and dark grey paint on black over dark red slip. Early Classic Nasca *h.* 7 in. (17.8). British Museum. Photo John Webb

168 Beaker; painted in red, purplish red, grey, yellow and black on white ground showing a demon between inner bands of geometrical design and outer ones of trophy heads. Late Nasca, Classic Period. South Coast. *h.* 7 7/8 in. (20). CMAE

169 Textile; part of border of mantle covered with solid alpaca wool embroidery showing outlines of small cats within larger ones. Paracas *w.* 4 1/4 in. (11). CMAE

170 Tapestry textile; rare type, in rose pink, light blue and yellow, with design showing a stylized monster worked in small beads strung on the warp. Nasca. *w.* of design 6 1/4 in. (15.5). CMAE

171 Clothing; lay figure dressed in richly embroidered mantle, turban and undergarments. Textiles from a Paracas mummy. National Museum, Lima. Photo Courtesy Dr Jorge Muelle

172 Markings on barren plateau above the Nasca Valley. Linear patterns have been formed by removing surface pebbles to expose the yellow sandy soil. Nasca Culture. Photo Hans Mann

173 Bowl; with feline head and tail and wavy rim, painted in red, black, white, orange and brown on pale brown ware. Early Tiahuanaco, Formative Period. South Highlands. *h.* 4 3/4 in. (12). CMAE

174 Beaker *(kero)*; upper band of stylized heads, lower of stylized felines, all in profile. Polychrome paint on red slip. Classic Tiahuanaco. *h.* 6 1/2 in. (16.5). The University Museum, Philadelphia

175 Relief; central figure from monolithic doorway holding staves. Tiahuanaco, Bolivia. Classic Period. Size of gate 12 ft × 10 ft (3.76 × 3.5 m.). Photo Abraham Guillén

176 Statue; kneeling male, wearing head-dress. Limestone. Late Formative Period. Pokotía, near Tiahuanaco, Bolivia. Photo Abraham Guillén

177 Statue; figure wearing loin-cloth and cap and carrying a human head. Stone. Late Formative

Period. Pucára, South Highlands, Peru. Photo Abraham Guillén

178 Potsherd; stylized feline head with vertically divided eyes. Design in low relief incised and painted in black and red. Late Formative Period. Pucára, South Highlands, Peru. Max. *w.* 10.2 3/4 in. (7). CMAE

179 Poncho shirt; with vertical bands of tapestry bearing abstract designs. The vertically divided eyes show the derivation from Tiahuanaco. Coast Tiahuanaco, Early Post-Classic Period. The Textile Museum, Washington

180 Process of stylization; from falcon-headed, staff-bearing attendant figure on the monolithic gateway, Tiahuanaco, to textile designs, Coast Tiahuanaco Culture. Drawings by Milton Franklin Sonday, Jr., from Alan R. Sawyer, *Tiahuanaco Tapestry Design*, 1963. Courtesy The Museum of Primitive Art, N.Y.

181 Cap; square, with peaked corners and geometrical decoration. Knotted pile cloth, wool, in red, turquoise, blue, buff, brown and white. Coast Tiahuanaco, Early Post-Classic Period. Each side 5 × 3 in. (12.7 × 7.6). Photo Courtesy Trustees of the British Museum

182 Double spout and bridge vessel; falcon-headed, staff-bearing figure with wings. Polychrome Coast Tiahuanaco Culture. *h.* 6 in. (15.2). British Museum. Photo John Webb

183 Bowl; with animal head, rudimentary limbs and tail in relief, painted with geometrical designs in black, white and red. End of Coast Tiahuanaco Period. *h.* 4 3/4 in. (12). CMAE

184 Face-collar jar; on neck, head of man wearing hat and ear-spools, on body, felines in pressed relief. Painted in washy black, white and orange on buff ground. Late North Coast Tiahuanaco style. *h.* 7 1/2 in. (19). CMAE

185 Relief; on wall of Chan Chan. Bands of birds, fish, and fantastic animals, and of scrolls and step ornament. Moulded mud-plaster. Chimú Culture. Later Post-Classic. Photo Hans Mann

186 Double spout and bridge ceremonial vessel; ornamental band on body, openwork crest on bridge, free-standing elements in the form of two monkeys and four heads. Hammered silver. Chimú. Lambayeque Valley. *h.* 7 2/8 in. (20). M. Mugica Gallo Collection. Photo John Webb

187 Drinking vessel *(Paccha)*; in the form of a man fishing from a reed raft. Black ware. Chimú. *l.* 12 1/4 in. (31). CMAE

188 Canteen; with pressed relief of jaguar on body, and two small handles. Black ware. Chimú. *h.* 9 in. (23). CMAE

189 Stirrup-spouted vessel with monkey on spout; man holding a child on a cubical base. Black ware. Against background of contemporary textile with brocaded fish and pelican designs. Chimú. CMAE

190 Beaker; standing male figure with, plumed head-dress and ear-spools, holding staves. Repoussé gold. Head-dress and ear-spools inlaid with turquoise. Chimú. Lambayeque Valley. *h.* 7 7/8 in. (20). M. Mugica Gallo Collection. Photo John Webb

191 Funerary mask; face with ear and nose ornaments. Gold, with stone eyes and traces of red and green paint. Chimú. Lambayeque Valley. *w.* 22 3/8 in. (57). M. Mugica Gallo Collection. Photo John Webb

192 Ear-spool; reversible design of two birds with a common body. Wood, with crenellated and polished edge, inlaid with coloured shell. Chimú. *diam.* 1 7/8 in. (4.7). British Museum. Photo John Webb

193 Ear-spools; central head with head-dress, surrounded by 10 similar heads. Thin silver, repoussé, Chimú. *diam.* 5 1/2 in. (14). AMNH

194 Ceremonial knife; blade with semi circular cutting-edge surmounted by the hollow figure of a deer, and danglers. Blade of base metal with gold plating, ornaments of gold. Chimú. Lambayeque Valley. *h.* 12 13/16 in. (30). M. Mugica Gallo Coll. Photo John Webb

195 Painted plain weave textile; fantastic faces in compartments separated by scrolls and chevrons. Designs in brown on buff ground originally white. Painted designs at this time show far less sureness of touch than woven ones. Chimú. Each panel. *c.* 2 3/4 in. (7) square. CMAE

196 Double cloth with design of pelicans in brown and white (below), and border of tapestry worked on gauze with pelicans within scrolled lozenges. Chimú. Size of detail shown 10 1/4 in.× 16 in. (26× 41). CMAE

197 Doll; representing fisherman and net. Slit tapestry face and warp-striped plain weave shirt. In pink, white, black, buff, yellow, green and pale lavender. Chancay Valley, Central Coast. *h.* 9 1/2 in. (24). CMAE

198 Warp striped textile; pattern of brocaded cats in blue, yellow and brown on dirty white. Chimú. *h.* 10 1/4 in.× 10 1/4 in (24× 24). CMAE

199 Large ovoid jar. Black-on-white decoration. Chancay style, Later Post-Classic. Central Coast. *h.* 17 in. (43.3). Photo Courtesy Trustees of the British Museum

200 Three bowls; all with textile-inspired designs in black, white and red. Ica style, Later Post Classic. South Coast. *h.* of largest 6 in. (15.2). Photo Courtesy Trustees of the British Museum

201 Machu Picchu; general view, showing low semi-circular tower. Inca, after 1450. Photo Hans Mann

202 Saccsaihuamán, Cuzco; lowest wall of zig-zag rampart of the fortress. Irregular 'megalithic' masonry. Inca, mid 15th C. Photo Nicholas Young

203 Statuette; alpaca with a hole in its back. Hard black stone. Inca. *l.* 4 in. *(*1 ₁.2). British Museum. Photo John Webb

204 Jar with lugs; polychrome with geometrical designs and snakes, lugs in the form of jaguars. Inca, after 1450. Region of Cuzco. Museo Arqueológico, Cuzco. Photo Abraham Guillén

205 Provincial aryballus; stylized plant design in black and white, the base red. Chile. *h.* 10 5/8 in. (27). CMAE

206 Provincial aryballus; with a pressed relief. Black ware. Chimú-Inca style. North Coast. After Inca conquest (*c.* 1470). *h.* 7 1/2 in. (19). CMAE

207 Aryballus; Cuzco polychrome decorated with geometrical pattern. Inca, after 1450. Photo Courtesy Trustees of the British Museum

208 Vessel with one handle; painted black, white and orange. Inca-Ica style. Ica Valley, South Coast. After the Inca conquest (*c.* 1480). *h.* 3 7/8 in. (10). CMAE

209 Poncho shirt; geometrical and feather designs, two small human figures within characteristic V neck. Vicuña wool tapestry. Inca. From an island in Lake Titicaca. AMNH

210 Statuette; llama with saddle blanket and girth. Cast silver with gold appliqué. Red cinnabar-resin inlay of saddle blanket restored. Inca. *h.* 9 1/8 in. (23.2). AMNH

211 Santa Maria funerary urn; stylized face on neck. Black and red paint on cream slip. Catamarca and neighbouring provinces, North West Argentina. After A D 1000. *h.* 21 1/2 in. (54.8). British Museum. Photo John Webb

212 Bowl; stylized face and linear designs. Red, white, and grey. Chilean diaguite. Near Coquimbo, North Coast of Chile. Late Period, after A D 1000. CMAE

213 Four tablets and two tubes for taking snuff; human and animal motifs. Atacameño region, Rio Loa area, North Coast of Chile. AMNH

214 Plaque; human figure between two felines. Copper, cast by cire perdue process. Aguada Culture, A D 700-1000. North West Argentina. *w.* 6 1/4 in. (16). CMAE

215 Statue; seated male figure blowing a trumpet, Lava. Highland Costa Rica. *h.* 6 1/2 in. (16.5). CMAE

216 *Metate*; slab for grinding corn, in the form of an animal. Stone. Costa Rica. *l.* 16 in. (41). CMAE

217 Miniature stool; stone. Province of Chiriquí, Panama. *h.* 3 1/2 in. (9). CMAE

218 Celt; angular human head and arms carved on upper half, blade ground to fine edge. Grey-green jade. Nicoya, Costa Rica. *l.* 4 7/8 in. (12.4). British Museum. Photo John Webb

219 Pendant; bird with snake appendages. Gold, cast by cire perdue process. Veraguas Province, Panama. *h.* and *w.* 4 in. (10.2). Fitzwilliam Museum, Cambridge

220 Tripod bowl; with animal's heads as feet. Nicoya. Polychrome pottery. Pacific Coast of Costa Rica. *h.* 5 in. (12.5). CMAE

221 Globular vessel with lugs; Alligator Ware. Two alligators sharing a central body within striped border, lugs modelled as animal heads. Black, red and white. Chiriquí, Panama. *h.* 7 1/2 in. (19). CMAE

222 Globular vessel; black negative painting over white and red. Chiriquí, Panama. *h.* 4 in. (10.5). CMAE

223 Quadrangular tripod bowl; with animal head and tail. Painted in black, white and red. Highland Polychrome ware. Costa Rica. *h.* 3 1/4 in. (8.5). CMAE

224 Figurine; squatting woman wearing brassière. Black, white and red. Nicoya Polychrome. Pacific Coast of Costa Rica. *h.* 6 1/2 in. (16.5). CMAE

225 Ovoid tripod vase; applied animal head on side, the forelegs forming two of the vessel's feet.

Painted in red, black and white. Nicoya Polychrome. Pacific Coast of Costa Rica. *h.* 11.2 in. (28.6). Photo Courtesy Trustees of the British Museum

226 Pedestal dish; characteristic pointed hooks and crocodile heads in red, black, white and purple. Coclé, Panama. *diam.* 11 1/2 in. (29). CMAE

227 Bottle; black, red and purple on cream. Coclé, Panama. *h.* 5 1/2 in. (13.5). CMAE

228 Statue; fanged human figure wearing cap and loin-cloth, and carrying staff and shield. Coarse stone. San Agustín, Colombia. *h.* about 4 ft (1.20 m.). Photo Courtesy Trustees of the British Museum

229 Shaft grave; view of interior. Stone, walls painted in several colours. Tierradentro region, Cauca, Colombia. *After G. Kubler*, 1962.

230 Figurine *(tunjo)*; flat, human figure with wiry details wearing head-dress, carrying staff and shield. Gold cast by cire perdue process. Chibcha, Colombia, *h.* 2 1/2 in. (6.2). CMAE

231 Three objects of precious metal; bell-shaped piece of uncertain use, decorated with a row of faces, gourd-shaped flask, and seated female figurine. Outer objects of *tumbaga* (gold-copper alloy), central one of gold. Quimbaya, Cauca Valley, Colombia. *h.* of flask *c.* 4 in. (10.2). Photo Courtesy Trustees of the British Museum

232 Bowl; pattern of geometrical areas and spots. Black negative painting over red. Quimbaya, Colombia. *h.* 3 3/4 in. (9.5). CMAE

233 Bowl; parts of surface cut away in champlevé technique. Red ware. Quimbaya, Colombia. *h.* 3 1/8 in. (8). CMAE

234 Head; with head-band, ear ornaments, and necklace stamped and incised. Pottery. Chibcha, Colombia. *h.* 13/16 in. in. (19.9). British Museum. Photo John Webb

235 Head; with elaborate head-dress, ear ornaments, and necklace stamped and incised. Pottery. Chibcha, Colombia. Max. *w.* 3 1/4 in. (8). CMAE

236 Statue; standing male figure wearing a cap and belt with two pendant strips. Manteño Phase, Integration Period. Manabí Province, coast o Ecuador. *h.* 4 ft (1.20 m.). CMAE

237 Bat; dolerite slightly shaped and incised. Manteño Phase, Integration Period. La Libertad, Guayas, coast of Ecuador. *w.* 8 3/4 in. (22). CMAE

278

238 Two vessels; simple forms with traces of iridescent paint and highly polished. Formative Period. La Libertad, Guayas, coast of Ecuador. *h.* of larger vessel 3 1/2 in. (9). CMAE

239 Three painted sherds; *(top left)* chocolate on yellow, Guangala, *(top right)* stylized pelicans in red and black on yellow, La Libertad, *(below)* red and black on yellow, La Libertad. Guangala Phase, Regional Development Period. Province of Guayas, coast of Ecuador. CMAE

240 Figurine; standing male, wearing ear-spools and nose-ring. Grey pottery. Manteño Phase. Integration Period. La Libertad, Guayas, Ecuador. *h.* 5 1/4 in. (13). CMAE

241 Stone-coloured pottery figurine; standing woman wearing domed hat. Bahía Phase, Regional Development Period. Esmeraldas, coast of Ecuador. *h.* 5 1/2 in. (14). CMAE

242 Hollow whistle figurine; standing male, wearing swept-back domed hat and holding a child. Red-brown largely smoked to dark grey pottery. Guangala Phase, Regional Development Period. Guangala, Guayas, coast of Ecuador. *h.* 12 1/4 in. (31.5). CMAE

243 Face-collar urn; limbs indicated by burnishing, face with heavy applied eyebrows and fangs. Grey-brown ware. Manteño Phase, Integration Period. Salinas, Guayas, coast of Ecuador. *h.* 17 in. (43). CMAE

244 Pottery figurine head; wearing domed hat, ear-spools and nose-ring. Bahía Phase, Regional Development Period. Said to be from Esmeraldas, but probably from Manabí, coast of Ecuador. Photo Hans Mann

245 Bowl; on low ring base. Black negative decoration showing outlines of two animals over red and cream.

Tuncahuán style, El Angel, Province of Carchi, North Highlands of Ecuador. *diam.* 8 1/4 in. (21). CMAE

246 Figurine; sexless, with topknot. Stone, grooved and polished. State of Trujillo, Venezuela. Department of Anthropology, Caracas. Photo Bela Sziklay. Courtesy Professor JM Cruxent

247 Pottery female figurine; characteristic Venezuelan type. State of Trujillo. Department of Anthropology. Caracas. Photo Bela Sziklay. Courtesy Professor JM Cruxent

248 Three-pointed stone; depicting a *zemi*. Puerto Rico or Eastern Santo Domingo. Length 9 in. (23). CMAE

249 *Zemi*; representing standing male divinity with grooved cheeks. The bark cloth loin-cloth probably a subsequent addition. Carved and polished wood with shell inlay. Carpenters Mountain, Jamaica. *h.* 3 ft 5 in. (1.4 m). British Museum. Photo John Webb

250 Stool with high back; in the form of a fantastic creature with human head. Wood, carved and incised, with gold inlay on eyes, teeth and shoulders. Hispaniola (Haiti or more probably Santo Domingo) *l.* 17 in. (43). British Museum. Photo John Webb

251 Two vases; alligators and abstract all-over designs. Pottery with brown or red slip with background excised from the design leaving it in relief. Marajó Island, Brazil. *h.* 8 5/8 in. (22) and 9 in. (23). The University Museum, Philadelphia

252 Deep bowl; white slip incised and retouched with red to produce angular S-pattern. Marajó Island, Brazil. *h.* 12 1/2 in. (32). The University Museum, Philadelphia

The maps for the book were drawn by Shalom Schotten

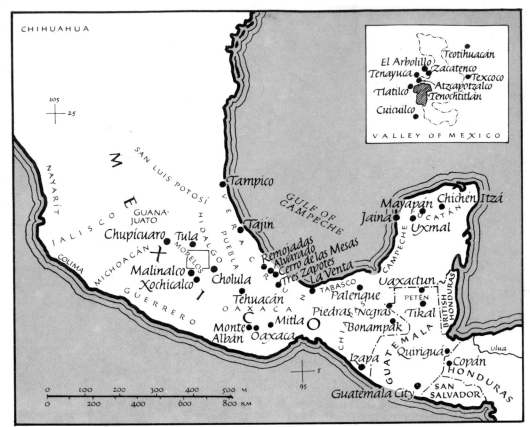

Map of Mexico showing the most important sites

Map of Peru showing the most important sites mentioned in the book.

Index

202, 205, *192-194*; influence on Inca pottery, 218, *205*
Chincha Valley, 209
Chipprak : rectangular towers, 210-11
Chiripa, 179; adobe houses, 180
Chiriquí, 229; miniature stool, 228, *217*; pottery, 234, *221, 222*
Cholula : Teotihuacán style funerary mask, 38, *28*; pottery, 69, 93, *81*; great pyramid, 49
Cholula Polychrome ware, 93, *81, 82*
Chongón : sculpture, 247
Chullpas, 211
Chupícuaro : cemetery, 97, *87, 88*
Cire perdue casting, 229, 238, 239, 250
Ciudadela (Teotihuacán), 36, *26, 27*
Classic Veracruz Culture, 71-6, *60-2, 64-7*
Coast Tiahuanaco Culture : spread of Tiahuanaco, 189-91; textiles, 191-2, *179-181*; pottery, 192, 194, 196, *182-4*; inlaid objects, 194; architecture, 194; decline, 196
Coatlichán : statue, 38
Coatlicué (Aztec earth goddess), 58; statues of, 59-60, *46*
Cochabamba, 182
Cocijo (Zapotec rain god), 86, *75*
Coclé, 228, 239; pendants and helmet, 229; pottery, 234, *226, 227*
Codices : Borbonicus, 67; Florentino, 67; Magliabecchi, 67; Nuttall, *83*
Colima art, 99-101, 91, *94-96*
Colombia, 227, 259, 261; gold helmets, 229; temples and sculptures, 237-8, *228*; shaft graves, 238; metalwork, 238-40, 250, *230, 231*; pottery styles, 241-3, *232-5*
Consuelo : statue, 79, *71*
Copán, 49; ball-court, 103, *97, 98*; stelae, 106, 108
Copper, 129, 130, 224, *122, 214*
Cortés, Hernan, 54, 68
Costa Rica, 227; carvings, 228, *215-217*; jade celt, 23, 229, *218*
Covarrubias, M., 22, 27, 71; quoted 64
Coxcatlán : statue, 59
Cuicuilco : tiered conical platform, 34
Cuismancu State, 207; architecture, 208
Cupisnique (Coast Chavín), 154, 160, *138, 145-7*
Cursive pottery, 169, *162*
Cuzco, 138; Incas settle, 211; Dominican friary, 212; Chimú artisans, 220

Cuzco Polychrome pottery, 217-18, *204-7*

Danzantes, Los, 25, 81, 82, 84, 152, *13*
Darién metalwork, 239
Diaguite pottery, *see* Chilean Diaguite
Diaguite region, 221
Digging stick, ceremonial, 164, *157*
Draconian pottery, 221

Ear-spools, 201, *192, 193*
Ecuador, 215, 241, 259; pottery, 244, 247-9, 252, *238-45*; cultural phases, 244; architecture, 244, 246; sculpture, 246-7, *236*; metalwork, 250-1; textiles, 251; the highlands, 251
El Arbolillo, 11
El Baúl : stela, 27
El Salvador, 22
El Tajín : ball-courts, 71; stone reliefs, 71, *60*; Pyramid of the Niches, 76
Epigonal pottery, 209 *see* Ica style pottery
Esmeraldas, 250

Feather work : Aztec, 67-8; Maya, 120; Preceramic Period, Peru, 141-2
Flares, 120, 122, *116*
Flint work, Maya, 122, *117*
Florero : Teotihuacán, 42, *34*; Zapotec, 84
Fortaleza Valley : Chimú terraced structure, 197
Fortresses : Chan Chan, 196-7; Marca Huamachuco, 194-6; Saccsaihumán, 212, *202*
Funerary masks : Teotihuacán, 38, 48, *28*; Chimú, *191*

Gallinazo (or Virú) pottery, of Peru, 158, 160, *149, 150*
Gold work : Chavín, 153-4, *143*; Mochica, 166, *160*; Chimú, 200, 201, *190, 191*; Central America, 229, 231; Colombia, 238, 240, *230, 231*; Ecuador, 250, 251
Gourds, carved, 140-1, *134, 135*
Grasshopper, basalt, 62, *48*
Greater Antilles : pottery, 256; *zemi*, 258
Gualupita : Olmec figurines, 23
Guangala Phase, 248-9, *239, 242*
Guayaquil, 247
Guayas Basin, Milagro Phase, 246, 249, 251

286

PRAEGER WORLD OF ART SERIES

PRAEGER WORLD OF ART PROFILES

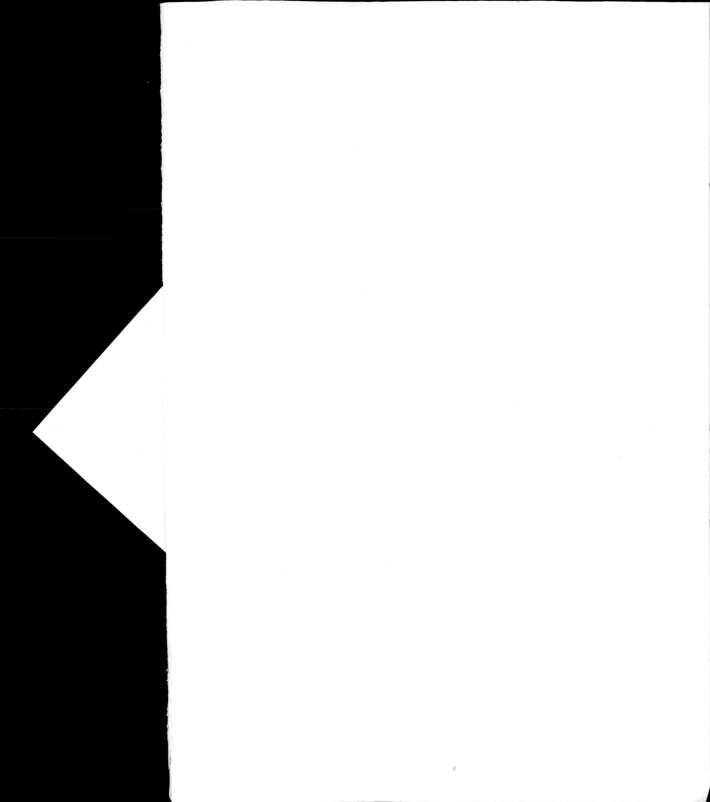

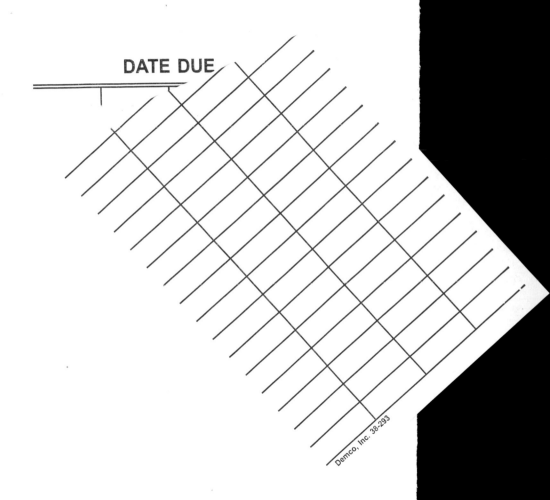

DATE DUE

Demco, Inc. 38-293